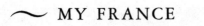 MY FRANCE

MY FRANCE

Politics, Culture, Myth

EUGEN WEBER

The Belknap Press of
Harvard University Press
Cambridge, Massachusetts
London, England
1991

Library of Congress Cataloging-in-Publication Data

Weber, Eugen Joseph, 1925–
  My France : politics, culture, myth / Eugen Weber.
    p. cm.
  ISBN 0-674-59575-0 (alk. paper)
   1. France—Civilization. 2. Politics and culture—France—
History. 3. France—Politics and government—20th century.
I. Title.
DC33.W37   1991
944-dc20

90-35780
CIP

For
Stephan and Agnès Guérin

Contents

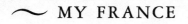 MY FRANCE

Introduction

In the beginning was the armor: Roman in horizontal bands, fish-scales in Crusaders' coats of mail, impregnable, impenetrable, picturesque. And lances, swords, shields, not to mention helmets—menacing with their nose pieces or somber slits for eyes, glorious in their crests: whoever wore such raiment and used weapons far more splendid than my wooden sword was worth investigating. I learned to read because I wanted to know about the pictures in my cousins' schoolbooks. The enigmatic lines of writing that streaked across the pages and around the pictures had to be mastered so I could discover what they had to tell. By the time I was five years old I could decipher them. This made available all kinds of recondite intelligence: posters, shop signs, magazines (less for the text, of course, than for the illustrations—but, still, what did these mean?), eventually stories. Especially stories. And, of all stories, history offered the most colorful, varied, rousing accounts.

Where I lived as a boy others had lived and fought: the Romans, and those whom they conquered, the Dacians. Many had trampled this dark and bloody ground where the Carpathian mountains curved west before they petered out near the Danube: Scythians, Thracians, Goths, Slavs, Hunnish tribes. But our local ancestors were Daco-Romans, so the schoolbooks said and so I was content to accept, even though some of my own ancestors remained barbarous (hardy, heroic, warlike, uncorrupt, Tacitus told us) quite a bit longer.

Many Romanians, especially among the bourgeoisie, drew ancestors from Greeks, Armenians, Poles, Germans. Nicolae Iorga, the great historian, was distantly of Greek descent. More recent Polish blood flowed in the veins of Corneliu Codreanu, who founded the Legion of the Archangel Michael, otherwise known as the Iron Guard. The kings were Hohenzollerns. But derivations of that kind attained no national conclusion, and sought none. Neither did we. I was satisfied to recognize my *morts* as Daco-Roman, with their splendid victories, no less heroic defeats, and their

1

impressive ruins—not least the bridge the Romans threw across the Danube at Turnu-Severin.

Though some of my *morts* lay in a different land—north of the mountains, in the land of seven (German) cities, Siebenbürgen—German vestiges never enthralled me much. I thrilled when I saw Fritz Lang's *Nibelungen*—both silent parts, during not-so-silent Sunday matinees ten years after their making. But it was the fighting that thrilled me, and the treachery. By the 1930s, when film began to bolster my fascination with history (and violence?), Italian mytho-history films offered richer fare, like *Scipio Africanus*, better befitting young Romanians. Besides, although my family divided between Germanophiles and Francophiles, the latter easily won.

Good Romanians go to Paris when they die. Those who can afford it get there sooner. Romanian culture was French-oriented and, in the upper classes, quite simply bilingual. This did not merely mean conversation at table and half or more the books on my parents' shelves, but the store of references, of dreams, of fantasies, at every level. The stamp catalogs of Stanley Gibbons were the ultimate authority of Anglophone philatelists; but in Bucarest Yvert et Tellier made the law. If I could get to Paris, I could visit the Invalides with its military museum, and with Napoleon's tomb, familiar from a picture postcard; I could also attend the weekly stamp-exchange near the Rond-Point des Champs Elysées. The seven-year-old's dream would be realized, in that precise order, at the age of twelve.

So my young self had more than one iron in the fire: films, stamps, martial arts at their most primitive, greed at its most gluttonous, and dreaming. Perhaps too much dreaming, since grades in school were not dreamy. Far from a prodigy, the child I was, and later the young boy, seemed then as he seems now remarkably unremarkable, except for reading—reading then, and later politics. (I do not know what else, other than politics, to call my vague dissatisfaction with the social hierarchy, the subjection of servants and of peasants, the diffuse violence of everyday life in a relatively peaceable country among apparently gentle folk.)

This odd unease would become slightly more focused when, at the age of ten, after a spate of nurses and of *fräuleins,* my parents got me a tutor. I forget his name, but remember he was slender, blond, very young, and, as I now realize, preoccupied with social justice. Was he a Socialist? There is no knowing, though socialism was almost as popular among university students of the 1930s as the proto-fascism of the Iron Guard. My uncles, however, were convinced of it when they heard me repeat some of the formulae my tutor uttered and which so conveniently articulated my own feelings. My liberal parents gave way to family pressure, my blond tutor vanished, leaving me to my own devices and to whatever books I could lay my hands upon: Karl May, Alexandre Dumas, Stefan Zweig, Victor Hugo, Homer, George Sand, Jules Verne, the Comtesse de Ségur, and every cheap paperback I could afford to buy from among those that hung from clothespins on ropes stretched along some fence: *literatura de cordel,* the Brazilians call it.

I remember the brochures, the gaudy covers, the sensational adventures, more vaguely than my mood of every day: boredom, tedium, leaden hours less leaden really than exasperating in their humdrum, insipid sameness. I wanted to leave Bucarest, leave Romania, get away. I wanted to fight the Italians in Abyssinia (I was ten) or, later, the Japanese in China (I must have been twelve). Anything for escape; and for a little action.

At an advanced age, something like sixteen, I read Alfred de Musset's *Fantasio* at school and recognized the cramped, confined, trammeled atmosphere I hated; the smalltown rebel who knows every cobble of every street, and every pair of eyes behind the curtained windows, who feels condemned to endless repetition, endless ennui, futile gestures, and a futile life. That was my feeling at ten, eleven, twelve, and it gave me the energy to nag my parents into sending me to school abroad. Not just anywhere, but as far away from Bucarest and Bucarest's commonplaces as could be managed. This meant not Germany, where my father and his relatives had attended university, not Switzerland where my mother had been sent to finishing school, not even France where "everybody went," but that most distant part of Europe: England.

England was exotic. And on the way to England one could see Paris too. Before the war put an end to the routine, I would spend school terms in England, Christmas holidays in Paris with my parents, summer holidays at home where I could show off my English tennis and my English flannels.

It may be the wintry weather and the badly heated hotels near the Opera that make my memories of prewar Paris so vespertine and, despite erratic shopping expeditions, rather melancholy. The city we explored in 1937, 1938, 1939 was nothing like the picture books and postcards illumined in Bucarest. The welcome it extended was grudging at best: officials were acrimonious, hotel staff sullen, bus conductors grouchy, shop assistants huffy, the crowds that thronged the glistening pavements glum. In retrospect, I realize those were the years when the hot air and hope were going out of the Popular Front, leaving fear and resentment behind. The ill-humor that filled the air like coal dust was primarily directed at other Frenchmen. But foreigners were not treated as innocent bystanders. They never are, of course: quite the contrary. But this time it was worse. Paris harbored numerous refugees, witness to a generous tradition. Now, these were linked to looming foreign conflict, and to internal stress. Stavisky, the revelation of whose creative thieving set off the riots of February 1934, had been an immigrant—from Bessarabia. The French had their own problems: why should they risk more bloodshed for distant folk that couldn't keep out of trouble? That was not my idea of international politics, though it might have been if I had been older. But it explains why strangers were not welcome, no more than I would welcome them during a family fight.

I suppose that we were not much more comfortable in France than Frenchmen were with each other. The image of Paris that I nursed through the war went with that experience, glossed by three images: shiny pavements, the Victory of Samothrace taking flight from her Louvre landing, and the carts of hors d'oeuvres proffered in restaurants, their lush offerings to my gluttony.

Back home, the summer of 1939 was drawing to an end when I walked out of a dark cinema into the blinding glare of a noontime street to hear the newsboys shout that Poland had been invaded. It must have been Friday, September 1. Sunday we listened to Neville Chamberlain making the Second World War official. Within very few days dedraggled Polish cars, burdened, mud-splashed and battered, were parked in the streets of Bucarest. For eight dreary months I was back at the Lycée Michael the Brave, waiting for my canceled English visa to be renewed. At last, on April 1, 1940, I could once again board the Orient Express for Paris and points west.

I was not the only April Fool. Paris never looked more radiant than that first week in April, its plateglass windows taped, its monuments sandbagged, its boulevards full of high-heeled trotting women, strolling men, and uniforms in various shades of khaki, green, and blue. I was most impressed by the strapping British soldiers ambling in twos, who sported brassards lettered MP. What young, handsome members of Parliament Britain boasted! And here they were, all in uniform.

Within a week of my return to Britain, on April 9, 1940, the German invasion of Denmark and Norway was under way. One month later it was the turn of Holland, Belgium, France. From Herne Bay, by the Thames estuary, my school friends and I bicycled to Ramsgate, to watch from the cliffs the host of boats shuttling from Dunkirk. In the next few days we could see their passengers hanging out of trains halted at Herne Bay railway station: haggard, scruffy, cheerful men getting their tea and buns. Within ten weeks of Dunkirk, Romania (which had lost two fifths of its territory and half of its population to Russia, Hungary, and Bulgaria) joined the Axis. However unenthusiastically this had come about, the British, under siege, now treated my homeland as an enemy power. My parents' money held in a British bank was frozen, and I found myself freer than I had ever wished.

The school holidays of 1940 were going to stretch out for me more than a year, until a wonderful woman, a distant relative, took the sixteen year-old in hand, persuaded a headmaster to take me in, and sent me back to school. There I dreamed only of getting into the army, and finally got my wish when I was eighteen, in 1943. Hopeless at maths or science and wonderfully clumsy, I judged that my best chance lay in the infantry, in which I had the honor to serve during four years. Discomfort and danger were relative and sporadic, the fighting most resembled American football which combines short spells of intense activity with long intervals for refreshment. After public school, the army offered less discomfort, better food, physical activity and adventure. Peacetime service does not sound much fun. Service in a good cause (there had not been a better in ages) gilds the gingerbread. I enjoyed military service but, by 1947, dreams of military glory had worked out of my system. I had learned many things: not least, how irresponsibly destructive young men can be for fun; and, like Fabrice del Dongo, how far experience is from our accounts of it.

By 1947, also, the time had come to cash in on the scholarships I had won before joining the army. I had read history, literature, politics, all my life. Now I would read them officially, at Cambridge. Not that I stayed put for long. Military gallivanting had sharpened my wanderlust, Paris was just across the Channel, French government scholarships as well as English ones spurred intellectual tourism. Besides, I had met a French girl whom I had to see again. In due course, she became my wife.

Whatever my infidelities to Cambridge, it was there that my intellectual life began. I had always been a bookworm and a scribbler. Given imagination and the talent, I would have been a writer of fiction. As it is, I have to use nonfictional sources to write—allegedly—nonfiction. At Cambridge what I read and wrote was more structured and directed, focused in the main on medieval history. Not always; not at once. When I left the army, I was so hungry for reading that I lapsed often into my old indiscriminate ways. By the end of the first year, Part One of the History Tripos (ex-servicemen could skip Preliminary exams) earned me no more than Second Class honors. That was when I went off for a year in Paris.

Cambridge tutorials had encouraged me to focus on specific questions, then to set out my findings clearly, cogently, elegantly if possible. The seminars I attended at the "Sciences Po"—the Institut de Sciences Politiques—expanded my horizons. Intellectual rigor could be infused with imagination, sometimes with eloquence. I always suspected that communication had to be in part seduction, that wisdom and fantasy could work well together. The French, who did not much relish fantasy in mainstream literature, found room for it in history. I returned from Paris determined to bring off a First. No First, no research scholarship to pursue the medieval

studies on which I had set my heart, no doctorate, no academic career. By
dint of applied work discipline the First followed, and so did the rest. Now,
for the dissertation.

I wanted to be a medieval historian. My dissertation would be about
Saxon settlements in Transylvania. Though I was worthless at Latin, dog-
Latin came easy, and so did German. In 1948 I had written a wildly erudite
undergraduate essay which a respectable journal actually printed some years
later.[1] But now it was 1950 and Michael Postan, the Cambridge medievalist whom I most admired, told me it was no use to think that I could get
at the essential sources in Romania. Instead, he offered me a post teaching
at Ibadan, in West Africa. Having just got married, I was tempted; but I
preferred to shift my dissertation plans. I would write on modern history;
better still, on contemporary times which, in those days, tended to end
with the First World War.

In their last undergraduate year, candidates for Part Two of the History Tripos prepared one special examination subject chosen from a long
list. The subject of my choice had been "The Third French Republic
from Boulanger to Dreyfus." Why not write my dissertation in that field?
Among a host of intriguing personalities of the period, Edouard Drumont
had caught my fancy, not just for the rabid antisemitism which, at that
time, still seemed to deserve exploration, but also by the conjunction of
Drumont's dim, lusterless personality and the catastrophically effective
influence that, for a while, he managed to exert. When I broached my idea
with Denis Brogan, he turned and picked up a heavy set of proofs: volume
one of Robert Byrnes's *Antisemitism in Modern France*. I took the pages home,
read, and realized that I was too late. Drumont still awaits a thorough biography but, at that time, it would have been difficult to better Byrnes. I
could not have done it. I only regret that Byrnes never wrote a second volume, to carry his narrative through the Dreyfus affair and beyond.

I had to find another topic. Did Brogan suggest it, did I invent it, did I
talk about it with David Thomson, my charming, nonchalant *patron?* I do
not remember. But there it was: I would write about "The Nationalist
Revival in France, 1905–1914": a nice monographic subject, accessible to
tyros such as I. In retrospect my research looks superficial, based largely on
newspapers, published documents, parliamentary debates, and much guess-
work. No wonder that critics found the finished work impressionistic—
meaning, I suppose, that it carried too many anecdotes and too little
analysis. In the end it was refused a Cambridge doctorate: a crushing experience at the time, but one which I have survived. The book is still in print.

Survival was facilitated by the fact that, in 1956, I joined UCLA—still
in those days thought of as the southern branch of the University of Califor-

nia, but already a splendid place to work. I had loved Cambridge, but there was no future there for me. I could have gone to the London School of Economics or to the CNRS in Paris (what a dream!) but, by the time firm possibilities surfaced, I had accepted a job in North America. I have never regretted it. Conditions may be different today, but in the 1950s academic advancement in Europe depended too much on patronage and politics. Whom you knew counted a good deal more than what you did. In the United States one did not progress by way of sherry parties—though a good stomach for martinis did no harm. Nor did one have to clock the death or retirement of senior colleagues in order to make one's way. There were old-boy networks in North America too, but there were so many colleges and universities that prejudice, influence, patronage, feuds, had little apparent impact on the profession. By and large, one was judged on the way one taught and wrote. That, to me, seemed ideal; and, when ideals flagged, the scale of academe offered alternative havens.

A mix-up over my visa forced me to leave the United States in 1959, the year when *The Nationalist Revival* was published. But exile was eased when UCLA gave me tenure and leave, the Social Science Research Council added a two-year Faculty Research Fellowship, and we set off for France. I thought that this time I would return with a book about the riots of February 6, 1934, or perhaps about the veteran leagues that played their part in those disorders. Instead, after months of hesitation, I focused on another participant in February 6: the Action française.

Like most of my kind and of my generation, I knew little or nothing about the right, except as bogeys, let alone about monarchism. Post-Dreyfusard nationalism had introduced me to the Action française, with its strange position of influence without power. The organization's more recent doings were tainted by association with Vichy and, so it seemed, with Nazism. Looking beyond accepted stereotypes revealed a more complex, nuanced, interesting picture. The politics of the Action française were no more a bloc than the French Revolution. Its personalities, too, were varied: often fascinating and sometimes attractive. To mention only those no longer alive: Emmanuel Beau de Loménie, Kléber Haedens, Gonzague de Reynold . . .

Personal sympathy does not necessarily make research more easy, but it helps to advance understanding. I realized, for example, something that was well known between the wars but that circumstances had since obscured: the intellectual fascination exerted at that time by the right in general and the Action française in particular. The time was all agog for new ideas. Impertinent, iconoclastic, these simili-royalists abounded with ideas (not necessarily good ones), and they expressed them well.

The true historian must, temporarily, join his characters, become a part of them, their mindset and their epoch. Sympathy may be too much to ask, but empathy is essential, not just looking at but "feeling with" times, people, and ideas. One did not have to approve a movement's politics or its actions to try to comprehend them, to place them in perspective and in the context of contemporary history.

Defeat, like fashion, can condemn to silence, to the blacking out (the French call it occultation) of people and events. Sometimes this is no great loss. In this case recent French history, which rests upon the dialog between left and right, was left unbalanced by the exclusion of one party. Had I not happened along, someone else would have begun to restore the balance. I was simply lucky, and I learned a lot.

One thing I learned was that, whatever the Action française was, it was not fascist. Yet in the 1950s and the 1960s these French royalists were identified with fascism as naturally as were Horthy, Franco, Salazar, and General Antonescu. I knew that Antonescu had bloodily put down the nearest thing to fascism in Romania, the Iron Guard; that Horthy did his best to keep out their Hungarian counterpart, the Arrow Cross. Simplifying stereotypes did not clarify issues, only confused them. A little discrimination seemed in order; *Varieties of Fascism* was the result.[2] Monarchism and fascism were no more identical than authoritarianism and fascism. Fascist or proto-fascist activities could be observed throughout Europe in between the wars, but certain societies, particular socioeconomic situations, were more fascist-friendly than others. France, for example, whose national identity was well-established, whose traditional right had an agenda of its own, whose middle and working classes never hit rock-bottom as their German counterparts did, never nurtured much of a fascist movement. Nor did England.

I found, as René Remond had done in his classic book *The Right in France* (1954), that much French fascist baggage and leadership came from what we call the left. In France, furthermore, the inspiration of the radical right was Bonapartist, that is, populist and authoritarian. Twentieth-century fascism, with its anticapitalist, often racist, overtones did not quite fit. And national socialism, not unknown to many Marxist regimes, could be traced back to organic nationalism, certainly to Maurice Barrès, who helped to formulate it. The point about all this is not how right I was. It is that, in the middle sixties, when fascism was still an undifferentiated notion and a label applied as readily to General de Gaulle as to Charles Maurras, a little discrimination did not come amiss.

I spent the middle sixties as chairman of the Department of History at UCLA, having little or no opportunity for research. So I wrote a textbook, *A Modern History of Europe,* which tried to offer a new synthesis but called for little research. I had been teaching introductory survey courses in Western Civilization since 1952 and wanted a text that married politics and society with cultural life in the broadest sense.[3] Narrative synthesis is the devil. Perhaps Theodore Zeldin is right, and pointillism is the only way to come close to historical reality. But pointillism may confuse those who know no history at all, who need a superficial picture that carries *some* sense and attraction before they can progress to more sophisticated understanding. I wrote for nonspecialist readers who have always, ideally, been those I wanted to touch. The book has done better in France than in the United States. Americans, wisely, shun textbooks; the French enjoy reading readable history.

In 1968 I moved to the University of Bordeaux, to spend two years as director of our University's French Center for Education Abroad. That was a revelation. I had read about France all of my life and specialized in its history since 1950. Yet all I really knew of France was Paris. France *was* Paris. Of course, I had seen many parts of the country as a tourist, but never had I experienced life outside the capital. I passed through Dieppe and Lyon, Dijon and Marseille, as, typically, I had passed through Bordeaux itself at the end of the war, transiting through Mérignac but never knowing that from one of the airfield's sheds Charles de Gaulle had sprinted to grab General Spears's hand and fly off to England and to History.

Now I found myself in a provincial capital, a little shabby but still grand, with a strong personality of its own, and with its own traditions whose very existence I had ignored. Here was a society with its own hierarchy in which Parisians had no place, great pride, and a particular culture that could not be known, let alone understood, from Paris. The same was true of other regions and of their capitals, all French, yes, but all sui generis. How could I call myself a French historian when I ignored so much of France?

And what was France? Great cities were all very well; they shared in the general history that one could read and that one wrote about, composed of kings, artists, writers, soldiers, industrialists, lawyers, engineers. Official history. Around these cities, however, behind the official history, lay less familiar terrain, invisible men and women in hundreds of small towns, on thousands of square miles of unexplored countryside: the vastness of what Frenchmen now call *la France profonde*.

As the French provinces had been subsumed in Paris, so this French countryside had also been lost from sight. Did it share the history of the cities, and to what degree? Did what we knew of France, so often based on Paris, apply to rural France as it did to urban centers? Or was there a *décalage*—a time-lag, a gap between the two? If that were so, could the differences be charted, their evolution traced? These were some of the questions that I asked myself, and their pursuit led to another book: *Peasants into Frenchmen*. Its gist was that residents of the country, France, lived in different historical time-zones until the late nineteenth century, and that France was only truly unified by the deliberate enterprise of the Third Republic, when social and cultural changes originating in great cities spread through all the land.[4]

As a generalization, this sort of statement can at best be only generally true. Even then, exceptions claim a hearing. Stretches of France had been Frenchified by the end of the eighteenth century, others entered the national community around 1851, whilst higher levels of cultural and material homogenization were only generalized in the 1960s. As with my writings on fascism, the point was not to be wholly right, but to draw attention to aspects of past reality that we had ignored. I can't complain: since 1976, the history of the peasantry and of their integration, political, cultural, and economic, has been receiving the attention it deserves.

I had accepted my appointment at Bordeaux to make quite sure that I would not be dragooned into continuing to serve as department chair. Unfortunately, the University of Bordeaux, whose history goes back to Roman schools, did not have much of a library. French universities had expanded to democratic scale, but their facilities had not kept up with their ambitions—one reason for the explosion of 1968. The rebels of 1968, however, were more concerned to improve the world than the facilities they used, which meant that they failed on both counts. Parked in a bald concrete campus next to the Haut-Brion vineyards at Talence, several miles from town, the Bordeaux University students with whom I talked seemed little concerned with bus services, dormitories, playing fields, even cafés conveniently situated. As for books, the French tradition suggests that you buy your own, which is why so many French own books while Americans use libraries.

I was more selfish than the students, or at least more demanding. Used to an imperfect world, I nevertheless needed a project that could be pursued with means available locally. My *Peasants* were still a hypothesis about a mystery. Fortunately, if Bordeaux offered no real library, it enjoyed another typically French facility for which the United States have no counterpart: a superior departmental archive. A little rummaging soon revealed that, among other local glories, Bordeaux had been one of the first cities in fin-de-siècle France to boast a rugby team. Interest in rugby, which I had played when young, led me to look into the coming of games and sports to France, and their relationship to contemporary ideology and politics. That opened up the question of physical regeneration (burning concern of a fin de siècle obsessed with decadence), of leisure, curism, tourism, and, not least, of the introduction of that incomparable harbinger of progress and emancipation, the bicycle.

All these excursions had to be suspended, first to write the *Peasants,* then to become Dean of UCLA's College of Letters and Science: a fascinating and amusing position in which I would have continued if it had not prohibited serious research and writing. So when an editor friend challenged me to write another book that would, as it were, wrap up some of the loose ends that I had carelessly left hanging, I resigned and wrote *France, Fin de Siècle.*

Fin de siècle is a book I enjoyed writing, and that many seem to have enjoyed reading. But, of all my books, it is the one I would most readily rewrite.[5] Written, at least in theory, to tie up loose ends, it is itself awash in them. The high art, architecture, philosophy, of the fin de siècle deserved far fuller treatment than they received. Above all, though, the question of religion got too short a shrift. After thirty years of teaching about the struggle that led to the separation between Church and state, it was exceeding strange that I should address the turn of the century with hardly a thought for one of its incandescent issues. Yet the idea did not occur to me until I saw the book in print: testimony to a mind more like a jumbly hayloft than an orderly library. The essay on "Religion and Superstition" represents my timid attempt to make amends.

Most of the essays in this collection reflect similar beginnings. Curiosity is the mother of invention. But knowing more, or thinking more about something, makes one aware of further possibilities. Interest in, familiarity with particular situations evokes observations one would not make otherwise. How curious, for example, that the battle song of the Army of the Rhine, born in Strasbourg, should have been made famous by southerners, many of whom knew but few words of French. Or, on another plane, just how fantastic are fairy tales, really? Could it be that reality is what many of them are about? And when did the image of the hexagon take shape? In what circumstances?

Statements once made and printed sometimes evoke debate. Were French peasants politicized after 1789, after 1848, or (as I incline to think) mostly toward the end of the nineteenth century? How swiftly did the new national identity replace long-standing local identities? What was the share of political propaganda and experience in bringing this about? I never take pen to answer published criticism, seldom join in public debate. On these particular questions I could not forbear, hence the essays on peasants and politics.

Working on the Action française, on fascism, on the fin de siècle, cast new light for me on other contemporary issues: alleged differences between right and left for example, the national socialist tradition in France, the difference, if any, between revolution and counterrevolution. It also colored my perspective on earlier antisemitism, my views on the relations between literature and politics, my interest in personalities.

History is about men and women who live in time and place. Time and place affect them, and they affect their times. Our picture of the whole depends upon its parts, the general makes no sense apart from particulars. Carrying sword or pen, shooting words or arrows, individuals mold or inflect events, institutions, trends. Biography is an integral part of the historian's art, whether attempted in one paragraph or in several volumes. Working with real people offers a rare chance to drive beyond abstractions. Balzac remarked that "in Paris men become *systèmes*—theories, abstractions, in the provinces 'systems' become men." And women. Good biographies turn even Parisians from abstractions into something more complex; they present dogma and doctrine not as monuments but as process, fluxive and instrumental; they suggest histories crowded with personalities, their shifts and their devices.

I have never ventured into biography, which takes a novelist's talent. But I have tried to place men in their time, or to discuss aspects of life by way of individual figures: the importance of private incomes through Maurice Barrès, the introduction of sports by way of Pierre de Coubertin, the experience of being a historian in the life of Marc Bloch.

Historians historicize. They take words, works, acts, figures, and place them in context, or try to. It is not irrelevant to do the same with the history historians write, whose tone and orientation reflects the age—indeed, the moment—of its writing. Quite a few of my writings and several of the essays below are inspired by some brief encounter between current politics and history: they take fugitive manifestations like the efflorescence of rightist movements in the 1950s and 1960s, or the debate about antisemitism, and try to locate them in a broader context. Others address issues that were ardently debated not long ago, but appear less contentious today. Some of the issues I raised in the 1960s had not been raised before. Today they are taken for granted. But when, at the Thirteenth Congress of Historical Sciences held in Moscow in 1970, I suggested that fascism and communism were not antithetical but *frères ennemis,* the suggestion struck many (and not only my hosts) as outlandish. Thus do times change, our perceptions with them, and the topicality of history-writing along with both. In a very small way, this collection is (also) a contribution to the historicization of history—one man's history.

But if current interests spawn a logical fallout, hazard also plays its part.

The essay on *nos ancêtres* springs from a discussion I had with Pierre Nora[6] about when the locution was born—not, of course, as a historical notion, but as a didactic and popular commonplace. Pursuit of its evolution revealed to me how nations (an eighteenth-century invention popularized in the nineteenth century) reforged foundation myths, first for adult consumption, then as childish fare, and the political role that such myths could play. Writing about the right, about fascism, about revolutions, raised questions concerning their ideological make-up, their relations with antisemitism, and with ideological neighbors in extremism. Some considerations on all these may be found in the last, fifth, part of the book. But disparate in inspiration as they are, I hope the essays come together in their focus on France.

Some French still act surprised that an American should take so active an interest in their history. I tell them that many Americans are interested in French history, that the Society for French Historical Studies alone has some two thousand members; its *Journal of French Historical Studies* almost as many subscribers. Of course, I am an American only by (mutual) choice. Before that I was happily English, my values and much of my culture come from the games I played, the war I fought, the schools I shared, with Britons. Before French history flowered in this country, first-rate historians were tackling it in Britain, where I began to learn it.

Before I became English, I had been Romanian. However uneasily I lived that destiny, it left its mark on me, and I am glad of it. For one thing, few twentieth-century historians of nineteenth-century Europe had the good fortune to be born *in* the nineteenth century. That was where Romania still lived between the wars: sophisticated prosperity and primitive backwardness, oligarchy, squirearchy, a "provincial" bourgeoisie still finding its feet and valuing the culture it was forging, striking discrepancies between social orders as between country and town. Social relations, manners, attitudes that others have had to learn from books I lived in my early years. Romanian francophilia, Romanian francophony, probably inflected my historical interests. Romanian experience certainly informed those interests.[7]

Many Romanians, in my day, dreamed of France; not many got there. My doing so was a matter of chance. Hazard determined that I would not do medieval history, as I had wanted, that I would turn to French studies, as I did not expect. It was by chance that Cambridge, in my day, held several distinguished French historians and offered an aspiring student an easy, obvious fallback. It was by chance that most of my works were subsequently undertaken, and that I wrote on this and not on that. Fortuitousness, contingency, and sheer good luck (not blind, because it followed orientation, preparation, determination and hard work, but still serendipitous) made me fall into France, just as one falls into love.

France must be a historian's paradise. As Rome to Catholics, it is our big rock candy mountain. Whatever one writes about the French will be attacked or praised, analyzed, criticized, censured, commended, berated or puffed, but never (or seldom) ignored. Not that any historian's views are so very important, but that history in France is part of the present, as it was of the past. History is past politics, but in France more than elsewhere, past politics are part of present politics and of contemporary arguments. All history is always contemporary history, present concerns always trespass on the past, but they do so in France more explicitly than in other countries. In memory, debate, public and private life, the past is a substantive presence. No wonder there are so many French historians. Exposure to France makes us feel relevant or, at least, less irrelevant than we are at home.

The French addiction to French history was something I ignored when I turned toward it. The obvious seemed sufficiently exciting. After the war, the most exhilarating kind of history was being done in France, home of the iridescent school of the *Annales*. It was in Emmanuel College library, around 1948, that I first devoured Lucien Febvre's *La Terre et l'évolution humaine*, published in 1922, and then Marc Bloch's *Société féodale*, which had come out in the later thirties, just on the eve of war. I hadn't even wandered in the desert, and here I was faced with fresh water, and a great caravan. Like the great films of the 1920s that dazzled my boyhood, books like these opened vast horizons. Here were new ways of doing history that brought the dead to life. Where historians used to stop on people's doorsteps, or timidly ventured to study or *salon*, Febvre and Bloch strode in to peer at bedrooms, kitchens, middens, and beyond them at ways folk thought and felt: *mentalités*.

Under their pens, history broke out of formal limits to enlist the skills and perceptions too often left to other trades—economics, ethnography, sociology, linguistics, folklore, technology—and to renew its old alliance with geography. More than just people came to life, endowed with a third dimension: mountains did too, rivers, seas, fields, ploughs, roads, crops, and horses recovered the active role they had played in past lives and still play in ours. Mills turned again, stirrups kept horsemen from toppling, yokes multiplied power, mines turned out wealth. The new history set places and objects dancing as in a fairy story or in the *Nutcracker Suite*. So did new writing styles, which gingered-up otherwise heavy fare. The tone, phrasing, rhythms, of Febvre and, later, of Braudel, even their punctuation, broke old rules, suggested new ones. The writing was as vital as the message, and as appealing.

The *Annales* have changed. Iconoclasm, novelty, generate their own conformisms. I never belonged to this, nor to any other "school," even those

I admired. But if French history today is doing well, we owe a great deal to the imagination of these twentieth-century pioneers, and to the stimulation their works carried.

I spoke of tumbling into France as into love. By now it must be clear the processes were not too dissimilar, with chance playing its part in both. Uncritical love is certainly naive and possibly unattainable for intelligent persons. A knowledgeable passion seems a more reasonable goal. This may be mere rationalization for the love-hate relationship that most historians, at least those of France, maintain with their subject. But knowledgeable or not, my feeling about French, dead or alive, is a passion—the desperate desire to encompass a kaleidoscope, a catherine wheel, a living multiform being, and to know it. In biblical usage, to know someone meant (among other things) to have sexual intercourse: the most profound, most intimate of relations. It certainly means not just to know but also to feel, to take possession and to make one's own, and to be possessed. It also means to understand in ways that go beyond explanation. To know, as Saint-Exupéry has put it, is to gain access to a vision. "Mais, pour voir, il convient d'abord de participer."

Participation is easier said than done. Historians, by definition, are travelers in foreign lands. Foreign historians are travelers twice over, and aliens to boot. When I first came to UCLA in the 1950s, my senior colleagues, who found nothing unusual about Americans teaching European history, were shocked at the suggestion that Europeans could comprehend U.S. history, let alone teach it. Such provincial prejudices have been overcome, in part by realizing how little we know about ourselves, let alone about our fellows, not least those other folk, long dead, whose unfamiliar ways we have the slenderest means of grasping.

It is true that foreign historians have peculiar problems. Striking a balance between empathy and detachment is never easy. Outsiders may find it particularly hard. Some of us fall uncritically in love with our quarry, some translate unfamiliar discomforts into equally uncritical distaste. We fear being taken for tourists, we want to pass for natives—at least, not to appear as outsiders. We affirm the mote in the alien culture's eye more readily than the beam in our own, or vice-versa. And yet we seem to manage, perhaps because the problems of historians working in distant lands are not different in kind, or greater, than those historians face who look at distant times. The past is a foreign country.

I always assume that my understanding of people or situations can only be as good as intuition and hard work can make it: in other words, imperfect. My vision of France is thus imperfect, just as the vision of French-born historians of France is bound to be. Elie Halévy, one of the great French students of English history, put the situation equably a long time ago: the foreigner overlooks local detail obvious to the native, but distance and detachment can sharpen his vision. What one loses on the swings, one wins on the roundabouts. Perhaps. But Halévy's law of imperfect objectivity does not dispense me from learning as much of the local detail as I can.

Getting to know France means reading everything about it. It also means, and that's the best of it, getting out of Paris with its sharp elbows and sharp tongues into localities where smiles come more readily and help-fulness is less exceptional. Departmental archives, less highly computerized than the National Archives in Paris, are more efficient, more welcoming, more interested in the treasures they hold and less adept at making their access difficult. Municipal archives may sit in a garret, but municipal officers, surprised by outside interest, are apt to welcome rather than reject it. The countryside is lovely, rivers run smooth and green, small towns offer more enticing walks and less of pretentious Japanese cuisine than big ones. This is no place to expatiate on offseason delights when most hotels refuse to heat their rooms and even hospitable archives close for lunch, casting the lonely researcher out into wintry streets. But a sense of place, of atmo-sphere, of detail, is worth even dyspepsia.

As one proceeds through France, the extraordinary variety of the land-scape confirms the variety of history. The leafy green of eastern valleys recalls the thick green shadows of Courbet's oils, the mere-bespattered wastelands of the Brenne illustrate the persistence of sorcerers in Bas-Berry, the poor lands of Creuse and of the Auvergne uplands explain the paradox of isolation and emigration. The cultural, hence oft political, break between plateau and river valley, sometimes no more than a mile apart, is readily apparent at Ornans, where the "new" cemetery Courbet painted stands a short walk between the Catholic uplands and the handsome Jacobin vint-ners' houses on the Loue.

France is one long paper trail of familiar references in unfamiliar places. Madeleines have become famous, but the dull town of Commentry where the pastries were born is little known, except by French men who passed through it on military service. Tourists enjoy the charms of George Sand's Nohant, but do not know (why should they?) that it was spared the worst of famine in 1847 and 1848 because local diet depended more on chestnuts than on grain. The fact that Clemenceau and the future General Boulanger went to the same Nantes lycée left its mark on French political history when Clemenceau made his old schoolmate Minister of War. So did French con-quest of the Franche-Comté where, the story goes, locals had themselves buried face to the ground so as not to see the French conquerors lording it above them. So has the long English presence in the Bordelais, which made claret England's traditional wine and which has kept Bordeaux as the most English town in France, even to the rain.

Anecdotes do not a country make, let alone history. But anecdotes suggest color, better still nuance, which mark local character, specificity, particularity. Therein lies the infinite aggregation of detail which, once elicited and ordered, makes History. Max Beerbohm once said, or is said to have said, that history does not repeat itself: it is historians who repeat one another. No wonder, if they ignore particulars for the general, trees for the wood. Abstract history is immaterial, bloodless, insubstantial. Its logic makes it an irresistible flood. Individuals may surface for a moment, their features flash, their gestures beckon, before they are engulfed again. In abstract history, human will, initiative, personality, give way to what Léon Daudet in another context called "la politique du chien crevé au fil de l'eau" (the politics of a dog's carcass carried by the waters). But humans, of course, manipulate history as much as they suffer it. Historians that leave no room for the exceptional, the contingent, and the human forget that the whole is less than the sum of its parts, that the particular is more interesting than the general because the particular is the microcosm without which generalities make no sense.

My friend Guy Thuillier likes to complain that historians, ready enough to rummage in other people's secrets, show little readiness to reveal their own. We speculate readily about our subjects' motives, but pay no heed to the motivation and inspiration of historians, let alone our own selves. That may be because it is simply safer to analyze people who are dead. We have trouble enough trying to understand what moved other folk, to seriously believe that we can fathom our own driving forces. But I do not think us slow to talk about ourselves, only reluctant to repeat banalities.

Banalities, today, are harder to avoid than in less vociferous and proliferous ages. All the good quotations have been quoted, most of the pregnant questions have been avoided for years. But the preceding pages are evidence of good will in facing questions like why I do history, and why I do the sort of history I do. The short answer is that I am incurably curious. Curiosity, reluctance to accept the accepted, a tendency to delve into stereotypes and commonplaces to see what lies behind them and what makes them tick, and a strong urge to tell others about what I find, this is what drives me.[8]

French culture favors my predilections. For the French, often enough to suit me, the exception does not just prove the rule, it *is* the rule. Within a context of cultural unity, the French as French *and* as individuals are utterly different from each other, vastly varied, and unexpectedly sui generis. There are so many versions of French history that it is hard to say just what

France may be or French history should be. Yet there clearly is a France, there evidently is French history—aggregations of variants and of infinite detail, creations of imagination, of faith, and of infinite effort. France and the French testify to the power of history—I mean the history that historians write—to forge the realities it imagines. And those who think that history exists only on paper had best remember that, as George Bernard Shaw wrote to Ellen Terry, "only on paper has humanity yet achieved glory, beauty, truth, knowledge, virtue and abiding love."

~ PART I

Assumptions

~ 1

Nos ancêtres les gaulois

Like camembert and vandalism, *nos ancêtres les gaulois* are part of the legacy of the Revolution. Gaulish ancestors, of course, had been acknowledged long before 1789. But, like the Vandals, they had been neither respectable nor politically significant. *Gaulois* had long evoked something boorish, churlish, rude; hence Fénelon's making François I declare: "Before me, all was rude, poor, ignorant, *gaulois*." [1]

Just as the term "Jew" is more loaded than a simple reference label for the Jewish people, so *gaulois* stood for more than the Gaulish branch of Celts. Queen Marie-Antoinette, for instance, was criticized for letting herself be painted wearing a *gaulle* or a *robe en gaule*—a simple chemise dress in the popular style, contrasting with more formal styles worthy of her standing. In the same vein, a few years into the Revolution, a provincial municipality described the books it had confiscated: "Since they are practically all *gaulois* [presumably old and illegible], it is impossible to read them." [2]

There had long been Gauls who lived in the territory that became France. But they had been conquered, first by Romans and then by Franks, with whom French history proper began: a history of master races, all of Germanic origin. [3]

In one of the great classic texts that were a part of schooling, Caesar depicted Gauls as brave but moody, foolhardy, capricious and fallible; Tacitus in *Germania* idealized the fathers of the Franks, in contrast, as hardy, heroic, warlike, uncorrupt. The late Middle Ages ascribed a Trojan origin to the Franks and, in early sixteenth century, Jean Lemaire des Belges broadened that provenance to include the Gauls, responsible for the foundation of Troy, from which Francus or Francion, son of Hector, had returned to his forebears' homeland. That was (roughly) when Etienne Pasquier (the first, apparently, to call Franks Frenchmen) wrote of the Gauls as "our good old fathers." By the time Pierre Ronsard published the first books of his *Franciade,* in 1572, the theme was a common one. But the heroes whom Ronsard cites are all Frankish knights nevertheless: Roland and Pharamond, Clodion and Clovis. [4]

By Ronsard's time, the romance of Amadis de Gaule had become wildly popular, and *Amadis* set the benchmarks of French chivalry, based on Breton, Gallic, and Arthurian myths. Yet Frankish nobility and Gallic chivalry were fused into a whole in which the Franks prevailed. Writing during the reign of Henri IV, Charles Loyseau, Seigneur de La Noue, made this very clear when he formulated the thesis of Frankish conquest and Gaulish subjugation. When the Estates General met in 1614, and President de Mesmes likened the three estates to offspring of the same mother, the nobility walked out in a huff. Allegations of brotherhood were insulting. There was as much difference, they shouted, between Nobles and Third Estate as between master and menial. That same year, a nobiliar publicist reaffirmed the Frankish origin of nobles and their monopoly of Trojan descent. "Thus may no man be called a gentleman," he logically concluded, "unless he be Turk or French." Gauls, once theoretically of equal birth, were being pressed back and down. At the height of Louis XIV's power, the history of France clearly begins with Clovis—a view that reappears in many works, not least in schoolbooks, down to our century.[5]

In the eighteenth century, when political interests explicitly took their stand on historical references, all parties to the struggle for power based their claims on some interpretation of the Frankish conquest. For the Comte de Boulainvilliers, still the best known—though little read—proponent of the dominant thesis, the Gauls became and remained subjects of the Franks as much by right of conquest as by the obedience the strong exact from the weak. Liberty and liberties were the prerogative of the Franks alone and of their descendants: the only ones to be recognized as nobles, that is, Boulainvilliers insists, as lords and masters.[6]

Henri de Boulainvilliers may have been eccentric. But his argument, however extreme, proved influential because it furnished a basic metaphor for claims and counterclaims, ever more shrill, ever more desperate. It served as premise for the nobiliar reaction—first against the crown that nibbled and crunched away their historic rights, but also against uppity commoners, subjects by definition because of their Gallic origins. As the Duc de Saint-Simon believed, as Montesquieu was to argue, the true body of the "nation" consisted in the (noble) heirs of Frankish conquerors, lords over the conquered commons of the land.[7]

Political and social institutions, hierarchy, laws, were all alleged to stem from the original conquest. By 1789 the assimilation of Franks and ruling classes was so common that, in his seminal pamphlet, Abbé Emmanuel Sieyès called on the Third Estate, descended from the Gauls, to send the aristocrats packing, back to their German forests. A few years later, in 1793, the Empress Catherine of Russia explained the situation in France in similar terms to Grimm: the Gauls were trying to chase out the Franks. Catherine thought the Franks would make a comeback, and she was right.[8] But by that time the Gauls had learnt how to assert themselves; and the barnyard rooster, vulgar but vigilant, had effectively challenged the fleur de lys.

The cock was not so triumphant as some would wish: Camille Desmoulins for one would have had it become the nation's emblem. About the time Desmoulins went to his death, in year II of the Republic, a correspondent of the *Mercure national et Révolutions de l'Europe* recommended returning to nature's pure, simple language, by learning to speak *le gaulois*.[9] But few would have known where to find that pristine idiom and besides, classical prejudice was too strong. The historical references of the Revolution were drawn from Athens, Sparta, Rome, not from Alesia. This was reflected in contemporary nomenclatry, dominated by classical heroes like Gracchus and Brutus, and one reason for it was simple ignorance. No one had bothered much to study unknown, inglorious ancestors—except by way of Caesar, who had defeated them. So while roosters postured on dishes and engravings, no sans-culotte seems to have changed his name to Vercingétorix or Brennus.

This would change. It changed because the contemporary vogue of Ossian made Celtic heroes fashionable, not least with General Bonaparte. It changed as well because the Gauls, having cast out the Franks or overthrown them, had to reassert their pedigree; to rediscover, reassert their history and their past as base of a new national history. Inalienable human rights were good; historical origins were better.

More broadly, too, the new nation state determined to abolish particular local identities had to replace them with a new national identity, substitute its version of national memory for venerable older versions that did not fit its end. Memory is what we make it. We are the sons and daughters of our history, but national history, the national heritage, had to be forged by debate, research, invention; had to be acclimatized, inculcated, catechized, made to compel belief, take hold of minds, until it was sanctified by habit. Historians were the clerisy of the nineteenth century because it fell to them to rewrite foundation myths; and history was the theology of the nineteenth century because it provided societies cast loose from the moorings of custom and habit with new anchorage in a rediscovered—or reinvented—past.

More than in our day, nineteenth-century history reached far past history books. It informed contemporary literature, art, conventions. It inspired private enterprise and personal erudition. Théophile Malo Corret de La Tour d'Auvergne was an authentic hero of the revolutionary armies whom Lazare Carnot and Bonaparte jointly named *premier grenadier des armées de la République* because he would accept no other promotions or rewards. In year V of the Republic, La Tour d'Auvergne published a study on Franco-Gaulish origins designed to rehabilitate the Gauls, "nos ancêtres," and resituate them, as he said, in that history of nations from which they had been erased.[10] When in 1800 he died in battle, the urn that bears his heart was topped by a *coq gaulois* rising upon a crown of laurel.

La Tour d'Auvergne's antiquarian and propagandistic activities reflect the lively contemporary interest which led (in 1805) to the foundation of an Académie celtique designed to study the origins of France in Celtic history. Soon provided with government patronage and subsidies, this was going to turn into the Société des Antiquaires de France. When, at mid-nineteenth century, Bouvard and Pécuchet plunged into Celtic archeology to learn about "les anciens Gaulois, nos aïeux," it was from these *antiquaires* and *érudits* that they drew their inspiration.

The topic might not have been so modish as to catch the attention of Gustave Flaubert's heroes if it had been left to *antiquaires* and *érudits* alone, which would have happened had Napoleon and his successors had their way. Unfortunately, as Catherine predicted, some of the Franks who made a comeback would not leave well enough alone. One in particular, the *ci-devant* Comte François de Montlosier, found it expedient to revise and publish in 1814 a work he had begun in 1804 at the behest of a Bonaparte, then still First Consul. The three-volume work branded most of Montlosier's fellow citizens as an alien race: freedmen, slaves wrested from their masters' hands, folk with whom the count's kind had nothing in common except, presumably, conflict. So the struggle between nobles and Third Estate became a tug-of-war between one ilk descended from free men and another, begotten by their subjects.[11]

Louis XVIII, like the First Consul, would have preferred to let sleeping races lie—or at least look on them as integrated, their conflicts settled, no longer relevant. But the Restoration was less an end to the Revolution than a counterrevolution, prelude to further revolutions. So the Restoration revived the political conflict quashed by Bonaparte and with it the search for historical justifications and metaphorical illustrations of the conflict.

The Ultras who rejected all of the Revolution forced relative moderates to defend it and to develop arguments that would legitimate not just particular gains, but the principle of revolution itself. It was in this context that the defenders of revolution, scrambling for arguments, recalled one argument almost inaudible in 1789, but which caught on much better a quarter-century later, because it fitted the romantic and national presuppositions of the new age: the Revolution as an ethnic conflict, the emancipation of conquered, subjugated Gauls, and their reassertion of their rights over oppressive Franks.

The theme surfaces in François Guizot, who was a historian before he became a political figure and described the Revolution as a real war between two hostile foreign peoples, a war in which the erstwhile vanquished finally turned the tables on the earlier victors. We hear it from La Fayette who, born near Le Puy, was proud of his Auvergnat origins. "I hope I am a Gaul," he wrote, "because very few Franks settled in the mountains of Auvergne. I prefer Vercingétorix defending his mountains to the brigand Clovis and his abominable successors." Not surprisingly, the secret society founded in 1832 that was to set off the bloody riot which followed General Maximilien Lamarque's burial called itself Société gauloise.[12] The tide of references lapped around other contexts—not least in Victor Hugo's *Notre Dame de Paris,* where the once-derogatory use of *gaulois* (as of Gothic) is turned around to glorify the old cathedral as truly *popular:* expressing native spirit, as opposed to fancy foreign styles.

The confrontation between Franks and Gauls appears most clearly and is most potently used in the work of a man largely forgotten today, yet tremendously influential in his time: Augustin Thierry. The bookshelves of Georges Clemenceau's country retreat at Saint Vincent sur Jard, in the Vendée, carry pristine bound sets of the works of Jules Michelet and of Henri Martin. Augustin Thierry's volumes are unmatched, and the disparate volumes show much sign of wear. We shall see how most political and intellectual figures of nineteenth-century France bore Thierry's mark, and had to take sides for or against his thesis. Enough for now to note the reaction of Alexandre Dumas when, in 1832, an old friend of his father's introduced him to the historian's work: "I read—wrong—I didn't read, I devoured the marvelous work . . . Then, without even having to open Chateaubriand . . . from the pen of Augustin Thierry grew a kind of new geography, each race flowed separately."[13]

Thierry, who was nineteen in 1814, had read Montlosier and had decided that the man, although an ideological foe, was right: "Internal war was postulated as a necessity of our history." He recognized that Montlosier was using a figure of speech to assert the claims of his privileged class, which Thierry calls a "nationalité privilégiée." But Thierry was himself an interested party in a debate that was far from academic, and he was persuaded that between his party, which stood for the present, and Montlosier's party, which stood for the past, there could be no reconciliation—only victory or defeat. "Always, whatever the form of events, there would be basically the same situation: two hostile people on the same land."[14]

Walter Scott's *Ivanhoe* (1819) is about the struggle of two hostile races,

Normans and Saxons, and their reconciliation. Thierry, though a great admirer of Scott, rejects reconciliation and hammers away at the racial antipathy that divides the French. Descended from the conquered, just like the Saxons in England, the Third Estate in France still had to wipe out the age-old conquest and avenge its defeat. Thierry's simile of two hostile peoples was meant to stoke the fires of conflict; the evidence suggests it did. And so it was that, against the Ultra challenge, a Gaulish nationality was officially claimed for Commons and Third Estate, and a racial metaphor became part of nineteenth-century revolutionary discourse and assumptions.

Historians know better than to think that historical doctrines have a lot of political influence. That is precisely why we must beware of dismissing historical arguments too lightly, especially when their veracity is irrelevant but their metaphorical punch is great. In the nineteenth century the division between amateur historians and professionals, between Gentlemen and Players, was not as deep as it is today (witness the records of Thiers and of Guizot), and a striking formula could have profound reverberations. Equally important, Augustin Thierry was not a mere study-bound intellectual. He was one of Saint-Simon's several secretaries, and wrote at least one of Saint-Simon's better books: the second part of L'Industrie entitled Politique.

I have no way of knowing if it was Thierry who suggested to the inventive count the analogy between gaulois and peuple that Saint-Simon uses several times; or if it was Saint-Simon (during the Revolution he had changed his name to Bonhomme) who reinforced Thierry in his race interpretations. A very serious witness, Duc Albert de Broglie, claims that it was Thierry who taught his generation the grounds for revolution.[15] At any rate, Thierry, one-time secretary to Saint-Simon, had a secretary of his own called Armand Carrel. It was through Thierry that Carrel met two other upwardly mobile young men, François Mignet and Adolphe Thiers, the three of whom a few years later founded the main liberal paper of the late Restoration, Le National, which helped to make (it was said to have made) the Revolution of 1830. It was Thierry, whom Carrel always regarded as his first master, who encouraged his young protégé to publish a History of Scotland that reflected Thierry's sympathies for conquered and oppressed races, as it did Carrel's belief that old struggles between races resurface in wars we euphemize as civil.[16]

Many will remember the unreconciled old aristocrat in Balzac's Cabinet des antiques, who dies after the Revolution of 1830 muttering "Les gaulois ont gagné!" And it is true that Gaulish symbols flourished under the July Monarchy, with roosters on top of flags, on the Arc de Triomphe, on the Colonne de Juillet, on the buttons and buckles of various figures of authority.[17] Gaulish cocks and Gaulish claims had been invoked by Hugo and by Béranger, they were going to be invoked by the provisional government of the Second Republic (on whose great seal a majestic lady is accompanied by a preening cock) as well as by those who challenged it. Written in 1850, when *démoc-socs* were groaning, Pierre Dupont's "1852" held out hope of better times: "C'est dans deux ans, deux ans à peine / Que le coq gaulois chantera . . ." (It'll take two years, hardly two years, for the Gaulish cock to sing.)

Most influential after Béranger, and much more explicit was Eugène Sue, about the only popular writer of the mid-nineteenth century to be widely read among the working classes.[18] In 1849 Sue began publication of *Les Mystères de peuple:* the tale of the Lebrenn family, dispossessed and enslaved first by Romans, then by Franks, and forced to reconquer their freedom bit by bit over the ages.

The *Mystères* were a political pamphlet: historical fiction shored up by authorial introductions that compared Franks and Cossacks, and by endnotes that urged readers to turn to the writings of Sieyès, Guizot, and especially of Thierry. The posh public ignored the work, the authorities more or less banned it, but workers seem to have read it. When, at the end of a long life of political struggle, Martin Nadaud—the mason from the Creuse, deputy in 1848, prefect in 1870—wrote his memoirs, he started out by tracing his family origins in the "great and powerful Gaulish race . . . enslaved by the double conquest of Romans and Franks."[19] Jean-Pierre Rioux, who edited Nadaud's memoirs in 1976, appears embarrassed by such *réminiscences livresques* about a "Gaulish race," and surprised by the number of working-class activists, even members of the Workers' International like Anthime Corbon and Benoît Malon, who were influenced by "curious theories about the permanent struggle between Celts and Franks."[20] It is almost as if these respectable working-class leaders had blotted their copybook by declaring a belief in Unidentified Flying Objects.

Yet it seems obvious that the race war metaphor, which fitted the preconceptions of the earlier nineteenth century, provided a convenient introduction to the subsequent formula of a class war. This must have become clear to Guizot, who soon turned the idea of race war into class war and the trial of strength between rival peoples into a struggle between contending classes. And I suspect that Marx, familiar with Thierry (whom he once called "Father of the Class War in French Historiography"), set out to stand the historian on his head as he claimed to have done with Hegel.[21] At any rate, we have no need to question the hold of race war theories on working-class leaders who had either read or read about Thierry's formulations; and who had almost certainly read Sue, as one can tell Nadaud had read him, because he cites him in support of his views.

But if working-class leaders should prefer Sue to Thierry, as the anarcho-syndicalist Emile Pataud preferred Alexandre Dumas to Karl Marx (and who could blame him?), there is another authority with which French socialists would be familiar, a man who had read Saint-Simon, Thierry and Guizot, and that was Pierre-Joseph Proudhon. His works are full of allusions to the basic ethnic conflict which, in Proudhon's view, was supposed to join the bourgeoisie to the people to which it belonged in pursuit of that revolution which they began together—but the bourgeoisie had failed and its task waited to be fulfilled by the people.

Beside Proudhon's works and casting a curious light on their spirit, is a letter he wrote from prison, when the Second Republic was on its last legs, to reproach Pierre Leroux for not being a true Gaul. George Sand's friend, Leroux, had the misfortune of being born on the banks of the Seine, not of the Doubs. But more than squabbles among rival revolutionists, Proudhon's words reflect a forgotten aspect of nineteenth-century discourse and belief. They also indicate how, given time, the message of race conflict could become a clarion call of class reconciliation that would be heard not only by Napoleon III, but in due course by the young leaders of the Action française.

> You have not heard as I have heard since childhood [writes Proudhon] the oaks of our druidic forests weep for the ancient fatherland; you do not feel your bones, kneaded out of the pure rock of the Jura, thrill in remembrance of our Celtic heroes, of Vercingétorix . . . you have not seen . . . Liberty appear to you under the traits of Velleda, the Gaulish maiden.
>
> You are not a son of Brennus: you cannot conceive that restoration of our nationhood which, beyond economic reform and the transformation of a degraded society, appears as the highest aim of the February Revolution.[22]

I shall not insist on the ease with which wars of national liberation can become wars of social liberation. What I mean to suggest is how the race war metaphor could be enlisted to a variety of ends, all highly significant in the gamut of political stances the French were to take up through the nineteenth century and, not least, at the fin de siècle. It is when a metaphor becomes a banality that it can prove most handy. It was used with increasing frequency by revolutionaries *and* reactionaries in 1789 and 1814, in the 1820s, thirties, forties, and fifties. It continued to be used because it could justify the continuation of a revolution that its enemies wanted to hobble, *or* the national integration with which revolutionaries triumphant, calling themselves republicans, eventually did hobble it, *or* eventually the counterrevolution of those who also wanted to transform a *société avilie* (degraded society) and revivify it with integrations and exclusions of their own.

Three examples should amply illustrate this Gallo-Frankish inheritance: that of the republican tradition, that of fin-de-siècle racism, that of the Action française. As in the Book of Genesis, it could be said that Augustin Thierry begat them all. The process is most striking (and least familiar) in the republican stream—or rather, in that republican delta where, by the end of the century, so many rivulets flowed together.

Let me begin with Jean Reynaud, who had been Hippolyte Carnot's alter ego when Carnot held the Ministry of Public Instruction of 1848. A Saint-Simonian who collaborated with Pierre Leroux in publishing the *Revue encyclopédique,* extremely influential among intellectuals, Reynaud was a fervent Gaulophile (or Celtomaniac), even mobilizing Mélusine, "cette illustre gauloise" (Jeanne Darc {sic} was another) in the national cause.[23] One of Reynaud's most faithful followers was Henri Martin, whose first serious work, published at twenty-three, was a history of France professedly modeled on the work of Guizot and Thierry; his second major book, in 1847, was dedicated to Jean Reynaud. Martin, who acted as the testamentary executor of Thierry, upon his death in 1856, became a major figure of republican historiography, of the Ligue de l'Enseignement, and of the Ligue des Patriotes. It would be around these organizations (especially the former) that the message of Gaulish ancestry was going to spread, carried not only by Henri Martin, but also and more so by a more attractive figure: that of Jean Macé.

Like many aspiring intellectuals of his generation, Macé, son of a carter, started out as a scholarship boy at the Lycée Stanislas. There he befriended another *boursier,* Jules Hetzel (whose father was a saddler). Both boys were taken under the wing of their history teacher, Theodore Burette, a close friend of Eugène Sue. Macé became Burette's "secretary," which really meant his research assistant and ghost writer through the 1840s. In 1848 he graduated to writing political tracts, populist, socialist, and patriotic. His *Petit Catéchisme républicain,* published that year, coined a phrase that republicans remembered for a long time: "Qu'est-ce que la Nation? C'est tout le monde."[24] Macé also collaborated with Hetzel, and sometimes with Jules Verne, in a number of popular publications—not least the *Magasin d'Education et de Recréation.* But history knows him best for his work on behalf of public libraries, of popular and adult education, above all for the Ligue de l'Enseignement which he founded.

The textbooks and periodicals published through the Hetzel connection (he had become an editor) spread the notion of Gaulish or "Celtic" patriotism—what a Marxist writer recently denounced as a *racisme primaire*[25]—

and when Hetzel pressed Macé himself for a simple, straight-forward history of France, Macé produced a short piece which Hetzel published by itself in 1881, under the title *La France avant les Francs*. It is a charming little book, in which Macé reasserts the true origins of France before its Frankish diversion.

We can therefore guess the kind of historical interpretation that the Ligue de l'Enseignement would favor. And it must be clear by now that this was not exceptional, at a time when many republican publicists, like Pierre Larousse for example, stood for Gaulish origins and a Gaulish populism that would speed French democratization.[26] What seems more interesting is how the Ligue, patriotic as well as populist in the tradition of romantic nationalism, reacted to the defeat of 1871. The men who made the Third Republic had grown up in the 1840s and 1850s (if not before). So it was the issues and inspirations of the Second Republic that had to be worked out in the Third. But if the 1880s and 1890s were marked by the patriotic populism of 1848, something new had been added by the experience of 1870: internationalism, pacifism, gave way to a humiliated and resentful activism, bolstered by suggestive references to Gaul's historical limits on the Rhine, and to a decadent Gaul conquered by barbarians from across the Rhine.

One aspect of Gaulish decadence were the internal dissensions associated with rebellious and destructive masses—those *barbares* so often denounced in 1848 and again in 1871. The analogy between savage, murderous rebels and the barbarian hordes that once destroyed Gallo-Roman civilization lived on into the Third Republic. But nationalism would redirect the focus once again on the German hordes from across the Rhine, and on the great task of national regeneration.

Popular education had been a republican priority since 1848, if not since 1789. In the 1880s it had to include physical and military preparation; and Macé, though he opposed a proposal to change his Ligue's name to Ligue des Patriotes, collaborated closely with his friend Paul Déroulède, who founded and led a league of that name. The fervently patriotic Déroulède had been brought up on nightly readings of French history and of Walter Scott.[27] Great admirer of Jean Reynaud (and probably, though we have no evidence for it, of Reynaud's Gaulish stories) he too expressed interest in reviving the conquering spirit of the ancient Gauls against contemporary Germans.[28] But Déroulède's vision of French history reflected less the confrontational teachings of Thierry than the integrationist version championed by Thierry's critics—among them Déroulède's great-grandfather, Charles Pigault-Lebrun.

That brings us to an influential variant of Thierry's conflictual metaphor: a model of invasion and conquest resolved and overlaid by time, assimilation, and integration. The first lesson to be drawn from French history, according to this version of it, was not race war but national synthesis. Under the leadership of men like Macé and Henri Martin, who eventually joined the Ligue des Patriotes, the Ligue de l'Enseignement urged the introduction in schools of military instruction, musketry training, and gymnastics. It also inspired the *programmes scolaires* that set the benchmarks for textbooks whose authors wished to use the national past to fortify the present and prepare the future. It was in this context that Hetzel published Macé's book on France before the Franks; but although "nos ancêtres les gaulois" constitutes the gist of his argument, that formula does not appear in it. It does not appear in the majority of schoolbooks of the Third Republic. Of one hundred and thirty I examined, one hundred and fifteen do not use either the locution, or any close variants. Nor does the great Lavisse ever use it.

The missing reference is easier to explain in the context of the rival tradition, publicly pioneered by Napoleon I, whose preferred founding hero was neither Vercingétorix nor Clovis but Charlemagne, the unifier: a tradition carried forward by Napoleon III, who patronized digs at Alésia but wrote a book on Caesar. Louis-Napoleon's last and greatest minister of education, Victor Duruy (who helped him write on Caesar), firmly believed that many races had joined to make the French people. Duruy's secretary and protégé had been Ernest Lavisse, of whom he wrote that "for the past thirty years I regard him as one of my children." In the fight between Gauls and Franks, Lavisse was a Roman or, better still, a Gallo-Roman like his patron Duruy.[29] And, obviously, Lavisse did not stand alone.

In the textbooks I examined, I often found qualified statements like "les gaulois nos premiers ancêtres," or "les gaulois nos vrais ancêtres."[30] This for the good reason that, by the 1880s, children were taught not conflict but reconciliation. If there had been conquest, something that is not always clear in the text, there was above all assimilation and integration. The fatherland was forged, the nation built, not by one race against another, but by a mixture of peoples. Romans civilized rude Gauls, Franks rejuvenated decadent Gallo-Romans. Thus the fulfillment of Gaulish claims Thierry and Sue had called for, the accomplishment of revolutionary efforts made in 1848 had been achieved, at least in textbooks. Gaulish swords were sheathed, Frankish axes buried. Just as the Third Republic claimed to have fulfilled the Revolution, so the *grands ancêtres* came together in its textbooks—although the Gauls were recognized as "nos *vrais* ancêtres."

This line of argument carried other advantages. The example of original ancestors—brave, inspiring, but primitive and uncouth—civilized by Rome and much better off as a result despite the discomforts of conquest, explained and rationalized the Third Republic's civilizing efforts in rural France, among them the education of the very children using the textbooks. It also justified the colonization of foreign peoples, especially the colonization of North Africa, which was also expected to benefit from French conquest, as France had gained from that of Rome. Conquest was painful but salutary and, in the spirit of the nineteenth century, progressive. Eugène Sue had already drawn the parallel between French and Roman imperialism.[31] Now this could be exploited, mostly by implication, sometimes explicitly, as in textbooks produced by historians of the left, but also in the writings of moderate republicans.[32]

But there is another, more directly political, aspect of the Gaulish tradition carried forward by Macé, Martin, and the Ligue de l'Enseignement. In 1848 the democratic party organized a committee to fight the elections of 1849 and called it Solidarité républicaine. The secretary of that committee was Jean Macé. Forty years later the president of Macé's Ligue de l'Enseignement would be Léon Bourgeois, who invented and preached the doctrine of Solidarity as the ideological program of the Radical party. *Solidarité* and *association* were key words of the 1848 left, which included not only Macé but also Proudhon, Charles Renouvier, and Jean Reynaud who (Jules Simon tells us) "believed in human solidarity and continued progress."[33] All were steeped in the literature of the Franco-Gallic school, for whom, as for Bourgeois, association was the prelude to reconciliation, and solidarity an equivalent of that fraternity without which the claims of liberty and equality could never be reconciled.

The Radical party of Bourgeois, Eugène Pelletan, and Georges Clemenceau was a direct heir of this 1848 tradition. From Gambetta's Belleville program of 1869, through Clemenceau's program of 1881, to the party declaration of 1905, the Radical program was going to reflect the basic principles of *quarante-huitard* republicanism. The revolution, whether in 1789 or in 1848, had not been made to establish some unimaginable dictatorship of the proletariat, but to open access to power to the Commons—synonym of Gaulish masses. Revolutions continued to be preached or made so that ever pettier strata of the bourgeoisie could accede to power, and ever lower social groups could accede to the bourgeoisie. The nation was everybody, everybody should have access to it. That, in 1848, had been the meaning of republicanism, of radicalism, indeed of Proudhonian socialism. That was what Jean Macé expressed in 1886: "Son of a carter, here I am, a senator. Am I of the people? Am I a bourgeois? That is the essence of democracy . . . no *castes*." Léon Bourgeois presumably expressed a similar view in his *Solidarité* of 1896, when he cited Proudhon as one of his predecessors and Macé's Solidarité républicaine as an inspiration.[34]

All this stresses the difference between radical and liberal thought. The latter, inspired by the Enlightenment, depicts progress as arising out of the spontaneous harmonization of diverse interests. The former, with its tinge of Jacobin interventionism, attributes progress to the will to draw the conclusions of national solidarity. Solidarity must be made to work by political action designed to repair injustice, create equality where inequality reigns, and deny no member of the national body access to education, association, perfectibility. In 1848 Charles Renouvier's *Republican Manual* had called for separation of Church and state, universal military service, fiscal reform, social insurance, worker associations, and cheap credit for people of modest means. The Radicals, who had branded their more moderate republican predecessors with opportunism, were going to be reproached with opportunism in their turn. Yet they must have felt that they had not done too badly by managing to carry out so many of the dreams of their youth (and of their mentors); not least the republic itself.

What has all this to do with Gauls and Franks? At first sight, nothing. A second look reveals rather more. Assertion of Gaulish descent stressed emancipation from servitude, or the need and moral duty to bring this about.[35] The political revolution of 1789 had been justified in these terms. Social revolt in 1848 was similarly justified. The congruence of early nineteenth-century Gallophiles with the republican, socialist, communist populists of 1848 is clear. The filiation between *quarante-huitards* and fin-de-siècle Radicals is suggested by one of Macé's pamphlets of 1848, *La Profession de foi d'un communiste,* which carries more than a foretaste of that *Solidarité* which Bourgeois, Bouglé and Gabriel Séailles sought to bring about. Credit, distributive justice, education, would seal Gaulish emancipation, establish a single national body within the borders of France, just because fraternal, fraternal because just.

Of course, the fin-de-siècle republic did not reign unchallenged, let alone undivided. Some of the challenges and divisions that it had to face also referred back to the race war analogy the Revolution ushered in. The most obvious instance of this is fin-de-siècle racism, which was a direct descendant of romantic history, even before a branch of this history allied itself with theories related to social conflict and to contemporary science or pseudo-science. I have already mentioned the Académie celtique and its offspring, the Société des Antiquaires de France. But Paul Broca, vicepresident of the Academy of Medicine, who died a senator of the republic after having formulated and institutionalized anthropology in France, had been a follower of Augustin Thierry. He would be denounced for it by

Vacher de Lapouge, who disapproved of Broca's national geology of successive races, one conquering and overlaying the other. A more up-to-date, allegedly more scientific, vision had the descendants of dark, small-brained, brachycephalic people reduced to servitude by blond dolicocephalic conquerors. Vacher did not like this version either, though he agreed that small-brained lowbrows had prevailed in France: "the first time in history that a brachycephalic people made itself autonomous," and this boded no good.[36]

More influential in his time than Vacher de Lapouge (whom Paul Valéry admired) was Jules Soury, the professor at the Collège de France whom Maurice Barrès liked to quote. Soury had picked up his notions of the national past from Ernest Renan, for whom he worked as "secretary" and ghost writer, and Renan thought very highly of Thierry and of Thierry's theories of race war, in which he saw "contemporary history brought to life."[37] A racial fundamentalist, Jules Soury is best known for his anti-semitism. He likened the invasion and conquest of France by Jews to the invasion and conquest of Gaul by the barbarians, and described both not as cause but as effect of French decadence. The barbarian invasions, thought Soury, had had a bracing effect in the long run. Perhaps the struggle against Jews would have the same effect, except for the fact that Jews were not opponents worthy of the Gallo-Romans, as the Germans were once and still remained.[38]

Less scholarly racists found romantic history a convenient pool to fish in. Stephen Wilson, who has written the most comprehensive study of fin-de-siècle antisemitism in France, cites Edouard Drumont as "one of the last proponents" of the two-races theory.[39] But Drumont is hard to pin down. In 1889 he pits Gauls against Germans all right, but in 1891 he appears to blame the Latin component of the French racial stew, and in 1914 he sounds as if, for him, real French history begins with the Crusades.[40] Less proliferous writers found consistency easier. When the cartoonist Adolphe Willette abandoned his Pierrots and Columbines to run as antisemitic candidate in 1889, the election poster he designed showed an ancient Gaul about to destroy the Golden Calf. Jean Drault, who founded the *Anti-Youtre* in 1891, called himself Noël Gaulois, the better to mark his national prejudices. More of an intellectual, certainly an aesthete, was Amadis Jacques de Biez, who helped found the Antisemitic League. He had learnt from Amédée Thierry (Augustin's brother) and Henri Martin that the French were not Latins but Celts, Gauls—like Christ Himself, who could not possibly have been a Jew.[41] In 1886 Biez's *La Question juive* coined the slogan "La France aux français," which was revived a century later by Jean-Marie Le Pen. Biez's book was dedicated to Drumont, whose *La France juive* appeared that same year; Drumont reciprocated in 1891 by dedicating his most anti-Latin book, *Le Testament d'un antisémite,* to Biez.

Like a great burr, the Jewish question and the prejudice it generates gathers around it whatever theoretical rationalization lies to hand, reactionary or revolutionary, social, Catholic or atheistic. No wonder, then, that racial theories brought grist to its mill. They could also generate equally fantastic identifications of Celts with Semites, the Gauls, like the Welsh, being no more than Phoenicians abandoned on a distant seashore: "colons, oubliés, méconnus et spoliés, de la race sémite."[42]

Less well known than antisemitism but more revealing of fin-de-siècle problems was the way in which the historical conflict of races was shifted to the regional level and made to reflect the rising tensions and antagonism between northern and southern France.

In the 1860s, Mistral and some of his friends had dressed the old conflict between north and south, langue d'oïl and langue d'oc, in more fashionable terms of race, to such effect that a northern *félibre* and leftist militant, follower of Thierry and of Henri Martin, had been moved to protest and to reassert the common Gallo-Roman ancestry of all the French.[43] But hostility to the republic, and to the alleged tide of southern politicians flooding into Paris, spurred a counteroffensive. Arguments of race were turned against meridionals who were denounced as alien and unFrench, less the Latins they liked to pretend than mixed breeds.

Professional antisemites like Biez, Jean Drault (who died in jail in 1951 after being condemned for collaborating with the Nazis), and Gaston Méry (who invented the term *raciste*) now turned their attention to the invasive southerners. In 1892 Gaston Méry published a novel called *Jean Révolte* with an epigraph, "Le Méridional, voilà l'ennemi." The book's back cover announced a forthcoming work by Drault and Méry to be called "La Gaule aux gaulois," and this slogan, along with the insistence that the Latin peril was as serious as the Jewish menace, provides the theme of the novel.

Jean Révolte, essentially, set out to rewrite the Thierry model of two antagonistic nations in one land. For Méry, the oppressed descendants of the Celts had been despoiled and beaten down by corrupt Latins (and their Jewish lackeys) who treated contemporary Gaul as a conquered country. The problems facing France rose not out from some fancied conflict between people and bourgeoisie, but from the domination of the Gaulish masses by a cosmopolitan elite. "The great social war of the fin-de-siècle will be not class war but race war." The revolt of native sons would restore "La Gaule aux gaulois." When Jean's *chartiste* friend objects that this slogan means nothing, since France is made up of superimposed races, including the Latin race, Jean replies that he knows his "formula" is false but does not care: enough for it to be "more or less true . . . it is a slogan." Boulanger, Gambetta, Drumont found success by using catchy slogans, why shouldn't Jean?[44]

Fascinated by the "celtisme intégral" of Jacques de Biez, Méry had written *Jean Révolte* in hope of a success that would bring him sales to match those of Drumont's *La France juive*. When the book fell flat, he accepted a job on Drumont's *Libre Parole,* just being launched in 1892.[45] Ignored by all, *Jean Révolte* would have sunk without trace, had it not been rediscovered a few years ago by Christian Amalvi.[46] The fact that Maurice Barrès owned a copy (alongside other works defending the Celtic tradition) probably reflects no more than the common Boulangist antecedents of Barrès and Méry. But knowledgeable readers will not be surprised to hear that, among a host of scapegoats he takes in stride, Méry also turned against the *école romane,* denouncing the likes of Jean Moréas and Charles Maurras as alien Moors.[47] This makes my point that the race metaphor could be used in a variety of ways. We must not let present attitudes, like our disgust with antisemitism, lead us to underrate the topical, circumstantial uses of race, of which the north-south antagonism provides a good example.

Méry also reminds us that racism is not an aberration but a natural point of view, easy to come by and attractive to use. Nineteenth-century usage tended to blur distinctions between race and profession (*la race des notaires*), race and class (*la race des paysans*), race and psychological type (*la race des avares*). It was easy to confuse nation (*race anglo-saxonne* or, as easily, *auvergnate*) or caste (*race des aristocrates*) with race, and endow all with allegedly peculiar characteristics. Identity should be identifiable. Like other contemporary writers, Balzac liked to establish social provenance by physical characteristics: the big feet of his low-class courtesans, the gentlemanly posture of Lucien de Rubempré who displayed the high arched foot of the Frank, the flat feet and thick neck of the *welche* Séchard.

Racism exaggerates and caricatures stereotyped characteristics, but it could not do this without references to some kind of substantive experience. And the first thing to remember about nineteenth-century racism is how evident, how often striking, differences were in those days: class, race, status, profession, regional provenance, were obvious in garb and in physique, in speech and behavior—far more so than today. So it is not surprising to find "race" invoked when people tried to explain history or current events, let alone when they tried to make a simple, attractive, political appeal.

The problem with racist arguments is not their plausibility. The problem, as we have seen, is that they can cut several ways. "La Gaule aux galois" would not appeal to proponents of broader national integration, let alone to the likes of Charles Maurras, whom it would exclude from the national community. Fortunately, by the 1890s, Gaulish exclusivism was on the wane. To show how this happened, I have to backtrack a bit.

When Philippe Buchez, the Christian Socialist who had been mayor of Paris and president of the National Assembly in 1848, wrote in 1859 about how the French nation had been forged, he complained that the mistaken thesis of conquered, subjected Gauls was being taught as the official version of national history.[48] But the postulate against which Buchez argued had never ruled unchallenged. Already in the 1840s Jules Michelet had broken from those he called *mes amis gaulois* to follow the trail of national integration. Under the Second Empire, the debate between partisans of Vercingétorix and those of Cesar heated up, with the deposed Louis-Philippe's son, the Duc d'Aumale, significantly taking the Gaul's side and Napoleon III the Roman's.[49]

Founding fathers are founding warriors. Picking the warrior hero to extoll as fountainhead of French history was an act fraught with politics, as legitimists knew who stood for Clovis; as republicans knew, for whom Vercingétorix symbolized not only populism and popular victory, but a demotion of monarchy in the national stakes. Like his master Napoleon III, Victor Duruy was well aware that scholarly research carried political overtones. It was for political as well as scholarly reasons that he disapproved of Henry Martin's Gaulish orientation. The extent of his displeasure was so great that when Martin died, he refused to stand for his academy seat for fear of having to sing his praises.[50]

Lavisse was not Duruy's only protégé. Another was Fustel de Coulanges, also a classicist, also hostile to Thierry's use of the past to comment on the present. Fustel had spent ten years teaching at the University of Strasbourg and was determined to match contemporary German academic domination of Roman history with a French research performance that would be even better. After 1870, this professional competitiveness took an out-and-out anti-German edge. Fustel thus emphasized the Roman contribution to Gallic culture and expressed his distaste for Frankish barbarians by admitting their destructive conquest but minimizing their effects. Four chapters of Fustel's magnum opus, first published in 1877, were devoted to showing how wrong Thierry had been. There had been no real conquest, no thralldom, no racial conflict. The French were ethnically mixed, but their cultural tradition was Latin, like their religion. Indeed, it was the Roman and Catholic tradition that took their captors captive and, in turn, Christianized and civilized the Germanic peoples as Rome had civilized the Gauls. There was no reason to criticize Latinity, now revealed as the source of French national character.[51] Attacks against it could be ascribed to German influence, a possibility seized with enthusiasm by Maurras and the Action française.[52] French unity, first forged by Rome, reforged by kings guided by the Church of Rome, was part of one long civilized tradition. As Louis Dimier concluded at the highly political celebration of Fustel's anniversary, which the Action française organized in 1905: "Thus no revolution at the origins of our history. No conquerors and no conquered. A quick fusion of the races . . . Peace among our dead."[53]

Why was the issue important? Why did it stay important for so long? In part it was because Thierry's version of French history, with its pattern of conquest and revolt, was recognized as a *Quatorze juillet littéraire* that ushered in, or justified, or inspired, the same tradition of conflict that the political events of July 14 had done.[54] *Théorie de guerre civile,* this "fatal legend"[55] had turned both history and the writing of history into "a sort of permanent civil war."[56]

The menace of past politics served up in a contemporary political sauce went beyond "mere" politics because, as Fustel understood very well, the *race* war theory concealed a theory—and magnified a reality—of *social* war. "It is," said Fustel, "born of class antagonism and it grows with that antagonism." A doubly dangerous opinion, therefore, and one that, just a few years after the Commune, "still weighs upon present society," spreading "nasty feelings of rancor and vengeance in people's hearts." Conceived in hatred, says Fustel, it perpetuates hatred—class conflict relaying and amplifying racial conflict.[57] The foundation of French political dissensions may not lie in historical interpretation, in "archeology," as Louis Dimier averred in 1905. But historical reference furnished their arguments and sharpened their barbs.[58] History, as revised by Fustel, was meant to blunt the conflict by turning it from intertribal warfare into a gigantic family quarrel.

That may be why Barrès insisted that the French were no race but a nation: *un pudding de pierre.*[59] And that is why, a quarter of a century after Barrès, the Action française's major historical statement, Jacques Bainville's *Histoire de France* (1924), began by affirming the assimilation and fusion of many races forming the French nation. Individuals, Barrès had taught, could adjust to the collectivity most readily, most "naturally," if their roots plunged into an ethno-cultural past that helped determine their true personality in the present. Nationalism was the acceptance of a determinism. But were the determining factors Celtic, Roman, or Germanic? Now, at last, two centuries of dispute were being reconciled—in historiography, but also in the schoolbooks and the public discourse that forge a people's consciousness. The answer was: all of the above. "La paix entre nos morts," as Dimier had said.

But peace in France is reserved largely for the dead; the living pursue their quarrels and controversies. French history continues to reflect and affirm political divisions as in the days of Thierry and Fustel, and historiography keeps on inscribing present politics retrospectively onto its versions of the past. The war between Franks and Gauls has died out, it is true, but only to be replaced by war between Gauls and Gauls. Curiously, as late as 1985, a *Fête gauloise* to benefit Le Pen's National Front featured the slogan: "La Gaule aux gaulois."[60] *Nos ancêtres* may be fading away, but in France the dead live longer than in other places.

2

Left, Right, and Temperament

Left and right. What is what? Who belongs to which? A question, here, of categories, definition, classification, so commonplace that we scarce give it a thought. Walter Theimer's *Encyclopedia of World Politics* tells us that left-wing parties are the progressive parties whose representatives usually sit on the left-hand side when viewed from the president's chair. The *Petit Larousse* explains "les partis les plus avancés siègent à l'extrême-gauche." But what, after all, is an "advanced" party? The position has become more ambiguous since the days of the Constituent Assembly in which "the progressives sat on the left, the moderates in the centre, and the conservatives on the right." Moderates may still sit in the centre, but on the wings the position is more nebulous and the distribution of the political spectrum increasingly uncertain.

Did Perón belong on the right because he was a dictator, or the left because much of his power rested on the unions? Should a nationalistic dictator like Nasser be on the right, or does his radicalism, his reformism, place him on the left? Does dictatorship automatically assign a man, a party, a regime, to the right and, if so, what do we do about Stalin or Tito? Does radicalism or revolution provide an automatic definition of the left, or does it allow for Kemal Ataturk and Nasser? We see there can be revolutions of the left and right, dictatorships of the left and right, planned economies of the left and right.[1] Can we find the criterion of the left in its popular appeal, its reliance on universal suffrage? But the most reactionary demagogues rely on popular appeal; and plebiscitarian dictatorships, like that of Napoleon III, like that of Hitler, rest on universal suffrage. We know at least, or think we know, that the left tends toward change and the right prefers to conserve: this puts Ataturk on the left, with Hitler and Porfirio Díaz, and Franco, Baldwin, Salazar, Poincaré, and Churchill in the same right-wing basket.

It would seem, in effect, that the label is smudging. We continue to use it but no longer know, cannot possibly know for sure, quite what it covers, quite what we mean. Even more than "big and small," "good and bad," left and right have become a matter of judgment not of fact, a matter of taste not definition. Unlike "big and small," however, scale only serves to confuse the issue for, while the bigger is more obviously big, more obviously different from the small, the extreme right is less obviously different from the extreme left. In politics, the two extremities have many things in common, and since when we talk of right and left we often think of the extreme examples that supposedly embody their most significant characteristics, it follows that by referring to the areas where these features are most confused, we merely make confusion worse.

All this is particularly true of France, where, notoriously, the nomenclature of political parties and figures has not kept up with changes in their orientation, in their nature, and in the nature of the country and its problems.

Men of the right—André Malraux, Pierre Mendès-France, Guy Mollet? Men of the left—Rochefort, Clemenceau,[2] Pierre Poujade? Parties of the right—governmental, respectful of the established order of things— the Radicals and the Socialists? Parties of the left—parties of the opposition—the Gaullist party of yore? And where does the traditional political vocabulary leave a party like the M.R.P. (Mouvement républicain populaire), both democratic and Catholic? Doctrines of the left or doctrines of the right: is it a *politique d'abord* that we might as well ascribe to Edouard Herriot as to Charles Maurras, a *France seule* which Communists evoke almost as often as nationalist demagogues, a Manifest Destiny touted in socialist congresses and capitalist banquets? Even the communist issue, far from simplifying matters, increases our perplexity and that of the French: Not all anticommunists are on the right, nor does the anticommunism of the right prevent its also hating the enemies of communism—Britons, Americans—or casting its votes along with the communist foe.[3] We know, indeed, that anticommunism has further confused the situation by driving all parties and opinions into a heterogeneous muddle which might almost have been designed to prevent a clear approach or solution to any problem.

This situation, this confusion, this obsolescence of categories and terminologies in current use, is not new. It can be traced back to the prewar years: to the establishment of the Radical party in moderate positions that suited both its parliamentary leadership and its middle-class electorate; and to the division of the erstwhile extreme left after 1920 between generally uncompromising Communists and increasingly moderate Socialists. To the satiated middle class, whose members had voted left not so many years before, first as a matter of political interest then as a matter of habit, the twenties and even more the thirties brought a great fear of communism that

made the right appear less obnoxious.[4] Less obviously, this reaction also
affected Socialists and syndicalists, whose anticommunism prevented any
enduring reunion of the left even when the Communists showed a concil-
iatory temper.[5] But the Socialist party's anticommunism did not reassure
erstwhile middle-class allies, suspicious of its economic doctrines and
repelled by its pacifism. Indeed, after 1917 or 1918, the pacifism of the left,
unwilling or less willing to squeeze the German lemon until the pips
squeaked, played no small part in its loss of sympathizers among a population for whom, all through the twenties, Germany and Germany's friends
were deeply suspect. In fact, some observers have inclined to attribute the
marked decline of the left after 1919 to this difference between the foreign
policy it advocated and the less enlightened sentiments of the French electorate.[6] We shall see that its causes lay farther back than that.

The issue of foreign policy, however, had a further complicating effect.
For, after 1932, all parties on all sides divided within themselves on the
policy to be followed toward the fascist powers; and toward Germany in
particular after 1936. The lines of political demarcation became increasingly blurred as "progressives," "reactionaries," and "conservatives" strad-
dled party lines over Abyssinia, Spain, and Munich. Socialists, Radicals,
and Conservatives split into "hard" and "soft" cliques[7], and after 1940 the
further division between resisters, collaborators, and wait-and-seers created
new groupings and orientations which, at least in the forties, seemed much
closer to reality than the classic labels of the past.

Considering the French political situation in the summer of 1946,[8] Jacques Fauvet concluded that "categories of right and left seem decidedly
obsolete." His opinion was shared by François Goguel, whose now classic
Politique des partis sous la 3e République (1946) proceeded on the basis of a
chronic division of French public opinion into two opposed families of
political temperaments. By 1951, Goguel had decided that 1946 marked
an end of the classic dualism of right and left.[9] With this, writers of the
right have long agreed. They had never ceased recruiting friends and readers
in circles of the traditional left and we have the word of one of the leading
intellectuals of the "new right," Philippe Ariès, that the postwar positions,
of left and right no longer make any sense at all.[10]

Yet as even the last few sentences bear witness, right and left continued
to be used to describe traditional characteristics, tendencies, and alignments—self-explanatory terms, which speaker and hearer, writer and
reader assumed as sufficient and valid. How confidently this was accepted
can be seen from a book like that by Jean Labasse—*Hommes de droite, hommes
de gauche* (1947)—which begins by asserting the existence of an "esprit de
droite et un esprit de gauche." If you compare governments of left and

right, argues Labasse, you cannot mistake the contrast of two economic policies, two social policies, two colonial policies, two educational policies, two foreign policies. There are minds of the right and minds of the left, spiritual structures of the right and spiritual structures of the left, and the division between them is as clear as that between blue- and brown-eyed people.

This is an attractive argument, conveniently schematic and appealing to what, since the nineteenth century, has become an established habit or point of view. Its flaws appear when one tries to define the two types. According to Labasse, (pp. 16–17) "the man of the right . . . prefers . . . to identify with liberalism rather than liberty . . . Mistrusting liberty, he may look favorably upon the so-called authoritarian regimes." A judgment such as this applied by 1958 as much to most Radicals as to Independents, increasingly also to the M.R.P., but only in part to the supporters of the old R.P.F., although it fitted the men they elected in 1951.

On the other hand (p. 13), "the spirit of the left is about protest and revendication against what is established . . . the spirit of the right, on the contrary, is about certainty, dogmatic assurance, anonymous constancy, respect." Yet the left-wing spirit so defined was to be found in the urban adherents of the R.P.F., in many Poujadists, and in part, though a shrinking part, of the M.R.P. It fitted only a small fraction of the Radical *marais,* and hardly at all an S.F.I.O. (Section française de l'Internationale ouvrière) *travailliste,* though it might well apply to many militants of the new U.N.R. (Union pour la nouvelle République). *L'esprit de droite,* on the other hand, describes the Communist party much better than many moderates, or the disenchanted adherents of the new right in 1957–58.

To continue, the chief characteristic of the left is said to be its love of, its identification with, the cause of freedom: "since the Revolution [this cause] definitely belongs to it . . . [Freedom] of nations like that of citizens. This is why only the man of the left knows how to speak of freedom." He does it, unfortunately, in a language that Africans abroad and political opponents at home fail to understand. We might compare these textbook definitions with the resolutions of the dissident Radical congress, meeting at Asnières in April 1957,[11] which called for the extension of military activity in Algeria and denounced in words worthy of Saint-Just "treason either open or insidious." We might compare them also with the Algerian policies of Socialist-led governments and with an endorsement of repression and war that could hardly be designed to further the cause of liberty—*celle des nations comme celle des citoyens.*

There is no profit in thus nagging poor Labasse, unless it serves to make clear the difficulties involved in using such vast, vague terms in vast, vague, undefined ways. A solution may be to update the traditional division or distribution of political parties. Labasse, for instance, considered the Radicals a party of the left, and this also seemed to be the feeling of Albert Milhaud in his *Histoire du radicalisme* (1951). Yet almost a century ago, Ernest Picard, a prejudiced but not uninstructed judge, held a different opinion. "The Radicals," he said, "are not a party but a coalition: they represent a way of getting on." [12] The resolutions of the party congress of 1904, drawn up by no less a man than Maurice Sarraut but less reminiscent of Gambetta than of Mr. Dooley, declare that the Radicals are against laissez-faire but for private property and also in favor of the state's rights to interfere in the relations between capital and labor. Juggling such as this leads one to think that when Edouard Herriot wrote that "to be radical is to revere reason" [13]; "to revere rationalization" would have been nearer the mark.

Pace Picard, not all Radicals were on the make; but few still consider them as belonging to the left. As *Le Monde* once remarked, the followers of Queuille and André Morice took up the positions of the "classic right." And the position of Mendès-France was not as clear, at least in French eyes, as one might think. [14]

If that is so, perhaps the left should begin with the Socialists? But, says Jacques Fauvet, even before the war "the Socialist party had become radical . . . From one end of France to the other, and even within the same province, [the party] forms the most diverse and self-contradictory alliances. It is less interested in *being* than in *having.*" [15] Dire words, which time was to bear out. Nor need Mollet's policies surprise those who remember the Jacobin heritage of the maire of Arras, and the patriotic tinge of Parisian socialism, on the whole more à la Rochefort than à la Marx. [16] There is no sense in forgetting, as we do all the time, the close connection between socialism or syndicalism and nationalism in circles where Proudhon and Sorel are still very much alive. But nationalistic and patriotic affirmations have, since 1944, been the staple of all parties beginning with the Communist—which is, of course, a complicating factor when one tries to sort out the attitudes peculiar to this group or that. At any rate, to the extent that the S.F.I.O. represented anything in 1959, it was labor—not the laboring class, for it was rather a party of school teachers, civil servants, and "bourgeoisified" industrial workers—but something like the *travaillisme* of the British Labour party, only a *travaillisme* without many *travailleurs*.

Torn between the nostalgia of a radical past in the opposition and the necessities of a moderate present in the governmental coalition, the Socialists bring to mind the M.R.P. trying to combine the heritage of Marc Sangnier and of the Catholic Church, an electorate that is primarily Catholic with intellectual cadres that are primarily progressive. There are the internal contradictions that lead us to find an M.R.P., often classed with the S.F.I.O. to the left of centre, taking up intransigent nationalistic positions over Indochina with Georges Bidault, as the Socialists did over Algeria with Mollet and Lacoste. We also find it collaborating with former Vichy supporters and surviving staffers of *Je Suis Partout* in the cause of an European Union and an E.D.C. (European Defense Community) that Socialists and Gaullists agreed in opposing. Is this mere coincidence? Is the M.R.P. really a party of the left? The right-wing press claims it is something else,[17] and the conjunction of Popular Republicans and dissident Gaullists in the investiture of Antoine Pinay leads one to think it may be right. Another reason to doubt the *gauchisme* of the M.R.P. is its attitude toward General de Gaulle. In the investiture vote of June 2, 1958, while only 42 Socialists out of 95 voted for the government which included both Mollet and Pflimlin, 70 out of 74 Popular Republicans cast their ballots in its favor. If this is any indication, we might conclude that while the S.F.I.O. is more than half left, the M.R.P. is almost all right.

But, once again, the difficulty lies in determining just what is right (or left). In his brilliant essay, *Les Français et la République* (1956), Charles Morazé suggested that, when you come down to brass tacks, the partisans of the right "prefer one man's authority."[18] As for the left, that defines itself by its opposition to such regimes of the right. If this suggestion is valid, then we should find the vote of June 2, 1958—a vote in which "l' autorité d'un seul" was very much at issue—helpful in determining the orientation of different parties. And, to some extent, this was actually so. The Communists, for instance, voted massively against General de Gaulle; the centrist Rassemblement des Gauches Républicaines (R.G.R.), M.R.P., Independents, Poujadists, and of course Social Republicans voted pretty solidly for him.[19] In between, however, things were far less clear: thus 42 Socialists voted for, 49 against, while 3 abstained; 24 Radicals voted for and 18 against; 10 U.D.S.R. (Mitterand's Union démocratique et socialiste de la Résistance) voted for, 4 against, and 6 abstained. Hence, according to Morazé's definition, the left is really certain only within communist ranks.

If, as the Fourth Republic neared its end, the limits of the left were debatable (or shrinking), may we conclude, at least, that the General's supporters belonged to the right? Yes, if all we want is a label under which to lump them. No, if understanding is our aim, for there was little enough in common between the members of this disparate group. The M.R.P., as we saw, had taken up an intransigent attitude over Indochina; the R.P.F. eventually condemned the Indochinese imbroglio and supported the attempts of Mendès-France to extricate the country from that disastrous war. The M.R.P. supported the European Defense Community, which was supported also by the extreme right, but attacked by the R.P.F. Many M.R.P. votes come from conservative Catholic quarters which have little in common with the brand of authoritarian or technocratic radicalism that characterized many of the General's followers between 1947 and 1952, still less with the reactionary Jacobinism of Poujadist electors; and differences like these may be found all along the line.

Some of the majority in 1957 and 1958, as in 1959, were technocrats, élitists, eager to hoist France into the modern world; others were democrats, reactionary in the most utter sense of the term, resentful of modern institutions and techniques that threatened their social position and their living. Further, many Gaullists and most Poujadists were antiparliamentary, while R.G.R. and M.R.P. defended the parliamentary system. In any case, the antiparliamentary wave that broke in Algiers on May 13 was not the creation or preserve of the right alone. Antiparliamentarism is as useful to the Communists, who have frequently invoked it, as to the authoritarian right. The General himself was no antiparliamentarian and declared his belief that government must be responsible to Parliament and that the source of power lies in universal suffrage.[20]

It would appear that antiparliamentarism can be of two kinds: authoritarian-progressive, as in the early days of a Boulangism with radical undertones; in the Gaullism of 1947, 1951, 1958; even in some of the hopes set on the Mendèsism of 1954–1956; or reactionary-defensive, as in the Action française or in Poujadism. Each of these categories, in turn, might be said to have a Jacobin and an elitist side, the one stressing democracy, the other stressing authority. But there is yet a third variant, represented by the opportunistic *ralliement* of Orléanists who transferred their loyalties from king to Parliament because the latter promised the political stability that was their main concern. Stability is still the main concern of their latter-day successors, and to defend their vested interests, social and economic, such men would not hesitate to abandon Parliament, and even the republic, for a more satisfactory form of government. In other words, though some of the General's support was idealistic or doctrinaire, much was opportunistic or *faute-de-mieux*. This does not make it unimportant, but alters its significance and indicates the friability of his endorsement.

For instance, among the Algerian *colons,* the General's support stemmed from a typical reactionary-defensive movement of the extreme right.[21] In metropolitan France his success may be visualized in terms of the traditional appeal in a crisis to nationally known figures with no *immediate* political attachments: Gaston Doumergue in 1934, Pétain in 1940, de Gaulle in 1958. Not necessarily an *appel au soldat,* this was rather an abdication (or opportunistic abandonment of tools that no longer serve their purpose) in favor of the plebiscitarian *caudillo,* of Bonapartism in fact if not in name.

But, if this is so, it should remind us of the other part of the *caudillo's* support and intentions—efficiency, reform, productivity, all extolled by the soldiers, technocrats, engineers of the right, opposed by the small shop-keepers, *colons,* peasant leaders and such. This contradiction within a possible right-wing coalition was apparent under the Second Empire, it was apparent at Vichy, it was apparent in 1959.

The dominant party in the first legislature of the Fifth Republic was the U.N.R. In the second and decisive ballot of the November 1958 elections it secured 4,769,052 votes, or 26.4 percent of the total, half a million more than the Moderate runners-up (23.6 percent), and over a million more than the Communists, who came in third place with three and three quarter million votes, or 20.7 percent of the votes cast.[22] But the 189 metropolitan deputies who carried its colors in the new Assembly had little in common beyond their allegiance to a father-figure who would not accept to be their leader. There were in their ranks liberals and reactionaries, regular officers, technocrats, colonialists, republicans and long-time opponents of the republic, men who sympathized with Pétain and men who fought him, men who served de Gaulle and men who opposed him, men who talked very much like fascists and men who had every mark of the conservative.

But if their coloring is manifold and their provenance diverse, their language is united in one respect: it is nationalistic. The interest, unity, and greatness of France pass before every other consideration. Yet this merely begs the question: the question of how such aims are to be achieved and, further, whether their pursuit will lead the U.N.R. toward their Moderate neighbors and the attitudes and policies of conservatism, or toward something else that the classic right cannot quite cope with.

There is, however, a clue for us in the nationalism of the U.N.R. and of an electorate that voted so many of its candidates into power. The tendency of French nationalists over the last century or so has been to form anti-party parties that attempt to unite or supersede all existing "factions." Whatever else this shows, it implies that their following is dissatisfied with existing parties—their structure, their doctrines, and their programs—and ready to seek satisfaction outside existing political avenues. Nationalistic movements sprang up in the Third Republic in the eighties around Georges Boulanger, in the nineties around the heroes of the Dreyfus affair, in the yeas before 1914 around Raymond Poincaré, in the thirties around Colonel de la Rocque and various rival but lesser proto-fascist leaders. Weak as they were in the nineteenth century, the twentieth finds the nationalists more numerous and politically effective; the Fourth Republic was strongly affected by them and they dominate the Fifth.

We may deduce that the growing power and significance of nationalistic movements is due to the increasingly unsatisfactory character of the available means of political expression, and this, in turn, to changes in the social and economic structure which had generated the classic political alignments and to which these were adapted. Contemporary studies of Asia and Africa suggest that the decay of traditional social and economic structures has played an important part in the development of their nationalistic movements. The same may be true of France, where the years to 1959 have seen an important socioeconomic revolution and the growth of a new class not catered for by existing political arrangements. J. H. Clapham argued that an "industrial revolution" began in France somewhere about the year 1895.[23] This, together with the more widespread political and economic developments that prompted both Georges Sorel and Edouard Bernstein to rethink the ideas of Karl Marx, accelerated the "embourgeoisation" of the proletariat, and over the years reversed the balance of forces on which Marx and his followers relied for the eventual success of the left. Although it has received little attention, this gradual integration of the "outs," of the economically underprivileged, does much to explain the rightward drift of Western politics in our time. However, the lower middle class it helped produce was, quantitatively, a new social phenomenon made up of working people on their way up the socioeconomic ladder and bourgeois on their way down (even if only relatively so). For these people, the class-conscious arguments of the classic left had no more appeal than the contented self-congratulations of conservatism. They were not satisfied with things as they were, but shunned the prospect of a proletarian revolution.

Unable to fit into existing political divisions which did not reflect their needs or aspirations, they rejected both and, ideologically speaking, tried, like Alphonse de Lamartine, to *siéger au plafond* (sit with the gods)—above the inessential struggle of factions which, meaningless to them, were considered *ipso facto* harmful to France. Here we have the roots of what, eventually, was labelled fascism and what, as a rule, provides the nationalist appeal. The new slogan would be unity, above and beyond parties. Mussolini said as much when he wrote the Doctrine of Fascism in 1932, but fifty years earlier the statutes of the Ligue des Patriotes had expressed the same idea: "Republican, Bonapartist, Legitimist, Orléanist, these are merely forenames. The family name is patriot." Barrès, Drieu la Rochelle, Maurras, de Gaulle, all heartily agree.

The nationalist ideology, in other words, although it has many affinities with that of the classic right (which is why when it wanes or fails its troops generally go to swell the numbers of the latter) is neither left nor right. It is part of the attempt to cut out new political avenues—to forge doctrines fitted to the changing realities of the sixty or seventy years before 1959. Its apparent confusions are due to the fact that the vast and growing group to which it appeals, the displaced persons of twentieth-century politics, are not a united whole, but divided into those who are clawing their way upward and those making desperate efforts not to slip down. But in the minds of men like de Gaulle or Michel Debré it becomes an ideology of movement; and Jacques Soustelle's picture of the U.N.R. as a party of movement is justified at least by his own hopeful concept: "France's economic and social evolution detaches ever greater numbers of the people, of wage-earners and urban workers, from the old formulas of Right versus Left. The country is ready to support a rational policy of [economic] expansion, with its corollary of social progress and its extension to ever more numerous sections of the population."[24] This may, of course, mean anything. Conservatives have talked like that and so have fascists. It is, however, an excellent example of the limitations of existing categories and labels, for it shows the difficulty of classifying a policy like Soustelle's.

So the right is not monolithic, neither is the left, and no slogan, label, or program can be so identified as to avoid all confusion. The Jacobin vocabulary and Jacobin mystique can be found at both extreme left and right. So can technocracy, so can elitism, so, indeed, can nihilism. There are communist peasants and independent ones; socialist shopkeepers, Gaullist and Poujadist ones; communist, Catholic, and Gaullist proletarians, intellectuals, and engineers. There are authoritarians of the right and left, imperialists of the right and left, "Europeans" and anti-Europeans of the right and left, enemies of communism and Americanism on both sides, enemies of the Church, of capital, and of the state. Can we, if this is so, find a more reliable criterion to replace the old, so confusingly, so strikingly, out of date?

Daniel Lerner suggests one possibility when he explains that "there exists in France a pervasive political sentiment called *gauchisme*. It is a sentiment because it entails no specific judgments on specific issues, but expresses rather a diffuse general hostility to the powers-that-be and things-as-they-are."[25] This is vague enough and vast enough, but does not help because on its terms communism and Poujadism have to be lumped together as they are by the simple *concierge* who, in casting her vote for Poujade, believed she was voting, as usual, to the left. The same holds true for the economic explanation, considered far more respectable but revealing itself no more helpful, since the industrial worker who seeks reform and the marginal shopkeeper who fears it have even less in common than the syndicalist and his employer, both of whom are at least part of the same world. Even so, a common interest in production does not range industrialist and proletarian side by side, a common poverty does not unite *travaillistes* and *poujadistes,* the common defense of property and private enterprise does not warm the small Jacobin or radical shopkeeper toward the great capitalist that drives him out of business.

Charles Morazé makes another distinction: "France of iron—France of the right. France of coal—France of the left."[26] But there is little congruence between the map he gives to prove his point and the seats gained by Poujadists in the elections of January 2, 1956. As in other instances, the crux of our difficulty is provided by what used to be the party of Poujade, hard to place on left or right. And this awkwardness becomes even more apparent when comparing Poujadist successes in the 1956 elections with the traditional political orientation of the regions where these victories were won. Of the six departments in which Poujadists obtained over 20 percent of the total vote, we find Isère, Vaucluse, and Gard to have been traditionally on the left since the 1870s, while Maine-et-Loire and Aveyron had been just as steadily on the right.

It may be argued that Poujadism was a passing phenomenon and that when it disappears, as it has in the elections of November 1958, its confusing influence must disappear as well. But while Poujadism itself may have passed, the attitudes it reflected will not disappear so soon. For Poujadism, transitory movement for a transition period, represented the struggles of marginal businessmen and cultivators against forces that endanger their livelihood, their values, their position in society. And it represented, too, one aspect of the French character, confronted with problems it cannot or will not understand, being dragged kicking and screaming into the twentieth century. There is nothing new in saying that most Poujadist votes were protest votes—the same has been said of the Communists.[27] The difference is that the communist doctrine and tone were fundamentally modern and optimistic—and this they shared with certain parties of the right, with the old R.P.F. and with the new U.N.R.—while the Poujadists were pessimistic and entrenched in an obscurantism that placed sentiment above reason.

It is true that, in effect, the old R.P.F., the short-lived U.D.C.A. or U.F.F. of Pierre Poujade, and the startlingly successful U.N.R., all appear as sentimental popular movements, popular leagues promising action. But that their strengths are different can be seen from the fact that the first drew most of its votes from the more dynamic parts of the country, the second found its support south of the Loire in the poorest and least productive areas, while the last, heir of the R.P.F. though it be, has taken something from both. The R.P.F. and U.F.F. reflected the problems of a transitional movement: the difference lay in the mood with which they faced them, a mood that enabled the one to dissolve as it did into already existing progressive or conservative channels, while the other could not. The hopeless quest, the insoluble problem of Poujade and his followers had to express itself in an explosive way. They disliked the present and refused the future. They defied the new world but could not live with it as opportunists can. And this is why their violence, their so-called Jacobinism, differed from the traditional brand familiar to the left.

Poujade, Stanley Hoffmann has told us, proposed a revolutionary revival: "le retour à l' idéologie révolutionnaire, au langage révolutionnaire." He appealed to the people and to the spirit of 1789.[28] But a neofascist journal, *Fidélité,* let the cat out of the bag: in February 1956, the organ of the Phalange française told its readers that the movement of St. Céré was the first and only in ten years to stir the cockles of its heart. "Pierre Poujade a l'âge de beaucoup des membres de la Phalange . . . Son langage violent, qui atteint le peuple sans effort, est le nôtre; c'est celui d'une génération qui a lu L. F. Céline"; a generation that read Céline and learned his nihilism, his hopelessness, his anger. In other words, action for action's sake, revolution for revolution's sake, here lies the difference between Poujadists on the one hand, Jacobins or Communists on the other; here, also, their similarity with Henri de Montherlant who, in *Le Solstice de juin,* declares that "Le combat sans la foi, c'est la formule à laquelle nous aboutissons forcément." And the evolution of Poujade himself, first elected R.P.F. councillor of St. Céré on a Radical list, friendly with his Communist colleagues on the council, brings to mind on a more intelligent though less effective plane the story of Drieu la Rochelle and his friends, turning this way and that, to communism, to fascism, to every—and ever more desperate—means of *action.*

Morazé has noted how in the south of France, where Poujadists have been most successful, the taste for extreme positions is often stronger than the attachment to left or right. Thus, a violently extremist right can wean extreme leftists from an allegiance or a leadership they judge to be too moderate. This seems to be borne out by the loss of communist votes in the very districts where the party of Poujade did well in 1956, especially west, southwest, and southeast.[29] However, we have seen enough by now not to let ourselves be tempted by schematic divisions. It is useful to interpret France in terms of iron and coal, north and south, east and west, fringes and centre; to contrast the dynamic north and east with the static country south of the Loire, to argue that there are differences between what used to be the Occupied Zone and the rest, or between the urban and the rural temper.[30] All such contrasts can be suggestive, as long as we do not let one of them take over and, alone, lead us astray.

Yet these categories and divisions persist; people continue to use them. They do so because, even obsolete, they still reflect certain differences and also because, though existing categories may be clumsy, nothing more convenient exists. Attempts have been made to devise new, more accurate, categories of political temper, temperament, or inclination. None so far seem to have caught on, but they do represent the results of the best thought on the question and may give us the answer, or at least a part of the answer, we seek.

André Siegfried's *Tableau des partis en France* (1930) sketches three major political tendencies: a left, republican and favorable to the little man; a right which defines itself by opposition to the left; and a capacious center whose essence it is to be governmental "and even more (yes, I think that is the true axle), [to seek] the preservation of the social order within the republican setting." A simple pattern of this sort is flexible and inclusive. However, on reflection it would seem that its definition of the left is cut to the measure of a Radical party that, even in the thirties, already belonged to the center. It ignores the Marxist left. As for the center's concern for the "cadre républicain," 1940 showed it to be of the mildest and so, perhaps, did 1958. Siegfried's generalization presents additional difficulties: in its terms Poujadists belong both left and right, Socialists both left and center, and many Gaullists, especially of the 1947–1951 brand, can straddle all three divisions. Not an inappropriate result perhaps in terms of the contemporary scene, but hardly wrought by a precision tool.

In 1932, Albert Thibaudet in *Les idées politiques de la France* selected six ideological "families": traditionalism, liberalism, industrialism, social Christianity, Jacobinism, and socialism. For Thibaudet, this system runs the gamut from conservatives on the extreme right, through the more broadminded, flexible, forward-looking liberals, past the new type of modern industrial capitalism ("a political system whose political point of view is subordinate to that of production"), past the Christian Democrat who tries to reconcile progressivism with a Catholic faith that in the thirties still defined men as un-left, through Jacobinism (mostly Radicals—"le parti de la Révolution") to the Socialists at the other extreme. At that time Socialists were, or purported to be, pacifists, and Thibaudet explains (p. 205) that "le socialisme seul est à peu près pacifiste." This would exclude a fraction of today's S.F.I.O. from that particular family. But there are other, more serious, difficulties about this scheme: for one thing, where does the extreme right fit in, the party of those who, in the words of Jacques Chardonne, "n'aiment que les trains qui partent?" Nor, in fact, does it seem that any of the present parties, except perhaps the M.R.P., would find its place clearly foreordained within the families of Thibaudet.

More recently, Morazé has proposed five tendencies drawn upon a more classic pattern: extreme left, left, center, right, and extreme right. Handy for following the evolution of parliamentary coalitions, this kind of classification tends to break down for the same reasons that apply to Siegfried and Thibaudet. Where Morazé is concerned, first R.P.F., then Poujadists, occupy the extreme right. In 1959 it would probably have been the U.N.R. But we have seen that none of these are necessarily the expression of classically right-wing attitudes.

An earlier work, Goguel's *Politique des partis,* had fallen back on only two political "temperaments" and sought to classify all variations within one of these two groups: that of established order, and that of movement. The fundamental division of outlook between the two derives from the fact that while members of the former take a pessimistic view of human nature and capacity to achieve the good life, adherents of the latter are optimists. This not only seems to place Liberals in the party of movement (and Christians *ipso facto* in that of order) but ignores the possibility, already quite evident in the thirties, let alone in the forties when the book was written, that a pessimistic view of the world may also lead to nihilism and total disregard of, contempt for, the established order.

Goguel himself does not ignore the frequent confusion of the two tendencies not only in the same party but also in the same breast. In spite of this, he feels that on the whole the opposition between the two tendencies remains significant and clear (p. 556). While this is true, it does not help our quest for further definition or precision. Yet Goguel tells us (p. 29) that, in lieu of *ordre etabli* he had first considered another label—*résistance*—only to discard it to avoid possible misinterpretations. If we were to readopt this other concept, we should have three categories, three parties, to play with: the party of movement, expression of optimistic humanism and inclined to radical change; the party of order, taking a pessimistic view of human nature but one which, because of its kinship with Edmund Burke's traditionalism, does not exclude change; and a third party, the party of resistance to change, of reaction, and violence. The first of these would accommodate Soustelle-minded men, Communists, and the Jacobin temperaments in most parties; the last category would fit many of the prewar leagues, certain Independents and dissident Radicals, and, of course, the Poujadists. As for the party of order, it is made to measure for men who prefer power to purity, for all the vested interests from *travailliste* to moderate, and for those masses tormented, in the words of G. E. Lavau, "by confused and contradictory aspirations that toss them between a traditional 'order' that is only intermittently satisfactory, and a new 'order' they cannot imagine clearly or fashion themselves." [31]

Another possible conjecture is thrown out by Jacques Dumaine's report of a talk with old Professor Langevin, in which the regretted Ambassador to

Portugal suggests that both optimism and pessimism take, according to temperament, either a static or a dynamic form. The static optimists and pessimists, both, are likely to proceed in negative fashion and achieve negative results. Their dynamic opposites feel, suggests Dumaine, "the precariousness of every happy state, of every favorable situation. Their original mood differs, but their aims tend to coincide."[32]

Neither of these variants would be far removed from the conclusions reached by G. Dupeux after his study of the Loir-et-Cher under the Third Republic.[33] Dupeux also divides political opinion into three: a satisfied Center and two dissatisfied extremes. What matters in this case is less whether the voters stand on the left or right, but more whether they are satisfied or not. One imagines that the dissatisfied would gravitate left or right according to their optimism or pessimism (as Goguel really suggests) rather than, let us say, because of the traditional orientation of their region or clan. The latter may well decide the particular label under which satisfaction or dissatisfaction, optimism or pessimism will express themselves. But parties and party labels, important as they are, are merely convenient molds for similar opinions. The opinions themselves, the tendencies or temper we describe today as left or right, meaning progressive, reactionary, republican, authoritarian, chauvinistic and the rest, these shape the molds—or gravitate to molds of the appropriate shape. And, in a system where most parties are coalitions, jellies, of frequently discordant opinions, in doctrine as well as in personnel, it is the opinions, perhaps even the inclinations, that we must try to define rather than the parties. This, in effect, is what Goguel, Dupeux, Langevin have attempted; and it seems to me that their psychological categories, rough as they are, serve better than our present ones: optimist or pessimist, static or dynamic, tells us more, much more, about the character of a man or group, than right or left. The new labels also need qualification; they are the most primitive of tools; but more suited to our time than the ones we have handled so far.

We see here a shift in the presentation and interpretation of political realities. While Maurice Duverger analyzes the machinery of political parties, Siegfried, Goguel, Lavau analyze their sociology, their psychology—not their doctrines, not their programmes, or hardly at all. If they proceed in this manner it is because they see in the parties merely the passing expression of certain sociopsychological and historical phenomena they happen, at a given moment, to represent. This is why "left" and "right" are no more use to them, because they are no longer real. Talk of movement and order, optimism and pessimism, may be no more accurate, but it is nearer reality, cuts closer to the bone.

What does all this mean for the parties, which after all, survive; what for French political realities? The gap between political reality and the forms available for its expression, the inadequacy of the latter, had become increasingly obvious throughout the fifties. Political parties must represent something concrete, in terms of interest, in terms of faith: maybe a regional, economic, or social reality; maybe—where religion still counts—a confessional one.[34] But very few French parties do, in fact, represent any such interest or faith. There are the *paysans,* who wield an influence far beyond their numbers, and there are the Communists. For the rest, conventional or "confessional" labels[35] serve largely to conceal the variety and unreconcilability of stronger interests beneath the surface, which break through again and again to wreck parties and party coalitions. As Drieu la Rochelle pointed out soon after the First World War, if there are no more real parties it is largely because there are no more classes with definite boundaries, values, characteristics. Instead of classes, there are only economic categories, with fairly similar *moeurs* and no spiritual differences. High and low, said Drieu, share the same elements, the same sentiments, the same vices. They have, in effect, become interchangeable. There is nothing to choose between them because, fundamentally undifferentiated, they afford no basis for a choice.[36]

Put another way, the one basis for choice is temperament, something that is determined by one's "famille spirituelle," better still, "émotionnelle." The passionate man will make for the extremes, the optimist for the left, and the degree of their political orientation will be determined by the intensity of their emotional inclination. That this may in turn (or in its fortuitous expression) be affected by certain factors determined by history, by geography, no one denies. But, in an increasingly undifferentiated world, political differences must become increasingly subjective, until even temperamental differences give way before pervading standardization. But this is not yet, we may still hope it never will be, and though the psychological argument is as far as one can safely go, one is tempted to venture one more remark.

If we look once more over the field in search of a criterion we may have overlooked, one will appear, the backbone of every political problem since earliest times. How to reconcile individual and society so that private and public good coincide? Nobody has solved it yet, though many have tried, but in the seventeenth and eighteenth centuries a doctrine developed which identified the good of the individual with the good of society and the good of society with the good of the state. In other words a parallel development takes place: freedom for the individual (or of arguments that urge it), and freedom, power, for the state. Yet state power is something which can only be exercised at the expense of the individual, at least of his freedom, if not of his comfort.

Much of the intricacy of French politics stems from the fact that, since

1789, every regime has striven to complete the centralizing policy of that monarchy which the Revolution both displaced and fulfilled. Essentially, the successors of Louis XVI took over from a *royauté fainéante* which had, since the beginning of the eighteenth century, failed to carry out its traditional purpose of enhancing the power of the state. This fact was, however, lost from sight behind a smokescreen of republican, liberal, and democratic verbiage, aspirations, and institutions. Hence a contradiction developed between the persistent reality of growing state power, seeking ever more power, and the equally growing elaboration of democratic forms and ideas. In a country less doctrinaire, or less dedicated to both of these parallel currents, the consequent difficulties might have been settled more easily. In France however, and most especially since the birth of the Third Republic, the result was a masked division between the avowed aims of political formations and their behavior when in power. This is everywhere the case to some degree, and platforms are understandably designed to run on, not stand on; but in France the difference between political language and political realities was more acute than most. Nor were the politicians themselves any less the dupes of their confusions. Rightists called for unity and freedom. Leftists for freedom and unity. Neither, when in power, failed to use or extend, either really or ideally, the central power of the state; neither could admit the fundamental identity of the two positions. Hence arose the necessity to emphasize *ideological* differences of largely theoretical nature, and the belief of students and observers that, even if there is not always a dualism of *parties,* there is nevertheless a dualism of *tendencies.*[37] The public had to be persuaded that there was, in fact, such a division because otherwise the political conflict between parties and cliques—all of which accepted (if only tacitly) the indispensability of the state and its expanding power—would have lacked all reality, and would have been reduced to a mere struggle for power between groups of men hungry for it and for its practical (material and psychological) rewards. But this *is* the reality of politics, and this is why, as both Goguel and Brogan have said of the interwar years, the coalitions of left and extreme left are formed for elections, those of left and right are formed in power. The Communists recognize it, so do the contenders for *l'assiette au beurre.* But the French public, and to some extent until quite recently French political scientists, were dissuaded from accepting this, were given the myths of left and right to play with and get excited about. These were becoming obsolete as early as 1906; their persistence for another half-century shows the power of ideas to affect and form opinion, but hardly much effort to see through the accepted theories and think them through afresh.

～ 3

In Search of the Hexagon

Montesquieu makes one of his characters declare that if triangles were to imagine a god, they would give it three sides. The French, though richly endowed, have not yet claimed six sides to their national character. Yet they have adopted the hexagon as a national symbol—a synonym for France, and its very image. To read the newspapers or listen to the news, the hexagon is as self-evident as "the Party"—or, at least, as the party used to be when the Communist party mattered. Yet few, if any, used the latter figure of speech before the Second World War, and fewer still thought of France as obviously hexagonal until the 1960s.

Today's familiar image would have struck mid-century Frenchmen as decidedly odd and probably out of place. If it existed when I learned the geography of France in the 1930s, or when I reviewed it again in the 1940s, it hardly did so as the conventional metonym that all could recognize, as all would do today. Somehow, between my youth and my middle age, an unexpected trope became a commonplace. When, how, did that happen?

Just how much of an innovation the hexagon represented, a little research soon revealed. The nineteenth century yielded a couple of mentions, notably in a large, illustrated geography of France which Jules Verne had published in 1868; but these did not read encouragingly. Théophile Lavallée, who contributed the French geography section of Jules Verne's tome, deplored the hexagon, which was furthermore *irrégulier,* as part of conventional limits, "broken, cut up, absurd, prejudicial to the greatness and prosperity of France." Nothing to boast about, but a makeshift. And the map of France that Lavallée printed carried no hint of a hexagonal contour. [1]

The same rather unsatisfactory image, though shorn of querulous overtones, reappeared in a textbook written in the 1880s by a Frenchman teaching in America, who told his students that French territory forms "a sort of irregular hexagon." [2] Only in 1894 did I come upon a clearly positive mention of France's hexagonal shape, which explained that the country's general contours are "symmetrical, well proportioned and regular."[3] The author, Pierre Foncin, is identified as inspector-general of secondary education, and this suggests a clue, or at least a coincidence. In 1887 Fernand Buisson, grand panjandrum of the educational establishment of the day, had brought out the second part of his great *Dictionnaire,* whose preface explains that it is not a dictionary of *words* but a dictionary of *lessons* "designed to provide the teacher with the essence of the lectures or of the course that he should consecrate" to the subjects of the curriculum. If you follow the hint, you will find that the article on "France (géographie)" begins with the hexagon, "which almost entirely circumscribes the national territory," and recommends that the first lesson should indicate its six summits: Dunkirk, Pointe Saint-Mathieu near Brest, the mouth of the Bidassoa, the Cap Cerbère, the mouth of the Roya near Menton, and the Mont Donon in the Vosges.[4]

Here we can recognize at once the source of the commonplace image-to-be, presented in one of the bibles of the republic's schools, at the very time when public instruction was about to become truly universal. Thousands of apprentice-teachers, millions of school children, would henceforth hear the lesson that Buisson's *Dictionnaire* recommends, would visualize the shape that it describes, would assimilate the image of a France that is "symmetrical, well proportioned and regular."

Curiously, however, this is a view which some of France's greatest geographers do not seem to share. Elysée Reclus, who also admired the "balance and elegance" of the country's shape, objectified it as a great octagon. While admitting with admirable equanimity that some see France as a pentagon and others as a hexagon, Vivien de Saint-Martin also preferred the octagon.[5] Vidal de La Blache, when he wrote a textbook, seems to have picked up Reclus's image, though with no precise polygonal reference;[6] and a reputable geographical encyclopedia of 1950 follows suit: "The shape of France," it says, "is almost geometrical: one can see it as an octagon, with four sides of land and four sides of sea."[7] But differences do not end here. The maps in Léon Mirot's fairly influential *Manuel de géographie historique de la France* give no sense of any hexagonal framework;[8] Emmanuel de Martonne prefers to speak of the country's "roughly pentagonal shape";[9] and the English have tended to see France as "roughly square-shaped."[10] Only the eleventh edition of the *Encyclopaedia Britannica* (1910) dropped the square for the hexagon, disregarding Vauban's advice to Louis XIV that he should square off his possessions ("faire son pré carré") and his preaching ("always square not the circle but the territory").[11] There is even a circular presentation in which the French Empire divided into 111 departments radiates out from its center at Bourges in the Cher.

The most interesting of these dissenters is Vidal de La Blache, the most influential of France's modern geographers, who really does not like formalistic games. Vidal's classic *Tableau* raises the question of France's geographic identity, but sheers away from questions of form in order to talk about function. France, he says, is the narrow end of a continental landmass, not quite an isthmus but a land bridge between two seas, and also between Spain and the rest of Europe. The land is wonderfully balanced and harmonious, as Strabo perceived long ago; but if you are looking for one word to sum it up, says Vidal, that would not be the definition of a contour, but *variety*. The most striking thing about the "General Physiognomy of France" (title of ch. 4) is the amplitude of differences.[12] The ensemble is actually a jigsaw, and the maps we are offered bear this out. They do not suggest any clear shape, but complexity, and the imbrication of French territory in a larger whole.

Vidal's refusal to simplify, his insistence that reality is complex, was not much use to elementary instruction, which is about simplification, or to vulgarizers interested in making difficult questions look easy. An elementary school public needs elementary points of reference, and ones that are easy to assimilate. A geometrical framework could render the country's shape easier to imagine, to memorize, to reproduce. It had been enlisted for the job since the seventeenth century, it would continue to be so used, and Nathaniel Smith has illustrated the variety of figures mobilized in the process: from circle and square, through a whole slew of polygons.[13]

Still, many works of reference avoided all of these. None of the classics—not Littré, nor Larousse, nor Robert—cites the hexagon, or any other polygon, as synonym for France. I found no mention of it in the *Dictionnaire de la langue française* by Hatzfeld and Darmesteter, either in the original edition (1890–1893) or in the revised edition of 1964, or in the *Dictionnaire de l'Académie* (1935). The 1962 edition of the *Grand Larousse encyclopédique* ignores this sense of the term; it first appears in the *Supplément* of 1969 as "la France limitée au territoire métropolitain." In 1972 the simile is recognized by the *Dictionnaire du français vivant:* "la France continentale." In 1976 the *Grand dictionnaire de la langue française* is more specific: "France insofar as it is reduced to metropolitan territory." And, one year later, the *Dictionnaire encyclopédique Quillet* (1977) would be more specific still: "Since 1962, one sometimes talks of the *hexagone* to designate France. This is a way of comparing metropolitan France reduced to its European dimension to the France before decolonisation which rules a vast colonial Empire."

I began this chapter expressing surprise that what I took for a commonplace turned out a novelty, and wonder how the latter had come to appear the former. Now that we are on the verge of an answer, let me stop and digress in order to point out another novelty: maps, or at least their contemplation and use by more than a tiny minority.

Just as the nation-state is a contemporary concept, the notion of its official limits is one too. Limits were always important at the local level, in matters of property and jurisdiction, and there they were known and described by a stream or steeple or other point of reference; but borders or frontiers of large entities were relatively fluid and left to administrators. Witness the great *Encyclopédie's* definition of France which, when it cannot call on large bodies of water, states without further detail that it abuts on the border of some neighboring realm, like Savoy.

Of course, medieval kings, like their subjects, had never seen a map of France (the first of these seems to have been drawn up in 1525); but the kings, unlike their subjects, had to be concerned with the actual extent and limits of their realm. Since, before maps, borders had to be described verbally, precision and simplicity both argued in favor of references that could not be contested, such as the rivers that played a large part in the treaty of Verdun (843). And the need for identifiable points of reference must have played a major part in the development of diplomatic geography, even when the rivers (and even more the mountains) were known to act far more as links than barriers. Hence, no doubt, the long tradition that culminates in Danton's well-known speech of January 1793, where he claimed the limits of the Republic as set up by nature: the Rhine, the Ocean, the Pyrénées, and Alps, all highly penetrable and attractive to roam or cross, as any tourist will testify. Thus it was that a practical convenience turned into rhetoric, and ended in the doctrine of natural frontiers. But before that happened, the tracing of such frontiers had to achieve some kind of corroborating record; and it is interesting that, in France at least, the hardening national state preceded the accessible record of its image.

It was during that conveniently vague timespan known as the Renaissance that maps began their two-pronged trip through modern history: the first as a form of decoration, source of wonder and delight for cultivated folk; the second as a utilitarian document useful in real estate transactions of every scale. Cartographers played an important role in this, but surveyors were no less important, furnishing most of the local cartographers in times when most cartography, concerned with the survey of particular estates, *was* local. Such topographers benefited from increasingly accurate surveying equipment, like the plane table and early versions of the theodolite, and from the refinement of the mathematics they needed to do their work. But those who looked at their maps, when it was not for fun, did not always know how to read them; and those who made the maps were chorographers (the *Encyclopédie* prefers "topographers") rather than cartographers. The basic unit they surveyed remained limited: by the interests of their clients, by the size of the plate that it was possible to engrave and print, and by the amount of topographical detail that one could squeeze onto such a plate without making the result illegible.[14]

Although the Renaissance gave maps to a few, and with them a new visual image to reflect upon when they could, the possibilities of these maps remained limited: the smaller the scale of the map, the less its accuracy. When a historian like Alphonse Dupront declares that in the sixteenth century "la France prend corps et âme,"[15] one feels inclined to add that body and soul might have been there (however different from what we imagine today), but there can have been no image of sixteenth-century France, for the image offered by a sixteenth-century map lent itself poorly to a kingdom's scale. A historian of early English cartography explains that military and utilitarian maps of that time were by nature piecemeal and did not provide an integrated image of the country as a whole.[16] A historian of French cartography finds as much across the Channel. Only general triangulation, Henry Vayssière tells us, would bring together "that cartographic archipelago that constituted the map of France of those times, made up of a multitude of disparate fragments."[17]

The large-scale map comes in with the late seventeenth century, with Louis XIV who, in old age "set out to correct his predecessors' disdain for French geography"[18]; with Jean-Baptiste Colbert, who might be called its patron saint; and with the seemingly endless Cassini clan so prominently connected with French map-making from the 1670s to the early nineteenth century. The heyday of the Cassinis, however, and of French map-making in general, lies in the eighteenth century, when scientific mapping from exact ground observation made its start, and speculative cartography, where

> Geographers, in Afric-Maps
> With savage-pictures fill their gaps
> And o'er unhabitable downs
> Place elephants for want of towns,

began to be abandoned. Furthermore, an admiring student tells us, "as in this great period France could not produce what she did not adorn, mathematical exactness went hand in hand with design." Artists like François Boucher tried their hand at embellishing the newly fashionable maps and when, in 1757, Gilles and Didier de Vaugondys, sons of the King's Geographer, brought out their father's *Atlas universel,* the engraving had been entrusted to well-known artists "and charming cartouches were designed to adorn the maps."[19]

One drawback of this is mentioned by a map historian, R. V. Tooley: the French "predilection for theorizing. They abhorred a vacuum, and so where no real knowledge was available, they filled in the gaps with theoretical conceptions, so that their maps were in effect frequently more misleading than those of their Dutch predecessors."[20] Another is that such products were extremely expensive. The publication of the Vaugondys *Atlas* was supported by the Court, led by Madame de Pompadour. Six hundred subscribers paid 126 livres each for its 108 maps, and some of them paid another 12 livres for a calfskin binding.

These details suggest not only that maps remained rare, a commodity for the very rich; but also that they continued to be multiple and disparate. The Cassinis completed the first national map survey in 1744, not on one sheet but on eighteen. The second survey, whose last sheets were published only in 1815, consisted of 180 maps. As if to confirm the enduring particularism that triumphed even over enlightened ideas, the second Cassini project was delayed by many provinces' insisting on getting their own maps rather than sharing in a general survey.[21] For my purpose here, though, the most interesting thing about the Cassinis' enterprise was that the map of 1744 was called "Description géometrique de la France," meaning that it was a scientific work based on triangulation.[22] And one is tempted to suppose that the geometrical map suggested the geometrical metaphor we started out with: not so much because contemplation brought into evidence some underlying contour, but simply because of the prestige that geometry, like other exact sciences, carried in an enlightened age.

But this is pure speculation. Nor should it be taken to mean, as some French historians seem to think with Bernard Guénée, that "the French" had got used to recognizing their country on maps; let alone that they were used to contemplating maps "since childhood."[23] Where, but for the favored few, were maps to be found anyway, and especially maps of *France*? Printed sources were few, and they remained so for a century. The splendid plates of the great *Encyclopédie* (1751) include not a single map. Until the end of the Old Regime, even the state did not possess a good map library; and the public would have no source of reference until 1924, when the map collections at Versailles were transferred to the Bibliothèque Nationale.[24] To claim, as Guénée does, that by the eighteenth century (the wonders above are attributed to the seventeenth) the French had any precise idea of the limits of the kingdom[25] is an anachronism that goes against the evidence. In 1789, the French borders were far from clear on paper or on the ground. Looking at Cassini's map, it is not easy to recognize the limits of the kingdom.[26] A map of the French *Empire* would finally be completed in 1805, and placed on public sale at four francs per sheet. But when, two years later, an engineer-geographer presented the authorities with the reduced-scale map of France that later became the *Atlas Napoléon,* this still consisted of a lot of separate sheets.[27]

As the nineteenth century opened, maps—especially maps of France—continued rare, and reading them an exceptional skill. The rivalry between the finance ministry, which needed *cadastres* (maps of landholdings) for fiscal purposes, and the war ministry, which needed maps for strategic and tactical planning, hobbled all large-scale cartography. And when the war ministry won the struggle, its project advanced with great deliberation: the *Carte de l'Etat-major,* not quite ready for the Franco-Prussian War, would be completed in the 1870s—a bit late for the soldiers, but a boon to conscientious tourists. (Most of the sheets were available for use in the war of 1870. Unfortunately, the maps provided to army staff were of Germany, while the fighting took place in France).[28] Still, the physical image of France and of its contours continued to strike contemporaries as a novelty. What a book on *The Making of France* describes as "those familiar features whose contours seem traced in advance"[29] was hardly familiar to most of the French.

History did little to help. An official report of 1890 on the teaching of history insisted on the importance of imagination and deplored the general neglect of visual methods in teaching, as a result of which "few students are able to interpret images." But the teaching aids the report recommended were exclusively verbal: books and tests.[30] Nineteenth-century history showed restricted interest in images (except of historical figures and romanticized scenes), and even less in that variety of images called maps. This was characteristic of the profession. In the Tempio Malatestiano at Rimini, Duccio's Clio holds a book. At the Palais de la Légion d'Honneur in Paris, Clodion's Clio holds a stylus: a cherub-secretary works for her on a nearby tablet. Neither needs a map; words suffice. As we know, if geography is about maps, history is about chaps.

Historical rhetoric was bent on creating its own verbal images. Narrative history did not want diversions to stanch the flow of the account. In the officially harnessed team where geography and history were yoked together in academic programs, geography played the subordinate part. When the *agrégation d'histoire et de géographie* was reformed as the century ended, out of four written examinations three were in historical fields. Even some geography books relied on verbal description alone. In 1813 Joseph Gibrat reedited his *Traité de la géographie moderne* and described its enticing virtues: "completely revised edition, presenting the old and new divisions of France and a list of diverse political changes that have occurred in the rest of Europe and the other parts of the world since the French Revolution, with a table of the longitudes and latitudes of major cities." But no map.[31]

Geography, on the whole, was much neglected. The explorations and discoveries of the nineteenth century fed a taste for it, but even there France lagged behind her neighbors. Pierre Larousse called for vulgarizations that made geography more accessible and above all for more instruction "among the laboring classes" so that no one in France should "lack sufficient knowledge of his country."[32] But this was slow to come, even in schools. A law of 1850 treated geography as optional in the elementary curriculum, a law of 1867 made it a required subject, but does not seem to have had much effect. Do not be misled by idealized engravings illustrating Alphonse Daudet's "La dernière classe." The patriotic teacher had no map to point to. It was on the blackboard that he wrote "Vive la France," while choking back his tears. Nor would anyone, then, have expected to see a wall map in an elementary school. Through the 1860s the evidence suggests that schoolchildren "see no maps, know nothing about their department or their fatherland," "ignore the existence of the department or of France."[33] In 1891, the same year that Vidal de La Blache brought out the first number of his *Annales de géographie,* the Sorbonne inaugurated what Lavisse greeted as a novelty: a home for its tiny department of Geography. As Maurice Barrès recalled of the 1880s, in a conversation with Jacques Millerand: "at that time, France was pretty vague."

Published in 1882, the first part of Buisson's *Dictionnaire,* which had nothing to say about the hexagon, of course, referred to the sudden impetus that the war of 1870 had given geographical studies. Such alleged precipitation remained relative, however, until Jules Ferry's decree of 1881 on the organization of normal schools, and the law of 1882, both of which in similar terms cited "Geography, especially that of France" among the subjects elementary schools must teach. This is when a publicist listing careers for bright young men, surprisingly follows "arts, letters and jurisprudence" with "geographical questions, so fascinating today."[34]

This is also the time when schools begin to be equipped with the crucial accessory they lacked under the empire, wall maps, and also with engravings of various parts of France. They could henceforth refer to the cartographic image of the fatherland, as well as to its landscapes and to its personalization in the bust of Marianne. By the time, before the First World War, when Gaston Bonheur inventories the walls of his country school, he can begin with "Vidal-Lablache's [sic] map of France."[35] This is just as well, because other maps scarcely appeared in overwhelming numbers. Bruno's famous *Tour de la France par deux enfants,* which is full of small illustrations and carries many maps of separate regions, offered no map of France until the 1905 edition. The 1884 edition had none. Vidal's textbook on *La France* contains no map of France as such. Of its 35 maps, four do show the whole country in order to indicate various climatic conditions, and five show separate portions of the French colonial empire. The remaining 26 refer to particular regions. For a book whose introduction declares that it is meant above all "to inspire the wish to see,"[36] the visual contents are slight, testimony to a long verbal tradition and to the enduring limitations of contemporary imagery.

Curiously, nineteenth-century Frenchmen had pioneered a sophisticated mapping technique that could easily have suggested the shape of hexagon or octagon from an early date. In 1830 Frère de Montizon, "Professeur de Chimie, de physique et de mathématiques," had published a "Philosophical Map of French Population" that showed only the country's outline and that of its departments, thereby inventing what geographers call the thematic dot map. This would soon be put to heavy use by Adolphe d'Angeville in his *Essai sur la statistique de la population française* (1836); it was then developed with great sophistication by an Inspecteur-Général des Ponts-et-Chaussées, Charles-Joseph Minard (1781–1870), turned statistical cartographer, whose first *tableaux graphiques* were published in 1844.[37] By 1878 maps made "according to the system of Minard" had become relatively common in governmental agencies and statistical circles.[38] But administrators and academics apparently did not mix. Geographers ignored Minard and his followers, perhaps because their maps took serious liberties with geographical position and cartographic scale; and the thematic technique now in general use remained confidential. A recent study has found reason to comment on the "curious fact that [Minard's] works have remained largely unknown to students of the history of cartography and geography."[39] The simplified outline of France did so, too, until popularized after the Second World War by outline maps standardly used in the *Cahiers de la Fondation Nationale des Sciences Politiques*.

One promising trail remains to be explored: that of travel and tourism, both of which flourished in the nineteenth century. Railways that burgeoned after mid-century encouraged the publication of travel guides. There were Adolphe Joanne's famous guidebooks, of course, but also cheap series like *Les Chemins de fer illustrés,* produced since 1858 for a mass circulation and selling at 25 centimes per booklet. But such booklets used strip maps to cover only single lines—like that from Paris to Fontainebleau— with the stops listed along a straight line. And many guides carried no map, using instead some linear image of the trail proposed, accompanied by more-or-less detailed descriptions.

Significantly, John Murray's *Handbook for Travellers in France* (London, 1892) included a clearly outlined map of France, in color. Yet the first editions of the *Guide Michelin,* published since 1900, offered only schematic partial maps, none of France; while the *Annuaire de route de l'Automobile Club Français,* which auto club members enjoyed since 1900, provided sectional charts and a primitive map of Europe (including France). Even the wonderful volumes of Ardouin-Dumazet's *Voyage en France* were slow to adopt maps. The first two volumes, published in 1893 and 1894, carried none; only the third (1895) began to include them. The third edition of 1910 would provide foldouts, and an outline map of France as well. By that time cyclists, motorists, and other travelers could draw on a variety of maps, all or most on separate sheets. But the *Livrets Chaix* continued to provide only schematic and partial plans of the country to accompany their railway timetables.

Not unnaturally, some of the earliest figures of speech evoked by train travel appear to be linear ones. Typically, in 1865, Jules Clarétie describes the way in which landscape appears from the train not as detail but as mass: "the whole ensemble in which there is life," and urges that we "not disparage the straight line" (of the railroad track).[40] There may have been a natural passage from trains and straight tracks to linear itineraries and travel plans, then to delineations of ensembles with a life of their own. But such relationships are purely speculative, nor do they bear on broader public acquaintance with large-scale maps.

My guess is that looking at maps, let alone deciphering one, became a normal part of French experience only on the eve of the First World War, with the growing popularity of the cycling Tour de France; and then with the war itself, whose campaigns so many followed at home or in the press. Until that happened, it would be safe to say that when the little children sang "la République nous appelle," the call was not to gaze upon a map. No French *mot historique* refers to maps, as the younger Pitt did before he died;[41] none of the poems that glorify the Republic's schools (the only ones, as we have seen, to house newfangled marvels) refers to maps either. They speak of benches and blackboards and *la règle de trois,* but above all they speak of letters, words, and books. The republicans recognized the need to inculcate a sense of national entity or sharpen it, and they recognized the importance of common allegories and national passwords which could create or reinforce identity: the flag, Marianne, the map of France. But their efforts in these directions remained mainly verbal.

This was so, in part, because their own schooling and experience had shown them the importance of words: "le verbe," as Victor Hugo said, "a tant d'importance pour le peuple." It was so, in part, because the popular culture of the nineteenth century, most of the century at least, remained an oral culture. It had not yet become a culture of images, as lithography and rotogravure were to make it even before the cinema and television. A good portion of the French population scarcely acceded to the printed word. The technical possibilities of print and publishing maintained the costliness, hence the rarity, of images of all sorts. In the quest for national symbols, the flag was more convenient: easier to see, to *read,* to assimilate. And after the flag, or beside it, the spoken word.

But there was the written word as well, and "culture" was not so much about images as about words; because words lent themselves not only to creating and recreating lacking images, but to abstraction, which was the highest level of reality. The hierarchy of knowledge, or perhaps of wisdom, was set in terms of a discipline's capacity to abstraction; and on this scale geography rated low: a kind of descriptive mechanics, even though here, too, a map was an abstraction of vulgar physical facts. It was not as abstract as words, however. Interesting though it could be, and admittedly useful, geography was only the rough, unformed underside of civilization. As Michelet's *Tableau de la France* explained, national entity finds its imperfect origin in geography, but is fulfilled in history. To begin with, "history is all geography," determined and imperfect, waiting to be molded by the will, the mind, and the hand of man until "history obliterates geography" and, freed of particular, material interests—"the miseries of local existence"—it reaches for "the high and abstract" unity of the fatherland: "cette pure et noble généralisation de l'esprit moderne."[42]

One might compare the evolution from the local and particular, to a higher and more abstract unity, to that which maps underwent in modern times. Vidal would not agree; he found concrete diversities and their inter-relations more interesting, and closer to reality as well. But the French intellectual tradition pointed away from the concrete (and confusion) to the abstract (and perfection). Michelet had insisted that the idea of the father-land, the greater fatherland that lay beyond and above the lesser fatherlands of village or of town, was an abstract idea; and Renan, considering the same subject, had stressed a similar concept: a nation is a spirit, a spiritual prin-ciple. A hundred years after Renan, Alphonse Dupront seems to share these views.[43]

It would be tempting at this point to argue that the tendency to abstraction led to the further abstraction of French maps, and that geom-etry, which (along with trigonometry) had helped to make maps possible in the first place, was enlisted to endow them with a less amorphous, more perfect expression: the further abstraction of an abstraction. A medium more perfect, a technique even more exact, than those concerned merely to reproduce appearance, would more rationally express reality, or better still transcend its disorder, by compressing geographical and historical space into geometrical space. In the occurrence, a hexagon. One could refer to the historical tendency of French cartographers, noted above, to improve their maps to match their theoretical conceptions. And one could refer to the utility of schematic, hence easily recognizable symbols, that would relate political limits and national identity in an accessible way.

There may be something to this, but the process I discern is more circumstantial. We have followed it from that long time during which no image of France existed at all (except as words could sketch it); to the time when cartography, or rather chorography, provided fragmentary images for use or decoration; to quite recent times when maps of France, all of France, became generally available and exposed to all. We have learned that pedagogic procedures included the suggestion of geometrical simplification as an aid to learning. Why then did not the hexagon—or some other selected emblem—pass from widespread experience into common parlance at an earlier date? Between 1900 and 1914, for instance, it would have furnished one more argument to advocates of a national revival and of the recovery of provinces whose loss dented contours manifest in mathematical terms as in historical destiny. After 1918 it could have testified to triumph, and justified the slackening of national energies that marks the entre-deux-guerres.

If the hexagon was not used this way, if it did not become a commonplace, this could have been in part because so many textbook maps, quite correctly, continued to *look* rather confused than clear, not a cut-out of France but her integration into her neighborhood, portraying not the country's artificially isolated shape but interrelations in which borders did not play a major part. This kind of graphic treatment (not necessarily predominant, but widespread), reflected the principles of a positivist geography that sought to eschew suggestiveness and tried to be more critical and "colorless": a task better carried out by informative detail than by simplification. It also approximates the dominant trends of turn-of-the-century graphics, whose images tend to merge into their surroundings rather than detach themselves clearly from a differentiated background.

But there was another, more important factor affecting the fortunes of the map of France: just when it was coming into circulation, the Republic found solace for the loss of Alsace and Lorraine and compensation for its truncated map in the acquisition of an overseas empire, last of a series. In 1884 already, Vivien de Saint-Martin expressed the feeling that "in all justice" the three Algerian departments, "simple prolongement transméditérannéen de la métropole," had to be counted as part of home territory. After 1890, the influence of the colonial party would multiply the number of history and geography books focused on French colonies, and references to the colonies in more general texts. Possessions, numbers and alleged riches overseas would mitigate diminution at home. "Another France" (Jaurès,

1884) provided a vast human treasury on which France could draw for all its needs (Vogüé, 1899).[44] The map of a new French Empire, or of a world where the Empire loomed reassuringly large, henceforth accompanied and sometimes overshadowed that of diminished France.

We hear a lot, and rightly, about the maps that marked the two lost provinces; less of the possible reticence such evidence of loss occasioned, and of the readiness to emphasize instead the compensatory success of ventures overseas. But even when the lost provinces had been won back, the sense of failure seemed somehow to persist. Concluding the vast enterprise of his *Histoire de la France contemporaine* in 1922, the very year he died, Ernest Lavisse had to admit that, after centuries of effort, France had failed to attain its "national borders" on the Rhine. Consolation for this was to be found in colonial accomplishment: "let us compare our lack of success in acquiring natural boundaries with the success of our colonial policy. Never has a country received a clearer indication of the route to follow." Let the French look to the seas, and beyond; let them establish an association with their one-time subjects, and "il n'y aura qu'une France, une plus grande France."[45] Within less than twenty years of this, with the metropolis occupied and dismembered, the unconquered colonies seemed to prove the wisdom of Lavisse's words. That greater France, which had enhanced the image of France, helped to preserve its existence. No wonder that in 1944 the office for national propaganda received instructions to concentrate on LA NOTION D'EMPIRE (sic). France, as the slogan had it, was not a country of forty million, but an Empire over a hundred million strong.[46]

Within a year, however, Empire had turned into Community; within twenty years more, it was no more an empire, but "un tout petit hexagone." In 1966 the *New Yorker*'s "Letter from Paris" referred to the country's "new intellectualized slang name of *Le Hexagon*" as a novelty worth reporting, while adding that "no one has ever talked about its shape before."[47] We have seen that this impression was false, and Nathaniel Smith has documented just how often people had talked about the hexagon before. But it was true that, now, the term had entered common usage sufficiently to be used in the titles of books, the headings of chapters, and even as a contemptuous epithet applied by the Algerian French to their metropolitan *frères ennemis*.[48] Before the sixties were over, even sedate dictionaries and encyclopedias had incorporated it.

The belated triumph was clearly linked this time to the shipwreck of the empire. Reflecting in 1968 on what loss of Empire meant for a France "since 1962 curtailed to the hexagon," Jacques Madaule found the "situation so new that we haven't yet digested all the consequences."[49] Time would reveal that not all of these were regrettable. The empire's existence "as psychically natural extension" of the French soil and dead[50] had broadened, but had also confused and obscured the clear figure of the fatherland. North Africa especially so close to the country's shores, could easily be regarded, as Lavisse regarded it, not just as a "prolongement de la France," but as an integral part of France.[51] This greater France, going in the fifties, irrevocably gone in the sixties, left only the hexagon of the metropolis, "of a geometry on the whole perfect—if diminished," but at least "undeniable."[52] Soon the pejorative connotations of the hexagon would be forgotten, its consolatory overtones of perfection would remain: "Reduced from now on to herself, even unto the sarcasm of its losses, when speech mocks the hexagon, [France] retains the perfection of its physical shape: that of a solar geometry."[53]

But amputation of the empire may offer only part of an explanation. For the "diminution" to which Dupront referred was taking place just as France was merging back into the neighboring Europe from which the development of the nation-state and the trenchancy of national rivalries had sundered her. In 1957 the Treaty of Rome established a European Economic Community which had been in the making since 1948. Suggestively, the first use of "hexagon" in a title is found in an article of 1956, written to show the relative nature of the country's limits.

Borders, insists Jacques Ancel in his admirable study of the *Géographie des frontières*—borders only appear on paper as a projection of internal preoccupations: "one doesn't revise borders—except by force. One modifies minds" (p. 2). Now, minds once intent on frontier posts were getting ready to abandon them. National borders were losing their brief primordial significance, the ideology of the national state (*pace* de Gaulle's holding action) was being overtaken by the reality of a more encompassing whole within which neighborly exchanges loomed larger than dividing lines. As fascination with identifiable borders—brief interlude between technological impotence and practical transcendence—waned, politicians and publicists discovered what the *Encyclopédie* had recognized: that a nation defines itself not by its linear borders, but by contrast with its neighbors. There was no need any longer to affirm national identity, just to identify it; and for this a symbolism not very different from that used for road signs would do.

I am inclined to believe that one reason why, for so long, no one referred to France as "the hexagon" the way popular usage refers to the presidency as "l'Elysée," was because the figure did not seem noble enough. Great notions called for great words—more solemn, certainly, than a schoolroom analogy; and use of the hexagon as allegory of *France* and of *patrie* could easily strike one as disrespectful. Before "hexagon" could enter the popular usage, the standards of public discourse had to change, and so had the exalted associations of the nouns it would be used to replace.

But an effective figure of speech must be not only culturally acceptable. It must be based on an effectively evocative figure of thought. Even while school had taught the geometrical contour of the map of France, graphic imagination had clung to the traditional idea of representation as imitation: vero-similitude. It was only after the Second World War that the general public and its more articulate servants became familiar with abstractions that dispensed with the mediating level of—more descriptive—signs. Nor, at this early stage of familiarization with them, were abstractions perceived in a positive way. Not surprisingly, therefore, the hexagon entered *public* parlances as a pejorative—or at least a belittling—term, suggesting less a destiny than a rump. Yet by 1966 already, the Gaullist U.N.R. had adopted the outline as underlying shape of its electoral posters, expected to carry a positive subliminal message.

In this connection, we know how quickly the pejorative associations of certain words tend to be forgotten: as in the case of Whigs and Tories. Etienne de Silhouette was Controller-General of Louis XV's finances during the Seven Years' War. When his political enemies gave his name to drawings that represented him in a few lines, they meant to symbolize the parlous state to which his financial policies reduced the French taxpayer. But when Silhouette died in 1767, his name had become famous for the cut-out profiles with which it remained identified; and the physiognomic calculations of Johann Caspar Lavater were going to be based on silhouettes, "which were thus recognized as having an epistemological status quite different from that of the conventional portrait . . ."[54]

Roland Bacri, himself a refugee from the Greater France that had for a while concealed the hexagon from sight, suggests that the career of our contemporary silhouette may prove as promising: "The Hexagon has its regions, which reason does not know hexagtly."[55]

~ PART II

Queries

~ 4

What Is Real in Folk Tales?

Near a large forest lived a poor woodcutter with his wife and two children. The boy's name was Hansel and the girl's Gretel. The woodcutter had little to eat, and once when a great famine swept the country, he was no longer able to earn even their daily bread. One evening when he was lying in his bed and tossing about and worrying, he sighed and said to his wife, "What's to become of us? How can we feed our poor children when we've nothing left for ourselves?" "Do you know what, husband," answered the wife, "the first thing tomorrow morning we'll take the children out into the thickest part of the forest. There we'll kindle them a fire and give each a little piece of bread; then we'll go about our work and leave them there alone: they won't find the way back home, and we'll be rid of them." "No, wife," said the man, "that I won't do. How could I have the heart to leave my children alone in the forest; the wild animals would soon come and tear them to pieces." "O you fool," she said, "then all four of us will starve to death; you might as well start planing the boards for our coffins," and gave him no peace until he agreed. "But all the same I'm sorry for the poor children," said the man.

The two children hadn't been able to get to sleep either, because they were hungry and heard what their stepmother said to their father. Gretel wept bitter tears and said to Hansel, "Now it's all up with us." "Be quiet, Gretel," said Hansel, "Don't worry, I'll get us out of this, of course." [1]

The stories that the Grimm brothers started to collect around 1806 were the sort of thing that peasants told at the *veillée* when they assembled in the evening around a fire. Bruno Bettelheim, who has studied such stories from a psychoanalytic point of view in a very interesting book called *The Uses of Enchantment,* [2] regards the story of Hansel and Gretel as a regressive fantasy:

> In terms of the child's dominant anxiety, Hansel and Gretel believe
> that their parents are talking about a plot to desert them . . . By
> projecting their inner anxiety onto those they fear might cut them
> off, Hansel and Gretel are convinced that their parents plan to
> starve them to death![3]

They lack "the courage to embark on the voyage of finding themselves," and
so the story is about "the debilitating consequences of failing to deal with
life's problems by means of regression and denial which reduce our ability to
solve problems."[4]

The naive historian who reads Hansel and Gretel might not have
thought of this explanation, especially when applied to little children who
show quite a lot of initiative in order to cling to a minimum of security or to
recapture it when it has been lost. And one reason why the historian might
not think of it would be that any story of cast-out children would strike him
as highly realistic and calling for very little interpretation indeed.[5] The
cunning analyst wants to go beyond the obvious, so one section of Bettelheim's book is called "The Fantasy of the Wicked Stepmother."[6] But that
interpretation simply ignores the grim everyday experience on which the
recurrent motif is based. Given the mortality rates, especially of women in
childbed, wicked stepmothers were not a subject of fantasy any more than
cast-out children.

Whether we take Hansel and Gretel or Cinderella, their basic themes
were utterly familiar to those who listened to them—pretty much into the
nineteenth century. Restif de la Bretonne's life of his father, who was born
under Louis XIV, describes the middle-aged widower marrying a young
servant who then proceeds to expel or exploit the daughters of his first marriage.[7] The memoirs of Jean-Roch Coignet,[8] born about 25 miles away from
Restif's village of Nitry in the same area of Lower Burgundy under Louis
XVI (in 1776 to be exact), describe a father who used three wives to sire 32
official offspring. Jean-Roch was one of the sons of the second wife. She
died; his father married the eighteen-year old servant who beat and starved
the orphans until the two oldest boys, aged eight and nine respectively, ran
away and hired themselves out as shepherds. Meanwhile, the two youngest
(a boy of six and a girl of seven) were Hansel-and-Greteled by their stepmother. One evening when the father was in the fields, she took them into
the local forest, as deep into it as she could, and left them there in the dark,
completely lost. After three days and three nights (during which they lived
on berries and cried a lot), they were found by a miller who took them in. So
they survived by sheer chance and then, again by chance, Jean-Roch (by
then a hard-bitten veteran of twenty-eight, well-launched on a military

career under Napoleon) discovered them twenty years later in Paris. Within three months of the reunion, the girl died, and one of the brothers followed her shortly, with Coignet noting that the hardships they endured in youth sapped their health and strength.

Another Grimm story, "Brother and Sister," sounds exactly like the experience of the Coignet children:

> A brother took his sister by the hand and said: "Since our mother died, we haven't had a single happy hour. Our stepmother beats us every day, and when we go to her, she kicks us out. Hard left-over crusts of bread are our food, and the dog under the table is better off, for once in a while she throws it some choice morsel. The Lord have mercy, if our mother knew that! Come, let's go out into the world together . . ."

For Bettelheim, who does not cite the whole passage and leaves out all the concrete reasons the children have for wanting to leave home, being pushed out stands for self-realization and having to become oneself. Just as in Hansel and Gretel, he chides the children trying to hold on to their parents even though the time has come when they should meet the world on its own terms. They need to transcend that primitive orality which we also encounter in Hansel and Gretel's infatuation with the gingerbread house.[9]

An apt comment on these perceptions may be found in one of the Grimms' nicest stories, "The White Snake," which is about generosity and its rewards. The hero rides through a forest,

> and there he saw a father-raven and a mother-raven standing by their nest and throwing their young out. "Out with you, you good-for-nothings!" they cried: "we can't keep up with your appetites any longer; you're big enough to provide for yourselves." The poor little birds were lying on the ground, fluttering and beating their wings and crying, "we helpless children! We are supposed to provide for ourselves, and can't yet fly! What is left for us but to die of starvation?"[10]

When, as in the seventeenth century, famine conditions imposed a diet consisting wholly of bad black bread, acorns, and roots; when despair could drive children to feed on themselves; and when, well into the nineteenth century, bad harvests could impel communities from poverty to destitution, "infantile dependency" was short-lived and "separation anxiety" well-founded.[11] And this is my argument: that *märchen*, the popular stories that we describe as fairy tales, can tell us a great deal about real conditions in the world of those who told and those who heard the tales.

It has been claimed[12] that fairy tales do not speak the language of everyday reality. The familiar formula "once upon a time" warns us that we're not going to hear about real persons and places. The Grimms even have a few choice beginnings, such as, "in days of yore when God Himself still walked the earth, the land was much more fruitful than it is now." And the opening of the first story they print, "The Frog King," is also illustrative: "In days of old when wishing still did some good, there lived a king whose daughters were all beautiful; but the youngest was so beautiful that the sun itself, which has, to be sure, seen so many things, was astonished every time it shone in her face."[13] However, a very rough count of the Grimms' 200 folk tales shows only 70 of them beginning with these timeless signals. If we also leave aside thirty more fables or riddles or nonsense stories, fully half of the total have more or less realistic openings, like that of Hansel and Gretel, which may suggest that they are about real people.

A careful reading of the collection reveals a number of recurrent themes: hunger, poverty, death, danger, fear, chance. There are many orphans; there are wicked stepmothers, stepsisters, and mothers-in-law; there are poor children who have to go out into the world; there are forests inhabited by woodcutters and charcoal-burners but also by wild animals and outlaws and frightening spirits—forests that provide a refuge, but whose darkness breathes danger, where it was easy to lose one's way or to run into trouble. For Bettelheim, the forest symbolizes "the dark, hidden, near-impenetrable world of our unconscious."[14] Perhaps, but it is also very close to the reality of people who, well into the nineteenth century, feared it as the repair of bandits and wild beasts, and as a place where it was easy to lose oneself.

As in real life, forests are places through which one wends one's way uneasily, especially if one is alone, a woman or child, not knowing what to expect from the dark solitude. The sounds of forest or wasteland are not part of the villager's familiar symphony; their dwellers do not participate in the net of relations that makes one feel secure.

Much has been made of the success of ballads and stories about outlaws and their adventures. However, these were meant to produce not the thrills of emulation but the delights of fear. Ghosts, too, remained an ever-popular subject for *veillées,* but no one claims their public aspired to be like them. The stories that Restif remembered being told by the servants and the shepherds of la Bretonne were about "witches, ghosts, pacts with the devil, excommunicated men turned into beasts, who eat the people . . . shepherd-sorcerers . . ." He stayed up late, after his father had taken off for bed, "to hear stories of thieves and specters, and they made such a strong impression on me that afterwards I did not dare go to my bed alone."[15]

Of ghosts the Grimms seem not to have heard, but their collection speaks to the frightfulness of robbers, and French folk tales also bear them out. Thieves, fear of thieves and of their revenge when foiled, inform more stories than do wolves and other wild animals. Connivance (or resignation) does not entail sympathy. Action, albeit defensive, risks retaliation.[16] An oft-repeated theme tells of the out-maneuvered thief, his hand cut off by a cunning lass, who returns to marry the girl, takes her away with him to savor his revenge, and finally fails, captured or killed by the heroine's relatives or neighbors, or by *gendarmes*. Robbers like Laramée are not popular, but nasty and alarming. When the *gendarmes* catch up with him, they burn him at the stake.[17]

The theme of the fiancé who is a bandit or murderer in secret also warns against allowing strangers to marry into the village community, as in "La Fiancée et les quarante bandits" where the heroine's suitor is *étranger au pays*. He claims a castle and vast riches somewhere else, but *il ne faut pas se fier au premier venu*, and "his riches, one did not see them." No one knew his family, nor did he offer to invite anyone to meet them or to see his property. So the girl goes off to see for herself, without the stranger's knowing, and ends by calling the *gendarmes*."[18]

A number of stories begin with the son or sons leaving home, very young, either to earn money or to escape the misery they knew. This is absolutely true to life well into the nineteenth century. The eight-year old Coignet guarding his sheep in the forest, the eleven-year old boy from the Pyrénées arrested in Paris in 1828 for selling engravings without a permit, and the twelve-year old boy a policeman noted among the rebels of 1832, all confirm stories like that of the three brothers who have nothing left to eat: "it can't go on like this," they said, "we'd better go out into the world and seek our fortune."[19]

In many a fairy tale (though far from all) such fortune eventually comes by marriage to an heiress. The ideal prize is a princess, of course. But the king, her father, sounds more like a landed gentleman or a wealthy farmer: he hires his servants in person, sees they are sent their meals out in the fields, watches them at work "through his castle windows," worries about their working too little or eating too much.[20] The wandering hero triumphs over suspicions (and bad faith) with magic help, of course preferably from his bride to be, but also because his need makes him rise to the challenges encountered. Note that, as a rule, he is not the heir to his own house but a younger son for whom marrying out offers the best chance to recover his original situation, or better it, with a status scarcely less favorable than his first-born sibling; not direct heir, but son-in-law.

Such situations could readily drive some aspirants to trickery, as we have seen above. In different circumstances, however, well-born youths or maidens may have concealed their origins in order to survive. Their honorable birth, unsuitable for kitchen maid or farm servant, was revealed when success made it relevant or when some other need called for self-justification.[21]

One hazard (among others) for those who wandered off: in the wider world, the language differed from one area to another, sometimes from one valley to another. Their speech, therefore, was probably meaningless away from home, and people had trouble understanding them. Like migrant workers today they tried to get by with a few words or phrases, and they often got into trouble. One finds this motif of senseless words or phrases being repeated in inappropriate situations in two Grimm stories, appropriately entitled "The Three Journeymen" and "Going Traveling," but it comes up most explicitly in a Breton story where three country lads go to Paris "to learn how to speak," pick up three French phrases, and get sent to prison for a murder they did not commit.[22]

It is then a hazardous world, and one in which chance plays a great part. In 1830, a fourteen-year old peasant lad from the Creuse called Martin Nadaud, who had been born exactly thirty years after Jean-Roch Coignet, is taken by his father for his first "campaign" in Paris as a mason.[23] In those days (and pretty much since Richelieu mobilized the peasants of Creuse and Limousin to build the great dike that would keep the English fleet out of La Rochelle), the men folk of certain villages spent nine to twelve months every year as builders in Paris, Lyon, or Bordeaux and earned the cash to make ends meet on the stony soil of central France.

Before he leaves, Martin says goodbye to his four closest friends who are also setting off to do the same work in Lyon. Of the five lads, three would die within a couple of years and Nadaud himself nearly died the very next year of a three-story fall from which he recovered, almost surely because his father refused to let him go into the hospital. Thus danger and death are very real, but so is the great rule of luck: being saved by someone, or making a chance encounter, or distinguishing oneself in a moment of crisis (in battle or at work) and starting to go up in the world. The *Red and the Black* is a monument to this sort of resistible ascension, and Julien Sorel was not wrong about the possibilities he could exploit. He was only wrong about not exploiting them to the full. Martin Nadaud was going to pull himself up by his bootstraps (let it be said that his first boots, at fourteen, turned his feet into a wound), and in 1849 his fellow-masons would elect him deputy of the Creuse.

The *Memoirs* he has left us carry a leitmotif of praise for the modern age: praise for the railroads "which ushered in the golden age"[24] when migrant masons no longer had to hike the 350 kilometers to Paris: praise for the superior diet which included meat (it is interesting to note that when the young Nadaud reached Paris it took him over a year before he could bring himself to touch meat which he had never eaten at home)[25]; praise for the rising wages and better conditions of life—especially for the poor. In the mid-1890s Nadaud declares that "our century is one the most marvelous in our history, as far as the rise of popular wellbeing is concerned."[26] History bears him out, and so does the memory of those old enough to remember the old days without meat or wine or schools or old-age pensions, not to mention access to light and water, and to hospitals where one need not be dragged against one's will because that is where people went only to die.

The fairy tales bear him out too. When characters in folk tales get gifts or ask for them, when they are granted three wishes and so on, their ambitions are very simple: they dream of better clothes and better places to live, but above all they dream of food—pots that will cook endless porridge, tables or tablecloths that set themselves with meals, fairy bread that cannot be eaten out of existence, cubbyholes that secrete bread and milk. A proverb of the poor Cévennes makes clear that food is the most prized of presents, and likely to be consumed at once: "He who appreciates the gift closes his teeth on it."[27]

When a white dove comes to the help of a girl lost in a forest, the bird gives her the key to a tree and promises that she "will find plenty of food." What she finds is "milk in a little bowl and beside it white bread to crumble into it, so that she was able to eat her fill."[28] The white bread would be a treat, but still that seems a very spare diet. The fact is that until the later nineteenth century the typical carnivores lived either in cities or in *châteaux* and palaces. That may be why we have a lot of legends about highborn ladies eating little children, just as Sleeping Beauty's mother-in-law wants to do in the Perrault version.[29]

In fairy stories only the wicked eat meat, like Snow White's stepmother who eats the lungs and liver of a boar thinking that they are those of the girl, or the wicked witch who plans to eat Hansel. As for the children themselves, when the witch serves them what we are told is a good meal, they get "milk, pancakes and sugar, apples and nuts."[30] That would have been a real feast, especially in a context of famine. In the Auvergne version of Hansel and Gretel, Jeannot is imprisoned in the pigsty to be fattened up and fed on pig's mash. Jeannette carries him the mash and he tries not to eat it, but "the stuff was too appetizing for hungry children." So it is not very surprising that, in another story, a king's daughter using peas to mark her trail has her plan foiled because "in every street poor children were sitting and picking up peas."[31]

The other thing the poor dream about is treasure: gold, silver, anything they could lay their hands on, precisely because they could lay their hands on so little or none. The nature of the descriptions bears witness to this—one character does not even know the value of coins at all and accepts farthings for dollars *(thalers)*, obviously because he had no previous occasion to handle either.[32]

Most poor people (which means most people) were riddled with debts, often handed down from father to son. Shortage of cash (and consequently usury) played a crucial role in the rural risings of 1848–1851 and did not cease to haunt the peasants until the First World War and its cash flow emancipated them. In one French story, entitled *Jean Le Laid,* a father sells his soul to the devil, then his daughters to Ugly John, all to pay his debts.[33] But if the image of usury is realistic, the theme of hidden treasure is realistic too in times when the ground, or a wall, or a well, were the only safe places for savings or plate. In the absence of banks, hiding one's capital or savings was the natural thing to do. No wonder that for every hundred charges of theft between fellow-villagers in eighteenth-century Languedoc, thirty-seven referred to objects hidden in fields, or by the roadside. Crumbling walls, abandoned cottages or wells, hollow trees or a chance digging could reveal unexpected wealth: hence the persistent traditions that fascinated all peasants and the quest for secret treasures—often involving magic techniques or the services of professional sorcerers.[34] In 1838 the Finistère Assizes acquitted a farmhand accused of theft, accepting his plea that he had found a treasure, supported by the common knowledge that the man was *devin* and *sorcier.* At Brignon (Gard), about half a century later, two local men cutting down an almond tree discovered a sack of gold among its roots. By then, explanations inclined to positivism: *"Belèu,* qu'il en reste encore dans les murs"[35]—so, no banks or vaults or safe deposit boxes, no credit, and little or no cash, or experience of it.

There is a splendid scene in Nadaud's *Memoirs* in which, in 1842, after years of hard labor to escape dire poverty and debt (with the shame attendant on the latter), the migrant mason returns home from a long stay in Paris with a trunk from which he first extracts fine presents for the family: wife, sisters, parents. Then comes a sack of 1,000 francs in 5-franc pieces, and a second, and great is the joy. Then Nadaud tells his wife to look and see if there is anything else in the trunk, and she finds a third sack, and then a fourth, and everybody begins to cry and kiss. Then comes the orgy: "We started to empty the sacks and to place their contents in 100-franc piles. The table was covered with silver pieces, blinding white. It was past two in the morning when we stopped contemplating what we called a fascinating sight."[36] The language is stilted, but the experience must have been stupendous, and it helps explain a lot of literary motifs that we no longer appreciate.

In folk tales the statement of misery, with which all were familiar, could lead to wonderful fantasies of resolution. There is one story in the Grimms' collection about "a little girl whose mother and father had died. She was so poor that she no longer had a room to live in nor bed to sleep in, and finally had nothing but the clothes on her back and in her hand a piece of bread that some kind soul had given her." Despite her straits, she gives the bread and the clothes off her back to people who are poorer than she is (or more enterprising), upon which the stars fall from the skies and turn into dollars which she gathers up. After which "she was rich as long as she lived."[37] Failing such rare selflessness, others sought the help of magic— not very different from what we find in tales. In 1776 Pierre Chambault of Nouan, in Sologne, was placed in the pillory on market day and then banished for having bamboozled a miller with the promise of a hen who would lay silver coins at her owner's will. The miller had paid 480 *livres* to acquire the bird.[38]

The fairy-tale world is a world in which no one can get rich except by miracle or crime. When a poor crofter in one Grimm story becomes prosperous and builds a house, his neighbors are convinced that he must have used foul means to do it, and he is summoned before the magistrate to explain his new wealth. As a matter of fact, the neighbors were right because the man was a trickster—but this, in the story, proved to be his salvation and the downfall of his neighbors beginning with the magistrate himself who ended up drowned because of their greed.[39] Evidently, in their world one could prosper only at someone else's expense (as the mercantilists correctly perceived): villages prayed that the hail should fall on the land of other villages, and people cast spells to translate milk from the udders of their neighbors' cows into that of cows in their own stable. It was a world where productivity is left to elves or dwarfs or other supernatural characters[40] who spin flax, or plait straw, or shovel mountains away, or sort peas like Cinderella's magic doves, while the hero sleeps or the heroine weeps.

The difference between the many poor and the exceptional few is reflected in looks and features: kings' daughters are visibly different—their hair is golden, their skin is white, they are beautiful, and only disguise (rags, caps to cover their shining tresses, ashes, blacking) can hide their natural nobility. Of course, the shoe-motif in *Cinderella* refers to small, dainty feet—an indication of ladylike refinement that would not be very practical for a peasant woman. Male features invite less comment, though several times kings or princesses object to the origins or the bearing of base-born suitors.[41] All this is perfectly realistic. Class standing was reflected in physique: there is evidence for it in the famous lines of Jean de la Bruyère about "certain wild animals, black and sunburnt and ghastly-looking," who have something like an articulate voice and when they straighten up show a human face.[42] The evil and the poor are often described as "black," the noble and good as "white." In the tale of Oc, *la brave Marinette* is "pretty as a new penny" while *la méchante Catinou* "had skin as black as a cricket and bleary eyes."[43] Whatever the symbolism, the fact is that only upper-class people could keep their face and hands white—and the equation between social and spiritual quality is soon made and widely accepted.

Reading Arthur Young, a century after la Bruyère, things had not changed very much on the eve of the French Revolution. And the situation for most of the nineteenth century is well-reflected in another Grimm story called "Eve's Unequal Children," in which God visits the household of Adam and Eve who have many children but decide to show Him only the handsome ones on whom he distributes rich blessings: they are to become kings and princes, nobles and merchants, burghers and scholars. As for those children who were ugly and misshapen, their parents had hidden them under the hay, in the stove, in the cellar, and so on. But since God was so good, Eve thought she would take a chance and bring them out too, and indeed God behaves very decently and blesses, as the text says, "the whole coarse, dirty, scabby, sooty troop." But the fate He allots them is to be farmer and fisherman, tanner and weaver, carter and servant.[44] So the poor themselves had a pretty good idea about their comparative looks.

Dress, of course, provides another mark of status and another contribution to the way people look. Ladies and gentlemen who do not dress right are not recognized for what they are. Heroines are only seen as such when they put on the right rich dress. That has not changed much! But one interesting detail is that even at the highest social levels fashions do not seem to change—which is not to say that they did not change in the real life of court and castle and burgherdom but that the folk public had no perception of it or of fashion as such. The prince who enters the Sleeping Beauty's palace after 100 years of quarantine finds nothing remarkable about its occupants except that they are asleep.

Compare this with Perrault's version of the Sleeping Beauty in which the prince cannot help noting that she is dressed like his great-grandmother, even though he takes good care not to say anything about it. And a little later, when they go to eat, we are told that the musicians played "old pieces, but very good ones, even though they had not been played for almost 100 years." Bettelheim finds such "petty rationality" frivolous.[45] But awareness of the chronological time is peculiar to certain types of society, and Perrault (who was a magistrate and a courtier) must have been well aware that his seventeenth-century readers would not fail to think of the changes time had wrought precisely because they lived in a society that took change for granted, whereas the contemporary peasant public did not.

By the time Washington Irving invented Rip Van Winkle, 120 years after Perrault, change-in-time is the whole point of the story with nature and humans thoroughly altered, the village changed, dress different, humans aging and dying.[46] All that after only twenty years' sleep! And the whole story is about history, about the evolution of men and societies in time. So we have quite a different notion of chronological time, which traditional peasant societies tend to ignore because it has very little to do with their conditions of life and work, as has the notion of change-in-time.

One thing that all social orders seem to have in common in tales as in real life is vermin: not just the fleas that plague even gentlefolk living in close proximity to horses and dogs (though only the peasants called getting up in the morning *"secouer ses puces"*), but lice, especially in the hair, which may be the origin of another locution, "dirty like a comb" *(sale comme un peigne)*,[47] and also the source of another motif to be found in folk tales, that of gold coins falling out when the heroine combs her hair.

One charming conceit that recurs in several stories is the relaxation that a little delousing can provide. When devils come home to grandma or kings rest with their enchanted brides, there is nothing they appreciate more than a little lousing before they go to sleep.[48] In one particular story, in which a king's son is given a series of impossible tasks, the youngest daughter of his tormentor (who is also a king) comes out into the fields to bring him something to eat (just as a farmer's wife would) and tries to cheer him up: "When he had eaten something, she said, 'First I'll louse you a bit, then you'll feel differently.' When she had loused him, he got tired and fell asleep." Whereupon, she performs a miracle and has a whole forest cut down. This is repeated three times until the prince has performed his tasks, after which they marry and she can louse him happily ever after.[49]

But marks of affection and helpfulness can become weary tasks when fair maidens are captured by dragons which, as all know, tend to a multiplicity of pates. In one such case, a young huntsman rescues not one but three princesses:

> He opened the door slowly and there sat one of the king's daughters with nine dragon heads in her lap and was lousing them. He took his hunting knife and hacked away. Then the nine heads came off. The king's daughter jumped up and fell on his neck, hugged and kissed him a lot . . . Then he went to the second daughter, who

had a seven-headed dragon to louse, and freed her too; likewise the youngest, who had a four-headed dragon to louse, he also attended to her. They all rejoiced greatly, and hugged and kissed him unceasingly.[50]

But the story does not end on this merry note because the brave young man who rescues the maidens is then betrayed by his brothers, who want to take the credit and the girls.

These stories are full of greed, envy, exploitation, and betrayal: step-mothers are terrible, of course, and stepsisters are pretty awful, but you cannot really trust your friends either,[51] or your spouse. Husbands beat their wives or condemn them to horrid ends, wives betray their husbands, and blood relations are no better: it is brother against brother, sister against sister, parents against their children. Hence perhaps a motif very popular in French folktales, songs, and sayings: "ma mère m'a tué, mon père m'a mangé"—not unrelated to certain ritual healing practices but, surely, not unrelated to experienced relations either.[52]

It would be preferable to attribute cruelty to step-relatives thus casting the responsibility for improper behavior on a stranger to the family. In theory, blood relationship should prohibit cruelty. In practice, the honor of the family and possibly its property, which could be forfeit by a heinous crime, were at stake. So, when in a Grimm story a little boy is invited to look into the apple chest and is murdered by bringing the lid down on his head, it is his stepmother who does it.

In one set of fifteen such French stories from the Dauphiné (where incidentally the lids of chests or kneading troughs are also favored) there is an occasional effort to explain the unnatural act by hunger: the mother's ferocity is due to misery; as for the father, he did not know what he was served.[53] But unlike our world, which excuses everything and understands nothing, this world always exacts retribution, and cruelty always receives a cruel punishment because folk tales, while not particularly moral, reflect the natural belief that punishment should follow crime—and that is what makes a really happy end: a wicked queen may be condemned to dance in red-hot slippers; villains will be slyly asked to name cruel punishments that will then be applied to them; and being rolled in a barrel full of spikes was particularly popular![54]

In real life retribution can also come in different ways, and our stories acknowledge this by indirection. The children, in due course, repay the treatment they have received. Hence moral tales are designed to persuade adults that it is in their own interest to be kind to their elders when they have become old and impotent.[55] This is the ambiguity of real relationships:

on one hand basic security can be found only in home, family, village: beyond these lay terrors, known and unknown. But the same terrors also lie in wait within the familiar circle, and a lot of folk tales acknowledge just how inescapable these are.

It is a frightening world everywhere, and one can do little to help oneself (or others!). Fairy bread never diminished, *provided* it was not shared with strangers, for generosity stopped at the family threshold. As far as we can tell from eighteenth-century Languedoc, it was unusual to invite passers-by to share one's food or drink.[56] Yet also (or perhaps therefore?) this is a world where the gratuitous gesture—kindness, selflessness—is the greatest virtue (perhaps because there is so little to give, perhaps precisely because it is so rare). No wonder that the generous heroes and heroines of many tales invited extraordinary rewards by their extraordinary actions. As another French proverb says, "Every fool has his good sense!" Apparent foolishness paid off, at least in fairy tales. On the other hand, in real life as in tales, a service requested (as by many a fairy figure) and performed (as by many heroes) created obligation. Hence the gifts or promises of eventual service extended by beneficiaries in our stories reflect the values of the working world.[57]

If we look beyond the commonplaces of everyday life (and I have far from exhausted them) can we discover an ideology which will give us a clue to deeper popular values? We can, but it is really no different from the dominant ideology, from the official ideology of Church and state. Like so much of popular culture, popular ideology appears mimetic. If it is not, then it reflects a coincidence of values which can be attributed to the fact that, *au fond,* the fundamental conditions of life are the same for all: a high death rate, a high incidence of illnesses and accidents, and fairly narrow limits to lived experience, compensated by frequent recourse to the supernatural. The world is finite, in space as in possibilities, and it is contingent, with fortune or misfortune playing a crucial role.

The good and the bad of the lower orders are little different from those of their betters. The work ethos is accepted by everybody, though it does not apply to everybody, since high birth, or success, of beatitude bring escape from labor. Hierarchy—social or supernatural—is affirmed by power and mitigated by luck. Folk wisdom and official values approve of reward and retribution, but experience, in which the relation between cause and effect remains unclear, suggests that many explanations are supernatural and that resignation is the ultimate wisdom.

Almanacs, the most widely distributed repository of popular wisdom, preach a stoic morality: prudence, submission, honoring the great (and to the small a lot of people are great). "Begin the year with resignation and live prudently" (but even "human prudence is helpless without help from on high"). "Forget what you cannot change." Mind your own business. "Do not judge what is not in your realm," and keep your mouth shut: "To keep silence in patience is a way of gaining favor."[58]

Patient Griselda, who endures every torment and injustice her husband heaps on her, is the model for a score of heroines: she triumphs in the end, which means that her husband stops playing nasty tricks on her, and that is probably the best that common people could expect. So it is not surprising that in a lot of folk tales enduring in silence is one of the most common tests a heroine (or even a hero) has to pass, often despite torment by witches or by devils. Power is arbitrary, people are mercurial, and it is probably impossible to justify oneself, anyway. For common folk, survival must often have depended on silence, and if it is well to be seen but not heard staying unheard may even help one to pass unnoticed.

If a common ideological basis makes some sense, there is yet another reason for the coincidence of popular and official wisdom and motifs: quite simply that folk thinking was colored, and often fashioned or refashioned, by what their betters thought or wanted them to think. The obvious agency of indoctrination here was the Church: Christian morality came to color the language and the thinking of even the humblest folk.[59] Yet, though I shall not dwell on this, Christian motifs in real folk tales seem ambiguous. Perhaps the clearest example of high culture turned to "low" can be found in the *bibliothèque bleue,* the little books bound in cheap blue paper covers that peddlers sold (along with almanacs and images) to be read or looked at by the common folk. The core of the *bibliothèque bleue* consisted of medieval legends about brave knights and fair ladies, legends mostly rewritten over and over since their vogue in the fifteenth century or so, but which in any version have nothing to do with the experience of the peasant public that inherited them and kept them alive when the sophisticated public had moved on to something else.[60] The interesting thing about these knightly tales is that they include a lot of the incidents and the motifs of folk tales, especially those found in the "once upon a time" sort. There are enchanted animals and forests and castles, giants and wicked stepmothers and nasty mothers-in-law, and treacherous brothers. There are wizards as well, though that very familiar figure, the witch (except as ogress), does not appear in knightly tales in which men retain the monopoly of what is, after all, a high-class profession. There is every reason to think that this sort of stuff trickled into the villages and the taverns, there to be reshaped to the needs and the mentalities of a popular public.

The *bibliothèque bleue* declined and died after mid-nineteenth century, about the same time that *märchen* went out; in both cases this happened because conditions changed, and because something better was becoming available, which the people took up as eagerly as they had taken up almanacs or images or knightly tales. Changing material conditions meant that the realistic substance of *märchen* no longer matched experience. Schools and military service were teaching the national language, and discipline and patriotism, so that the stories about people who could not make themselves understood away from home lost their old meaning except in places like Brittany; the deserters who figure in a number of tales were no longer heroic; the violence was now frowned on as disorderly and immoral—and the Grimms themselves in their second edition dropped a bloody story about children who play at killing each other.

The new national institutions also taught hygiene. The use of soap was generalized, as taxes on soap were abolished in the later nineteenth century. Lice were getting scarce, and only philologists remember that in Occitan the little finger was called *kill-lice*. Forests were cut down and roads were built through what was left of them, so fear of wolves, of forests, and of other vast waste places no longer figured as a fact of life. There were more police. Money circulated more, and so did people.

Even more fundamental changes took place: famines became rare as agricultural productivity increased (the last great European famine flared in mid-nineteenth century), and local subsistence crises (which were really *transport* crises) disappeared as railroads became capable of carrying food to places where it was lacking. After mid-nineteenth century diet improved. Poor people, especially country people, remained far more herbivorous than their urban betters, but they did eat meat and drank wine. The caloric intake rose, and hunger became a private affair, no longer a recognizable public issue.

Mortality rates fell too. Up until the eighteenth century, adult mortality followed by remarriage might be compared to divorce today. It certainly furnishes one major theme of folk tales. Now, the family gradually became more stable and affected the better integration of children and also the nature of current fantasies. To take only one example: when the nineteenth century opened, expectation of life for women in the Lower Burgundy of Restif and Coignet was about twenty-five years. By mid-nineteenth century this had risen into the forties; by 1900 it hovered around fifty-two. There would be a lot fewer orphans and stepmothers, just as there was a lot less hunger and want. The practical need that had made for speedy remarriage grew less urgent. During the seventeenth and eighteenth centuries three or four out of every five widowers remarried within the year of their spouse's death. By the twentieth century not quite one in five bothered to do so.

Meanwhile, the control that ordinary people could exercise over life increased. By the nineteenth century cattle were no longer left to look after themselves as best they could. They were fattened, selected, *bred*. Men presided over their couplings and came to look on breeding as a technique like any other. If animal life could be regulated, human life could be regulated too. By 1840 the peasants in certain French rural communes were having half as many children as their forebears three-fourths of a century earlier. There were fewer parents forced to accept Death for a godfather because they had so many children that no one else was left to accept the charge.[61]

So what had been realistic detail became distant and unreal. The morality that had made sense in its own terms no longer quite fit conditions and possibilities as they were now perceived. Endogamy became less oppressive, and stories about robber bridegrooms no longer warned against the dangers of marrying away from the familiar community. Escapist fantasies became less necessary and also less relevant because the fantasies themselves were changing with the times. The storytellers perceived this, and by the latter part of the nineteenth century they treated fairies and goblins and werewolves only as *past* realities: their grandfathers knew them, yes, but they left the region about the time of the French Revolution.[62]

It was not just that the wisdom of the folk tale was no longer useful. Their relative entertainment value also declined as the folk moved out of the do-it-yourself era into the new market of an industrial age. As the nineteenth century wore on, homemade amusements were discarded along with homemade clothes. Both could be found in the market now, and not only were they available but they could also be afforded. Sensation, excitement, amusement became available in print, in images, in access to urban facilities or to developing centers of rural sociability and fun—cafés, cabarets, and so on. Home crafts were declining and more homes enjoyed some kind of light and (even better) heat, so the *veillées*—the evening work bees at which most of the tales were told—declined. Meanwhile, the stories that could be heard in school or read in schoolbooks were more varied, more impressive, more prestigious than the old tales.

The world was being domesticated. Mysteries were explained away. A nature that, only a short while before, could only be handled by analogy was being analyzed into working parts. Manure took the place of magic. Time became an element of everyday life, novelty was both available and desired (the press brought news, and new sensations), and change was perceived not only as a fact of life but as desirable. As Nadaud insisted, change was progress. The press, the schools, the public speeches, and one's own life, confirmed this. In such a context the images that the old tales offered were no longer familiar or acceptable. Their wisdom became nonsense and superstition—which is precisely how it had been denounced for centuries by voices and authorities the public steadfastly ignored as long as the old wisdom still made sense. Now the services the yarns had rendered were no longer required, indeed could be dispensed with on every sort of level. They could be relegated to the world of children, along with fairies, fair maidens, and brave knights, to become the entertaining fictions that the educated classes had long appreciated as such.[63]

~ 5

Who Sang the *Marseillaise?*

The battle song of the Army of the Rhine was born at Strasbourg, on April 25, 1792, from a suggestion that Mayor Dietrich made to a young officer among his guests, Captain Rouget de Lisle.[1] The song Rouget composed was sung in Dietrich's salon the following evening; and three days later, on Sunday, April 29, it was played by the band of the National Guard and sung for the Lyons volunteers of the first Rhône-et-Loire Battalion,[2] who paraded that day on the Place d'Armes in Strasbourg. It was a great success; Mrs. Dietrich, the mayor's wife, wrote to her brother about it, describing it as *"du Gluck en mieux,"* and within a few days it had been put into print—which facilitated its distribution throughout the land.

On June 17 the song was heard at Montpellier, and within a few days a delegate of the Constitutional Society (that is, of the Girondists) of Montpellier carried it to Marseille. The delegate was Mireur, who was destined to become a general of the Republic; for the moment, he was trying to encourage the Marseillais to respond to a Paris appeal for 500 men "qui sachent mourir": and since he was not beyond using audio-visual aids in a tricky task, on June 22 he sang the new song at the end of a constitutional banquet.

People sang a lot in those days—popular deputations would visit the Convention and sing patriotic songs of their own composing, which rather hampered proceedings; and Danton had to intervene several times to establish that the Convention was *not* a place for singing songs.[3] But banquets were, and this one met with great enthusiasm.

The very next day, the new song was printed in the local press, and also on a separate broadsheet of which the volunteers of the Marseille Battalion, then being raised with some difficulty, received several copies each. They would sing the song and distribute copies of it, on their march to Paris, which took all of July. They may also have shouted snatches of it when they helped to storm the Tuileries, on August 10. At any rate, the song became known as the hymn or the air of the Marseillais.

This raises an intriguing question: who sang the *Marseillaise?* Or, to put it differently: how was it that the *Marseillaise* was sung in French? In 1792, by all accounts, French was as foreign to most *provençaux* as to Senegalese a century later. As a matter of fact, it was unfamiliar to most people within the borders of France. The Abbé Grégoire, who undertook a vast official survey of the question in 1790, concluded rather hopefully that three-quarters of the people of France knew *some* French. On the other hand, he admitted that only a *portion* of these could actually sustain a conversation in it, and he estimated that only about 3 million could speak it properly—while fewer still, of course, could put their French in writing.[4]

We can take this as a rough guide, although I think Grégoire was a bit sanguine. But it is well to remember that, south of the magic line that runs from Saint-Malo to Geneva and divides northern, francophone, developed France from the rest of the country, the non-French speakers were much more concentrated than Grégoire's estimates suggest. In 1824, a third of a century after the *Marseillaise* was born, the official *Statistique des Bouches-du-Rhône* recognized that the normal speech of the middle and lower classes was Provençal, and added: "it will take a good many years, perhaps centuries, before the French language becomes commonplace."

Just as most Neapolitans nowadays can produce some English if they have to, the ordinary people of Marseille understood enough French for whatever aspects of their business would call for it, but they seldom spoke the language. This suggests that the volunteers were a bit exceptional—which they must have been, since they numbered a little less than 500 out of a population well over 100,000, and had to pay their own way! We do not know how many of them really did pay it, or had it paid for them; and precise information about them is oddly hard to get. But we do know that they were led by young men of the upper classes—who would be, by definition, bilingual; and we know that they included a good few people whose trade edged them toward a knowledge of French: ex-soldiers, journalists, port workers and artisans, or simply drifters.

A writer of the 1840s claims that true Marseillais were few among a rabble of foreign elements; and while he is a hostile witness, it is certain that Marseille itself had become a foreign element in its region—a great cosmopolitan trade center. Outsiders and other mobile types would be more likely recruits for the battalion: they would be more available mentally and physically, they would be more likely to know or understand French, and it is significant that Michelet wrote about them as "alliés et amis du parti français."[5]

However, Michelet recognized that the battalion included also "rude men of the people," and this may account for Lamartine's remark that the masses of people who saw them on their march to Paris were struck by "leurs langages étrangers mêlés de jurements."[6] They also improved on Rouget de Lisle by producing a Provençal verse of their own, which was pretty strong stuff:

> March on, God's arse
> March on, God's fart
> The emigrés, by God
> Have no more idea of God
> Than old monarchist priests.[7]

But obviously what was remembered and noted wherever they passed were the words in French.

By autumn of 1792 the hymn created in the far northeast, disseminated from the south, was sung throughout France—"by all the troops and by the children," specified a report of October 1792, which pointed to the chief agents of its penetration. When Kellerrman wanted a *Te Deum* sung on the battlefield at Valmy, to celebrate his victory, the minister of war wrote back prescribing instead the *Hymne des Marseillais,* "que je joins ici à cet effet." This was certainly connected with other political considerations, but it also reflected the official campaign of frenchification. In 1790 the famous *fête de la Fédération* had included a *Te Deum* sung in Latin, with the responses provided by "the people." This had produced criticism of such official use of Latin: "Parlons en français."[8] "Chantons en français" was the same thing, and the *Marseillaise* was used to that purpose. But the circumstance also suggests that for populations traditionally used to singing canticles or responses in Latin (or dog Latin) which they could not understand, a French refrain to a much livelier tune would present no greater problem.

The paradox, of course, was that the new national hymn (as it became in 1795) was linked to a city whose people did not speak French nor, in the case of many of them, feel themselves to be French. But even those who did not speak French could sing it, and singing endowed them with the gift of tongues.

For example, here is a true scene which took place at Bellegarde, between Nîmes and Arles, one day in the 1850s. The poor of a whole parish go off to glean at the break of dawn, and as they go they are singing their own songs. Then, in the midst of this unschooled, thoroughly *patoisant* mass, one man starts to sing *Partant pour la Syrie,* in French; and the whole crowd, we are told, joins in the culminating verse of this song that Queen Hortense had composed at the first Napoleon's court:

> Faites, reine immortelle,
> Lui dit-il en partant,

Que j'aime la plus belle
Et sois le plus vaillant![9]

Batista Bonnet, the man who tells us this and who tells us how as a little boy he joined in the singing, went off to be a soldier and serve for six years until wounded in the Franco-Prussian War; and he knew French so little at the end of this, at age twenty-seven, that when he decided to stay on in Paris and try to work there, he had to take French lessons "à 40 sous l'heure."[10]

Bonnet was no exception, and in a way that is what I want to stress. In 1893, according to official figures, about a quarter of the 37,000-odd communes in France spoke no French. Their population accounted for seven and a half million out of the 30 million souls in France. About half a million out of 4 million children between seven and thirteen spoke no French; another million and a half could speak or understand but could not write it—a strong suggestion that they knew it badly. And the reports of academy inspectors inspecting teachers' Normal Schools through the 1870s and 1880s show that the children's teachers and apprentice teachers knew it badly too.

To put this differently: French was a foreign language for a large minority of the country's inhabitants. And almost half of the children who would reach adulthood in the last quarter of the nineteenth century were taught French, if and when they were taught it, as a foreign language.

The Revolution and the Empire had perfected the administrative and legal unity of French territory; but cultural integration, cultural unity, still had to be imposed on a vast and stubborn (or, rather, indifferent) diversity. My reference to the *Marseillaise* was intended to stress the superficiality of certain symbols, the relatively narrow range of their effects, and the depths still unplumbed where everyday life went on, where the *pays* or *patrie* still stood for a limited valley or parish or land, and where it would take a long time before symbols like the *Marseillaise* reflected any real identification with a wider culture—the culture of France as we read and learn about it, the culture of French, of Paris, of the schools.

The subject is immense and few have bothered to scratch at it. The accepted dogma has France forged either by the "*quarante rois qui en mille ans ont fait la France,*" or struck out at a heat in the furnace of the 1790s. A variant of this prefers 1848, or 1849, or 1851. And yet Jacques Duclos, born in Béarn in 1896, only learned French after he went to school. And when he was called up for military service there were peasants around him who did not speak French at all. Around 1903, just when Duclos was going off to school, a travel writer called Ardouin-Dumazet was trying to find his way in a village in the monts d'Ambazac, not far from Limoges. He could not find a single person who could understand him (or who would, which culturally amounts to the same thing). So he went on and, outside the village, in the fields, he found the men at work—and they could speak in French, having learnt enough of it at school or in the army to get by.

I mention this story because it is not about the Pyrenees or about Flanders, where under the Third Republic priests like the Abbé Lemire had to learn Flemish in order to exercise their ministry; or about Brittany, where in the 1880s the rector of the Academy of Rennes suggested in an official report that the French should do what the Germans were doing to "our poor Alsace-Lorraine." The monts d'Ambazac are in the very center of France, and their speech is the speech of Languedoc. But I mention the story also because what schooling there was in country places until the 1880s was directed to the boys, and was therefore bound to have only superficial effects in societies where women and older people were left outside its ken, and where the business of life outside school, in the home, in the streets, was necessarily conducted in the local speech.

Clearly language, the form of speech in which we conduct our transactions, in which we enshrine our wisdom or speculate about our experience, is crucial to culture and to mentality. Those for whom their speech (and hence their thoughts) was something else than French, could never be really French, could not be (as long as this state lasted) really thoroughly part of the modern nation of France—at least no more, or little more or more significantly, beyond the level of taxes and conscription, than they were part of humanity.

Now, it is fairly clear that they aspired to participate in French culture, at least in terms of what they saw of its external expressions. French was a Sunday language, just as meat (for those lucky enough to have it) was a Sunday dish. *Habits mangeant viande* and *habits de messe* are both terms for a Sunday suit. French, remarked an officer riding through Hérault in 1828, was a *langage de parure et de cérémonie*. And there is a lot to show that he was right. Thus, until the end of the century, peasants addressed their betters in French. At dances, the invitation and the first approach are still made in French. In old *noëls,* the shepherds speak dialect, but the angels speak French. And Agricol Perdiguier tells us that at Morière, near Avignon, in the 1820s, the peasants who spoke only *patois* nevertheless resented being given a sermon in *patois* and not in French at a First Communion ceremony: "It struck us as common, trivial, unworthy of so great a ceremony." [11] As with the songs, as with the Mass, how much you understand is secondary. What matters is the melody, the sense of the act.

Speaking French, or giving oneself French airs, was a symbol of social promotion—or at least of aspirations in this direction. And this was understood by village society that both mocked and envied the *Franciot,* the *Fran-chiman*—or whatever he was called in various places. French reflected a superior other-ness, like that of squire or priest or teacher; and so it was perceived by the villagers, as can be seen from a story that Albert Dauzat told about the peasants in Puy-de-Dôme who got uppity as the nineteenth century dawned and began to give their children French names, in imitation of their local squires. In 1820 the priest of Vic-le-Comte asked a little girl her name: "Marie," she said, "Marie! But that is a young lady's name, not a name for a peasant. You must be called Miyette or Mayon." And the little girl answered: "I'm as entitled to bear the Holy Virgin's name as any lady." [12]

French was dignified, suspect, and superior. It was also urban, modern, "civilized." It provided the terminology of innovation and modernity, and it provided certain more or less abstract notions for which traditional language had not catered. So that little *Janed* of the Breton song, who is tired of service and wants her freedom, sings: "Mé zo skuiz o servicha / La mé houl và *liberté*!"

But French provided or helped provide something else as well; this was an image or self-image that I can best describe by referring to a book by the English Africanist Terry Ranger. [13] The book is devoted to the history of a dance mode called *Beni,* which had developed on the Swahili-speaking coast of East Africa, in places like Mombassa and Dar-es-Salaam. As *Beni* progressed into the interior, into the back country, it carried with it the aura of Swahili civilization. It was sung in Swahili, it came from the great Swahili urban centers, and Ranger quotes a local informant: "People who could sing in such a dance were esteemed very highly as Swahili, even though his or her spoken Swahili was very poor."

French songs, city songs, were similarly regarded. And, in a period of national integration, when public policy and private interest seem to coincide, at least on this score, songs (like those of Béranger, immensely popular in the 1830s) helped the singers pick up elementary notions of the national language, perhaps encouraged them to learn more of it, but also bolstered their self-esteem. In the small urban centers of Provence workingmen had their own singing societies, where they made up their own songs in local dialect. But we are told that they avoided public performance of "songs in the vulgar tongue." [14] Thus, when the Prince-President Louis-Napoleon visited Aix in 1852, the local authorities tried to organize a performance of Provençal songs for his benefit. But they could not. The choirs sang fragments from operas and comic operas (very likely they sang *Partant pour la Syrie*), and they sang original French songs by local composers. But they would not sing in Provençal. It may have been cultural snobbery. But is was probably also a refusal to be cast into an exotic and implicitly demeaning role.

This *mimétisme,* this sociocultural mimicry that affected many more realms beside that of song, could also be used to didactic ends—not only to spread the use of French, but to spread the mentality approved by official culture: to moralize, to civilize, to soothe the savage breast. So national integration also involved a war of songs. Before they turned to collecting popular songs, like butterflies on pins and just as dead, educated men pursued them with their ire. In the 1860s an excellent folklorist of Lorraine, Xavier Thiriat, wrote about the Vosges, insisting on the vulgar character of native songs (in dialect of course!) as opposed to "those coming from big cities and written in our time," which he found "well-inspired and true expressions of noble sentiments." [15]

Feelings like this were strongest among professional carriers of civilization and literacy: the teachers. Popular songs, like other forms of popular culture, were best the soonest shed and replaced by something finer. And one of the first ways in which teachers intervened as publicists for noble sentiments would be in the realm of conscription—which normal people loathed, and which called forth popular comment that was either tearful or bitterly satirical and sarcastic, like the well-known product of three stocking-makers from Languedoc:

> Monsieur le Maire et le Préfêt
> Ce sont deux jolis cadets.
> Ils nous font tirer au sort
> Pour nous conduire à la mort. [16]

This sort of thing had to be countered, and it is interesting that about the only songs in French that became part of the village *répertoire* after the 1850's were patriotic conscript songs like:

> Partons, partons, vaillants conscrits,
> Partons, la fleur de la jeunesse!

produced by *instituteurs* and such like propagandists. The next step would be moralistic. In the 1860s we find a Pyrenean schoolteacher, in Ariège, complaining that all one hears in the countryside are coarse and impure songs: the singing that would improve morals, refine feelings, enoble the spirit, develop intellect, was completely ignored. Schoolteachers, he said, must realize that it is their duty, nay their mission, to propagate such songs. They did.

In 1864, the department of Aude reported with pride that "the lewd songs that wounded even the least modest ears have been replaced by the religious and patriotic choirs of numerous *orphéons* . . . due to schools and to the initiative of teachers."[17] Under the Republic, virtuous but isolated efforts of this sort turned into a nationwide campaign. Jules Simon, who was minister of public instruction in 1872, had often been struck, he wrote to Ambroise Thomas, the composer, "to hear nothing but very vulgar songs at workers' or peasants' get-togethers." He and others set out to provide remedies on the model of German ones, because they had noticed that in 1870 the Germans, whatever region they came from, could join in song, and they wanted to "teach little French children this means of uniting and of glorifying their fatherland," sentiments which, incidentally, most little Frenchmen ignored—at least in the areas I am talking about.[18]

In 1864, a school inspector in Lozère had expressed indignation after visiting schools where he could not find a single child to answer questions like: "Are you English or Russian?" or "What country is Lozère in?" And he added bitterly that, in most of the children, "thought does not go beyond the limits of the poor parish in which they live." The great educational campaigns of the 1880s were directed against this sort of thing, and among their more effective armaments were new song books that followed German models for school use. Lay elementary schools put great stress on singing lessons which could inculcate a sense of the fatherland, of civilization, and of moral ideals. And the effects of this become clear when, by the mid-eighties, we hear the hills of backcountry Cantal echoing no longer with lewd ditties, but with the songs of Déroulède, yelled out by enthusiastic schoolboys. In 1894 one of the great educational apostles of the day, Félix Pécaut, noted that songs learnt at school were beginning to replace (*sometimes,* he added cautiously) among adult youth "the bad songs that had been too current in France." This was terribly important: "C'est la patrie, c'est la civilisation, c'est aussi un certain idéal moral."[19] In other words, we are talking about culture and about the process of replacing one culture, one set of cultural equipment, by another.

The *Marseillaise,* with which I started, plays only a marginal role in all this. But it does provide a symbol of the process, and a special case. At Jemappes, it played the soldiers of Dumouriez to victory, and after that it became associated with the great battles of the Republic: Hoche had it sung at Wissemburg, Bonaparte crossed the Saint Bernard with it, and in 1795, after Thermidor had delivered Rouget de Lisle from prison, an official decree made it the national anthem.

Under the Consulate and the Empire, the *Marseillaise* seems to ebb, although it reappeared at the Berezina, at Waterloo, and above all during the Hundred Days. After that, it went underground, of course, but it rose again in 1828, in Auber's opera, *La Muette de Portici;* and it marked the revolutions of 1830, not only in Paris but in Brussels too. But Louis-Philippe (although he provided a pension for Rouget de Lisle, who was old and ill) did not really like it very much. It was too closely associated with *cannibales*,[20] and this was confirmed in 1834, when the insurgents of the rue Transnonain adopted it, after which it was largely suppressed until 1840, when, at the height of the Orient Crisis, the government permitted its singing, thus providing the cities of France with a perfect way to express their chauvinism.[21]

War and Revolution, War *or* Revolution, was what the *Marseillaise* represented. And in 1848, naturally, Rachel brought down the house every time she sang it wrapped in a *tricolore*. Just as on March 28, 1871, the Commune would be proclaimed at the Hôtel de Ville to the strains of the *Marseillaise*.

So the song was loaded with political implications, and it was a party song. We read about a bloody political riot at Tarascon in 1850, where the Reds, says the police report, cried out ferociously (no doubt in dialect!) while singing the *Marseillaise*. It was banned under the Second Empire, but an Ardennes workers' song, which represents the journeymen going off for a Monday's drinking the country, also called for it:

> And if one of us should know it,
> Let him sing the *Marseillaise*![22]

Obviously some people did know it, because in 1858, when the garbled news of Orsini's attempt to murder the Emperor reached a little village in the Pyrenees, and people thought the Emperor was dead, the deputy mayor sang the *Marseillaise*, because "now we are all free."[23]

It was difficult to build up the myth of Napoleonic glory and stifle its most rousing battle song. Around 1865, in far-off Aurrillac, Frère Hilarion, who taught history in the local high school, communicated his own enthusiasms to his students. "One day, as he was telling us about the volunteers of 1792, he was carried away by his enthusiasm into singing us a verse of the *Marseillaise*. Suddenly, we were all on our feet, pale and shivering, drunk with the glory of our forefathers. We took it up, in full voice." Arsène Vermenouze, the royalist poet who recalled the scene many years later, had learnt to play the trumpet then, simply in order to play the hymn.[24] So, when the Empire fell, and especially during the siege of Paris, the *Marseillaise* was back very quickly,[25] often with new verses. The Commune would also have its own version, written by the wife of Jules Faure, herself born a Castellane, which did not prevent her from writing:

> Chantons la liberté,
> Défendons la cité,

Marchons, marchons!
Sans souverain
Le peuple aura du pain.[26]

Down again, up again. . . . The *Marseillaise* could not be the hymn of the *ordre moral*. Indeed, it was the symbol of opposition to it; in 1877, when Marshal MacMahon visited Roanne between the 16 May and the October elections, his reception would be troubled by a crowd of workingmen belting out the subversive song.[27] But the republican political victory in 1879 once more reinstated it as the national anthem. And by 1900 or so, that is what it had fully become, with even the band of the *Ecole des Frères* at Pont l'Abbé, in darkest Brittany, concluding their program with it, and having to repeat it to public acclaim.[28]

By that time, too, the workers whose fathers had sung the *Marseillaise* were learning to sing the *Internationale*. The general acceptance of what had long been prized as a fighting song had softened its implications. As late as 1880, the *Marseillaise* was still the favorite song of striking workmen. After 1884, Michelle Perrot tells us, the *Carmagnole* began to offer it serious competition.[29] By 1890 it had overtaken it among working people, and the first strains of the *Internationale* were being heard in socialist meetings. A new factional song had replaced the old one that was now recognized as a symbol of national unity.

Before that happened, however, the song had to cover some ground. Not only in terms of politics, where the right took a very long time to accept it (we know all about that!), but in terms of culture, of significance: because you will have noticed that, like most expressions of the official culture, the *Marseillaise* remained largely an urban affair, and that even when "the people" sang it, it was in towns that they sang.

Perhaps I can best make the point with one of the mass of popular patriotic songs that blossomed with the *République des républicains*. In 1882, a ditty called *Le Fils de l'Allemand* represented a German officer in Lorraine asking a peasant woman to nurse his baby.[30] And the woman proudly answered:

Và, passe ton chemin, ma mamelle est française.
N'entre pas sous mon toît, emporte ton enfant.
Mes garçons chanteront plus tard la *Marseillaise,*
Je ne vends pas mon lait au fils d'un Allemand!

The point here is not only the reference to the *Marseillaise,* but the fact that, at that time, the countrywoman would most probably express herself in *patois*—something that the Parisian author of the song ignored, of course. And, as long as she did, French could hardly be a *langue maternelle,* with all that this implies for the sort of patriotism our *chansonnier* was interested in. Identification could only shift from the familiar community to a broader one, the cult of the local fatherland could only be transferred to more abstract entities, when speech confirmed and suggested new values and new identities.

Of course, this is not what the song was about. We know that the *chansonnier* wanted to make the point that Lorrainers continued to feel more French than German—and very possibly he was right. He would certainly be right in suggesting (but it never occurred to him that the issue arose!) that the generation born around 1880 would indeed sing the *Marseillaise,* and that they would find in it a meaning as great as the songs of their own *pays,* or perhaps greater. But my point has been to suggest that such feelings were *not* there, in much of the countryside, in 1882, any more than they had been in 1792. Both the French language and French sentiments had to be inculcated. They had to be taught. In January 1884, a teacher's magazine called *L'Ecole* recommended that teachers should teach their students the *Marseillaise,* "whose words are as ignored as its music is famous." And it would be the schools that taught both the French words of the *Marseillaise,* and the French sentiments—the French identity it stands for.

By the end of the century, the warlike, patriotic, revolutionary song of one political faction had, in effect, become the song of France. And it carried not only the language of its lyrics, but a potent identity. "One sings the *Marseillaise* for its words, of course," said Maurice Barrès in 1902, "but one sings it especially for the mass of emotions that it stirs in our subconscious."[31] In an age of oral culture, it is unlikely that anything but a song could have wrought so much.

～ 6

Religion or Superstition?

Superstition is the religion of others: their credulousness about beliefs we do not share. Religion is the belief in gods that some hold false, behavior or practice others consider contrary to reason, but that provides a bond (*religio*) among its votaries. So religion and superstition are two sides of the same coin—at least in this particular perspective on nineteenth-century France.

The eighteenth century opened the way to heterodoxy, but only for a minority, most of whom knew or learned the virtue of discretion. But the Revolution sent the Church tumbling and, with it, the public disciplines and restraints which kept superstition—that is, nonconformity to official religion—in its place: in the shadows. After 1801, even after 1814, Catholicism was no more than the religion of a majority of the French, the Church that once enforced it represented one opinion among others. More overtly than ever, at least within living memory, piety took many forms. René de Chateaubriand had warned that witches' lairs would open when the temples of the Lord were closed. But witches had been around for a long time; and when the temples of the Lord reopened, sorcerers and soothsayers were still around to challenge their offerings, their prophecies and ceremonies. Never, it seems, at least in modern times, were religion and superstition more active in France than during the heyday of irreligion and anticlericalism.

Betting on horses that have won, accounts of the age emphasize irreligion and its struggle against traditional beliefs, but pay less heed to widespread religious preoccupations, let alone persistence. We acknowledge the nineteenth century's fascination with religion, from piety to faddishness, but minimize the relevance of an obsessive religious quest. Even historians of *mentalités,* myself included, have tended to play down less obvious linkages between broader religious activities, culture and politics. The late eighteenth century's revival of millenarian beliefs, and the conjunction of millenarianism and mundane politics, offer a good example of the sort of thing we know but gloze over.

The Revolution of 1789, and even more its brood, had been about changing mankind and altering human nature. Even when it foundered, revolutionary experience suggested a radical transformation in progress, and changes of cosmic significance just around the corner. Apocalyptic speculation was reinforced by circumstance. E. P. Thompson has referred to the chiliasm of despair. There was also, of course, a chiliasm of hope: specific or diffuse, present terror bred hope of future regeneration. Even the persecution of the Church suggested the coming of the Joachimite third age. Fourscore years ago, Albert Mathiez described such messianic expectations of a new Jerusalem: the vision "of an age of gold placed in the future and no longer in the past." [1]

The conjunction of revolution and chiliasm was crucial. In a work published in 1975, Clarke Garrett made the point that revolutionaries and millenarians both affirmed the possibility that heaven could be built on earth. Nor were the two currents clearly divided, either from each other or from Christian thought. There were those for whom accomplishing the political revolution advanced the realization of divine will. Garrett devotes a chapter to Suzette Labrousse, a holy woman and prophet from Vanxains,[2] near Ribérac in Perigord, for whom the Revolution ushered in God's regeneration of the world, and who unsuccessfully tried to get the Pope to collaborate with the divine design. The constitutional bishop of Dordogne, meanwhile, edited a *Journal prophétique,* "dedicated to showing that the Revolution was the herald of the millennium,"[3] sometimes in very practical ways that remind one of Charles Fourier: the weather would improve, the land bear richer fruit . . . Only the seas of lemonade are missing.

The Church soon jettisoned such encumbrances. Some anticlericals stuck with them. Those whom Frank Kermode nicely described as religious anticlericals could not do without them. Hence the apparent paradox that makes early Socialists religious (or superstitious), often in a millenarian vein. Explorers of literary marginalia are acquainted with the strong current of romantic mysticism that ran through Restoration to July Monarchy, drawing its sources in Swedenborg and Saint Martin, Mme Guyon and Mme de Krüdener, to Lamennais, Esquiros, Buchez, Quinet, Alphonse-Louis Constant, and developing fashionable themes of eschatological thought: a new last age, the end of days, the cult of woman as redeemer, Christ—no longer the Revolution's *sans-culotte de Nazareth,* nevertheless a harbinger of social salvation. This is the inspiration of a wordy, pretentious, excruciatingly bad book by Philippe Muray, somewhat reminiscent of James Webb's *Flight from Reason.* Serious students would do better to shun Muray and turn to Auguste Viatte's classic *Sources occultes du Romantisme,* or to his more accessible *Hugo et les illuminés de son temps.*[4] Yet beneath Muray's verbiage, a lean article struggles to escape. Its argument: that the occult was unavowed progressivism, socialism a form of occultism that prefers not to think about its origins (or foundation myth, or basic nature). The common factor of socialism and the occult is magic, in the sense that Flaubert had in mind when he pointed out that magic believes in immediate change by virtue of the formulas it employs, exactly like socialism. Thus a metaphor becomes an argument, and Muray insists: "without the occult the triumph of socialist [ideas] might not have been as complete."[5]

The thesis is interesting, though Muray claims undue priority in its formulation. "Socialisme et occultisme. Une question jamais posée."[6] The subtitle of Gérard de Nerval's *Les Illuminés: Les précurseurs du socialisme,* which Muray himself quotes without the publication date, 1852, suggests that the idea had occurred before. Garrett raises it too. But Garrett is more restrained; he lacks the baroque boldness of an author ever ready to treat metaphor as evidence. Garrett has "resisted the temptation to look for secret or unconscious millenarians among the principal actors of the French Revolution."[7] If only Muray had resisted as stoutly. Instead, he yields to every far-fetched suggestion. Robespierre is Messiah; Jacobins refer to him as Savior; his admirers liken him to God; "his icon hangs in cottages"[8]—a dubious assertion before the advent of cheap prints, but reminiscent of Che Guevara in Bolivia. Contemporary gossip does not make a case.

Guilt by allegation becomes proof by association when Muray trots out Catherine Théot, an aged prophet consulted and adulated by a few disciples, attractive to nosy neighbors, *mondains* interested in eccentrics, and police spies. For Muray, Robespierre's involvement with Théot (alleged and dismissed in the Convention just before Thermidor) raises no doubt: "Royalists, *magnétiseurs,* Jacobins, everyone comes to see her."[9] Naturally, Robespierre had his special armchair reserved by her side. A look at Garrett's chapter on Théot explodes the mummery. No mesmerism, no magnetism, no Robespierre; some royalists (but not *as* royalists), and Jacobins—mostly to observe and denounce the prayer meetings conducted by Théot. This places in perspective Muray's description of his book which, he tells us, offers "a history of the literary nineteenth century complete with rigorous periodization [actually, a capricious farrago], an approach to the key question of how past religions turned into universal socio-occult beliefs [diverse affirmations with no documentation], and finally a novel, a sort of novel."[10]

This last is true. And, though the historical novel seems long, it presents the times and their literary and political personalities in an unaccustomed light, stressing a side of them that we knew but to which we have not given much thought. Muray reminds us how strong the millennial, chiliastic, eschatological currents were in early and mid-nineteenth-century France, how pervasive the interest in the occult, how permeated progressive political and literary milieux were by these currents. "Wherever one turns, one stumbles on a Messiah." [11]

For the swarm of *illuminés,* Emmanuel Swedenborg was one of the patron saints. Dead since 1772, he had left behind the vision of our universe as a forest of symbols, Baudelaire's "temple ou des vivants pilliers / Laissent parfois sortir de confuses paroles." He had done more: he had traveled among the planets, had seen the dead, had plumbed the world of spirits and attended the last judgment. In his wake, Swedenborg's disciples would seek the key to the secrets of the universe, the host of obscure oracles announcing a new era and the coming of a "social" religion. Although Swedenborg affected many, Fourier was probably not one of them. But Muray likes chains of influence: Swedenborg influences Fourier who influences Flora Tristan who quotes both in support of her feminism. [12] But Fourier would have been irritated to see his system of analogies attributed to Swedenborg, and Tristan appreciated Fourier not for his esotericism but for his social phantasies and, above all, for his stout championship of women.

For Muray, feminism is connected with suspect inclinations toward vegetarianism, theosophy, and pacifism. [13] It was certainly a rather eccentric notion, yet not so strange in times when social justice was still confused with charity. A number of the nineteenth century's utopian prophets shared it. Fourier, Auguste Comte, Prosper Enfantin believed in the liberty, equality, in certain ways the superiority, of women. The image of the suffering woman, especially the suffering mother (the Virgin mother best of all, symbol of salvation for the Christian soul), could easily turn into a promise of worldly redemption, a vision of woman as instrument of social progress. Ill-married or prostituted, deprived of legal and intellectual rights, condemned to procreate in pain, woman is crucified as the Christ was crucified and shares his redeeming role. Swedenborg had spoken of a hidden key to the secrets of life. Mary or Magdalen, woman holds the key to a new mankind, and that key is suffering charity, loving suffering. Better still, in the Abbé Constant's *Dernière Incarnation* (1846) Christ returns to Paris to preach socialism, and he holds out the vision of a fusion of the sexes in an androgynous socialist realm where men and women will be no more, only strength and tenderness, grace and energy, integrated in one being.

In this context, one appealing figure deserves to be drawn from the shadows, to whom Muray alludes very much *en passant:* Ganneau, sculptor by trade and founder, in the 1840s, of a philosophical religion that insisted on equality of the sexes and sought to fuse the male and female principles into one. The religion's name, *evadisme,* fused Eve and Adam; and Ganneau's title as high priest, Mapah, was a conflation of MAter and PAter. Evadisme foundered in 1848, leaving behind a few pamphlets now in the Bibliothèque Nationale, and some traces in the mind of men it briefly attracted, like Jules Verne's editor, Hetzel, and the future *communard* destined to die a deputy of the Third Republic: Félix Pyat. Muray does not mention evadisme, nor does he make clear just who the Mapah was. He is too fascinated by the absurd aspect of such cults to notice how easily the transition could be made from a socialist union of the sexes to a socialist union of classes, how naturally one image of suffering redeemers could (and would) be substituted for another.

Although feminism was a good deal more than queer cultishness, a propensity to cultishness does mark the times. Muray reminds us (he is not the first) how many nineteenth-century reformers dabbled in the esoteric, if not in the occult: Saint-Simon for one, who ended by proposing a *New Christianity* (1825). Olinde Rodriguez, Alphonse Esquiros, and Prosper Enfantin, heirs of Saint-Simon, helped make philosophy "a suburb of the occult."[14] Even Auguste Blanqui, before his death, committed *L'Eternité par les astres* (1872). Emancipated from formal religious observance, new believers sought new systems to replace the old, adopted the language of the old to present the new.

One day, Esquiros and his friend Adolphe Constant, went to see the Mapah. They had gone to scoff, they stayed to pray: "Having heard him we thought it would be beautiful if we could find the last word of the revolution and tell it to the world."[15] Esquiros exalts the great revolutionaries in *L'Evangile du peuple* (1841); he becomes a representative of the people in 1848 and publishes his socialist vision of the future: spiritualization of matter, purification by suffering, reincarnation on earth, then among the stars.[16] Constant, once trained for the priesthood, shifts from admiration for Christ as the great reaper "armed with a scythe" to new models: St. John, "the songster of the Apocalyptic revolution," Lucifer, angel of light and principle of Liberty reconciled to Christ by Mary.[17] The occult sciences would show the way. Constant, having become Eliphas Lévi, foretells the marriage of Christianity and socialism as a preliminary to the millennium.

Most of the figures cited so far could be dismissed as marginal. Less so George Sand, whom Renan once described, not unfairly, as the aeolian harp of her time, vibrating to every intellectual and political breeze. For Muray, Sand is a "Joachimite-socialist" and for once he is not awry. Invited to become the female Messiah of Saint-Simonianism, Sand declined. But her good friend Pierre Leroux, a democratic Christian in the illuministic vein, was keen on the Revelation of John and on the other revelations attributed to Joachim of Flora, whose idea of an elite charged with the conversion of the world at the dawn of a new age of Holy Spirit and brotherly love attracted much sympathetic attention. It was under Leroux's influence that Sand wrote *Spiridion* (1839), whose hero, Angel, saves from his pious mentor's tomb the manuscript revelation of a new religion, compound of Lamennais and Pierre Leroux. Socialist, occultist, *Spiridion*—revised, clarified and further Joachimified in 1842—fascinated Renan and pleased Michelet and Quinet, for whom the gospel of Joachim of Flora spoke to the heart and mind, when that of the Church spoke only to the letter.

Paranormal phenomena were related. Swedenborg's world of spirits and symbols permeated by divine light, Mesmer's transmission of universal forces through a subtle invisible fluid, spiritualist belief that departed souls communicate with mortals, all fumbled for a hidden key to the secrets of life and death. Muray has a lot to say about animal magnetism: a subject which Robert Darnton treated with greater elegance (and economy) in his *Mesmerism* (1968). Muray may not have read Darnton (it is not clear just what he did read) but he elaborates Darnton's point. Magnetism appeared an alternative science, just as promising but more accessible, and more immediately exciting. Balzac, Hugo, Théophile Gautier shared the fashionable belief in invisible fluids that carried the forces of life. Flaubert's *Bouvard et Pécuchet* turned their attention to it, and his *Dictionnaire des idées reçues* ridiculed it along with other contemporary absurdities. But it was not easy to dismiss it. Magnetism was evoked from the pulpit of Notre-Dame, prestigious men of science were intrigued by the potential extension of mere natural science: among them Camille Flammarion, the astronomer, Cesare Lombroso (professor of psychiatry at Pavia), who busied himself raising the dead, and Edison, alleged to have developed a telegraph system for speaking with the dead. Better known is the case of the James brothers, William and Henry, whose father had been fascinated by Swedenborg and Fourier, of Conan Doyle, and of other literary figures like Nerval and Sainte-Beuve.[18]

The occult sciences (a term Eliphas Lévi first used in 1856) were defined by Joseph Grasset, a Montpellier neurologist: "those facts which do not yet belong to science [but] can one day be part of it." Nothing supernatural, as Victor Hugo put it who turned to turning tables after the drowning of his daughter Léopoldine—just the occult continuation of infinite nature.[19] At the century's closing, still, an apology of spiritualism begins with the affirmation that spiritualism is a science, "indeed *the* science," and predicts that "we shall soon manage to photograph thought, the psyche, the *périsprit*."[20] Having discarded religious miracles, the enlightened turned to the miracles of science.

Occult forces were a convenient resource for those who sought to explain phenomena others considered supernatural. We are not surprised to hear from Muray that in 1848 *Le Journal du magnétisme* took the side of Revolution. Or to find the man who would later call himself Eliphas Lévi, seconded by his fiery young wife, presiding at a Club de la Montagne where he declares: "We will boil the blood of the aristocrats in the boilers of the Revolution and make blood pudding to nourish the starved proletarians."[21] Muray omits this scene, though it brings grist to the mill of an occultist-socialist conjunction. Nor does he mention that a disciple of the Mapah, Sobrier, had fired the first shot of the February Revolution.[22] But 1848 secreted other revolutionary forces. In March that year, in upper New York State, the Fox family discovered the possibility of communicating with the world of spirits. Spiritualism, table-turning, rapping, automatic writing, ectoplasm, eventually telepathy, a flood of messages flowed in upon the century, and many mediums were recruited among veterans of 1848 or victims of Bonapartist repression. The greatest spiritualist of the time, Allan Kardec, founder of the *Revue spirite,* seems to have shared their turn of mind.

The relation of occultism and politics (especially left-wing politics), however tenuous, was going to feed the belief, current in Catholic circles, that the Church's political enemies were in league with Satan. Figuratively, revolutionaries who disestablished the church, persecuted the Pope, executed the king, were clearly *suppôts de Satan.* Their affinities were revealed when the Estates General associated the left (hitherto linked to negativity and evil) with progress and other allegedly beneficial forces. The connection was further confirmed as many Romantics presented fallen angels as heroic, Promethean or, at least, sympathetic. Proud rebels, first to revolt against the established order, first to struggle against unjust authority, first victims of oppression for having dreamt of better things. For the Restoration, liberty was diabolic. For the partisans of revolution Satan, angel of revolt, was also Lucifer, the carrier of light. For some of its foes, democracy looked like demonocracy; and the religious wars that ravaged nineteenth-century France reinforced that impression. Soon, masonic dens of republicanism and anticlericalism became temples of Satan—quite literally so for many ecclesiastics and for Rome, in the fin-de-siècle revelations of Léo Taxil. In 1895, having disclosed the iniquities of the Church, Taxil turned coat to tell the dreadful tale of the devil's personal manipulation of masonic politics from headquarters sited under the rock of Gibraltar and in Charleston, South Carolina. The Church knew he spoke true. For those who worshipped Satan, "King of the disinherited," God was a tyrant and usurper.[23]

Curiously, the enemies of the left, who had never been backward in their own recourse to the supernatural, were as embroiled with the occult as their foes are alleged to be. Not so curious, really, if we follow Muray, for whom occultism, socialism, and antisemitism go together for mid-century *mages* like Eliphas Lévi, as for more up-to-date figures like Drumont of the *Libre Parole* and his acolyte Gaston Méry.[24] Since (at least in one of its aspects) antisemitism was an offshoot of socialism, as Jews were not only predestined enemies of Christendom but usurious bloodsuckers and enemies of the people (quite literally in cases of ritual murder much publicized at the time), their relation to Satan was evident. Their relation to the end of time was also predestined, at least for those of millenarian bent like Drumont and Léon Bloy, but also for the Assumptionist Father Bailly, editor of *La Croix,* for whom antisemitism necessarily preceded the conversion of the Jews, after which would come the end of time.[25] *On prend son bien où on le trouve.*

Unregenerate Jews stubbornly refusing to help the millennium along are a problem, of course; but the sources of fin-de-siècle antisemitism are so manifold that Muray sagely does not insist. Less wisely, he has nothing to say about the fin-de-siècle epidemic of magic and satanism. Since much of this was related to reaction in literature (Joséphin Péladan, J.-K. Huysmans) or in politics (Drumont), and inspired by a reactionary occultist, Eugène Vintras, Muray's discretion is understandable.[26] Reactionary occultism ill fits his original argument. Yet the persistence of occultism and its appearance on all sides of the political spectrum suggest the widespread influence of what we too easily dismiss as simply silly. So do its recurrent themes: regeneration, social and individual; science and proto-science; conspiracy or counterconspiracy; activities and forces acting below the surface, invisible to the uninitiated but fundamental to understanding and control of an increasingly opaque world.

For Muray, one example of the century's obsession with the supernatural was what he describes as "le typhon de marisme" that broke upon it—mariolatry as part of the messianic-feminist explosion he traces elsewhere.[27] Apparitions of the Virgin Mary were hardly confined to the nineteenth century, let alone to France. But for the purpose of this survey we can turn to two illuminating studies that touch upon them: the older by Thomas Kselman, *Miracles and Prophecies in Nineteenth-Century France* (1983), and Michael Carroll's more recent *Cult of the Virgin Mary* (1986). Both deal with some of the major apparitions of the Virgin: at Paris in 1830, at La Salette in 1846, at Lourdes in 1858, at Pontmain in 1870. Kselman emphasizes economic, social, and political analysis. Carroll favours the psychoanalytic approach. Each, it seems to me, makes a suggestive contribution to the historical and human understanding of events, and their books can be usefully read together. But neither exhausts the possibilities of historical interpretation, in which private experience acquires meaning in social context, and general considerations are illumined by specific conditions. Without any more pretension at exhaustiveness than Kselman or Carroll exhibit, I want to suggest some factors that deserve more attention than either provides.

On the night of 18 July 1830, Catherine Labouré, a twenty-four-year-old novice of the Sisters of Charity of St. Vincent de Paul in Paris, was awakened by her guardian angel who led her to the convent chapel, where the Virgin Mary talked to her about the dangers that would soon befall France. The Virgin appeared again to Catherine on 27 November, telling her to have a medal struck in her honor. The first 1,500 medals were delivered in June 1832. According to Gérard Cholvy and Yves-Marie Hilaire, in less than four years over eight million medals would be struck, by 1842 about a hundred million. Carroll discusses Catherine's "hallucination" in the context of Catherine's double loss, first of her mother, then of the mother's sister who had raised her. He also tells us that she went to bed on 18 July "in a state of great emotional intensity." The following day was the feast day of St. Vincent de Paul, and on the 18th each sister had been given a morsel of the surplice once worn by St. Vincent. "Catherine tore hers in two and swallowed one of the halves." [28]

Carroll does not remark how Catherine's action reproduced an age-old preservation rite, followed by Christians since the Middle Ages and maintained in religious and magic ritual since. More important, it seems to me, he fails to place events in their historical context. July 1830 saw the culmination of a constitutional crisis that came to a head in the revolution of 27, 28, and 29 July that toppled Charles X. The last legislative elections of the Restoration began on the 13th and ended on 19th July. Feelings against the Church, associated with the policy of reaction, were running high. During the *Trois Glorieuses* the archbishop's palace would be sacked, the sacristies of Notre Dome desecrated, Jesuit headquarters at Montrouge attacked. Churches had to close for a few days till passions abated, priests no longer dared show themselves in the street wearing ecclesiastical garb, while the archbishop of Paris, Mgr. Quélen, denounced as a public enemy, went briefly into hiding.

Stress and crisis continued through the summer. After much uncertainty, November 1830 (the month of Catherine's next vision) saw the installation of a new government; but the climate of insecurity persisted. France was boiling over with revolt and the Church was in dire straits. In February 1831 serious riots broke out around the church of St. Germain l'Auxerrois, culminating in the sack of that church and that of the archbishopric itself.

Between November 1830 and January 1831 the Virgin had appeared to

Catherine a number of times before Catherine's confessor was sufficiently impressed to petition the archbishop to authorize the minting of her medal: a request presumably discussed, perhaps even received, after the archbishopric had been sacked for a second time in eight months. The medals were being struck just when the cholera hit Paris. Prime Minister Casimir-Périer died of the cholera in May 1832, the first medals were delivered in June 1832, and their phenomenal success cannot be separated from their use as images of preservation, any more than Catherine's emotional state can be separated from the echoes of current events that reached her convent in the rue du Bac.[29]

From Paris, we move on fourteen years to the apparition of the Virgin to two shepherd children in the wild mountains of Isère, near La Salette. Kselman relates the Virgin's apocalyptic statements to the economic crisis of 1846.[30] Carroll thinks that the boy's "hallucination" "was an attempt to gratify an unconscious wish to harm his stepmother, which derived from the intense hostility he felt as a result of the abuse he had suffered at her hands."[31] Neither view is implausible. On the one hand, economic conditions in 1846 were pretty terrible. On the other, many fairy tales reflect the sufferings of orphaned stepchildren and the fantasy retributions they long to inflict.[32] Some forge fairy tales, others hallucinate. But there is, surely, more to the situation.[33]

The Lady who appeared at La Salette was crying—perhaps, as the shepherd boy thought, because she had been beaten as he might have wished to beat his wicked stepmother. But the message she delivered was that of a *père fouettard,* not very different from the sort of sermon the children could have heard in church: God's name is being taken in vain, Sunday is not observed as a day of rest, only old women go to church, there is dancing on Sundays and eating of meat in Lent, the young make a mockery of religion and throw stones at girls who go to church. No wonder there is dearth, and there will be worse to come if folk don't mend their ways.

Carroll and Kselman do not delve into local detail. If we look into that, we find that, at La Salette as in other villages, tensions between parish and priest ran high. The priest was sixty-four, an advanced age for those days, and accused of drivelling in the pulpit. We do not know what the drivel was, but at Corps, a few miles away, in whose jurisdiction La Salette lay, indifference to clerical injunctions was rife, Sunday attendance low, dancing "scandalous," the faithful worked on Sundays, did not keep feasts, insulted the priest, blasphemed, behaved badly in church when they went there. They were admonished about it. It is not unreasonable to think their next-door neighbors were too, and that much of the Virgin's language echoed the admonitions of local priests.[34]

The swift devotional reaction of the undevout population round La Salette could have been accelerated by the terrible economic conditions of that winter. But it could also be seen as an affirmation of local originality against Corps next door, and of local autonomy over the routine injunctions of official authority. The sympathetic hearing the children received from clerical authorities (contrasting with the caution shown in Paris and in Lourdes) reflects appreciation of an opportunity to take difficult populations in hand and advance their re-Christianization.

Now we move on again, to the west of France. In January 1871 the Franco-Prussian War was drawing to a miserable end. On 18 January the king of Prussia had been crowned German emperor at Versailles. An Armistice would be signed on 28 January, when the siege of Paris ended in capitulation. Since October 1870, the shock of French defeats had spawned holy missionaries and visionaries carrying a message of hope among Catholics and royalists. In the west, desultory fighting continued, as German troops pursued the French broken at the battle of Le Mans.

That was the situation when, on the night of Tuesday 17 January, the Virgin rose like a star above a cottage in the little village of Pontmain. Her message was a message of hope: prayer would bring delivery and fulfilment of entreaties. Pontmain was not threatened by the German advance, but thirty-five village lads were fighting the Germans (or running from them)— specifically, as Carroll reminds us, the elder brother of the boys who first saw the Virgin. An illusion, therefore, prompted by a conjunction of anxieties, and specially by fear for the safety of a beloved brother.[35] Why not?

But why not more? Pontmain lies in fervently White, fervently Catholic country. Charrette's white flag embroidered with the Sacred Heart had flown over his Breton volunteers facing the Germans only weeks before. Pontmain is spiritually in the Vendée, a few miles from the Breton border, in Maine. St-Ouen-des-Toits, the parish where Jean Chouan's revolt began in August 1792, is only twenty miles away. Fougères and its forest, bastions of *chouannerie,* lie fifteen miles across the Breton border. Jeanne Leroyer (1730–1798), in religion Sœur Nativité, spent a holy life full of visions in the Franciscan convent at Fougères; and her revelation, published in 1818, identified the Revolution with the reign of Antichrist.[36] At Pontmain, war would look much like a holy war, a village scarcely threatened by the enemy would have a greater number of its sons in danger and its sentiments more deeply engaged than one might expect to find in the largely indifferent countryside.[37]

Further consideration reminds us that this is a region fertile in visions and cults. Michelet in *La Sorcière* places the witches' favorite haunting-grounds in *marches* (border areas), *landes* (moors), dark forests, briar and brush, *déserts* (wastes) and, above all, *nos marches de l'Ouest*.[38] Pontmain fulfils his conditions. As at La Salette (and to a lesser degree Lourdes), the place-names around it suggest poor land: bracken and brush, wolves, untilled land, moors: Fougères, Landivy, Désertines, Louvigné du Désert, La Tannière, La Futaie. Deprivation, isolation, repression, make visionaries and fanatics. In places of this sort religion is more binding, social conformity more pervasive, visions—or illusions—are easier to share.

On a more pedestrian level, as Kselman reminds us, miracles procure for poor parishes a source of revenue.[39] The Pontmain basilica to Notre Dame de l'Espérance was still unfinished in 1903, providing work in the midst of underemployment and, of course, tourist income. The same goes for La Salette, where the miracle was followed by miraculous economic effects and where new village priests quickly instituted a long-distance novena service, the income from their mail-order prayers being divided between clergy and locals.

So apparitions are overdetermined, just like the apparently absurd beliefs of so many urban progressives. They may not make much sense in a twentieth-century perspective, but they make more sense in context than Muray allows, or than more narrow interpretations suggest. One closes the books of Kselman and Carroll with the feeling that the "backward" populations of rural France managed their emotional and material problems not too badly, and agreeing with Kselman's conclusion that "the number, significance and visibility of miracle cults and prophetic movements in France . . . suggest that our understanding of France's modernization must be revised."[40]

But so much attention paid to the Virgin risks spoiling our perspective. Mary is a favorite of official religion; and that sort of religion, like politics (or feminism, or mesmerism) is an urban product. Country people worship the Virgin, of course—or rather their particular local Virgin, but they prefer their saints. As with the wooden Christs that hang from the cross in the country churches of western France or of Quebec, plain and heavy-featured in the image of those who adore them, the peasant prefers a saint he can recognize. Someone, for example, like the sixteenth-century Ste. Germaine of Pibrac, near Toulouse, whose story is exemplary. Germaine was a sickly child, scrofulous, and with a withered hand. Ill-treated by her stepmother, fed on scraps, she slept in the stable, or in the cupboard under the stairs, where she died at age twenty-one. She had herded sheep since the age of nine. One winter day, her stepmother accused her of taking some stale bread from the breadbox and ordered her to show what she held in her apron. Germaine opened the apron: it was full of spring flowers. Not long after that she died, leaving a story with the makings of a fairy tale as much as of sainthood. There are plenty of holy Virgins in Toulouse: Notre Dame du Taur, Notre Dame de la Dalbade, Notre Dame de la Daurade, but it is the Santa Vierja de Pibrac whom (Cholvy and Hilaire tell us) the women of the Toulouse region invoke in hard cases.[41]

The Virgin indeed plays a minor role in Judith Devlin's *The Superstitious Mind,* where she appears, in a host of distinct and localized incarnations, as Our Lady of Lan-Karé, of Kernitou, of Le Crann, Revercourt, or wherever. They are a lot like squires' ladies, each a local patron or benefactress, related to the others but hardly the same person, whatever priests may say.

Devlin's book is about the persistence within a purportedly rational and pragmatic civilization "of a mass sub-culture characterized, on the intellectual level, by irrationality and confusion and, on an emotional level, by fear and instinct."[42] Credulity regarding the supernatural ("agency above the forces of nature, outside the ordinary operation of cause and effect"), irrational fear of the unknown or mysterious, mark the superstitious minds that Devlin sets to plumb among French peasants. Yet Devlin questions the pejorative definitions. Just how supernatural did the supernatural appear to those who invoked it? Can it be dismissed as perverse irrationality? Was it irrational, was it confused, did it address agencies outside the ordinary operation of cause and effect? No more, surely, than contemporary urban attempts to comprehend, solicit, and utilize hypothetical forces—mysterious enough, but not inaccessible to faith, persistence, and a kind of logic.

First, and basically for Devlin, the supernatural "was in fact . . . assimilated to the natural and harnessed to its needs."[43] What some dismiss as superstition *was* religion—the fears, obligations, and expectations that bind us to gods and to each other. In this light, nineteenth-century religion, at least that of the common people, was not about God and his purpose for man. What bound people together were "common beliefs and ideas that reflected the economic and social restrictions on those who held them."[44] An inarticulate society with no access to more effective techniques translated need, greed, frustrated ambitions, and the search for comforting explanations amidst acute discomfort into commerce with the supernatural: a familiar exchange of goods and services between the relatively powerless and the relatively powerful.

The test of such intercourse was efficacy. The religion that flourished wrought miracles, brought health and even wealth, transformed life, alleviated monotony and suffering. Its marvelous powers operated practically in a next world for which the dead were buried with their false teeth, and variously equipped with bread, cakes, wine, plate, toys, sweets, walking stick or crutches or umbrella, or coin to pay for further facilities.[45] But the marvelous powers of popular religion were not confined to the next world or the passage to it. They counted here and now, and saints were its chief agents. Saints filled roles nowadays assigned to doctors, psychiatrists, marriage guidance counsellors and social workers, insurance agents, private investigators and security services. They righted wrongs, cured illnesses or sped them to resolution, watched over soldiers, travelers, children, and folk in distress, protected against thieves, hail, storm, fire, spells, evil spirits, or conscription.[46]

Benign apocryphal St. Bon had his miraculous fountain at Blesnan. Apocryphal or not, saints could heal, but also resolve awkward situations. In Normandy, St. Va-et-Vient intervened to make the sick recover or die, rather than hang on as a burden to relatives. In Moselle one prayed to St. Maur (*mort*) to speed the going of a dependent. In the Vosges, St. Vivra, St. Languit and St. Mort fulfilled similar functions. They could also be invoked for more obviously maleficent ends. In the Cher, at St. Mauvais's fountain, you could pray for the demise of enemy or rival. Bretons consulted Notre Dame de la Haine, near Tréguier: three aves in her honor would cause an enemy to die within the year. A variety of "religious" rituals—*messe de Saint Sécaire, messe sèche, messe de mâle-mort, messe du Saint Esprit*—so common in the early twentieth century that sermons were preached against them, offered ways to rid oneself of those hated enough.[47]

In the society Devlin studies, God and His saints are as aggressive, vindictive, malicious, as those who invoke them. If improperly approached or treated with less than the deference they expect, they are apt to turn nasty. Ideally their wrath works against the powerful and rich, but it may also affect the thoughtless who dismiss them too easily or forget to pay their dues. On the other hand, when entreaties, bribes or cajoleries don't work, worshippers may adopt the *manière forte*—threaten or punish—to draw the saint's attention; and they do so with no apparent fear of retaliation. Some of these rites invoke sympathetic magic, as when saints are pelted with mud, nails or water to inspire cures or other interventions.[48] Others are punishment for failure, urging better performance in the future. Statues, icons, relics, are whipped, thrown into rivers or wells, penned up, stood on their head, or turned face to the wall.

This is familiar territory: man makes God and his court in his own image; no wonder he treats them in consequence. But Devlin goes well beyond. The rites she describes, like throwing mud at a statute of Saint Laurent to obtain a cure for eczema, are only "tenuously connected with the desired results," and those who go through them do not regard them as mechanistically functional aspects of a process of cause and effect. Sympathetic magic does not work like homeopathic medicine, rather like catharsis. For it to function, its efficacy does not have to be evident: it operates at a level which is crucial but hardly visible.[49]

Magic, says Devlin, "was a psychological technique with social rather than scientific overtones." It furnished people with ways of expressing and sometimes overcoming disorienting feelings, of satisfying their dreams. And witchcraft (which subsumes Church-related magic techniques) "provided a social theory of misfortune," the means to undo damage and avenge it.[50] Fairies, goblins, elves, will-o'-the-wisps are rooted less in legend and retrograde illusion, more in real conflicts and problems. *Fades, ondines, carrigans, dracs* and other *follets* crystallize, then help dispel, worry and stress. They console and reassure the vulnerable and despised—for example, orphans afflicted with unkind stepmothers or siblings. They provide alibis, not just for coming home late or having spilt the milk, but for unavowable feelings like the dislike of children who could be identified as changelings, or dislike of one's family if the "changeling" was oneself. Apparitions, prodigies, dragons, serpents, ogres, genies, *vouivres,* discouraged children from wandering too far afield, adults from exploring for the hidden treasure of others, and all from blundering into the hideouts of robbers and smugglers. But they addressed another level of reality too. In a society fearful of physical disaster and short of analytic vocabulary, legends allowed people to voice feelings about their environment, provided harmless expression for "divisive and corrosive" impulses, reassured the vulnerable, helped express and exorcize anxieties and yearning and regrets.[51]

Devlin stresses the search for consolation and satisfaction in fantasy, the search for relief from a multiplicity of pressures, including boredom. Miracles and visions flourish in a context of need and misery. Illustrative of this idea is the popularity of the miraculous resurrection of stillborn babies long enough for them to be baptized; a merciful suspension of the natural order that affords a small triumph over suffering. She is quite right, as the vogue of *sanctuaires à répit* attests, and their lessened attraction by the century's end, along with diminished interest in the sacrament of baptism.[52] Neither vogue nor decline, Devlin would say, can be explained simply in terms of public health or of the politics of religion. I agree. Such extraordinary events helped salve a lot that only miracles could cure. They also afforded breaks from monotony, surrounded humble folk with unwonted prestige, provided opportunities to express inarticulate feelings of anxiety and rebellion.[53]

This was also where pilgrimages to shrines near and far came in as search for relief from trouble (admitted) and ennui (unformulated). The more difficult ordinary life, the more readily people flocked to shrines, eager to witness the miraculous transformation of an otherwise unyielding reality, and to believe the miraculous message of new and better things to come. Better times could only come, of course, after repentance, after apocalyptic changes, after the inauguration of a new order of things that simple people know is not for them, at least not for their time. So apocalyptic prophecies too, popular as catharsis, are whittled to manageable proportions: specific miraculous interventions at some shrine, celestial letters, amulets, charms put to malevolent or beneficial use. Like storytellers, prophets, visionaries, and healers reflect the needs and dreams of their contemporaries, mostly poor contemporaries. What they offer is not extramundane, abstract, unrelated to reality. On the contrary. The successful visionary or witch must provide hope and opportunity for evasion here and now.[54]

Visions, easily dismissed as fraudulent, or as the symptom of a diseased mind, might well be attempts to draw attention. They were also taken up as emblems of hope and attempts to escape from ordinary life. In a world of deprivation where psychosomatic disorders were common, hysteria, possession, offered forms of escape accessible to the most vulnerable, cracking under "the pressures and tensions of their physical and social environment."[55]

Spells were frequently invoked by hysterical girls to justify deviant behavior. Visions or cases of possession could prove catching and spread to whole neighborhoods, endowing humble people with unfamiliar importance and with a temporary sense of power, providing novelty and excitement in the midst of dull routine. Devlin recalls a classic case of epidemic possession that swept the alpine village of Morzine in the late 1850s, affecting some 120 people, mostly children and women: in other words those most deprived and least independent. At Morzine, blasphemy and physical violence went with rebellion against God, parents, mayor, priest, even the bishop of Annecy. This particular revolt against a harsh social and economic order only died down in the mid-1860s, when the forces of authority (police, soldiers, threats of hospitalization) intervened.[56]

Like much of traditional medicine, such doings, Devlin believes, were not really meant to work, heal, save, make things better. She is inclined to view them as placebos which participants conspired to treat as real. She takes for example the respect accorded to the hawthorn which, sharing some of the properties of Christ's crown of thorns, protected from lighting or spells, and even afforded salvation to those who without it might die unshriven.[57] Prayers addressed to the hawthorn—or to stones, streams, trees—were not invocations to an object endowed with anthropomorphic qualities. Like whistling in the dark, they provided a measure of relief, however illusory.

Spells, of course, were meant to produce positive effects as well. They could be used to summon the devil (or a representative of the devil, usually in animal shape), preferably at midnight, preferably at a crossroads. And spellbooks carried awesome powers that could be used to terrorize feeble imaginations, as Charles Nisard put it at the time.[58] Nisard's remark recalls Burke's view of superstition as the religion of feeble minds—when religion is simply the superstition of the successful. It reflects the urban sense of superiority, it ignores contemporary urban predispositions to savor the terrors of magic and, more surprising in a scholar like Nisard, it disregards the tendency of illiterates to regard all books as *grimoires,* unintelligible, hence mysterious. Witness the village teacher driven out of a parish in the 1830s: "il aurait été lapidé comme un sorcier. Un Virgile était cependant tout son grimoire."[59]

Devlin knows better. She reminds us that demonology and inventive magic exploit perennial fantasies of fabulous treasures to be found, of improving one's social position in extraordinary ways, of realizing the extraordinary dreams of people whom poverty confined to dreaming. Folk tales, too, represent more than illusion or wishful thinking. They provide us (like magic) with the "vocabulary of discontent":[60] poor boys, poor girls, orphans, younger sons and daughters, deprived, ill-treated, triumph over circumstances, acquire status, luxury, success, unthinkable in real life. The impossible becomes possible. Ste. Germaine of Pibrac found satisfaction in her goodness. Poudounette, the Breton Cinderella, reaps reward and revenge by being good: she marries a marquis.

But goodness is only the half of it. As often as not, trickery, swindles, deception, guile, cunning, slyness or sheer luck permit the hero or heroine to gull, dupe, cajole, flatter, lure, ensnare, beguile God, the devil, ogres, robbers, even Death himself. For fairy stories are about reality; and so is magic. Devlin observes how much magic turns on treasures, love-potions, exemptions from military service. A twentieth-century study brings grist to her mill and demonstrates the lively survival of good spells designed to bring a good number in the draft lottery, as of bad spells to make an enemy or rival draw a bad number.[61]

For, of course, if personal interest comes first, in situations where goods are limited, my good is your harm, profit comes at the expense of someone else. Like Jules Michelet, Devlin discerns that "hatred and envy lay at the heart of witchcraft."[62] The tendency to ascribe one's personal misfortune to the malevolence of others was a sort of wish fulfillment in reverse. Spells and accusations of spells reflect social and family relations that are often strained, jealousies, rancor, tensions, generated within close-knit poor communities in which discomfort and competition for bare necessities are a frequent source of ill will and strife. Sorcery and countersorcery exhibit this, and exacerbate it. Old women, beggars, marginals (shepherds, charcoal burners), exploit a reputation for magic power to provoke fear, and are resented, feared, hated in return. The magic violence of the vulnerable provokes the brutish retaliation of the terrified. Into the twentieth century men and women would be beaten, tortured, shot, or brought to court, or have their barns and houses burnt, in this encounter of mutual resentment, intimidation, and vengeance.

But witchcraft has its positive side. The fear of God may inspire justice and charity; so may the fears of other powers. According to Evans-Pritchard, fear of spells is the beginning of wisdom; fear of reprisal can inspire good deeds or at least mutual tolerance. The moral of many a fairy tale is that one should be kind to the weak and helpless. The same moral can be drawn from tales of spells, often regarded as a punishment for failing in one's duties to neighbors, beggars, relatives, lovers, inferiors.[63] Wielded as an instrument of primitive justice, a spell could threaten reluctant debtor or exigent creditor, reward or punish where no other sanction could be hoped for, thus encouraging generosity or moderation if only out of prudence. Hence the great rule of French country life: no hubris. Avoid the envy, jealousy, resentment of others; do not be overbearing, do not show off, do not excel too visibly, do not triumph over your fellows, for a spell may humble your pride.

What is interesting about the spells discussed by Devlin is how much they borrow from official ritual: the importance of prayers, religious devotions, even of being in a state of grace. Pragmatically, magicians function like substitute priests or minor saints. They too are intercessors to whom one has easy recourse. They too procure wives or husbands, make spouses love each other, or hasten their demise. They recover lost property, find treasures, help avoid conscription, treat the sick, break charms, win lotteries, cure livestock, predict the future. It is less surprising, then, that some of their prescriptions—*paters, aves,* candles, masses—differ so little from orthodox supplications.[64]

In magic rites the devil materializes, but so does the Virgin. Both take monetary transactions for granted, as did the priests who charged for their services, for the chairs in church, and often figured as principal usurers of their parish. Of course, devil and Virgin take on predictable form, fashioned by folklore, convention, snippets of popular literature and imagery, recollections of the Church's teachings. Devlin points out that the Virgin seen by Catherine Labouré in 1830 wore a white dress *taillé à Vierge.*[65] And the Ladies of La Salette and Lourdes dressed much like *enfants de Marie:* the former looks as she can be seen in devout pictures, dressed in white, beribboned, crowned with roses; the latter all in white, with veil, blue sash, and roses at her feet.

Virgin, devil, priest. The greatest sorcerer, the one with most—or with the only—books, with access to the best-confirmed powers, was the priest. Montaigne and Voltaire, like Devlin, connect superstition with fear. But what more fearsome beliefs than those of established religion; and where could they be heard more fearsomely expressed if not by the priest in church, or on a mission? Black witches brought harm with the help of the devil. The priest was a white witch who did good with the help of God: he lifted spells, he exorcized demons, he repelled storms and hail and cleansed the land of vermin, he prayed for rain, bountiful harvests, fertility and healing. He could charm the trout by muttering his Latin. How far could his powers extend? Even books of miracles could perform miracles, religious texts or a semblance thereof could serve as amulets to be worn or, at critical junctures, swallowed. So could scapularies (see Catherine Labouré). In 1908, a clerical review, *L'Ami du clergé,* questioned about swallowing holy images to obtain a cure, answered that the practice was acceptable, though only with clerical approval.[66]

But priests who had the power to exorcize could also say a dry mass (no water, wine or candles) to dry up an enemy. They could levitate at dusk on to the roof of those who did not pay their debts or tithe, and recite a book backwards to set off trouble and odd happenings in the house. They could drive off storms or hail, or make them fall on the neighboring parish; or they could attract them, ruin their fellow-villagers to avenge a slight or punish irreverence.[67] Devlin knows how much accusations could hide "natural" antagonisms, everyday squabbles over tithes or fees or moral conformity or precedence in seats and in processions.[68] Further, since priests (like the priest at Corps) kept threatening their congregation with dire punishments, it was not unreasonable to attribute catastrophe to them when it occurred. If plague or defeat in war were presented as manifestations of God's wrath, why should not priests appear as Prussian agents or *semeurs de peste, metteux de choléra,* eventually responsible for the phylloxera as well?

The same was true of doctors, also witches, also more costly than the traditional *rebouteux* and competing with them for popular confidence. If doctors found employment during epidemics, why shouldn't they be held responsible for them? *Cui bono?* If cholera killed more poor than rich, why shouldn't the rich and their catspaws have provoked the cholera to hurt those who, wishing so much to hurt them, attributed their own malevolence to those they envied? Suffering and anger turn to a primitive logic to focus on culprits for their plight: the stuff of modern political campaigns in which similar myths are served with a different sauce.

It is not difficult to follow Devlin in conclusions that point to the heritage of traditional fantasies and popular imagery "manipulated to justify personal resentments and animosities, to exculpate the guilty and inculpate their victims, to reinforce prejudice." This, she says, would be channeled into the politics of the twentieth century, which reproduce the taste for blaming others for misfortune, the inclination to reallocate responsibility for difficulty and disaster, the old hostilities to wealth and power, the tendency to self-deception and self-justification, the delight in collective celebration and evasion through myth.[69]

All this is suggestive, especially when Devlin insists that superstition is not unreasonable, but rational in its own terms, offering pilot charts to navigate the shoals and rapids of precarious life. Devlin is not quite sure how rational the "superstitious" peasant mind really was. "The evolution towards rationality was gradual . . . primitive and logical thought could . . . coexist in one mind."[70] But primitive *was* logical: the two did not conflict. The supposed confrontation between common sense and magic was actually a conflict between different kinds of magic and between different kinds of common sense.

The context within which all this unraveled is presented and analyzed in an excellent *Histoire religieuse de la France contemporaine,* by Gérard Cholvy and Yves-Marie Hilaire. As I began by saying, though reestablished by the Concordate of 1801, the hold of "the religion of the majority of the French" had been much weakened by the Revolution. Before 1789 the church presided over all the great occasions of life: birth, marriage, death, and also the First Communion—that great rite of passage into the adult world. The church watched over the parish and over the conduct of its members, it helped the crops increase and cattle prosper, it taught and healed and preserved from harm. After 1789 it had to compete in all these realms with the secular power. Rites of passage were removed from its hands. Birth, marriage, and death were registered by secular authorities and, after 1882, the First Communion too would be overshadowed by the school-leaving certificate. Divorce, though abolished from 1816 to 1884, had been legislated once and would be reestablished. Sunday was no longer the unchallenged day of worship and of rest. It had been secularized, and attempts to resacralize it after 1814 encountered indifferent success and managed only to stir up the politically potent opposition of tavern-keepers and employers. The proportion of unbaptized children, 7.4 percent in 1865, increased to 28 percent in 1885.[71] The Church had been inescapable in everyday life. After the Revolution it became an issue, sometimes a nuisance, before being marginalized. Meanwhile, its unquestioned hold had been broken, or at least weakened. This, one may speculate, is what makes the nineteenth century so rife with superstition, with occult cults, with counter-religions. All had existed before 1789; now the difficulties of orthodox religion gave them a chance to flourish—no longer underground, but visibly, at all levels of society.

Part of the problem of official religion lay (and was reflected) in the shortage and insufficient training of its personnel. In 1815 the Catholic

Church was woefully short of priests. Tens of thousands of ecclesiastics had left it in the previous quarter-century, some to retirement, some to civil life, some to anticlericalism, some to dabble in the occult. Few had been replaced. Thousands of vicarages stood empty and, in those that did not, nearly half the incumbents were over sixty—an advanced age in those days. Julien Sorel had a promising future. He could have had a great career, like many a lower-class lad unfit for harder labor. And the attraction of holy orders would be the greater in times when celibacy was not exceptional: in Pas-de-Calais, Hilaire reminds us, in 1851 30 percent of the population between thirty and thirty-four years of age remained unmarried. This changed only toward the century's end and in the early years of the twentieth century. Alternative opportunities for social and economic promotion in schoolteaching and in the civil service cut ordinations by half in the score of years after 1868. Economically enforced celibacy also shrank: in Pas-de-Calais from roughly one-third to about 18 percent of the thirty–thirty-four age group.

But, even while early nineteenth-century conditions loomed fair, the peasants being trained and rushed into the breach the Revolution had opened faced an uphill task. The generation born after 1785 grew up in religious ignorance, uncatechized, unsermonized. The short contemporary life span (twenty-eight for men, thirty-two for women) meant that, through the first decades of the century, a majority of adults lacked the religious background of their elders.[72] No wonder that religious practice was more slack; but also more vulnerable to heterodoxy, to enthusiasm, to individual or popular interpretation, to superstition.

Cholvy and Hilaire mention the *Petite Eglise* only briefly, and numerically they are right: politically, statistically, it remains an irrelevance. But it illustrates some of the problems faced by a Church divided and disorganized by a decade of persecution. The Concordate of 1801 confirmed a number of the Revolution's reforms: new dioceses; abolition of religious observances, fasts, and holidays; above all acceptance of many "juring" priests who had taken the oath to the Constitution; and, sometimes, replacement of those priests who had resisted it. In places, reticence turned to resistance and, eventually, to schism. In the Vendée, the Lyonnais, and elsewhere, communities of old believers held out against both Church and state. *Illuminés, purs, fidèles, rigoristes* in Vendomois, *blancs* or *bleus* in Forez and Charolais (after the royal colors), *enfarinés* in Rouergue, Auvergne or the Dombes (from the rice powder on their old-fashioned tresses): simple folk who remained true to the Church when the Church ceased to be true to itself. The name that best reflects their stance is that of the *décidants* of Bas-Poitou, whose Christian decision soon turned to dissidence.

In communities of this sort, when the old unreconciled priests died, laymen like Pierre-Augustin Métay of la Foye (where Vendée and Deux-Sèvres meet) became *chefs de prières*. Persecuted, recalcitrant families and communities continued to observe more—and more rigorous—fasts and to celebrate more religious holy days than their Catholic neighbors. They used (and use) a pre-Revolutionary missal, instructed (and instruct) their children from a Catechism promulgated by eighteenth-century bishops of La Rochelle; their dead are buried in a separate section of the cemetery, dissident graves facing west, Catholic ones to the east. They found more tolerance among republican laymen: "C'est des gens qui nous laissent tranquilles, on était libre . . ." So their children went to public (secular) school, as at Le Pin in the *bocage* country of Deux-Sèvres; and their votes were cast for anticlerical radicals, as at Courlay—a dissident center even today.

It might be worth observing that the Bas-Poitou, where the largest dissident communities survive, lies in the heart of the Vendée militaire. Equally important, it once was part of the diocese of La Rochelle. Stretching from south of Angers to Rochefort, this had been a Protestant stronghold into the eighteenth century, before becoming a fortress of Counter-Reformation Catholicism. Saint-Laurent-sur-Sèvre, where Louis-Marie Grignon de Montfort, the great missionary of the west, died in 1716, remains a favorite pilgrimage site for old believers. But the resistance and survival of the *Petite Eglise* testify as strongly to Protestant habits of resistance, and persistence in adversity, as to the success of Counter-Reformation missions. Protestant resistance to the *dragonnades,* pastors concealed and prayer meetings held in hidden places, were played over in the 1790s, and then again in the nineteenth century, before dissidence came to entail no more than social marginalization.[73]

So the Church, though restored, had to face many problems.

Amidst anarchy of observance, private enterprise thrived. Witness the Abbé Ferdinand-Toussaint-François Châtel, ordained in 1818, placed under interdict in the 1820s, then consecrated bishop by another eccentric: Dr. Fabré-Palaprat. Fabré-Palaprat was a chiropodist who proclaimed himself Grand Master of the Templars and Sovereign Pontiff of the Primitive Christian Catholic Religion: essentially, as described in his *Lévitikon* of 1831, the Church of Johannite initiates as opposed to the mass Church of Peter's unenlightened followers. Like Fabré-Palaprat, Châtel too wanted to return to the simplicity of primitive Christianity and liked to refer to the Apocalypse of John. He described himself as "fondateur de l'Eglise unitaire, évêque par l'élection du peuple et du clergé," and achieved a modest success in the 1830s, when the fortunes of the orthodox establishment were low. Several villages of the Paris region threw out their priests to install his adherents, who said Mass in French and did not charge for chairs.[74] Here was popular religion running wild.

The crisis of the Terror had revealed the basic interests of parishioners left to themselves. In the absence of priests, rites of passage had been performed by civilians, propitiatory ceremonies had continued when needed, guardian saints had been defended. In August 1793 the municipal council of the not very pious parish of Saint-Chinian (Hérault), where five priests were to be massacred a few months later, asked for a procession to pray for rain. At La Ferté-Gaucher (Seine-et-Marne), where the Jacobins had caused "the Virgin and the saints to cry in churches," the peasants rioted, sacked the Jacobin club and forced the authorities to replace the statues in their church.[75] Attachment to the Church was focused on practical and protective activities—and on representatives of divinity expected to carry out such functions.

Amidst anarchy, the restoration of religious discipline would not be easy. Clergy trained under the Restoration were not strong on learning. As Julien Sorel found in the seminary at Besançon, the Church distrusted intellectual achievement. As the chronicler of one seminary found cause to comment, the Church would rather see "its domain labored by donkeys than have it lie fallow."[76] But there was an element of suspicion there too: too much learning was dangerous, an invitation to speculation, questioning, doubt. Saintliness was better than bookishness.[77] That may be why Cardinal Manning found the French episcopate "chiefly remarkable for their goodness."

But the new saints in a surplice were better at scourging than forbearance. *Qui aime bien châtie bien.* In a country where dialects still used the term for fear to express respect, their God was a God of fear, their faith excessively austere. Piety condemned the Devil and the Flesh together. In 1830, Paul-Louis Courier's *Pétition pour des villageois qu'on empêche de danser* was much more than a *jeu d'esprit*. Dancing, especially Sunday dancing, became and continued a burning issue in many a village. The God of the thundering priest looked increasingly like (Pierre Hamp *dixit*) "a machine to screw poor people." The priest, often a peasant himself, "always ready to abuse his parishioners, to scold them, call them rubes, peasants," became the storm-centre of village conflicts. What went on in church was equated with fear, with punishment and hellfire, "thoroughfare from a miserable life to an eternity of suffering."[78]

Rejected when possible as oppressive, intrusive and increasingly irrelevant, religious observance lived on as superstition: protective, part of simple folk's armory of self-preservation. In Burgundy, where Philip Gilbert Hamerton lived in the 1860s and 1870s, religion for the peasants, at least the men, was "a sort of precaution which may not turn out to be of any use, but which it is as well to take . . . si ça ne fait pas de bien, ça ne fera pas de mal." In Bourbonnais, Emile Guillaumin's *Simple Man* testifies to a similar frame of mind, skeptical but prudent, hence trying "to please the Master of the Elements, who held a great part of our interests in his hands." [79]

Occasional conformity did not imply devotion, not even belief. It reflected a reasonable concern for everyday interests in the preservation of which the Church played a part. But such concerns focused on just those aspects of observance that critics denounced as obscurantist and superstitious, and this placed the Church in a quandary. Should it play the card of popular religion, and retain or regain the masses by its hold on their everyday hopes and fears? Or should it purify religion of superstitious accretions, insist on a God-centred faith indifferent to material profit, the here and now? In the event, Church policy (if one can speak of a policy amidst a diversity of tactics and personal opinions) reflected both tacks. Against rationalists and free thinkers the Church opted for miracles, prophecies, and local devotions. Against the utilitarians in its midst it denounced backward superstitions that competed with official faith. The first confirmed the criticisms of its enemies and sharpened their contempt. The latter lost it the support of the popular masses.

When local notables joined hands with clerics to discipline or repress disturbing popular religious activities focused on the healing functions of good fountains, stones, statues, bonfires; when priests explained away werewolves and apparitions with as much eloquence as local schoolteachers; when they hesitated to bless livestock or a *repas des morts*, they encouraged doubt, disaffection, or quite simply indifference. The old tradition of ringing church bells against storms provides a fine example of a sticky wicket. Priests who continued to allow it could be denounced for ignoring natural science. Priests who refused to countenance it provided opportunities for anticlerical mayors to insist on the traditional protective ritual and disparage the reluctant priest. Rigorism, skepticism, and attempts at rationalism, all reinforced this dilemma.

The wonders of modern science did not help. In one encounter the priest reproves the farmer for forgetting Mass, then comments on the contents of the farmer's cart: "Chemicals? But they are very bad, they burn the soil." "Monsieur le curé," replies the peasant, "I've had Masses said and got no profit from them. I've bought chemicals and it worked. I'll stick to the better merchandize." Ominous words, but not as decisive as they sound. Guillaumin's Tiennon believed in liming *and* in prudent observance. So did many others who continued to reinforce the magic of science with that of the Church. From Minerve (Hérault) the priest reports that no man observes Easter, but "curiously" all men and youths join in parish processions. [80]

Modern medicine appears in the same light. Urban observers cheered its advances against the redoubts of rural benightedness. They had a point, but the advance was halting. In 1882, at Abondance (Haute-Savoie) a priest opened the stomach of a dying mother to baptize the fetus. In 1883 a teaching nun at Saint-Malo-des-Trois-Fonts attributed epilepsy among her students to "a spell cast on her school by those who wish it ill." In 1885, near Redon (Ille-et-Vilaine), another teacher-nun brought three of her girls to kiss the face of a girl dead of diphtheria: two died. In 1891, near Châteaulin (Finistère) a stepfather strangled his eleven-year-old stepdaughter and told her mother that, if he was not caught, he would have Mass said, go round the chapel on his naked knees, and undertake a pilgrimage to Sainte-Anne-de-la-Palue.[81] Anticlericals had a point. But doctors remained few and healers numerous. Even if one overcame suspicions of newfangled remedies, and if one could afford them, a Mass would do no harm, nor would a healer. Hence traditional techniques and new ones were not mutually exclusive.

Nor did schooling, even universal instruction after 1881, have radical effects. As Cholvy and Hilaire point out, literacy and religious instruction went hand in hand. So did literacy and religious detachment. It was Flaubert who observed that when people ceased to believe in the Immaculate Conception, they would start to believe in turning tables. J. B. Durand, nineteen years old, judged at Limoges Assizes in 1883, provides a living footnote to *Bouvard et Pécuchet*. Durand had been the first boy from Monsibre (Corrèze) to be sent off to school. As a result, we are told, he reads immoral books and obscene novels, distils undrinkable alcohols, scours the ruins of Muratelle castle in search of buried treasure . . ."[82]

No wonder that a contemporary priest concluded that the uprooting of old beliefs "to which the clergy contributed as much as modern philosophism," had "ruined faith without crushing superstition"; and he cites "this shameful procession of animal magnetism, spiritism, somnambulism, turning tables. It's no use hiding behind a mask of science and changing the definitions—the reality is still the same!"[83]

As the hold of orthodoxy relaxed, first in town, then in the countryside, religious aspirations adjusted to modernity. Before spiritualism there had been *le parleur aux morts,* now there were mediums. As Cholvy and Hilaire tell us, in the north small superstitious sects proliferated among the dechristianized lower classes; in the republican south *lo que fa parlar los morts* took the place of the *armier,* the messenger of souls. Ernest Ferroul, holder of a medical degree from Montpellier, socialist, immensely popular deputy and mayor of Narbonne, was *spirite*—spiritualist and medium.[84]

Still, newfangled practices, religious or superstitious as one wills, did better in town than in the country. Religious practice shrank everywhere as opportunity for personal choice expanded, as material wellbeing grew and, along with it, alternative sources of diversion and reassurance became available. But conformism is social, hence local. Those who left hamlet or village for an urban centre exchanged one conformity for another. Those who stayed, by and large conformed to regional patterns of religious detachment or attachment, or of militant anticlericalism. In most cases, however, as founts of traditional dread tarried, as famines, dearths, wolves, rabies, plagues, *grandes peurs,* turned into history, religious practice became a personal choice, its magic appeal focusing less on communal interests and more on practical or personal concerns. A remarkable ethnological study, Alban Bensa's *Les Saints guérrisseurs du Perche-Gouët* (Paris, 1978) tells what happened next.

Every other work I quoted is broad in scope. Bensa's monograph focuses narrowly on one aspect of popular observance in a restricted region, less than 250 square miles between Chartres and Le Mans. Yet his findings open vast horizons, because what we see foreshortened in his tale is the relation between Church and popular religion, between the magic of lay folk and of priests, first operating then withering; and, declining with it, the popular interest in religious sanction which clerical participation had maintained.

The crux of a study that provides rich footnotes to Cholvy, Hilaire, and especially to Devlin, lies in the search of common men and women for magic that will work. The culture Bensa plumbs values efficacy above everything. "It works or it doesn't work." The healing saints whom Bensa studies (and they are all he studies) have to be made to work. Traditional intermediaries offer their services as diviners or intercessors to see that they do: *voyageuse, reveuse, dormeuse, somnambule.* Such professionals, vicariously performing healing rites on behalf of their clients, subsisted in 1970. Some lived from the income their functions brought, others used it as additional income while working their farms alone or *en famille.* When one such *voyageuse* is taken to court for illegal practice of medicine, she is acquitted. Her local prestige is great. Not only common people, but priests, châtelains, and physicians turn to her in difficult cases of spells and witchcraft (*dèsenvoûtement* and *mauvais sorts*). She presides over the ceremonies surrounding the midsummer Feux de Saint Jean, and priests place her at the head of religious processions.[85]

Ideally, though, one does without intermediaries. The *voyage,* of course, can be performed by a particular postulant, alone, in procession, or in an organized pilgrimage. The thing to remember is that a saint's healing powers are related to time and place. For example, from the sixteenth century to the nineteenth, Sainte Mabile's fountain near Brou healed fevers and other maladies. A local squire built a cross beside it, but no other official recognition came: no priest, no Mass. Yet pilgrims and *voyageuses* still trudged to the fountain in 1972, the locals cleaned the spring and kept the scrub in check around the cross, the cult subsisted (then at least) without official sanction. On the other hand, saints who are forced to move will make transport difficult or simply shift back to their original home, as Sainte Barbe did when displaced from her oratory to the church of Marolles-les-Buis nearby, returning by herself to the field where her chapel now stands.[86]

If site is crucial, so is date. The pilgrimage to be effective has to be made on the exact day of the saint's feast, not the preceding Sunday or the following one. For over a century local priests have tried to meld saint's feast and Sunday Mass. Popular response remains "very reticent." If the saint is not celebrated on the traditional day, his or her pilgrimage dwindles in importance, and the faithful divide, some observing the saint's own day, others that chosen by the priest. Bensa cites the example of one parish where, between 1912 and 1953 most of the locals maintained the traditional date, only newcomers to the parish following the priest's choice.[87]

Where this sort of break occurs, the results for worship are dire. At St. Lubin near Authon, the local church ceased to serve during the Revolution and the parish was attached to nearby Authon in 1802, after the Concordat. But the pilgrimage to St. Lubin continued popular. Until 1960, the vicar of Authon would come to St. Lubin on 14 March and 15 September to recite Mass and read the scriptures. Then he began to celebrate the saint's days in Authon parish church, the Sunday following. The feast's attraction waned, St. Lubin's statue was moved from its twelfth-century site to Authon and, by the 1970s, his worship was a memory.[88]

At La Bazoche-Gouët the great pilgrimage to St. Gourgon, whose false relics had been brought there from Rome in the seventeenth century, went hand in hand with the major annual fair. In 1970 a new parish priest tried to "fight against superstition," shifting the celebration from 9 September, a weekday, to the following Sunday—a decision that disturbed not only habits of worship but the commercial connection of the feast. At La Bazoche-Gouët the struggle about when St. Gourgon's day should be celebrated was still going on when Bensa wrote his book. But there as elsewhere, when fair and pilgrimage no longer coincide, both decay.[89]

Shifting the date of ceremonies affects their efficacy. So do other changes in ritual. In 1848, at Combres, where the patron is St. Antony, the parishioners wanted to oust their priest because on 17 January he led the saint's procession leftwards round the church, not right as it should go: "les processions à gauche, voyez vous, dam! on dit que ça fait mourir le monde plus vite." The feud between concerned worshippers and parish priest accused of sorcery and of bringing bad weather fostered anticlericalism and brought about the decline of an important local pilgrimage centre. Today there is no more pilgrimage at Combres.[90] But the issue is still alive elsewhere.

At St. Eman—original of Proust's Guermantes—the patron saint of the parish is specially good for rain: "on vient de Beauce chercher la pluie du Perche." The pilgrimage to St. Eman, abandoned in 1963, would be taken up again in 1971 at the request of many parishioners supported by the Société des Amis de Marcel Proust. In 1972, however, the priest, refusing to turn around the saint's miraculous fountain, took the procession round the church instead. Whatever literary sightseers thought, "les gens n'étaient pas contents." No wonder. How could a healing fountain heal in such conditions? As for rain, for St. Eman to bring it his bust must be dipped three times in his spring, then carried round the church with its face to the West. Turned east, the saint's face brings sunshine: distinctions that self-respecting modern priests despise, when they do not ignore them.[91]

By now probably most of the population do so too. If they remembered them so long it was not only because in magic practices ritual details matter, but because saints and their observance were an integral part of the agrarian cycle, their feasts concentrated when the local work schedule made them most convenient,[92] their personalities similar to those of their worshippers. Like kings in fairy tales, who survey their fields and send their daughters out to bring the hero lunch, saints are close to home. As their parishes fight each other, so do neighboring saints, and St. Lhomer throws large stones at St. Laurent. Like feudal lords they are combative and vengeful. St. Evroult heals white sores, but may also inflict them—as he did upon the priest of Mignières who laughed about his powers.[93]

What we behold is the standard supernatural exchange of goods and services: healing against worship, aid against attentions and deference. The people need the saints, but saints need their popular clientele as professors need graduate students. Their influence and prestige depend on it. Like professors, the saints resent indiscriminate appeals to too many colleagues and react by leaving the help requested to another, so that nothing is done. They demand sustained devotion, not just one-time appeals or a perfunctory *ex voto*, and may react to slights by causing a return of the *mal* they cured. And they expect honorable treatment: at Soize in the 1830s, St. Gille, being transferred from his original chapel to the village church, kept the oxen that pulled his cart from crossing a ford until an improvised procession came to greet and escort him to his new home.[94]

Site, Bensa makes clear, is crucial not just as locus of miracles, but as centre of a cat's cradle of interrelated factors. There is local pride and the boost it gets from association with a saint, as nowadays with a football team. There is also *situation*—in forest, at crossroads, best of all near borders or boundaries between parishes or provinces, between cultivated land and forest or waste, between fields remade by human labor and the dangerous forces of the nonhuman realm.

The above-mentioned Authon, for example, is close to the Sarthe, which is known as a *pays de sorciers et de dèsenvoûteurs*.[95] La Bazoche-Gouët is at a physical transition between hilly country and pasturage, on the verge of the Beauce. We may recall that Pontmain too is set in a borderland, close to forests and springs, and to "deserts" dear to hermits and smugglers. Such places are nurseries of witches and saints, both of whom draw on the inspiration lodged in particular localities.

The Church, however, is supra-local, indifferent or hostile to local interests. The priest, who occupies a key position in the exchange of magic goods and services, can foster such activities or stifle them. In Bensa's survey he appears in a negative role. Not only do Perche priests shed their magic and insist on being like other men; they shed the crux of their function. As religious practice wanes, the clergy tries to purify the faith of the remaining faithful, fights unorthodox practices, condemns the past and its superstitions. For the Church, saints are intercessors to whom God lends his powers. For the peasants it is the powers that matter, and those who [appear to] wield them or refuse to do so. Religion is a stock of merchandise sold in a local store. The storekeeper is the priest; the church is his store. "The priest has his business, I have mine," says one of Bensa's peasants.[96]

If men do not attend Mass on Sundays or even at Easter, they attend the saint's day and the pilgrimage, because that gives them what they want. Like the old man at Moulhard, near Authon, who does not trouble to remove his beret and grumbles when Mass goes on too long, they wait to approach the statue of St. Marcou or another and to proceed with healing rites. In the back of the church one hears "je suis pas venu pour le Bon Dieu, mais pour le saint." There lies the difference. Saints do not evoke Christ, but healing and protection.[97] For the priest, popular traditions are marginal to his ministry. For his parishioners they are essential, and the priest's ministry can easily become marginal. When the priest shows no interest in what interests the peasant, their businesses no longer coincide. When the village church no longer fulfils its practical functions, it becomes irrelevant.

This is the process Bensa traces, as the French say *en filigrane:* the persistence of traditional practices and their crumbling, less under the impact of modern technology than under that of clerical hostility. Characteristic of how this works is the Church's attitude to the healing powers attributed to the *marcou:* the seventh son, preferably the seventh son of a seventh son, endowed with thaumaturgic powers just as kings had been, but more durably than kings. Since the sixteenth century at least, *marcous* have been connected with Saint Marcou or Marcoul and priests have insisted on the saint's role in the healing process: "example of the church's struggle against popular traditions," comments Bensa, and of its *volonté de récupération.*

But recuperation is not enough. At Moulhard, mentioned above, the Perche's best-known pilgrimage shrine to St. Marcou, the 1860s saw an attempt to supplant the saint by placing the church under the patronage of the Virgin Mary and by favoring her feast (15 August) over that of the native saint (1 May).[98] There is no evidence that the campaign worked, but it illustrates the Church's tendency to take over the practical aspects of pilgrimages and other pious activities, to reclaim their therapeutical or protective functions, to separate devotion to a saint from practical agrarian or other applications. As medical practice develops and becomes more effective, the Church concentrates therapy in a few great centers like Lourdes, and focuses on faith. The cult of saints itself becomes more official and less practical. Attempts are made to replace the cult of interloper saints, like St. Marcou, with more acceptable devotions, preferably to the Virgin; which also replace the local and specific by more distant, more universal objects of devotion.

On the other side of France, in the Ain of the curé d'Ars, "the monumental and affective omnipresence of the Immaculate Virgin had dealt a hard blow to old local devotions," including old-established marial sanctuaries. One cannot help wondering whether the marial offensive of mid-century, partly inspired by the Virgin's romantic popularity, was not above all an attempt to displace traditional observances—superstitions embarrassing to a hierarchy aware of the criticism to which they exposed it and eager to discipline its unruly faithful.

Only relatively successful against local saints, the new cult of the Immaculate Mary eclipsed local marial sanctuaries, including the *sanctuaires à répit;* it overwhelmed many limited local cults, and replaced collective practices by the personal devotion to a tender, loving, private presence. The great marial apparitions we surveyed and the publicity they received reinforced this trend, transferring piety from the parish level to a transcendent object, just when patriotism too was being transferred from the *petite patrie* to the *grande.* Church and state, at loggerheads about politics, were at one in their efforts to uproot popular culture. However, while national patriotism found justification in economic and cultural interests, the economic and cultural interests that had maintained religious attachment at the parish level began to wither when detached from it. Philippe Boutry concludes: "In this process the parish loses some authority; it loosens the bonds of the faithful, who until now were ruled by their diverse religious opinions."[99] The services of the Church, devalued from within, were losing their hold; and, as they did, so did the institution whose major role had been to provide them.

Curiously, some of Bensa's closing observations recall the remarks of much earlier observers. Bensa is struck by his informers' use of the imperfect tense. They say "In the old days . . ." or else "In Orne they believe . . ." or "It doesn't exist any more, but you still find it in such and such a place." A hundred years before Bensa, Laisnel de La Salle had heard old storytellers in Berri closing their tales with "Ce sont là des contes de vieux; les jeunes s'en amusent." Emile Littré, too, was struck by the slow but irresistible obsolescence of the supernatural. "Henceforth miracles appear only to those who begin by believing in miracles."[100] Yet those who believed in miracles continued numerous, the obsolescence of the supernatural proved less irresistible than some took it to be, and the young were laughing less heartily than it seemed, or else they changed their mind.

Should we view the decline which Bensa chronicles in that perspective? Or have circumstances changed so irretrievably, at last, that the old beliefs have no leg left to stand on? The books reviewed suggest a Scottish verdict: Not Proven. As far as one can tell, official religion always overlaid, masked, overlapped with, a host of practices that sometimes competed with it and sometimes used its facilities for their own ends.[101] When it did not ignore these, the ecclesiastical hierarchy devised its own strategies to cope with them. It persecuted, co-opted, tolerated, condemned, tried to take over, squeeze out, eliminate, incorporate "superstitious" practices. Witness the miracles, prophecies and apparitions Carroll and Kselman discuss. The "superstitions" meanwhile adjusted and adapted just as actively, not only to religion but to changing circumstances and conditions. Witness the evolution of superstitious minds and the way modern medicine and psychology tried to come to terms with it. For Devlin, magic practices are strategies of impotence. Such strategies altered as the nature of insecurity, the sources of fear, the objects of desire altered. They did not survive, they did not disappear. Muray's book displays the—mostly urban—superstitious mind assimilating scientific advances and political challenges. Bensa shows how rural communities adjusted to radically new material conditions and intensified cultural pressures. The situation that was moving to a close in the nineteenth century is still moving to a close in the twentieth. Religion and superstition, sœurs ennemies, rather like Siamese twins, are not through dying.

PART III

Traditions and Politics

～ 7

The Second Republic, Politics,
and the Peasant

There has been a running debate, some of it explicit, some implicit, about the rate at which French country people of the nineteenth century were integrated in the national political process, about the major factors and stages of this integration, and the degree to which country people assimilated the rules and values of the political game which they were called to join.

One view of the French nineteenth-century situation was expressed by Karl Marx in 1852, who found peasants to lack political interest or initiative. Two score years later Friedrich Engels repeated the observation,[1] and many an administrative report from the provinces confirmed their impressions during the intervening years. When the peasants were not described as indifferent or apathetic, they simply voted as their betters told them. Dependent and submissive, they were citizens in name only: savages more like cattle, to which a guidebook of the 1820s compared them; barbarians in the midst of civilization, as Engels found them at mid-century.[2]

A more positive impression has been advanced by the authors of two seminal works: Philippe Vigier on *La Seconde République* and Maurice Agulhon with the influential *La République au village* (1970). These works and others represent the Second Republic as chiefly responsible for the politization of simple people, not only in towns, but in the country too: the efforts of the "red" opposition to Louis-Napoleon's ambitions carrying urban arguments into village and hamlet, the success of their propaganda evident in growing governmental concern about "subversion," and in the rural risings that followed the president's coup of December 2, 1851.

That view is not completely new. Already in 1865 Eugène Ténot described "the peasant" on the eve of December 2 as committed to democratic politics.[3] Two score years later, Georges Renard expressed the same veiw in his volume on the Second Republic in the *Histoire socialiste:* this was when "peasant democracy, awakened to political life by the revolution of 1848, enters the fray."[4] Contemporary scholars are more specific: Vigier, who quotes Ténot in a similar vein, comments that the rural populations which had mostly greeted the new regime with indifference, would rise in their thousands in December 1851 to defend "la république des paysans" against Louis-Napoleon's *coup d'état*. Whatever their earlier unconcern, by 1851 the Alpine southeast, at least, bore testimony to the "prise de conscience politique des masses rurales."[5] Better still, recent American writings have tended to argue for an ideological penetration of the countryside during that period. According to John Merriman,[6] what began as "an urban ideology of social reform," achieved rural acceptance and, in the guise of the democratic and social Republic, became "a rural as well as an urban ideal." The repression of the 1850s would drive the new republicanism underground, but only to lie dormant and to wake again in the late 1860s or the seventies. A subtler and more encompassing interpretation is Ted W. Margadant's *French Peasants in Revolt: The Insurrection of 1851* (1979), a thorough and imaginative study arguing that the widespread risings of December 1851 provide proof of rural integration into a "modern" model of national politics, and the details of their preparation show how this was achieved at a time and to a degree not usually recognized.

Other interpretations have run the gamut, placing crucial developments in the 1880s and after;[7] or even suggesting, as have recent contributions to the ethnologically oriented *Etudes rurales,* that (in one sense) they never took place at all, and that village politics have continued *sui generis,* with values, aims, and points of reference steadfastly different from those of urban-dominated national politics.

Each of these theses carries some conviction and reflects a part of the truth. I am particularly impressed by the argument for long-lasting stability presented by Claude Karnoouh, Jean-Claude Boutron, Claude Mesliand and others, for whom "politics" in the villages, national politics that is, continues to "come from outside," while the phraseology and institutions of the central power mask the persistent reality of local concerns and "the attempt to [maintain] local autonomy."[8] My only answer to them would be that although their facts convince, they remain a matter of degree. Rural politics continues a question of clans and personalities to an extent incomparably greater than can be found in its urban counterpart, but it is not autonomous, nor is it perceived to be. National issues, even as camouflage for local ones, cannot be avoided; local (and personal) affairs, once largely autonomous indeed, are forced to ride on national forces. To some extent this had been always so, but for a long time that extent was so slight that a sense of autonomy was warranted and the wider world could properly be viewed as largely irrelevant. Then, at some point, village and hamlet not only lost their political "autonomy" but became aware of the fact. Such awareness would make a deal of difference, and all parts of the French countryside live with it by now.

The question just when this happened is hard to answer. In a realm where local factors loom so large and particular experience overshadows the general, no one interpretation can tell the story whole. But since the mid-nineteenth century is the first arguable (and forcefully argued) time for which the claim is made. I shall examine the merits of the theory that explains the peasant risings of 1851 by their participants' "republican convictions,"[9] thus holding for fairly widespread politization of rural France in the three or four years before December 2.

Politics, of course, is an ambiguous term. Interest in, concern with, the affairs of the community have never been absent from village or parish. But to the nineteenth century (as to its predecessors) politics was about the state; and politicization was the awareness that national affairs were of as much concern to the individual and to the locality as those of the local community were; indeed, more. Politics meant national politics, implied levels of (apparent) abstraction absent heretofore and an interpretation of specific local issues in more general terms. Politicization meant first of all the recognition that village affairs were directly affected by powers and forces well beyond the village, then action in consequence: in elections, in Parliament, in Paris, in a political and economic marketplace wider by far than anything the village had considered before.[10]

What did the events and experiences of 1848–1851 contribute to a process of politicization that would bring rural France closer, at least, to the attitudes just described? In March 1848 Charles de Rémusat returned from Paris to his country estate at Lafitte, not many miles from Toulouse: "no part of France was less politicized." Yet even there, "without understanding anything, the peasants well knew that what had happened affected the poor, that they would count for something, and that their condition would change."[11] In a number of places, as we know, this impression led to attempts to accomplish that change at once, and in the most straightforward terms. Not far from Rémusat's Lafitte, a small-scale *peur* terrorized the south of the Haute-Garonne through March and April of 1848. The villagers of the Barousse, in Hautes-Pyrénées, encouraged by the change of regime, rose in a classic *jacquerie* directed against usurers, forest guards and other oppressive figures. The miserable and angry mountaineers destroyed government registers, but also school books—symbols of an oppressive system—and appeared to threaten nearby small towns that represented oppression in a more general and traditional sense. It was from the towns that the repression of the Barousse revolt proceeded. Their national guards marched against the rioters, dispersed them, arrested a hundred or so, and brought them back, roped together in twos and threes, to be marched through St.-Gaudens *au son de la Marseillaise.*[12]

Was that politicization; or old grievances, old-style reactions and old-style repression, set off or facilitated by new-style national events? As Agulhon observes (in another context), while the educated looked to elections to ensure social progress, the uneducated felt that "the exercise of social democracy began at once."[13] That is one way of putting it. At any rate, since the uneducated were the vast majority, those who looked to elections faced pressing problems.

The little towns, especially the bigger little towns like Rémusat's sous-préfecture, Muret, were touched by Paris notions. The villages were not. George Sand agreed on this with Rémusat. "How do you expect the rural populations to understand from one day to the next that their parish pump is not the center of the world? The revolution has caught us short. The elections come too fast, especially for the peasant who does not think fast."[14]

Something had to be done about this, and the Republicans did it on two levels. On the didactic front, special delegates were appointed or sent out as proselytizers: the minister of public instruction, Carnot, called on schoolteachers to become the propagandists of the democratic Republic—some of these heeded his call[15]—and electoral clubs were set up wherever possible, "the better to judge the particular value of candidates."[16] But the missionary delegates sent out by the Republic often sent back discouraging reports. "Most country people," wrote one from Montastruc (Haute-Garonne) in April, "know practically none of the candidates," and worse, care little about their new electoral rights.[17] They had to be enlightened more directly, and the Republicans set out to do that too. As a local historian has put it, "it can be said that the authorities exert some pressure on the electorate."[18]

The Second Republic took its governmental prerogatives seriously. The elections were postponed. Mayors and municipal councils were removed and replaced all over the place. The phrase that recurs in local studies of this period is "hecatomb of mayors"—like that of 170 of the 208 communes in the Puy-de-Dôme.[19] Mayors would tell their charges how to vote; friendly mayors prepared friendly voters.[20] But however determined the Republicans, things did not always go smoothly. Thus at Cusset (Allier), deposed Mayor Arloing, a notary and a member of the General Council, refused to give up his post, ignoring or forcibly expelling several official messengers until a military detachment finally forced him out in mid-March.[21] Elsewhere, things looked better. From Nohant, George Sand reported that her son, Maurice, appointed mayor by the new authorities, found only friendliness and confidence, although he had "to work to enlighten nine hundred charges and two hundred electors who all say 'Vive la République, down with taxes,' and will not hear anything else." Even so, "if only every parish, like Nohant, would place absolute confidence in a tested friend!"[22] But one could not always know in what notable, in what friend, the trust would in the end be placed. A year after these high hopes, George Sand was bitter: "Les gens de Nohant ont voté comme des porcs."[23]

One can think of several explanations. One is suggested by Rémusat's comment on the 1849 elections, when it seemed that (Alsace apart) it was in the poorest and most backward areas that "a bad air of socialism, even of communism, seems to infect and spread through the population." True, in general, the big cities leaned towards democracy. But elsewhere, "in 1849, demagoguery is by far out of step with civilization."[24] So, a relatively enlightened electorate (if, *pace* Sand, that of Nohant might be so judged) could actually have voted in terms of its perceived interests.

More likely, though, what Sand had described not long before as "une population à l'état d'enfance," because of their primitive understanding of politics, approached the situation in terms of their experience: savings exhausted, credit tight and ruinously expensive, no means to cover their backs or to repair their homes, "that does not make them love the little Republic about which they don't understand a thing." The little Republic, for the peasants, "was taxes and tight credit."[25] Their reaction to this seems nowise infantile, though many listened to the siren songs of those who promised them an end to all their troubles. In Creuse the attorney-general of Limoges deplored "the unfortunate influence of *veillées*," where publications sent from Paris by migrant masons were read and discussed. Near Brive, in Corrèze, he reported "socialist lectures delivered live and loud in the marketplace." Everywhere, an "incessant, mysterious, indistinguishable socialist propaganda."[26] And yet, if one believes the attorney-general, the peasants who voted in such numbers for the reds had no real understanding of the reds' "political" ideas. Such country folk were against the rich, they had voted against *lo listo de lo ritso* (as the *démocs-socs* had dubbed it), they hoped for a share of bourgeois property; and the accusation of being *des partageux,* so often rejected by the reds, was taken as a promise by sharecroppers and tenant-farmers eager for property of their own. The peasants hoped, of course, to see an end to debts and taxes—*their* debts and taxes. Witness the fact that, when the red electoral victories became known, some sharecroppers refused to pay dues and taxes. But, above all, claims the attorney-general "for them, expropriation is the point of all these so-called egalitarian systems."[27] After all, why not? When Adam delved and Eve span, who was then the *gros bourgeois?*

The fears of the *nantis* were exaggerated,[28] but largely because the hopes of the poor were impossible to realize, not because the hopes were not there, had not always been there (however vaguely, in the realm of fancy and folktale), and were not being fed by radical promises. In November 1850, Dr. Victorin Mazon of Largentière spoke at Laurac (Ardèche) about what the new world would entail: "the poor will pay practically no taxes, salt will be sold at 5 cents a pound, the rich who now dine on their chickens will be justly reduced to eating only the potatoes that the people eat."[29]

John Merriman has written of the radicalization of the Limousin between February 1848 and May 1849—a prelude presumably of later, similar radicalizations of other rural areas.[30] But what did such radicalization entail? Was it more than the liberation and encouragement of traditional and well-founded resentments against exploiting and usurious townsmen, against encroaching outsiders, against misery and unusually hard times?[31] Was it what Charles Tilly once described as a reactionary and localized protest, or what Charles, Louise, and Richard Tilly in a later work refined into the concept of pre-political action?[32] To put the question differently, how démoc-soc were those who voted démoc-soc; how much (and what) of the political ideology of their "party" did they know or care about?

I shall eventually argue that it was little indeed—nor do I consider that disgraceful. For the moment, let us search for more evidence. In August 1849 at Eaux-Bonnes in the Pyrénées, Nassau Senior asked his guide if the Republic was popular: "O yes, he said, we all voted for Louis Napoleon." In a village of the Hautes-Pyrénées he found the mayor (who had also voted for Louis Napoleon) quite indifferent to politics, quite ignorant of the departmental representatives. This in a part of France whose villages he judged "by far the most civilized I have seen on the Continent except in Holland and Switzerland."[33] Halfway across the country, among the "fanatical and ignorant" ardéchois, mayors and officials were no better versed.[34] In Gascony one hears what to the nineteenth-century French historian will soon become a familiar litany: "The country populations are utterly indifferent to political struggles that have nothing to do with either their interests or their habits."[35] Even in 1851 the attorney-general of Aix, writing about that eminently political document, the petition for a revision of the Constitution, uttered a salutary warning: many of those that signed it would as readily sign a petition to opposite ends. "Do not take a signature as having a political significance. They do it by amenity and political indifference."[36]

There were the clubs, of course, and many sprang up in very small localities. In the Vaucluse, a historian of the department's politics affirms that every commune had one in 1848. But they were not consulted when it came to drawing up the republican ticket headed by Agricol Perdiguier.[37] Peter McPhee has shown a similar efflorescence of clubs in the Pyrénées-

Orientales.[38] We have a description of the club at Thuir by the man who ran the local school, Sauveur Morer: it included "several friends of mine; almost all landowners, the new justice of the peace, the new mayor and his deputy"—the elite of the town's Republicans. Its daily meetings attracted "people of every condition: besides the members of the local administration and the judge, numerous *propriétaires* and landworkers." Morer would read the newspapers "and comment on their leading articles to make them understandable to all."[39]

Maurice Agulhon attributes much of the cultural-political development of mid-nineteenth-century Var to the most popular clubs there—the *chambrées*—through which national ideas filtered into the villages and whose members "opened themselves to novelty, to movement, to independence."[40] We do well to remember, however, that the villagers of lower Provence, by Agulhon's own admission, behaved more like city than like country people, and that their model of political impregnation would be more urban than typically rural.[41] Besides, there is an aspect of such clubs that has attracted little or no attention, and that surely deserves a thought. In February 1850 the attorney-general of Aix, a bitter foe of *chambrées*, which he treats consistently as troughs of political perdition, reports on five *chambrées* of Puymoisson of which two—La Fraternité and Les Descaladaires, "composed of men belonging to the exalted opinion"—had been ordered closed. The official inquiry would show "that local hatreds alone had dominated these gatherings where one had become red only by opposition to the commune's administration which held the other three *chambrées* under its influence."[42]

It was not ideas that inspired the *chambrées* of Puymoisson, but local divisions and "local hatreds"; and the exalted opinions for which their members were denounced were simply opinions different from those of other fellow villagers. A later report from the same source provides an even clearer picture: "power rivalries and municipal ambitions establish two parties in every village," explained the attorney-general of Aix on June 3, 1851. "One of these parties professes the government's principles, the other upholds those of the political opposition. All the malcontents join the *chambrées*."[43] We have seen that not only *mécontents* joined *chambrées*, but the rest makes sense. So the political—ideological—coloring was incidental. Which need not mean it could not prove effective, but suggests caution in the assumptions we make.

It is hard to tell the effect of clubs (open or secret) on the politically uninitiated.[44] The humble may well have enjoyed an extension of traditional sociability, especially in the company of their social betters. But how many of the latters' ideas rubbed off on them and in what form? One may as easily imagine that such unwonted extensions of sociability helped establish new or closer personal relations which would be simply variants of quite traditional kinds of deference and allegiance.

Pierre Joigneaux, well placed to evaluate the impact of *montagnard* indoctrination efforts, did not think much of them. He saw the clubs as platforms for mediocrities, "when they could have served instruction." In the countryside, the clubs "were cold": a few men of good will, most of them incapable of improvisation, limited themselves to reading official proclamations and newspaper articles.[45] The reminiscences of Morer seem to bear him out. In a village that never saw a newspaper, the novelty must have been attractive. The political effects remain dubious—and certainly difficult to discern.

What evidence we have is thus hardly conclusive. Arguments have been advanced for the effectiveness of red propaganda, in clubs and elsewhere, based not only on the December risings but on the assumption that exposure to political debate must have left some mark. That, however, is not entirely certain. In mid-1851 a company of sappers suspected of republican infection was posted in disgrace from Montpellier to Rodez. The Republicans of Rodez initiated a number of its noncommissioned officers into the Jeune-Montagne before the company was posted on to Paris, where it would take an active part in the operations of the *coup d'état*.[46] How deeply affected were the *sous-officiers* who had joined the Jeune-Montagne? More to my point, perhaps, is what happened—or what failed to happen—in the Allier, where the chief secret society was La Marianne, which recruited most heavily among the miserably exploited peasants of the western part of the *arrondissement* of Moulins. The areas of Gannat and La Palisse, where Republicans were best entrenched, were not touched by it. Yet after December 2, the lands of the Mariannes, dominated by noble landowners and by their stewards, remained quiet.[47] Their peasantry, whatever its clubability, lacked leadership. Insurrection was left to those parts of the department where republican notables led the risings.

This recalls the crucial roles notables played and the frequent coincidence between the absence of republican notables and the absence of republican risings. Agulhon insists that by December 1851, in a lot of places, leaders from the common people had taken over from the bourgeoisie.[48] That depends on what we recognize as *cadres populaires*, and I would argue (and will argue subsequently in greater detail) that the leadership functions of the lower orders remained slight throughout. But Agulhon himself tells us that at La Garde Freinet (Var) most of the radical leaders were the offspring of wealthy landowners (who had made money in cork manufacturing).[49] As for the insurgents who briefly held Digne in December 1851,

Philippe Vigier has listed their leadership: Buisson, the most "popular" of them, *liquoriste,* owner of a small enterprise and mayor of Manosque; Charles Cotte, lawyer at Digne; P. E. Aillaud, *huissier* at Valensole; Ailhaud de Volx, *garde général des eaux et forêts,* who, having been fired for his political opinions, returned to his native village of Château-Arnoux and turned the wholly rural canton of Volonne (practically devoid of large estates, hence of rival notables) into a bastion of his revolutionary ideas. Among the lesser figures Vigier cites a lawyer, a landowner of Gréoux, and a goldsmith of Forcalquier. Not a very vulgar band, and not a peasant among them.[50]

My point here is that even when secret societies or individual agitators were active in the countryside, one should be wary of reading too much into their activities or, indeed, of overestimating their influence among the peasants.[51] Thus in Aveyron, in December 1851, when the Republican Casimir Moins set out from Villefranche to march on Rodez, his own friends accompanied him but he could scarcely raise any peasant from the villages on the way (the one exception was a *marchand colporteur*) until Privezac, "where he had friends because he came there to hunt every year." On the other hand, when Moins' insurgents reached Rignac where the mayor was a notable of opposing views—Dr. Colomb—they were routed by Colomb's "peasants and friends." Personal relations, personal loyalties—the account has a feudal ring.[52]

Then too, how many *peasants* did red—or republican—proselytism actually touch? The Marianne's strategy, for instance, was to stay away from towns and *bourgs* and highways, where the gendarmes could get at them. Hence their meetings in isolated, lonely spots where risks of surveillance and surprise were small. But the recollections of a Marianne leader of the Yonne show that, in Morvan and Puisaye at least, the society's centers of activity were still small towns and most of its members artisans or petty bourgeois. Of the six men initiated at the same time as he was (in a forest clearing), not one was a *cultivateur: rentier, propriétaire,* lumberman, carpenter, mason, hairdresser, the estates cited to show the society's diversity also suggest its urban (or suburban?) nature. Similarly, of thirty men at a secret meeting well away from town: "c'était l'élite des artisans établis dans la commune."[53]

Eugène Ténot would also show the democrats spreading their views in "the small towns, the multitude of *bourgs* . . . In these small centers, among these half-city, half-peasant folk."[54] The bourgeois and the artisans of the *bourgade* would then carry the exciting message to the country folk. The argument is plausible, when we know how many landworkers lived in suburban agglomerations and imagine the relative facility of relations between peasants and "these half-city, half-peasant folk." But again, how easy were such relations? And how effectively was the democratic message carried? At Beaune, after receiving news of the *coup d'état,* the would-be insurgents sent emissaries to rouse the countryside, but without effect: "they only managed to carry with them a few inhabitants of communes very close to Beaune." These turn out to have been employed by republican militants—like the three workmen employed by him at Savigny that were brought to town by C.-M. Naigeon, a well-off tailor and *chef du comité des campagnes (en fuite).* After all this, the only verdict I can glimpse is: not proven.[55]

Without a doubt then, the revolutions of 1848 echoed throughout France, unto its remote corners. In many rural areas, though, they were perceived in archaic terms: distant doings signifying an opportunity to settle local problems—forest or pasture rights, personal or communal feuds, the burden of taxes or, sometimes, of usurious debts. Did the propaganda of 1849, and more especially of 1850 and 1851, alter this locally oriented vision of politics, open new horizons, fulfill the didactic purposes of the red activists? Whatever we hazard on this score can only be an impression based on a variety of sources, none unprejudiced. But with this warning kept in mind throughout, my answer for the countryside would be: not very much. Margadant has argued for "a basic shift from local to national symbols of group identity," as the "reactionary" peasant disorders of 1848 and 1849 were "replaced by collective actions with a distinctively modern component of national political ideology."[56] On the basis of some of the impressive documentation he provides, one may well ask whether this "distinctively modern component" was perceived in its own terms, or in terms of local factions and tensions to which it contributed a fresh supply of symbols and gestures that would be assimilated only by habit and accumulated experience over time.[57] Red, *démoc-soc, montagnard* propaganda was effective in one respect: it linked concrete resentments, as that against taxes (and especially against the new tax of 45 centimes), with what went on in Paris; and it suggested that action on the local plane, whether by voting or in defense of the Republic or the Constitution, could bring some solution to these and other ills. But Paris remained vague and distant; Republic and Constitution continued as abstractions difficult to conceive and as oddly imagined sometimes as their defenders: La Martine, or Le Duc Rollin.

So what did politics mean to the peasants? Two witnesses from opposing camps agree: of course there are turbulent and ill-disposed men (reds, no doubt), reports the attorney-general of Grenoble about the Hautes-Alpes in 1850, but their ideas cannot get very far. "Woods, pastures, flocks are the constant objects of [the people's] thoughts." All they care about are the forest laws. "Politics are wholly a matter of interest and do not reach, so to speak, beyond their mountains."[58] A red agrees. Around Dijon, where Gustave

Lefrançais was exiled in 1851, Joigneaux's radical *Feuille de village* suited the peasants because "it treated politics chiefly in terms of cutting taxes, especially those that weigh on wines—the chief business of the area."[59] So if we leave aside their entertainment value, politics became interesting when connected to traditional local concerns.

This need not be a bad beginning. Self-interest, more or less enlightened, might well account for all the files that bulge with reports of subversive activities. A closer look suggests (I am not the first to say so) that these reports too need to be approached with care. Red slogans could often sound quite terrifying, replete with references to Robespierre, guillotines, and shootings, but—leaving aside their anachronism—their appeal to peasants without a prior family attachment to the Jacobin cause appears slight. Red songs and slogans were bandied about by urban enthusiasts but were not likely to raise much echo among the peasant folk. Thus in July 1851, at a village feast in the Basses-Alpes, we hear that reds from nearby Barcelonnette began to sing songs like the *Marseillaise* and the *Chant du départ* in a café. When gendarmes harassed them, they appealed to the surrounding peasants for support but seem to have got none.[60]

Yet the authorities were only too ready to look on traditional gang or village fights as political "rebellions."[61] When we know that hardly a village feast or fair passed without *rixes,* some very bloody indeed, we need not wonder that a participant or party in the melée might appeal to new-model factions or use their imprecations. Trivial incidents could easily acquire a political coloring. In July 1851 again, at the gates of Bédarieux (Hérault), a dozen drunken reds returning from a tavern took a shortcut across a private property and picked a fight with shepherds guarding it. This standard clobbering, in which one townsman was injured, immediately acquired political significance.[62] Like personal conflicts, labor or local ones were easily painted red. At Voiron (Isère) friction between an employer and his workers led to a gang of local youths marching about brandishing sticks hung with bacon-rinds. The employer, aware of local custom, played down the incident; gendarmes (and perhaps local reds) played it up, till it ended in a judicial file.[63] Zealous officials easily exaggerated: was that really a clandestine meeting at Saint-Romain-de-Lerps (Ardèche), in September 1851? "It is possible that hunters were taken for socialists," suggests the sous-préfêt of Tournon.[64]

Some magistrates warned against hasty (mis)interpretations. In June 1849 the attorney-general of Aix explained that the political charges brought against the mayor of Flassans (Var) were beside the point. True, the mayor had gained much influence over local peasants by promising to divide the common lands, but the ensuing disorders "avaient plutôt une couleur de coterie que de politique."[65] We shall soon see the crucial role of factions and the political coloring some were led to adopt. But there were other ways of getting into trouble. In spring 1851 the court of Besançon spent two months investigating complaints against the parish priest of Arc-en-Gray (Haute-Saône) for his "red" sermons attacking the authorities and the respectable local bourgeoisie. It turns out that the priest, a Legitimist, resented the way local employers forced their people to work on Sundays. His critical sermons had become "red."[66] At Saint-Barthélémy (Isère), a minor local figure was imprisoned on a charge brought by the mayor but soon released when the charge was dismissed. Back home, drinking with his friends, he began to shout "Long live the Reds! Down with the Whites!" The attorney-general believed he did it "to give himself importance and probably also in order to disguise under a political appearance the charges brought against him."[67]

The same magistrate reports another typical case: at la Cluze-ès-Paquieu, the assistant mayor denounced the subversive remarks of a certain Duclos. Investigation revealed Duclos to be decent enough, a good neighbor, but a drunkard and a bit of a loudmouth, "an object of fun for the whole neighborhood; he is not regarded as a serious man and everyone, even the children, enjoys getting him excited." Unfortunately for him, when the assistant mayor circulated the petition for Constitutional Revision dear to Bonapartist hearts, Duclos refused to sign, remarking that the man would do better to pay his debts than to get people to sign petitions. "It takes little more," commented the disabused attorney-general, "to excite a village hatred which in private persons leads to violent recriminations and which M. l'adjoint de la Cluze has turned into official exaggerations."[68]

Even if they had picked up subversive ideas (and it does not sound as if Duclos had), people like these were not likely to be taken seriously by their fellows any more than the man denounced as the chief red of Guémenée (Loire-Inférieure), a tough and drunken timber-worker. The court report on him reads as if his fellow villagers knew his ways, while the gendarmes and their superiors took him and his windy words seriously.[69]

Who then, were the true subversives, the rural leaders and their most active converts who spread political views around the countryside? A list of the president's political enemies, tried after the December 2 coup in Loir-et-Cher, gives us a classic idea. Of twenty-one men condemned to being shipped to Guyana, Algeria, and other noisome spots, three came from Blois, five were tavern-keepers, and two were millers by trade, well placed to influence their neighbors. Six were artisans (three carpenters, one shoemaker, one printer, and one weaver), one was a schoolteacher (and lapsed priest), one a public works contractor, and three were farmers or farm laborers. With the list of those condemned to simple exile we come to the minor village notables: four doctors, one pharmacist, one notary, one tax collector, and a justice of the peace, with the note: "He exerts considerable influence in his district, because of his fortune and his lineage and family position."[70]

Others have commented on the activity of militant taverners and artisans and on the unjust discrepancy of having the heavier retribution fall on such acolytes, leaving the leaders to the comforts of an exile they could more easily afford. I would point out the evident hierarchic division between the two groups and suggest that the comment on the justice of the peace above states the essentials of rural leadership.

Before we tackle the leaders, let us glance at teachers, whose later political influence might make them candidates for our attention at this time. John Merriman examined their political role rather thoroughly and concluded that "French schoolteachers did not become political men en masse during the Second Republic."[71] That being so, their contribution to any politization of their neighbors would be at best sporadic and seems to me quite slight, not surprisingly so if we recall the figure of the priest-pecked schoolteacher in Buvard and Pécuchet's Normandy village. The reports of school inspectors, department by department, leave an impression less of deliberate action than of accident. As a result of their command of suddenly significant skills such as reading, writing, and sometimes rhetoric, a hitherto insignificant social category was propelled to the fore. This unexpected importance proved irritating to those who were used to treating them as menials; and heady for a few, mostly younger, dominies who seized the opportunity to give themselves importance. But nonconformist political militancy can hardly have been frequent. As the school inspector of Basses-Pyrénées reported in 1850, "most of them are Republicans as country people are Republicans, that is to say because we are in a Republic."[72] When allegiance became a matter of debate and choice, it would have been difficult, perhaps impossible, for minor public figures of this kind to escape involvement. Whatever their wishes, they would be tempted or forced to side with one local party or another. Even so, I suspect that the scant show of teachers among the proscribed of Loir-et-Cher reflects not only a general reluctance to become involved, but also the relatively low social position from which leadership would not normally flow.

Some teachers, like Gérard Basilet of Menet, near Mauriac, headed the reds in their village. But their radical proclivities, their attacks on the priest and the rich, possibly also their personal character, had got them into trouble even before 1848.[73] Other teachers, perhaps less exceptional, got into hot water as a result of village feuds. The popular and influential teacher of Orignac (Hautes-Pyrénées) had been in his village for thirteen years. His standing was clearly related to "investments evaluated at about twelve thousand francs, result of his work as teacher and as *expert*."[74] Presumably land surveyor, did he also function as village usurer? In any case, the mayor got the teacher fired, the mayor and the new teacher were subjected to violent *charivaris,* the gendarmes despatched to give them aid and comfort were ambushed under hails of stones, and a typical local brouhaha grew into a major affair whose political overtones are less clear than its local sources.

Sauveur Morer of Thuir (Pyrénées-Orientales) is cited by John Merriman as one of the schoolteachers whom the revolution thrust into the limelight and who suffered in its wake.[75] Morer's own *apologia pro vita sua* leaves a different impression. A self-made man, the *instituteur* of Thuir soon became a village notable allied with one of the local clans—that of the Aragos. His school prospered. Although involved in the usual intrigues of local politics, he did not suffer after December 2, even though his republican convictions apparently prevented him from taking the oath of allegiance to the new regime—at least for a while. In 1853 the prefect wrote to praise his educational ideas, in 1854 he was elected to the Société agricole, scientifique et littéraire of his department, in 1855 he began to act as *secrétaire de mairie*, and in 1857 he fell victim to typical clan intrigues unconnected with any politics but local ones.[76] Not a good example of political initiative.

Rural leadership, whatever the political persuasion, was provided by local notables, almost all of them landowners. Naturally, few such figures at the grassroots were nobles (fewer still among republican sympathizers), and their prestige did not run far—just far enough to be effective. But they were honorably known, they had the means that provided the opportunity and the leisure to study, travel, read and talk; and they were personally respected. Thus in Allier, Gaspard Delarue, medical officer, landowner at Theil: "influential in the region by his position and intelligence . . . he has abused this influence to pervert not only his commune, but all surrounding ones."[77] Thus in Puy-de-Dôme the figure of Mr. Hardy, a well-known landowner in the arrondissement of Yssoire, whose comfortable circumstances enabled him to maintain connections between local enthusiasts and the Republicans of Clermont; or the wealthy ex-mayor of Ambert, Lavigne, whose family connections with the descendants of the *conventionnel* Magnet preordained his fealty.[78] Along with the landowners and generally coinciding with them went the professional and administrative cadres of the little towns or, often, their sons. Though Merriman's *Agony of the Republic* emphasizes the activity and growing importance of the lower orders, his pages are sprinkled with notable leaders like Alexandre-René Dethou, mayor of Bléneau (Yonne), "a worthy man who tried to help the little people"; and Louis-Florent Chauvot, "a wealthy and educated proprietor" also of the Yonne and a member of its General Council, though obviously an eccentric who had married a working woman without the blessing of the church.[79] Jacques Bouillon, who like Merriman has written on the Limousin, stresses the role played by such men in the red successes of 1849— "local notables who belonged to the republican opposition under the July Monarchy and who then turned to more advanced theories, even socialist ones," such as the leading figures of the democratic movement in the little towns of Creuse, where most of Martin Nadaud's political friends were in professions like law, medicine, or teaching. At Saint-Junien, "pourtant fort ouvrière," the red leader was a young law graduate, son of the local justice of the peace.[80]

Another judge's son appears at Antraigues (Ardèche): Firmin Gamon, son of the Justice Emmanuel Gamon. Helped by a teacher and by a doctor from Vals, Firmin Gamon tried to raise the canton of Antraigues but succeeded only in sacking the home of the little town's mayor, Salomon, who was *en conflit d'intérêts* with his father. "We owe to this wretch," railed Salomon, "all the miseries of our district. He has upset everything by making use of his standing and influence as son of the justice of the peace and brother-in-law of a prefectorial aide."[81]

Philippe Vigier's discussion of *montagnard* successes in the Basses-Alpes also suggests that opposition to notables came from other notables. Having established that in the politics of that region, dominated by family rivalries, *la politique* played only a minor part through the 1840s,[82] Vigier discerns a turnabout around 1850 or 1851. Yet the evidence he marshals and that the archives provide permits a different interpretation. The politics of Digne were the clan politics of two families: the Fortouls and the Duchaffauts—the latter, royalists turned republican because their rivals were Orléanists. Local republican leaders like Charles Cotte and Julien Sauve, both lawyers of Digne, were friends of the Duchaffauts, who had come into their own in 1848. The only plebeian (and the only true personality) in republican ranks, Langomazino, a carpetbagging workingman from Toulon, had risen to leadership—as the procureur of Digne explained—"en s'appuyant sur des rivalités de famille." The Fortoul clan, for its part, would be represented by a younger son, Hippolyte, elected deputy in 1849 and who counted on Louis-Napoleon (whose minister he would become) "to reestablish his family's power in the Basses-Alpes."[83]

What the prefect of Hautes-Alpes wrote about his department applied to its neighbor and certainly to many others:

> In the three little towns of Embrun, Briançon and Gap, one finds only parish-pump notables whose influence does not extend beyond the limits of their town or *canton*. There is no district more

wrought by divisions and jealousies among local folk. All contest each other's status, all vie for the least appointment, for the slightest favor, with unimaginable fury. Every village has its Guelfs and its Ghibellines, and it is impossible to get the notables ever to agree on a question of personalities.[84]

This was the way things were under the July Monarchy, said the prefect, and nothing had changed since February 1848.

When one bears in mind the crucial importance of personalities (in both senses of the term), it is interesting to reread Eugène Ténot's account of December 2 and to see how such figures stand out. Scarcely a situation he describes in which the "energy" or "influence" of a man be he of the left or right, does not prove temporarily decisive.[85] Saint-Gengoux, Saint-Sorlin and other communes of Saône-et-Loire are aroused by Dismier, "un démocrate influent dans le pays," who raised five or six hundred men, entered Cluny unopposed, then marched on to Mâcon and defeat. In the Hautes-Alpes, "the bourgeois were the activists of this movement. Lawyers, doctors, accountants, merchants, shopkeepers marched off with their rifles, at the head of each group." (In one village, the leader was the *curé*.) In the fighting at Crest, "in the first rank of the insurgents on the dike we noticed a young man from one of the best local families, M. Vernet from Bourdeaux." To cite all relevant examples would entail re-citing most of the book. And when the expected leader does not intervene, Ténot mentions the exceptional occasion. Thus at Bessones (Gers), northwest of Mirande, "the rising was the exclusive doing of peasants. Whilst everywhere else they had awaited the signal of some member of the bourgeoisie, [here] they rose spontaneously and, led by some of themselves, took the road to Auch."[86] Here, the exception proves the rule: a tribute to a deferential insurrection, if ever there was one.

In Bourbonnais, the only cantons that voted en masse for Ledru-Rollin as president were Bourbon, Donjon, and Lurcy-Lévy.[87] In these centers, a historian of local politics tells us, "public opinion was directed by energetic men, such as Rocheton, notary and mayor of Lurcy-Lévy, who owed their influence over their fellow-citizens to their intelligence and their strength of character." "Educated, intelligent and respected" in official eyes, Rocheton was recognized as dangerous "because of the influence he exercised on the people of the region." He would be arrested on December 3—a move that probably accounts for Lurcy-Lévy's failure to stir.

The only real resistance to the *coup d'état* came around Donjon, where it was led by the Terrier clan (brothers of the representative from Montluçon, Barthélémy Terrier) and their allies, who even briefly occupied the subprefecture at Lapalisse. Adolphe Terrier was notary at Donjon, Felix Terrier took care of the family estates. Around them, a network of landowners and professional men—like Gallay of Neuilly-en-Donjon, unsuccessful candidate to the Assembly who would become mayor of Donjon in 1870, and the Prévérands of Lanax and Montaiguet—brought up their peasant contingents on December 4, while Felix Terrier tried to raise Bort, "where he had a property which had permitted him to exercise a certain influence on the workers." But once the little peasant army had taken Lapalisse, some fifteen miles away, it found itself in alien territory. The locals refused to take sides, and when the Republicans tried to raise the surrounding countryside by sounding the *tocsin,* those peasants who came were "mostly without arms and moved rather by curiosity than by desire to support the insurrection." Over and over, a peasant *dépaysé* proved a peasant *dérouté;* and that was almost as true of their leaders.

The court records of Riom furnish the portrait of a typical red notable: Philippe Fargin-Fayolle, known as Sommerat after one of his family properties, younger brother of a local lawyer and *montagnard* representative to the Assembly. As the village priest testified, "M. Sommerat enjoyed immense influence in the region and could direct several communes at his will. I believe that he owed his influence to the force of his political convictions, to the disinterestedness and the generosity of his character." Good father, good neighbor, convincing—even "seductive"—in his talk, helpful, everyone praised Sommerat's good deeds. His "proverbial generosity" and his "thoughtless hospitality" were cited as major causes of his financial ruin, despite a comfortable inheritance. Another reason for insolvency was that his political interests left him little time to keep up his domain at La Chapelaude, not far from Montluçon. But the people loved him: "I think that on his orders they would have gladly jumped in the lake," says the postmaster of La Chapelaude. One of his friends, Claude-Victor Vincent of Boussac, sounds much the same: "mauvaise tête et bon coeur." Charitable, Vincent did not hesitate to give his clothes to the poor or spend his money to succor needy friends. He too had wasted his inheritance and lived with his mother, working her land when he could, but spending most of his time in politics.

Such types may seem utopian, highflown, or simply addlepated from our perspective—as from that of their enemies—but the impression they leave is frequently that of strong, respectable characters, such as Auguste Bravard, architect at Issoire, "homme doué d'une grande énergie et d'une fermeté de caractère peu commune";[88] or the radical idealist, Paul Belougou, conseiller-général of Bédarieux since 1848: "hard on himself as on others, he lives on 1 franc 20 a day" (a poor farm laborer's wage).[89] Some followed the rule of Saint Dominic; others, like Vincent above, or another Bravard—Toussaint—of Jumeaux-sur-Allier, also a "dangerous demagogue" of the Puy-de-Dôme, that of Saint Francis. Ferdinand Raspail testified in 1862 that while studying medicine in Paris, Toussaint Bravard had shown himself generous and spendthrift. But almost all his money went to needy friends, several of whom he put up at Jumeaux when they needed help. *Officier de santé* in his canton of Brassac-les-Mines, he treated all the poor free—a note one finds repeated in other similar cases.[90]

Such are the typical virtues encountered among popular leaders, both of the right and left; whether in a Legitimist like Charles de Lazerme, conseiller-général of the Pyrénées-Orientales, or in his republican opponents like Arago or Pierre Lefranc, men "of absolute honesty and incontestable honorability."[91] Yet what did such decent, well-intentioned men tell the peasants when they tried to rouse them? In June 1849 Fargin-Fayolle was one of the *montagnard* deputies who tried and failed to defend the Republic by starting an insurrection. Wanting to help, his brother, Sommerat, briefly mobilized the peasantry of his canton—Huriel. The eight to nine hundred men who finally gathered on an Allier moor, at la Brande des Mottes on June 15, were told that Paris was in flames, that at Montluçon "on égorgeait tout le monde," and the Mountain was fighting on the people's side against the tyrants (the "infamous royal government"). The couriers who sought to rouse the peasants on Sommerat's behalf told them that the fatherland was in danger, that the enemy (generally unspecified, but sometimes the Cossacks) were about to invade France, that they had to come to the aid of Montluçon and Paris, and, significantly, "that those who did not obey would be punished as traitors."[92]

The affair of la Brande des Mottes fizzled out. But thirty months later, the brief December rising in nearby Limousin rehearsed similar themes: *tocsin,* revolutionary eloquence, inflammatory but confused appeals. "Your turn has come to work no longer. Let the bourgeois take your place." "Tomorrow we shall be fifty thousand in Limoges; it will be the finest feast you've had in your life." Those reluctant to join were threatened or tempted: there would be free food and drink for all. "Tomorrow we shall celebrate the great carnival; here is the peasants' republic, tomorrow we'll have the harvest feast!" The same report continues: "In the midst of the insurgents one notes Master Delassy, member of the General Council, ex-justice of the peace, the most influential man in the canton. He arrives on horseback."[93] Like Sommerat. Like Sommerat, also, we read in the later trial record, he was "an honest man, well-loved in his district but fiercely republican . . . subverted Chateauneuf; rode on horseback at the head of the band that was to march from Linards to Limoges."[94] Condemned to be transported to Algeria, his sentence was commuted to exile.

In Ardèche, on the night of 4 to 5 December 1851, the men of Chomérac and Saint-Vincent de Barrès, carrying what arms they could find, moved on Privas, following those who said: "Let's go to Privas: we'll burn the prefecture, the mortgage bureau, the tax collector's office, the barracks." One of those arrested explained his motives: "We wanted to uphold the people's rights.—What do you mean by the people's rights?—I don't know a thing about it." Another was more to the point: "Nous marchions pour faire diminuer les contributions et les patentes."[95]

The prefect of Hautes-Alpes, who with three hundred men had just delivered Sisteron (Basses-Alpes), reported on "the revolt which had managed to stir up several thousand peasants who had been led to believe . . . that the authorities did not want to recognize the acts of Louis-Napoleon."[96] Same note in the Drôme where "in many communes the people had risen in the name of Louis-Napoleon; in others they believed they were fighting against the rich, who were accused of being royalists."[97] Vigier, who sees the movements he describes as above all political, nevertheless declares that most of the peasants and even the artisans who marched on Digne and Crest ignored the Constitution and "politics in general."[98] One has to choose between the leaders of the insurrection who "insisted on giving their movement a sense that was above all political," and the representative from the Drôme pleading in 1852 for the "simple farmers . . . incapable of clear political ideas," who did not understand the significance of their rebellious acts. Vigier has made his choice—the wrong one in my view.[99] To attribute more limited aims and motives to the peasants who marched behind insurrectionist leaders is neither derogatory nor patronizing. On the contrary: it abandons the notion that an abstract political ideology is superior to the limited, matter-of-fact interests (and loyalties) those peasants followed who knew what they were about.

My conclusion is that the peasants, some peasants, had indeed been brought into national politics; but they had been carried there by traditional leaders—men whom they respected and trusted, and whom they followed because they took their word. Local notables committed to a particular ideology or political stance mobilized their allies and their clients who trusted or obeyed them in a feudal sense. The allegiance, the personal relationship, were surely more important than any ideology that they were made to serve.

I do not mean to suggest that matters were quite so simple. For one thing, few communities were really undivided in allegiance. Vigier has sought to emphasize the contrast between regions like Isère, Vaucluse, and parts of Drôme, where a wealthy and educated local bourgeoisie is supposed to have divided into *parties,* and regions where before 1848 political life came down to "rivalités impitoyables entre coteries de notables de faible envergure."[100] In my eyes this distinction does not hold. Divisions and rivalries were the rule wherever a local monopoly of influence did not obtain;[101] ideological or "political" divisions were the preserve of the educated minority and, to a lesser extent, of their acolytes;[102] nor were the "ruthless rivalries," which Vigier tries to circumscribe in space and time, left behind in 1848.[103] Indeed, I have argued elsewhere that in these divisions lay the source of "politics," and that national politics entered the provinces and the countryside by way of local feuds whose origins lay in the recent or quite distant past.[104]

Moreover, each local situation was a concatenation of particular factors. One look at the history of the Yonne lumber floaters and at the tangled labor relations of the Yonne waterways will show that the bitter Clamecy rising of December 1851 had little directly to do with the *coup d'état* and a lot with the long-standing griefs of lumber floaters, whose agitation, strikes, and troubles with the local lumber merchants went back almost two hundred years.[105] In a market town like Bédarieux (Hérault) which had been legitimist in 1848, economic conditions had shifted many working people to the left by 1850. For Gérard Cholvy, three causes contributed to the rising that made the revolutionaries masters of the little town for nearly a week after December 2: first, the deteriorating economic situation; then, the role of the general councillor whom we have already encountered—Paul Belougou, "proprietaire aisé de sentiments franchement républicains;" last but not least, strong local hostility against the gendarmes who had been putting down the widespread poaching. It was the gendarmes' stupid behavior that really set off the trouble in Bédarieux, says Cholvy,[106] and it is well to remember that events of general significance may stem from very particular (and sometimes unexpected) causes.

The same point holds for the tendency to overestimate the mutual reinforcement of local and national politics. This is not to underrate the role of local factions and associations, but to place them in perspective by asking whether personal allegiance led as straight to political allegiance as some like to suggest. How far—and especially how fast—did "voluntary associations and informal friendship groups" go in turning traditional loyalties "into a tenacious political movement"?[107]

The social cohesion and (its counterpart) the social pressures that loom behind local factions represent grassroots realities: structures of socioeconomic dependence and interdependence which also govern the sociable associations whose role political historians now treat with due respect. But whilst it is clear enough that such relations could lead to politization, it is not really clear that such "voluntary associations" (taking both terms in their most encompassing sense) readily become action groups "for class-based political movements,"[108] or that their contribution to politics and to politization went much beyond their contribution to traditional sociability and interdependence.

When a countryman, peasant, or artisan, said "I go with my patron," or "I go with my pals," or "I go with my family," or "I go with my neighbors," he said nothing new. Such traditional attitudes did indeed help usher those who shared them into the more complex world of national politics. But not consciously. The question is one of degree: like other traditional relationships, sociability was mobilized for political purposes. But in 1848–1851, these were the *political* purposes of others. It would take time and a longish *rodage* before this changed, before the supralocal political attitudes were assimilated and internalized. What the experience of 1848–1851 contributed to this process was a degree of acceleration and the sort of personal experience which made certain individuals and communities readier to perceive the opportunities of a modern political system and its relevance to them. But only in due course.

Agulhon's own balanced account of resistance to the *coup d'état*[109] shows that it stemmed from essentially local issues and grievances. But Agulhon—like Vigier, like Margadant[110]—concludes in favor of the political character of the risings. It is evident that—based on my definition of politics, which is similar to that obtaining in 1848 or 1851—I do not share his views. Not because the facts and the impressions he and his like present are not valid, but because they do not strike me as comprehensive *enough* or sufficiently qualified. Historical reality is a jigsaw which, I daresay, none can really reconstruct. But insistence on any one motif of the jigsaw gets in the way of its completion or comprehension. As I have indicated, to insist on the "modern" dimensions of the peasant movements of 1851 ignores the long survival of more archaic conditions and attitudes that governed them. Notably, it leaves aside the personal factors, hardest to trace, let alone to pin down, whose function I have tried—however superficially—to suggest. History is about people. It remains incomplete when it fails to recognize this, or to situate its characters as fully as possible in space and time, *Cherchez l'homme!* should be the slogan of political as well as social and economic historians.

Historical interpretation also falters when it sets standards inappropriate to the time. There was no particular virtue in sharing the often admirable values of Republicans, of Democrats, of Radicals. The peasant's own sense of why he acted is difficult to discern, but if he marched simply because he was from Poujols, or because his neighbors or patron urged him, that too would be normal—and perfectly sensible in the circumstances of that time.

The scholar's final trap is probably that refined form of *hubris* that grows from thorough and conscientious archival research. Archives are like the yellow pages: if you know what you want to find, it would be surprising that you do not find it. Enough material, and you have made a case. *Your* case, marked by your working hypothesis and your *coup d'oeil*. But the most convincing case is incomplete; and the better documented it is, the greater the risk of forgetting this.

That is no criticism of *histoire à thèse*. Angels often rush in where fools fear to tread. Much of the best history is written from—and to assert—a particular view. That is precisely what deserves remembrance when we read it and, still more perhaps, when we write it.

~ 8

Another Look at Peasant Politicization

Villages, the student of a Japanese hamlet recently remarked, are rather like a stage where most of the action goes on with the curtain down.[1] Historians prefer the curtain up and the lights on. They have tended to leave the crabbed evidence of the village to more frugal colleagues in ethnology and political science. As a result, students of Asia, Africa, and Latin America know more—or have more publications to read—about the peasantries of these continents than do the historians of peasant life in modern Europe. And rural studies in European history are closer to center stage for earlier centuries (and for the twentieth, where ethnologists and political scientists set the lead) than for the nineteenth. In French history, in which so much original work has been done, scholars have concentrated on the period before 1800. André Siegfried's *Tableau politique de la France de l'Ouest sous la Troisième République* (1913) remained a lonely monument pretty much into the 1960s, when several impressive publications appeared.[2]

The 1970s welcomed richer fare. Following Philippe Vigier, a number of scholars came to see the brief tenure of the Second Republic as a crucial time of rural politicization, when, in Charles Tilly's words, "the national state won a durable victory over local power-holders and traditional particularisms."[3]

Some years ago I wrote a book about how the peasants in certain parts of nineteenth-century France, still largely indifferent to the national state and to the urban-led world around them, were gradually lured into that "modern" orbit; they were, in other words, integrated into systems of values and activities that had long remained, or appeared to them, irrelevant.[4] I argued then that personal considerations reigned supreme over local politics, in which ideologies played very minor roles, but that, by the turn of the century, new conflicts and solidarities—now on a national scale—had penetrated, new possibilities had been apprehended in regions indifferent to them a generation or two before. What I did not sufficiently attempt was to describe the personal and interpersonal dimensions of a process, predictable

159

enough in itself though scarcely traced before, by which the language, gestures, and perceptions of national politics penetrated the countryside.

Other authors have lately considered this question in greater or lesser detail. Uncertain of the extent to which politicization had advanced, albeit haltingly, in the backward Limousin by 1880, Alain Corbin has seen it in the guise of a left-wing tradition that reflects economic quandaries and social tensions at the grass roots. Tony Judt, writing about the more urbanized villages of southeastern France at the turn of the century, has attributed the shift of some villagers toward socialism to practical experience and economic difficulties. The novelty in the Var of the 1880s and 1890s was that more peasants now glimpsed the solution to their local difficulties in national "political" action. Other historians—Pierre Barral, Maurice Agulhon, and Siegfried—have also equated, each in his own way, the electoral advances of the left, whatever its label, with politicization. Yet such a view, however justified, still seems to beg the question. Politicization is not about moves to the left (or right) but about an awareness that alternatives exist, that choices are possible, that "political" activities are not about irrelevant abstractions but are closely related to social and economic concerns that are local, personal, and immediate. So voting left does not, per se, prove politicization. It can just as easily reflect the survival of social cohesions and of traditional views rooted in the past. And the enduring political traditions—red, white, or blue—that have become established in regions like the Vendée, Var, or Limousin argue even more convincingly for persistent immobilities than for socioeconomic—and hence political— evolution.

Alain Corbin remarked that, at least until 1876, electoral results in those areas of the Limousin that were more exposed to national currents (the villages that, for example, sent migrant masons to Paris and other large cities) turned out "slightly less unfavorable to the right,"[5] which provides an indication, one would think, of the greater likelihood of individual self-affirmation in places where the traditional pressures and limitations of rural life had eased. Greater participation in market economy, more opportunity for individual enterprise and enhanced awareness that this opportunity exists, relaxation of social constraints, and the appearance of alternatives— all work *not* to politicize but to create conditions in which politicization can take place. The key question, then, is whether we can mark the passage from what Corbin has called the "territorial" (localistic) stance to a broader vision of national society and national affairs. To do this properly, we need access to the records of some thirty-six thousand communes. But can we at least determine a few major factors and stages of this passage? Can we date a few turning points? And can we go beyond the statistical to the personal and the local?

I want to emphasize the personal factor. Occurring at the level of village, hamlet, and farm, the political acculturation of the peasantry should also be seen as a multitude of individual evolutions in which personalities played a part. That part is no less crucial for being so hard to trace. I do not mean to deny the significance of other factors but to suggest the more modest context within which they evoked interpretation and response at the individual level. Fresh forays among the documents may suggest just how national politics initially were grafted into local issues, which were dependent upon relationships of clans or kin or friends with their sociabilities and their feuds.[6] Narrow interests could open the way to broader perspectives, but only in the service of individual or locality.

But first we must consider the problem of chronology, easy to overlook since the various localities and regions of France were at different stages of political evolution at any given time. Very roughly, political rivalries among the notables left the populace unengaged (except for local aspects) at least into the 1860s. Even so, one may well ask how much ideology and what Alexis de Tocqueville called "politics properly speaking" entered into the electoral activities of the enfranchised. "Very little, infinitely little," the deputy of Valognes assured his friend, Gustave de Beaumont, in 1842.[7] This only started to change in the 1860s, as factional conflicts were nationalized by a growing awareness of national politics (war, military service, tariff measures) impinging on local life. Beginning in the later 1860s and culminating in 1877, freer (or at least livelier) elections and a greater variety of candidates introduced real competition for the popular vote. Finally, during the 1880s, the peasants learned to use the ballot to improve their economic position, and those who competed for their vote learned to promise concrete returns, on whose delivery they would be judged. At that point, alignments based on interest (such as those for which Judt has argued in the Var) came into their own, and the process of acculturation appears to have run its course.

Reality was, of course, far less systematic than all of this might suggest. As late as 1913, Siegfried recognized that many Frenchmen did not regard as essential "the great problems on which the country divides and by which it orders the direction of its destinies." Rather, they were "moved by reasons that are local, special, and often incomprehensible to an outsider."[8] In the provinces, politics were a function of private relations. Since 1848, at least, publicists, ideologues, and government servants had sought to shift politics from this "trivial" plane. They would have liked to find questions of principle, not merely the petty warfare based on local animosities between hamlet Montagues and village Capulets. In fact, only too often, "questions of principle [gave] way to questions of personalities."[9] What was said of Die, in the mountains of the Drôme, was true of many another small town in 1865: "Idleness and pride have long since rent the upper bourgeoisie and divided the region into coteries, whose leaders become the representatives of a political party in order to give themselves more importance. But convictions play only a secondary role in their choice, and the flag they flourish always conceals personal animosities." [10]

Twelve years later, in 1877, the Third Republic faced its first great trial: President Marshall MacMahon replaced the republican government with a minority cabinet, dissolved Parliament, and held new elections in an atmosphere redolent of 1851. [11] At Saint-Julien-de-Civry (Saône-et-Loire) the schoolmaster described the village caught in the new political crisis in terms similar to those used to depict Die. The village was torn, but were there well-defined political parties? Certainly, "if one considered only the labels" that defined the hostile camps; certainly not, if one looked for other differences between them, all of which lay "in hostilities, hatreds, rivalries, profound jealousies." This dichotomy between the labels and their substance continued to be true throughout much of rural France at least until 1914. [12]

Increasingly after 1830, national administrative intervention altered local politics but initially did little to elevate them above narrow social rivalries, which provided the highway for the eventual infiltration of national politics into the provinces. First reaching the "intelligent" or "enlightened" minorities and finally the masses, national alignments came to define local animosities. The periodic reports of departmental prefects and attorneys-general (*procureurs-généraux*) show how personal and local rivalries with no political overtones provided a focus (or inspiration) for political opposition and how men with no intention of opposing the regime were gradually cast in this unintended role. [13]

This transformation is especially evident in elections for municipal offices and for the departmental General Council. Frequently apolitical in character, these elections were the obvious proving grounds for men with wider political aspirations; as such, they cannot be ignored when considering the general political scene. Many were disputed by candidates ready to side with the government in order to obtain its support or at least its neutrality. By favoring one candidate, the authorities ran the risk of alienating his opponent, turning a merely opportunistic or otherwise indifferent notable into an open enemy of the regime. [14] In the middle and later 1860s, as political activity intensified, reports reflect a growing awareness of the problem. In the southwest, where every parish seemed divided into rival "parties," such local divisions "with no political character" were affecting electoral results and attitudes toward the government. In the center of the Empire, the attorney-general of Riom stressed "the considerable role played by personal and parish pump rivalries, particular interests and feelings," in the electoral struggles but added that such "shabby motives" afforded the opposition an opportunity to "spread political ideas among the people that they had hitherto ignored." And at Die, where the prepolitical coteries had adapted national issues to suit their own ends, the opposition, which was initially apolitical and local, soon became political and republican.[15]

Well into the Third Republic, however, rural elections were marked by the comparatively slight importance of political opinions. Indeed, the continuing importance of personal relationships may help explain the durability of many local potentates—scions of families "whose sole interest [had] always been the public good"—who remained ready to serve "whatever regime availed itself of their services." Not that the regimes had that much choice. In the Haute-Loire, from the First Empire to the opening decades of the Third Republic, eighty elections turned around thirty names. In other words, for well over three-quarters of a century, except during the years 1848–1850, thirty families provided the high political cadres of the region.[16] As Proudhon foresaw, universal suffrage was counterrevolutionary, at least initially. But although feudal-style patronage (noble or bourgeois) was widespread, its effectiveness was limited. Large landowners in small villages set the political coloring of the community. That coloring changed with time and varied from place to place, but for peasants to accept the landlord's politics as long as employment and social security depended on anything as "unimportant" as a vote made good sense.

Mayors, justices of the peace, constables, or highway inspectors were naturally—and rightly, too—regarded as fountainheads of troubles or favors. In 1865 an official writing from Brittany noted how eagerly rural electors went to vote—in sharp contrast to the numerous abstainers in more politically lively urban centers. Such civic punctiliousness, thought one magistrate, stemmed from "the influence the mayor can exercise in their private affairs." The peasant did not necessarily know the man he voted for; indeed, most often he did not. It sufficed that the mayor knew him. Reporting home from the Vosges in 1877, Jules Ferry rejoiced to find the peasants "cured of the sickness of fear." He was talking about a particular kind of peasant (*demi-bourgeois, indépendants par situation*); and while the existence—and evolution—of their kind should not be ignored, many more retained "a sort of superstitious fear toward the owners of the land."[17]

Fear, respect, sympathy, dependency. For most of the 1860s and 1870s, men like the Baron de Veauce, elected deputy of the Allier in 1863 (as he had been in 1852 and 1857) by 17,930 votes out of the 19,061 votes cast, remained typical: "Born at Veauce, landowner at Veauce, mayor of

Veauce, and quite simply Veauce. A little feudal baron."[18] There were many like him elsewhere. As late as 1898, the Marquis de Lauriston, mayor of the small community in Loir-et-Cher, which even today has almost no roads, declared with confidence, "At Villefrancoeur there are no politics." What he clearly meant was, no one questions my word. The evidence suggests that even in the twentieth century many electors continued to vote for the man they knew, or as the man they knew told them to vote.[19] If, by then, some voters picked up ideas that they had ignored in earlier days, they persisted in voting for something represented by someone: a notable and what he represented.

What he represented was often the *pays* and its "immemorial" orientations. The commonplace that more votes are cast *against* than *for* appears to be borne out by the long political history of local contentions: the antipathy between neighboring parishes; the hostility of rural areas toward the country town; the antagonism between village or *bourg* and the isolated hamlets and farms around it; or the dissensions of clans and factions based on family connections, service relations, or chance hostilities.[20] Such local allegiance and local loggerheads could not but affect behavior in the subsidiary realm of national politics. In Saône-et-Loire, around 1900, village rivalries drew "even stronger dividing lines than political rivalries, to the point that they often" muddled national politics. All over France many small towns (and their hinterlands) have been rivals "from time immemorial." To repudiate a candidate merely because he was supported by another town, whatever his political label, was common. In Savoy, the little towns of Bonneville and Cluses, about fifteen miles apart, have disputed the leadership of the Faucigny area ever since the fourteenth century. Both towns voted left, unless one town could vote against a candidate identified with the other. When that occurred, as it did in a famous election of 1897, the rival town voted enthusiastically the other way, unto its farthermost parish.[21]

The politics of these endogamous societies appear little different in spirit from their family alliances. As proverbs warned against choosing a mate away from home, so electors were reminded that they could only judge a candidate's worth if they knew him personally. He should be born in the area, live in it, "be bound to it by family bonds and everyday relations." This particular statement dates back to the days of the *monarchie censitaire,* which often honored such requirements in the breach. Stendhal's *Lucien Leuwen* testifies to the occasional success even then of what more recent days describe as *candidats parachutés.* In Isère, as the Empire drew to a close, Riondel, the mayor of St.-Marcellin, triumphed over forcible government opposition because the local patriotism of the cantons of Lower Isère gave him "an impregnable position," according to the subprefect, "leaving all political considerations aside." Yet in the "more advanced" cantons of Rives and Beaurepaire, which might have been expected to support him even more strongly on ideological grounds but where he was less known, the official candidate regularly gained more votes than he. In Savoy, the valley of Tarentaise and the hills of Maurienne have long opposed each other whenever possible. In the election of 1872, the candidate of the left was a Dr. Jacquemoud of the valley town of Moutiers, in Tarentaise. His opponent was an ironmaster from the hill town of Randens in Maurienne. Most of the left-wing parishes in Maurienne voted right, against the "man of the valley"; and a number of right-wing Tarentaise parishes voted for the republican candidate, Dr. Jacquemoud, because he was their local man.[22] Just two examples among many; but this fixation on an *enfant du pays* was not unreasonable since the nearer to home the candidate, the more responsive to home needs he could be. Throughout the Second Empire and even into the Third Republic, regardless of the political coloring of a commune or canton, the candidate who lived there or whose family lived there could garner 60, 70, or even 80 or 90 percent of the vote.

What changed, when it did change, was the nature of the service a local patron rendered or the popular perception thereof. In a disputed election in 1876, in Haute-Garonne, the tone is still similar to that of mid-century. The supporters of Comte Adhémar d'Ayguesvives denied allegations of fraud; their candidate got his votes because he was very honorably known in the canton of Castanet, "because his family had owned properties there and still enjoyed great consideration." At a less exalted level, the mayor of Rebigue, accused of using the influence of his official position on behalf of Ayguesvives, replied, "If I enjoy any influence in the canton of Castanet, it is solely due to my family position and to my landholdings, not to the modest and obscure functions with which I have been entrusted." He also explained that his political opponents, who had testified against him, were his personal foes as a result of petty conflicts: one because the mayor had not saved his son from military service, another because he would not give him a job, the third because he had not leased him a piece of land.[23] True or false, this reflects the grassroots realities of political partisanship. As the prefect of Haute-Loire had written in 1854, "There is no rivalry, no neighborhood squabble, that does not degenerate into open quarrels and suits, no quarrel not envenomed into hatred to be transmitted from one generation to the next." Such statements provide more than a hint of the grounds on which people chose sides. A family, a village, a social or professional group might have been red or white because it had acquired national property in the 1790s, had taken communion from a constitutional priest, or had benefited from or suffered in the Revolution, and these attachments became solid, hereditary, intertwined with the material interest related to an economy of clientele and patronage.[24]

This development was more readily apparent in the towns than in the villages and the countryside, where social cohesion remained stronger, alternative patrons (or opportunities of self-affirmation) more rare. The Revolution of 1848 and its aftermath began to change the bonds of both towns and the countryside, sometimes radically. Old motives and old factions subsisted, but their protective coloring took on new hues. Jean Dagnan, the historian of mid-century Gers, claimed that "universal suffrage awakened the countryside to political life." He showed villages dividing into reds and whites, "deux camps qui voisinent haineusement." But the political divisions merely fed on prior hatreds: "their discord is alimented by local intrigues and coteries, by family divisions." As some school-teachers no doubt found, it became increasingly difficult to avoid choosing sides. A novel of 1860 makes the point clear:

> Two parties, the White and the Red, struggle endlessly in the villages of the Midi. Willy-nilly, whatever a newcomer's indifference, he is enrolled in one of the two camps . . . A simple quarrel with a member of his party is enough to cause a peasant to desert his camp. Politics are always the pretext of the disagreement, whose true cause really lies in some measly material issue.[25]

So by the 1860s, at least in the circumstances described, villagers had a choice: they could choose between parties (that is, between clans), and politics offered one opportunity to do so. Another novel (this one written by a village schoolteacher in the 1890s) describes how that might work. In the Languedoc village of Antonin Lavergne, the absence of a republican leader had left the field to the conservatives (note the modern political terminology!):

> At last M. Guibal entered the field. Even though his family held Conservative opinions, he . . . openly declared himself the opponent of M. Lauret and his ideas. For many years, a veiled enmity divided the Guibals and the Laurets, who, even in the days of the First Empire, jockeyed for power and supremacy in Saint-Michel. Hence much friction and bad blood between the two families. Since then, the *bourg* divided into two camps: but political questions were excluded. After the fall of the Second Empire, the father of M. Guibal constantly opposed old M. Lauret in this way, while courting the Reds. [At his death, the son changed tactics.] Reso-

lutely, he declared himself Republican; he was followed by his friends and became the party leader. Yet politics continued for a long time extraneous to these local competitions, only formally referred to . . . One was for M. Lauret or for M. Guibal, rather than Conservative or Republican.[26]

In this light, village politics of the Third Republic look more like those of the Italian city-state of Romeo and Juliet than like the France of Jules Ferry. The voter's clan, the voter's leader, the voter's vote were designated by memories and decisions that remained obstinately local, whatever the superficial homage paid to the new national idioms. During the election of 1889, when the issue was eminently modern phenomenon of General Boulanger, a local candidate in the Gironde was denounced by the Conservatives and supported by the Republicans because he was the grandson of a *sans-culotte terroriste,* who, even worse, had made money by buying "nationalized" property *(biens nationaux).* Further north, in Brittany, "One is Red or White, but one is necessarily one or the other. . . . Being born in a given family, in a given part of the parish, one inherits a political ideology."[27]

Survivals of this sort were found at their most explicit in Corsica, where French officials and travelers never ceased to marvel at local anachronisms. One voyager noted in 1914 that there were "no political opinions in Corsica." He did not mean that the Corsicans were uninterested in politics but that they evinced no interest in French politics, which they did not consider their own. Their politics were very active indeed and affected local life in every possible way, but they were local, conducted in Montague-Capulet fashion and based on a system of patronage and clientele. Clients paid uneconomically low rents on the lands they held, lodged with the patron when they came to town, often asked for small loans without repaying them, sold the patron products he did not really need, and appealed to his influence when in trouble. In return, they voted for him faithfully and, if necessary, supported him with their guns. "If you live outside Corsica, you can follow a general policy. On the spot, these generalizations do not exist."[28] Note the exchange of services, the inescapable circumstances, and the irrelevance of alien generalities that have nothing to do with the local situations.

Corsica, in its stubborn anachronism, seems to have little to teach in the context of French mainland politics. But it was a museum of the values and processes of an only slightly earlier age. And similar situations abounded on the mainland—whether at Plozévet, where "M. Le Bail is Republican, hence we are Republicans because my father's family has belonged to the Le Bail clan for two generations"; or at La Réole, about forty miles upriver

from Bordeaux, where from the 1880s to the Second World War local politics were dominated by the clan conflicts of Larozistes and Chaignistes who
struggled for supremacy, directly or *par candidat interposé,* for three generations and thirteen elections.[29] As in Corsica, whoever wanted a road surfaced, a school built, a subsidy granted, a contract awarded, a loan made, or
a job offered had better vote right—and be lucky.

As I read the evidence, which is admittedly patchy, the ideological and
extra-local aspects of national politics remained the preserve of traditional
leaders—great or petty notables—who used them for traditional ends.
Only gradually did the country people themselves adopt the new terminology, let alone new ideology, or perceive its relevance to their concerns.
Even then, the extent to which local categories and local conflicts were
simply rendered into a political language is difficult to determine; national
alignments were often merely used to validate and support local interests
and local divisions, in which political reality continued to lie.

One significant exception to this apparent rule concerns the Church:
national (and international) ecclesiastical conflicts were quite swiftly and
meaningfully translated into local terms. No historian of nineteenth-
century France has ignored the importance of the clerical-anticlerical
struggle, but only in the last decade have scholars like Maurice Agulhon
and Ted Margadant stressed the major role this struggle played in the
nationalization of local conflicts and the political education of populations
not accessible to ideological argument on other terms. Yet although recent
monographs (rightly) stress the conflict's historical role in the formation of
the left, some attention can usefully be directed to its contribution, quite
simply, to the generalization of faction where occasions for it had otherwise
been rare.

The sociopolitical importance of religious conflicts lies not so much in
the divisiveness that set neighbor against neighbor but in the factionalism
that set squire against squire and priest against priest, dividing authorities
that were considered a single unit, that spoke with one voice, and that
wielded a natural power in different circumstances natural to heed. The
acquisition of national property during the Revolution and the retribution
visited upon the buyers of this, mostly ecclesiastical, real estate after 1815
drove communities and families to the left, or into clericalism (generally of
the right) to cover their tracks. However compromised in the terror and
counterterror of the revolutionary era or the white reaction of the Bourbon
Restoration, these families, hitherto politically uncommitted, were forced
into new political commitments for purely practical, not ideological, reasons. When not willing or able to melt into conformity, descendants of the
farmer enriched by an opportunistic purchase or of the squire who had done

well under the Convention or Directory while (or because) his fellows suffered, provided a potentially new leadership in scores of rural communities. As the century progressed, tension also grew, here and there, between priests of vulgar extraction, limited in education and manners, and the *châtelains* ("squires" or "petty nobles") or other notables, who treated them as inferior dependents. Grudge, resentment, or vexation led some *curés* to set up as rivals of the *châtelain* or the mayor or to join some rival faction. More often, a local notable, an *acquereur de biens nationaux* or descendant of one, headed an anticlerical or antinoble party.

As regimes kept changing, differences between the political sympathies of priests and notables became increasingly likely to occur and, worse, increasingly evident, especially when official ecclesiastical policy went counter to the established sympathies of political patrons. Conflicts of authority had been rare at the grass roots. Under the July Monarchy, however, differences surfaced, with the clergy strongly suspicious of Adolphe Thiers and especially of the "Protestant" François Guizot; at that time a multitude of parish priests got into hot (or tepid) water for refusing to sing the *Domine salvum fac regem*. Conflicts grew more frequent in 1848 and 1849, when universal suffrage, which propelled the humble masses into prominence, also invested their mentors with a new influence. Priests, far more than lowly schoolteachers, were the obvious beneficiaries of this new potential for leadership. Quite a few took up political positions that set a patron's teeth on edge, raised a portion of the community against them, and opened religiopolitical feuds that sometimes lasted for generations. Friction between local notables and the priest—with their respective factions that often arose from causes unrelated to religion or politics (school, the upkeep and decoration of church or presbytery, the parish budget, questions of precedence)—could also turn a parish into a political hotbed.[30]

Such conflicts became more frequent still under the Second Empire. Cutting across custom and material interests both, the Roman Question determined the political attitudes of the clergy, whether turning new Bonapartists against their traditional legitimist protectors or sparking priestly hostility to a government unaccustomed to opposition from such a quarter. This led to open clashes between *cure* and *château* or between *cure* and *mairie*—sometimes, to clerical opposition to both at different times. Such built-in conflicts offered village priests opportunities for self-assertion for which many (especially of the younger generations) seemed to long. And noble patrons found it difficult to admit that a local priest's views should diverge from their own, whether he (before 1859 and in 1863 and 1865) supported an Empire they scorned or he (after 1871) opposed the regime they supported. In the Pas-de-Calais, for example, the nobles of St.-Pol were legitimist, but an "influential fraction" of the clergy were "clearly favorable" to Napoleon III.[31] These conflicts also offered unexpected opportunities to mayors and other local officials at loggerheads with the parish priest to settle old scores in the guise of political action.

For the half-century after 1860 the local stance of churchmen was more freely determined by new kinds of rivalry and friction, and their national politics were guided by the distant interests of papal policy. The priest as a free, or, at least, an unpredictable agent in politics was a newfangled phenomenon, and a troubling one. It was difficult to ignore priests like the one at Drouges (Ille-et-Vilaine), who told his congregation, "You must not vote for the government's candidate, you must not listen to the *gendarme,* or to the *cantonnier,* or to any [public] agent."[32] Here was a category of popular propagandist no regime, and no grassroots public, could disregard—and one that, I suspect, did more to factionalize the country and to spread awareness of extra-local conflicts by tying them to local doings than the *montagnards* of 1849 had done.

After 1870, and especially after the fall of Rome, many clerics were more hostile to the Bonapartism they blamed for the "unpardonable" event than to the new Republic, and Bonapartists returned the antipathy in kind. This is no place for a survey of clerical and anticlerical attitudes. But it is worth remembering that priests' conflicts were not only with anticlericals. Priests could also be found opposing the conservative municipal council at Listrac (Gironde), quarreling with the white mayor of Cazedarnes (Hérault), feuding with the *châtelain*-mayor of St.-Jean-de-Cole (Dordogne), or even coming to blows with the local notary and president of the parish council at Boisse (Dordogne).[33] Predictably, the heightened tensions between different categories of notables were not only sensed by local populations but also reflected in their attitudes. These tensions, of course, grew worse with the formation of the Republic. But the real clash between Republicans and the Church came in 1877, when the Holy See appealed for aid from the French episcopate and from France in its conflict with the Italian kingdom. The republican refusal to be dragged into a foreign quarrel (or their exploitation of the useful issue this offered) led to the crisis of May 16 and to elections fought with Gambetta's *new* slogan: "le cléricalisme, voilà l'ennemi." We know all about that but less about the measures with which the Church sought to counteract its problems.

One result of the clergy's more consistently embattled stance toward the end of the nineteenth century was its increasingly deliberate entry into politics. "The mission of the clergy," wrote the bishop of Périgueux in 1904, "is to introduce Catholics into politics en masse." His statement may have been unusually explicit, but it came very late in the process of peasant politicization. The widespread campaign to persuade believers that voting in legislative or municipal elections was a religious duty was surely more significant than its more picturesque and, often, more familiar aspects: public damnation of political opponents, denunciation of pacts with the devil, sexual deprivation of politically peccant husbands, and so forth.[34] But these, too, contributed to the politicization of simple people—either by using idioms that were especially accessible and likely to impress or by the irritation and hostility they caused.

Another aspect of the same campaign may be viewed as more defensive in character. As early as the 1870s, the growth of anticlericalism and especially of religious indifference encouraged social Catholicism even among the least socially minded, with campaigns against Sunday work, so men could attend Mass, and for free seating in churches, so attendance would not be discouraged. More important still, charity wisely distributed was used to reaffirm poor people's confidence in their betters and to advance what a Béziers medical man described as "l'oeuvre chrétienne des élections."[35] Thus, Christian charity was enlisted in conservative politics as republican enlightenment was enlisted in anticlerical politics. The two clashed, which they were meant to do, as in the 1880s, when manuals of moral and civic instruction by authors like Jules Steeg and Paul Bert were placed on the Index of Prohibited Books.[36] Some priests refused to admit children using the books in school to First Communion, with predictable results on village tempers.[37] Didactic inculcation of prejudice and its divisive fallout marched on.

To this, the Catholic publicists contributed. The 1890s were marked by the appearance of regional editions of *La Croix*, which appealed to country people not only through their local news furnished by village priests and practical advice about hygiene and crops but also by their tone. *La Croix* was republican and patriotic, but it opposed capitalism, financiers, speculators, Jews, and foreigners. Combative advocates of the Catholic cause, the paper's writers were forceful participants in the religiopolitical debate and advanced interest in politics by making both religion *and* politics more lively and intriguing. Like their competitors of the *mauvaise presse*—*Dépêche de Toulouse, Progrès de Lyon, Petite Gironde, Petit Parisien*—such papers were introduced by long-term, free "trial" subscriptions, followed by subscriptions at reduced prices. Whatever their rural readership, and it continued to be low until after the First World War, around 1905 most village priests read and recommended *La Croix*. By then, however, the political struggles of the preceding years had developed a taste for even stronger fare: *La Libre Parole, L'Autorité.*[38] Clerical politics opened the door to national politics.

All of this has taken me far ahead of my tale, but not away from it. Like the *démoc-socs* of the Second Republic, priests carried their ideologies and their peculiar politics into areas where these had been unknown. But the conversions of mid-century were never so lasting as those achieved two or three decades later, when continuity of endeavor found a material context to support its aim.

What the Second Republic left behind in limited circles, even in the countryside, were the open wounds of the repression that began in 1850 and culminated in the aftermath of December 2, 1851. The great Revolution and the Old Regime had left their imprint too: deeply etched memories and family alignments that did not easily diminish. During the Second Empire and much of the Third Republic, tithe and *corvée* retained their power to horrify and mobilize to electoral ends. So did resentments produced by 1851. In 1856 the subprefect of Béziers reported both unhealed, with the "personal, family and party hatreds" they had caused likely to last a long time in a region haunted by "the hatreds and discord of 1815." Those hatreds were certainly still there in 1870. The Empire, which sought to dampen political tensions among the peasantry, had done little to assuage resentments among its erstwhile opponents in the middle and lower-middle classes. Teachers, postmen, tax collectors, and *cantonniers* denounced and revoked under political pretexts—as whites before 1849 and reds thereafter—had learned political lessons that they earlier had most probably ignored.[39] During the winter of 1858–59, after Orsini's unsuccessful attempt to murder the emperor, some two thousand suspects were arrested, over four hundred of whom were transported to Algeria.[40] Such political hatreds as had subsided in the intervening decade were revived by the renewed brutalities and suffering of those months.

These actions do not seem, however, to have reverberated far among the peasantry. Few, like Jean Fontane of Anduze (Gard), continued to be "constrained to political inactivity but dreaming always of revenge" through the decades that followed. Perhaps the political interests awakened in some villagers during the Second Republic did indeed lie dormant under the Second Empire, awaiting only the chance to spring back to life. Yet the evidence I have seen suggests less a prudent dissimulation than an absence of sentiments needing to be dissimulated.[41] The Empire did not foreclose all opportunities of expression for the political classes, however fruitless these might actually have been in practice. But I have seen nothing to indicate that the silent masses kept silent because of repression rather than out of indifference.

This is the context in which we should look at a process of political evolution as varied as the multitude of parishes and clans making up that jigsaw—France. The Second Empire's contribution to the politics of notables was the official candidate, who was selected by the government's representatives and supported by the government's not insignificant resources and prestige: "a light that opinion needs to guide it amid party intrigues." Through the 1850s the light shone largely unimpeded—its effects, as Quentin-Bauchart explained, "straightforward and free of pitfalls."[42] The peasants needed firm leadership. Opponents impertinent enough to enter the electoral lists were treated cavalierly: their posters were prohibited or torn down, the men distributing their voting bulletins harassed and sometimes jailed, their complaints ignored. In the following decade, in small parishes at least, shouting one's support for the wrong candidate could earn the voter a beating followed by imprisonment. Officials of the *Ordre Moral* saw things no differently: in 1877, the subprefect of Mauriac (Cantal) instructed all mayors of his district that distributors of republican tracts were acting illegally and should be arrested and conveyed at once to Mauriac. As a prefect of those days insisted, "Il faut imposer le bien."[43]

Given a peasantry absorbed by work and reasonably satisfied with its returns, the policy worked. Many villagers who stirred to defend the Republic in 1851 probably came to believe the government's argument that they were misled, since they were not personally affected by Napoleon's coup d'état. Social superiors, who might have enlightened them, had been eliminated or held their peace.[44] Then came the gradual relaxation of the 1860s. Although the liberal Empire was introduced only in 1867, villagers could after 1859 again hear their betters speak with several voices, offering alternative leadership and courses of action. Republican candidates appeared in the elections of 1863 and by 1865 and 1866 magistrates were reflecting on the "emancipation" of the electorate. Electoral results were still attributed (and probably with justice) to "petty local passions" and hence often dismissed as "politically" insignificant. Yet it was recognized that "universal suffrage is no longer, as it was a few years ago, in the hands of the administration," for voters had come "under the direction of other influences." Public opinion, "even in the countryside," was "awakening"— increasingly "determined to find its own direction."[45]

Patchily but portentously, growing prosperity was beginning to emancipate rural populations from traditional dependencies—and absorptions. Like the offspring of the successful Var farmers turned cork manufacturers in the 1840s, whom Maurice Agulhon has studied, the sons of thriving Languedoc wine-growers now sought to assert their independence from the local gentry. Hitherto "white," they signaled their newfound aspirations (and their up-to-dateness) by flaunting republican sympathies. Established forms of sociability provided them with a ready forum, and the burgeoning labor shortage provided them with a potential following of journeymen emancipated from the landowner's sway. Where such conditions obtained, the villager with pretensions or a grudge now had somewhere to turn. In 1858 the attorney-general of Montpellier noted the trend, only just beginning, philosophically: "les jeunes veulent être de leur temps."[46]

Adjustment to this novelty did not come easily. The sensitive Charles de Rémusat, Thiers's future minister of foreign affairs, had realized as early as 1863 that electoral success now called for unwonted effort, for a far greater investment of time and energy than before. He was ahead of his time; but other astute observers soon recognized the "urgent" need to work on the electorate, not intermittently but constantly, from well-established *local* bases. If constituencies were to be won, or held, they had to be nursed. As early as 1861, a magistrate noted that at Marcheux (Doubs) the governmental candidate, M. de Conegliano, was resented because, though a local landowner, "he rarely sees his electors." The local electors had turned to a rival "who spends his life among them." New expectations were taking shape, and wise politicians drew the consequences. Rémusat's brother-in-law, Adrien de Lasteyrie, settled at Lagrange (Seine-et-Marne) where in 1863 he had run a close race against the official candidate. Auguste Casimir-Perier, elected to the General Council of the Aube where he owned considerable property, took a house in Troyes and spent all winter in the region in order to prepare for the 1869 elections.[47] Gone were the days when Godefroy Cavaignac, recognized and feted in a country inn, could refuse to shake hands with local radicals because, as he explained, he did not know them.[48] When in 1869 the Marquis de Grammont was elected in the arrondissement of Luxeuil (Haute-Saône) and his peasants flowed into the *bourgs* to celebrate, the attorney-general of Besançon reported ruefully that "the marquis himself, intoxicated by his triumph, mixed with the popular rabble." Others of less exalted nobility, like Flocard de Méprieu, mayor of Sarmérieu and deputy of the Isère since 1852, even went so far as to lead the local fire company.[49]

A new step toward democratic politics was taken in 1868, when electoral meetings were authorized under fairly strict conditions. A mass of official reports speaks to the concern felt by police and magistrates about the appearance and extension of "ostensibly" private meetings and about the surveillance and harassment to which opposition figures were subjected.[50] As yet, however, only local notables were affected. Meetings by personal invitation scarcely touched the humbler electors—and certainly not outside the industrial centers.[51] News of effective political campaigning nevertheless spread to fairs, taverns, and *veillées*—even into Haute-Savoie where tales of Jules Favre's oratory evoked the admiration of mountaineers who had never heard him. "We must be careful to vote for [him]," they said. "At least he's not dumb." Immediately effective or not, this feature of political contests became increasingly significant; politics as entertainment attracted a rural population woefully short of diversions and eager to break the monotony.[52]

At any rate, the later 1860s showed evidence of a new—and recognizably political—sensibility to issues of wider import. Given a little time, mused the attorney-general of Aix in November 1868, attitudes hitherto limited to urban centers would trickle into the countryside, and the opposition views of a politicized urban middle class "would progress rapidly among the rural population." The peasant was more reluctant to accept administrative suasions, reported the attorney-general of Dijon a few months later. It was not that the peasant had developed political views but that he wanted to assert himself; thus, he tended to prefer the opposition. His colleague in Besançon summed up the evolution:

> Parliamentary ideas, once discredited, have regained [public] favor . . . the movement that began among the upper classes is affecting the masses: the practice of universal suffrage and the reading of newspapers have altered their frame of mind. They understand the power that elections give them and insist on using it as they please. We shall henceforth have to take this new tendency into account.

One magistrate in Toulouse even went so far as to consider the uses of a new war in turning opinion away from "these sterile and irritating questions of internal politics."[53]

By late 1869, in the midst of official reports that confirm the continued lack of interest in country people, nuances began to appear: "Our countryfolk have not departed from their usual indifference," advised the attorney-general of Limoges. "Generally illiterate and until now practically indifferent to the political impulse spread by the press, they are really only interested in promoting their own material well-being, selling their products, and improving the means of communication, whose constant development leads them to appreciate governmental activity." Here are new themes that gained in importance with the years, themes not unrelated to a novelty, already noted in this essay, which struck the attorney-general: "the importance the peasants are beginning to attach to the exercise of their electoral rights."[54]

Economic expansion and affluence were propelling once isolated regions into the national market, suggesting new needs and possibilities directly related to the national government and hence to electoral politics, which the rural areas had once ignored. Electoral politics catered not only to self-interest but also to dignity, suggesting novel possibilities for self-

affirmation. The farmers around Bordeaux, for example, were "very flat-
tered to find themselves the object of the visits and the consideration of
candidates who came to ask for their votes. Some peasants, imagining
themselves very enlightened about their rights and their [new] importance,
took advantage of this . . . to thwart the local authorities." These were
mere forest murmurs. As the attorney-general of Chambéry explained, the
problem was not that of getting the "peasant agitated about political issues
during an electoral campaign" but of finding someone with "reasons to do
it. . . . In the end, the bourgeoisie alone has the enlightenment and the
money needed to move the masses."[55] The bourgeoisie soon entered the lists
en masse but began by finding, if we can believe *La République de l'Allier* of
September 26, 1870, "rural populations unenlightened, scarcely literate,
and obey[ing] in politics more instinct than reason."

So we must not exaggerate isolated developments or the perceptions of
timorous officials, excessively sensitive to anomalous displays of defiance.
Republicans continued to insist on the peasants' political ignorance and the
need to undertake their political education. More important, perhaps, and
certainly more immediate, republicanism remained an urban phenomenon,
lacking militants at the grass roots. Indeed, had there been more republican
notables (or other enthusiasts), the Republicans would have felt less keenly
the need to educate the peasant into political autonomy. And the plebiscite
of May 1870 seemed (and seems) to bear out those who saw the rural electorate as scarcely politicized.[56] The *candidature officielle* itself continued well
into the 1870s. Yet it did not work as well as it once did. "Our good peasants," remarked a Bonapartist in 1874, "are easy to lead only when one
leads them where they want to go."[57] That may always have been the case,
but now it had to be reckoned with. Slowly—in some places very slowly—
the traditional notables left the countryside;[58] meanwhile, a new figure
entered the scene. "The politicians are invading France," declared a publicist in 1879. "The term is new, because the phenomenon is new."[59]

More clearly than under the Empire, effective local patronage came to
be seen as dependent on broader connections—to the Paris world of banking, press, and politics, which provided publicity for local grievances, support for municipal needs, or favors for private electors. The availability of
such connections and the perception of their significance dominated the
gradual shift from simple factional alliances to interest-group politics.[60]
Influencing this slow evolution was the republican campaign to win over
the indifferent or unfriendly masses, without whose support prospects were
bleak. In the Nièvre, where the countryside was "under the tutelage of the
great landowners and dependent upon them," a republican politician, who
was the son and grandson of republican notables, insisted that in 1870 rural

electors "had no personal opinions; they expected to be told." To move public opinion from the Empire to republican ideas, "a whole education of the electoral body" was needed. Very quickly the Republicans set out to improve their position, especially in the rural regions, "by enlightening rural electors on their rights and duties in electoral matters." Result: "at no time was political life in the department so intense."[61]

Political life had been equally intense in the period after the Revolution of 1848, but it had been restricted physically (fewer villages had been touched by it), culturally (illiteracy and a sense of irrelevance limited its impact), and practically (real alternatives were few). At that time Republicans and Bonapartists had sought to indoctrinate villagers and draw them into the political game. I have argued elsewhere that conditions were not ripe, that the context of political activity under the Second Republic was still archaic, and that modern ideas wilted in an alien world where they were only perceived, if they were perceived at all, in outmoded terms.[62] Since that time, more roads, railways, and schools had been built, and opportunities for urban employment had begun to moderate the endemic underemployment of country people, improve their wages and autonomy (however relative), and lighten their dependence on landlord and neighbor.

Such generalizations only apply, where they apply, in the most general sense. Years, sometimes generations, passed before the peasant felt their effects and drew their political conclusions. But the Second Empire and the ten to fifteen years that followed laid down a material base for the evolution of modern politics. Thereafter, the efforts to mobilize the peasants had the advantage of continuity, and the voting public was better prepared to listen to, and to perceive the relevance of, ideas no longer entirely strange and unrelated to local and individual interests. Even so, the countryside did not spontaneously enter the wider political arena but needed to be dragged there. As the attorney-general of Chambéry had predicted, someone had to invest the money and the energy necessary to move the masses. After 1870, all urban political groups turned to that task: the Republicans in order to establish solid rural positions, the Conservatives in order to retain theirs. Political exposure creates political experience and under the Third Republic, especially in its first decades, such experience did a lot to advance the politicization of the countryside.

The most significant results were produced by the sharpest political crises—during elections that were fiercely contested and when contestants scrambled for support in quarters previously ignored. Comparing the election of 1877 to that of 1871 in the Nièvre, Massé concluded that the Conservatives "owed their relative success [in 1877] to the means they used to bring to the polls a large number of electors *who had not voted in the preceding*

elections."[63] But the most marked results were achieved in the elections of
1889, which seem to have mobilized parts of the countryside as never
before. It is true that adverse economic conditions contributed to this mobilization. The agrarian depression of the 1880s had soured many on republican patronage, previously accepted as more serviceable than that of
Bonapartists or Legitimists. Hard times sharpened the farmer's expectation
of material returns from his vote. But the political activity itself was surely
as important as the ends to which it was deployed; and, again, as in 1877,
an activist "Bonapartist" approach (now enriched by the infusion of American campaign practices) sparked unusual interest and participation.

In districts where they ran, Boulangist candidates and their propagandists went everywhere. The copious campaign chests of the Boulangists
meant that villages never before touched by political debate (their political
orientation had always been taken for granted) were now riven by rival arguments and new divisions. Thus a Boulangist candidate in Corrèze, who
decided to bypass a particular village assumed to be adverse to his candidacy, reversed his decision on learning that he had a chance there and was
gratified to find supporters. Because political orientations were confused by
republican and legitimist alliances with Boulanger, people who had steadfastly and "naturally" voted republican, clerical, or conservative had to
reconsider their allegiances. At the same time, Boulangist propaganda
sought to relate local interests more closely to national issues. As a result, a
hostile witness averred, the idea spread to "the humblest cottage . . . that
governmental action could modify everyone's way of life." This was a revolutionary notion to communities where, for centuries, government had
been regarded as a distant, hostile force. "For a very long time in this area,"
a local official in the Pyrénées had reported in 1850, "country people have
taught the children to consider the government, any government, as their
natural and personal enemy."[64] This fundamental attitude had to change
before national politics could gain attention. Relating government to the
fulfillment of the people's needs made politics relevant and connected parliamentary elections with self-interest.

A more immediate result of Boulangist campaigns, however, was the
appearance of rural syndicalism. In Cher, Nièvre, and Allier, the Boulangists focused on the peasantry, especially on lumbermen hurt by deteriorating economic conditions but hitherto indifferent to politics. Until then,
Louis-Henri Roblin (one historian of their unions) has claimed, agricultural
workers and lumbermen regarded political debate as "a question of men
rather than of doctrines." Lumbermen had never before thought that, for
them, their work, and their pay, the form of government could have any
importance. Newspapers were only read in the industrial centers or by the

more well-to-do in the countryside. Public meetings did not attempt to address the rural workers. "With Boulangism everything change[d]"; Boulangist successes in central France in 1889, Roblin pointed out, were followed closely by the spread of peasant strikes and unions (1891) and the eventual electoral success of Socialists and Radical-Socialists (1892).[65]

Two points are worth noting about this. The first, perhaps a minor reminiscence, is the similarity between the effects of Boulangism, "which left a prodigious echo in the popular consciousness," and those of demo-cratic socialist propaganda two score years before. Writing in the aftermath of the 1890s, Amédée Dunois, who had been involved in these events, insisted on the great hopes they had evoked: "All honestly imagined that the time of salvation was near and that the miseries, the oppression, the humiliations of all kinds . . . would end forever." The eschatological belief in a brave new world that could begin at once, so prominent in the peasant aspirations of 1851, was soon again evident in the appeals that swayed and mobilized unsophisticated country people, introducing—or re-introducing—them to *political* activity. The second point is that although local political figures who had sided with General Boulanger lent the lum-bermen a hand, their movement was a peasant movement with peasant leadership. Its very lack of order and of coordination (in 1891–1893 lum-bermen on the two shores of the Allier ignored the others' activities, and there seem to have been as many strikes and autonomous syndicates as there were forest regions) testifies to its origins. The lumbermen were no more artisans than were the harvesters; they were journeymen, working in the local farms when they could find work, especially in summer. As a local senator explained, "le bûcheron, c'est l'ouvrier rural, c'est l'ouvrier agricole."[66]

In those parts of central France where farmland and forest are closely interlaced, most small farmers and day laborers made ends meet by seeking forest jobs during the winter season. Since the last years of the Empire, the local landlords who employed them had given way to urban lumber mer-chants. Harder times and growing competition among dealers led to deteri-orating working conditions and growing friction between employers and their peasant work-gangs. Workers' grievances opened their ears to Bou-langist arguments, and they were the first to unionize and strike in the early 1890s. They struck again in 1898–99, in the context of a would-be "na-tional" movement. By that time, their ideas, carried out of the forest by fellow agricultural laborers, had affected sharecroppers and farmers in nearby areas. Leaving aside the original impact of Boulangist agitation, the important thing here is that the syndicalist contagion spread over the countryside. Syndicates had existed before—some founded by landowners and large farmers, others by or for urban workingmen—but peasants previously avoided them. As one peasant syndicalist explained, "landsmen and urbanites or villagers reciprocally ignore each other; the peasants obstinately refuse to join organizations founded by the workers of *bourgs* and towns; the socialist papers of Montluçon disapprove of [the peasant syndicates] and [the peasants] feel that the CGT approaches things from the urban workers' point of view."[67]

Thus in 1900, almost a decade after the lumbermen had first tried and failed, the peasant-sharecroppers of Bourbonnais set up their own syndicates, the first of them at Gennetines and at Chézy (Allier), "unrelated to political or religious inspiration." None of these ventures was very successful; by 1909 or 1910 most of them had collapsed or lingered on only in the guise of reading societies or buying cooperatives. Still, despite their deliberate attempt to stay away from politics, the organizations helped initiate their members—and their neighbors—to political life. Their direct economic impact was slight, but their efforts to mobilize Parliament, government, administration, and the national press reflected their dependence on national authorities and spread awareness of politics as something that went far beyond local resolution of issues. At the same time, when the syndicates collapsed, they left behind a new sympathy for socialism, whose representatives had defended them in Parliament. In Allier, where the sharecroppers' syndicates had been active though short-lived, Socialists made strong gains in the 1910 elections and retained their rural support in 1914. One historian of the Bourbonnais has attributed this support to the similarity the peasant found in socialist and syndicalist aims and hopes and the absence of dues and public commitment (hence, possibly, jeopardy) attached to socialist allegiance.[68] By the twentieth century, electoral politics had the distinct advantage not only of costing less but also of offering an opportunity to exercise one's will (that is, the right to vote) without letting on what this will was (that is, for whom one voted).

This conclusion suggests that, before World War I, the pressures and conformities of country living inflected political activities there. Nevertheless, political life in the county was more active and better recognized than it had been a generation or two earlier. Obviously, this evolution was gradual and sporadic, appearing in different places to different degrees. The historian's problem is to follow it.

Some political scientists have suggested that abstentions from voting can furnish a rough index of politicization. But abstentions are just as likely to furnish indications of commitment and discrimination. Take, for example, the case of Louis Olivier, a bailiff of Lesneven (Finistère), who declared to a parliamentary commission that he paid no attention to the campaign of 1897, "having no candidate of his opinion," and did not even go out on the day of the vote.[69] Olivier was a sheriff's officer in a small town, but people in rural communities, though less articulate, appear to have shared his views. There, as in urban districts, the abstention rate was markedly higher when the vote was a foregone conclusion; and it was especially high when many voters could not find a candidate of their political stripe. Even under the Second Empire certain white royalist parishes in Vendée, villages that had taken an active part in the risings of the 1790s, showed two and three times the abstention rate of their neighbors. They were no more isolated than neighboring villages but had no Legitimist to vote for; rather than vote for a Bonapartist, they abstained. At La Réole (Gironde), which was equally rural, over 37 percent of the electorate abstained in 1871, and over 40 percent in 1873. Then, in 1874, a Bonapartist candidate dared to show his head, and abstentions fell to 21 percent. By 1877, when political excitement was at its height, abstentions had fallen to 14 percent.[70] If abstention is an index of political apathy, it is sometimes ambiguous: people who abstain for lack of a suitable candidate may go out to vote against an unsuitable one.

Though equally impressionistic, I prefer the evidence found in the investigation of parliamentary commissions inquiring into allegations of electoral fraud, because it goes beyond the outside observer's judgment with which students of a popular and often illiterate public are condemned to content themselves. These files contain testimony from witnesses whose political observations are seldom otherwise recorded. What the files reveal is an evolution that was uneven, certainly, but palpable; the peasants, once granted the vote, gradually learned to treat it just as their enfranchised predecessors had done under the *monarchie censitaire;* as a source of personal and communal advantages. As early as 1847 Duvergier de Hauranne reported their astute observations: "Why shouldn't we sell ourselves for money, when the bourgeois sell themselves for jobs?"[71] Once they began to sell themselves for money, they came to recognize the possibility of more profitable returns.

But that took time. Threats, menaces, bribery and corruption of various kinds, or simply forcing electors to vote correctly had all been common under the Restoration and the July Monarchy. They continued to be so under the Second Empire (and probably under the Second Republic before it), despite the decree of 1852, which provided that those convicted of intimidating electors into abstaining or casting an unwilling vote were subject to a minimum of one year in prison and a large fine. This decree hardly seems to have affected the spirit of electoral campaigning, especially in rural areas, where by the 1860s fraud was taken for granted by all. In some villages, mayors avoided even the pretense (and bother) of balloting, confining themselves "to certifying the presumed operations" and the desired result.[72] More often, however, mayors simply substituted ballots of the candidate they favored or counted the votes as they pleased. Complaints were prevalent that more votes were counted than had been cast— Finistère, in 1869, for example: at Lacumolé, 256 electors but 264 votes; at Trévoux, 285 electors but 304 votes; and at Arzano, 442 electors but 462 votes—or that votes that had been cast were not counted or were counted only for the official candidate—for example, in 1863 at Corcone (Gard) 24 cast but only 12 counted; in 1869 at St.-Radégonde (Gironde), 69 cast but only 23 counted; that same year at Montbéraud (Haute-Garonne), 41 cast but only 5 counted.[73] When such complaints were raised, officials ignored them, and government spokesmen dismissed them as normal corruption. Twice the minister refused comment, arguing that discussion would be contrary to the *secret du scrutin*.[74]

Alexandre Pilenco, the first student of electoral fraud in France, concluded that direct administrative intervention of this sort became extremely rare after the 1880s. Perhaps. At any rate, in the opening years of the Third Republic rural societies were still subject to the bonds of economic dependence and social deference and to straightforward intimidation by national or local authorities. In 1876 and 1877, for example, police confiscated copies of the *Dépêche de Toulouse* in Luchon marketplace and frightened off those carrying the paper; employers *on both sides* often expected their workers to vote for the candidate they favored, although not all went so far as the gentleman of Pontivy who circulated an official notice to that effect;[75] and victory *farandoles* and *charivaris* enlisted traditional forms in the service of novel activities that were guaranteed to confirm and deepen the divisions that politics espoused. In Brittany, but not only in Brittany, references to widespread unfamiliarity with the French language and also to illiteracy were abundant. At St.-Barthélémy (Morbihan) the mayor sought to mislead illiterate peasants, distributing ballots to them under false pretenses: the mayor gone, "the woman, Le Nedelec, who could read, saw that M. le Maire had deceived them." There were numerous allegations of illiterate voters taking the ballot of one candidate for that of another or being guiled into voting for a man other than their own.[76] And there were still more cases of outright interference with electors—mayors, priests, or notables thrusting ballots of their own candidates into electors' hands, opening folded ballots, taking ballots away from unwilling voters, throwing ballots away, or simply refusing to accept legitimate ballots.

Such practices seldom reappear after 1877 outside the most backward regions—like Morbihan, where, as late as 1902, priests and landowners retained their age-old power and where laborers and domestics were marched to the polls, each holding his ballot in one *raised* hand.[77] More generally, however, straightforward brutality had given way to ruse or to more familiar forms of seduction. The first references I have found to buying votes date from 1862 and 1863. They testify to a new sharpness of electoral contention, which official pressures alone could not resolve. Some peasants attained a measure of autonomy and decision that a generation earlier only their betters enjoyed. Obviously, menace was more economical than purchase.[78] The sale of a vote is no warranty of political awareness, but it does suggest that the voter had some freedom to choose and that a vote had value—a notion capable of translation to another plane.

The cash value of votes varied. Precise figures are seldom given, but those I have seen suggest that in the 1860s votes ran between ten and twenty centimes in Brittany, while in the Marne "two francs per vote is not expensive but more than is necessary." By 1881 at Pontivy (Morbihan), where many votes had been bought for three to ten francs each, and where whole Republican villages were alleged to have been turned around, the subprefect expressed surprise at the low cost of political loyalty in the region. Generally, the price of votes seems to have reflected the bitterness of electoral combat, so that in 1869, in the hotly disputed first district of the Pyrénées-Orientales, men were getting up to ten francs a vote; and peasants did not take long to realize the possibilities of such situations. "They offered me ten francs," said one witness. "I refused. Then my son said to me, Take it anyway. You'll vote as you please."[79]

During the 1880s and 1890s, the practice of treating and "corrupting" electors gained ground. The poorer the region, the more prevalent the problem. In the legendary elections of the first district of Brive (Corrèze) in 1893, the rich Mielvaque de Lacour, whose platform had no political coloring whatever, did best among poor villages of the *châtaigneraies,* his republican opponent in the more prosperous wine-growing areas.[80] Yet it would be wrong to regard bribery and corruption as limited to poor and backward regions. The Alps and Pyrénées head the lists, but the records show that such practices were rife before 1902, and to some extent up to 1914, in departments from Aude to Manche to Pas-de-Calais, from Dordogne and Ardèche to Vienne and Seine-et-Oise. They were only curbed by the law of March 31, 1914, which prohibits gifts in money or kind as well as promises of favors or jobs. Until then, open bribery continued to be evident, particularly in Brittany, where the economic dominion of great landholding families by the twentieth century seems to have required the support of cash and copious libations. The cost of Breton elections was notorious, and the quadrennial inflow of petty cash (and the outflow of tipple) came to be relied on as a contribution to the local economy. At Kermoroch (Côtes-du-Nord) "the commune" supposedly "belonged almost entirely to M. le Duc des Cars." Yet the "influential" duke's "influential" steward had to pay handsomely for his peasants' votes.[81]

Such customs dated back at least to the 1880s—testimony, again, less to the generosity of Breton magnates than to the bitterness of some electoral conflicts and to the venality of the peasants. As an old electoral hand testified in 1902, "Our Bretons quickly turned the exception into a precedent . . . made it into a tradition; since then, electoral campaign signifies drink and money to them." It may be that carousing had preceded pelf, especially since Brittany took its time to enter a money economy. In 1869, it seems, "cider and the pope sufficed to gain all of the votes of Morbihan."[82] At any rate, I am inclined to hazard that, there as elsewhere, payment in species rather than tipple came later, occurred more rarely, and disappeared sooner.[83] Drinks, however, had to be offered even if a candidate was running unopposed: "a dry election" drew no voters. No wonder a Pyrenean inquiry concluded that "electors have to walk or ride five or six miles to attend a meeting. How could you send them back without a drink?" On the whole, a philosophical attitude prevailed. As the reporter for one parliamentary commission declared, "In conformity with Breton electoral custom, [the voters] drank with M. Brune and they drank with M. La Chambre; the parties are even in their alcoholic largess . . . While blaming intemperance, the members of this commission do not consider themselves empowered to reform the mores of the department of Ille-et-Vilaine."[84]

Even so, there are scattered indications that a new sense of civic dignity was emerging. Lies and dissimulation had long been the nonconforming peasant's only recourse, whether against his fellows or against his betters. Centuries of experience had perfected attitudes that could be adjusted to electoral situations as they appeared. Folk tales reflect the yokel's ambition to trick the devil or any of the devil's surrogates: city folk, social superiors, or simply enemies. The peasants had no problem about "singing the right song" and doing as they pleased, when the occasion offered.[85] Gradually, however, democratic propaganda spread abroad the sense that there was something wrong about the very need for subterfuge. Free men should vote freely, and their votes should count and should be counted. When, in 1869, the results of the Haute-Garonne elections were skewed by heavy fraud and official intervention, the peasants clearly understood that their opponents had not *won* their victory, but *stolen* it.[86]

Interest and pride are hard to disentangle. Dressing in Sunday best to cast your ballot is a small indication of pride. But as one rural representative wrote Thiers in 1873, "the peasants [had] understood the value of their vote," so that they began to exhibit "the sentiment of political freedom." Increasingly courted by betters who had long ignored their existence, let alone their significance, smallholders were conducting a small revolution of their own. Some time passed before they claimed mastery of their own territory, but their growing civic pride is unmistakable.[87] In September 1893, Audeguil Pierre of Saint-Antoine (Corrèze) testified that he had refused drinks offered by an electoral agent—"being not merchandise but a man." Another farmer sent a letter, in fine calligraphy and execrable spelling, written "par mon petit qui va en clace," to tell the commission of inquiry "que je saient un homme qui et republiquin." Most revealing, perhaps, are the inscriptions traced on the walls of the extraordinary dream mansion built between 1879 and 1912 by a village postman in the Drôme. Ferdinand Cheval, of Hauterives, insisted that his feat was "the creation of a peasant" who gloried in his labor and found happiness in the honor of achievement. Creativeness, honor, glory, valiance, pride—once the preserve of their social superiors—were values to which peasants also could now aspire.[88] Seen in this perspective, the vote was but another component of a new self-awareness.

As more electors became interested in exercising their voting rights and as open repression or fraud became more difficult, personal corruption (buying or treating) became a symbol less of subjection than of emancipation. So, perhaps, did the violence of organized gangs hired to keep electors from the polls. The harder it became to buy or intimidate electors, the more important the transitional role of physical violence. With official violence on the wane, private enterprise entered the field. In 1893, in the first ward of Brive, several groups of toughs under the leadership of picturesque characters—Alfred Larue *dit l'Hercule,* Peuchaneil *dit Barbe de Fer,* Aubignac *dit le Zouave*—broke up meetings and discouraged the faint of heart. A decade later, lower Brittany became sufficiently emancipated to follow suit. In 1903, at Plougoumelen and Biedz, eight members of hired sailor gangs were arrested and tried for terrorizing the electors.[89]

Other aspects of electoral campaigns also evolved. In the 1870s it was still possible to incite panic among what one witness described as "decent but credulous" communities with false news of rampant revolution: the Midi in flames, red flags flying over ruined churches, and massacred priests. At Bouloc (Haute-Garonne) the Legitimist-Bonapartists promised that if the Republicans won priests would be defrocked, private property would be divided, churches would be torn down, and society would be lost. At Massouins (Var) the priest warned his flock that after a republican victory there would be no more burials in holy ground and no baptisms of infants and there would be damnation for those who had voted republican. At Pontivy in 1881, circulars in the Breton tongue took "advantage of the intellectual and material isolation of the Breton people" by announcing the return of the Comte de Chambord and the approaching end of the Republic. In the second district of Poitiers (Vienne), the Royalist was denounced as standing for the guillotine, bloodshed, and Henry V; the Republican as a warmonger whose success would mean mobilization for all men to the age of forty. In some places it was asserted that war had already been declared and mobilization begun. The false rumors appealed to the well-established rural phobia against military service but also rested on the untimely coincidence that men in the army reserve were just being called up for their twenty-eight-day obligatory service. Yet even while threats of war were being bandied about, new themes could be heard in scattered villages. At Civray and Availles, candidates argued about education, Republicans promising free school for all and anti-Republicans predicting prison for parents who would not send their children to school.[90]

Michael Burns has demonstrated how the Dreyfus case with its national themes—antimilitarism and support for the army, antisemitism and nationalism—and personalities—like Emile Zola—entered the consciousness of small rural communes, affecting their rituals (during Carnival or draft ceremonies), their imprecations, and their propitiatory rites. Antisemitic posters displayed at fairs linked Jews to usury, grain speculation, and hoarding. Rural Gers returned three antisemites to the Chamber in 1898. That same year the mayor of a small village, Baigneux, in Loir-et-Cher attributed the agricultural crisis to "the wild speculations of the cosmopolitan Jewish gang."[91] In the recent past, inexplicable troubles had been ascribed to supernatural forces or to the dark machinations of landlords and governments; now they were explained by city-forged formulae.

"Rural credulousness" appears in the sources through the 1880s but I have found no reference thereafter. Wider perceptions spawned novel allegations. A witness from Morbihan in an inquiry of 1902 declared that he was called a *dreyfusard*, "which is the worst insult in our regions." Here the Dreyfus affair evidently symbolized the diabolical forces that menaced decent people and the Church. During the 1893 elections in Ardèche, a republican candidate was exorcised by a Jesuit priest on the grounds that he was possessed by the devil. His opponent, Eugène-Melchior de Vogüé, was much hurt by reminders that, during 1846–1848, his grandfather "avait noyé le blé pour affamer le peuple"—had speculated on the price of grain, a painful memory still alive in many peasant homes. In the same election Vogüé referred (apparently with some effect) to his role in establishing the Franco-Russian alliance, and his opponent felt that this "exercised considerable action on people's minds."[92]

Justified or not, this sort of campaigning suggests a widening of local horizons and a new awareness of factors to which the peasants had once been indifferent: urban myths, foreign relations, or tariff policy. Country folk continued to be like hedgehogs, suspicious of wide-roving foxes, but the hedges they ranged now ran far afield. Even folk tales reflected this new awareness of a wider world and the entry of politics into everyday village life. Another "we" appeared, another *pays* took shape; and both were larger. So was their context. The impact of imported grain upon domestic grain prices also widened the horizons of villagers. As early as 1881, a villager at Genouillé (Vienne) criticized a candidate "for having opposed the entrance of American grain into France, thus making ours rise to forty francs." When surveyed in 1898, the village mayors of Eure-et-Loir attributed their economic difficulties variously to insufficient tariff protection, imports from Russia, Germany, and the United States (especially wheat), the rapid development of backward countries, and French reluctance to abandon outmoded production.[93] Admittedly, these were notables—however minor—in a relatively well-situated department. But the same year, a poor farmer's son from Ygrande (Allier) could write a dialogue, "Le Blé d'Amérique," for the local paper. A few years later, the same Émile Guillaumin, now an established writer though a farmer still, published a novel in which a peasant discussed crops and prices with two passing tramps who knew a great deal about national and international conditions: "Bah!" said one of the tramps, "it's not because the crop in central France has been a bit below average that you can expect higher prices; we got a good yield from the North and West; and from America and Russia one can get all one wants." "And from Algeria," said the vagabond Misery, who had served there.[94]

Adult access to information, through printed matter, grew notably in the 1880s and 1890s with the education of their young. The father of another of Guillaumin's characters, an illiterate farmer, subscribed to two papers "as soon as [his son] was able to read properly." "Quelle joie pour lui de se faire lire le journal!" Of course, many (perhaps most) peasants still could not understand those interested in the news the paper brought: "what did not affect them directly remained strange, distant, suspect . . . 'As if for people like us that means anything,' they said."[95]

But even villagers now realized the concrete importance of "governmental favors": "to have better roads, to obtain a dispensation from or a postponement of military service for a son, to get a relative hired in an administrative service or a *bureau de tabac* for oneself, to receive compensation for crops ravaged by hail or cattle decimated by disease, or simply to avoid official vexations—here are powerful reasons . . . to vote for the governmental candidate and to show the greatest zeal in supporting his ideas," wrote a historian of poor, back-country Cantal.[96] That was precisely the criterion for electoral support established by bourgeois electors of the 1840s: "our roads, our railways, the taxes, the upkeep of [public] buildings—what have you done for them?"[97] In nearby Lot, still in 1905, "our peasants belong to whoever gives them a living." This had become the motive that led them to shift from Bonapartist to Republican in 1889. They "have got into the habit of being with the government and receiving its favors." They may have learned that lesson sooner (they had done so in Auvergne) from migrants who disseminated the conclusions they had picked up in the hard school of Paris: to serve one's home interests, one "has to use the only weapon that is effective today, the political weapon."[98]

The old-fashioned patron-client relationship continued, but the actors had changed. The leading roles were no longer held by local notables in a position to provide work or help in need. Their place had been taken by those best able to secure governmental intervention. As Emile Guillaumin wrote grudgingly to his sharecropper-readers, "Despite its vices and its shortcomings, one has to admit that the make-up of Parliament affects our daily life. That certain politicians have spoken about sharecropping in Bourbonnais is not a matter of indifference. It does not mean that things will change tomorrow, but it does mean that, if those concerned wanted to do so, they could change something more easily."[99]

The peasants had accepted the Republic, had become republican, for reasons not unlike those that had made them accept the Second Empire: higher cattle prices, free schools, a shorter term of military service, old age allocations, and so forth.[100] More important, though, they had become aware that national and international events had an impact on them; that villagers could, however slightly, *affect* parliamentary politics and thereby their own lives; that their efforts, if they were willing to make them, could bring about *some* change. Here, surely, were new perceptions and possibilities that testify to a degree of politicization that is recognizably modern—that is, a political awareness not very different from our own.

~ 9

The Nationalist Revival
before 1914

Students of the history of the Third Republic frequently assert that the years before 1914, and especially from 1911 to 1914, were a period of nationalist revival,[1] a somewhat exceptional period when politics were dominated by a novel concern for national unity, prestige, and power; by calls for order, tradition, and discipline; and by catchwords connected with all these things. I propose to inquire first into the social aspect of this apparent change in the ruling ideology of the Republic, and then into the background and nature of the nationalist movement.

To begin with, it might be well to touch very briefly upon the attitudes and sympathies of the different social classes, insofar as these can be apprehended. Any acquaintance with the life and literature of the time should convince us of the reality of class consciousness and class divisions, sometimes of a very meticulous kind. However, the main division in this case will have to be classic almost to roughness, and examine the aristocracy, the middle classes, and the rest.

At the beginning of the twentieth century, the first of these had not lost all political and still retained a great deal of social influence, particularly in the countryside. Purged of its eighteenth-century skepticism, the nobility had moved through royalism to Catholicism, the defence of the Church having proved a better proposition than the restoration of the monarchy. The great bastion of their power lay in the west—especially in Anjou, Maine, and Vendée—where they still made elections in the twentieth century much as the Earl of Brentford made them for Phineas Finn at Loughton in the nineteenth. This aristocracy, whether legitimist or *ralliée,* was fundamentally antirepublican, patriotic by tradition, and not at all "nationalist" in any party sense. The constructive part of the nationalist platform they had always advocated as a matter of course, unless they had taken it for granted to the extent of not thinking it worth the mention. The rest was probably a matter of indifference to them. They naturally showed some interest in the "integral nationalism" typical of the new mood, and of that vociferous representative of the new mood, the Action française. But where their power was absolute, as it was in the west, they had no need of it, and could afford to ignore it in political practice. It was in the southwest of France, where their influence was thin, that men like the Marquis de Lur-Saluces and Mgr. de Cabrières, good Legitimists as they were, saw in the nationalism of the Action française a useful channel for their policies.[2] In western *towns,* where the Action française did wield some influence, there was not alliance but competition and struggle that caused the right wing to split, and the weaker party—in this case the Catholic middle-class—won against the stronger aristocratic faction by securing the support of the new Nationalists.[3]

This serves as a useful reminder of the influence of the Church, even where its power is not predominant. Such influence as the Church retained had been exerted in the early 1890s on behalf of the Republic to bring about, however half-heartedly, the *ralliement* by which an important section of the Catholic right left the royalist camp and accepted the established order. But the institutional traditions and the class connections of the leaders of the Church made it, and them, lean heavily towards the right even before pacifist Radicals had provoked their enmity by their anti-clericalism. Throughout the life of the Third Republic ecclesiastical influence appears openly, though not officially, on the side of nationalism. It was the Catholic alliance in the more specifically Catholic parts of the country (Normandy, Brittany, Basque country, Catholic areas of the Cévennes and the Vosges) which gave the Nationalists heart. But once again Catholicism was the local reality, nationalism only its occasional political expression—and not the only one.[4] Whatever forms Church power might take, however ferocious the family quarrels in which it might indulge, it remained Catholic, and Nationalist if this was consequential to being Catholic.

This official right wing of aristocracy and Church hardly alters their orientation in terms of political attitudes and language during the twenty-five or thirty years before 1914. The early twentieth century finds it on much the same positions which it held a decade before, and which it will hold a decade and more later. There is little or no question of change or development about it: the most we can say is that it awaits the swing of the pendulum which will restore its ideas to the favor of political fashion.

The second of our social classes, tremendously diversified, shading off into its rivals at both ends, should provide most of the material for a study of contemporary politics and political opinions, as it provides most of the personnel of the political, intellectual, and administrative worlds. We need not consider those few members of it, *grands bourgeois,* like Casimir-Périer or Pouyier-Quartier, whom only the nobility know (as they know themselves) not to be of their own. Below them *haute* and *moyenne bourgeoisie* had in common a snobbery which made the sanction and frequentation of the aristocratic world one of their dearest aspirations. Vulgar academicians, ignorant of social niceties, may have considered the drawingroom of Mme. Verdurin (in M. Proust's *A la recherche du temps perdu*) to be the height of fashion. But Mme. Verdurin herself knew better, and did her best to shed her awkward Dreyfusist connections in order to pass like the proverbial camel through the eye of the Guermantes needle.

It was, however, less the social aspirations of the bourgeoisie than a new community of interest which made it move toward positions which the aristocracy had held for forty years. The events of 1848 had done much to shake the Voltairianism of the bourgeoisie, and 1871 had confirmed this tendency. At first religion had been good for the people, then it had provided for the children's education, at last it had appeared as that essential element of moral and social discipline which seemed so signally lacking in modern democracy. It was also worth considering that by going to church and to church functions one could meet the local *châtelain,* and even perhaps penetrate into the little world of the nobility. Nobility and bourgeoisie met in defense of the Church, as some of them had met in defense of the General Staff, and common political interests sometimes opened doors which neither economic nor cultural considerations could open before.

But beyond political, material interests also drove the bourgeoisie from the ranks of the party of movement, as François Goguel has called it, into those of conservative defenders. In the years after 1871, layer after layer of the middle class came to the conclusion that enough had been done to alter the face of France, and that further change should be opposed. The old bourgeois aristocracy (if the term be allowed) of the country towns had its day with Thiers and MacMahon, disapproved of Jules Ferry's anticlericalism, and went into opposition with Jules Simon in the eighties. Their fellows of the industrial and commercial world, survivors of what men still called the *Gambettisme d'affaires,* did not follow them for another decade, until the defeat of the moderate Méline and the critical years of the Dreyfus affair persuaded them of the primary importance of social defense with all its implications.

The middle and lower-middle class, the real Third Estate, took longer to come round. It harbored few of the social ambitions of the upper layers, and was easily persuaded into a "radical" policy as long as this radicalism stuck safely to democracy and anticlericalism. The appearance of working class demands was however enough to frighten them away—not from radicalism which was by then no more than a harmless label, but from further reform. This class was not only anti-Socialist but anti-state, and one of the reasons for such an attitude is expressed in Pauline Bergeret's words to her father: "The State, father, is a pitiful and ungracious man seated behind an office counter. So you understand that one doesn't feel like stripping for him."[5] Thus though by 1905 it was the radicalism of this class which dominated government and Parliament, its mistrust of the state power toned down any program of social reform and turned it quietly into a conservative force.

In its lower reaches, this layer merged with the working class; and this lower-middle class of small shopkeepers, shop assistants, and office workers—afraid of oppression from above and of losing their identity in the proletariat below yet without exactly abandoning the hope of forward movement—offered by its vulnerable and incoherent nature just those opportunities, just that temper of mind, on which all the Boulangisms and all the demagogues could try their hand. A program like that on which Anatole France shows us the Nationalist Lacrisse riding to victory in the ward of the Grandes-Ecuries, could appeal to all these groups:

> Defend the national army against a gang of lunatics. Contest cosmopolitanism. Uphold the rights of fathers threatened by government plans for university reform. Avert the collectivist menace. Connect the Grandes Ecuries district to the Exhibition by a tramway. Improve the municipal water service.[6]

It seems fairly clear that, by the early years of our century, the middle class, whether notables like the Siegfrieds of Le Hàvre, or people on the edge of the working class like the market-gardeners of Bobigny on the outskirts of Paris,[7] had left the reformist republican camp—had left "the party of movement." They tended either to obstruct changes which they feared would endanger the established order, or to attack the established order to secure vague but violent changes. The paradoxical result was that both these tendencies brought grist to the Nationalists' mill: the conservative because it found in nationalist energy a not unattractive reassurance, the cataclysmic because it was tempted by their equivocal programs and by the passion of their demagogy.

One section of the middle class cannot well be included under any of these categories, and that is the great and growing body of state employees who were beginning to develop not only a strong feeling of common interest, but also a concrete syndical structure—in the civil service, the teaching professions, and so on. Their traditions were strictly bourgeois, but perhaps due to the centralization of their services, the low level of pay, the size of the organizations of which they were a part, or the analogy of their working conditions to those in great industrial enterprises, their sympathies went to the parties of movement and social reform, sometimes indeed of violent reform.

When speaking of "the rest," one nods in passing to a great indifferent mass of town and especially country dwellers, whose parsimony as a rule outweighed patriotism and social spirit, and who swayed with the wind of the active, vocal minority, and of local tradition. We cannot, however, ignore the influence of the increasingly organized workers' parties, largely united by the S.F.I.O. in the political field, though the Independent Socialists (more independent, most of them, than socialist) were also important. Though any Syndicalist would claim that parliamentary Socialists did not represent the working class, they interested it enough to secure ever greater electoral support in the years before the war, and to frighten all the defenders of property and of the established order with the prospect of an impending *Götterdämmerung*.

Varied as these groups and interests were, they had one thing in common—a basic or growing distrust of the system of government which some of them condemned for being too harsh and others for being too weak, which Royalists and Socialists condemned on principle, and others because it seemed unable to secure for them either the stability or the opportunities they desired. Men who were in temporary possession of the levers of power may have believed that the system could work well enough, and there were those who—like Barrès or Jean Jaurès—thought that any radical change would probably be for the worse. Nevertheless, whether change appeared as a threat or as a promise, it was bound to affect a growing section of the politically significant minority, the men who made opinions and sometimes policies.

Such men would count among their number leaders and militants of political parties; writers and journalists; bodies representing or creating certain vested interests such as the unions, the *Institut,* or the *Université;* and also individuals whose opinions were weighed by the position they occupied in government or society. These leaders of opinion considered themselves, and were treated as, a social and intellectual élite, an élite which owed much of its cohesion to family relationships or student friendships. Cousins and in-laws spread the old-boy network from party to party, from salon to salon; and where no *cousinage* existed, a student camaraderie that amounted almost to free-masonry might make up for it. Thus nearly 95 percent of the men appointed to the diplomatic and consular services between 1907 and 1927 were graduates of the Institut des Sciences Politiques. Here we have a small group of able and influential people who, for the greater part, shared a vested interest in the established order and who eventually came to look upon Raymond Poincaré as their standard bearer, and to agree upon standards which (even when they were called Poincarist) were in effect nationalist.[8] The thing worth noting is that slogans of national unity, discipline, confidence and power were not new, not original, did not have to be invented.

The Nationalists' idea of the superiority and strength of France, an idea to which one could appeal in order to perfect national unity and self-consciousness, an idea which could be exploited for politically significant ends, was already a tradition to be remembered or revived. After 1871 nationalism in France had become associated with the left; chauvinism had been the preserve of the uncultured, of the masses. The Jacobin tradition of the left was not dead. When the twentieth century opened, everyone still remembered its latest eruption in the Commune, and in the efforts and peregrinations of Léon Gambetta.

Gambetta had been considered dangerous in case his *revanchard* intransigence would endanger the peace of France. But Gambetta's thought evolved as did his position, and increased power brought with it increased inclination to compromise. His political heirs, first Jules Ferry, then Jules Méline, sought for peace without forgetting that much of their moderate republican support lay in the patriotic and vengeful eastern departments. Since the danger of war lay on the Rhine, they concentrated their efforts on reconciling colonial and financial expansion with a policy of *détente* toward Germany. This gave their supporters the satisfaction of French successes without the dangers of a German war. Ferry and Méline were moderate men, and a positive policy along such theoretical lines as the Nationalists advanced at the time could not be expected from them. This left the nationalist and *revanchard* arguments as convenient weapons in the hands of the opposition. Nationalism remained a Radicals' preserve for many years: Boulanger, for one, rose first to power, then to notoriety, with radical support. Many of his followers were Jacobins and *revanchard*, lower-middle class men of little or no property. His chief enemy was Jules Ferry. Boulangism is typical of such nationalist movements as had to rely on a single leader, on the enthusiasms and prejudices of individuals rather than of groups, and on uneasy deals and alliances that might keep them going.

When faced with the opposition of established parties Boulanger collapsed, and his fragile structure collapsed with him. It was not Boulangism that survived, but the ideas on which it was built and on which it had relied for its success. Where Boulangism lived on, it was not through some virtue of its teaching, but because it was itself the transient, if convenient, expression of a tendency which took different forms and labels, sought different support, but remained fundamentally constant in character and aim. And it is worth noting that it was in the regions most inclined toward that tendency—in the north, in the east, and in Paris—that Boulangism reaped some of its most interesting successes with the General's triumphant elections in the north and in Paris, the electoral victory of young Barrès at Nancy, and the eventual defeat of Jules Ferry in his own Vosges constituency.

This spirit lived on. The Panama scandal of 1892 was the Boulangists' getting back at their victors of 1889. It has been said that the Dreyfus affair was the last effort of the Boulangist spirit. This attributes too much importance to one manifestation of a tendency that was much longer lived. We learn better if we look at *L'Appel au soldat,* in which Barrès makes his young hero, Sturel, vow after the General's fall: "Nous retrouverons des autres boulangismes!" Sturel would not have been too old to take an active part in the nationalistic activities of 1911–1914, and many of Sturel's old companions did. His creator, Maurice Barrès, carried his ideas through the years, giving them first coherence, then a name. The name came when, in 1892, he first used the word "nationalism" in an article concerning the then-current debate between partisans of the classical French tradition, and "romantic" admirers of Tolstoy, Ibsen, and Maeterlinck. The transition from literary nationalism to political nationalism did not take too long.

The Dreyfus affair offered the doctrine an opportunity both to spread and to affirm itself. It was then, in 1899, that Barrès defined his idea of nationalist:

> He is a man who relates everything to France, who judges everything, even the abstract truth, in terms of French interests. The assertion that a thing is good or true begs the question "In relation to what is this thing good or true?" Otherwise one might as well say nothing.[9]

The nationalism of Barrès was republican, traditionalistic, respectful of the established order even when he disapproved of it. Out of the Dreyfus affair, however, inspired by Barrès but differing from him on many points, grew another nationalism. It was a rebellious nationalism, antirepublican, whose assertive traditionalism rejected a whole century of French tradition, revolutionary because royalist, and chauvinistic by reaction against the foreign elements that it felt were swamping French life and culture.[10] In the mood that prevailed in the prewar years the activities of these Nationalists had their clear share; their preaching heightened the defensive tone of France, and also the aggrievedly offensive tone of Germany. Effect and cause were so clearly interconnected that they are even now inseparable. Paris too must be granted its proper importance, for there the movement was in great measure concentrated. Nor was this surprising or new: the city had been revolutionary when the government was conservative, radical when the government was moderate; Boulanger had flourished to its cheers in 1889, anti-Dreyfusard nationalism ten years later. It would always be radical in its own fashion: before 1914 it was destined to see the greater part of the new nationalistic ferment. Again, this is understandable from a class point of view: at a time when France seemed threatened by the foreign enemy, the Nationalists stood most explicitly for French greatness and the power to affirm it; at a time when the social order seemed threatened, the Nationalists spoke up loudly if not clearly against those who attacked it. "The best people" would not condone their vulgar and violent methods, but they would look upon them with discreet sympathy. The solid bourgeoisie would find little good to say for their hooliganism, though its student sons would join the Camélots du Roi or chant nationalist slogans. However, those lower middle classes uneasily teetering between bourgeois respectability and the disgrace of proletarianization—small shopkeepers, shop assistants, clerks, butchers (there should be a chronicle of the part played by butchers in the annals of nationalist leagues) and so on—could and would be more decisive about it, and the vote was not their only means of expression.

Here was a numerous public, relatively stagnant, relatively backward, opposed to changes which might threaten the established order and its own precarious social position, yet impatient of the established order which appeared weak, indecisive, inefficient, hardly a trustworthy champion of internal order or national prestige. "Respectable men" revolt against the corruption that would be the country's ruin and that could so easily be attributed to foreigners and foreign ideas. "Little men" revolt too, against the growing oppressiveness of state and money power, and become anti-semitic "because the Jews have all the money." It is all rather complex, hardly ever clear, but clearly good material for nationalist agitation, which offered a ground upon which persons moved by vague and contradictory aims and dissatisfactions could meet with profit. But though numerous, such people do not contribute much to national opinion. "The best people" do. And the most influential of these were in Paris.

We know, of course, that in terms of political and cultural activity, Paris has long been the centre of France. If Saint-Phlin leaves it for his native Lorraine and a life of political insignificance, his fellow-*déracinés* remain, as did his creator Barrès; as does also Jules Romains' country-born Jerphanion who may talk of his native soil, but who makes his life in Paris and remembers his childhood home chiefly for electoral purposes. M. Bergeret, unhappy and ineffective in the provinces, comes into his own when he is transferred to Paris; and the correspondence of Charles Péguy shows to what extent banishment from the metropolis troubled men who were, or wanted to be, active in political and cultural life.[11] As Versailles under the monarchy, so Paris under the republic was the place where things could be done, where men could get on, *la foire sur la place* of a myriad social, economic, and cultural activities. And so, however much he might talk of Lorraine, it was in Paris that Barrès produced himself; and the spell of the sorceress Martha was not strong enough to keep other *félibres* beside Maurras in their native Provence. They were right to come, for in the countryside things had changed little since Renan recorded his impressions of the electoral campaign of 1869 in Seine-et-Marne. As for the little towns, communes whose activity has been so well described in Roger Thabault's excellent study of his own Mazières-en-Gâtine, their fate, like that of M. de Gromance, was settled in Paris. Their political ideas hardly less so.[12]

It would be a mistake, certainly, to think of French public opinion in the prewar years as one, coherent, united sentiment, gradually rising against the ever more clearly perceived and ever more resented threats from abroad, from within, or both; even though broadly and superficially this is the very picture of events. Obviously, public opinion is never wholly united, never wholly coherent, and seldom rises to a pitch of passion without being influenced—that is, without the use of propaganda. Such propaganda came wholly from Paris, through the conversation held there, the newspapers published there, the appointments made there, and the public speakers who went out from there (even if they were not by any means all Parisians themselves) all carrying a point of view forged and current in Paris. The two or three village notables, and anybody else who read or listened, were the local counterpart of the *minorité agissante* at work in Paris. But the provincial editors also read the Paris papers, maintained a Paris office if they could afford it, subscribed to a Paris news agency if they could not, and the Paris Letter was a staple feature of the local newspaper. The most widely read provincial newspaper, *La Croix,* was itself little more than a copy of the Parisian *editio princeps,* and even great provincial dailies like the *Dépêche de Toulouse* or the *Progrès de Lyon* read like brothers or echoes of the Paris press.

All this was important. And it would be difficult, also, to overestimate the significance and the influence of contemporary literary production— especially at its most accessible, most popular level, that of the novel and the play. A great deal of attention has been devoted to French writers' reactions to the crisis of the times, but students have focused with determination on evidence furnished by what are largely self-conscious documents, whether contemporary or *ex post facto:* diaries, correspondence, essays and articles, memoirs published later, and so forth. Yet the literary forms most likely to affect and reflect general public opinion—particularly popular novels—have been rather neglected.[13] True, the evidence is clearer, less ambiguous, more accessible too, in the important contemporary investigations of opinion in literary and student circles,[14] in the critical essays of men like Brunetière, Lamaitre, Capus, and Faguet; in the mass of politico-literary writings by Massis and Sorel and Maurras and Daudet and Bainville and Barrès; above all, perhaps, in the brilliant work of Charles Péguy, full of reflections of (and on) the contemporary scene.

And yet there is a good deal left of evidence and propaganda: even if we only mention the plays of Hervieu and Brieux, Emile Fabre and Jules Lavedan and Paul Bourget; even if we remember only the novels of Barrès and of Ernest Psichari, of Romain Rolland and Paul Bourget, and the solitary but important work of Roger Martin du Gard, an essential document for the student of the new atmosphere. Written in 1912, published in 1913, the changes of the time are emphasized in it because they appear emphatic to the author. And it was natural that Barois, the idealistic writer-politician formed in the Dreyfus period, should be struck by the change of temper among the young. Open *Jean Barois* anywhere and you will find a running chronicle of contemporary intellectual attitudes: open it at the chapter where Barois grown old interviews the young representatives of the new nationalist and Catholic middle class, and you will find the stuff of the times. The emphasis falls heavily on the catchwords of the period: "Discipline, Heroism, Renaissance, National Spirit"; *"La France nouvelle, la France de la menace allemande, la France d'Agadir."* Order must replace anarchy. Positive knowledge must replace vague philosophizing. The reader is told that one of the young men is in Normale-Sciences, not Normale-Lettres, and that the other studies law and political science: more "positive," useful subjects than the philosophy which Barois' generation would have chosen. They are stern, firm, and positive, without the weaknesses of dreams, or humor, or self-doubt. Even their regard for tradition and religion, which they see almost as one, is of a positive sort: traditional (that is Catholic) morality must be restored because of its disciplinary virtues.

This last point is borne out by the evidence of Henri Massis who has presented the Catholic revival of the time as part of a trend towards authority, hierarchy and discipline, rather than of a search for ultimate truth. It agrees with the testimony of M. Petit who speaks of Paul Claudel as being "au premier rang des poètes qui voient dans le catholicisme la grande école d'énergie." It fits in with the ideas of Ernest Psichari.[15] The whole discussion in Barois is paralleled in Agathon's *Les Jeunes Gens d'aujourd'hui,* and in Emile Henriot's *A quoi rèvent les jeunes gens (Enquête sur la jeunesse littéraire),* both published in 1913—the same year as du Gard's novel. Henriot's *Enquête* quotes a lot of young writers (G. Duhamel, J. Copeau, J. Boulanger, A. de Tarde, H. Clouard) much to the same effect as the interlocutors of Jean Barois. And Julien Benda, when he later writes *Un Régulier dans le siècle,* confirms that "tout un monde littéraire ne voulait plus savoir que l'âme 'française,' les vérités 'françaises'." [16]

In *Aux écoutes de la France qui vient,* also published in 1913, a Protestant youth leader, Gaston Riou, declares: "Two men above all represent Young France—Charles Péguy and Romain Rolland." [17] Péguy in those days was not widely read, though Romain Rolland himself has very appositely written that "a whole young French generation joyously marched toward [war], and at the head of it Péguy marked the step, with the marseillaise of Marathon." [18] But in *Jean Christophe* Rolland himself, having written a novel in which a whole generation discovered its own reflection, cannot but describe the new mood and the effects of the new nationalism—the new Catholic revival which affects Aurora and Georges; the reaction against Free Thought and toward war and chauvinism that hurts Emmanuel grown old; and Jean himself cannot escape the impression that Europe "offrait l'aspect d'une grande veillée d'armes." Colonel House, one cannot help feeling, was somewhat less perspicacious.

With Ernest Psichari we come to an ideal type of quite another sort; a patriot of good family, a grandson of Ernest Renan, a Nationalist, an admirer of Maurras, a soldier by choice, a Catholic by conversion, the very image of the perfect youth of the Nationalist Revival. His evolution can be traced through his two novels: *L'Appel des armes,* (1913) exalting the order, discipline and patriotic virtues of military service, and *Le Voyage du centurion* (1915) exalting the superior order, discipline and spiritual virtues of Christian service. In connection with Psichari, we might also notice Paul Acker whose novels are clearly vehicles for the discussion of militarism and antimilitarism, and of the new patriotic attitude that alone can save France from her decadence. [19]

With Acker, however, we touch the demarcation line between the writers who depict and those who propagandize; and the most influential of these latter at this time was without any doubt Paul Bourget with his "campagne de restauration nationale" [20] Antidemocratic attitudes played an important part in the Nationalist Revival, and so did the need felt by some to preserve or restore the social and moral order threatened or affected by the "prevalent anarchy." The work of Bourget affords an excellent illustration of these themes. The divisions and discords of the Dreyfus affair had inspired him to try his healing pen on the nation's wounds. The inspiration of his social and political concepts comes, like that of Maurras, from Comte, Bonald, Le Play and Taine; and his *porteparole* characters, like Victor Ferrand in *L'Etape* (1902) are eager to cite their authority. *Un Divorce* (1905), *L'Emigré* (1907), continue to preach the virtues of "travail, famille, patrie," social order and traditional values. The point is carried to a vaster public in the plays whose series begins in 1908 (some of them novels adapted for the stage): *Un Divorce, L'Emigré, La Barricade, Un Cas de conscience, Le Tribun.* The influence of the plays was the wider for being published also in the theatrical supplement of *L'Illustration* which would carry them automatically to the marble table-tops of many thousands of right-thinking families. The influence of the literary figure was enhanced by that of the political columnist, a regular contributor to *L'Echo de Paris.* And there are other— Barrès, Bordeaux, Bazin, *revanchard,* patriotic, traditionalistic, *professeurs d'énergie.* Léon Daudet, better in his chronicles than in his novels; Charles Maurras—a poet, an essayist, a pamphleteer, but as a novelist only a novelist *manqué.* But Anatole France, whose *Histoire contemporaine* so brilliantly reflected an earlier period (as did the *Roman de l'energie nationale* of Barrès), gives us nothing or only a few flashes for this later time in *La Révolte des anges,* and nothing at all to compare with the adventures of M. Bergeret.

And if all these throw relatively little light on the activities of the nationalist movement itself, they throw a great deal on the nationalist mood, on the revival of patriotism, of national self-confidence and self-consciousness; on the new insistence on order, discipline, moral values, and the positive virtues; on the fashionable reaction against free thought, socialism, empty values like justice and truth,[21] internal divisions (those created by anybody else), and generally the pernicious anarchy that had been born in 1789 and that had triumphed in 1902. Words against words perhaps. But Carl Becker has taught us how to identify the climate of opinion of a time by the words it favors most. By this token, the weight of literary evidence for the years before 1914 confirms the contemporary impression of a national and patriotic revival.

It might fairly be asked how far Paris reflected France or, better still, how far it reflected on France. True, in the 1850s Paris "glimmered before Emma's eyes in an atmosphere of vermillion." But just because Mme. Bovary over-indulged her literary tastes, may we assume that then, or half a century later, the provinces were devouring the products of the Paris presses? We probably may; there is evidence to show that the novels of Barrès and Bourget were popular, Jules Renard finds cultivated men in the Nièvre who know more than he of what goes on in Paris, and certainly the correspondence between Alain-Fournier and Jacques Rivière shows that there were then, as ever, circles in Bordeaux quite up to date on Parisian activities. Here is more proof of the focal importance of Paris, to which the Rastignacs and the Julien Sorels, the Pécuchets and the Sturels of the twentieth century still looked for inspiration, for opportunity, and (though often under protest) for leadership.

No doubt parliamentarians still glanced toward their wards with moderate apprehension, and ran their constituents' errands in Paris ministries.

But the movement for parliamentary emancipation was already under way, and proportional representation, designed to free the deputy from too close dependence on his electors and place him under even closer dependence to party headquarters in Paris, was itself significantly enough part of the platform on which a "nationalist" coalition fought and won the elections of 1919. Paris was winning.

The new tendency toward patriotic emphasis is no less significant for being largely concentrated in a few regions which had long entertained it anyway, and in certain very active and articulate Parisian circles. Localized as it seems to have been, it is important enough to affect the parliamentary behavior of sound anticlerical politicians like Thomson and Messimy, the public behavior of grand old representatives of the republican camp like Ernest Lavisse and Anatole France, the orientation of one-time Dreyfusist strongholds like the Ecole Normale.[22] It is obvious enough to be noticed by all interested observers, both foreign and French.[23] And it is apparently strong enough to keep in power a president and a government who, if they did not actually seek war, yet accepted it as a part of their plans for France and for the future. But it is new only in a very limited sense; it is really a revival of attitudes never altogether abandoned, an emphasis on terms which fashion had slurred over for a while. What novelty there is in it lies in Paris. And that never was any novelty in France.

So we are justified in speaking of a nationalist revival in the sense of that term; the problem remains that of defining the nature and the source of a movement which was undoubtedly there.[24] And this problem arises, as must already be clear, from the confusion caused by different groups and individuals apparently moving together toward a common "nationalist" goal. The movement appears most clearly in dramatic events such as the election of Raymond Poincaré to the presidency in January of 1913, or the passing of the law prolonging military service from two to three years in the summer of the same year. But it manifested itself over a much longer period of time in fostering the mood that became first apparent and then apparently dominant as the nationalist revival. Its makeup was not always clearly understood; many good Republicans merely recognized behind it their traditional antagonists—Clericals, Monarchists, and Nationalists: "Boulangism in 1889, Nationalism in 1899, Nationalism again in 1908," wrote Le Progrès de Lyon on January 3, 1909, "but integral nationalism— that is to say monarchism. The Republic is undergoing its decennial crisis." And the very next day, Louis Vaugeois, elaborated the same idea in the Action française:

So those forces of sentiment that Barrès demonstrated (and rightly) in 1900, as limp and inert when the idea of Monarchy was presented to patriotic crowds, here they are, there's no denying, welling up in those same crowds during the last few months. It is impossible to say otherwise if you are in good faith. At the Salle Wagram [the other day] the same people were crowding round Réal del Sarte [a royalist champion], as had crowded round Mercier and Rochefort in 1906–1907. And when the slightest allusion to Dreyfus, to the Jews, brought the whole hall to its feet, brandishing canes and fists, that was no more, no less, than the thrill of "nationalism": the very same spirit as of 1899.

He might have added "and of 1889."

It was easy to confuse the nationalist movement with its noisiest and most active representatives who, to all but those forces themselves, seemed one with the traditional enemies of the Republic. But in fact it was much more than that: as Georges Sorel very sensibly told one of his friends, "One doesn't stir the masses with journals that print 500 copies." [25] The vocal Nationalists were not powerful, and hardly significant, politically or socially: where they could muster four or five thousand demonstrators for an occasion, the Socialists would gather 150,000 when they really tried. [26] And the good people who, Princess Radziwill writes in May of 1909, bunched together portraits of the Pope, tricolor flags, and effigies of Joan of Arc [27] can be cited in connection with the newly prevalent nationalist mood, but hardly in connection with the integral nationalism of the Action française.

We should understand the situation better if we consider the idea of Henri Bazire who, writing at the end of 1911, pointed to the birth of a "new nationalism." He attributed it to external causes and in particular, to the general impression that Germany would never allow the country to live in peace:

> Before the revelation of the foreign danger, a new nationalism is born . . . It does not stem from transports of enthusiasm, nor from a political movement, but essentially from an awakening of patriotism, and of reasonable patriotism at that . . . [28]

Nationalism and patriotism were used as equivalent terms, for that was how they appeared to him:

> People will say "your new nationalism is so close to patriotism that it dissolves in it, it is an average of the public spirit which will more or less penetrate political parties, but which produces neither a positive program, nor a specific plan of action . . . You're simply talking about atmosphere, *ambiance*." And why not?

His article was the first attempt to analyze the new atmosphere. It called forth confirmation and warm agreement from readers and friends. And the spate of investigation which flowered during the spring of 1912 led Bazire to reiterate his opinion: the new nationalism was different from the old; it overflowed the limits of the old parties and looked beyond the anxieties of internal politics.[29] The same cries and the same canes might rise in the *salle Wagram,* but the mood that impressed foreign observers was to be found elsewhere too—in the press, in the schools, in the tone of the theatre and the publishing trade, in the Elysée beginning in 1913, and the army, and the Palais Bourbon.[30] It was therefore more than just the bright flare-up of nationalist embers.

Now F. Hertz has explained in his *Nationalism in History and Politics* that certain contemporary triumphs of extreme nationalism "were facilitated by the attitude of many statesmen and politicians who were not in sympathy with their aims, but either believed that it was too dangerous for their own position and that of their partners to take energetic measures against them, or even considered them as necessary evils." And this illuminates the tolerance, the sympathy, the support which old-style nationalists received from the new, it indicates the real forces behind the nationalist revival, and it helps to clarify the confusion between its various components. "The typical nationalist attitude," writes Hertz, "is to assume that national power and prestige are the best keys to all the treasures of the world, and that a strong State alone can solve the social problems and secure the best possible conditions for the development of national civilizations."[31] This helps to point out why conservative and nationalist programs cannot really be one: the conservatives aiming at the conservation of states, liberties, privileges, situations; the nationalists aiming rather at the creation of new ones, "with prestige and power as the supreme goals." But it also shows why the superficial observer at a time when moderates and nationalists emphasized the importance of strong government and national prestige could not see much difference between their respective programs. Why, in fact, patriotic conservative *poincarisme* should look very much like patriotic extremist *nationalisme*—to all but a few who, like Poincaré or Maurras, were in a position to know better.

The apparent unity, then, of the nationalist movement and of the nationalist mood in the years before 1914 is partly due to a confusion of catchwords, a concatenation of common slogans emphasizing patriotism, order, tradition, and discipline, a general tone whose coherence is more apparent than real. If we look closely we may distinguish an alliance of different tendencies, survivals, interests, and tactics; and the sometimes-only-tacit collaboration of different men and groups leading to striking results, joining in striking policies, agreeing on striking measures, emphasizing first a latent then an elated patriotism. But the patriotic tone which characterizes the period after 1905 was not new; it was, as we have seen, the same old thing *monté en épingle*. Neither Barrès nor Bourget waited until the prewar years to adopt it; Péguy was a rabid patriot even when leading the Dreyfusist bands of the Ecole Normale down the hill of Sainte-Geneviève; Brunetière's ardent nationalism never wavered; when Jules Lemaître joined the Action française in 1908 it was no new departure for the ex-pillar of the Patrie française. People like these did not need clowns like Jean Richepin to show them the way. The way had already been traced, and the men who followed it in 1914 had themselves laid some of its milestones in 1889 and 1899.

Thus to many of the people they affected—old Monarchists, steadfast Catholics, unreconciled Boulangists, unrepentant anti-Dreyfusards—the slogans of the new nationalism had long been familiar. Others had been shifting gradually to an appreciation of their use. Some were moved, as Bazire has told us, by the revelation of foreign danger. And some, perhaps among the most politically significant, merely saw them as handy slogans in a difficult political situation in which internal and external pressures were complicated by the demagogic demands of the current political system.

A movement, then, the nationalist revival? Only in the sense Professor Heberle tells us that we may sometimes use it, of "trend" or "tendency." A public opinion? Certainly as he defines it—"The prevailing publicly expressed opinion on a matter of public concern, which can claim effective validity in a society."[32] Effective? We can have little doubt of it when we survey the French political scene before 1914. But vague, incoherent, tangible but indefinable—and almost impossible to explain outside the detailed story of events. In that case, "vous allez encore nous parler d'ambiance?" After all, "pourquoi pas?"

PART IV

"Let Us Now Praise Famous Men"

~ 10

Pierre de Coubertin and the
Introduction of Organized Sport

Watching the Olympic Games of 1968, remembering that they had been reinvented by a Frenchman three-quarters of a century before, I found it odd that the chief sporting manifestation of our time should be attributed to a nation not overly given to sport, one whose athletic tradition hardly compares with those of her English or German neighbors, one in which games of every kind were beginning to spread only as the nineteenth century ended.

An early legend attributes the origin of Olympic games to Pelops' triumph in a chariot race which he had won by bribing his rival's groom. But we cannot assume that this symbolic coincidence of *mores* lay behind the nineteenth-century resurgence of rites going back to the second millennium BC—even though the pediment of the great temple of Zeus at Olympia depicts this appropriately equivocal sporting victory.

The man responsible for the revival and for the paradoxes it suggests—Baron Pierre de Coubertin—could not at the time of this writing be found either in the *Petit Larousse* or in the *Encyclopedia Britannica*. Given the paucity of material, these pages are a simple reconnaissance of uncharted terrain, suggesting some ways in which sporting activities fit and illuminate other aspects of the *fin de siècle*.

The first thing we can do with Coubertin when, having surmounted the initial obstacles to documentation, we discover he was born in 1863, is to place him in his generation. There he finds himself in the company of Maurice Barrès (b. 1862), Romain Rolland (b. 1866), Léon Daudet (b. 1867), Charles Maurras (b. 1868); and exact contemporary of one of the most revealing characters in French fiction: Roger Martin du Gard's Jean Barois.

The coincidence between Coubertin and Barois goes beyond birthdates. In 1896, the year of Coubertin's great triumph in reviving the Olympic Games at Athens, Martin du Gard's hero was founding his periodical, *Le Semeur,* designed to assert a new élan "against a tired, enervated world."

There is no suggestion here, and no reason to think, that du Gard, writing in 1910–1912, gave any thought either to Coubertin or to Olympic activities scarcely noticed even in the French sporting press.[1] But the coincidence serves a useful purpose. It reveals the possibilities of a particular social group at a privileged moment in time; the challenges that some members of this group perceived; and how they reacted to them.

Pierre de Coubertin was born in his parents' *hôtel* in Paris, rue Oudinot, half-way between the École Militaire and the parish church of St. François-Xavier. The family was wealthy, ultra-montane, and legitimist. The mother, a Mirville, was pious, elegant, busy; the father, Charles-Louis, Baron Frédy de Coubertin, a mediocre if fashionable academic painter. Life swung between Paris, the maternal estate at Mirville, close to Bolbec in Normandy, the family chateau at Saint-Rémy-en-Chevreuse, the annual visits to Rome, the occasional pilgrimage to Frohsdorf, where the Comte de Chambord was still worshipped as Henri V.

Frédys (descended from patrician di Fredis) and Coubertins had been nobles in France for a long time; the Mirvilles prided themselves on descent from a son of Louis VI. Past alliances (among others to a descendant of Cyrano de Bergerac and to the Bertier de Sauvigny family) related Pierre to most of the noble Faubourg. Yet he felt little sympathy for what he called "the cretins of the Faubourg Saint-Germain." Too many of his peers (like his own father) had opted out of the world around them. And in return the world ignored them. No longer resented or persecuted, the nobility was left to itself and to the public's occasional surprise that it continued to exist.

In 1879, a meeting with the Comte de Chambord convinced the adolescent that the Restoration was an empty dream. In 1880 he completed his studies (he had been a brilliant student) at the fashionable Jesuit College of the rue de Madrid. He studied law unenthusiastically, was fascinated by the lectures he attended at the Ecole des Sciences Politiques, joined the Republican group in the miniature parliament of the Conférence Molé, boxed, fenced, went out a great deal. Listless, dilettantish, he was looking for a way, a purpose, which neither "the systematic right" nor the *"extrème gauche pleine d'inconnus"* could furnish. He found them first in the philosophy of Frédéric Le Play, whose views on the reconciliation of worker and employer carried attractive overtones of *noblesse oblige*. The possibility—the duty—of emancipating and integrating the working classes always remained one of Coubertin's concerns, but the focus of his attention soon shifted to a field where laborers in the vineyard were markedly fewer. He would devote his life to promoting the revival, the rejuvenation of France; but he would turn especially to youth: "I shall put some color in the cheeks of a solitary and confined youth, [toughen] his body and character by sport, its risks, and even its excesses."[2]

The way in which he came to this self-assigned task, the extent and the limits of his achievement, provide the subject of the following pages. More broadly speaking, however, Coubertin's was a personality that clearly fits into the golden age of the idealistic rentier-intellectual. Without going beyond the 1890s, we shall see that the introduction of organized sport in France also fitted the tendencies of the time, and fitted them on several different planes.

In his teens, Pierre de Coubertin had been fascinated by Hippolyte Taine's *Notes sur l'Angleterre,* which had been published in 1872 and which he seems to have read about ten years later. What especially caught his attention was Taine's description of the physical side of English education: athletics and games. At this point, the nineteen-year-old youth, like his older contemporaries, seemed eager chiefly to make up for his country's recent defeat by whatever moral rearmament education could impart.

But this was not all. One of the great apostles of applied positivism, Taine thought that the best system of government—or of education—is one that conforms most closely to nature. One implication of this arises from the observation that nature has made men *un*equal. Nearly a hundred years earlier, a revolutionary had grumbled that God was an aristocrat. Nature, too, was an aristocrat by inclination; and so was Taine. His *Notes sur l'Angleterre* set out to show that the existence of a superior class, its moral and political influence, and the acceptance of this superiority and influence by the nation as a whole, were sources of stability, of social energy, of national power, and success. What made this class superior? Its character and outlook, themselves forged by an educational system in which the physical counted above the intellectual, and the moral ahead of the physical. A physical and moral elite was what Taine sketched, what Coubertin found exciting, what he set out first to investigate and then to create.

The young nobleman had been destined for Saint-Cyr and an army career. But there seemed to be no opportunities for glory in the perspective of the early eighties. Peacetime soldiering, the monotony of garrison life, appeared unattractive. He decided that he would make his name in another field, by some "great pedagogical reform." Taine had quoted *Tom Brown's Schooldays,* a French translation of which had appeared in 1875. Coubertin, who had read it at the time in the *Journal de la jeunesse,* picked it up again, reread it with Taine's arguments in mind, and became a devotee of Thomas Arnold of Rugby. Arnold was dead, but his heritage lived on. So in 1883, at the age of twenty, the young Coubertin embarked on his first pilgrimage to the sources of his faith. Having visited Eton, Rugby, Gladstone, and other monuments, he returned a confirmed Anglomaniac.

Coubertin was not alone in believing that Anglo-Saxon power and success rested on a recently built educational system aimed not, as in France, at discipline, but at the gradual emancipation and self-revelation of youth. But his observations persuaded him that the whole English system was built on sport, particularly on team sports, and that it was impossible to achieve the same end by any other means. What France lacked was *virilité scolaire*. "Here was the one recipe for national greatness to which over several centuries none of our governments had thought to direct its attention and its efforts." He would go to sport as some of his contemporaries went to the people.[3]

At once, Coubertin began to campaign for the introduction of sports and athletics in secondary schools. Still in his early twenties, his connections, his conviction, his persuasive tact, helped to secure the support of a great many personalities, including the influential Octave Gréard, Vice-Rector of the Académie de Paris, and, better still, of the Minister of Public Instruction, Jules Simon, who in 1887 agreed to head a Committee for the Preparation of Physical Exercises in Education. The Committee—officially set up in 1888—backed individual initiatives, encouraged clubs already in existence, publicized the new cause, and guaranteed its respectability. The real work was left to its secretary: Coubertin. His missionary zeal had found an almost virgin field.

Organized sports on the English pattern, chiefly running and ball games, had made their timid appearance only in the 1870s. The Havre Athletic Club, founded in 1872, and destined to introduce rugby football into France, had begun as an almost purely English venture. In Paris, a Club des Coureurs had been started in 1875; the Racing Club in 1882, and its great rival, Le Stade Français, a year later. But these societies were exceptional, isolated, and affected only few. Such clubs as existed lived perilously close to extinction. Outside their quasi-confidential activities, the score was meagre indeed.

Where English schools were nurseries of sportsmen, French ones ignored the very idea of team games or athletics. A lycéen's daily timetable covered eleven hours of class or preparation in *étude*. Lycées were sunk in routine, bound by anachronistically rigorous rules. In 1889, the twenty-seven-year-old Maurice Barrès dedicated his second novel, *Un Homme libre,* "aux collègiens de France, victimes d'une discipline abominable." That same year, the report of a subcommittee on educational reform chaired by Henri Marion, professor of philosophy at the Sorbonne, pleaded for liberalization. The repressive discipline of the lycées should be modified, free exercise and open air games promoted, young people encouraged to "exercise *self-government*" (in English), form their own groups and clubs, "train themselves for free life by adherence to an order of their own making, and obedience to self-imposed laws." The response to such advice went little further than a ministerial circular of 7 July 1890, granting permission for students to talk during meals in refectory, on walks, and during periods of exercise.[4]

But more was amiss than deadening discipline. Learning could be exciting, but its tendency was not toward action but abstraction. What mattered in the educational approach of the 1880s and 1890s, was not the learning acquired but the *process* which trained the mind. Students of Latin or Greek, for instance, were not expected to end up knowing those languages or the societies which they represented and which their classics depicted, but to have exercised their minds by the gymnastics involved in the learning process. The physical training sessions, which regulations required them to attend when the lack of facilities did not prevent this, were also given for an ulterior purpose, not for any pleasure they might provide. Games, on the other hand, were ends in themselves, their uses seldom recognized, their pleasures suspect, their dangers—to health, discipline, and self-control—feared. Official efforts in favor of physical education had only added a little more drudgery to the loaded programs of national education. The notion of games organized by the students themselves was alien to the Napoleonic discipline that ruled most of the schools.

A distinguished geographer recalls the "intoxicating impression of freedom" he enjoyed when games were permitted in the provincial lycée of his youth. But such freedom was limited by facilities, and still more by conventions. Even where games came to be tolerated, they had to be closely supervised. Thus, when in 1890 the teaching assistant supposed to accompany the team of a Paris lycée to a match against another school fell ill, and the team captain offered his word of honor that he would look after his fellow players, "My friend," answered the headmaster, "how do you expect me to take the word of a schoolboy?"[5]

All this, seven years after the beginning of Coubertin's efforts, illustrates the difficulties in his path. To quote Barrès once more, writing on the youth of lycée and university, "who in 1883 would have offered them a method designed to form not scholars, but men?"[6]

Possible initiatives were discouraged by physical circumstances. Most lycées were overcrowded. In some, wooden barracks were being set up in courtyards to furnish classroom space; in others garrets and corridors were brought into use. What schoolyards there were, were small, dark, squeezed between buildings. When in 1891 Charles Péguy, then a senior boy at the Lycée d'Orléans, persuaded his headmaster to permit the older boys to play football, this had to be done on the boulevards during the noon break.[7] It is significant that the first teams were set up in institutions that disposed of exceptionally spacious grounds: Lycée Michelet at Vanves, Lycée Lakanal at

Sceaux; or in distinguished private schools like the Ecole Alsacienne or Monge, described by Sarcey as "the model lycée of tomorrow's university." It would be their students who, with the support of Racing and Stade, organized the first schoolboy competition, a paper chase held at Ville d'Avray on 4 July 1888 and greeted as a public event by the summer press. The first breakthrough of organized games in Catholic schools also came in suburban institutions, first the college of Juilly, then that of Albert-le-Grand at Arcueil, where space could be found for playing fields.

Obviously, space was never the crucial factor, and some lycées, like that of Briançon, would rent a yard some minutes walk away if they felt the need. The Jesuits, who encouraged their students to play games and even joined in them, showed no interest in Coubertin's initiative because they did not wish their charges to be thrown together with young people from secular schools, as they would be in football matches. In contrast, Fr. Didon, the great Dominican educator who, after 1890, helped to introduce competitive games at Arcueil, was a remarkably liberal theologian, often in hot water for his progressive views, and, significantly, well-versed in contemporary German and English thought.

To begin with, then, sporting activities and especially their insertion in a pedagogic program were looked on with suspicion and treated very gingerly. Even the authorities of the Ecole Alsacienne, first to permit the foundation of an athletic association among their students, fought shy of attracting public attention to this aspect of their activities. They seemed to fear, reports Coubertin, that it would hurt the good reputation of their school. Given this mood, Coubertin needed all the moral support his committee could furnish. To combat the vulgar connotations of sporting activities, he would have to invoke the snob appeal that could attract parental approval and interest. Coubertin's energy and social connections enabled him to mobilize fashionable figures, and turn athletic competitions into modish concourses. Presidents of the republic were persuaded to patronize meetings he organized. Headmasters who did not turn up at their students' games days were liable to miss an impromptu appearance by Lesseps or Carnot. By 1889, this policy showed its results in the foundation of the Union des Sociétés Françaises des Sports Athlétiques (U.S.F.S.A.). By the early 1890s several score athletic associations existed in lycées and colleges, most of them affiliated to the U.S.F.S.A.[8]

Another proof of success lay in the fact that—within weeks of the paper chase at Ville d'Avray—Coubertin's campaign had conjured up a rival, one that challenged it on nationalist grounds: Paschal Grousset's Ligue Nationale de l'Education Physique.

Grousset is a very interesting figure, both because of his background and because of his connection with sport. Son of a college teacher, journalist under the Second Empire, collaborator of Rochefort, he was to become the Commune's Delegate for Foreign Affairs. Exiled to New Caledonia in 1871, he escaped three years later and made his way to England, where he lived until 1881. Amnestied, he returned to France, earning his living by his pen. In 1893, the Twelfth Arrondissement of Paris returned him to Parliament, where he continued to sit as a Radical-Socialist until his death in 1909. Elected with the help of the bicycle vote, drawing strong support from *La Bicyclette* which had mobilized the good people of Picpus and Bercy with slogans like *"Cyclistes aux urnes!"*, he repaid them with a bill on the rights of cycles and other "vehicles with human traction," before introducing one of the first proposals for an income tax.

In due course, Grousset was to become a keen Dreyfusard and to write two pamphlets about the Affair. Before the Dreyfus affair, however, nationalism was still a sentiment of the Left, and the old communard was no exception. He had made part of his living with a long string of books about school life in England and elsewhere, books for and about young people, advocating fresh air, physical exercise, and the revival of traditional sports.[9] He must have felt that Coubertin was poaching on his preserves and, what was worse, brandishing foreign examples where native ones should do. In July 1888, therefore, Grousset published a series of articles in *Le Temps,* supporting the notion of sport in schools, but condemning the importation of English games and ways when the French would do better to seek their models in antiquity rather than across the Channel. "Let us be French; let us be so passionately, even in little things; let us be so above all in weighty matters like the education of our sons, if we want France to survive in the midst of the wild beasts that roar around it . . . There are no unimportant concessions: avoid useless ones."

Of course, the year 1888 (and especially the summer, when Grousset launched his campaign in *Le Temps*) was a period of intense political activity, with a number of by-elections being fought chiefly round the controversial ambitions of General Boulanger. It was in the wake of Boulangism that patriotism ceased to be an apolitical article of faith and became a political issue. Not that Coubertin and his friends lacked patriotism. But Grousset appealed to it, and its vocabulary figured prominently—and conveniently—in his arguments.

Clearly, sport was good; but should be taken. Grousset favoured the "noble jeu de paume" over tennis, and preferred to call football *barrette*—a term temporarily adopted by some lycées, like Janson de Sailly, but not very useful, since none could discover quite what the rules of the ancestral ball game had been. He proposed reviving the medieval student festival of the *lendit* in annual athletic events; and *lendits* actually took place in 1889 and 1890, great competitive pageants for the *jeunesse des écoles*. He even proposed the instauration of Olympic Games on a national scale in France, to encourage sporting activity.[10]

Grousset's campaign soon ran out of breath. *Lendits* disappeared, first from Paris, then a few years later from those provincial towns where they had caught some local imagination, had offered the opportunity of one more celebration. The Ligue prospered for a few years in places like Bordeaux, Pau, Montpellier, Besançon, and in certain Paris lycées, where personal enthusiasm promoted its activities; then collapsed or merged into other sporting activities. The Olympic notion was taken up on a different scale by Grousset's rival. What endured longest were the nationalist accusations he had brought against Coubertin. Having enlisted traditionalism in the service of patriotic revivalism, Grousset elicited quite a bit of support. *Le Temps* (5 June 1890), referring to some regattas U.S.F.S.A. had organized, censured M. de Coubertin who "is fighting to acclimatize in France the English system of team training," while Grousset's Ligue applied "the very French respect for the individual" by furnishing each rower his own skiff and oars.

Throughout the 1890s, the U.S.F.S.A. (and Coubertin) had to defend themselves against repeated suggestions that *their* sports were English and hurt the practice of truly national sports. As late as 1901, Philippe Tissié, leading figure of sport in the southwest, rehearsed the same accusations: "Having copied the Germans, we now copy the English. From one day to another, we unlearn our Frenchness."[11] And when, that same year, J. J. Jusserand published his *Sports et jeux d'exercice dans l'ancienne France,* his massive study was also an attempt to show the national origin of games accused of being un-French.

This rather puerile squabble over what was still a very thin field reflected more than mere chauvinism. The political divergencies were more profound than that. It is not surprising that Grousset's Ligue had as president the great chemist, Marcellin Berthelot, father of one of the founders of the Racing, and as vice-president Georges Clemenceau, a votary of the *folle bicyclette* like his fellow-Radical Grousset: personalities well to the left of those identified with the Coubertin-Simon Committee.[12] Nor need it surprise us that an ideological struggle should take place over control of sporting initiatives, given the function envisaged for them.

When in 1887 Racing and Stade first set up the Union des Sociétés de Courses à Pied de France, the first club's powerful secretary, Georges Saint-Clair, explained that this was not meant simply or solely to sponsor the development of athletic activities, but "to create a school where the will develops and is strengthened, a school which will forge the man of action, the man who knows how to will, to dare, to undertake, organize, govern, and be governed." [13] At about the same time, Edouard Maneuvrier, active in educational reform circles and author of a book approved by Coubertin, was preaching the formation of "a democratic elite"—without which, he argued, society could not operate or the bourgeoisie maintain its positions. "The urgent task," he concluded, "the democratic task *par excellence,* is therefore the regeneration of our aristocratic educational systems. To reform an army one must begin with its cadres; in the same way, we must begin to forge democracy from the top." These and similar views were to be expressed in the conclusions of the official commission appointed to recommend reforms in secondary education. The fourth subcommission, chaired by Maneuvrier, advised that school breaks should be devoted to active physical education. There should be less premilitary training, more games, more athletics, more fresh air, more self-governing sporting societies and student associations. [14]

Better known than Maneuvrier and more influential was Edmond Demolins (1852–1907), like Coubertin a disciple of Frédéric Le Play, and editor of the chief organ of Le Play's sociology, *La Réforme sociale.* Demolins valued Coubertin and shared his admiration for England and for Arnold. It was in his review that Coubertin had published a series of articles on English education with which he caught the attention of Jules Simon. What Demolins appreciated about English schools was that they trained their pupils for physical fitness, self-reliance, initiative, and adjustment to the modern world, turning out not scholars, dandies, or dilettantes, but all-round men. Like Maneuvrier, like Coubertin, he considered educational reform an urgent task and one that must be undertaken from the top. In 1899 he put his theories into practice, opening the Ecole des Roches, in the Normandy countryside, patterned after progressive English boarding schools like Abbotsholme and Bedales. [15]

Admirable though they were, l'Ecole des Roches and the other schools whose foundation it soon inspired were extremely expensive. Boarders paid 2,500 francs a year, day-boys in such places as accepted them some 1,800 francs. "No doubt," admitted the headmaster of the new Ecole de Guyenne that opened in 1905 in the fashionable Bordeaux suburb of Mérignac, "by its high boarding-fees [the school] is directed towards the rich, hence aristocratic. But it can be democratic in spirit." Whatever the spirit, fees equivalent to an *instituteur's* yearly pay were certainly aristocratic. So was the school's board. The aristocracy (of money, if not of birth) was preparing to struggle for life in democracy, or thought it was. And this brings us back to Coubertin himself.

Pierre de Coubertin wanted to form (or to re-form) a moral being, inner-directed, autonomous within an ever-more-encroaching world: something closer to an ideal prototype than to an actual person operating in a recognizable social context. Reading Coubertin, his ideal sporting type appears as real (or as related to reality) as Huysmans' des Esseintes. And while the two types seem very distant from each other, one cannot help remarking that *A Rebours* appeared in 1884 and that the rise of organized sport in France was contemporary not only with the development of aestheticism and art for art's sake, but with Nietzsche's formulation of the aspiration to go beyond laws and standards, to enlist effort and will to create superior humans, to become supremely human, a kind of language that Coubertin could well accept.[16] A kind of language, too, that we recognize in the writings of Maurice Barrès, breviaries in which young dilettantes learned to admire that "passionate taste for human energy" which feeds "the constant effort to create oneself, to the point of substituting one's own conception of the world for conventional reality, in brief of recreating the universe."[17] Barrès was no great admirer of sport, but the quotation, representative of views he often repeated, is also a good description of one aspect of organized games—refuge from, reshaping of, an unsatisfactory world.

Paschal Grousset had known or sensed what he was up against. Coubertin *was* a reactionary figure, albeit an enlightened one. He stood with Gladstone, whom he admired and whose approval he sought; with the Mill of the essay *On Liberty,* insistently and persistently treating human beings as ends rather than means. But he also stood with Le Play, in whose name he declared: "Inequality is more than a law, it is a fact; and patronage is more than a virtue, it is a duty."[18] He suspected what he regarded as the dehumanizing forces of state, and science, and press. He recruited his committees by co-option, and ran them at his own expense with an iron will and a velvet voice.

Sport played an important part in what Coubertin described with a fencing term as possible *parades* against the industrial civilization that he disliked and feared. Industrial civilization stood for the four Sancho Panzas of the Apocalypse: greater comfort, specialization, exaggerated nationalism, and the triumph of democracy. Sport and education could provide remedies to all these evils and counter them to foster a human progress which Coubertin conceived as the unlimited development of individual capacities. Such development could come only after the young had been converted: to sport, to games, to exercise, and to the self discipline which alone could forge sound characters in healthy bodies. The young must be lured onto the playing fields; and this, reasoned Coubertin, could be done only by the example of champions, by the glamour of achievements that many would wish to emulate. Only great exploits would fire the imagination of the young, attract them to the stadium, the track, the court, the swimming pool. It was not that Coubertin wanted to recruit players in great numbers in order to seed out champions, but that he sought champions whose influence would inspire the young to play. The individual exploit was a recruiting agent. What better stage for such exploits than competitions carried to an international level, surrounded by all the excitement and publicity of great official functions? Grousset's *lendits* could reappear, reshaped, in the pageantry of the revived Olympics. Rereading his *Souvenirs d'Amérique et de Grèce,* published in 1897, in the wake of the first Olympic Games of 1896, one is tempted to see in this recreation the greatest of Coubertin's *parades,* the most astute publicity move for the expansion and popularization of sports.

These sporting activities, however, affected only few. The capacities they developed were those of members of a restricted group: restricted by birth, by education, by wealth, by the opportunities all these afforded. A publication of the early 1890s, referring to the delight with which the press greeted the physical regeneration of the "jeunesse universitaire—flower of French youth," regrets that this covered only a tiny minority. Physical exercise was a good thing, but those who needed it most never got it. If athletics and ball games "brillent dans l'ombre des manèges des riches écoles . . . le peuple les ignore!" [19]

One of Coubertin's circulars of 1894 insists on the supreme importance of preserving "the noble and chivalrous character of athletics," of defending them against professionalism and the spirit of lucre. But his stubborn insistence on amateurism, perfectly appropriate to the purpose he had in mind, raised yet another barrier between "true" sportsmen and the mass of ordinary men. In the end, as *L'Équipe* once explained (12 January 1955), "only schoolboys are true amateurs because they play for fun."

Games, in this perspective, are antiutilitarian *par excellence:* quite useless in the material sense, unproductive, and gratuitous. Free, separate, uncertain, regulated, fictitious, games are ends in themselves. They leave behind no harvest, no gain, no work of art, not even any ruins. And none could be more gratuitous or nonutilitarian than the sport of fencing on horseback that Coubertin spent his life trying to get accepted by the Olympic committees he headed. If one considers that games are excellently suited to the consumer society that people talk about today, being simply the accumulation and expenditure of disposable effort, then one may say that sports were a commodity suitable for the consumption of the rentier class that flourished in late nineteenth century France and apt to be particularly attractive to their young who had time and energy to spare.

The economic situation permitted the *fils de famille* to satisfy his whims at a low price, whether indulging in a *soubrette* or a *plaquette*. The general atmosphere hardly encouraged the young and the potentially active to turn toward economic activities as such. The most dynamic discovered that advancement lay in noneconomic enterprises: writing, politics, speculation, entertainment, the university. And the situation that suggested this also made it possible, by creating the lower prices and providing the higher revenues that sustained large sections of the middle classes. It is in these broad but numerically limited circles that one finds the young men of independent means who staff most of the intellectual activities of the time, like Barrès, Daudet, and Maurras, or like Jean Barois and the circle of friends who joined him in founding *Le Semeur*. And lesser lights confirm the pattern.

Maurice LeBlanc (b. 1864), son of a wealthy Norman textile manufacturer, spent some reluctant years pretending to manage one of his father's factories while trying to break through to literary fame. Before achieving success in 1907 with the fictional figure of Arsène Lupin, LeBlanc published one of France's first sporting novels. *Voici des ailes* (Paris, 1898) glorified not the aeroplane but "the new friend that destiny has granted man"—the bicycle that gives us wings to rise above the vileness of the world. Tristan Bernard (b. 1866), another provincial in easy circumstances, started off in the *Revue blanche,* founded a shortlived publication of his own, then moved to the editorship of a cycling review. Before achieving success with *Les Pieds nickelés* in 1894 and becoming a well-known author and playwright, he had launched the first great indoor bicycle stadium in France: the Vélodrome de Buffalo, built on the site once occupied by Buffalo Bill's circus. More revealing still is the career of Charles-Louis Baudry de Saunier. Born in 1865, he broke off his law studies to found a literary review, *Le Roquet,* for which Willy and Jules Renard occasionally wrote. Toward 1890 Baudry took up cycling and published four books about it, culminating in *L'Art de bien monter la bicyclette* (Paris, 1894). Then, around 1897, following the trend of fashionable taste, he abandoned the bicycle for the automobile, producing a number of guides on driving before he became editor of the *Revue du Touring Club de France*.

Devoid of these modish and opportunist aspects, closer to the idealism of Jean Barois, were men like Coubertin, or another disciple of Le Play, Albert de Mun, whose major endeavor was moral and political. It is not irrelevant that Coubertin's activities were made possible only by a private fortune that it took a war and forty years of spending to exhaust, and by social relations that facilitated initiatives impossible to less well-connected zealots. But such explanations do not go far enough. These circumstances made his undertakings possible; they did not preside over their conception, which stemmed from the reactions that more generalized conditions roused in his particular temperament.

Looked at in the perspective of the fin de siècle, Coubertin's dream reflects the romantic elitism of a nineteenth-century aristocrat fascinated by Darwin, by Taine, above all by Dr. Arnold; the Arnold beside whose tomb he sought inspiration on several occasions, the Arnold who wanted to instil in his Rugby charges religious and moral principles; the behavior of a gentleman; intellectual aptitudes. In that order.

The good thing about such traditionalism was that it enabled Coubertin to claim that he was a nonconformist—and to do it with absolute sincerity. There is a familiar sound about his closing words to the international congress which he persuaded to endorse the principle of reviving the Olympic Games. The Congress had been called in 1894 by the U.S.F.S.A. (General Secretary Pierre de Coubertin) "to study and propagate the principles of amateurism." A vast and elegant public, seventy-nine delegates from thirteen countries including the United States, ministers, academicians, luminaries of the university, the Church, and the *gratin,* presided over by Baron Chodron de Courcel, sometime French ambassador in Berlin and now in London. It had been held—as many functions Coubertin sponsored were to be held—in the great aula of the Sorbonne, among the potted palms, the recitals of music and poetry, and the frescoes of Puvis de Chavannes, that guaranteed the respectability of athletics. "Those of the old school," Coubertin told his hearers who came from nowhere else, "have lamented our holding our assizes right here in the Sorbonne. They have realized that we are rebels, and that we shall end by overthrowing the worm-eaten structure of their philosophy. And that is true, gentlemen, we are rebels."

There is no evidence of opposition to the congress or of criticism of its doings. The president of the republic smiled upon it, the Academy of Paris welcomed it. Its sessions did not threaten the established order, did not quarrel with the republic, did not criticize the rising democracy. But the feeling of nonconformity lent it a special sense of virtue and the vigor that rebels enjoy even when they are rebellious in name only. Coubertin's nearest approach to nonconformity at this time was his emphasis on the pacific and internationalist character of his enterprises, as when he advocated the reestablishment of Olympic Games as "the best of internationalism," and argued that the best battleground for universal youth was the playground.[20] But such views themselves were the views of his peers and odd only in the respect that Coubertin had jettisoned the legitimism and clericalism of the conservative tradition in which he had been born, retaining only the internationalist and pacifist aspects along with the code of honor.

Yet convention deprived of some of its familiar aspects can look unconventional. Tadpoles without tails look very different. Coubertin meant what he said, and that mattered.

To the current elitism of the contemporary upper classes Coubertin opposed another brand of elitism, more in tune with the times because more activist, more competitive, and also, at least apparently, more open and accessible.[21] Competitive games reflected a society which stressed competition in most fields. England, first to accept the competitive principle in economic life, first to introduce it in the recruitment of its bureaucracy, was also the first to idealize it in sport, to edulcorate it with notions of sportsmanship and fair play, to turn it into a social convention. Other modern societies had to follow suit or face grave risks. Rastignac's apostrophe to Paris: "Et maintenant, à nous deux!" is that of a player about to enter the ring, but a player determined to win, whatever the means, whatever the effect on the game, on the rules, or on others. Rastignac is the professional champion, for whom the games is a means, not an end, and the values he represents (or accepts) are precisely those that Coubertin and his friends wished to counteract. The games they sponsored were meant to provide such satisfactions that the end of play would be not its justification but merely its final point.

A society where competition ruled in business, elections, examinations and *concours,* where winning at any price appeared essential but where the dice were too often loaded, discovered a mitigating factor in the regulated competition of sports. Aleatory in the real world, the rewards of effort and merit were codified and (almost) assured in the reconstituted world of track and field, where ideal, sheltered conditions permitted official values to be honored in the observance rather than the breach. And, lest even these conditions were too hard to bear, the proviso was added in a famous address to the participants in the London Olympic Games of 1908, that "it is less important to win than to take part." A sentiment more memorably worded in Grantland Rice's verse:

> For when the one Great Scorer comes
> To write against your name,
> He marks—not that you won or lost—
> But how you played the game.

Good, aristocratic injunctions which, if heeded, would take some of the pressure off contemporary society. Reminiscent of Knut Rockne's remark, "After the church, football's the best thing we've got."

As it happened, the leading personalities of the sporting world insisted on keeping sport out of politics, and political issues out of sporting life.

"All political or religious discussions are rigorously forbidden," declare the Statutes of the Ligue Girondine de l'Education Physique, drawn up in 1889: "Furthermore, the League forbids itself any political or religious activity." Athletics, another art for art's sake, could provide activity without action: an excellent refuge for a certain kind of internal emigration that today we describe as nonparticipation.

This cautious and conservative point of view found concrete expression when, at the height of the Dreyfus affair, *Le Vélo,* France's only sporting daily, blotted its copybook by showing too much sympathy for the condemned officer. To preserve the basic principles of apolitism, a group of wealthy "industrialists and sportsmen," including the Comte de Dion, Baron de Zuylen de Nyevelt (president of the Automobile Club de France), the Comte de Chasseloup-Laubat, Edouard Michelin, Adolphe Clément (great bicycle manufacturer and French distributor of Dunlop tyres), subsidized the publication of a rival daily, *L'Auto-Vélo,* whose first number appeared in October 1900.

While *L'Auto's* editor, Henri Desgranges, was a sporting enthusiast with no apparent political ideas, his backer's political neutrality was clearly inflected toward the right. The Michelins had already acquired the authoritarian reputation they retain today; Chasseloup-Laubat's army connections made him an early and pugnacious anti-Dreyfusard; while Dion, even more notorious for his reactionary views than for the automobiles he built, had got himself arrested at Longchamps for his part in the anti-Dreyfusard demonstrations of 4 June 1899 against President Loubet. Like certain dinner tables, athletic activities were to constitute that privileged domain which, providing its own end, would prosper best by excluding the potentially disintegrating influences of the outside world. As Thomas Arnold once wrote to a friend, "The state of public affairs is not inviting, and I rejoice that we take in no daily paper."[22]

While noting the political possibilities that such "sportsmanship" held out, it is necessary to absolve Coubertin from all but the most Arnoldian of its motivations. One might go further and credit him with a perceptiveness that went beyond reaction, convention, or tradition. It is a commonplace to say that the long spell of European peace that ran (for France) from 1871 to 1914, was highly unusual. It is almost equally commonplace to note that, in the twenty or thirty years before the First World War, the most vocal advocates of pacifism were Socialists, Marxists, and working-class groups which proposed an alternative to foreign was in internal class warfare, replacing international by civil conflicts. One wonders in this context whether the experience of a prolonged period of peace was not in some ways unnatural and, practically speaking, uneasy—most especially for that group, a small minority but strategically placed and highly articulate, whose incomes or whose parents' incomes protected them from struggles and left them a great deal of leisure and energy to spare.

Written in the wake of the Second World War, a suggestive essay by John Bowditch argued that Bergson's *élan vital* was a rationalization of national weakness, a kind of contemporary myth.[23] The argument might perhaps be reversed, treating Bergson's notion as the expression of an over-flowing vitality around him, quite literally around him in his own social class and among the students he taught: a superabundance of unused energy, producing a will-to-action that burst out in the political struggles of the fin de siècle as in the literary and artistic movements of the time. Like nationalism, Fauvism, Cubism, and Futurism were all expressions of this unexpended energy, which also led to an increase in youthful violence and rebellion, and which a number of contemporary observers connected with the sheer need to blow off steam somehow, steam that could be jettisoned, in the course of play especially, by people to whom few other forms of effort were normally open.

"The glories of our generation are unquestionably André, Bouin, and Carpentier," declares the athletic hero of Jules Jolinon's *Joueur de balle*.[24] "Small glory, you will say. Is there any other at our age? Are we permitted any success in art, in politics, in science? Do not old men seize on all the openings, close every issue, cling to every last seat? Is it not decreed that we are worth nothing before our thighs have withered? Is it not settled that youth has no other talents than muscular ones?"

As long as one bears in mind Jean Giraudoux's friendly remark that a sporting life is a heroic life in a vacuum, there is no contesting the liberating effect of competitive games on those who play them. What the schools of the bourgeoisie offered at this time was disinterested culture, as remote as possible from practical, utilitarian education, designed rather to differentiate its beneficiaries from the unprivileged masses than to train them for life. The games Coubertin promoted fitted this nonutilitarian schema, yet permitted the manifestation of personal merit in activities that were simple and whose ends were clear. They encouraged self-affirmation but at the expense of no particular interest, transferred the principles of free enterprise to a collective plane, reconciled individualism and social spirit, all on an innocuous level even more separated from the surrounding world than the elite circles and institutions from which they drew recruits.

However, like the education that lycées and universities imparted, games scarcely trained for life. The liberation they provided seldom went beyond conventional limits. Reminiscing in 1918 about his rugby-playing days as a lycéen, Pierre MacOrlan remembered the watching girls and "their confused feeling that the young men in their English-style gear were no longer, at least for eighty minutes, under the control of their parents. Girls, even bourgeois girls, have an inclination for those who can reach a freedom to which they do not themselves aspire." Freedoms such as these were just what a bourgeois doctor would have ordered. Offering a reality-substitute for a minority of the ruling minority, they added yet one more abstraction to the abstractions in which French education and public life already revelled. As Barrès once said of his own life, they provided "not a race towards some goal, but a flight towards elsewhere."

From a way of broadening and cleansing the lives of men, Coubertin's dream turned into an escape from real life, a provision for social adjustment, and, eventually, a gain-producing activity. The forces it had been designed to foil assimilated it. The ulterior motives which first inspired state sponsorship of physical education in the schools came to justify a similar adoption of organized games, mitigated only by continuingly scarce resources. By 1933, Huizinga's commencement address at the University of Leyden referred to sport as a sterile function which had quite discarded the ludic factor. The easy freedom of earlier days, with their fantasies and improvisations, had been left behind. In the new era, declared an expert, one no longer had the right to fun. The new ideal now was to improve men's productivity.[25]

As for Coubertin, his greatest successes were obtained beyond the borders of the country he had hoped to rejuvenate. The Olympic Games themselves, whose international committee he presided over until 1925, were a dubious success when matched against his ideals of peace, international understanding, amateurism, and an aristocracy of merit. The French took to Olympics very slowly. The Games of 1900, meant to be held in Paris in the context of the Universal Exhibition of that year, foundered before the antagonisms of rival or unsympathetic cliques. For the only time since 1896, the Games turned into a mere series of athletic events, symbolically presided over by the president of the Union des Sociétés de Tir. This was to be atoned for in 1924, when the eighth games were actually held in Paris, leaving their mark on men like Montherlant, and on the city which still retains the Olympic Stadium at Colombes. Yet French youth, whom Coubertin had set out to *rebronzer,* would not begin to get brown in the air and sun until after the Second World War. The French masses, appreciative enough of spectator sports, scarcely took part in them until after the social laws of 1936.

The question must be asked why the sporting activities and, above all, the sporting spirit that Coubertin so valued, failed to catch on in France beyond restricted circles. But any answers, at this stage, can be only tentative and superficial.

In nineteenth-century England, the practice of sports had become a didactic method of social integration. It was deliberately used to inculcate a particular set of socially approved attitudes, first in the schools of the ruling minority, then at all accessible levels of the public. The values which sports helped to generalize were widely accepted. In a deferential society, not riven by profound ideological conflicts, they colored the language and the behavior not of particular groups but of the nation. At the most obvious level, notions derived from games, sports, and athletics—sporting behavior, fair play, respect for the rules of the game—became part of the English character, as the English conceived it and as outsiders perceived it.

French conditions rendered such developments impossible. Like Arnold's, Coubertin's had begun as a private, isolated, didactic initiative. Like Arnold, Coubertin directed his appeal to the young of the ruling elite. But in France this elite did not exist unchallenged and admired. Social emulation had given way to political competition. The dominant ideology was not one of reconciliation but of struggle. The educated minority was divided by political, social, and religious differences. Success in one quarter caused hostility in others, support by one faction sparked off the criticism of another.

A professedly elitist and aristocratic enterprise like Coubertin's could hardly elicit the support of political opponents. Grousset's opposition illustrates this fundamental breach. The social background of the first sportsmen and of their supporters seemed to justify suspicion, and their ideology confirmed it. Political neutrality was already associated with conservatism. In any case, what they had to offer had no wide appeal. Few ambitious *bourgeois* of the Third Republic aspired to be *gentilhommes*. They sent their sons to school not to become Christian Gentlemen but to pass examinations; the competition they envisaged conformed to rules other than those of sportsmanship. In such conditions, athletic sports were condemned to social insignificance;[26] surrogates for the energies of the favoured few, irrelevant luxuries to many, they might eventually furnish spectacles for the popular masses. Their moral overtones, alien to the needs and conceptions of the Republic's rulers, were soon left aside.

Little wonder, then, that like most prophets, Coubertin reaped little honor in his country. When he died in 1937, he must have been one of few Frenchmen left undecorated. His fortune had been spent on his work, lost in the war and subsequent depressions. He was poor. In 1935, at seventy-two, he had looked for a paying job and failed. His house in the rue Oudinot, where he had been born and married, had to be sold in 1918; the family château at Mirville was abandoned in 1930. In the last years of his life he lived in hotels, and in an apartment placed at his disposal in the headquarters of the Olympic Institution at Lausanne. That is where he died at the age of seventy-four, a few weeks after Lausanne had elected him an Honorary Citizen. The citation referred to "the disinterested and magnificent initiatives which have contributed to developing, throughout the entire world, the influence and renown of the generous ideas appertaining to the French spirit." The generosity of the French spirit did not extend to remembrance.

It was later, in 1964, that steps were taken to commemorate the fiftieth anniversary of the reestablishment of the Olympic Games, and also the hundredth anniversary of Coubertin's birth. There were ceremonies, speeches, and a plaque was placed in the aula of the Sorbonne where, in 1894, Coubertin had won his greatest victory. Paris and a number of French cities named streets, squares, and stadiums after Coubertin. But Coubertin was dead.

~ 11

Inheritance, Dilettantism, and the Politics of Maurice Barrès

In his *Journal 1950,* Julien Green records the story of the French writer at Oxford giving a lecture on Maurice Barrès. "There are three Barrèses," he says: "The Barrès of the *Jardin sur l'Oronte,* the Barrès of (I've forgotten which one), and the Barrès of Charmes." At the end of the lecture, a student inquires: "Could you give me the Christian names of Barrès's two brothers?"

Si non e vero . . . at least the anecdote suggests both the widespread ignorance of Barrès these days,[1] and his diversity.

The life of Maurice Barrès (1862–1923) reflected most of the major trends of the Third Republic: the spirit of *revanche;* the populist explosion of Boulangism on whose surge Barrès became, at twenty-seven, the youngest deputy in the French Chamber; the Dreyfus affair in which he was a leading protagonist of the anti-Dreyfusard camp;[2] the rise of a modern, radical and social nationalism, which he was the first to formulate,[3] and the *bourrage de crâne* (brainwashing) of the First World War, in which he played a prominent part. On the literary plane, meanwhile, Barrès's *culte du moi* was one of the great influences of the fin-de-siècle. Though (or because) the rebellious individualism of his beginnings eventually turned into organic collectivism, Barrès (elected to the Académie française in 1906) remained until the eve of 1914 one of the great "modern" writers; not only in French eyes, but also in the opinion of the rest of Francophone Europe. Louis Aragon admired *Les Déracinés* as the first modern political novel, nationalist predecessor to socialist realism. Paul Léautaud, who detested his politics, still found him the greatest writer of his day.[4] His works molded the sensibilities of two generations, including such widely differing figures as Maurras and Mauriac, Malraux and Jouhandeau, Montherlant and Drieu la Rochelle. Finally, in a fitting paradox, the first man to formulate a proto-surrealist rebellion in the 1880s (Jacques-Emile Blanche refers to his "dadaïsme avant la lettre . . .") would be condemned "for treason" in a notorious surrealist "trial" in 1921. Barrès had predicted this in an ironic essay of 1890 where the man of letters was fated to end "definitely spurned by the young men of letters who would appear thirty-five years hence, and whose self would differ from his own self." [5]

Multiplicity, or contradiction? Barrès's nationalism and his exoticism are easily reconciled. There is no necessary contradiction between the inventor of fin-de-siècle nationalism and the romantic lover of Venice, Toledo, and the Jardin sur l'Oronte. But other incongruities remain. We see the *prince de la jeunesse* of the 1890s, leader of the moment's generational revolt, becoming a symbol of reaction twenty—even ten—years later. We see the "anarchist" writer whom Fernand Pelloutier met in 1893 when he arrived in Paris, and to whose *Cocarde* he contributed in 1894–95, choosing the part of "order" in the Dreyfus affair, [6] even though the founder of French syndicalism continued to respect him thereafter. And we see the detached ironist, whose life is a spectator sport, turning to commitment. [7] Above all, though, we see the supreme, persistent egoist in whom others, from Pelloutier to Jérome Tharaud, could recognize themselves. "He was only interested in himself," remembers Tharaud, "he only talked about himself. And himself was ourselves." [8] How could this individualist invent and formulate the collectivist nationalism with which we associate him? How can we reconcile the young Barrès, passionate and progressive, with the reactionary image that most recall today? I suggest that Tharaud's remark provides us with a clue.

The *nous-mêmes* of Jean and Jérome Tharaud were *lycéens:* students from the Collège Sainte-Barbe and the Lycée Louis-le-Grand, attending a Thursday afternoon lecture by Barrès at the Odéon, a lecture that was supposed to be about *Tartuffe,* which Barrès opened with the words "Ignace de Loyola était un de ces rastaquouères [dubious adventurers] comme on en voit au Café de la Paix" and which continued in this vein to the delight of the assembled *potaches.* Not one word uttered about the ignoble machinations Molière had etched, nor of Tartuffe himself, only about the noble hidalgo and his methods for creating in oneself and at one's will the highest spiritual developments. It sounds like fun, and also like the sort of prank that made Barrès so popular with the young.

But who were these young? At the time of the lecture Tharaud recollects, that is in 1890, [9] there were in France about 2,300,000 boys between eleven and seventeen. Less than 60,000 of these—2.59 percent—attended a lycée or a college. They had been fewer still twenty years before, when Barrès attended first the Collège de la Malgrange, then the Lycée de Nancy from which he graduated in 1880. [10] But they would be hardly more numerous on the eve of the First World War. Here was a small, privileged elite, offspring of a privileged elite, trained to continue as the same:

rulers-to-be, set apart by their education and by the private means their parents and they themselves enjoyed.

These were the sons of lawyers, doctors, industrialists, property owners and civil servants, above all of that extraordinary group so numerous in the late nineteenth century: *rentiers*. In 1880, for example, among the boys in Paris lycées, precisely one third of the parents gave their profession simply as *rentier*.[11] We tend to think of *rentiers* as retired people, which is quite true. It is useful to remember their prevalence and their relative youth. When money retained its value and inflation scarcely counted, it was not difficult to save and to plan ahead. A striking number of men retired from business, trade, army or professions at an early age, during their forties, to live off savings or an inheritance. A sound observer of small-town life before 1914 found one of its most striking aspects in the large number of young people "qui sont déjà retirés des affaires."[12] Many, however, never seem to have faced regular work at all. They managed the family property, which generally occupied a few hours every week or month to collect rents on farms or urban real estate; and they struggled against boredom as best they could. Barrès's father appears to belong to this class; the son of an army officer who had married into a solid Lorrainer bourgeois clan and settled at Charmes when he retired, aged forty-nine. Auguste Barrès studied engineering at the Ecole Centrale, married (at twenty-one) the daughter of his home town mayor, and lived over seventy years leaving no evidence of any steady work, only of comfortable circumstances.[13] Whatever the formal training of such men, their chief profession was simply to inherit. Such were the *nous-mêmes* whom Barrès addressed at the Odéon.

These lycéens and their parents, two or three percent of their generation, were the ruling class or, at the least, its nursery. No civil servant and scarcely a member of Parliament lacked the *baccalauréat*. When, just before the first World War, Robert de Jouvenel satirized *La République des camarades*, he was talking about a fraternity that had grown up on the benches and in the yards of lycées. The program and degrees of secondary education built the fortifications of the bourgeoisie: barriers that kept out unqualified candidates to power, levels that forged a community transcending minor ideological differences. Thus when, around 1908 and 1909, royalist Camelots, and red agitators met in prison, they could fraternize in part at least because of their similar backgrounds. Victor Méric, an extreme left-wing Socialist, had long conversations in jail with Maurice Pujo, and no degree of sarcasm can hide his appreciation of Maurras's intellect. Méric's father had been senator of the Var, his grandfather a republican notable: he belonged to the aristocracy of the Republic. He could afford to be a red. Pujo, for his part, remarked in the *Action française* on this similar culture that made all the difference, so that "however opposed we might be on political matters, we could often agree on others."[14] In the same way, Tharaud remembered Barrès's appreciation of Jean Jaurès and attributed it vaguely to many reasons, of which the only ones he specified were "the manners, the politeness, of a man from the upper-middle class. Despite all that separated them, they faced one another as two men of the same class." *Classe,* of course, referred to quality. But one cannot help feeling that class alone would count as much.[15]

The general situation would not change until after World War I. Exceptions to it were so rare as to have little impact. Apart from a small number of socialist deputies, the exceptional cases consisted largely of scholarship boys sufficiently few to be easily digested, like Péguy, Herriot, or that Burdeau pursued by Barrès's ire. And we shall shortly see that Barrès's rage against his onetime professor of philosophy, the scholarship boy who became a cabinet minister, was not unconnected with Burdeau's ascension. Meanwhile, it is quite clear that we are talking about a ruling class.

Barrès was a typical member of this class, a spokesman for several generations of *héritiers,* a representative figure of a privileged time for privileged people—specifically, the years of economic stagnation (or depression, depending whom you read) that run roughly from 1880 to 1905, when prices fell, fixed incomes rose, and dilettantism rose with them. Lack of economic opportunity strengthened a natural distaste for work. Young men who in earlier times might have entered some sort of career, now made haste more slowly. I have suggested that the number of secondary students grew little or not at all between 1880 and 1914. In effect, their number *decreased* from 73,200 in 1881 to 69,200 in 1913. Yet during that same period, the number of *University* students quadrupled.[16] Once again, absolute numbers remain quite small. But, where the faculties of the 1870s numbered less than ten thousand members, by 1914 the count has risen above 42,000, most of them in letters and in law, the classic refuge of those who don't know what they want to do and don't want to do much about it.

Numerically and in terms of status a new sub-class appears within the bourgeoisie: eighteen to twenty-five-year-olds, doing nothing in particular, but distinguished by a common status—that of student. Given this alibi, or that of paid or unpaid sinecures, or none at all, young men of independent means sketched the first outlines of a youth culture whose chief characteristic, then as now, would be freedom from necessity.

In a general sense, this freedom marks the fin-de-siècle. When we look back on its works, we see necessity—in the shape of familiar restraints, formal or material—repudiated, neglected, or ignored. Where the traditional bourgeois felt they had to keep up appearances, their offspring now insisted that one must create them. I do not refer to works that may be most characteristic, but to those that are today considered the great expressions of its art and thought. It is not the massive Zola that we remember, with the ponderous unfolding of his determinisms, but the more fragile worlds of Huysmans and Mallarmé; not the tangible Taine but the buoyant Bergson; not the academicisms of Detaille or Bonnat but the eccentricities of Gustave Moreau. Oddly enough, it is the products of affluence that we recall: refractory to constraint, stressing unsubstantial, immaterial things in a coarse, substantial age, suggesting gratuitous and voluntaristic acts against the stringencies of matter or of reason, affirming subjectivism over positivism, and the decadence sensed by a few over the progress that many rejoiced in.

There is a discrepancy about the fin-de-siècle (or in our history of it), and it rests in the contradictions that I just pointed out. I am convinced that, on the whole and for most people, this was a busy, optimistic age. A recent study of prize-giving speeches that mirror prevalent values well show them to have been sanguine and convinced of progress. The poorer classes had reason to think that things were getting better. Not that they were satisfied, but conditions *were* improving, many could feel it, and even the new political and syndical organizations voiced not despair but hope. Where, then, does all the talk about despair come from, and decadence, and dismay?

It comes from the representatives of this privileged group, who took their impatience for despair, their boredom for suffering, and the conformism of family and provincial life for decadence. It comes from young men like Barrès, eager to escape inactivity and routine restrictions; hungry for action, for emotion and fame, for something to do, for a foothold in the real world. It finds an echo among his fellows—*lycéens, collégiens, étudiants,* to whom his earliest works were dedicated, and among others who were or wanted to be like them. Here were a growing number of physically mature but socially irresponsible persons, fated to suspended animation. Free from material pressures, deprived of the excitement, however petty, of getting on, these young are bored and listless. Their values are not those of the working crowd. *Elan,* for instance (dash? enthusiasm?), matters more than sense. Feelings, the more intense the better, are precious, even when they hurt. Happiness is rather gross, and success seldom worth the price it calls for. Like Sturel in *Les Déracinés,* one might "desire a thousand things" but not wish "to yield to the conditions they impose." After all, what could the effort bring?

One could speculatively describe two contrasting cultures, representing Necessity and Anti-Necessity: the one marked by realism, rationalism, logic, the emphasis of form over content, stability, and utilitarianism; the other by fantasy, sensibility, subjectivism, emphasis of content over form, gratuitousness, and art (for action) for its own sake. One or the other will dominate a given social group or a particular time. Anti-necessity goes with aristocratic pretensions, with a certain fading of energies or of the will, with uncertainty of social purpose, with leisure and experimentalism. It also goes with the means that suggest or make them possible. This is quite clear in the first book Barrès published. "Your masters, their books, and their long-winded speculations," a philosopher tells the hero of *Sous l'oeil des Barbares*, "gave you an excellent vision, a world from which the idea of duty (effort, devotion) is absent—except as voluptuous refinement . . . [The world] is an orchard where you have only to satisfy yourself, quite frankly, by a thousand gymnastics (I assume you have health and some *rentes*)."[17]

Health, by all means; but, above all, *rentes:* here is the formula of fin-de-siècle privilege. Without it, in one form or another, no education, no calling, no career. The heroes of Roger Shattuck's *Banquet Years* (even Jarry, even the Douanier Rousseau) had all enjoyed either a secondary or a private education. The political careers of the time were launched by private money. In 1879 Benjamin Clemenceau sold one of his farms so that his son could buy his own newspaper, *La Justice.* Déroulède pulled the strings of a restive Ligue des Patriotes as he did its purse-strings, which were his own. A respectable Nantes lawyer, Waldeck-Rousseau, became a successful politician and prime minister by dint of his wife's inheritance. Charles Péguy founded his bookshop with his wife's dowry. Lucien Herr, librarian of the Ecole Normale and gray eminence of socialism, used his inheritance to save Péguy from bankruptcy. Marc Sangnier's *Sillon* was a private enterprise, like the *Revue blanche,* like *L'Humanité,* and scores of others. In November 1884, Barrès's own *Taches d'encre,* described itself as a *brochure de luxe.* "Printed with selected type on a paper that the most successful novelists of our day could envy," remembers a friend,[18] it scorned the common herd, set its cap at a select elite ("nous autres, désouevrés et amis de la littérature"), and proclaimed the one-man staff's "revolt against necessity."[19]

There wasn't much necessity to revolt against, hence the possibility of revolt. Hence also, at least in part, its motive: a fat boy's misery, as Barrès himself explained when he looked back on the completed statement of his *culte du moi:* "The problem of the modern young man is lack of energy; not finding anything that will interest him."[20] Solution: let him learn to know himself, to be himself.

What is he? Well, he is, first of all, a man who knows the value of money. This is a different bourgeoisie from its predecessor of the early nineteenth century, which had had to ape the aristocracy and pretend that money did not matter (one pretense few nobles bothered with). When

Sainte-Beuve wrote his *Lundis,* on the eve of the Second Empire, he indicated the bad taste of Fontenelle because the philosopher had referred to money as a source of social wisdom. Then came Offenbach's Empire, and Haussmann's, and the open admission that money counts and could, indeed, be counted. The bourgeois manners did not change, but the great Naturalists had cleared the way, and a young ironist could now permit himself to articulate their solid base—and his own.

There is in *L'Ennemi des lois* (1893) a reference to a child "qui avait connu la désillusion des mains pleines." Perhaps Barrès was the first, or one of the first, novelists of affluence. Perhaps emancipation from necessity was still new enough to warrant notice. At any rate, Barrès did not ignore its prime condition: in order to be free, to be yourself, to flee from the barbarian others *and* escape them, a man needed money. "Ayez de l'argent et soyez considéré," he had insisted in 1885.[21] *Un homme libre* (1889), written during his Boulangist campaign at Nancy, is unequivocal: "For without money, how to develop one's imagination? Without money, no more *homme libre.*" On the other hand, "given some alcohol and red meat at one's meals, and money in one's pockets, one can endure all contacts."[22]

Better still, of course, avoid them. With 14,000 *francs de rente,* eight or ten times the salary of an *instituteur,* Philippe and Simon, the two friends in the book, buy a remote country house where they can meditate in peace; to avoid base thoughts, ordinary chairs are banished from their retreat for "no thinker ever combined anything respectable outside an armchair."[23] Not only a room of one's own, as Virginia Woolf demanded, but a comfortable one as well. After all, "what would be the use of having read so many volumes at 7fr 50, in order to love (or think) like everybody else?"[24] The conclusion is obvious. And the last novel of the trilogy, *Le Jardin de Bérénice* (1891), closes with the hero, Philippe, soliciting the concession of a suburban race course, because the only refuge from the world lies in "solid material independence . . . Money, there is the haven for spirits concerned with the inner life."[25]

But haven from what? Who were the barbarians whom Philippe fled? In one sense, everybody other than oneself: "Qu'on le classe vulgaire ou d'élite, chacun, hors moi, n'est qu'un barbare."[26] But this intransigent formula has to be qualified.

Barrès—at least the one who created Philippe—was a Socialist. What does this mean? It means that his search for self-affirmation, action, social criticism, his combativity and his opposition to established order, led him into the camp first of General Boulanger, then of a socialism much less precise and less homogeneous than we have come to think of it. Louis Madelin, the historian who knew the young Barrès in the days of Boulangism, remembered that his ideas were vague but his need to act and fight was real.[27] Barrès himself remembered Boulangism as "a tumult and a fever." When the tumult subsided, Barrès found himself among the score of left-wing Boulangists washed up in the Chamber.

With Boulanger in exile on the island of Jersey, the men who, like Barrès, had called themselves "Revisionists" now became "Socialist Revisionists." For us, declared Barrès in an ambiguous phrase, "our Jersey is Socialism."[28] Did this mean that, for him, socialism was exile and defeat? Hardly. The equivocal drift of Boulangism, navigating uneasily between right and left, had been resolved by defeat. Barrès and his fellow-survivors were clear about what to do. Before the end of 1889, Barrès pushed his electoral committee at Nancy toward "the great task of socialist reform."[29] *Elu des ouvriers* against the opportunit establishment of Nancy, by popular votes that came indeed mostly from artisans, industrial workers, and the young,[30] he spent his first parliamentary term (1889–1893) collaborating closely with the Socialists, and eventually running for re-election as a Socialist (and losing). Friends and enemies identified him as a Socialist: thus, Charles Maurras who wrote to him in December 1896 about "la conduite donnée à votre parti par les Millerand et les Jaurès."[31] In Parliament, he opposed indirect taxes—"l'impôt sans justice"—supported old age pensions, limitation of daytime working hours for women and children and elimination of night work, credits for striking miners, amnesty for socialist and syndicalist militants; and he called for state socialism, inspired by German social legislation.[32]

There was little fundamental difference between Barrès—*frondeur*, elitist, populist, concerned with social justice and reform—and most other Socialists in the Chamber: some also elitist in the tradition of Blanqui or Guesde; also reformist in most cases; also regionalist, because municipal socialism was paying off; also patriotic and "national" in the Jacobin vein,[33] and also in many cases strongly antisemitic.

Barrès himself was only a moderate antisemite, especially when compared with the acute antisemitism of many Blanquists and of the *Revue socialiste* (not to speak of baying Christian Democrats and Social Catholics!).[34] Most important, he saw very clearly that, when the crowds howled against the Jews, "it is 'Down with social inequalities!' they really mean. What do they care about the 80,000 Jews of France? All their ire runs against the formidable organization of capital that dominates them . . . State socialism is the indispensable corrective to the anti-Jewish formula. It gives us a beautiful dream."[35] Obviously, antisemitism was no driving force for Maurice Barrès, though few Lorrainers could be really free of prejudices so deeply rooted in the small towns and in the countryside of eastern France.

One is inclined to think that, without the Dreyfus affair, Barrès's career might well have taken a different turning. But the decision that shocked Léon Blum has to be explained. It was not antisemitism that made Barrès an anti-Dreyfusard. Antisemitism had not kept him from consorting very closely with Blum and the *Revue blanche* group before 1897 (and it did not keep hitherto antisemitic Socialists out of the Dreyfus camp). Barrès's patriotism could have carried him against the party of order as easily as toward it, as Blum obviously expected and as would have been in accord with Barrès's earlier adventures. The decision, it seems, was hardly one of principle. I believe that the Dreyfus affair simply precipitated a prior disaffection the roots of which lie in the Neuilly-Boulogne elections of 1896.

Barrès had run for election in the oddly assorted constituency of Neuilly-Boulogne in 1893,[36] and had enjoyed the support of his socialist friends, notably Jean Jaurès, whose doctoral dissertation (completed in January 1893) he had just praised with great enthusiasm. He was defeated, but he tried again in 1896. This time he found himself opposed by a rival middle-class Socialist, Louis Sautumier, a livelier and younger man who enjoyed the support of the parliamentary Union socialiste. There was little ideology and much intrigue about the Sautumier affair. Its convolutions, as fascinating as they are unedifying, would lead far from my argument. More to the point, the Socialists of the *Petite République* backed Sautumier, not for ideological, but for financial reasons. Between 1894 and 1896, Sautumier had become the financial mainstay of Independent Socialists: "All the candidates of the *Petite République* revolve around the rich deputy," reads one police report in March 1896. "Tout le monde l'avait tapé," remarks another in November. The *Petite République,* like other socialist publications in financial straits and socialist candidates seeking aid in municipal elections as far as Le Havre, all relied on his support. Were they short of funds? "Bah! M. Sautumier payera encore."[37]

Barrès, who had married a rich young woman in 1891,[38] and who would henceforth be independently wealthy, could (or would) not compete on such terms. When Sautumier won, Barrès deeply resented what he regarded as the desertion of his onetime friends. This was compounded later the same year when the twenty-seven-year-old Sautumier committed suicide, and when no suggestion followed that perhaps Barrès might try again, this time with socialist support. It is true that Sautumier's secretary did suggest that Barrès might take up his succession, and Barrès briefly announced his candidacy in December, but he soon stood down, on learning that the *Petite République* would not support him. Another socialist candidate ran in his place and lost.

Barrès remarks somewhere in *Les Déracinés* that the only things men never forgive are personal slights. This was one such case; and the grievance rankled. In November and December 1896, his *Cahiers* assumed a somber tone; the bitterness against Jaurès is evident. A year later he still remembered his "betrayal."[39] One may imagine that, when Blum appeared in December 1897 and asked him to take sides, Barrès chose the friends that had not let him down, men like Déroulède and like Rochefort, whose *Intransigeant* had supported him throughout, over those who had failed him.

No one could then know that a squabble over alleged legal irregularities would become *the* Affair. In December 1897 it was still only "cette irritante affaire qui nous divise."[40] But, as it developed and as tempers rose, Barrès could once more enjoy the passionate atmosphere, flush with the heat of battle. It is interesting to note, nevertheless, that in 1898 he returned to Nancy to run on a platform of "Nationalism, Protectionism, and Socialism," only to be defeated by an extreme antisemitic candidate. His successful opponent, running under a moderate label, and supported by the clergy, garnered the votes of the moderate bourgeoisie. Barrès got mostly the working-class votes of Nancy-Est.

By this time, after the publication of Zola's *J'Accuse* (January 1898), nationalism and socialism had become hard to hold in harness. Barrès dropped the socialist component of his troika and henceforth stressed protection—an issue close to the hearts of industrial workers who were threatened by cheap foreign labor, especially at Nancy, so near to Germany and Belgium; an issue that matched a wider protectionist mood: rural, industrial, and social too. J. E. C. Bodley, writing in the same year 1898, quoted the remark of the economist, Frédéric Bastiat, that protectionists are Socialists who have 50,000 francs in *rentes*. The rapprochement is suggestive, and wickedly so for Barrès, whom marriage had promoted from solid comfort to riches. Yet we have to remember that Barrès was for labor protectionism, demanding for workers and peasants the advantages enjoyed by big business and farming enterprises, and seeking to protect his working-class electorate from the competition of foreign labor imported by employers to break strikes and lower pay-scales: a protectionism many Socialists did not disavow.

At any rate, whether advocated by Jules Méline, another easterner, whose name remains associated with the protective tariffs of 1893, or by Barrès, French nationalism would henceforth appear defensive, like the attitude of the class that spawned it. Raoul Girardet has categorized this nationalism, which Barrès would articulate at the height of the Affair and which would survive at least until Vichy, as right-wing and conservative (contrasted to its Jacobin predecessors) that turns out to be largely "a meditation upon a decadence."[41] The formulation is striking; but it deserves to be qualified.

First, it is well to remember the antecedents of this turn-of-the-century nationalism: the Parti National of the Boulangist left, its radical sources, its socialist connections. Then, even if the socialism of the 1890s is dropped from the label, the populist, collectivist, anticapitalist and antiliberal inspirations remain in the formula and, I think, in the mentality. Such aspects of nationalism would revive not only in the young Action Française of the prewar days, *ouvrieriste,* Proudhonian, and sympathetic to Georges Sorel; but also in the *non-conformistes des années trente,* who aimed to transcend traditional oppositions and fuse (or de-fuse) the factions in a new order of things; and in the social leanings of the Gaullist left, which was regionalist and as eager for social and industrial integration as for social peace. Lastly, while nationalism has become associated with conservatism (at least in France, though hardly in the Third World), I find Girardet's description of it as conservative to be misleading. Nostalgic seems to me a better word, and one that illuminates its origins as well. For a nostalgia for things past was just as much a part of fin-de-siècle socialism, as it might have been of reactionary movements. About the socialist and syndicalist workers he had known before 1914 (and we should remember just how few they were), an old working man recalls: "their confused dream carried them less towards the founding of a new world than to a return to forms of life they had known or heard tell about; and, the years and distance blurring the bad aspects, made the past appear a new Icaria."[42]

Thus the inventor of the *culte du moi* did not need to do violence to his creed in order to become, first a Socialist, then a Nationalist—each self-defined, elitist, *sui generis.* Each philosophy grew out of the tension between detachment and commitment, each tried to place the self within a context where it could find a personal fulfillment. Each, also, was directed to a somewhat general audience which had the particular characteristic that it did not come too near. Which brings us back once more to our friend Philippe, and the *barbares.*

The interesting thing about Philippe is that he resents those nearer to him more than those farther off. The unwashed, as he explains to an engineer whom he dislikes, hardly bother him. On the contrary, "the people" is something he can plunge into and emerge refreshed, energized. That is where "the creative energy, the sap of the world, the unconscious" lie.[43] Philippe had discovered the noble savage, one he could appreciate the more, the less he socialized with him. The middle-class intellectual of that day consorted very little indeed with lower-class people. Philippe's creator even less. Jérome Tharaud, who was Barrès's secretary for the ten years preceding 1914, noted that his employer would no more have thought to talk to a peasant in the Lorraine countryside than to go into a Paris shop. This is a style of life we hardly imagine today: one in which a successful writer and politician could totally ignore what a worker, a peasant, a servant, a teacher, a soldier, might be. As Tharaud observed, "He did not want to know them."[44]

Of course, he did not need to know them. And a police report of 1889, relating Barrès's electoral campaign at Nancy, where most of his electors were working men, relates how, after a rally, Barrès would go off with the Prince de Polignac and a couple of local scribblers to sit in a café and chat while, in the same café, his fellow-Boulangist campaigner, Gabriel, a base-born fellow, sat and talked with a group of workers in the opposing corner.[45] He might admire noble savages, but he found little he could say to them.[46]

It wasn't "the people" whom he feared, or that he consciously rejected. It was another social class, though class is too vast a term for a subdivision: those de-classed transients whose threat he felt acutely, those socially displaced persons to whom he gave the name of his first great social novel: the uprooted, *Les Déracinés*.

Published in 1897, *Les Déracinés* tells the story of seven young Lorrainers who graduate from the Lycée de Nancy and go up to Paris to seek fame and fortune, when they would have done better to stay home and be themselves in the familiar world where they could do some good. Uprooted, in Paris they lack the firm base and the immediate purpose they would have had at home; and those who do not return eventually go to pot in one way or another. Those who do worst among them are the poorest: Mouchefrin and Racadot especially, who are *boursiers:* scholarship boys like Bouteiller, the teacher who is responsible for their unwanted pretensions, their unhealthy ambitions, for the divorce between their nature and their artificial notions. All three end badly.

Albert Thibaudet has pointed to the social prejudice such predestination reflects, to the real or relative success Barrès vouchsafes to the better off, to the favor he shows the scions of the upper middle class, offspring of solid bourgeois families. And it is true that old man Racadot had made his fortune buying and selling cattle, dishonestly at that; though one is expected to doubt that anyone could engage in petty trade (especially of a sort Lorrainers associate with Jews!) and remain honest. Mouchefrin's family is needy; his father sold his land to set up as a photographer in a small town, and he doubles as electoral agent of the opportunist deputy (an unfortunate job, comments Barrès) on whom he depends for favors. Renaudin, son of a very petty civil servant, is left penniless when his father dies and is driven to venal journalism and blackmail. The implication is that you cannot preserve honesty or honor when you are short of money or too eager for it; when, in effect, you lack independence. We are back at Philippe's conclusions: the philosophy of the *héritier*.[47] A very realistic view, and one shared by Paul Bourget who, in one of his critical essays, found that the crux of *Madame Bovary* and of Stendhal's *Red and Black* lay in the difficulties social displacement created: Julien is a peasant who has received a bourgeois education; Emma is a peasant who has been brought up as a bourgeois. No wonder they went wrong. Social prejudice? Of course. Not prejudice directed against peasants (or workers) whom one can ignore but prejudice against those newcomers who by their ambitions, dissatisfactions, and uneasy yearnings threaten the stability of the *héritiers*.

The fate of Barrès's characters reflects reality in reflecting prejudice; indeed it was this very prejudice that would help their foundering. And the prejudices in turn reflect the conflict between the mordant and the torpid sections of the middle class: the hustlers and the drones. What no one has remarked, in any case, is that Mouchefrin, Racadot, and Racadot's mistress, the sluttish Léontine, represent a menace Barrès had discerned long before: the menace of unfulfilled expectations among men educated perhaps beyond their capacities, certainly beyond society's capacity to employ them.

One paragraph outlines the strangely modern situation of the 1880s when 730 graduates in Sciences and Letters competed for six teaching posts a year. The state provided 350 fellowships, while providing only the six places for which 730 candidates already competed. Here, says Barrès, was a particular class taking shape under our eyes: a proletariat of graduates. Their quality was irrelevant. What mattered, as the baron de Reinach is made to say a little later, was that they were *déclassés*. "Have you calculated how many graduates, each one remarkable and full of appetites, come to Paris every day? There's your danger: the overproduction of merit."[48]

The theme was not a new one for Barrès. He had argued it a decade or more before *Les Déracinés*, before his literary and social success might lead him to defensiveness and reaction. Once upon a time, he said in an essay of the 1880s, France knew two political parties: the men of twenty and the men of forty. That was, presumably, when the ruling class was still restricted and its conflicts were mainly generational. "Today . . . more and more, the question comes down to this, which is serious, those who have and those who want to have." He was not talking about the workers. The problem he had in mind was defined by the title of his essay "Le Quartier Latin." "In this restaurant, close to the round-breasted girls, wreathed in the smoke of indulgent cigars, whatever [ideological] nuance they parade, all will always be accomplices in pleasure. But out of miserable pot-houses, at this same hour, students emerge, also young, and needy, who lick dusty cigarettes and climb up to their lofts with soured hearts and tainted stomachs. Thence comes the danger."[49]

This danger materializes in the crime of Racadot and Mouchefrin, who murder a rich woman for her jewels, to pay the debts of the political paper Racadot had founded. But it comes to life in a scene where two of his better-off companions confront Mouchefrin in his sordid attic, after Racadot's arrest. They tell Mouchefrin they will defend him, when Léontine, Racadot's mistress, pipes up: "Voilà! . . . notre malheur servira à quelque chose pour ces messieurs." *Ces messieurs* had, indeed, helped bring Racadot and Mouchefrin to their end, and Barrès makes no bones about their exploitation of their social inferiors. At this particular point, however, he used Léontine to emphasize the relations between his heroes and the class that she and Racadot and Mouchefrin represent. "The only possible relation between misery endowed with a critical spirit and the culture of the leisure class," comments Barrès, are exploitation *and* resentment.[50] Exploitation may be in the nature of things, but the resentment is sharpened by an awareness that the less educated lack. It is the critical spirit, the *esprit d'analyse* inculcated by an inappropriate education, that makes these people resent their misery, suggests recourse to socially dangerous means to overcome it, and equips them with the kind of know-how that makes them dangerous.

I must insist on this, because, if Barrès may be said to have become a reactionary, his kind of reaction was different from what we imagine today. The standard motive attributed to reaction is fear of the working class. One finds a classic formulation of this view in George Lukács's *Roman historique,* an analysis in which he explains the late nineteenth-century "liberal turn against the people" as based in "fear of the proletariat, of the proletarian revolution." That is not true. There was no early turn against the proletariat. There was little fear of proletarian revolution between the crushing of the Commune in 1871 and the rise of revolutionary syndicalism in the late nineties or early 1900s. "Alienation from the people," argues Lukács, "turns into hostility towards the people." The question is: "what people?" For many, as for Barrès, alienation from peasants, poor and the working masses facilitated ideological sympathies that greater familiarity might easily have stifled. The menace they discerned lay closer to home.

Barrès's theme reappears under the pen of Georges Sorel. Using a term probably coined during the Dreyfus affair, Sorel denounced "ces intellectuels, mal payés, mécontents ou peu occupés," whose true vocation it was to make trouble by exploiting political issues.[51] For respectable men of property and for their sons the enemy was not among the working class, which so far had not appeared as a distinct threat, but among the lower middle class and in its sons. The *nouvelles couches* Gambetta had exalted—"this world of small property owners, small manufacturers, shopkeepers . . . the salesmen, the jobbers, the small entrepreneurs, this sort of training ground for noncommissioned officers of the great democratic army"[52]—look very different and very dangerous in Barrès's writings, as indeed they did in his eyes.

Here is the familiar conflict between *héritiers* and *hommes nouveaux*, and it helps explain why Barrès could quite easily combine sympathy for workers and peasants with resentment of vulgar (and threatening) *arrivistes* and money-grubbers. But if he loads the dice against them in his pages, this reflects less the author's prejudice than his estimate of the world he lived in. It comes to the same thing, perhaps. Yet in some respects this estimate was sounder than that of his then and later critics. And this is because, while he addressed the indolent and the idle, Barrès himself was neither of these things. Attacking Barrès for his anti-Dreyfusism, Lucien Herr once referred to his "provincial patriotism" behind which lay, said Herr, not only the chauvinism of a border province, but the primitive hatred for all that is different—for aliens and *horsains*. Curiously, Barrès recalled the incident, but rewrote Herr's analysis into a derogatory reference to him as "a typical product of small French towns." The description was just; the attribution was not. But Barrès recalled the phrase, to pride himself upon it, and in this he was right.[53] His provincial background taught him a great deal. He recalled it whenever he could, experience reinforcing the common sense that made him the first French patriot to encourage Alsatians and Lorrainers to stay at home, maintain their heritage (and that of France) even at the cost of serving in the German army, even at the risk of fighting their own kin.

Au service de l'Allemagne, published in 1905, features a chapter entitled "Un héritier," where Dr. Ehrmann, the Alsatian hero, explains: "I am an heir; I have neither the wish nor the right to abandon riches already created." Not only material riches: cultural ones too, a social context and a social position that are his by right, above all by right of birth because he is (something rarely noticed nowadays) his father's son. But birthright and its prerogatives are not limited to aristocratic societies, or aristocracy to nobiliar lines. They are a part of stable societies, where being someone means being someone's kin, where being someone's son (or cousin) has a distinct meaning, as it has to Ehrmann, who can talk to the humblest people wherever he goes in his own *pays*. "My father is highly esteemed in the Haut Rhin; I have relatives everywhere; people know our name . . . My *pays* is a field of action cut to my measure."[54] Sound sense (what would Ehrmann be in Paris?), the sort of sense that recurs in other situations.

Even that most fantastic of Barrèsian characters, in the most confusing of his novels, *La Colline inspirée*, the heretical priest Léopold Baillard, is above everything else a peasant, his passion for the hill of Sion "a peasant lust to own land," his missionary labors and those of his brothers producing more than spiritual fruit: "the three brothers were making gold. It's the most beautiful thing anywhere."[55] Looking at Barrès, the painter, Raffaelli, once discerned dreams in his right eye; down-to-earthness and *practicité* in the left.[56] The dreams in the right eye changed; the practical sense Raffaelli glimpsed in the left persisted beneath superficial variations.

If I insist on practical, pedestrian aspects it is because they are basic. Barrès was an heir, with the advantages but also the predicaments of an heir, peculiar to that brief time when the triumph of the middle—more especially the upper-middle—classes began to set their teeth on edge.

In his introduction to a little book on the Third Republic, Pierre Barral explains that, since 1848, the direction of political life had remained almost entirely the monopoly of the *messieurs,* the same *messieurs* that Léontine mentions so bitterly, owners of established fortunes and holders of social authority. Many opponents of the Second Empire—many beneficiaries of the Third Republic—were such "heirs of a patrimony that guaranteed comfort if not wealth, heirs also of a tradition of which they considered themselves to be the guardians."[57] But, by the 1880s, and especially by the 1890s, such heirs, better off than ever before, were on the defensive. The growing challenge of ever lower orders, the intrusion of masses into a political world hitherto restricted to the few, challenged their position. The *héritiers* had reason to fear for the *héritage,* cultural and material both.

This produced reactions: elitist educational practices, or the introduction of sports, attempted to distinguish the ruling classes from their challengers and train them to maintain themselves. Escapist doctrines, increasingly personal and subjective, sought to evade the issue. Decadent irresponsibility, often connected with drugs, avoided it altogether. Some men, finally, tried to formulate public and private philosophies to actually come to grips with the situation. Barrès was one of these. First the *culte du moi;* then Boulangist socialism (which has been thoroughly documented by now[58]), and later still, organic national socialism or national collectivism were the results of his awareness, fear, concern. Yet, whatever shape they took, they failed because they had not been tempered in necessity, absence of which was a major component of the predicament that Barrès sensed but could not allay.

As with contemporary enthusiasts of sports for the young, the action that Barrès recommended—personal, social, or national—was a surrogate for reality. He knew enough to recognize his quandary, but not enough to solve it. Like André Malterre, the idealist *Ennemi des lois,* "given his education, he could not restrict his ideal to a campaign for the belly, though he knew well, by God! that for the miserable the first need is bread, meat and alcohol." As a matter of fact, Barrès knew just as well that there were other material wants to be remedied, almost as urgent. As a deputy in the 1890s he had steadfastly supported the socialist struggle to make syndicalism work, improve hours and conditions of labor, implement safety measures, create pensions and accident compensation. But such material ends could scarcely seem essential to his kind. "We, who never wanted for necessities, need something better than a humanity where one does not starve. Material needs once satisfied, it remains to provide our sensibility with those psychic satisfactions it demands."[59] A generous socialism, perhaps, but one that seeks to transcend gross realities, and so avoids them.

Civilizations, Paul Valéry once said, are structures of enchantment: systems of convention that make a certain sort of life possible as long as they are sufficiently unquestioned. In the enchantment of the Third Republic, words were equated with acts. It may be characteristic that when the great Gambetta died, the places where he had made his finest speeches were engraved on the monument that was raised to him, much as Napoleon's victories were listed on the Arc de Triomphe. If one could believe that words and deeds were one, then issues could more easily be avoided even by those who came quite close to formulating them. Identification with a prevaricating creed displaced inner anxieties onto appealing causes. This could be done (or done more easily), because it was done in a climate without real tension, where gerontocracy and economic stagnation deepened the divide between youth and manhood, where action seemed as removed from concrete results as growing up was from maturity. Substitutes for action, serving a particular need, the systems that Barrès devised were surrogates for reality.

They did their job by shaping a philosophy of action for action's sake, of actions meant to give the illusion of action the way Gambetta's speeches were endowed with the sense of military victories. Once again, Barrès himself sensed this when he wondered aloud why all the ardor and enthusiasm of his young *déracinés,* who had just vowed over Napoleon's tomb to embark together on a Napoleonic fate, should lead them to decide to found something as un-Napoleonic and vicarious as . . . a newspaper.

Barrès himself had opened the first number of the only national newspaper he ever edited, *La Cocarde,* with the statement that "un journal . . . c'est une action." And this was true, up to a point, especially in circumstances where unorganized or loosely organized parties left the molding of opinion to a political press whose protagonists wielded unusual influence. Still, the discrepancy between the aim and the gesture remains striking. It would have been odd if Barrès had failed to feel it.

To equate a newspaper with action was to shirk the issue—and the action. With all their ardor, these young people could only slide off into rationalizations. At least the poor among them were after money. Barrès understood that they must make their way. But for the rest of them, commitment was gratuitous; and it was scarcely commitment: "they will fight for nothing, for the fun of it," Barrès explained. But if that was all they will fight about, they will fight windmills. Their struggles, while they might be serious, would not be about serious things. The interests in dispute, unless they were personal, were not really their own and could be dispensed with. The ideas they supported had been espoused only in a marriage of convenience and could be discarded.[60]

Barrès knew what he talked about, and what he disapproved of with half his mind, because it was just how he himself behaved. Free of the rules of necessity, one's chief concern was how to keep amused. But, as Barrès confessed to Jules Renard, "on ne s'amuse qu'à faire autre chose." Not persistence but variety kept interest alive. The only consistency we find lay in the circumstances that encouraged such a life. "Barrès fait de la politique comme Jules Favre [the politician] fait des vers," Jules Renard had noted. He had gone into politics for the experience: not with the particular purpose to serve a concrete end, not in pursuit of an ideal, not even for self-advancement. He sought the sense of action, the excitement, and the observations he could draw from it. Of course, he meant what he said; but what he said had less a social or political meaning than a personal one. His was a sort of sport for those who, like himself, no longer called to answer to necessity, were hungrily available for any "glorious adventure frivolously engaged."[61]

~ 12

About Marc Bloch

On March 8, 1944, at place du Pont in Lyon, the Germans arrested an aging gentleman, rather short, gray-haired, bespectacled, neatly dressed, holding a briefcase in one hand and a cane in the other, whose papers identified him as Maurice Blanchard. The following day, the Gestapo raided the dressmaker's shop, on the rue des Quatre Chapeaux, where Blanchard rented a room. One of the women who worked there had apparently denounced him. The officers found a radio set and enough papers to suggest they had seized an interesting prize. For several weeks Blanchard was beaten, tortured, subjected among other trials to the humiliating and suffocating torments of the cold bathtub, and brought back unconscious to Montluc prison, his wrist and his ribs broken. Sent to the hospital with broncho-pneumonia, he recovered and was returned to prison.

A few months later, on June 16, with the Germans beginning preparations to clear out and eager to liquidate their holdings, the little man and twenty-six others were loaded into a truck, which drove up the Saône toward Trévoux—a road, the Nationale 433, more familiar today to those seeking out the restaurant of Paul Bocuse at Collonges. A young man in the truck was crying and Blanchard reassured him: "They're going to shoot us—don't be afraid, it doesn't hurt. It will happen fast."

A bit past Trévoux, at a place called Les Roussilles, a little short of Saint Didier-de-Formans, the prisoners were unloaded and shot in groups of four at the edge of a field. Incredibly, one of the twenty-seven survived both the shooting and the coup de grace and managed to crawl to safety during the night to tell of their last moments. So the twenty-six bodies were found and identified on June 26; among them was Maurice Blanchard, delegate of Franc-Tireur to the regional directorate of the united resistance movements (M.U.R.) and editor of a major underground publication, the *Cahiers politiques,* whose real name was Marc Bloch, one of the great historians of our age ("the greatest historian of modern times," according to J. H. Plumb). Writing to Fernand Braudel in a German prisoner-of-war camp to announce the death, Lucien Febvre provided a characteristic epitome: "The loss of Marc Bloch is irreparable. All this end of his life has been magnificent." He had succeeded in acting out his aspirations, not only as a scholar, but as a citizen and as a man—a success that is not given to many of us.

Marc Bloch, who was born in Lyon in July 1886, was fifty-seven years old when he died. His father, Gustave, was professor of ancient history there, but he soon moved to Paris, to the Ecole Normale Supérieure and the Sorbonne. That was where Marc grew up—between his parents' apartment on the avenue d'Orléans (now avenue du Maréchal Leclerc) and the *quartier des écoles* where he attended first the Lycée Louis-le-Grand, then the Ecole Normale Supérieure where he studied (including a year's military service) from 1904 to 1908. The Left Bank would be his home for all his Paris life, and his attachment to it was reflected in the choice of his noms de guerre in the Resistance: first *Arpajon* from the little train that, until 1936, clattered along the boulevard Saint-Michel to the Halles; then *Chevreuse,* sticking to the Ligne de Sceaux; and finally shifting to *Narbonne* only when the other two names had been found out and rendered useless.

In 1908 Bloch passed his *agrégation* examination in history and geography and went off for a year to German universities, then dominant in medieval history, followed by the plum of a three-year fellowship at the Fondation Thiers. Then came his first teaching posts, in provincial lycées: Montpellier, 1912–13; Amiens, 1913–14. He started to publish, to plan his doctorate, and to establish his long-standing relationship with England. Then came the war: the moment when, as Lady Sackville put it at the time, "Ce sale Kaiser, voilà qu'il a upset le milk."

For Bloch, as for many of his generation, the war came as an exciting development. He was exhilarated by the national mood and shared in it. Back in the army from the first days of war, he thoroughly enjoyed the experience. Apart from two months in a hospital, three months' sick leave, and fifteen days at base camp, he continued on active service, nearly always in the infantry, from August 2, 1914, to March 13, 1919, and left the army with four citations, the Légion d'honneur, and the Croix de Guerre.

When the war broke out, Marc Bloch was no callow youth: twenty-eight years old, he was a grown man, well embarked on his career. It is important to note that he enjoyed what he later described as "four years of fighting idleness," and his peculiar historian's eye sharpened his appreciation. As he recalled about the heavy fighting on September 10, 1914, "My curiosity, which seldom abandons me, had not left me." So he observed the differences in the colors of the smoke associated with different shells (the time shells are ocher, the percussions black), he remembered passages from Tolstoy, and he noted small details: the potatoes rolling out of the kit bag of a dead sergeant major, the extraordinary weight of corpses. But one major consideration overshadowed all others, and it would be made clear on the day in 1915 when, convalescing from that typical trench disease, typhoid fever, he began to write his *Souvenirs de guerre:* "*I had the honor* [my italics] to take part in the first five months of the 1914−15 campaign."

It is not surprising that an intelligent and able man, professionally confined to paperwork and talk, should welcome the opportunity to test himself in action. But Bloch, like many of his generation (at least at that time), had a strong sense of personal honor—a quality that runs the risk of being lost from sight in a time like ours, which does not always recognize this form of self-respect.

We are talking, of course, about a generation that had grown up with a strong sense of what are nowadays described as "bourgeois" values: honesty, probity, effort, order; and of the civic virtues that went with them—virtues in which Bloch's father, the historian of the Roman republic, strongly believed. We are also talking about the strong patriotism nursed in a family of French-Alsatian Jews who had left Alsace when the Germans occupied it, and for whom the national and the republican commitment were one and the same thing. And we are talking about a man who, under a calm, restrained exterior, held strong feelings about right and wrong along with the will to be true to himself. Unless we give due credit to Bloch's sense of honor, we shall understand neither his success in war, nor his return to the army in his fifties, nor his later commitment to the Resistance.

In any case, the little *prof binoclard,* less than five feet five inches tall, did very well as a soldier. In the Battle of the Marne he learned how to dig trenches; he learned how to supplement his weak eyesight by using his ears; he became a real poilu. Sergeant, then sergeant major, second lieutenant in 1916, he ended the war a captain covered with wound-stripes and citations. Meanwhile soldiering, with its built-in idleness, offered opportunities for reading. His pocket diaries contain lists of history books in English and French, sprinkled with other matter: Walt Whitman's *Leaves of Grass,* Saint Augustine's *Confessions,* Dostoevski's *The Insulted and Injured* (twice). By 1917 there was also a brief work plan for his doctoral thesis. Demobilized in 1919, Bloch took advantage of the special facilities offered to veterans and crossed his last academic hurdle with an abbreviated version of what, in normal circumstances, would have demanded many more pages and many more years. By the end of 1920 he had his doctorate. Meanwhile, since 1919, he had been teaching at the University of Strasbourg, where he would become the titular Professor of Medieval History in 1927.

Thereby, however, hangs a tale. One of Bloch's teachers at the Ecole Normale had been Christian Pfister, the son of modest winegrowers from

Beblenheim, whose parents had sent him out of Alsace in 1871 to finish his education in Paris at the Lycée Louis-le-Grand, where he met and befriended another *interne* called Raymond Poincaré. The two boarders, one from Alsace, one from Lorraine, struck up a friendship that never flagged. In 1919, with Poincaré president of the Republic, Pfister was appointed to a chair in the new showcase University of Strasbourg. In 1927, with Poincaré as prime minister, Pfister became rector of the university. Bloch's academic fortunes were not unrelated to those of his patron. Intellectual merit is not always enough by itself—it needs luck, and the right circumstances. Bloch often combined the three, and this is a point to which I shall return. But Pfister, a good, solid medievalist, also contributed to, or reinforced, other aspects of Bloch's mind: he was a burning patriot, he was a model of minuteness and integrity, and he was fascinated by regional history—the first professor in France (at Nancy) to hold such a chair, that of the history of eastern France, from 1886 until he was transferred to the Ecole Normale on the eve of Bloch's arrival there.

This brings me to a point that deserves to be made because, while it does not explain Bloch's career, it helps to illuminate it from the social historian's point of view: Bloch was fortunate, and he was privileged. He was born with an academic silver spoon in his mouth, the son of a great figure in the university (I have heard Bloch described as *fils d'archevêque*). This not only gave him good connections and a good start in a very competitive trade but also the opportunity to acquire an unusually broad cultural background and unusually broad academic relations. He traveled early, and he traveled widely, to a degree quite unusual in a rather restricted and constricted profession. On the eve of war, in 1914, he was on holiday in Switzerland. When the riots of February 1934 threatened the republic, he was lecturing at the London School of Economics and drinking port at Oriel. In March 1939—when he was called up, like other reservists, for the second time in six months—he had to rush back from Cambridge. So, when Bloch advocated comparative history, he did it not only from the point of view, exceptional in his time, of one who had been able to pursue it in the only provincial university in France with a decent library and a more than provincial perspective, but also from the position of someone who had been able to pursue the necessary documents in a wide variety of libraries and collections. Bloch's great paper of 1927, in which he argued for comparative history, was delivered at an international congress in Oslo. In it, drawing a parallel between enclosures in England and Provence, he revealingly added: "Mais ces textes, il faut songer à aller les chercher."

If documents are to be sought out, you not only have to think of going to look for them, you also have to have the means to do it. In a modest way,

Marc Bloch always had the means to approach the ends he had the brains to conceive. After his marriage in 1919 he had a level of income and support that most of his colleagues lacked. Simone Vidal was the daughter of a successful engineer, *inspecteur des ponts et chaussées,* and descended from a family of engineers and manufacturers related to the Dreyfuses. She made two crucial contributions to Bloch's life and to his work. Clearly, she made him happy—indeed the couple was so united that their six children (or some of them) sometimes felt they were not really wanted. Simone acted as her husband's secretary, helped in his research, transcribed his manuscripts, and seems to have been his favorite interlocutor. She also made him independently wealthy, which was not entirely an advantage because it seems to have excited the envy of his colleagues, but which gave him elbow room, a freedom of time and movement that must have been unusual in his profession at that time.

This can help to explain the torrent of writings that the prodigious Bloch poured out, especially through the 1920s and 1930s. Were it not for its quality, the quantity of his output would not be important. But given the quality, quantity becomes highly relevant, especially as a factor of the range and impact of the message that the writings carried. Beginning in 1911, Bloch never ceased to publish reviews, not only of French works, but of books and articles in German, English, Spanish, Italian, Flemish, Latin, of course, and the occasional Scandinavian language. His own first article in English appeared in 1925, in Spanish in 1926, in Italian in 1928. From the beginning—when he reviewed H. G. Wells's new history of the world in 1922—but especially in the 1930s, his interests were omnivorous: in space, where he reviewed works on Africa and China and Japan; in time, where ancient slavery or the fabrication of matches in the nineteenth century were grist to his mill; and in disciplines, where he showed serious interest in anthropology and sociology, politics and linguistics, geography and psychology, folklore and museums.

The mere numbers remain impressive. Bloch's bibliography for 1934 shows 121 articles, notes and reviews of works in five languages; that for 1935, eighty-seven. Even in 1943, when he had become active in the Resistance, he published thirty-one reviews, including several of German books. I did a superficial count of the *Annales* for 1934, and found twenty contributions by Bloch in the January number, running from a paragraph to several pages; twenty-seven in March, four in May, fourteen in July, twelve in September, four in November. All this while, presumably, he was finishing off the two volumes of his *Société féodale* (which came out the following year) and keeping up the German historiographical bulletin of the *Revue historique.*

The briefest of Bloch's notes is thoughtful, critical, full of throwaway points. Virtue unaccompanied by severe intellectual criticism, he wrote, always risks turning against its dearest aims: if Saint Louis went off to crusade in Tunis, it was probably because he had no atlas. A good, international interlibrary loan system would do more for comparative studies than a lot of wise advice. The Bibliothèque Nationale needs to get organized, get on with the cataloging, keep up serials, use chariots to distribute books to readers (a service that was eventually introduced in the 1970s).*

Bloch was, of course, very organized, *"un esprit tres ordonné."* In a letter to Febvre, after his return to England in 1934, he describes the vices of the parliamentary system that had given way before the riots of February 6, 1934: "a horrible and puerile mixture of flabbiness, false chumminess, bad work habits, and total lack of intelligence." Here was a mirror image of the virtues he respected, which turn out to be his own: strength of character, reserve, work, discipline, and intelligence.

But in considering Marc Bloch's achievements, I am inclined to think that only through a mixture of monomania and unusual facilities could he have achieved so much research and reading, so much thinking and writing, while simultaneously preparing the annual lecture courses against whose demands he never ceased to argue. As a historian he was a man possessed—never without a book in his hand. Even in the Resistance he always carried a book and used it to keep his notes in cipher. He was never without a work in progress. Always writing: his great meditation on the defeat of 1940, *Etrange défaite,* poured out all molten between July and September 1940; his discussions of the historian's craft, *Apologie pour l'histoire,* drafted during 1942 and 1943. As a private person, he was a very comfortable bourgeois, living in a Paris penthouse at Sèvres-Babylone just beside the Hotel Lutetia (later from its headquarters in that same hotel the Gestapo organized the looting of his apartment and removed his library en bloc), protected from interruptions (including those of his children) that would have interfered with his work. Monomania and the means as well as the talent to satisfy it make an ideal recipe for great work. One without the other might have been a waste, but one supporting the other gave us the many-faceted plenitude that we can still admire.

*(Another innovation he suggested, still awaited today, would be to stop limiting the number of request bulletins allowed in a single day.)

The B.N. was always Bloch's bête noire: "No question about it," he wrote to Febvre, "a few hours of work at the *British* [Museum] inspire the irresistible desire to build in the square Louvois a vast pyre of all the B.N.'s regulations and to burn on it, in a splendid auto-da-fe, Julien Cain [the director], his librarians and his staff . . . also a few malodorous readers, if you like, and no doubt also the architect . . . after which we could work and invite the foreigners to come and work."

One interesting result of a deliberate reading through of Bloch's work from its beginnings is the impression of consistency one gets—both in style and in the dominant themes or approaches—despite its great variety. Development turns out to be a broadening of scope, an enrichment of sources, a ripening rather than a change. One realm where this shows well is in Bloch's style, which may not be extraordinary today but which stands out, as does Febvre's (though Febvre's style is more peculiar and recherché), in the impression it gives of ease, assurance, lack of constraint. Bloch's first great book, the learned study of the healing kings entitled *Les Rois thaumaturges* (1924), reads almost like a story—to my mind, like a detective story. I do not think this detective story aspect of Bloch's history has been remarked on, not even in Robin Winks's compendious *The Historian as Detective* (1968), and yet that seems to be the gist of the *histoire problème* on which he liked to insist.

In July 1914, as a young professor delivering the awards speech at the Lycée d'Amiens, Marc Bloch had explained that historians are judges of instruction charged with a vast inquiry of the past. Like our colleagues from the Palais de Justice, he said, we collect testimony, which we use to try to reconstruct reality. This model of a magistrate—embodying an investigator's probity, ingenuity, and quest for a manifold, multifaceted truth (approximate, uncertain, but which one must encompass as best one can)—this high sense of imaginative professionalism keeps coming up in Bloch's work. It was there in the first course in economic history he delivered at the Sorbonne in 1936, when he insisted that history is never a finished product but a process, with the historian the slave of the evidence that past ages have left behind. It comes up again in an article of 1921, on the appearance and circulation of false rumors during the war just ended ("an immense experiment in social psychology"), in which he mobilized the critical methods and the information of a medievalist to analyze a familiar contemporary subject. And it reappears a few years later in *Les Rois thaumaturges,* where his earlier analyses of perception and of collective mentalities were pressed into the service of recondite scholarship. (It surfaces, too, in a letter of December 1935 where, after complaining bitterly about the movie fare offered in Strasbourg at Christmastime, he dreamed of a big article on the cinema. Bourgeois cinema, he notes, is becoming increasingly vapid, but it remains "one of the most marvelous cultural and social barometers we have." The *Annales* should find someone who can do justice to the subject. Its "artistic" and "psychological" aspects are beyond the *Annales*'s scope; but the birth of the industry, the passage from scientific discovery to industrialized entertainment, *"cette révolution du spectacle* for people who hardly ever went to the theater and never to the *café concert,"* deserves the historian's attention.)

And yet, like Marc Bloch, the true historian is more than a detective.

The detective's work is to unravel a particular situation, to discover how it came about. To do this he tries to understand the motivations and hence (at least at times) the personalities of the characters involved. He becomes, so to speak, a playwright in reverse, seeking to discern the unfolding script from a rather garbled account of its conclusion.

But the historian seeks to become a character in the play whose tale he tells—before he tells it. To use another simile, he is (ideally) a cultivated traveler arriving in a foreign land he has read much about, foreign but not entirely strange, and yet all the stranger because, although familiar with much and with many he encounters, he is continually surprised at gestures, attitudes, and activities he had not expected, or that he finds more complex, more obscure, than he had thought. Fascinated by the workings of this society, which he refuses to abandon after a swift tour of monuments, land-scapes, and eating houses, he settles in it and learns what the natives have picked up simply by being born and living there. Although he becomes a naturalized member of the society he adopts, he cannot take it for granted. A certain distance sets him apart and suggests questions that would not occur to natives, a constant posing of riddles that can only be resolved by experience, deduction, and informed curiosity.

This surely is what Bloch meant when he said that history is nothing but a succession of problems. Yet he who says problems implies selection, discrimination among facts, and ample perspective. This, of course, is the essence of Bloch's style, which insists that without the past there is no understanding of the present, but that conversely the present illumines the past. He uses a thousand little traits taken from a marvelously diverse reality to reconstruct, bit by bit, a general picture more exact but also more nuanced; and he warns that, before going from the particular to the general, you need a broad survey that will tell you how to classify and interpret apparently minor facts.

Like the investigating magistrate's, the historian's task is difficult and demanding, his subjects stubborn in their semidarkness. "Only the use of crosslighting *(un jeu de feux croisés)* can hope to shed some light on them." Hence the need to knock down the partitions between disciplines *(abattre les cloisons)*, which inspired the foundation of the *Annales d'histoire économique et sociale*. This periodical was designed by its founders as an *agent de liaison* between geographers, economists, sociologists, statisticians, and histo-rians—and also political scientists such as André Siegfried, whom Bloch managed to lure after much effort to speak for an interest in contemporary matters, an interest still rejected by the historians of the 1920s. The first number of the *Annales* came out in January 1929.

The preliminary correspondence, about the title and so on, shows

Febvre insisting on the social and Bloch on the economic aspect of the
Annales (which at one point Bloch even suggested calling *L'Evolution économique*). Bloch also stressed the need for the journal to reach out beyond the
higher seats of academe, to lycée professors, to *érudits de province,* to members of learned societies, even wanting to send these groups a special publicity notice. So, there was the interdisciplinary and comparative approach
that we now hear so much about. But also much thought was devoted to the
nuts and bolts of scholarship and academe. Erudition is all very well, but it
teeters on the verge of sterility if it does not plunge its roots in observation
and experience. "Most people seem to go about with their eyes closed, they
don't bother to look." *Regarder:* to keep eyes and mind open all the time was
Bloch's recurrent message; to recognize the difference between classifications and realities, the tension between traditional classifications and new
relations; to show that what some formulas (or histories) represent clearly
was actually complex and confused. Equally important was it to be atten-
tive to the material world, the flesh and blood of creatures working in real
fields, feeling real weariness, hunger, pain; the adventures of the body, as he
called them in *La Société féodale*—how can you pretend to understand men if
you do not know how they feel physically?—and so on.

Away with rural histories whose heroes do their plowing with charters.
Bloch praised André Allix's study of the Oisans because the author had
nothing of the deskbound scholar about him—he had spent nights in
barns, he had spoken to the locals, he had plunged into the physical and
human reality of his subject. Such essentials ignore disciplinary limits; the
facts you look at "should have a human value," not a departmental pigeon-
hole. In this context, his criticisms of Allix are as revealing as his praise:
Allix did not consider distances in terms of time, hence of the changed
experience that roads and rails produced; he did not talk about the postal
service, which was an "essential element of economic and *intellectual* revolution." You can see that while suggestive, exciting to some, such an
approach would be disturbing to others—the more so when it went side by
side, increasingly hand in hand as it did with Bloch, with more direct
attacks on academic dovecotes and on the doves within them.

Bloch's writings, like his lectures, are littered with criticisms of his colleagues—that is, of practices characteristic of many of his colleagues
(though practices fortunately quite unknown in our time). He did not mind
honest mediocrity unless it preened itself, but he denounced preten-
tiousness and pompousness, and "that most deplorable professional iniq-
uity: drivelling." He suspected the original sin of French intellectuals: the
tendency to wrap themselves in what the *Canard enchaîné* calls *paroles ver-
bales*—verbal words.

In the realm of the positive sciences or of techniques, an idea only
has value as an image or abbreviation of concrete facts. Short of
that, it is no more than a label that covers a bit of emptiness . . .
there is no worse danger for a teacher than to teach words instead of
things.

Along with this, and equally irritating no doubt, went Marc Bloch's
unrelenting criticism of the educational system. Bloch's first attacks on the
history curriculum go back to 1921; his last can be found in the third
number of the clandestine *Cahiers politiques,* dated August 1943. In between,
he raised the subject tirelessly (some may have thought naggingly), notably
in his Oslo paper of 1927, where he described the *programmes de licence* as
"garroting" higher education, and again in a major statement of the *Annales*
in March 1937, in which he placed the crisis of history teaching in the context of the contemporary social and intellectual crisis. He argued that the
existing system was hung up on exams and routine, stereotyped, unimagi-
native, and constraining; it discouraged initiative and stifled originality. It
forced candidates to cram and professors to prepare ever-changing courses
on sterile, isolated subjects, with the result that they could not do research.
    Bloch repeated the same indictment more sharply six years later, when
he claimed that the defeat of 1940 was a failure of both intelligence and
character, and that military disintegration and collapse reflected educational
disintegration and failure. The examination mania had turned tests of
achievement into achievement itself and had produced generations imbued
with the dread of initiative, the avoidance of disinterested curiosity, the cult
of success, and, instead of any taste for knowledge, an appreciation of successful cheating and sheer luck. The cures and answers Bloch suggested for
all this make melancholy reading today, especially when one realizes how
little was done after the war, and how little was actually achieved after
1968. But Bloch (who probably hoped to become minister of education
after the liberation and get on with university reform then and there) could
not know that the period from 1940 to 1945 was just another instance when
history reached a turning point and failed to turn.
    Views of this sort, especially when they were strongly held and pun-
gently expressed, did not endear him to all his colleagues, some of whom, at
least so I have been told, already considered him cold, distant, and both
timid and hypercritical. The enmities he stirred up would hurt him later
on, as when, in 1941, his wife's health suggested a move from Clermont-
Ferrand to the sunnier climate of Montpellier. The dean of the faculty at
Montpellier was Augustin Fliche, the church historian, who apparently
made no secret of his antisemitism. But Fliche also disliked Marc Bloch for

personal reasons (specifically, a bad review), and these must have entered into his opposition to the move and to his making Bloch's life at Montpellier more uncomfortable than it need have been. The same kind of thing helps to explain Bloch's repeated failures to achieve his dream: an appointment to the Collège de France, the only faculty where personal research could be at one with teaching and reflected in it.

Marc Bloch always wanted to be at the Collège de France. Perhaps the same could be said of most French academics, but Bloch really deserved to be there. It has been argued that antisemitism entered into the opposition to his appointment, and I think both he and Lucien Febvre believed that to be so. While that is the sort of thing that cannot be proved or disproved, nonetheless in the 1930s Bloch's Jewish origins could easily have figured in the thinking of his colleagues. They obviously did so figure (in a preventive, defensive sense) in Febvre's appreciation of the situation. But Bloch's repeated failures to obtain an appointment at the Collège seem to have simpler, though not necessarily more straightforward, explanations.

The archives of the Collège de France show Bloch signaling his interest in a chair as early as 1928, when the chair of numismatics became vacant and he wrote the *administrateur* to say that, although he did not want to be a candidate at that time, he believed that his kind of work (which he claimed to be alone in doing) "deserves to have its place one day in our great foundation of free scientific research." That day came in 1933, when Camille Jullian, the professor of "national antiquities," died and, with the new year, 1934, the struggle for Jullian's chair began.

Chairs at the Collège are shaped to their incumbents, but their allocation also reflects some faculty consensus about fields and subjects that deserve support. Jullian, while he lived—and his friends after his death—wanted his succession to go to his student, Albert Grenier, an older man than Bloch, also a professor at Strasbourg, and very much in Jullian's field. But in February 1934, Etienne Gilson officially proposed that Jullian's chair should go to Bloch and that it should be devoted to the study of comparative history. Since the comparative history of European societies Bloch wanted to pursue "could not be conceived today in the rigid framework of our universities," the candidate explained, "it seemed natural to propose its creation to an institution that traditionally welcomes scientific novelties." That was a slight exaggeration. The world, Bloch liked to think, belongs to those who love new things. The Collège did not. Since its founding by François I, the sympathy for innovation had grown slack; the traditional academic postures had hardened. Gilson belonged to the *Annales* group whose leader, Lucien Febvre, was also a member of the Collège. Febvre was considered a bit too pushy to make a good campaign manager, so he held back as much as he could. But everyone could see that the personal contest between Grenier and Bloch reflected a contest not only between two academic clans, but between two views of history and two quite different schools.

More important in the immediate context was the fact that Bloch's candidacy split the history camp and placed it in an awkward situation vis-à-vis the scientists, themselves divided among partisans of statistics, chemistry, and experimental psychology, but still capable of coming together for pragmatic ends. Furthermore, the psychologists (who could expect to end up with the science votes), although also divided between two candidates, were agreed on the title of the chair they wanted. The historians, in disagreement about Grenier and Bloch, were also in conflict about a chair for national antiquities or one for comparative history. Since the vote on the chair preceded the vote on who should fill it, Bloch's intervention appeared to jeopardize the historians' chance of cornering the chair.

In mid-March 1934, the faculty of the Collège met to decide the issue. The debate began. Bloch's supporters spoke first, followed by those of Grenier, among them a chemist named Camille Matignon. When Matignon finished, he was followed by one of his friends, a well-known classicist, Eugène Albertini. "But hardly has he spoken a few sentences than the sitting is interrupted, at 3:15, by a tragic event. M. Camille Matignon, suddenly taken ill, falls unconscious; he dies a few moments later in the midst of his colleagues." So the discussion was put off for a few weeks. But the year was 1934 and the country was in the midst of a political crisis, which was also a financial crisis. On April 4, the decrees were published by which the Doumergue cabinet cut the budget, including the budget of the Collège de France, by 10 percent—which meant that neither Jullian nor Matignon could be replaced.

By the end of 1934 two more professors had retired, and "a benevolent application of the decrees" allowed the Collège to keep one of the four chairs it had by then lost. So the faculty met again on Sunday, January 13, 1935, the historians split as expected, but the Grenier party seems to have made a deal with the scientists. By the fourth ballot, comparative history was left with just one vote; national antiquities had reached the necessary majority of twenty-two, and experimental psychology came second with nineteen votes, which meant that it could expect to get the next chair—as indeed it did—the following year.

A year later Bloch returned to the fray, this time aiming for Charles Simiand's chair in labor history. Simiand was an economic sociologist or, if you prefer, a social psychologist, and a co-editor of the *Annales sociologiques*—which is interesting in light of all the fuss that has been made about

Bloch's fascination with Durkheim. But the Collège had a new administrator, Joseph Bédier, connected to the traditionalist Ecole des Chartes and hence not particularly friendly to the *Annales* even though Bloch had, as a student, attended the courses of his school. More important, some of Simiand's friends felt that Bloch, who had criticized Simiand in a major article only eighteen months before, would not make an appropriate successor to the colleague he had manhandled. But lo! The chair of economic history at the Sorbonne, next door, was about to fall vacant because its holder, Henri Hauser, retired in 1936. So Bloch withdrew his candidacy and set his sights on second best. Since he had not quarreled with Hauser or with too many other historians at the Sorbonne, he won the position, the only economic history chair in France at the time (his appointment would be signed by Léon Blum's minister of education, Jean Zay, another casualty of the approaching war). It was obviously a triumph mitigated not only in terms of prestige but also and above all in terms of professional possibilities.

So the annual round of *cours de licence* and *cours d'agrégation* continued. It did not seem to slow down Bloch's writing, however—or his proselytizing on behalf of a new history. Looking at the lecture notes for the first undergraduate course in economic history that Bloch taught at the Sorbonne in 1936, one finds them to range from Carolingian days to the nineteenth century, with the lecturer never satisfied with actions, always seeking to establish motive. History is but the many-stranded story of change. The invitation to approach it as a complex, dynamic process shines through even more clearly in one of Bloch's later courses, delivered in the 1940s at Clermont-Ferrand and Montpellier. We still have the big sheets of yellow paper covered by Bloch's impossible handwriting and by that of his wife— the opening of the first lecture is typical: "Why begin an introduction to Economic History by a sketch of monetary history? Because coin [*monnaie*] is essentially the instrument and the measure of exchanges, and economic life is, above all, founded on exchanges." The concrete reference leads to an analysis that is not static but dynamic.

By that time, the war had come and gone. Bloch had served again, again enjoyed the opportunity for action, however frustrating or desperate the conditions, again won a citation—his fifth. As "the oldest captain in the French army," which is the way he described himself, he had gone through the catastrophe in Flanders and had been taken off the beach at (let's call it) Dunkirk by an English steamer named the *Royal-Daffodil*— describing the setting as they sailed away as being "under golden skies colored by the black and fawn smoke from a burning refinery." With his mates, he was shipped from Dover to Plymouth in a single day and then embarked again for France, where the troopship arrived off Cherbourg at dawn on

June 1 and had to wait until port officials opened their shop after 9:00 A.M. Impotent and furious, he had watched the final collapse, before discarding his uniform jacket for a civilian vest and going home to the family farm at Fougères in the Creuse. It was there, between July and September, that he wrote his finest book, *Etrange défaite,* an almost lyrical outpouring of controlled rage.

The fascinating thing about *Etrange défaite* is its disciplined anger: used to fuel not rhetoric but analysis, hence more effective than rhetoric could be—again, not words but things. Sloppiness, slipshoddiness, a system designed to dilute and hence avoid responsibility had marked the French campaign. But, above all, the German victory had been an intellectual victory over people (over *a* people?) who refused to learn from experience, who refused to think. What was the use of French military education, he asked, if it prepared one for anything except for war? But military education was not alone at fault. The whole educational system had to be blamed, even the primary schools—which he generally appreciated, but which had committed "the worst sin": inculcation of a negative view of the fatherland.

For the moment, *Etrange défaite* was buried in the orchard at Fourgères to await better days. Bloch went back to teaching until suspended from his job in November 1943. As a Jew, he would have been fired in October 1940 but for a special measure that recognized, not his military services, but his "exceptional scientific services to France." He seems to have been in touch with the first resisters in Clermont-Ferrand; he certainly joined the Combat network in Montpellier and helped it to organize the surrounding region. As soon as they were old enough, he sent his two eldest sons to join the Free French forces, which they did after the usual spell in a Spanish jail. It may be that as a Jew, rejected by his government and by many of his fellow Frenchmen, with his life threatened by the Germans (and perhaps not only by the Germans), resistance or flight were his only alternatives. Such a choice would help account for the large number of Jews among the small number of resisters, especially before 1943. But in Bloch's case resistance was also, perhaps above all, the inevitable consequence of a personal humiliation, which reflected the national humiliation that had wounded the honor of both himself and France. A review of Anatole de Monzie's *La Saison des juges,* entitled "La Vraie saison des juges," in the November 1943 number of the *Cahiers politiques,* rejects the possibility of reconciliation, of indulgence extended to traitors and enemies, of a *paix blanche.* "The punishment of traitors does not only answer to a profound and legitimate need of the popular conscience . . . for us it will also be . . . the only way to avenge our national honor."

By 1943, back in Lyon, which was, of course, the resistance capital of

France as well as his own birthplace, Bloch had become a full-time underground organizer (he used archival research as pretext for his travels) and,
soon, a leader of the Franc-Tireur group. As we know, and like most others,
he did not last long. Within a few months he was arrested, tortured, and
killed. His wife had died in Lyon while he was in prison. In 1977 Bloch's
ashes were transferred from Saint Didier-de-Formans (Ain) and buried near
Fougères, in the cemetery of Bourg d'Hem, in the rolling countryside he
had come to love. On his gravestone, the only memorial is the phrase he had
chosen for himself: DILEXIT VERITATEM.

No one demonstrates better than Marc Bloch that the great historian
contributes, not a model, but the suggestion of a new way of going about
our business, not a *vision,* but a *view;* vision surviving at best as a document
of its times, the view adding to historical understanding. There is not so
much history that we can learn from Bloch today. His history has become
part of the history we have learned already—to such an extent, indeed, that
reaction may be timely, if not already underway. The local and national pro-
vincialisms against which he recommended supranational and comparative
studies may be ready for fresh explorations; the trivializing personalization
of history that he denounced has been replaced by the equally trivializing
emphasis of collective phenomena. The sins of kings-and-battles history
against which he inveighed through his participation in social groups and
doings cannot justify the obliteration of individual men, let alone of heroic
figures that have caused history to tilt. And the pedantocracy he prosecuted
now rules in his name.

But it would be naive to dismiss Bloch just because we have already
learned his history. There is more to history than a story, however richly we
go about its telling. "The distant past," Bloch wrote only a few months
before he was arrested, "inspires the sense and the respect of differences
between men, at the same time as it refines our sensitiveness to the poetry of
human destinies." In this context all pasts may be considered distant; all
meditations upon other lives and times to inspire and refine.

The essential that is left of Bloch's writings is his style, and there he
remains idiosyncratically singular and fascinating. Herbert Butterfield,
very much a representative of our time, has suggested that half-truths are a
good way of writing trenchant history. Bloch proves him wrong. He knew
that truth was inaccessible, perhaps indefinable, but he pursued it as and
where he could; made very clear the possibilities, the thrills, and the failures of his quest—*our* quest.

PART V

It Takes All Kinds

13

Nationalism, Socialism, and National Socialism

"I wanted to reconcile the movement of social emancipation which is rocking the whole world, and the national fact. I tried, for myself and for my friends, to gather in a general synthesis these two currents that have shaken the twentieth century. Both have been forced to change, and perhaps they will manage to establish a connection."

It was on Friday, November 18, 1960, that a tense, spare, fair young man with a crewcut, Jean-Jacques Susini, born (like Nazi power) in 1933, spoke up and rocked the boat—or, rather, the court, the courtroom, and his fellow-accused, who were bent on greater discretion, at the Procès des Barricades in Paris. He came back next day to eat his words and to restore an atmosphere of vigorous but calm and essentially law-abiding patriotism, without political overtones: the atmosphere his comrades of the Algiers barricades wanted to create and his judges asked only to believe.[1] But he had spoken for many, even of his political opponents, and expressed a point of view which, increasingly popular in postwar France, has never in our time been absent, though always underplayed, from the country's political tradition.

Since the different manifestations of nationalism combined in varying proportions with social concerns have their importance in the story of the last three French republics, I have set out to examine this neglected aspect of modern political fumbling. The result is not an exhaustive study of all the national socialist movements France has known; that would demand a book.[2] The aim of the following pages is, rather, first to trace the persistence and the nature of the national socialist tradition, and then to analyze its inherent contradictions through some of the better-known or more representative of these movements.

There is one sense in which the defeated are always wrong—or, at least, insignificant; a sense in which events decide the names and the ideas that survive and triumph and deserve our attention because of their survival, because of their success, and because of the part these make them play in our history and in our lives.

261

But if persistence is any criterion, then some defeated ideas must have their positive significance too, if only because they keep cropping up over and over again. And then, their persistence must be taken as the expression of enduring realities (ideological and material); and their failures, or apparent failures, must be examined to understand why the forces that recurrently arouse them are incapable of, or insufficient for, apparent success. Or, alternatively, to ascertain whether a measure of success has in fact been achieved, but so discreetly as to deceive all but the most careful observers with an appearance of failure—failure which is no more than the withering of the flower that has achieved its purpose and cast its seed.

If one adopts this latter point of view, it becomes obvious that French political language and habits of thought have been profoundly affected by the work of men and movements sometimes ignored, and even officially condemned (for example, Charles Maurras and the Action française); and it is arguable that the real influence of national socialist ideas has little to do with their apparent lack of success.

Almost a hundred years ago already, speaking in 1896 over the grave of a typical nationalist buccaneer, the Marquis de Morès, Maurice Barrès had taken care to explain that Morès was both nationalist and socialist. As for himself, said Barrès, he never feared to insist upon the intimate union of nationalist and socialist ideas. So much so that when two years later he stood for election at Nancy, his program was headed "Nationalism, Protectionism, and Socialism," and his supporters were the members of the Republican Socialist Nationalist Committee.

The Socialist Nationalists were unsuccessful in 1898. But in a republican and traditionally patriotic province like Lorraine such a label, when sported by one of General Boulanger's bright young epigones (Barrès was then only thirty-six; he had been nine years younger when first elected in 1889 on the Boulangist ticket) was not surprising. It found its place in a tradition illustrated by Pierre-Joseph Proudhon and perhaps even by Gambetta—to go no further back—and one which would be continued by a number of men whose first steps on the political ladder led up socialist rungs, and whose "social" mentality accompanied them, as it did Alexandre Millerand, René Viviani, Albert Thomas, in their later careers.

Men like Millerand were mavericks and opportunists to whom labels meant little and ideologies sometimes less: "men of government" who saw and tackled immediate problems, both personal and national, in immediate and empirical terms. But the occasional and opportunistic combination or alliance of social and patriotic ideas which these men represent is not relevant to our quest. Mentioned *pour mémoire,* they may be left aside.

The connection of socialism and nationalism has existed for a long time;

it is like one of those common-law unions which practice and habit render commonplace and extremely unremarkable. Less so, if only because theoretical discussion has insisted upon their incompatibility, is the ideological alliance of the two, an alliance that interests us here and that, as stated, has never lacked supporters in France since the days of Barrès.

The supporters have been diverse. They range from Gustave Hervé, the impertinent schoolteacher whom Aristide Briand defended for suggesting that the flag's place was on a dunghill—the same who counseled in 1935 and 1936 that c'est Pétain qu'il nous faut, all the way to Maxime Blocq-Mascart of the Conseil National de la Résistance and the Conseil d'État, and, of course, to Jean-Jacques Susini, successor of Pierre Lagaillarde as president of the Students' Association of Algiers.

The first meeting of socialist and nationalist seems to have occurred in the pages of a Barrès's short-lived periodical, La Cocarde (published from September 1894 to March 1895). It grouped such unlikely companions as René Boylesve and Charles Maurras (both later of the Académie française), Frédéric Amouretti, Camille Mauclair (contributor, during the last war, to L'Appel of Pierre Costantini's Ligue française), and extreme syndicalists like Augustin Hamon and Fernand Pelloutier. As resolutely social as they were national, members of the editorial committee (Cocarde, Jan. 17, 1895) greeted President Casimir-Périer's resignation as "one of the moments of the Social Revolution that is slowly taking place . . . and whose accomplishment no power can henceforth prevent." The journal's biographer, Henri Clouard (who later made a name as literary critic), found it "exactly socialist in that it led a relentless struggle against economic liberalism and called for organization of labor and the suppression of the proletariat, that is to say, its integration in society."[3]

The appreciation of the young admirer, then an active follower of Charles Maurras, reveals one characteristic of these nationalists' social concern; interested above all in national unity, they reject class war in favor of class integration, without, however, approving a capitalist and bourgeois order they despise. It was this rejection of bourgeois order—and bourgeois democracy—that provided the basis of the next significant rapprochement which took place at first in the ranks and the tendencies of the royalist Action française, then between the monarchists and the followers of Georges Sorel.

It is not generally appreciated that Action française, which never hid its reactionary views, had before 1914 been extremely interested in questions of social reform and in the possibility of attracting a working-class public it vigorously wooed with posters, with meetings, and with tracts. "We are nationalistic and consequently social," Maurras had declared in the third number of the daily Action française (March 23, 1908). This continued to be so in theory, even when concern for social conservation got the better of concern for social progress,[4] and it was to this that Thierry Maulnier referred when, on the eve of the Popular Front, he told the conservative readers of *la Revue universelle* that "the battalions of Action française had been at the beginning of the century the harbingers of this new Right which, not satisfied with being the party of resistance, meant to be—it too, it *above all*—the party of movement."[5]

It was perfectly true, as Thierry Maulnier reminds us, that Maurras's critique of individualism and liberalism led him to positions very similar to those of Socialists, who were, like him, concerned with a public good superior to the private; like him, too, aware that a society whose members are left to themselves tends toward anarchy and the tyranny of the strongest.

Where Charles Maurras differed from the Socialists was not in matters of social *concern,* but in matters of social *order*—denouncing their egalitarian myths and their belief that authority stems from the mass when, to him, authority is clearly established only by the natural hierarchy of competence and birth. Maurras, then, opposes socialist democracy; he also opposes socialist internationalism. In his great *Dictionnaire politique et critique,* under the heading "Socialism," we read: "There is opposition, contradiction, between egalitarian and international Marxism and the protection of nation and of fatherland. But a socialism that has been freed of democratic and cosmopolitan elements can fit nationalism like a well-made glove fits a beautiful hand."[6]

Such a hand-in-glove relationship would be tried (and found wanting) before the First World War in the stormy courtship of Charles Maurras and Georges Sorel.

We know that about 1907, Sorel began to ease away from the syndicalist movement from which he had expected so much. As the syndicates showed a growing inclination to cooperate with political parties, Sorel found them just as "greedy," just as "hungry," as the reviled bourgeoisie. Within a few years the old theoretician came to agree with Croce that "socialism is dead," and to appreciate the potential public that Action française circles offered him. On April 14, 1910, the *Action française* published an article by "the most powerful and penetrating of French sociologists" on "the Awakening of the French heart" (Péguy's *Mystère de la charité de Jeanne d'Arc*). This was followed on September 29, 1910, by an interview with Sorel, in which the latter declared his turn toward "reaction."

It was in this mood that projects were mooted for a review, to be called *La Cité française* (note the undertone of Fustel de Coulanges, dear to nationalist hearts) and run jointly by syndicalists and nationalists. Sorel even went so far as to draw up the project of a manifesto: "This review addresses itself to the men of reason who have been sickened by the stupid pride of democracy, by the humanitarian bilge, by the fashions come to us from abroad." Then, the *Cité* having fallen through, in the spring of 1911 appeared one of the most intriguing of national socialist reviews: *L'Indépendance*.[7] Its steadiest contributor was Sorel, a patriotic, nationalistic, antisemitic Sorel, who compared France's struggle against the Jews to America's struggle against the yellow peril,[8] and flourished in the company of the Camelots du Roi.

But the more intellectual among the Camelots could not be satisfied by Sorel's rather anarchic criticisms. They want to clear up the persistent confusion between liberty and disorder, and they want an opportunity for national socialistic studies of economic problems. In answer to their demands, in December 1911, the Cercle Proudhon holds its first meeting under the presidency of Charles Maurras. A month later appears the first *Cahier du cercle Proudhon*. Its contributors—and founders of the Cercle (Georges Valois, Henri Lagrange, Gilbert Maire, René de Marans, Édouard Berth)—all agree that "democracy is the greatest error of the past century," the enemy of culture and productivity both. Democracy is responsible for the exploitation of labor, as it is responsible for destructive capitalism. And soon thereafter, in 1912, whilst a special number of the *Cahiers* is dedicated to Sorel, his disciple Édouard Berth publishes *Les Méfaits des intellectuels*, which reveals nationalists and syndicalists at one upon the necessity of destroying the capitalist regime, of restoring monarchy, and (on the way) of reconciling Sorel and Maurras in "a new and fertile synthesis."[9]

Soon after World War I, which destroyed these hopes by reinforcing the established order and decimating most of the *Cahiers'* leading spirits, Drieu la Rochelle (who had been attracted by the eager activity of those halcyon days) could still write of the fascist climate around Charles Péguy and the Action française in 1913, of young men of Lyon who called themselves royalist socialists, of other young men, drunk with heroism and violence, who dreamt of destroying both capitalism and parliamentary socialism. As late as 1936, Pierre Andreu, another survivor of these golden times, would lament the ruined hopes of "1913 Fascism."[10] A few months later, a contributor to the same review also found the essence of fascism in "prewar social nationalism and syndicalism" and the tendency to oppose syndicalism and fascism absurd.[11]

In the meantime, however, the dragons' teeth of prewar activity had sprung up more numerous and more resilient than ever their early sowers seem to have expected.

It was in the spring of 1916 that Gustave Hervé, who had shortly before changed the title of his crusading paper from *La Guerre sociale* to *La Victoire*, first tried to launch his *socialisme national*. This was, at the time, something of a damp squib. But shortly before the elections of 1919, which would prove so disastrous to the left, Hervé and a veteran socialist lawyer, Alexandre Zévaès, who had just defended the murderer of Jaurès before the Seine Assizes and got him off scot free, tried to make a fresh start. As Zévaès explained in *La Victoire* of August 8, 1919, this national socialism drew its inspiration from the old French socialism of Fourier and Saint-Simon, Considérant and Louis Blanc, Lamennais, George Sand and Eugène Sue—not from German intoxicants like those produced by Marx and Engels.

The mixed bag into which the two partners dipped was a romantic one, and it seems that some names were cited more for the purpose of invocation than for that of explanation. The moment did not, in any case, prove propitious; the electorate was bent on relaxation, the entrenched forces on a return to business as usual. Nationalism rode into power with the cohorts of militant conservatism, who looked forward to going back, saw victory in terms of Fourteenth July parades extended to Alsace and Lorraine, and squabbled endlessly over the extension of republican anticlericalism to the newly liberated provinces. Hervé's notion fizzled out along with *La Victoire,* the organ that was supposed to help sell the idea.

More distinguished patrons of the national socialist conjunction appeared a decade later when, in 1933, Jean Hennessy's funds and Alfred Fabre-Luçe's ideas came together in the Parti Social-National. Heir of a name famed among drinkers and of the fortune that went with it, Hennessy entertained ambitions which appear in retrospect to have been in inverse proportion to his capacity of fulfilling them. During the war he had backed Gustave Téry's Jacobin *L'Œuvre* which, having been launched with the slogan "Imbeciles don't read *L'Œuvre,*" had prompted Maurras to remark: "Imbeciles don't read *L'Œuvre,* oh, Hennessy—they just pay for it!" When *L'Œuvre* failed to serve his ends, Hennessy managed to secure control of a briefly famous newspaper, *Le Quotidien,* founded "by honest people, for honest people" and which had slipped out of such gentle hands soon after helping to decide the elections of 1924. Apart from a certain predilection for progressive circles, ideas mattered little enough to Hennessy. But he needed to establish himself as the providential man the country required to resolve the problems of the ambient recession.

Bearing this in mind, it is interesting that such an ambitious opportunist should consider a combination of nationalism and socialism a suitable vehicle for his plans. Maybe it was the formula's success next door, in Germany, that helped convince him. Certainly his resident ideologist, himself the scion of a family closely connected with the Crédit Lyonnais, had found in Germany reassurance—if not inspiration. He was reported as expressing firm accord with Hitler. And *Candide* (June 1, 1933) could only comment suavely what a good thing this was, because now France need only wait for Fabre-Luce to seize power, after which its difficulties would be resolved.

Fabre-Luce never made it; nor, really, did his fellows. But there was no reason why a brandy-manufacturer should not aspire to dictatorship, when a perfume-maker could—and did—and used his fortune trying. François Coty spent the last ten years of his life backing fascists and would-be fascists whose Mussolini he hoped he might become. The first of these, Georges Valois, was responsible in 1922 for the translation and publication of the first book explaining fascism to a newly intrigued French public: Pietro Gorgolini's *Le Fascisme*.

Student of Proudhon, friend and peer of Georges Sorel and Edouard Berth, Valois was a dynamic, self-taught economist, a thinker of great vanity, originality, and talent. Before the war, he had mixed in the curious circles we have described above, and also in the group or groups that turned about Péguy and Sorel, and which a familiar described in 1911: "One would still like to call them socialists, but this is merely out of habit. In fact these antidemocratic syndicalists head straight for the Action française."[12] Valois had been one of those who went, in the belief that the royalist movement would help realize his plans for socioeconomic reform on corporatist lines. To him, "Nationalism plus Socialism equals Fascism." His ideal was to persuade workers to act together, regardless of traditional labels and divisions irrelevant to their true interests. His greatest success in the middle twenties was the debauching of the Communist mayor of Périgueux, whom he persuaded that communist activity could be carried out on the national plane, a point of view which led that gentleman out of the Communist party into fascist ranks before returning him to obscurity and oblivion.

Valois himself left the Action française in 1925, because he sought a more lively activity, both national and socialist, than Maurras' movement could furnish after the war had drained it of its most social-minded members. He tried to gain his ends with a rather mixed team (including Jacques Arthuys, Philippe Barrès, and a wealthy oil-man, Serge André) in the pages of *Le Nouveau Siècle* and the ranks of a French *fascio*, directly and unequivocally inspired by its transalpine forerunners.

It is hard to imagine today the enthusiasm with which veterans flocked into the ranks of the new organization. Disgruntled by the financial crisis of the times, disillusioned by a world very difficult for heroes to live in and in which no one asked their advice, dreaming of an orderly, comradely, and "pure" society, the cream of *anciens combattants* donned the blue shirts of the Faisceau and marched in its parades. Communists came to join them, and also syndicalist leaders like Loridan, who had made his name organizing the powerful textile unions of Roubaix-Tourcoing-Lille, and very bright young men like Philippe Lamour.[13] So much so that, for a moment, Parliament, banks, and unions felt the touch of fear before the activities of this lively and active opposition. Then Poincaré reestablished the franc and, by 1928, the fascist threat (which Léon Daudet never ceased to call the *Fesso*) disintegrated under the blows of royalists and republicans, capital and labor, all of whom it had briefly scared and who, much aided by the Faisceau's own loss of impetus, abetted by a newly indifferent public, had combined to get the better of it.

Valois himself vegetated on through the thirties: we find him at one time close to Trotskyite circles, later at Vichy, later still deported by the Germans to Bergen-Belsen, where he died shortly before the liberation of the camp—the waste of a good man.

François Coty, for his part, did not despair; he had many irons in the fire, and many leagues. Typical of these was Jean Renaud's Solidarité française, which showed itself particularly combative on February 6, 1934, but which, being less a group of doctrinaires than one of mobile toughs, need not concern us here.[14]

In 1933, however, a lesser companion of the defunct Faisceau, much decorated Marcel Bucard, founded the Francistes whose fascism was more self-consciously national socialist. Characteristically, in the spring of 1934, we find the party organ declining an invitation to join a nationalist coalition, denying that francism could be considered a right-wing movement, and sneering at the idea that there could be anything in common between Francists and "conservatives and reactionaries" like Jean Renaud, Taittinger (of the Jeunesses Patriotes), or de la Rocque.[15]

Dissolved in the Popular Front's offensive against armed leagues, the movement was resurrected by the Germans after 1940. Arrested in the Tyrol, where he had sought to hide after following his German patrons in their rout, Bucard was condemned and shot in 1946. To this brave, unintelligent man, who had worked for Hervé on *La Victoire,* for Valois in *Le Nouveau Siècle,* fascism—and Francism—drew both its elements and its spirit from the left; because "being the opposite of Marxism, it is much nearer socialism—understood in the sense of social justice—than it is to bourgeois conservatism which it holds in horror."[16]

Much of francist activity consisted in disputes with a rival body of the same name, recruited by a certain Henry Coston who after the Second World War made a pretty income out of scissor-and-paste compilations like *Le Retour des deux cent familles* (Paris, 1959). Throughout the thirties, and under varying titles, Coston directed a *Libre Parole* in the tradition of Edouard Drumont, now daily, now monthly, now weekly, only less vivid and also far less read. [17] His Francistes, who claimed to be the true Francistes because they preserved and cherished the true old antimasonic and anti-semitic ideas which Bucard was accused (rather unjustly) of neglecting, also called themselves the Parti National Ouvrier et Paysan, and kept up a "fascist guard." Fortunately for Coston, his fascism was more of the pen than of the knuckle-duster variety; his fascist guards (that had no Coty money to recruit with) dissolved before he could sell them to the Germans, and this probably saved his life after the war.

But all these were costly enterprises. Coty died ruined. His pretorians disappeared, some into lasting obscurity, others into suspended animation, others into the ranks of rival but similar organizations. For in the middle thirties there was no shortage of openings in France, in leagues and parties all of which professed that nationalism was social, and socialism necessarily national, most of which would have endorsed the words of then-fascist Jacques Debu-Bridel: "We are anticapitalist because we are national and anti-Marxist . . . Our doctrine has its roots in the soil of France. The very term of national socialism can be found in one of our dearest masters: Barrès." [18]

I should remark in passing that the most successful league of the thirties, even though it came to call itself, not unsignificantly, Parti Social Français (P.S.F.), does not fit into the national-socialist category. Colonel Count de la Rocque was a respectable, law-abiding man, respectful of the established order at least to the extent of accepting its subsidies. Most of his followers, like himself, were frightened by the Bolshevik menace, exasperated by economic straits and problems they could not begin to understand, anxious about the country's future and their own. But soup-kitchens and parades are not enough to make national socialists, and the Croix de Feu or P.S.F. simply do not qualify as anything more than patriotic conservatives.

Even without them, however, the crop is rich enough; Jacques Doriot, Marcel Déat, each deserves a study in national socialism. Both were anti-communist with a strong "social" tinge—less theoretical for the mayor of Saint-Denis, more so with Marcel Déat.

Doriot's Parti Populaire Français (P.P.F.) acted after 1936 as a catch-all for social authoritarians of every imaginable background: many ex-Communists, of course, who had left the party in the wake of Doriot himself, and ex-Socialists like Paul Marion, but also straight fascists: Victor Arrighi and Fabre-Luce from Hennessy's Parti Social National, Popelin and Maud'hui dissatisfied with the Croix de Feu, Claude Jeantet and others of the *Je Suis Partout* team from the Action française, and a host of others, not least questing intellectuals like Drieu la Rochelle, Ramon Fernandez, Maurice Duverger and Bertrand de Jouvenel. As the latter himself has told us, most P.P.F. men were inveterate joiners, league-hopping in search of salvation.[19] They evidently thought to have found it in the forceful man who proposed to tear away the disfiguring mask of capitalism, reveal the true face of France, and free it for its civilizing mission among the backward nations.[20]

Déat, for his part, had made his way into politics by way of the École Normale Supérieure, and his mark in 1933 at the Socialist Congress held at the Mutualité Hall in Paris. The speeches which he and his fellow-socialist deputies, Adrien Marquet and Barthélémy Montagnon, delivered on that occasion, argued in effect that the reigning plutocracy could be removed only by a revolution that French Socialists have lost from view, a revolution that is essential even if it should be a fascist one.[21]

Déat had already outlined his views two years before this in a remarkably perceptive book, *Perspectives socialistes* (Paris, 1931), published by none other than Georges Valois. The book insisted on the need for union with other opponents of the capitalist order, rather than purely socialist action on classic and isolated lines. Ten years later its author, whom his 1939 refusal to die for Danzig had made acceptable to the Germans, founded a party destined to carry out his ideas of 1931 and 1933. The Rassemblement National Populaire (R.N.P.) was founded in 1941 and died in 1944. During the first of these years it was colonized by the gangsters of Eugène Deloncle's prewar terrorist Cagoule, revived by German warrant under the promising label of Mouvement Social Révolutionnaire (M.S.R.). Once he had got rid of the M.S.R. gang, however, Déat drew his followers chiefly from the ranks of the academic and journalistic left: men like Francis Delaisi, Georges Albertini or, again, Ludovic Zoretti—who had set up the C.G.T.'s Centre d'Éducation Ouvrière and helped to found the International Teachers Union. This R.N.P., reflection of Déat's earliest theories, was like its maker interested in a modern socialism: national, popular, and authoritarian, anticapitalistic but not antisemitic, and anticlerical not on principle but only within the limits of immediate needs. It is particularly interesting in our context, however, as an instance of a national socialist movement, drawing its inspiration and its cadres from the left where most of the others drew theirs either from the right or from the sort of authoritarian opportunism we tend to associate with "the fascist temperament," but reaching much the same conclusions as the others.

It is easy to understand why Léon Blum should be appalled by the heretical prospects he could glimpse in the speeches of his fellow Socialists: he could foresee their logical end in a national socialist camp that events identified with Germany, Hitler, and death. But if they got there in the end, it must have been in good part because the S.F.I.O. Socialists persisted in ignoring that reality of our time which fascists accepted—more than accepted, felt in their bones: the need to *do* something and to feel that something was being done, the will to motion for motion's sake, to action for action's sake, to revolution for revolution's sake.

Pierre Lassieur has expressed this sentiment very well in *Le Roman d'un condamné à mort* (Paris, 1950), which is simply the fictionalized life of Robert Brasillach whom execution (for collaboration, in 1944) turned into one of the literary right's most patented heroes. For Lassieur as for Brasillach, whose boy-scout enthusiasm at Nüremberg rallies, at *Je Suis Partout,* in the Spanish holocaust or in the vaster one that followed remains the most striking thing about him, fascism is a great romantic adventure. Not reason but feelings drag him along the road of passionate action. In the words of Pol Vandromme, fascism offered the men of the right what communism offered to those of the left: "the banners of revolution, the exaltation of the clan, the prestige of the leader, of his guard, and his standards." Taken for a policy, it was really, says Vandromme, "a sort of morality of style." And in his life of Robert Brasillach[22] he insists on this fact that, for the best of them, for the purest and most disinterested, for Brasillach himself, fascism was never a doctrine, "mais un grand mouvement de fièvre."

Much the same can be said, not in praise or in excuse (for feverish activity or attitudes in public matters end too often in disaster) but as a factual observation, of many who adopted the communist religion between the wars. And it may well be that the professional politicians who reinvented national socialism in the France of the thirties—whether at the Socialist Congress of 1933 or, soon thereafter, at Saint-Denis, while they were neither boy scouts nor irresponsible journalists driven forward by the impetus of their polemics, did also feel the touch of this prevailing fever. A Marquet, a Déat, sensed the need for something—*not* more coherent, more logical, more theoretically perfect, but on the contrary more incoherent, more attuned to the moment's complex demands. They sought a sort of revolutionary glamor, a revolutionary promise, that would not rest upon—and only upon—a body of doctrine still cherished only by faithful doctrinaires and irrelevant to the tendencies of the public and the needs of the moment.

This is probably what Pétain's aide, Dumoulin de Labarthète noticed "chez les néos" when he wrote of a combination of the English Labour spirit, of the Millerandism of 1912 (when, with Poincaré, Millerand, then minister of war, had incarnated the current nationalist revival), and of the mentality of those radicals who, in the days of Boulangist fever, had held the bridle of the General's black horse.

From Boulanger to Déat, by way of Barrès certainly, and perhaps of Millerand, seems a strange and crooked road. The explanation is furnished by another traveler upon it, and one whom we have already met—the bright young critic who in 1934 contributed a preface to the French edition of Moeller van den Brueck's *Le Troisième Reich*—Thierry Maulnier. Fascisms, Maulnier tells us, have come into being because liberal democracy has shown itself unable to cope with the vital problems that face it: "What creates fascism is the fatal, evident disintegration of liberal democracy." [23]

Loss of hope in the possibilities of existing order and society, disgust with their corruption, produce a revolutionary mood in which the only issue lies in catastrophic action—but always with a strong social tinge: "I place my only hope in the continuation of socialist advance through fascisms," writes Drieu. "For the necessary subversion, the élites of disinterestedness will be reinforced by the élites of despair," declares Thierry Maulnier. "Both violences are necessary; it is up to us to join them." And Jean-Pierre Maxence: "All that is left to Frenchmen is the revolution of disgust." For that he calls insurgents of all parties to join "the front of a reconciled youth for bread, for grandeur and for freedom, in immense disgust with capitalist democracy." [24] From this angle, as from many others, fascism looks very much like the Jacobinism of our time.

There is no doubt that, at least in France, it was the failure, real or apparent, of the established order to guard itself and its dependents which created and recruited the troops of fascist reaction. But the appearance of these troops may also be cited in evidence of the middle classes' determination to defend themselves. No serious observer feared a fascist threat in the France of 1923. But by 1924 the threat had materialized. And the speed with which leagues blossomed in 1924 and 1925, only to wither on the branch in 1926, once Poincaré had managed his financial stabilization, may just reflect the healthy readiness of threatened capital first to recruit and then to demobilize whatever support circumstances required.

Nothing is more significant in this respect than the reaction that followed the first demonstration, after the first world war, of the revived left. The elections of 1924 had brought defeat to the conservative forces elected in 1919. In November 1924, great working class demonstrations accompanied the highly symbolic transfer to the Panthéon of the remains of Jean Jaurès. The flood of cloth caps and shabby clothes behind the red flags of workers' delegations convinced the middle classes that Herriot's Cartel government was either incapable of defending their interests, their property, their very existence, against advancing Bolshevism, or else unwilling to do it. There followed in quick succession the creation of the Jeunesses Patriotes, of the Ligue Républicaine Nationale, of the Ligue d'Ordre et de la Conservation Sociale, of Valois' Faisceau, and of other, lesser bodies by the score, mostly provincial and mostly short-lived. As one of their communist opponents would comment in a pamphlet of 1926: "This is the moment, above all, when the true fascist movement begins. The bourgeoisie wished to raise an organization that could withstand us, that could stop the drift of the petty bourgeoisie, attract it, and oppose us by force."[25]

Movements of this sort are the pure expression of reaction. A social class or a body of men think their interests threatened and organize to defend them. There is nothing "social" about such a reaction, hardly even a pretense. But while social reaction and social thoughtlessness have made their contribution to fascism, and while, as we have seen, fascism has often been identified with national socialism, even by those who should know best, it is possible to distinguish between the two, if only at the doctrinal level. For, while what people say about their ideas does not always match what they actually do, it does reflect their assumptions, which they usually respect—if only in the breach.

Now, between fascism and national socialism there is a first and very obvious difference in that the former has always rejected theory in favor of practice, and relied largely on the attraction of that "fever" to which Vandromme referred. The fascist ethos is emotional and sentimental; at that level, the ends of action count less than action itself, and the forces that lead men into the fascist camp can be enlisted on any side whatsoever, provided they are given an opportunity to indulge themselves—the more violently, the better. This indiscriminate nature of the fascist personality appears in figures as far apart as Darnand, Doriot, and Drieu la Rochelle, who might have been a lot of things and were, indeed, by turns, first one thing, then another.

The national socialist, on the other hand, is very theoretical indeed. He may use theory merely to rationalize, but he respects it. Whatever he may pretend, words and ideas count for him as much as actions, and sometimes they replace them. What Valois or Déat seem to have sought was a new *system* which, unlike old ones that had been tried and found wanting, would serve to rebuild or repair the failing structure of the state. The state—here is the crux of national socialist thought. Whether his origins are on the ideological left, like those of Hervé or Déat, or on the right, like those of Thierry Maulnier, the national socialist considers that the unit of action is the nation and the means of action is the state. He does not, like the Socialists, affirm faith in an international brotherhood that never existed. He does not, like conservative nationalists, seek the disintegration of central power and its liquidation for the profit of provincial and peripheral interests.[26] He recognizes the need for reform, and reform in a collectivistic direction; he realizes that such reforms need a strong central authority to carry them through and that, as things stand, they can only be envisaged within the limited sphere of national sovereignty.

The fact remains that public opinion is far more particularist than international-minded, that local particularisms affirm themselves ever more strongly even within federalist or national schemes, and that an appeal to national (or local) pride and national (or local) interests is more likely to succeed than one to any kind of other-regarding altruism. Besides, it seems increasingly clear that human society is not one, that higher wages for African workers mean higher prices for European ones, that more liberty for poor Arabs tends to mean less for poor Frenchmen (and vice-versa), and that while the world *may* be capable of the rational organization that would eliminate such friction and inconsequence, it is quite unwilling, freely, to take the steps such an organization would necessitate.

And so, the national socialist builds a doctrine upon the observation that in practice socialist organization and reform has been national— whether in Russia, England, or China, and that what countries need in order to repair, reform and reconstruct themselves is not more freedom but more power: power to secure freedom from outside interference, and also to impose what is called for by the General Will . . . that General Will which, as Rousseau has told us, is not necessarily the will of all, or even that of most.

For a nation to repair itself, it must be united. And the unity must be achieved, if not by persuasion, by force. But here force is only a means, and not a necessary one: the end is unity. Georges Valois was certain that "in my father's house there are many mansions." So was de Gaulle.

Many political groups and many politicians in the 1950s and 1960s preached or practiced national socialism without knowing it, as Monsieur Jourdain did prose. But the only group that clearly and self-consciously represented the doctrine (for M. Susini represented no group) were the Jeunesses Socialists Patriotes (J.S.P.), who expressed their views in a hard-to-find publication called *Patrie et Progrès*. With Léon Boutbien, member of the S.F.I.O.'s directing committee, ex-Ambassador to Israel P.-E. Gilbert, and Maxime Blocq-Mascart, founder of the *Parisien libéré* and director of several large companies, we have here a section of the "left" different from that which François Mauriac tried to catechize in the pages of *L'Express*. Their program, as presented in the first number of *Patrie et Progrès* (November 1958), rejected capitalism, proposed the nationalization of banks, the suppression of business profits, and the confiscation of property destined for too conspicuous consumption, like the villas and the yachts of M. Boussac.

Since 1958, their posters, rejecting both the intellectualism of the antinationalist left and the opportunism of the right, expressed these views in concise slogans: "Economic planning, national independence, *Algérie française*." The ritual call for this last alienated some personalities otherwise close to their views—like Léo Hamon, ex-senator and professor of law. But it implied no sympathy for conservatives like Pinay and Bidault, still less for "senile" generals whether they rattle their swords or their pens. To J.S.P., *Algérie française* meant solidarity with the younger cadres of the army and civil service interested in planning, building, and reforming both at home and overseas. They counted among their number an impressive proportion of distinguished young technocrats, both civil and military.

The J.S.P. ideal is probably close to those national technocracies that are installing themselves here, there, and everywhere, but piecemeal and imperfectly because their existence and the need for their existence cannot be recognized either in communist or democratic countries, in liberal or socialist ideology. Patriot-socialists, on the other hand, seem to want to plan ahead on the basis of an open admission of facts elsewhere denied or ignored, to prepare an authoritarian, technocratic revolution for the France of tomorrow. It remains to be seen whether the open expression of such heretical views will pay, and whether men who menace so many of the interests and prejudices vested in the present system (and in its gradual evolution) will ever get very close to the levers of power. (They have not.)

But the proliferation of ideas such as theirs (France even knows a small but articulate National-Communist party) offers food for thought. There is, as Susini said, and as we too often and too wishfully forget, a national fact. And there is a movement, indeed there are a great many movements, of social emancipation that are tearing through the world and tearing it apart. These are the two great, the two chief, realities of our time. To envisage one without the other is too easy and too wrong. They can be tackled only when they are reconciled, and this can be done only by thinking them through to the point where synthesis need no longer be impossible.

While many Western governments practice policies that might be described as socialistic, at least loosely and in part, and practice them on the national plane, this unconscious or necessary national socialism presents us with a twofold problem. It is clear that, everything being equal, a camouflaged or fumbling policy will always be less successful than a deliberate and acknowledged one. It follows that a situation where national-socialist aims can be admitted, and the best means of attaining them envisaged in function of these aims, is preferable to the familiar embarrassed rationalizations and excuses designed to defend reforms from the accusation of being "socialistic."

Socialism, in any case, has become a practically meaningless term. It is, in certain cases, a pejorative label to stick on undesired men or measures; in others, a popular description of desired but undefined reforms. It applies best to measures carried out following a general plan and involving a redistribution of national income and influence within the nation, according to decisions made by specialists in the service of a central power. Considerations of humanity and social justice play a smaller part in this kind of technocratic planning than they did in the original socialism of the nineteenth century. Material comfort and socioeconomic opportunity are desired for all, but for utilitarian reasons and within the limits of more general interests in which the good of the community may not, and often does not, coincide with the immediate good of single individuals. Rousseau and Robespierre, Marx and Maurras, all understood this just as well as the theorists of Bolshevik revolution; but the roots of European socialism lay in humanitarian rather than utilitarian concerns. This duality of inspiration has served to confuse most discussions in our time, for the simple reason that humanitarian socialists have nearly always hidden, even from themselves, behind a thick cloud of utilitarian doctrine. They try to justify their charitable intentions with pseudo-scientific rationalizations, disguise moral judgments behind the vocabulary of positivistic analysis, and practice the piecemeal reforms which their humanity suggests.

Once we distinguish between humanitarian socialists and utilitarian ones, the situation becomes much clearer. There is little to prevent the latter from operating on the national and, if convenient, the nationalist plane. We may not like what they do, but at least we shall know a little better what we (and they) are talking about.

Humanitarian socialism is almost necessarily pacifist and internationalistic, because the same concerns that make men care for their fellows at home apply to human beings everywhere. It is idealistic, because it is founded on sentiment and on ideals; it will therefore do best in fairly prosperous societies where a margin for luxury exists. This kind of socialism tends to collapse before sterner realities, when self-interest at the individual level or that of the group gets the upper hand. Its adherents, then, have the choice between martyrdom (usually on a small scale, ineffective but self-satisfying as it seems to be in the case of conscientious objectors) and conformity ("we shall suspend our pacifism until the war is over"). Useful as a palliative, and also as an educative force, this kind of socialism is useless at times of crisis.

Utilitarian socialism, on the other hand, is opportunistic and empirical, doctrinaire only for technical reasons (not the least dangerous sort), and inclined to consider men and women only as part of groups which are the significant units of political calculation. Where the former socialism is sentimental, the latter tries to be mathematical. And given this approach, there is no reason to wonder at apparent changes in orientation, such as can be found aplenty in Soviet history for instance, even though there matters are confused by a Marxist religion that imposes forms of speech and of exegesis which can mislead both faithful and outsiders.

This, then, is the solution to one part of the problem, or at least to its better understanding; national socialism is possible when the socialism in question is of the utilitarian kind, as capable of cold empirical opportunism in its internal politics as nationalism has always been in external politics.

The trouble with French national socialists is that while pretending to be coldly and ruthlessly utilitarian, they were in fact being romantic and sentimental. Their occasional ruthlessness itself was part of their terrible trappings, a disguise, a *mise-en-scène* designed to persuade themselves and their beholders that they were really serious, and capable of passing from words to deeds. All this is very confusing for, at first sight, the difference between authentic and synthetic toughness is hard to tell, when both flaunt Machiavellian theories and murderous activism. The difference, however, appears upon reflection.

The utilitarian, for instance, concerned with efficiency, considers "action" from the point of view of minimum effort and will just as soon avoid violence if he can gain his ends without it. The romantic considers the value of the gesture and its excitement even more than its results. His desire to appear strong and consistent may lead, at times, to mere acts of self-justification, dangerous to him and perhaps to others. There is bravery in Robert Brasillach's continuing to stand with the men of *Je Suis Partout,* whose extreme collaborationist ideas he no longer shared after 1943. But it is a gratuitous, schoolboy bravery, the loyalty and pride of one "qui ne veut pas se dégonfler," who will not let the side down even though it is wrong and drags others along the wrong road.

It is doubtful whether the values that presided over the charge of the Light Brigade should dominate our actions, more doubtful still whether we have the right to inflict them upon others. Insistence upon playing the game in such circumstances may be admirable according to the code of chivalry, but it is a game one plays chiefly to satisfy one's own idea of oneself. A private individual may act according to his code, may try to live up to a model he has set himself. When a public person does so, whose words and deeds can influence others, the question arises whether he has a right to selfish actions that fulfill his code of honor; and whether such acts are more honorable than any indulged in for reasons we generally hold in contempt. Fortunately, the question is not one that concerns us in this context. It is enough to say that a great many French national socialists found themselves driven on, not by cool-headed calculations, but by winds of sentiment and passion they were either unwilling or unable to control.

It is no wonder, either, that—to nourish their dreams of authoritarian force—they had from the beginning indulged in every kind of theatrical dodge. There is no need to dwell on the love of uniforms, especially shirts, that afflicted almost every movement of this kind: the blue raincoats of the

Jeunesses Patriotes, the green shirts of Dorgères' Front Paysan, the blue shirts of Valois' Faisceau, then of Bucard's Francistes, the gray shirts of Adrien Marquet's followers in the Gironde, all the way to the handsome SS garb of the Milice. It was a fever to which even Déat succumbed and, just as in 1943 he advised his followers to join Darnand's Milice (the idea was to infiltrate and take it over!), so in 1940 his abortive projects for a single national party included uniforms that turned around more shirts and *bérets-basques*.

But let us consider a group that remained immune to uniformity; a group whose pride lay in the empirical Machiavellianism of its leaders: the Action française.

The essence of A.F. arguments lay in readiness to grasp power by any available means—even legal ones. For forty years, after 1899, in the pages of daily, weekly, and monthly publications by the dozen and books by the hundred, they discussed at length, in great detail, and with the utmost cogency, just how power might be seized, how they would go about it, the reasonings and ruses they would use to get their way. They proclaimed their Machiavellian views in every *salon* and on every rooftop, so much so that from being Machiavellian they soon began to seem naïve.

The wolf never greeted Little Red Riding Hood with roars of "WOLF!," but many members of Action française did little else. The feeling that they were dangerous conspirators was so exalting that they had to share it and, shared, it became more intense, though far less justified. The prolonged and public discussion of the revolution-to-come came to replace the revolution itself. And when certain hotheads went off on their own to plot and plan in secret, A.F. went out of its way to ridicule them by calling them Cagoulards.

Certainly, the leaders of Action française were right in thinking that their task was didactic, not conspiratorial. The point is that they insisted on the second as well, to satisfy the sentimental needs of their followers—and probably their own, as well—for something more exciting than mere history and logic.

This insistence that he is Auguste Comte, when he is really d'Artagnan (or perhaps Porthos), is the characteristic and the weakness of the French would-be nationalist socialist. This is the only kind that concerns us here; for the conservative nationalist is more conservative than nationalist and, as such, prefers maneuver to theory; while the mere socialist has a theory that is equally vitiated by d'Artagnanism, but of quite a different order. It is perhaps in the nature of the modern romantic to visualize himself as a cool-headed, hard-hearted positivist. A Provençal poet has taught him how essential it is to be so; and, since Charles Maurras, no self-respecting nationalist would be anything but rational. Yet the lyricism pierces through the sober surface, the cloven hoof of passion peeps beneath the vestments of positivism, and, in the end, our national socialist returns to the great nineteenth-century tradition of sentimental, adventurous romance—national and social because a hundred years ago national and social activity was considered romantic. With Chateaubriand's René he calls on long-awaited storms to rise. And this is a tendency—and a tradition—that none has incarnated better than Edouard Drumont.

It is significant how many of the would-be national socialists of the twentieth century have trodden in the footsteps of Drumont. Everything that Coty touched was full of him: from Valois to his biographer, Bernanos, and on. "The nationalist formula is born almost wholly from him," wrote Maurras when Drumont died, "and Daudet, Barrès, all of us, started upon our voyage in his light."[27] Bucard's *Francisme,* according to a recent commentator, was in effect "Drumont retouched by Mussolini." If Bucard and Coston disputed his heritage, if the Action française was full of men whom he inspired (beginning with Léon Daudet), some of the reason for this may lie in the "social" and anticapitalist nature of Drumont's thought. For, if Drumont's great success of 1886, *La France juive,* was a reactionary book, the reaction it expressed was against the money power, against what the Duc d'Orléans would call "anonymous and vagabond wealth" and its corrupting effects upon society and the state. His point of view was close to that of contemporary socialists, who also equated moral and political action, to whom antisemitism seemed natural at a time when Jew was synonymous with usurer or banker, and Rothschilds and Péreires were the symbols of high finance.[28]

Drumont's *Libre Parole,* "ce curieux journal qui est lu par des curés et des communards,"[29] was founded in 1892, partly on the proceeds—moral and material—of his most "social" book, *Le Secret de Fourmies* (Paris, 1892). Fourmies was the small northern town where, on May 1, 1891, government troops had shot down striking miners, their women, and their children so that, wrote appalled observers, the gutters ran red with blood. The lines that Drumont penned about one of the dead, the young working girl Marie Blondeau, furnish a perfect example of his approach and his appeal:

> The child of the people had begun her day by working from the very first rays of light, and the light was not yet gone before she fell under the lead of other children of the people, like herself . . . She was literally scalped, the whole top of her head was torn off; the *curé* gathered the bits of her brain scattered on the pavement, but no one ever found the magnificent fair hair of which she had been so

proud. Legend pretends that this hair was stolen and sold. It probably went to deck the bald head of some old Jewish baroness; and some ruined gentleman, playing the comedy of love before the crone in the hope of a loan from her husband, may, in a *boudoir* of the fashionable quarter, have covered with his kisses the fair remains of the murdered working lass.[30]

This is a collector's piece, not because such passages are rare in the chronicles of purple prose, but because it provides such a good instance of the *genre*. Drumont, here, gives us everything: the pure and suffering poor, the Jewish profiteers, the corrupt aristocracy, the lie indirect—based on fact (death of Marie Blondeau) and on assumptions (disappearance of her hair); and, finally, the assumptions being treated as fact, the feeling that such horrors as he has imagined should not go unpunished by men with any sense of chivalry and justice. Social indignation here, like antisemitism, becomes a question of *noblesse oblige,* and thus acceptable to men who might otherwise reject it.

Except during its conservative-Catholic period, when it was run by Henri Bazire and Joseph Denais, *La Libre Parole* would stick to the social romanticism of Drumont: its national enthusiasms fed on firm belief in a plot-theory of history that made it see everywhere the ill-hidden hand of Judeo-masonic treachery in the service of corrupt and corrupting capitalism . . . and, of course, vice-versa; its social concerns exasperated by hatred of the common capitalist enemy, busily planning the perdition of the proletariat and the ruin of France.

It seems today that antisemitism is no longer the absolutely necessary concomitant of national or socialist activity. But old habits die hard, so do old prejudices, and the Jew reappears as symbol of the rootless and probably subversive alien where, before, he had stood for occult money power. Nationalists and socialists would do better to realize the irrelevance of the so-called Jewish question to their concerns; as for ourselves, antisemitism continues to furnish an easy means of superficial identification for old-fashioned nationalists and nationalist doctrines.

But if antisemitism is irrelevant to the true concerns of nationalists and socialists, it is hardly irrelevant to their failure. It appears, above all, as the classic red herring which—with the suggestion of obscure malevolent intrigues by powerful and hidden plotters—can turn from its course a social analysis that threatens to pierce through the nonsense-curtain of press and pretense. And, once we begin to understand the significance of antisemitism in this role, we can understand the fate of national socialism much better. For the prophets and tenants of national socialism needed money to become effective on the public plane, and they got this money from men whose interest it was that these leaders should not become effective in ways harmful to their patrons. The enemies of anonymous and vagabond fortune were encouraged to pursue their quarry in directions as insignificant as they were superficially exciting. *The Protocols of the Elders of Zion,* still seriously referred to in some circles, furnished the prototype of such conspiracies. The Jews, with their supposed racial community, formed the core of a vast international underground that also included Masons hidden behind mysterious rites, and certain secondary or maverick financiers.

Thus men who started out with the excellent idea of tracing and neutralizing the doings of diversified and irresponsible money powers that weigh upon the destinies of their nation and of the world, were quite literally led astray: taken over, or persuaded to campaign on side-issues which combined glamor for the public and innocuousness for the interests they might have threatened. And every would-be-socialist league found its national-minded backers eager to support campaigns that would combine the excitement dear to activist hearts with the uselessness demanded by the money interests they represented. There were Berliet and Georges Claude for the Action française, Jacques Taittinger for the Jeunesses Patriotes, Coty & Co. for a swarm of proto-fascist enterprises, and the nameless millions of business money, oil money, textile money, sugar and alcohol money, gas-electricity-and-other money, that flowed into the coffers of newspapers and parties ranging from extreme right to almost extreme left, with only one end in view: the domestication of men and movements which, whatever their professed opinions, could in the end be used for the concrete ends of invisible and irresponsible money interests.[31]

True, most men, and most movements too, asked no better than to be domesticated: the naïveté of some, the cynicism of others, the second-rate abilities of many, go a long way to explain the facility with which the nationalist enemies of capital became its mercenaries.[32]

The antimasonic campaigns of Vichy are a good example of how inability and unwillingness to get to the bottom of things can be disguised into a semblance of forceful and effective action. These campaigns did serve one purpose, however: that of exploding the masonic myth. The myth of Jewish power (and especially Jewish cohesion) has proved harder to exorcise. Its absence from such recent national-socialist thought as that of Déat or of the J.S.P. may be due to an effort for renewal in nationalist quarters, to recruits from sections of society not until now affected by middle-class antisemitic prejudices, or to the fact that the patrons of fictionalized diversions (some of whom are and have always been Jews) no longer consider antisemitism *de bon ton,* it being too likely to explode in their faces.

But the heritage of Drumont has remained to confuse the issues, and to subordinate efficacy to morality (or, really, simili-morality) in the manner of an earlier age. It encourages the romantic nationalist, more interested in gestures than in doctrine, to pretend that doctrine matters; and the social-minded nationalist, more interested in doctrines than in gestures, to believe that gestures matter. What is worse, it offers a vast treasure-trove of simple and fascinating explanations, as full of obscene enemies and fair maidens as a Gothic romance, and about as historically accurate. The Jews, the Masons, the various enemies of the people, are still presented as facile but convincing reasons for difficulties which have other, and otherwise perceptible, causes. They excite, they mislead, they sentence to failure perfectly well-meaning people whom tradition has condemned to begin their social studies with the works of the Master—or of his pupils.

The worst of this is that, of course, the plot-theory of history is right; as right, that is, as any partial theory of history can be—an indication, a hint, of things to look for. One has only to read Beau de Loménie, or Augustin Hamon, or even the *Canard Enchaîné,* to sense that things go on within the old-boy network which historians hardly ever manage to approach. These things are no less important for leaving behind them no evidence that serious historians will (seriously) consider until it is more than three hundred years old. But where Drumont is so terribly mistaken and misleading is when he assumes a peculiarly effective fraternity among Masons or Jews . . . or Protestants—and, hence, a group significance that is not there. His act is a variant of the practice of the popular press, whose intimate insipidities concerning Stars, Queens, and Babies direct attention upon what is irrelevant and inessential and, by their emphasis of private and passional factors, discourage or deflate all accurate analysis of public affairs. Instead of serving up the secrets of some princely alcove, Drumont pretends to offer those of politicians and of financiers. His readers, conditioned to take group solidarities for granted (racial, national, class solidarities that they know and understand), accept the analyses he offers and, with them, many of his other ideas. The analysis is mistaken whenever it seeks to generalize on the basis of isolated facts, the ideas are out of date, and the Drumont tradition can only lead them into error.

This has been the fate of nationalists who have operated within it, that is of all French national socialists with the exception of Marcel Déat, whose theory has always been better than his practice.

Thus, when M. Susini elaborated his national socialist ideas, it was "in the context of a revolutionary war," in which the Army was envisaged as "an army of missionaries and crusaders, of fighters for a revolutionary cause of general significance." This cause, which is the salvation of the West, could not be successful without profound political and social changes which would adapt France to the movement that affects the world.[33]

If we did not know this as the style of soldiers and activists who have read Mao Tse-Tung and have adapted, if not adopted, his ideas, we should recognize in it the language of Nazi salvation through a new order in Europe. Of course, the similarity is not fortuitous when we know that Joseph Bilger, the Nazi-like Alsatian, had by 1960 graduated to the General Secretariat of M.P. 13 (Mouvement pour le 13 Mai), and that sometime-SS men of the L.V.F. (Légion des Volontaires français) provide the cadres of youth movements that open their meetings with Nazi songs and *stimmungsmusik* designed to create (or recreate) the proper mood. On another level, the F.E.N. (Federation of Nationalist Students), set up on May 1, 1960, to oppose the antinational activities of the reigning left-wing students' union, proposes an ideology which "inspired by Barrès, Maurras, Drieu la Rochelle, and Brasillach," aims to set up "a national, authoritarian and popular State."[34]

We find ourselves once more in the realm of patriotic and social mysticism, harking back to the classic masters who propose the cult of the dead, the logic of hierarchic authority, the glamor of comradeship, of action, and of a new heroic order. Yet it is not the theories of these masters that the F.E.N. invokes, for they are more different than alike, but their shades. In 1960, they cite these disparate names as Zévaès had cited others forty years before, in order to conjure up not so much ideas as a mood. The air-raid sirens, the tramp of heavy boots, the cannonades, and marches on magnetic tape that furnish the *stimmungsmusik* of their less intellectual fellows, are here replaced by selected quotations . . . or no quotation at all, since the names alone evoke and represent the correct feelings.

Once more, in one more generation, the same recurrent reaction, the patriotic anxiety and fervor, the superficial social awareness, summon up the same recurrent reflection that confuses morality and politics. It was perhaps inevitable that this should be so, since reactions to the present are conditioned by memories of similar conditions and similar reactions in the past. History ensures that men, when faced with problems that torment them, seek suggestions in the intellectual luggage of their kind. In the case of modern French nationalists, this is almost wholly nationalist-romantic and has been so from the beginning. The nationalist movement has been marked in certain grooves by the peculiar adventures of recent French history, indeed of the military, industrialized, modern Western state, and in these grooves it is likely to dwell, repeating the popular slogans of the nineteenth century, the antisemitism of a superficial socialism, the sentimental calls for reconciliation and for justice, the army lore of the Dreyfus affair— all (or almost all) in excellent prose.

But there is little about such movements to be taken seriously (except the tragedy they reflect). In the last analysis, too few of their leaders, perhaps none, are really ready to die for their cause—*by themselves*. Schoolboy diversions, violent and even murderous manifestations, splendid rhetoric, and a great deal of invective cannot hide the fact that the activists of today, like those of yesteryear, are only too often play-acting. Until 1961 the white Algerians had not, in six years, produced a Sinn Fein (on any scale worth talking about), let alone a Haganah. There is no evidence of will or ability to face realities and cope with them. In the last resort, one appeals to the *Deus ex machina* of army, or police, on whom success depends. All the rest is a terrible, tragic pretense, whose despair is no less dreadful for the stupidity behind it.

The plot-theory of history has turned its adherents into romantic conspirators, sometimes dangerous, sometimes fascinating, generally uncomfortable, but no more effective than their predecessors.

It is hard to tell as yet whether a group like the J.S.P. has understood this. They seem to want a more utilitarian socialism and a nationalism brought up to date. Within a social order shaken and partly disorganized by rapid industrialization, by even more rapid urbanization, by economic difficulties and unsuccessful wars, and by the civil war of the early sixties, they direct their attention not toward the classic proletariat, but toward others whose stake in the existing social order has been weakened by recent developments. They look to young people in schools, colleges, and technical institutes, and toward what they call the frustrated classes of the nation. Not small businessmen and industrialists threatened by modern developments, however, but the very representatives of what they consider the coming order: first of all, the officer corps—frustrated by apparently useless struggle in Africa and Indochina; then the police—upset by contradictory orders and constant criticism; then the cadres and technicians—ill-equipped, ill-rewarded, and ill-satisfied.

They reject both "the sclerotic bourgeoisie" and "the working masses obsessed by economic problems." They look to the army, "alone to keep its head when all about are losing theirs," and to technologists who, in and out of uniform, will be the artisans and the masters of tomorrow. Theirs is a national-technocratism that has abandoned the phrases and the panaceas of yesteryear for what may be fresher formulas. The step is important, for it reflects the continued interests of responsible and patriotic Frenchmen in solutions on national socialist lines, but adapted now to realities which traditional nationalists never really grasped.

The J.S.P. itself is probably only a straw in the wind, to be blown into oblivion by gusts of change. But the new awareness it represents may be an indication that the French, like their neighbors, begin to adjust their theories to national-technocratic developments throughout the world.

14

Jews, Antisemitism, and the Origins of the Holocaust

The Holocaust is not about antisemitism, but it is (and it is about) the fallout of antisemitism.[1] When one asks about the origins of the Holocaust, one really asks how an infection latent in Western Christian society for centuries could become a murderous plague just when that society had become least Christian and most orderly. And the answer to this sort of question must refer to cultural tradition.

Societies produce stereotypes (which are the height of artifice), and then consume them as commonplace (which is the height of naturalness). That is how bad faith can pass for good conscience. That is how religious distinctions and cultural stereotypes can lead to murder—which is not an unusual case in history but unusually gruesome and shocking when practiced on the scale that marks the Holocaust.

Hence the desperate attempts to understand or, more correctly, to comprehend—in the sense of taking in and rendering intelligible—a phenomenon so inapprehensible by its nature. Let me say at once that understanding something (or understanding just a bit better) is simply the satisfaction of a curiosity. I do not believe that, in the popular phrase, to understand all is to forgive all. Indeed, it is one of the weaknesses of contemporary thinking to act as if one could understand all, and as if one could or should forgive all. We cannot explain everything, and we understand even less.

Others have tried before us, of course. So much has been written on the subject that it is hard to say anything new—anything that is not already a platitude. A dip into even one or two representative books—say, Rudolph Loewenstein's *Christians and Jews,* or Hannah Arendt's *Origins of Totalitarianism*—will provide all the basic interpretative themes: Jewish peculiarity and particularism; the association of Jews with the death of Christ, with usury, and with dark-mysterious-implicitly threatening forces; the ubiquity of the Jew as *other* in so many places and at so many social/economic/cultural levels; and finally the resentment against Jewish pretensions and upstartness. These are also the basic explanations that I should advance for anti-Jewish sentiment. And I shall treat them in due course.

More interesting, though, and more debatable, is another point I want to raise: it is that antisemitism does not necessarily imply genocide, or even mass-murder. But a desire for riddance of what is regarded as alien and potentially menacing can lead to such conclusions, as may be seen in a well-known document, whose accuracy is debatable but whose contents are revealing. In Book I of *Exodus* (I, 7–10), Joseph, under whose aegis the Jews had prospered in Egypt, dies:

> And the children of Israel were fruitful, and increased abundantly, and multiplied, and waxed exceedingly mighty; and the land was filled with them.
>
> Now there arose up a new king over Egypt, which knew not Joseph.
>
> And he said unto his people, Behold, the people of the children of Israel are more and mightier than we:
>
> Come on, let us deal wisely with them; lest they multiply, and it comes to pass that, when there falleth out any war, they join also unto our enemies, and fight against us, and so get them up out of the land.

Pharaoh, as we know, tried persecutions of all sorts and when these did not work, he began to have all the male children killed at birth—which is the beginning of the story of Moses.

A few hundred years later the story repeats itself, and the text is even more suggestive. In the Book of Esther (III, 819), we find the Jews in Babylonian exile, that is, essentially in Persia:

> And Haman said unto King Ahasuerus, There is a certain people scattered abroad, and dispersed among the people in all the provinces of thy kingdom; and their laws are diverse from all people, neither keep they the king's laws: therefore, it is not for the king's profit to suffer them.
>
> If it please the king, let it be written that they may be destroyed . . .

A rather similar decision, though more piecemeal is reported by Tacitus for the reign of Tiberius: send the men of military age to Sardinia to fight the bandits. "If they perished as a result of the unhealthy climate, it would be no great loss. The remainder would have to leave Italy if they had not abjured their profane rites before a set date."[2]

And why all this? Why such extreme measures? The sources suggest the extent to which apparently modern arguments and criticisms were articulated hundreds of years before Christ. For one thing, the Egyptians and their friends had to find an explanation for the embarrassing events of the twelfth century (whether they had occurred or not). And so in the third century BC we find the Egyptian Manethos, and also the Greek Hecateus of Abdera, accusing the Jews of contagious maladies, subversion, rebelliousness and lack of piety[3]—and these are all dangerous to the realm; but they also accuse them of *misanthropy* and *misoxeny*.[4] And here we come to the crux of the matter, especially when we read that the Jews, chased from Egypt for their lack of piety, perpetuated in Jerusalem their hatred of men/of mankind/of strangers: "This is why they instituted special laws, like never to sit at table with a foreigner and to show them no kindness."[5]

Here is one leitmotif, one major theme among many, that one runs into all the time: in the first century BC, Posidonius of Apamea thinks that "[the Jewish race] alone of all nations refused to have any social relations with the other people and considered them all as enemies."[6] More explicit is Philostratos of Lemnos, another Alexandrian Greek, writing around 200 AD:

> For this people had long raised itself not only against Romans but against humanity in general. Men who have imagined an unsociable life, who share with their fellows neither table nor libations, neither prayer nor sacrifices, are further from us than Susa or Bactria, or even the farthest Indies.[7]

Finally, Juvenal repeats some of these charges but makes explicit two of their implications: suspicion growing out of a sense of mysterious doings among the suspect; and resentment of a people that insists on having its own way and does not participate or share in some of the essential aspects of its neighbors' lives. Juvenal accuses the Jews of spurning Roman law and revering only their own, which he says, Moses passed on "in a mysterious volume: not to show the way to the traveller who doesn't practice the same ceremonies; to point out a fountain only to the circumcised." And to spend the seventh day doing nothing, "without sharing in the duties of life."[8]

One last quotation, to show how many familiar themes had been developed 2,000 years ago: in 59 BC, Valerius Flaccus, a corrupt Roman official who had served in Palestine, was accused of having appropriated the gold that Jews all over the Empire sent for the upkeep of their temple. Flaccus hired Cicero, who was the best lawyer in town; and Cicero argued that, in confiscating the Jewish gold, Flaccus had merely opposed a barbarian superstition and an uneconomic drain on Roman resources. And here again a familiar note creeps in. Flaccus, says Cicero, in effect, *a bien mérité de la patrie,* because it takes a brave man to take on the Jews: "You know how numerous their gang, how they support each other, how powerful they are in the assemblies . . . to despise in the interest of the Republic this multitude of Jews . . . is proof of a singular strength of mind."[9]

So here we have a people (or sect) whose insistent particularism arouses strong resentments—which will be further reinforced by Christian experience and Christian tradition. And this brings me to my first component of modern anti-Jewishness: religious indoctrination.

I shall not insist on it, because it is obvious; yet it is basic.[10] By the nineteenth century, traditional religion was no longer a dominant component of high culture—sometimes not even of official culture. But religious tradition was; and religious tradition in its most basic form shaped the mentality and conditioned the reflexes of most people—especially simple people.

One thing everybody knew was that the Jews had killed Jesus. The crime and its implications were reiterated in liturgy and catechism, generation after generation and year after year, at the very least in Easter Week services which often included the wreaking of symbolic retribution on the Jews, either during the Tenebrae service on Maundy Thursday, or on Good Friday. Symbolically, beating "the Jews" with hammers or cudgels or fists; extinguishing them with candles; burning them in bonfires—these were practices that survived in France around 1900, and elsewhere, I suspect, longer than that.[11]

The memory of alleged Jewish crimes was also preserved in the legends of a number of saints whom the Jews were supposed to have martyred, like St. Hugh of Lincoln, or St. Verney in Auvergne—who had been crucified head down by local Jews—whose official or officious worship lent authority to the legends of ritual murder that kept reviving into the twentieth century.[12]

In 1892–93 a French friend of the Jews, Anatole Leroy-Beaulieu, wrote a book about and against antisemitism, in which he remarks that "races conserve for a long time at the instinctual level repugnances whose cause they do not really know very well."[13] I am convinced that the firm base of visceral antisemitism in the West was laid down by this long-persistent conditioning that made suspicion and condemnation of Jews integral parts of prejudices and aversions that could be evoked almost at will. Two references to Hannah Arendt's work will illustrate this.

At one point, talking about the time of the Dreyfus affair, she says: "There can be no doubt that in the eyes of the mob the Jews came to serve as an object lesson for all the things they detested."[14] The point is well made, but it begs the question: could that have happened without preparation? If Dreyfus had been an Armenian, or even a Turk, could the press campaign against him have achieved so much so quickly? The ground had to be prepared, and Arendt herself tells us about the preparation, though that is not her purpose in this passage: "For 30 years," she writes, "the old legends of world conspiracy had been no more than the conventional stand-by of the tabloid press and the dime novel, and the world did not easily remember that not long ago . . ."[15] One may notice here a rather haughty disparagement of the most widely diffused creators and expressors of popular lore, because they are cheap and vulgar; *and* the mistaken assumption that "the world" did not easily remember, when in effect it had never forgotten.

This sort of protective self-delusion is also found in Rudolph Loewenstein's preface to his book, where this very able analyst refers to his surprise in 1940 (having completely identified himself with France for many years) "suddenly to find himself morally rejected by his adopted country because he was a Jew."[16] It is difficult to understand how an intelligent man living in the France of the 1930s could find his rejection by his adopted country *sudden*.[17] But, whatever the psychological interpretations, it is hard to miss the readiness with which potential rejection becomes actual. Which makes antisemitism an excellent recruiting agent.

Hannah Arendt perceives a "grand strategy of using antisemitism as an instrument of Catholicism."[18] This is very debatable—and the more so because the idea was first mooted by the anticlericals, notably in a famous open letter of Emile Zola (January, 1898), where he argues that antisemitism was the Church's handle for rechristianizing the masses. The Catholics, said Zola, were trying to regain popular support by founding workers' clubs and organizing pilgrimages, but belief would not return. It was only when they started to appeal to antisemitism that they began to win back the masses. The People, says Zola, still do not believe, "*but is it not the beginning of belief to make them want to burn the Jews?*"[19]

This brings me very conveniently to my second argument, because the idea that, while antisemitism may be beside the point, it can be put to use—an idea which Zola attributed to the Catholics—was also explicitly shared by the Socialists. It was a Socialist who condemned antisemitism as the socialism of fools. But plenty of Socialists also believed that it could be useful in winning them a hearing, in introducing the politically illiterate to integral socialism. One of the great figures of the French left (Augustin Hamon) said this quite explicitly in an interview of 1898: "With the petty bourgeois especially, anti-Judaism is the road to Socialism . . . the stage through which the petty bourgeois passes before becoming a Socialist."[20] But for the left as for the Catholics, anti-Jewishness was far more than just a recruiting device: the utilitarian argument itself probably the rationalization of more profound sentiments.

Until a few years ago, to talk about an antisemitism of the left seemed like a contradiction in terms. By now we know more about the equation of money power, banking, capitalism, and usury, with Jews; and how this notion was symbolically incarnated in the Rothschilds. The fact is that, in France at least, most of the great anti-Jewish works (great in size and impact, of course, not in content, which is largely a farrago of nonsense!) came from the left; Fourier, Proudhon; and, in a major key, Toussenel, Chirac; even, in some ways, Drumont. Which is understandable if we remember that, through most of the nineteenth century, the historic left was *against* what we used to call progress, that is, the development of capital and industry.

The left probably remained the most vociferous source of attacks on Jews until the 1890s, with frequent antisemitic articles in officious publications like the *Revue socialiste,* where the use of terms like "parasites" and "microbes" was nothing exceptional.[21] In 1894, *Le Chambard socialiste* (March 24) still called the Jews *youpins.* The popular rebellion against the hardships of the modern world found in the Jew a convenient symbol. But I would argue that the economic component of antisemitism is not crucial in itself—only as alimented by, and alimenting, basic cultural tensions and (again) cultural stereotypes.

For example, one cannot help being struck by the epidermic nature of prejudices that came out even in the opponents of antisemitism, like Anatole France, or Marx's son-in-law Paul Lafargue who, when he attacked Drumont could not find anything better to call him than a "dirty Jew"![22] Jean Jaurès himself allowed himself derogatory remarks about *la juiverie,* notably about the Jewish race, "subtle, concentrated, always devoured by the fever of gain."[23] And if one reads Marx's notorious essays on the Jewish question (of which the second is the only really hostile one) one will find that their interest does not lie in their anti-Jewish statements, but in the fact that Marx, like his contemporaries, identified the Jew with "gross and unrelieved commercialism"—with "huckstering" and money-grubbing.[24]

If Marx is considered a hostile witness, let us take a more acceptable figure: Bernard Lazare, himself a sephardic Jew from Nîmes and one of the heroes of the Dreyfus affair, contrasts *israélites de France* and *juifs* (of whatever race) and describes the latter as "dominated by the single preoccupation of rapidly making a fortune . . . by fraud, lying and trickery." If only antisemites would become specifically *anti-juifs,* he says, a lot of Israelites could join them. As for the French Israelites, they should leave the Alliance Israélite Universelle and work to stop "the continual immigration of these predatory, rude, and dirty Tartars (East European Jews) who come to feed upon a land that is not theirs."[25] Lazare changed his mind about these things, but his first position is revealing. Nor was Lazare's view an isolated one, because as late as the winter of 1898–99, when the leading antisemitic paper in France, *La Libre Parole,* launched its notorious subscription to build a monument to Colonel Henry (the man who forged the papers incriminating Dreyfus), quite a few Jews sent contributions, including one who described himself as *"un israélite dégoûté des juifs."*[26]

Whatever one may think about Lazare's description of these "rude and dirty" strangers, it is a fairly mild reflection of a widespread reaction to people whose looks, speech, and behavior were so alien and in consequence so easy to perceive as ugly, grubby, unmannered—essentially uncivilized because essentially different. Even a friend like Leroy-Beaulieu had to admit that "It is true that the race is neither strong nor handsome." And he repeats: "The race is not handsome," before he goes on to quote a young Russian woman: "They are so ugly that they deserve all their troubles."[27] Leroy-Beaulieu attributes Jewish unpopularity with "so many women" to their ugliness. But the remark, insofar as it is significant or revealing, does not necessarily apply to men alone. Karl Marx once described a boring woman he met during a visit to Germany as "the ugliest creature I ever saw in my life, a nastily Jewish physiognomy."[28]

In this context it is useful to remember that Jewish emancipation itself carried very equivocal implications; that its advocates had seen emancipation in terms of assimilation—a contractual demand for fusion in exchange for freedom. This vision had been inspired, it is true, by belief in the rights of man; but the rights of man not so much to *be* what he will, but to *become:* secularized, homogenized, "civilized," like his fellow-citizens.

To the extent that Jews refused the implications of this tacit understanding; to the extent that they hesitated or tarried; to the extent that unassimilated Jews tarred the assimilated with the brush of their difference (their "ugliness"), the promise of emancipation itself turned into a new source of resentment and criticism—and even into the source of a certain liberal antisemitism.

We are talking of an age and of societies that are culturally imperialistic, for which cultural integration and homogenization are basic principle and active practice. And here are the Jews—who, on one hand, take some time to assimilate and, on the other, are continually irrigated by fresh streams of immigrants whose presence and whose strangeness help to stress their difference-by-association.

And so another factor of irritation is the insistent persistence of cultural difference, of Jewish particularism, or apparent particularism willy-nilly, whose results, again, are well reflected when Leroy-Beaulieu has to admit and to justify the incomplete integration and assimilation of the Jews. The change from Jew to Frenchman or Englishman, he says, "has been too sudden to be complete." They have sometimes for us "something that jars— something discordant"—"a look, a word, a gesture, suddenly bares the old

Jewish base . . . Scratch an Israelite, one of my friends said to me, and you will find the ghetto Jew. That is not always true. What we take for the Jew is often only the stranger . . . What one does feel coming through in the civilized Israelite, is not so much the Jew as the parvenu . . . Parvenus! Most of the Jews we know are certainly that." And he lists their characteristics: pretentious, conceited, vain, lacking distinction or elegance or tact, revealing bad taste, bad manners, bad breeding, their excessive ways, their tendency to be either overfamiliar or overdiffident, the trouble they have in showing the measure of men of the world.[29]

The justice of such charges is quite irrelevant; the fact that they reflect the perceptions of a friend and defender is not. But this aspect of the Jew—which Leroy-Beaulieu cites as a venial drawback, only to explain it as a passing phase—brings tremendous grist to the mill of the antisemites. Hence my third point, best introduced with another quotation from Hannah Arendt: "The antisemite tends to see in the Jewish parvenu an upstart pariah."[30] The upstart pariah is at the center of many a hostile paroxysm and, given the guilt-by-association syndrome, all Jews who act as if they think themselves the equals of their fellows may be so considered.

Here is another opportunity to articulate griefs founded in feelings that remain inarticulate. Jewish emancipation creates passional problems not very different from those aroused by the legal emancipation of the Blacks, which was roughly contemporary. Here are people who (until Louis XVI abolished the practice), paid the same tolls on entering towns as those charged on cattle.[31] This group, so traditionally and so obviously inferior, is declared equal to all. What is worse, its members declare themselves to be equal and act as if they believed it. Indignation at such pretensions made North Africa (where Jews had been a particularly despised and disadvantaged community) a hothouse of antisemitism, both French and Muslim. It also contributed to European antisemitism—whether at the benign level one can find in Leroy-Beaulieu, or at the bumbling redneck level, or at increasingly explicit levels—a fund of more or less articulate indignation, also very available, also very easy to exploit.[32]

Were one trying to be exhaustive, one would have to include every personal maladjustment which could find expression in some anti-Jewish rationalization. That is not my purpose. But I would add that antisemitism proved useful not just for diverting social tensions, but for arguing the case of national unity against the divisions and dissensions that could be declared artificial and attributed only to Jews or to their influence. To those who wanted to avoid or play down class issues and antagonisms, antisemitism could be useful, because it translated economic resentments and claims from a class to a national or racial context. Other national groups beside the Jews could provide scapegoats for economic distress and social crisis, but Jews were the most widely available and traditionally designated villains of the piece.

So, in this context, anti-Jewishness was not merely the identification of a scapegoat, but a rallying-cry in the precise sense of the term: the assertion of unity and community, in terms of an appeal to common stereotypes and, hence, at least by implication, to common interests more powerful than any divisive factor.

Here we have an out-group whose inferiority and whose noxiousness have become a cultural commonplace; and whose cultural difference, reaffirmed by themselves and by their critics, is a constant irritant, a constant reconfirmation and reinforcement of prejudice, and an invitation to further rejections. Any deliberate campaign—whether motivated by concrete resentments or private paranoia—could build on prejudice, could make the latent manifest or, at least, could expect to be greeted with understanding. There was nothing extraordinary in the fact that Jews should provide an object of prejudice and persecution, whether continuous or sporadic, according to circumstances and to the interests a given situation suggests. What is extraordinary is that they managed to survive so long.

It is not even illogical to take antisemitic attitudes to one possible conclusion, which is the elimination or extermination of the rejected outgroup—especially when the Church, which needed their presence, was losing its grip![33] The Old Testament provides precedents; and so does history.[34] The only thing about such precedents is that the means of execution available in premodern times (whether for Pharaoh, Louis XIV, or the Young Turks) were imperfect. And the execution of almost any scheme tended to be piecemeal and incomplete at best!

On the other hand, premodern societies, living on the margin of subsistence, offered great incidental opportunities for the destruction of rejected individuals or groups, because any such that were placed "without the law" tended to be removed from access to food, to shelter, to the means of keeping alive. Mortality rates were already very high. They were vastly higher for the outlaws. This meant that the mere decision to destroy, however inefficiently executed, tended to have self-fulfilling effects.

Modern society, by contrast, could be far more exhaustive and efficient. Its dominant values operated against the destruction of human groups, at least in times of peace. But when such moral prohibitions were suspended, destruction could be surpassingly thorough. It also had to *be* more thorough, because the modern policed state had mitigated the operation of natural processes of selection and destruction. No modern society could accept the kind of disorder that its predecessors took for granted, and that permitted these "natural laws" to operate. Nor would modern sensibilities accept it. Even if it had been possible, the social hygiene of the modern policed state could not tolerate great numbers of people starving in public places, dying in ditches, bleeding on somebody's threshold; corpses cluttering up the sidewalks or the highways; the impediments to shopping and traffic; the possibilities of infection and disorder; or even, simply, violence as private enterprise.

If an out-group had to be eliminated, the *ad hoc* possibilities of earlier times, occasions built into the premodern economy but also into the nature of premodern society and state, were excluded. Social hygiene prescribed something more orderly, and something that could proceed without contaminating the regularities of policed society. Natural forces could no longer be trusted to operate "naturally": first, because they no longer did; but also because if they did they would be far more destructive of the social fabric than in the earlier, looser context of the premodern state.

So there is a logic to concentration camps and to extermination camps. If extermination is going to take place, it has to take place in isolated centers. This was not a consideration in more bucolic days.

One can see this clearly if one compares other great massacres of the twentieth century with that of the European Jewry. All but this last have taken place in backward, undeveloped societies. In India, in Bangladesh, in Cambodia, in various parts of Africa, hundreds of thousands of people at a time have been massacred by traditional means; or simply driven out by the millions. They are patchy but impressive examples of what artisanal methods can achieve when the preservation of social order is not a high priority. An excellent illustration of my point, however, is what happened to the Turkish Armenians in 1915.

It is a good illustration because Christians living in Turkey were also a subject, inferior race, and traditionally designated as dogs.[35] The reformed state of the Young Turks had declared Christians and Jews to be equal citizens with Muslims. But the nationalist passion for Turkification also demanded the extinction of separate communities, including the Arabs, but especially when, as in the case of certain Christian communities, these existed as distinct colonies and cultures.

The war of 1914 provided opportunities for extreme action that would have been difficult in times of peace; and the geographical situation of the Armenians on the Russian border designated them for this sort of action. Precisely what the Turkish government, the Turkish authorities, wanted to do to the Armenians remains the subject of debate. What they did do is less debatable. The men were disarmed and then butchered. U.S. Ambassador Henry Morgenthau tells how at Ankara all Armenian men between fifteen and seventy years of age were sent off on the Cesarea Road, bound in groups of four and massacred by a mob of Turkish peasants "in a secluded valley" where "their bodies, horribly mutilated, were left" to be "devoured by wild beasts."[36] The young and the old and the women were deported, mostly on foot and mostly to various desert places. Morgenthau reports that out of one such convoy of about 18,000 souls only about 150 women and children reached Aleppo. Fridhof Nansen makes this 350, but he tells us about another convoy from Erzerum which had 11 survivors out of 19,000.[37]

The description of what happened to the convoys is very repetitive; a few extracts taken from German and American witnesses, mostly missionaries, will convey the gist. Here is one American in 1916: the deportees were driven to die by the roadside, left to bleed to death, or to commit suicide, many women and children were raped, many others were sold cheap or given away to peasants. Arnold Toynbee and others mention that hundreds of thousands died of hunger, thirst, exposure; or, if turning from the road, were shot or speared, hunted down by Kurds and Turkish peasants.[38] Another German eyewitness writes about the deportees driven into the great limestone deserts of Asia Minor, into the wilderness and semitropical marshes of Mesopotamia, barefoot, part-naked, starved; about newborns buried in dungheaps, severed heads rolling about the roads (and there are photographs that can compare with concentration camp ones!), "fields strewed with swollen blackened corpses, infecting the air with their odors, lying about desecrated, naked"; and about those who were driven into the Euphrates bound back to back."[39]

As in the India of 1946–47, river-crossings were favorite places for massacres. One report says: "In a loop of the river, near Erzinghan . . . the thousands of dead bodies created such a barrage that the Euphrates changed its course for about 100 yards."[40] And everybody notes the intolerable mess along the routes: dead, dying, sick people spreading epidemics around them, bodies unburied or only half-buried with vultures and dogs tearing at them, occasional corpses thrown in wells, and so on. I am not trying to insist on the horrors, but on what would seem to us the disturbance involved, and to show how much can be done just by encouraging private enterprise when the circumstances are right. But one has to notice, too, that these haphazard methods missed a lot of people. Thus Toynbee estimates that there were about 1.8 million Armenians in Turkey when the war broke out, and that about equal numbers "seem to have escaped, to have perished, and to have survived deportation in 1915."[41] That is scarcely thorough. And even this limited success depends on high tolerance for disorder, and the availability of large waste spaces.

It is hard to tell how much of the slaughter was deliberate and how much just to be expected in the semiprimitive Turkish context aggravated by the wartime breakdown of almost everything. But one can see that it could be quite destructive in its way.[42] One can also see that it could never have been tolerated in a Western country—especially in that model of the policed state which was Germany!

I conclude that if a society determines to eliminate an out-group today, the logic of that determination suggests that this be done in isolation; and the technological and administrative means at our disposal are bound to make the process itself very efficient. Platitudes perhaps, but platitudes to which a lot of Armenians probably owe their lives.

One last consideration arises: before the Jews could be isolated and exterminated, they had to be divested of the human qualities that emancipation and liberalism had proclaimed they shared with other members of modern societies. There were certain things one could do to people in the old world, and that people did to each other all the time before didactic civilization put its mark on us, that one could no longer do after the nineteenth century had humanized and sensitized our sensibilities. There were certain things Turks could do to Armenians that Europeans could not *normally* regard except as crimes. So there were things one could not do to Jews, and murder was certainly one of these. The rights of man, however diffuse the concept, were also the rights of Jews, so long as Jews were recognized as men and women. This is where the logic of the situation demanded that the Jew be dehumanized. And the didactic and exemplary process of isolation and dehumanization was able to draw on the whole treasury of prejudice and resentment that has been chronicled.

But then, if the Jew was less than human—and harmfully so, of course: a microbe or a parasite—it was not enough to expel him from society, from this country or that. One had to rid the world of him. The logical conclusion of his dehumanization was his extermination. The rest is history. And, to the extent that it has become a part of history, it suggests that the humanization and sensibilization of man may have been a transitory phase: the generalization of particular and limited experiences treated as irreversible by people who took the exception for the norm.

The question remains, and it continues to obsess or fascinate our time: how could an apparently civilized society, an ordered modern society, produce and condone the mass murders that we describe as genocide? I believe that this is a false question. If an earthquake leveled a city and killed most of its inhabitants, we would say: "How could this happen?" Scientists could answer our question in terms of general laws and particular conditions, but that would not satisfy us because our words are really an expression of shock and horror at the very notion of such destruction—and of destruction on such a scale!

The fact is that the question of Jewish genocide can also be answered in matter-of-fact terms, too banal to satisfy. Tragedies on this scale seem to defy the trivialization that explanations inflict upon them, and almost reject the attempt to explain as a sort of insult. That may be right, because explanation is sometimes advanced as an exorcism (and that is an evasion), or as an excuse (and that is inexcusable). But explanation is also advanced at times as if it could help to prevent similar tragedies in the future. And it may be a last question one might wish to consider—whether that is not a form of naiveté.

~ 15

Revolution? Counterrevolution?
What Revolution?

Almost any discussion of fascism is bound to involve consideration, explicit or not, of its revolutionary or counterrevolutionary nature.
Fascists claimed to engage in a revolution. Their opponents denounced
them as counterrevolutionaries. Most students divide unevenly about this:
many consider the fascists' counterrevolutionary role self-evident, a few
prefer to begin by taking the fascists at their word, some still judge the
charges unproven.

At any rate, the debate suggests the high symbolic, hence passional and
practical, value of terms like revolution and counterrevolution, increasingly
loaded, in intellectual and political intercourse, with an ethical burden that
even the mass media perceive. The revolutions of the eighteenth century
stood over the cradle of the modern world; the modern world remembers. It
is a long stretch from the fall of the Bastille to the launching of a revolutionary new detergent, but it is worth the trip. As Sellers and Yeatman
would have said, revolution is a good thing. One never hears of a counterrevolution in automobile design, though one might be in order. Better
accentuate the positive. As a result, the struggle for political advantage
involves minor but important skirmishes for semantic advantage. Like the
hero in a Western movie, the movement that comes in riding on revolution
can, as a rule, expect our sympathy.

I shall suggest that, as of today at least, the issue is wrongly joined.
Like left and right, revolution and counterrevolution have become anachronistic stereotypes, real because installed in vocabulary and minds, but
confusing as categories for understanding and scholarly analysis. Misleading, above all, because for a long time now the notion of revolution has been
interpreted in one sense only, implying automatically that movements
directed to other ends (opposite, or simply different) could not be described
as revolutionary, and might well be counterrevolutionary, whether they
wanted to be or not.

The very word "revolution" suggests the great modern prototypes:

298

French and Russian. These more than suggest, they impose, a model of what revolution should be because it once was, of expectable actions and stages to which revolutionary developments should conform: the last throes of the dominant classes, the first phase of a bourgeois revolution overtaken by more popular challengers, duly put down in a Thermidor easily leading to Brumaire. Moderate change, radical advance, repression, and their dialectic, always open to further challenges. Interpretation provides the recipes of expectation; sometimes of action too. History is born of history. From Marx's title, *The Eighteenth Brumaire of Louis Bonaparte,* to Trotsky's description of the Soviet Thermidor when Stalin takes power, through Crane Brinton's *Anatomy of Revolution,* patterns are formulated and roles are prescribed where coming players (or reporters) learn their parts.

A French politician and historian, writing about the student revolt of 1968, refers to barricades, red flags, "the Faculty buildings resembling the Smolny Palace (sic) in Petrograd, the lecture halls [resembling] Soviets." [1] And André Malraux, writing in 1972, summarizes the twentieth century in one image: that of a truck bristling with guns. Obviously, the Russian Revolution again, and one of the most familiar images of it.

Some responsibility for this lies in organized history and the generalization of historical knowledge, making available that pattern of revolution to which revolutionaries will henceforth conform. Those that fail to conform are not revolutionaries. "The revolutionary knows his revolution as the wretched knows his want," writes André Découflé, author of a work generally regarded as one of the more sensible treatments of a touchy subject. [2] But the wretched knows his want precisely because he lives in it; the revolutionary seldom does more than imagine his revolution. And those contemporary revolutionaries who, in the perspective of history, still claim to know their revolution—in its unfolding beyond means to ends—must be naive indeed.

But history, storehouse of images and recipes that it is, does not exhaust the revolutionary's resources. Gracchus Babeuf could tell his readers, and later his judges, that the Republic was worthless: "But it is not the real Republic. The real Republic is something we have not yet tried." [3] The point, frequently made since Babeuf, proceeds from hypothesis to fact, and even against fact. Thus in Découflé: "The hypothesis of the revolutionary project excludes the destruction of man, since it is [aimed at] his regeneration; and, in fact, it does not destroy him, despite the horrible enterprises of some of its managers. Beyond all the propagandas, the present chronicle of the Soviet Union bears abundant witness to this." [4]

I like Découflé's reference to the managers of revolution, a handy and expressive term and a revealing one. But it is odd to find, in a book published in 1968, the reaffirmation of an ideal which remains entire though some of its managers betray it, the deliberate denial of historical experience by affirmation of its contrary, and all on the basis of an original hypothesis stronger than any observed fact. The Revolution survives all revolutions.

Far from fearing facts, the hypothesis consumes them, that is, it assimilates them to its needs. Boris Porchnev turns the peasant rebellions of the seventeenth century into evidence of class struggles in the early modern period. Découflé hails Eric Hobsbawm's *Primitive Rebels* as a work on *revolutionary* phenomena, despite its French title: *Les Primitifs de la révolte.* Even social rebellion of a primitive kind must be mobilized for revolution.[5] Such topical imperialism, perfectly dispensable in Marxist terms, conceals the difference between revolution and rebellion (a difference Hobsbawm himself in no wise ignores) and deprives the critic of a category he could find useful in refining his terms.

Découflé does distinguish between insurrection, which finds its end in itself, and revolution which is *transhistorical,* "situated in the realm of duration, temporal site of immanence"; and this permits the keen observer to distinguish between an insurrection, however long-drawn-out, and a revolution, however brief. Thus, the "revolution" of 1830 was actually an insurrection that lasted eighteen years, while the Paris Commune of 1871, though only a few weeks long, can be identified as an authentic revolution, just like—the Crusades![6]

It is Découflé's modest claim that such a conception helps to avoid a lot of shopworn debates and endows "the category of revolutions with an unusual extension and strictness [of definition]." To the uninitiated, the extensibility of the category and its flexibility appear more striking than its strictness of definition. Events are promoted, excluded, or denied. The Crusades, of course, are there in honor of Alphonse Dupront who (re)invented them, unless they are there to fill the gap left when strict construction eliminated the Agricultural and the Industrial revolutions. But what about the Revolution of 1830, demoted to a mere insurrection, yet very much a revolution to its contemporaries: change of regime, of the symbols of state, of the flag, of political personnel . . . isn't all that enough, until next time?

Clearly, no. Political revolution is not real revolution, not the transhistorical sort. The social aspect is missing when all we get is a change of guard (and of uniforms) among the privileged elites. The wretched continue in their wretchedness. They continue to be exploited: by their exploiters in their time; by intellectuals who have discovered the plus-value of poverty, in ours.

Old-style revolutions ignored the poor.[7] Aristocratic and oligarchic societies made aristocratic and oligarchic revolutions. The poor were enlisted as cannon fodder. Their occasional uses did not entitle them to higher ideological rank. War is waged by soldiers, of course. It is not *about* soldiers, or for them.

Then, from objects of the revolution the poor became its subjects—and its energetic force. The French Revolution said it was about the people. It was not; or only in a special sense. But it did involve mobilizing the masses in a new and now doctrinally necessary sense that could not exist before "the people" had become the subject of politics. And Gracchus Babeuf, more memorably than many, identified "the people" with the poor people, and the poor people with the majority of the people,[8] a view that contemporary circumstances largely warranted. This new doctrine, due like others to survive the conditions it reflected when it was formulated, would soon coincide with economic and social changes that suggested yet further appeals and further mobilizations.

So, the Revolution, which had been about political power for people who were far from poor, was said to be about the poor, about the poor ceasing to be poor and, even though its efficacy as a means to this end remained dubious, the myth took shape. The poor as energizing agents of real revolution turned into the poor as dynamizing ideal of prospective revolution. They had been other ranks in the armies of the revolution; now they became its flag.

Not everything, of course, went as one might wish. Thus the Revolution that had been supposed to precipitate the participation of excluded social groups (Third Estate, and so forth) in the body politic, actually operated by the violent exclusion of other social groups (aristocrats and to some extent, although unplanned, the clergy). This pattern would be repeated on subsequent occasions. Fraternity henceforth would be affirmed by exclusion (of bourgeois, aliens, Jews); just as Justice became the act of taking from the old haves and giving to your supporters. Not, perhaps, the most desirable way of ensuring upward mobility or the redistribution of wealth, but effective enough up to a point.

In any case, the masses that cheered and hooted, stormed and stared, were a necessary stimulant and fuel of action. Revolution came to them less as a promise of better things, though it was that too, than as a gigantic holiday and adventure. For many, its goings-on were the first spectacle they enjoyed. And one of the greatest luxuries Revolution afforded was the opportunity to see their "betters" humbled. Like the peasants of Languedoc who welcome late-summer rains, good for their corn, bad for their landlords' wheat, with "il pleut des insolences," the people welcomed the chance to be insolent in its turn, to see its "betters" cut down to size, not excluding its revolutionary emancipators, carted through hooting streets that cheered them days before.

So, after all, the people could be wrong.[9] At the very least, its instincts could not be trusted—not, at any rate, when untaught. For Saint-Just, "the people is an eternal child"; and Robespierre said as much. Lenin would build or rebuild a doctrine and a party on this conviction. His *What Is to Be Done?* (1902) shows how the spontaneous development of the workers' movement has simply led to its domination by bourgeois ideology. This had to be remedied, a different ideology had to be provided. In due course, in places, it was.

But was this other ideology—creation of rebellious bourgeois and intellectuals—necessarily more revolutionary? I suppose so. More popular? Hardly, since it denied the possibility of government of the people by the people, and did this more deliberately, with a clearer view of the matter, than Saint-Just would or could have done. This is an issue we need not stir again, except to point out that the superior revolutionary capacity of a movement has little to do with its popular character or representativeness. Quite the contrary: the Leninist argument since 1902 has been that the more popular the movement, the less revolutionary it is likely to be, hence the less objectively representative of true popular interests. A form of elitism no less elitist for coming from the conventional left.

So the people, the poor people, already dubbed *proletariat* by Rousseauist and revolutionary antiquarianism, could continue to enjoy its heroic role, but (a big but) only the role that had been written for it. This is worth bearing in mind, but the point I wish to stress is different: the role in question, sketched at the end of the eighteenth century, written and rewritten through the nineteenth century, falls far short of changed realities in the twentieth-century West. When a neo-Marxist declares in 1973: "The proletariat, producer and not consumer, is the absolute and inalienable ethical order,"[10] he is not only talking nonsense, but anachronistic nonsense. I doubt whether any human group, now or at any time, has been specifically invested with the mission of political liberation and social salvation for mankind. Many such groups have claimed and still claim the daunting responsibility. But that is no excuse for those trained to critical thinking to abandon the thoughtful examination of such claims. Clearly, political messianism and other cargo cults of the West are no monopoly of what we call the right.[11]

A moment always comes, however, when revolutionary revelry must give way to discipline; the joys of insolence, the privileges of disorder, to the order of new privileges. The generous, self-indulgent revolution becomes a stern disciplinarian, sterner than the tyrant it displaced. By January 1794, unexpectedly early, the Committee of Public Safety advises its representative in the Calvados to moderate his zeal: "Today we are less concerned to revolutionize than to set up the revolutionary government." The fateful words are out. The revolution is made, or can be suspended. It is time to turn it into a regime: the managers of revolution into managers of the state.

This is where the rot sets in. Joseph de Maistre was right. In the end, all governments are monarchies; no matter what you call them, all governments are aristocracies. The young Chateaubriand had said as much in his reactionary essay on revolutions: "What do I care if it be the King or the Law that drags me to the guillotine? . . . the greatest misfortune of men is to have laws and a government." [12] Chateaubriand, writing in exile, had little sympathy for revolution. But many nineteenth-century revolutionaries faced that same quandary and failed to solve it: the state is always counter-revolutionary, yet without the state how can a revolution be carried through? Can anything be built except on the ruins—not of the enemy's camp so much as of one's own? Revolutionaries set out to make or remake history. Their opponents say that history is already made, or in the making, and waiting to advance on existing lines. The revolution succeeds, affirms precisely what its opponents used to say, and sets up a government to make sure it is done. That government, like every modern state, will seek the monopoly of violence, conforming not only to Max Weber's thesis on that score but to the more grandiose rule de Maistre decreed: "all greatness, all power, all subordination, rest on the executioner: horror and bond of human association." Remove the executioner and order disintegrates, powers collapse, society disappears. But society must be rebuilt, so it must be the revolution that disappears. A twist of the wrist, then, and the revolution has been juggled away. A great deal has been done. A great deal has been changed. The power of new rulers and freer trade in one case; the power of new rulers and the expansion of productivity in another. Electrification without soviets.

One other novelty of the modern revolutionary tradition is a reversal in the classic relations between state and revolution. [13] Where once upon a time making a revolution meant overthrowing the state, in the new situation it is the state that makes the revolution, becomes identified with it, so that opposition to the state is opposition to revolution. A revolutionary state is a contradiction in terms. But even a socialist state, or one so called, very soon disappears behind administration, institutions, police machinery, bureaucracy—or rather, it becomes simply the flag that flies over the towering office building of the state.

At this point, presumably, the revolution institutionalized is ready for the challenge of another revolution that will break the frozen flow and set the great glacier of history on the move again. In this respect, a succession of revolutions is but part of the same vast forward movement (necessarily forward, in whatever direction it may face). This may have been what Proudhon had in mind in his toast to the Revolution of 1848: "properly speaking, there haven't been several revolutions, there has been only one and the same revolution." The revolutionary wheel turns, but each revolution of the wheel propels it farther, each halt only a pause, each apparent failure a spur to further advance. *Ce n'est qu'un début, nous continuerons le combat!* As Babeuf affirmed, the Revolution, the Republic, may be worthless, but the true revolution is still to come, the common weal remains to be achieved. Even a "revolutionary" state, controlled by revolutionary leaders, can further the interests of this immanent force. The revolution is a constant of history.

Perhaps. But all this begs a question: what revolution? "La révolution," says Proudhon, "est en permanence dans l'histoire." Not revolution in general, not any particular revolution, but *the* Revolution, identified, vaguely perhaps but enough for all to know, as Babeuf knew it, as Découflé's revolutionaries know it. Reference to revolution, says Proudhon, is necessarily reference to progress. But where does progress go? What is "forward"? Toward what does the revolution advance?

Toward the left, of course. It is no good to say that this has become, more than it ever was, an uncertain point of reference. The wretched are still on the earth. Their emancipation can be the pole star of revolutionary progress. If history tells us anything, it is that "revolutions and revolutionaries are leftist."[14] There can be debate as to whether the revolution belongs to gradualists, organized revolutionaries, radical leftists. There can be no revolution from other quarters. Any such suggestion is counterrevolutionary by definition.

The term counterrevolution itself evokes, as Joseph de Maistre noticed, violent action in an *opposite* and hence related sense to that of *the* revolution: "a revolution (the OED tells us) opposed to a previous revolution or reversing its results." The counterrevolution is condemned to a reflected identity only. It exists in terms of the revolution it opposes and seeks to reverse. Revolution is the positive term; without it, no counterrevolution.

De Maistre, who understood how awkward such a definition can be if you are saddled with it, sought to escape it. The monarchy reestablished, he insisted, though it is called counterrevolution, "ne sera point une révolution contraire, mais le contraire d'une révolution": not an opposite revolution, but the opposite of a revolution. He seems to have been right. If a revolution is more than the violence that it involves, a project for radical change, an attempt at precipitate movement, then the monarchy restored, which conceived no such course, was not revolutionary even in a counter-revolutionary sense. The Restoration was not a revolution against the previous revolution(s), but an attempt to restore the state of things and the rate of evolution, the speed of movement, that had preceded revolution. It wanted to be the opposite of a revolution. That is what, insofar as it could be, it was.[15]

If the Restoration, while antirevolutionary, was not counterrevolutionary, other regimes and movements in later years did adopt revolutionary methods to counterrevolutionary ends—that is, deliberately directed to opposing or reversing a particular revolution. Louis-Napoleon's government appears a case in point, typically adopting not only revolutionary methods but also some of the measures extolled by the revolutionaries with whom it competed. The Action française was counterrevolutionary: explicitly so. Hungary after 1918 was revealingly torn between antirevolutionaries (Horthy, Bethlen) eager to maintain a regime the very opposite of revolutionary, and counterrevolutionaries (Gömbös, Imrédy) ready to adopt the revolutionary panoply the better to fight what had become a *révolution introuvable*. Franco's insurrection fits the same bill: beginning on the pattern of classic nineteenth-century Spanish revolutions against the "revolution" of the Popular Front regime, cannibalizing the would-be revolutionaries of the right, and adopting their most visible symbols (as King Carol II of Romania was to do) as a façade for the longest-lasting of antirevolutionary counterrevolutions in captivity.

Can we ever untangle this skein? Many actions described as counter-revolutionary turn out to be simply repressive, though no less odious for that. Charles Maurras said that revolutions are made before they break out. That was the rationale for their preliminary repression. But such repressions did not, as a rule, involve revolutionary means. The Cagoule was scotched in France by fairly straightforward police methods. The Iron Guard in Romania was gutted by police and army terror only slightly beyond the country's past experience. The monopoly of violence was reasserted before it slipped away; in some places (Soviet Russia) even before it could be challenged. Both revolutionary and counterrevolutionary regimes rest foursquare on de Maistre's *bourreau*. But is this preemptive counter-revolution, as it has been called? Hardly. It is self-preservation of a conventional sort and, of course, an occasional excuse for the equally conventional elimination of political opponents. And the constant confusion of simple opposition with revolutionary, antirevolutionary, or counterrevolutionary action, a confusion that has its roots in fact, fantasy, theory and reality, allows whoever wills to give a dog a bad name before attempting to eliminate it. As Saint-Just explained to Robespierre in December 1793, measures of public safety are justified by the existence of counterrevolutionaries. No more counterrevolutionaries, no more need for public safety or for the dictatorship that is its instrument, *provided* human weakness does not lead people—the people?—into "that maze in which the revolution and the counterrevolution march pell-mell."

An illustration, here, not only of the ease with which the image of counterrevolution can justify preemptive repression, but of the difficulty of disentangling revolutionary from counterrevolutionary strands. Only the initiated can tell them apart. But the voice of revelation that addresses the few must, by others, be accepted on faith. No wonder that almost any action, movement, or regime can be interpreted as one wills and that Girondists and Enragés, Proudhonians, Trotskyists, and Kronstadt sailors have been made to bear the brand of counterrevolution. In Bolivia, for example, where revolutionary activity was very much the order of the day, Trotskyist leader Guillermo Lora denounced the leftists whose radicalism leads only to counterrevolution, while a top figure of the pro-Soviet Communist party dismissed Lora's own party as the best ally of reactionary forces.[16] Nor need we be surprised to read that "the most accomplished contemporary form of the counterrevolutionary project" is North American-style democracy.[17] One does not have to claim a close approach to integral democracy for North American regimes to recognize the prejudice of such a phrase, that can pass unexamined (and often does) only in minds where the case has been prejudged.

Even denunciation of neo-capitalism does not preserve one from the counterrevolutionary snare (increasingly reminiscent of those children's stories where one character after another tumbles down a trap). The pastures of objective perdition are broader than those of the Lord. Marcuse and the Freudo-Marxists have in their turn been denounced as counterrevolutionaries whose cultural terrorism finally leads to neo-fascism.[18]

In the last resort, counterrevolution does not even deserve rational interpretation. For Découflé, it "seems to come less under the jurisdiction of sociology than of psychoanalysis: it borrows the modes of revolution and does its best to create its reflected image, determined as it is to take up the contrary position on every score." A few lines later, Découflé refers very sensibly to Jung's remark that the most dangerous of revolutionaries is the one we carry in ourselves. But this is a predicament attributed to counterrevolutionaries alone. He insists rightly on the anxiety that drives them to extremes, but never on the anxiety that haunts successful (?) revolutionaries, once set in the seats of power.[19] And nary a word about *ideological* divergencies that may set revolutionaries and counterrevolutionaries apart.

For the latter alone, doctrinal persuasions must be the rationalizations of unadmissible drives.

Analyses so one-sided are unsatisfactory even in their own terms. Equally important, placing the interpretation of counterrevolution on the psychoanalytic plane minimizes other factors (social, economic, and so on) and denies the existence of ideologies or doctrines deserving rational examination on their own account, and concerning their evolution or corruption, just as we do with revolutionary ideologies. One side is human and rational, the other is human only in its travesties: a sickness. Thus, one both begs the question and avoids it.

Let us fall back on a more serious work. In 1971, Arno J. Mayer's *Dynamics of Counterrevolution in Europe* set out to examine the concept and to fit it into an analytic framework. My first and chief criticism of the work is that it accepts unquestioningly the Marxist stereotype of *one* revolution in our time, in terms of which counterrevolution must necessarily be defined. In other words, while Mayer's Marxism is explicit, his definition of revolution is implicit. It thus avoids any suggestion that not only counterrevolution is in need of definition, but revolution too. Mayer's general thesis, with which I disagree, is thoughtful, honest, and forcefully argued. It is therefore with the most sensible exponent of the dominant stereotypes that I take issue.

Mayer distinguishes between conservatives, reactionaries, and counterrevolutionaries. Reactionaries scorn the present for a lost, regretted, past. Conservatives, like Metternich, believe that stability need not mean immobility. Counterrevolutionaries are pretty much what we designate as fascists or radicals of the right: egalitarian, dynamic, adept at mass politics, often similar to "the hated revolutionary rival," yet only pseudo-revolutionary at best, intending "to create the impression that they seek fundamental changes in government, society and community,"[20] but actually anchored in the established order, values, and aspirations. Counterrevolutionaries pretend to represent an alternative revolution; they are, in effect, only an alternative to revolution. "In style, method and appearance, their break with the politics of compromise and mutual concession is very radical indeed. But in all other major respects the counterrevolutionary project is in the nature of a stabilizing and rescue operation disguised as a millenarian crusade of heroic vitalism."[21] True, conservative or reactionary antirevolutionaries (so often the most visible of counterrevolutionaries in everyday politics and parlance) may turn against Mayer's revolutionary counterrevolutionaries, as King Carol of Romania turned against Codreanu. But this does not affect the ultimate kinship of all three categories in one objectively counterrevolutionary camp. Thus, having begun by brushing aside the threadbare confusions of the past, Mayer arrives at a more refined version of the same.[22]

We shall meet some of his arguments shortly. But first, a crucial statement—crucial not only to Mayer's thesis but because it represents a widespread point of view: "Counterrevolution is essentially a praxis. Its political doctrine is in the nature of a rationalization and justification of prior actions. It is a pseudo-doctrine."[23] If counterrevolution is only the mirror image of revolution, this makes perfect sense. It is the violent start of reaction to the revolutionary challenge. Doctrine comes later and, dominated by this same challenge, it can only become a distorting echo of its original reactions: anger and fear.

So far, so good. But only for that counterrevolution, for those counterrevolutionaries, whose "project is in the nature of a stabilizing and rescue operation" for the established order. And that, unless we fall back on "objective" interpretations which should then include all those denounced for diversionist and counterrevolutionary strategies, lets out a number of fascist movements, not least German National Socialism, much of whose history was but the acting out of some fantastic doctrines.

But these are pseudo-doctrines, "inconsistent" (what political ideology is not so in practice?) and instrumental. This last suggestion, of ideology as an instrument of manipulation, confuses the concern of most modern politicians to find the most effective formula for selling their case and themselves, with the ideological constructs embodying their vision. Hitler was possessed. Obsessed. His obsessions were not "calculated and instrumental." It turned out that they worked that way. But Hitler's doctrine was the instrument of his dreams. The doctrine, the movement, then the people he ruled, became the means of their realization. The threat of communist revolution was only one aspect of the national deterioration he sought to stem and to reverse. To deal with this he planned a revolution that was not opposed to, but other than, the model most current at that time. Since another revolutionary project already held the field, his was an alternative, not a counterrevolution. Codreanu also postulated a fundamental change. He encountered no revolution in his way, only the established disorder. As for Mussolini, I incline to think that the revolutionary threat, scotched or at least defeated by Giolitti's Fabian tactics, seemed less a foil than a convenient pretext. For none of these was counterrevolution, in the ordinary sense of the term, the main concern.

Another example and one less debatable may clarify my case. Mayer appears to place the origins of counterrevolutionary ideology in a reaction to socialist challenges.[24] Wherever this may have been so, it was not so in France. There is no evidence that Boulanger, Barrès, Maurras, were particularly concerned with fighting socialism.[25] Boulanger made the most of the Jacobin tradition that inspired both Socialists and Radicals of his day, Barrès was a socialist fellow traveler between 1889 and 1896, Maurras' chief quarries were elsewhere. All addressed themselves first and foremost to what they saw as problems of public morality, vitality, and unity. They may have been deluded. They were not insincere.[26]

It is too easy to dismiss their old-fashioned patriotism, their new-fangled nationalism, as convenient derivatives for pressures they (or cleverer men) discerned but could not meet. What they (and cleverer men) thought they discerned was a flabby, deteriorating society. They worried about it. Divisive "revolutionary" movements that preached class struggle were one aspect of this social decay, but hardly their dominant concern. And social justice, which Socialists called for, was also a concern of theirs, because they thought it necessary to the renovation, revivification, unification that they sought. Much of what they said now has an irrelevant ring. We have discerned, we think, other more crucial seams and strains in the fabric of society. My only point, right here, is that their doctrines were not "calculated and instrumental." Nor were they counterrevolutionary in intent, except (but I do not think that was Arno Mayer's meaning) in the case of Maurras, who, of course, rejected everything that had happened since 1789.

This illustrates the need to be specific, placing events in their context, which alone can show what was revolution, counterrevolution, some other kind of revolution, or no revolution at all. If, as Mayer thinks, the reactionary and conservative coordinates of counterrevolution are central to its identification, then we must discriminate between counterrevolutions that may adopt a revolutionary façade, and alternative revolutions that have been found to adopt a conservative façade. Perhaps a reference to the old-fashioned categories of Movement and Resistance (coined for the July Revolution by André Siegfried) could help in this. Because it can suggest that movement may turn against (post-)revolutionary regimes, and that the latter may find themselves resisting movement. Only one thing is sure: there is no *juste milieu,* the very notion of it is eccentric. The more so as politics operate less in concentric ripples than in disorderly swings—toward extremes. And the motions of extremism matter more than its directions.

Fascist revolution in Italy, Nazi revolution in Germany, were carried out—like their forerunners in France and Russia—against the flabbiness and the failures of the existing regimes. Horthy and Franco led actions opposed to "red revolution" in one case,[27] and to a Popular Front regime in another. They are thus properly counterrevolutionary. Rex, in Belgium, was neither revolutionary nor counterrevolutionary: it was political adventurism dressed up in currently modish fancy clothes which happened to be fascist by historical coincidence.[28] And Salazar established his power, like Antonescu, in traditional terms.[29] It is worth repeating that repressive authoritarian regimes may borrow the rhetoric and methods of the class revolution, as others borrow the rhetoric and techniques of the alternative revolution, in order to cloak their inertia or their uncertainties. In both cases the revolutionaries will be eliminated, or put out of the way, by Franco, Antonescu, or Stalin.

The confusion becomes patent when all such action against revolutionaries or revolutionary forces is treated as one single phenomenon. In effect, most antirevolutionary action, especially of the preemptive sort, is taken by conservative forces worried by threats against their order or their systematic disorder. Police repression, military action, or coup d'état may be carried out against national revolutionaries as against Marxist ones. And given the tug of war for possession of the revolutionary label, is it not always clear, let alone admitted, which side in the conflict is counterrevolutionary.

Which side is revolutionary and which counterrevolutionary in Berlin 1953, Poznan 1956, Budapest 1956, Prague 1968? Or when Moscow and Belgrade, Belgrade and Tirana, Moscow and Peking accuse one another of counterrevolutionism? History will tell if we cannot. But the "direction" of history and hence its reading can change. In 1939 or 1940 many feared with reason that it would confirm the racist dogma of triumphant Nazism. Genetics and biology rather than sociology would have framed the mythology of the new age. Who could believe that they would have failed to do so very competently? Revolution, we are told, is the recognition of historical necessity, surrounded by a dike of inertia, confronted by counterrevolution. But history is what happens, invested with value only by those who perceive it as good or bad. Like plague or drought, a revolutionary movement is history because it is in history. So are its rivals, its opponents, its victims and its beneficiaries. The Spring of Prague proved abortive; the armies that crushed it got their way. Who stood for revolution? Who represented history?

Is revolution, then, like beauty, only in the eye of the beholder? Who is to say which is the real revolution and which the sham? Mayer shows no doubts, but he does not address the question when he explains that "revolution is more productive of human growth, betterment and dignity than counterrevolution,"[30] because this only holds for some revolutions, or some parts of some revolutions. We can attempt a list: 1789–1792, but not the Terror; 1848 (but which?) but not 1830; the early days in Cuba, but not the repression that followed (and, most recently, in parts of Eastern Europe). Every man his own historian. And even if the revolution is one block, as the famous phrase insists, the doctrinaire will make sure just what is cemented in it. Which brings us back to the subjective selectivity that we denounced to start with.

We should abandon the notion of one revolution, identified with only one direction or theme, and replace the question "what is revolution?" by the question "what kind of revolution is it?"

In a war we do not say of one side that it wages counterwar. Yet use of the term counterrevolution[31] suggests an authorized version which, misleading as to the motives and ends of movements that do not conform to an approved pattern, implies (though seldom explicitly) the superiority of, the virtue vested in, one kind of revolution only. Because we remember it as great, many believe that it was good. Since revolution equals good, counterrevolution equals bad. Hence the importance of dubbing what we consider bad as counterrevolutionary, a description as illuminating as the label "fascist" freely applied to conservatives, liberals, and portions of the left. When, in the end, fascism and counterrevolution are treated as one, as if identity was self-evident, confusion is complete. Yet the evidence at hand, far from justifying confident affirmations, seems to suggest we should proceed with caution—our strongest weapon, doubt.

What are modern revolutions about? The original formula tells us: liberty, equality, fraternity, or death. But, as Saint-Just realized as early as 1791, liberty once conquered is easily corrupted into its opposite. Equality is either equality of opportunity, rightly criticized as basic inequality, or it entails injustice and constraint. Fraternity is the vaguest and also the most delusive of the terms. It may reflect the elation of the original release from the constraints of order, but I doubt it. Is it there to compensate for the too evident absence of order, or to replace a missing father-figure with a more accessible brother? Latecomer to the original revolutionary duo, fraternity is an invocation, as if for rain at the height of drought; but also a logical outgrowth of the egalitarian ideal: authority is no longer the father, but the brother—a wiser, more experienced, elder brother, standing shoulder to shoulder with you in the struggle, before he is metamorphosed into Big Brother. The figure of authority, thrown out by the door, climbs back through the window. Finally, death: sole of the revolution's promises that it is certain to be kept, whatever its orientation. Bystanders remembered that when, at the feast of the Supreme Being, on 20 Prairial, year II of the Revolution, the symbolic figures of Atheism, Discord, Ambition, and False Simplicity were consumed on a symbolic pyre, the statue of Wisdom that the flames revealed was black with soot.

We might note in passing that for Marx and Engels liberty, equality, and fraternity are fine, but hardly serious, since Marx and Engels rejected ideas such as morality, truth, and justice. Marxism, like its contemporary,

Phrenology, is a science, not an ethics. The revolution it talks about is part of a historical mechanism, hence purged of values. We have just seen how seriously to take such claims.

Revolution and counterrevolution today both stem from the democratic doctrines of the eighteenth and nineteenth centuries, and from the breakdown of their political outgrowths. While true counterrevolution is the offspring of revolution, revolution is the creature of the regime against which it rises—even to the pettiest things. "I went to the Convention," notes Chateaubriand, "and saw M. Marat; on his lips floated the banal smile that the Old Regime has placed on everybody's lips." Marat's smile, like Marat's ideas, had been acquired before the Revolution. It was the Old Regime that taught Robespierre his self-possession, Saint-Just his strict demeanor and his romanticism, so many deputies their courtesy and manners, Girondists and Jacobins their composure in the face of death. Superficial? Perhaps. But suggestive of more important carry-overs.

When Mayer sees the mainsprings of communism and fascism as "drastically different, possibly opposite,"[32] he is wrong. The great revolutionary creeds of the twentieth century were (among other things) all inspired by Social Darwinism. Nationalism, fascism, communism, all reflect belief in the survival of the fittest: in terms of nation (or of race, itself a confused notion of the nineteenth century), or in terms of class. This is why, at least one reason why, the distinction between fascism and communism is relative rather than absolute, dynamic rather than fundamental. Both are originally urban ideologies, devised and propagated by middle-class intellectuals seeking to appeal to underprivileged and badly integrated sections of society. Both react against liberalism, its injustices, its inefficiencies, its decay; and both are its offspring.[33] Neither represents a revolt of the masses, though both seek to incite one. As the studies by Lasswell and Lerner indicate, Nazi and Communist elites show striking similarities in recruitment and in evolution. The revolutions they make are, in both cases, "operated by frustrated segments of the middle classes who . . . organized violent action to gain what they had been denied."[34] The fascists benefit from "the interested collaboration of the old cadres"?[35] Have Communists not done so? Who offered the Red Army, or the French revolutionary armies for that matter? How far do the administrative, technological and intellectual establishments of popular democracies, so-called, depend on the old cadres and on their scions? And the newcomers become a "new class" much like the one they displaced.[36] This is not what André Malraux had in mind when he declared that every communism that fails calls up its fascism, every fascism that fails calls up its communism;[37] but it is in these terms that the phrase makes good sense.

Mayer is right when he suggests key differences, structural and other, between communism and fascism. They can all be revolutionary, though different.[38] Both preach monistic solutions, establish orthodoxies, define heresies, march to specific ideologies—in Karl Mannheim's terms: "systems of representations that pretend to offer complete explanation of social phenomena and permit discovery and advancement of solutions required by problems of social change." They do not only start from a similar gnostic base. They also end in a would-be total system: legally unrestrained government, mass party, rigid ideology, pseudo-elections, systematic terror, state monopoly of mass communications, and a centrally directed industrial economy. Isn't this fundamental similarity between totalitarian creeds and systems at least as important as their differences of view?

I do not seek to labor points that have long been made, though familiarity is no excuse for indifference to them; and I am not aware of convincing arguments raised against those who find the fundamental similarities of communism and fascism to be highly significant. My purpose here is not to estimate the moral worth of either, even by implication, but to discern their relation to revolution and counterrevolution, and see if the question itself makes sense.

The fact that both communisms and fascisms are violent and monistic in no way proves that they are the same. Merchants of absolutes can hawk different wares. One may be free to choose between them. The question then comes up: is the direction of choice more relevant than the fact of choosing? The answer depends on the importance attributed to the choice. Is it on the level of buying a new car, or on that of saving one's soul? In this case, the right choice, viewed as a matter of life or death in the struggle for life and for history, is crucial. Both communism and fascism regard as intolerable and intolerably decadent the society which, having created values, tires of them, detaches from them, examines them, organizes uncertainty and tolerates doubt. Both communism and fascism affirm and structure belief. Even their denials are affirmations in reverse. There is no qualitative difference between affirmation and denial, which makes it possible to shift quite naturally from one to the other, and explains the counterrevolutionary aspects to be found in the propaganda of both.[39]

Propaganda alone is not all they share: also racism, torture, mass murder of genocidal proportions, ideological contortionism; is there much need to insist on similarities that some continue to deny and others to consider superficial? The interest of such characteristic coincidences is not to mark them, but to see why and how they happen, what in the nature of a movement or a situation leads to this blemish and not to another. It isn't so much the state terrorism of modern revolutions that bears witness against them, as their inability to invent ends different from those of the regimes they claim to fight. The similarity of their means may be superficial. Yet it is precisely at the level of means that we place the difference between revolutionary and nonrevolutionary creeds. We cannot escape our methods, and methods are often imposed by the situation, by the demands of the project. The revolutionary project, the revolutionary situation, have their corruption built in. One may well feel the justification of the project, the exaltation of the action. But it is well to note their implications too. We have failed to draw the conclusions of our findings for far too long.

Communism and fascism differ, we are told, because they appeal to (and benefit) different social groups. This is far from proved. I have argued the contrary case in a number of publications;[40] data concerning leadership of the rival movements appears to support my interpretation; and I suspect that there has been even more hypocritical dissembling about the attitude of German workers toward Nazism than there has been about the resistance of the middles classes. Finally, the argument itself is based on the unproved assumption that true revolution can only stem from a chosen class—or else represent it, an even more dubious view. Even if this were true, doctrinally speaking, just what is the difference between a national socialist revolution partly based on peasants, and a national communist revolution largely based on peasants? When Mao and Castro find room in the Marxist Hall of Fame, why exclude Strasser, or Hitler? The answer is obvious? Not in these terms. In all cases, tactics take precedence not over strategy only, but over ideology too. Tactics are the locomotive of revolutionary history. What really matters is making the revolution. The revolutionary knows or thinks he knows what will come of it. The doctrine is there to tell him. Or he doesn't care. But what comes of the revolution matters less than the event, the making of revolution. Belief in revolution for its own sake is one more thing radical left and right seem to have in common.[41]

Yet they opposed each other. This cannot be denied; it need not be. Fascist revolutions were in effect directed against Communists—not exclusively, but also. In this sense, which has been treated as decisive and which is almost accidental, fascisms were counterrevolutionary: revolutions against a rival revolution. They did not seek, as the Enragés or Babeuf had done, to carry one revolution beyond a given stage; but to carry another revolution in a different direction, to define its aims (often similar to the other's) in terms of other principles, to define its foes (often similar too) in terms of different values. The coincidences so many have noted[42] were denounced by Communists and their friends as camouflage; they were to be stressed by the Communists' enemies to smear the Communists. No one thought to remark that it is possible to react to similar problems in different ways—even on the immoderate plane. Revolution had been preempted: like the *frigidaire*. Ironic, when one remembers that the Jacobins were nationalists. Convenient, in terms of the way the rival revolutionary movements oriented their appeal.

By doctrine and deliberate choice, communism focused its appeal with narrow intensity. This was (and it is oddly ignored) the basic doctrinal difference between it and fascism which, convinced that the social reality was a national one, accused Marxists of splitting the nation and thus weakening it. The fascist net was cast more widely. This has been cited as proof of reactionary opportunism. I incline to see it as a more appropriate response to modern conditions.[43] The debate remains open. But I note that, having at long last read the statistics of thirty years earlier, Communist parties had in the mid-seventies extended the working class well into what was still denounced as the bourgeoisie; and doctrinaire internationalism had taken second place to the hard realities of national (and nationalistic) sentiment.[44] It is the tribute that virtue must pay to vice.

Digressions are hard to avoid. But every digression contributes to my case that fascism, too easily described as counterrevolutionary, is not a counterrevolution but a rival revolution: rival of that which claimed to be the only one entitled to the label, and which is still accepted as such. As Jules Monnerot has written, and he is in a good position to know: "for the fascists, communism is not subversion attacking the established order, it is *a competitor for the foundation of power.*"[45]

If fascism was a rival revolution, what was revolutionary about it, what was it revolutionary about? As far as I can tell, revolutionary projects differed. I have tried to outline that of Codreanu in Romania.[46] In Italy, the fascist leadership conducted its own Thermidor, and revolutionary élan seeped off between the seats of power. In Germany, however, national socialism proposed and embarked upon a *sui generis* revolution, and one that was recognized as such by men as different as Hermann Rauschning, Denis de Rougemont, and Jacques Ellul.[47]

It is still objected that national socialism was not a revolution because it did not destroy capitalist economic structures and change the relations of production. But, on the one hand, it showed that control was as effective as formal nationalization. On the other hand, communist experience suggests that a total change in the relations of production finally leads to results that differ little as regards the relation between producers and the industrial machine. Decisions are still made in one place and executed in another. It would be a help if available facts could be discussed outside models constructed over a hundred years ago. Finally, the objection illustrates my earlier point: inscription in the category "revolution" is only possible within limited terms. Certainly destruction of capitalist economic structures is a revolutionary achievement. It does not prove that other lines of action, not entailing this, cannot be revolutionary too.

How would the German situation look, as presented in Nazi perspective? Here was Europe's "proletarian nation," encircled by enemies, ruined, powerless, despoiled of its past glories, rebelling against defeat, against the world that caused it, against the forces to which it attributed its straits. The Nazi Revolution would build a causeway through the ambient corruption, the loss of confidence and self-respect, the collapse of public (and private) morality, the decadent culture that wore the Germans down and made them flabby, weary, and weak. It would reshape man. Manual and intellectual labor would be linked, personality reforged more through service than through schooling, art would become militant and committed to an ideal rather than to negative incoherence. The virtues would be revived: self-denial must replace self-indulgence, self-sacrifice would displace bourgeois selfishness, public spirit would rise where individualism flourished, school and work would contribute to moral, social and political indoctrination. The Nazis were inspired by communism, perhaps; witness the concentration camps with their pious slogans: *Arbeit macht frei*. But they were also fired by the practice of successive French republics, by nationalist tradition, and by more recent cultural revolutions energized by violence and youth, led by a hero leader, inspired by the certainty that if you could first (re)create man, social and economic changes will necessarily follow.[48]

This is an attitude that has often been described as typical of fascism. It seems to belong in other revolutionary traditions. Malraux has spoken of Saint-Just as one who passionately hoped to change man by constraining him to participate in a transfiguring epic. The basic "fascist" themes, including epic project, theatrical transfiguration, and constraint, appear in the French Revolution as naturally as in China or Cuba of the 1970s. So does the theme of death and transfiguration: in the Commune of 1871, in the novels of Malraux, in the proclamations of Che Guevara, or in Régis Debray's likening of Che's passion to that of Christ.

The action-for-action's-sake aspect of fascist movements reappears in leftist movements of the 1960s. The student movements that cluster around the year 1968 appear inspired by the thought that first comes action, then an idea of what to do with it. In Latin America, some revolutionary groups develop a mystique of violence for its own sake, comparable to that of the declining Iron Guard. In Colombia, one such organization called itself La Violencia.

Incapable of solving, sometimes even of comprehending, the problems that they face, such covenants have recourse to what Ellul has called (in another context) *le terrorisme simplificateur*. Revolutionary war, says Régis Debray, is a sort of destiny for men who have chosen it in order to endow their lives with meaning. Should we attribute such adventurism to social origins and objective counterrevolutionism (remembering that Lenin dismissed leftists as petty bourgeois overwhelmed by the horrors of capitalism), or attribute it to despair—the kind of pessimism often ascribed to fascism? "Pessimistic as to the issue of the struggle we undertook," writes Debray of Guevara, "disillusioned by the way the revolutionary cause evolved in Latin America,"[49] his revolt was a *mystical* revolt, a Christ-like self-sacrifice. It is reminiscent of Albert Béguin's description of the classic road to fascism: "the way of the revolutionary who has remained revolutionary, but who, by experience of failure or innate propensity, has come to despair of men."

To despair of them, perhaps, but also to bring them a kind of hope that seems inaccessible otherwise. And so, around Valle Grande, in Bolivia, where Che Guevara's body was brought after he had been shot to death, thousands of photographs of the Che joined the other pious images on local peasants' walls, and tales of miracles wrought by him were heard throughout the countryside.[50] Evidently, despair and redemptive action—even without hope—are not the preserve of fascists alone, but of other revolutionaries too.[51] Nor are they necessary characteristics of revolutionism of any sort, which readily admits dissatisfaction with men and things as they are, the more forcefully to assert the possibility of changing them.

True, the Nazi revolution was oriented not only against the order of Weimar, which it denounced as disorder (a self-fulfilling prophecy to which Nazis contributed a great deal) and which went bankrupt through its own devices; it was also against modern society itself, or what it denounced as such: the devaluation of values, the destructuring of structures, the liquefaction of familiar references, "a state of anomie unknown until that time."[52] Nazi criticism did not limit itself to liberal society and economy, collapsing all around and which, when it worked, worked to demean mankind. It reached out to their concrete incarnations: industrialism, bureaucracy, the mechanization of life, the bourgeois spirit denounced as the essence of meanness, mediocrity, and modernization. Familiar themes today, more difficult perhaps to denounce as purely reactionary than they were at the time.[53]

At any rate, whether we like it or not, whether we trust it or not, the Nazi revolutionary project is clear enough. It is all the more evident in its revivification of the *fête révolutionnaire,* the exhilaration of the great ceremonies and displays that the first Revolution inaugurated, the elation of living a vaguely defined but emphatic adventure: dawns when it is a joy to be alive.[54] Sacrilege? It may seem so to us, scarcely to the participants. If revolution is about the people, this was as close to a revolution as Western Europe has known in the past century. And most Germans seem to have perceived it as such at the time.

What were they being promised? The Nazi Revolution held out the ultimate revolutionary promise: *changer la vie*, an absurd project unless associated with *changer l'homme*, Nietzsche's *noch nicht festgestellte Tier*. Mayer warns us[55] that this too is typical of counterrevolutionary leaders, who "place greater stress on profound changes in attitude, spirit and outlook than on economic and social structures." He may be prepared to apply this judgment to men like Régis Debray and Che Guevara too, for whom the true end of communism is the creation of a new man; and to Découflé who seems to adopt Rimbaud's famous words as his slogan. And if he did, Mayer might be right. He would at least be consistent. At any rate, the project that aims to change life and man implies constraint. It did so for the idealists who sat on the Committee of Public Safety. It has done so since. Theories about the revolution are one thing; the practice of revolution is another. Revolution in practice is still another. These are platitudes we sometimes forget.

The Nazi Revolution, like other revolutionary projects, proved self-defeating. We have not dismissed other revolutions for that. Babeuf did not do so. Découflé does not do so. Perhaps all revolutions are false: they lead elsewhere than they claim. Why should one revolution be more false than others? In any case, how far does even the best-reasoned revolutionary project reflect the revolutionary perception of the masses? Especially the best-reasoned! Our understanding of this remains on the most impressionistic level. This may be why we fall back on sociological or theoretical analyses which, in their different ways, provide something we think we can get our teeth into: the security of apparent fact or logical structure. All that we do, too often, is treat assumptions as solid points of reference: wax fruit for working models of the real.

I do not think it has been often said (although the evidence is not exactly lacking) that most popular perceptions of revolution tend to be reactionary. We have not given enough attention to the nostalgic side of revolution which, when encountered, tends to be dismissed as an irrelevant primitivism similar to the coccyx. Yet a nostalgia for things past informs most visions of the future, if only because imagination has to build with blocks made of past experience, personal or vicarious. We enter the future backwards. The French Revolution itself was conservative, reactionary, aiming not to abolish but to restore (see Tocqueville), and only inadvertently revolutionary (see Hannah Arendt). It executed Louis XVI because

Charles I had been executed. It looked back wistfully to the ancient world, and pushed its antiquarianism so far as to revive the notion of the *proletarian,* which Rousseau had fished out of the depths of Roman history. Much nineteenth-century revolutionism was consoled or sparked by nostalgic fantasies and yearnings, which survived in fin-de-siècle socialism as they did in explicitly reactionary movements.

In a way, all revolution is reaction. Not only in the original sense of the term: an action reacting against other actions or against a state of things; but in the sense that it draws so many references from the past. Is it so clear, when we look again, that reactionaries demolish in the name of the past (tradition), while revolutionaries demolish in the name of the future (progress)? Is the reality quite so simple? And, if it were, what matters more in the end: the demolition, or the ideals in whose name it is carried out?

Is not, after all, revolution simply the realization of *revolt,* that is of revolt or reaction against conditions or acts that are revolting, so that the only definition of revolution would be: the violent and successful embodiment of one sort of reaction which, in due course, becomes another sort of reaction. This is a question that becomes most pressing in our own time when, most of the traditional revolutions discredited, the torch of revolution seems to have passed to newer nations.

Mayer has avoided discussing the independence and national liberation movements in the Third World.[56] Not surprisingly, since such discussion would reveal profound deviations and confusions in the Marxist doctrine of revolution. Yet in the 1960s and 1970s the movements and regimes of national liberation have been the chief representatives of revolution, the chief targets of counterrevolution, and any discussion of the two terms that avoids them begs far more questions than it faces.

Reference to the Third World is essential, because it places our question in perspective. Nowhere does the ambiguousness of the "revolutionary" definition appear more evident. Nasser, surrounded by petty bourgeois or middle-class aides, many of whom were, like himself, once close to fascist-style ideas, adopted a "socialist" position in 1961 and was recognized as such by the Russians, who declared that backward countries, sparing themselves the dictatorship of the proletariat, can pass directly to socialism under the leadership of progressive national forces which include the anti-colonialist bourgeoisie. This novel interpretation meant, in effect, that Marxist doctrinaires could endorse "national revolutions" being made to set up a national state on the nineteenth-century pattern, create a nation, and institute all the most conventional characteristics of the society against which revolution is supposed to take place in the West. It meant endorsement of dictatorships and coups d'état that had little to do with Marxist theories, and also of millenarian revolutionary ideologies that had even less. It presented doctrinal quandaries (like that which François Bourricaud outlined for Peru),[57] when in newly developing countries the industrial working class turned out to be a privileged class.

The notion of the privileged proletarian, launched by Frantz Fanon in *The Wretched of the Earth,* has often been applied in Latin America, whose writers seem to have coined the term "proletarian aristocracy." In such circumstances, revolution was forced to seek its partisans among the peasants and the urban sub-proletariat—the very social groups whose support was once supposed to prove the counterrevolutionary nature of fascism, and whose revolutionism tends toward nationalism anyway. All of this has led to the development of intricate and seemingly paradoxical patterns of opposition and of doctrinal heresy.

Inspired by Cuban example and by long native tradition, "leftist" revolutionaries argue that a numerically weak working class, tending to reformism and "aristocratized in fact by the relatively high salaries paid in large concerns," precludes adherence to the Marxist-Leninist model; and that, in any case, proletarian hegemony over predominantly peasant countries would be an aberration. "The vanguard class in Latin America," declares Debray, "is the poor peasantry, united under the conscious direction expressed in student ranks." More orthodox opponents of such "petty bourgeois intellectuals" argue that politics cannot be treated as a simple arithmetical operation which holds majorities decisive; and that, faced with a peasantry that is "backward and hardened in its ways," the proletariat remains "the revolutionary class par excellence." As for the Indian Revolution, on behalf of the most oppressed majority of Latin Americans, this is no more than a racist notion designed to drive a wedge between exploited people whether in country or town.[58] In the end, the advocates of *foquismo* and of a "people's war" appear more like primitive rebel leaders of guerilla bands, while their doctrinaire critics seem fated to revolutionary inactivity.

Such divisions are less interesting than the achievements and the fate of attempts at national revolution led by those national bourgeoisies that the Russians have come to approve and the leftists to abhor. In Bolivia, for example, the M.N.R. (National Revolutionary Movement), founded during the Second World War, has been denounced both as fascist and as communist. Its checkered career, which runs from revolutionism to collaboration with "imperialism" and American business interests, shows it as a powerful force for change, unafraid of violence, and responsible for "irreversible structural changes" in Bolivian economy, society, and politics. In its time, and to the extent possible at the time, admirers of Guevara tell us, the M.N.R. "carried the Bolivian people through the first stages of a revolution without precedent in Latin America."[59] Yet by the later 1950s the M.N.R. had decayed into corruption and opportunism. A more recent representative of revolutionary nationalism, General Juan José Torres, supported by nationalists, socialists, and orthodox Communists, harassed by Trotskyists, Maoists, and "leftists" who denounced him for refusing to arm the people, could not survive the tug of war between more and less radical revolutionary groups, each accusing the other of objective counterrevolutionism, and was to be swept out by a right-wing army coup in 1972.

Other examples could be cited. But perhaps the point has been made, *not* that would-be revolutionaries disagree among themselves, something that Lenin knew perfectly well, but that there are many ways of attempting a revolution, and even of making one. In conditions prevailing throughout most of the Third World, just as they did in Romania between the wars, the "revolutionary patriotism" of Castrism, the "revolutionary nationalism" of Bolivia or Peru, the "struggle of national liberation" with its economic implications can be very revolutionary indeed—especially where, as a Bolivian writer has put it, the nineteenth century is not yet over. This is why the debate between the national left, which places anti-imperialism first, and more orthodox doctrinaires who give priority to class war, is very revealing;[60] because the emphasis laid on anti-imperialist struggle, which is simply an aspect of nationalism, shows a perfectly logical direction to which revolution can turn. Likewise, the decay of the M.N.R.'s revolutionism indicates a very natural tendency, to be imputed not to bourgeois corruption but, as we have seen, to built-in factors that manifest themselves in all revolutions, whether they end in the contradictions of an Institutionalized Revolutionary party as in Mexico, or a new class as in Eastern Europe.

Even when a successful revolutionary leader converts to the authorized version, as Pepin did to Rome, and for similar reasons, the original revolution seems to harden into something else. Cuban peasants in 1959 thought that the liberty the new revolution brought meant freedom from work, as well as from their old masters. They were fast enlightened. Their duty was to work even harder to build socialism. There were no more latifundia and no more sugar barons, but the peasants had to carry workbooks like all other workers: the infamous *livret de travail* that stained nineteenth-century capitalism and that survived in the Soviet Union at least into the 1980s. Absenteeism was punished; strikes were banned, salaries frozen, holidays diminished. The chief enterprise of modern states—propaganda—was massively increased, sometimes as education, a guise that can be traced back to the French Revolution and beyond but hardly confused with freedom. The distinction between the center of decision and the executants persists. What we see in Cuba is a centralized, bureaucratic, police state, basically similar to other modern states, though more to some than to others. Does this go counter to Castro's revolutionary ideals? It does. Does it make the Cuban experience less revolutionary? It does not.

The same point can be made concerning Colonel Qadhafi, the Libyan leader. Qadhafi, who must be counted as revolutionary in the Libyan context, is clearly a reactionary in his ideology. He was, indeed, denounced as a "fascist dictator" by the Popular Front for the Liberation of Palestine (Paris *Herald-Tribune*, 20 August 1973). What are we to make of this?

Once it has abandoned the Marxist model of revolution stemming out of capitalism and industrialization, once it has adopted the abridged version of precapitalist societies hustling straight into socialism, revolution becomes not the resolution of a developed society's contradictions, but the accelerator of evolution toward development (and toward the contradictions development must bring). In this perspective, socialism is no longer a revolution creative of socioeconomic progress of a special kind, but just a way to do more quickly what capitalism has done elsewhere, or has not done fast or well enough. The exploitation of man by state replaces the exploitation of man by man. The difference blurs between the developmental revolutions (Mexico, Bolivia, Cuba, Egypt, Algeria) cited by Edgar Morin,[61] and the developmental dictatorships of Borkenau and Nolte. Mayer was right. Our findings, it would seem, do dilute his heuristic construct and blunt its cutting edge. But if a heuristic approach serves to apprehend some kind of truth or bring us nearer to it, perhaps that's just as well.

No wonder, then, that fascism is included in the category of developmental revolutions by qualified observers, together with the national revolutions of undeveloped or developing countries. We remain uncertain whether either kind or both should be labelled growing pains, revolution, or counterrevolution, unless it be preemptive revolution—a favorite for coups d'état from all quarters since the Ides of March. Only one conclusion seems clear. One cannot exclude fascists and Nazis from the revolutionary category of our times because of the equivocal nature of their rhetoric and their reformist hedging as they jockey for power, without applying the same standards to most "national revolutions" of our day. So, either the latter are fascist—in which case the fascist model is shown to be actual and appropriate to present circumstances; or they are revolutionary, despite failure to measure up to Marxist definitions, and then the fascists are revolutionary too.

Who can gainsay that Qadhafi, Nasser, Castro, Khomeini, are (were) revolutionaries, their regimes radically different in essentials from preceding ones? The point is not that they have betrayed some ideal pattern of revolution but that, despite nonconformity to the dogmatic pattern, their particular role, action, effects, proved very revolutionary.

There is no revolution to betray, because there is not one version of revolution only; and the contortions of Marxist theory reveal not its capacity to assimilate, or to adjust to, practice, but its anachronism.

Nor is it so much that the Marxist-inspired model of revolution involves us in time-consuming aberrations, as that it is beside the point.

Revolutions, revolts, rebellions, riots, risings, mutinies, insurrections, tumults, troubles, disturbances, coups d'état and civil wars figure in present history as in that of the past. The first rebels were angels. The first rebellion the Fall. We shall not be rid of the ilk in the foreseeable future. Perhaps we ought not to be. In any case, they exist, they demand our attention. Treating them in terms of one doctrine, relevant though it was in its time, suggestive though it remains in ours, lessens our grasp of the problem, limits our capacity for comprehension, increases the possibilities of confusion. Incantations hobble analysis. Even the restrictions imposed by terminological conformism pass into our thinking and hamper it. Political terminology becomes a political fact, intellectual terminology becomes a factor of intellectual activity. When we describe something as revolutionary or counterrevolutionary, half the interpretative process has been performed already, the other half will reflect what went—or, rather, what failed to go—before.

Yes, revolution is a continuing historical fact; but the context and objectives of revolutions change. Nineteenth-century revolutions, modeled on that of 1789, were supposed to be for freedom (constitutional, legal, of press, speech and economic enterprise), for the nation (patriotic and nationalist) and the state (a more efficient one, preferably a republic), against tyranny (and monarchy). Twentieth-century revolutions, on a model suggested by Marx and then revised by Lenin, are supposed to eliminate the bourgeoisie (not monarchy), to further the consciousness, unity and struggle of class (not nation), to take over the means of production (rather than free them for private exploitation). The relations that had to be changed in this second case lay in the sphere of economics (production), not of politics (the constitutional reflection of economic realities). There was a world of difference between the two revolutionary projects. And Marx, when he came along to say that the changed context of his time called for a changed revolutionary project, could appear irrelevant in terms of the ruling ideology and terminology and counterrevolutionary to the tradition-directed revolutionaries of his time, in the same way as one who today denounces the Marxist project and its derivatives as anachronistic when they are applied in a context very different from that of their formulation.

The socialist revolutionary project spoke of and to an industrial society, dominated by the steam engine, by the conditions of life and labor industrialization generated, and by their expression in liberal, individualistic doctrines and competitive economic organization. All this is gone or disappearing in the West. Which is not to say that want and war, injustice or exploitation, national rivalries and overweening states do not endure. But socialism has shown itself no more capable than other systems of solving such persistent problems. In any case, the point about Marxist analysis is not how correct it is in general terms, but how apt it can prove to provide a dynamizing (revolutionary) interpretation and inspiration in specific historical circumstances. Highly appropriate to the needs of certain industrially developing societies, like those of late-nineteenth-century Western Europe, Marxist analysis in conditions like those that prevail in most Latin American or African countries seems restrictive or confusing, condemning would-be revolutionaries to ideological contortions and to awkwardness in practice. Meanwhile, and especially in developed countries that set the pace throughout the world, social mutations from the secondary to the tertiary sector, economic mutations from ownership to management, ideological mutations as the age-old rule of necessity wanes, have all wrought profound changes. New major problems take shape and call for new solutions: growth, the explosive pace of change, technology, automation, demography, mass media, information and propaganda. Many progressive circles view progress as the modern equivalent of the Fall. If only we could be left to die of our ills, they cry, not of our remedies! What has Marxism to propose about all this? The ideal of the nineteenth-century revolution: *travail, famille, patrie,* more industry, more productivity, eventually more goods to be enjoyed. On such grounds, less revolutionary systems can match and improve on it.

An anachronistic doctrine of revolution hampers its strategy, restricts its tactics and, finally, hamstrings its theory too. In the context of today, reference to socialist or communist theory increasingly suggests the absence of revolutionary theory. This is clear enough in those neo-Marxist variants, neither new nor Marxist, which substitute the poor for the proletariat, the struggle of poor against rich for the struggle between classes (specifically between industrial proletariat and bourgeoisie), the wars of nations for the wars of classes. If such revisionists ignore Marx's views on this score, it may be because reference to Marx would reveal their views as far from Marxist or, more simply, because they ignore Marx. At any rate, viewed in the light of such doctrinal decay, fascism is just one more recent avatar of revolutionary myth,[62] disputing this with ideological rivals with a prior hold upon it; the very assertion of its revolutionism a tribute to the evocative power of the notion.

It is a tribute, too, to the enduring power of millenarian dreams and to their actuality. For this is what survives in positive as well as negative stereotypes of fascism and communism. If fascism really was the ultimate spasm of capitalist society on its last legs, the need for it must be past today when capitalism, however uneasily, rules the world. The communist revolution, in its ideal form, has shown itself hardly more relevant or more possible. Both fascism and communism have failed, in their own terms, to achieve the fundamental revolutionary dream: *changer la vie*. Yet, at another level, that is beside the point, and the persistence of the issue proves the persistent relevance of revolution as a cause.

The very notion of changing life or man is an inheritance of 1789 and after, the apprehension, novel for mankind, that things can be made different from what they have always been. *Belief* that change is possible, fundamental change, even more than the *fact* of change, is characteristic of the modern age. Revolutionary projects answer that belief, which constitutes the chief objective condition of their being. In this perspective, revolutions propose first to define, then to accelerate, what they say should happen and what without their intervention would not happen, or would happen otherwise. They express the general situation less in their content than in their form and, above all, in the crucial affirmation that radical change is possible and should take place. Fascists and Communists may find themselves revolutionaries without a revolution (we haven't quite got there yet!), but the "revolution" as part of the contemporary situation, of the modern view of life, is ready to adopt almost any guise that can express it.

This raises a different question: Do revolutions really change, or do they transform, modifying institutional or ideological expressions of fundamentally similar structures? We know that revolutions wreak great changes, overthrow a regime, break with a given order or state of things. But does this represent a passage from one state to its contrary, or to another form, shape, avatar, of the same? This is not idle speculation or even simply an aid to theory. For it would seem as if most modern revolutions are made not to abolish the existing society and state of things but to seek integration in them.

The French and the Russian revolutions were made against tangible groups: aristocrats, bourgeoisie. Whom are the new revolutionaries to eliminate? The bureaucrats? Who is their bourgeoisie? Only the workers know quite whom they should redefine as such from time to time, and they do so only because their avenging arm needs to point out some object for their wrath, some enemy in order to ensure their semblance of subsistence as a class. Sorel had sensed this vanishing trick when he tried to make workers fight to force the bourgeoisie to stay bourgeois, which was essential if the bourgeois were to continue to provide one of the two irreducible terms without which (*in ille tempore*) the dialectical evolution would have broken down. No class war, no clash, no synthetic issue into a new society: and that is just what happened. Over the years the bourgeoisie, that Protean monster, far from being eliminated by its successors-to-be, trained and indoctrinated them to assimilate the dominant culture and its values. Not counterrevolution but integration, appropriation, of the revolution, of revolutions, of revolutionary ideas, mark the practice of the last hundred years.

This holds in the long run, of course. In the short run, society reacts violently to challenges it can't absorb. But brutal reactions become rarer as we go along. For revolutions are primitive, and primitive rebels are increasingly isolated, assimilated, or entertained to death. So those who take the place of the "bourgeoisie" take up only its succession. The new society is not the opposite of the old, but its prolongation and its heir. Undeveloped countries want to industrialize. Developed countries want more of what they have already for more people: immediate satisfactions, regular work, or less work, continuity, security, predictability, comfort, more efficient facilities, and fewer traffic jams . . . Pursuing the benefits of productivity, bowing to its demands, the parties of Movement and of Resistance both revolve among restricted options. What kind of revolution is there left to make when all revolutionaries propose in the end to establish similar values?

Some time before the March on Rome Mussolini found occasion to remark, apparently with some surprise, that one could be both revolutionary and conservative. An incriminating remark? Certainly an actual one. As misery and exploitation grow less intense in the West, more complicated elsewhere, the revolutionary project becomes less concrete. In the wealthy West, revolution turns more toward intellectuals and dissatisfied members of the middle classes than to the underprivileged who are not revolutionary but reformist. But a less radical public demanding more costly public services (housing, education, health, social security) can prove more dangerous to the established order than the more vehement (ideological) radicalism of its predecessors. In Bourricaud's Peru, Sendero Luminoso maintains the dream of avenging revolution—destructive for destruction's sake, while other revolutionaries, turned ex-revolutionary, pursue a dream of development: industrial, educational, above all urban. In Lima or in Moscow ideals grow increasingly close: no more classes, only consumers. All revolutions now are oriented not to change existing standards but to enjoy them.

In the beginning was inequality, injustice, hunger, and want. Humanitarianism and political action remedied this (a bit), but only by relying on greatly increased productivity. Man in his numbers and in his way of life depends on technological efficacy and control, seeks to advance by increasing this dependence. What revolution will change this? We are, as Jacques Ellul insists, the prisoners of our technology, the captives of our means. We may diversely estimate this predicament. It may not be a predicament at all, and I for one am far less moved by it than Ellul seems to be. But it is a fact. Consumer society has consumed the revolution. The advances of modernity—production, consumption—have changed the data a would-be revolutionary must consider. Since it is doubtful that revolution now can do much to alter relations of production, perhaps it will return to the more modest project of altering relations of authority.[63] But, judged according to current stereotypes, this would scarcely qualify as revolution at all.

Perhaps the sort of revolution that goes beyond the immediate event, the merely spectacular, is nowadays unlikely. At any rate, what is currently accepted as revolution is not of that sort. The would-be revolutionaries of today would do well to look away from their anachronistic models, which they have abandoned in practice anyway, and try to invent a revolutionary project appropriate to the contemporary context. That is not my concern. But history suggests that such a project must go beyond the spectacular aspects of life, unlock the gate that leads from the familiar to the unexpected, release history to move ahead to a new and unpredictable stage.[64] Marx understood this; and the revolutionary categories that he proposed corresponded to the society of 1850, as it had not yet learned to see itself. But it is not the structures of 1850 that revolutionaries should attack today. Such an attack could still make sense in the first half of the twentieth century, when nineteenth-century structures lingered on. That was when fascist and communist revolutions, rooted in nineteenth-century criticisms and ideals, attacked the surviving structures and their conservative, anti-revolutionary, or counterrevolutionary defenders. The offensive of the revolutionaries and the ensuing conflicts were part of the preparation of the changes we have lived. They grow less relevant as the modern mutation gains ground throughout the world.

We know too much nowadays to explain very much. We certainly know too little to explain anything thoroughly. But as long as our notions of historical change continue to turn on terms as imprecise as revolution and counterrevolution, they remain blocked, and focused on problems already left behind.

Notes

For books published in Paris, the notes will show only the date of publication.

Introduction

1. "An Introduction to the Study of Saxon Settlement in Transylvania," *Medieval Studies,* 18 (1956).

2. It was published at about the same time as *The European Right* (Berkeley, 1966), written with my friend Hans Rogger.

3. It is a natural tendency to write textbooks that will fit one's teaching. Thus for this same course I prepared *The Western Tradition* (born in 1959, fourth edition 1990), and for my courses in intellectual history I wrote *Paths to the Present* (New York, 1960).

4. It is interesting that volumes three and four of Georges Duby's great *Histoire de la France rurale,* 1789–1914, and 1914 to the present, appeared in 1976, the same year as my *Peasants into Frenchmen.* Certain questions and interests may be in the air even when scholars ignore one another's enterprise.

5. I would not touch any of the other books. Not that they are perfect, but I have nothing to add. René, Abbé de Vertot, had finished writing his *Histoire des Chevaliers de S. Jean de Jérusalem, appelez depuis . . . Chevaliers de Malte* (1726), when he received a tardy note about the siege of Rhodes, which he dismissed: "J'en suis fâché, mon siège est fait."

6. I also owe to Pierre Nora the French translation of my *Action française,* and the incentive to put together *Satan franc-maçon,* which he published in 1964.

7. My Romanian background taught me, for one example, about the excitement that fascist-style movements could stir. As a boy I thought of the Iron Guard as a dark menace, but found in their rhetoric, their activism, their shows of force, attractions that were hard to ignore.

8. Perhaps indiscretion, too, plays a part in this historian's craft. Reading my headmaster's correspondence upside down while standing before his desk proved excellent training for deciphering historical documents in later years.

1. *Nos ancêtres les gaulois*

The writer thanks Mr. Christian Amalvi, Conservateur of the Bibliothèque Nationale for his helpfulness. Readers should thank the Bibliothèque Nationale for a cascade of strikes in Fall 1988, without which these notes would be twice as long.

1. Fénelon, *Dialogues des morts* (1718).

2. Guy Thuillier, *La Bibliothèque municipale de Nevers* (Nevers, 1983), 44. When, in 1821, the *Encyclopédie des dames* launched an *Histoire de France,* the first volume, by Sophie de Maraise, contained references to Gauls as clean, but rude (*grossiers*); 4, 18.

3. When Michel Hennin published *Les Monuments de l'histoire de France* in 1856, his history begins in 481 AD with Childeric, father of Clovis, originator of "la première race." See vol. I, 24; vol. II (1857), 1. Four score years before him, Jacques-Philippe Le Bas's *Figures de l'histoire de France,* (n.d., probably 1778 or 1779) begins with Pharamond and the Franks. One plate shows Pharamond promulgating the Salic Law "which recalls our Germanic origin."

4. The best general description of the mythology of French origins remains Jacques Barzun, *The French Race* (New York, 1932); Alfred Lombard, *L'Abbé Du Bos, un initiateur de la pensée moderne* (1913) is also useful. But see Jean Lemaire des Belges, "Les Illustrations de la Gaule et singularités de Troie," published in 1512–13, in *Oeuvres,* I–II (Louvain, 1882); Pasquier, *Recherches de la France* (1560), I, i, 3–4; Pierre de Ronsard, *Les Quatre premiers livres de la Franciade* (1572) and the verses addressed to the Queen in his *Discours de la misère de ce temps.*

5. Charles Loyseau, *Traité des seigneuries* (1608), 5 and *Des ordres de la noblesse* (1613), 27–28; for President de Mesmes, see Barzun, *French Race,* 104–105; for French and Turks, Claude Malingre, *Traité de la loi salique* (1614); Père Daniel *Deux dissertations préliminaires pour une nouvelle histoire de France* (1696).

6. Comte de Boulainvilliers, *Histoire de l'ancien gouvernement de la France* (Amsterdam, 1727), 33–36.

7. Duc de Saint-Simon, *Mémoires,* ed. Cheruel (1872), II, 367; Jacques Godechot, *La Contre-Révolution* (1961), 10; Montesquieu, *L'Esprit des lois* (1748), xxx, especially chaps. 23 and 24, as well as Lombard's comments in *L'Abbé Du Bos,* 472. Barzun, *French Race,* 223–224, points out that the Jesuit *Dictionnaire de Trévoux* followed the Boulainvilliers line, while Voltaire ridiculed it. For the continuing debate see also Emmanuel Louis Henri de Launay, Comte d'Antraigue, *Exposé de notre antique et seule légale Constitution française* (1792), 24 and *passim.*

8. Abbé Emmanuel Sieyès, *Qu'est-ce que le Tiers Etat?* (1820 ed.), 70; *Lettres de l'Impératrice Catherine II à Grimm* (St. Petersburg, 1878), 536, 581.

9. Champfleury, *Histoire des faiences patriotiques sous la Révolution* (1867), 260; Jean-Claude Bonnet, ed., *La Carmagnole des Muses* (1988), 180.

10. La Tour d'Auvergne, *Origines gauloises* (an V), vi–viii. But see 210–214 and *Le Moniteur,* April 4, 1797, where it turns out that the Franks were also Celts. *Correspondence de La Tour d'Auvergne* (Bourges, 1908), 277–278.

11. Comte de Montlosier, *De la Monarchie française depuis son établissement jusqu'à nos jours* (1814), I, 136, 149, 155, 163, 176; II, 146.

12. François Guizot, *Du Governement de la France depuis la restauration* (1820), 2–3; Marie-Joseph, Marquis de La Fayette, quoted in Etienne Taillemite, *La Fayette* (1989), 13; Perreux, "La Conspiration gauloise," *Bulletin de la société d'histoire moderne,* June 1923, 368.

13. Alexandre Dumas, *Mes Mémoires* (1968) v, 99, 103. The friend was Etienne J.-F. Cordellier-Delanoue, like Dumas's father a general of the Revolution and the Empire.

14. Augustin Thierry, *Considérations sur l'histoire de la France* (1840), 172–173.

15. Albert de Broglie, "Du Caractère général de l'histoire civile de France," *Revue des Deux Mondes,* Jan. 15, 1854, 270.

16. Armand Carrel's *Résumé de l'histoire de l'Ecosse* (1825) opened with an introduction by Thierry, reminding readers that the Scots were Gauls or Celts, and of the way "l'ancienne lutte des races" resurfaces in "wars qualified as civil" (ii, xiii). In 1823 Carrel's ally, Adolphe Thiers, had published the first volume of his immensely popular history of the French Revolution, which repeated the story of barbarian conquest followed by the subjection of the "immense population." *Histoire de la Révolution française* (5th ed., 1836) I, i, 3–5.

17. The fullest account of gallinacery is to be found in Arthur Maury, *Les Emblèmes et les drapeaux de la France: Le Coq gaulois* (1904).

18. Godson of the empress Joséphine, Sue had been christened after her son, Eugène de Beauharnais.

19. Martin Nadaud, *Mémoires de Léonard, maçon de la Creuse,* ed. J.-P. Rioux (1976 ed.), 21. Nadaud cites the authority of Eugène Sue (25) but gets the title wrong: what he calls *L'Histoire des prolétaires à travers les ages* is actually *Les Mystères du peuple,* which is subtitled *Histoire d'une famille de prolétaires.* Reading Sue must have led him to Thierry. For Nadaud refers in passing to "un Gaulois, Fréret," allegedly cast into the Bastille for having praised "our Gaulish fatherland." He could have picked the reference to the obscure Nicolas Fréret only from Thierry's *Considérations,* which ushered in the very readable *Récits des temps mérovingiens* (1840).

20. J.-P. Rioux, ed., *Leonard, maçon,* 9. In this context, see the garbled version "of the two-race war, between the Frankish and the German [race]" upon which French reactionary thought allegedly fed for several centuries as presented in Bernard-Henri Lévy, *L'Idéologie française* (1981), 130. This would be fine but for the fact that the two races at odds were never Franks and Germans, and that the metaphor fed revolutionary thought far more than its reactionary counterpart.

21. For Guizot, see Paul Bénichou, *Le Temps des prophètes* (1977), 23; for Marx (writing to Engels on July 27, 1854), Ruth Leners, *Geschichtschreibung der Romantik* (Frankfurt, 1987), 41. One of the pioneers of Marxism in France, the *féministe* and *communarde* Paule Mink (1839–1901), named her illegitimate son Lucifer Blanqui Vercingétorix.

22. Pierre-Joseph Proudhon, *Oeuvres complètes,* (1924), II, 392.

23. See Jean Reynaud, "Les Fées" of 1844, reprinted in *L'Esprit de la Gaule* (1864 ed.), 338.

24. Coincidence or contemporary commonplace, Charles Renouvier's better-known *Manuel républicain de l'homme et du citoyen,* published that same year (1848) puts the idea in much the same way: "Le peuple c'est tout le monde."

25. Jean Chesneaux, *Une Lecture politique de Jules Verne* (1971), 152, finds in Jules Verne not only echoes of utopian socialism in the tradition of 1848, but a sense of "Celtic patriotism"—hence the *racisme primaire.*

26. See André Rétif, *Pierre Larousse et son oeuvre* (1975), 11–12, 160. Not only Republicans looked to national origins for inspiration. When two Berrichon noblemen, De La Tremblais and De La Villegille, published their *Esquisses pittoresques sur le département de l'Indre* (Châteauroux, 1854), they wrote of the Brenne's druidical forests as harboring their ancestors *(nos aïeux).* A few years later, Grillon des Chapelles, *Esquisses biographiques du département de l'Indre* (1862), I, 3, refers to "[nos] ancêtres, les Galls ou Gaulois." So now Gauls were *ancêtres* to nobles, too.

27. Camille Ducray, *Paul Déroulède* (1914), 6 and *passim.* Déroulède's mother was the granddaughter of Charles Pigault-Lebrun, so they probably read his *Histoire de France, abrégèe . . . à l'usage des gens du monde,* 8 vols. (1823–1828) which takes issue with the race-war theory.

28. Paul Déroulède, *Propagandes* (1913), 86, 87. When Déroulède's *Chants du paysan* was awarded the Jean Reynaud prize, this gave him particular pleasure.

29. *Histoire de Jules César* par l'empereur Napoléon III (Naumbourg, n.d. 1865?); Victor Duruy, *Notes et souvenirs* (1901), I, 225; II, 312. But see A. Parménie and C. Bonnier de la Chapelle, *Histoire d'un éditeur et de ses auteurs: P.-J. Hetzel* (1953), 497, for a letter from the twenty-six year old Ernest Lavisse to Hetzel, proposing a "very simple" new history of France, which would go easy on wars and insist on progress. "Je ne perdrais pas de vue les humbles que j'aime comme les aimait A. Thierry que je sais par coeur."

30. For example, Pierre Foncin, *Textes et récits de l'histoire de France* (1873), 5. For the record, the first appearance I found of "nos ancêtres les Gaulois" used verbatim was in an article by Edgar Quinet in the *Revue des Deux Mondes,* March 1, 1855, 933.

31. Sue, *Mystères,* I, 19, compares the Gauls reduced to slavery by Romans to the blacks reduced to slavery in the colonies; I, 21, compares Roman Gaul to French Algeria.

32. In 1884 Jules Ferry's right-hand man, Paul Bert, wrote an introduction to Jules Renard, *Histoire de l'Algérie racontée aux petits enfants* (Alger, 1884) which presented Algeria's colonial experience as a replay of Gaulish experiences and compared Abd-el-Kader to Jugurtha and Vercingétorix. Like them, the Algerian leader "represented the cause of independence . . . his memory deserves our respect." (75, 156). The handsomest example of an oft-repeated theme is offered by an article of Charles Braibant in *Le Temps* of April 11, 1937, reprinted in *Un Bourgeois sous trois républiques* (1961), 408, where Braibant, who has compared French colonial populations and territories to Roman-colonized Gaul, continues: What are we but emancipated "natives"? "Les indigènes des Gaules, civilisés par leurs conquérants, ont formé quand ils se sont rendus libres un peuple nouveau."

33. Jules Simon, *Mignet, Michelet, Henri Martin* (1889), 312.

34. Edouard Petit, *Jean Macé* (n.d.), 455; Léon Bourgeois, *Solidarité* (1896), 5–6.

35. In 1793 or 1794, under the Convention, the citizens of Paris petitioned for the abandonment of "the infamous name" recalling the Franks who had reduced the French to servitude, and a return to the name of *Gaulois*. Armand François Comte d'Allonville, *Mémoires secrets* (1841) IV, 8–10, quoted in Marc Bloch, *Mélanges historiques* (1963), I, 95.

36. Vacher de Lapouge, "Observations sur l'infériorité naturelle des classes pauvres" in *Race et milieu social* (1909), xxvi, 62–63, 231.

37. Jules Soury, *Une Campagne nationaliste, 1899–1901* (1902), 31–32; for Renan's view of Thierry, see his *Réforme intellectuelle et sociale*, ed. Alain de Benoist (1982), 16, 35, 113, 116–117, 120. According to Leners, *Geschichtschreibung*, 23, Renan, who around 1850 had worked with Thierry, spoke of him as "his spiritual father." He was particularly pleased that it was Thierry's seat to which he succeeded in December 1856, when he was elected to the Académie des Inscriptions.

38. Soury, *Une Campagne*, 8, 199, 201.

39. Stephen Wilson, *Ideology and Experience* (East Brunswick, N.J., 1982), 467.

40. Edouard Drumont, *La Fin d'un monde* (1889), xx, xxi; *Le Testament d'un antisémite* (1891), 12, 13; *Sur le chemin de la vie* (1914), 38.

41. Raphael Viau, *Vingt Ans d'antisémitisme* (1910), 9–11; Jean Drault, *Drumont, La France juive et la Libre Parole* (1935), 42, 67.

42. Baron Magrath de Moyecque, *Les Gaulois nos aïeux* (Morlaix, 1881), 6–7, 38.

43. Eugène Garcin, *Croisade du provençal contre le français* (1869), 5, 13 and passim.

44. Gaston Méry, *Jean Révolte* (1892), 67, 305, 157, 26.

45. Drault, *Drumont*, 85.

46. Christian Amalvi, "France du nord et France du midi," in *Sources*, 12: 67–71.

47. Méry, *Jean Révolte*, 120.

48. Philippe Buchez, *Histoire de la formation de la nationalité française* (1859), I, 9.

49. Duc d'Aumale, "Alésia," *Revue des Deux Mondes*, May 1, 1858; Louis-Napoleon, *Vie de César* (1864). The latter had already broached a *Vie de Charlemagne*, in 1841.

50. Duruy, *Notes*, II, 282. He could not bear to justify Martin's first title for his *Histoire de France*: "d'après la méthode d'Augustin Thierry, de Guizot et de Michelet." A few months later he stood for the seat of Mignet, whom he could stomach better.

51. Fustel de Coulanges, *Histoire des institutions politiques de l'ancienne France*, I (1877); III, xi–xiv.

52. Frédéric Amouretti who, with Maurras, had penned the *Déclaration des jeunes félibres fédéralistes* in 1892, "avait la passion de Fustel de Coulanges." Louis Dimier, in *Le 75e Anniversaire de Fustel de Coulanges* (1905), 24.

53. Dimier, *75e Anniversaire*, 58.

54. Quoted in Leners, *Geschichtschreibung*, 24.

55. Paul Bourget, in *75e Anniversaire*, 13.

56. Fustel quoted by Dimier in *75e Anniversaire*, 49.

57. Fustel, *Les Institutions*, I, 452, and in *Revue des Deux Mondes*, May 15, 1872, 242.

58. Dimier in *75e Anniversaire*, 56, quite possibly inspired by an article on "L'Organisation de la justice" that Fustel published in *Revue des Deux Mondes*, Feb. 15, March 15, August 1, 1871, where he declared: "ce sont nos théories historiques qui nous divisent le plus; elles sont le point de départ ou toutes nos factions ont pris naissance, elles sont le terrain ou ont germé toutes nos haines" (538). One does not have to agree with this overestimation of scholarly pursuits to appreciate the importance that could be attributed to them.

59. Barrès, *Scènes et doctrines du nationalisme*, V, 33.

60. *Libération*, Oct. 21, 1985, for Le Pen's *Fête gauloise*, and the slogan on party badges. Also Allain Rollat, *Les Hommes de l'extrême droite* (1985), 15. Curiously, the Gaulish reference seems to have survived on the left as well. Interviewed in 1983, Bernard Stasi, a leader of the liberal Démocrates sociaux, complained that the left placed its electoral victory of 1981 "dans le droit fil des combats que le peuple français mène depuis Vercingétorix pour son indépendance, pour sa liberté, pour son bonheur." Marie-Laurence Netter, *La Révolution française n'est pas terminée* (1989), 203. Echoes of Eugène Sue!

2. Left, Right, and Temperament

1. Not Marx but Mussolini—and Keynes—introduced the planned economy to the twentieth century.

2. Maurice Martin du Gard, "Drieu la Rochelle," *Ecrits de Paris*, December, 1950, 75, quotes Drieu after a visit to Clemenceau in 1922: "il m'a dit que, s'il pouvait recommencer sa vie, il serait d'Action française." "Je ne vois pas Clemenceau royaliste," objects du Gard. "Maurras est un vieux républicain, comme le Tigre, comme nous tous, marmonna Drieu." Compare Drieu la Rochelle's *Comédie de Charleroi* and *Plainte contre inconnu*, in which his own indecision, his own dissatisfaction with these unreal categories are made evident.

3. The "Politique du pire" is too notorious to call for comment. From another viewpoint, Jacques Dumaine, *Quai d'Orsay* (1955), 86 comments on the American error of oversimplifying their interpretation of French politics: "Simplistes, ils considèrent que deux blocs s'opposent en France et que l'un fera crouler l'autre. Ainsi méconnaissent-ils la tendance au mélange hétérogène qui est la caracteristique de la vie politique française."

4. In some cases the fear of Bolsheviks even worked to the advantage of Nazi Germany. See A. de Chateaubriant, *La Gerbe des forces* (1937), 97; P. Reynaud, *La France a sauvé l'Europe* (1947), I, 94 ff.; J. Carcopino, *Souvenirs de sept ans* (1953), 23.

5. See P. Reynaud, *La France*, 125; J. Paul-Boncour, *Entre deux guerres* (1946), III, 147. I am not judging an attitude for which there seems to be much justification, but merely stating the facts.

6. See Casamayor's column in *Esprit,* July–August, 1958, 124.

7. Thus, G. Champeaux, *La Croisade des democraties* (1943), II, 246, cites among the publications which he found "resolutely and integrally pacifistic," at the time of the Munich crisis both *Action française* and *Le Temps;* both *Petit Journal* and *La République,* both *Je Suis Partout* and René Bélin's *Syndicats.*

8. Jacques Fauvet, *Les Partis politiques dans la France actuelle* (1947), 71; see also Jacques Laurent, "Pour une stèle au docteur Pétiot," *La Table Ronde* (May, 1948).

9. François Goguel, *Géographie des élections françaises de 1870 à 1951* (1951), 103.

10. An inquiry launched by the Nationalist *Nation française* in January 1957 showed that a certain proportion of its readers came from "the left." A teacher in the Nord wrote: "L'Action française a, pendant cinquante ans, cherché ses partisans à droite, alors que c'est à gauche qu'ils se trouvent pour la plupart." Philippe Ariès, "Litanies bêtes," *Nation française,* May 20, 1957. See also Edgar Faure in *Combat,* Feb. 3, 1958; Paul Sérant, *Où va la Droite?* (1958), 159. The fact is that the Action française had for quite a while, especially before the First World War, tried to fish in syndicalist waters with results that might have been less poor but for its persistent monarchism. Though there is little to substantiate the teacher's opinion, it would be interesting to see what sympathies the chauvinism and antisemitism of the extreme right has evoked among workers, peasants and, of course, in the once-radical lower-middle class.

11. *Monde hebdomadaire,* April 4–10, 1957.

12. A. Milhaud, *Histoire du radicalisme* (1951), 67. Picard's judgement is borne out by Edgar Faure's experience in 1945, when his choice between standing as a Radical in Paris or M.R.P. in Vaucluse was governed by no particular conviction besides the feeling that his chances would be better as a Radical in Paris. He lost. See Dumaine, *Quai d'Orsay,* 27; Faure himself, quoted in *Combat,* Feb. 3, 1958; also the case of Jacques Ducreux, Radical deputy of the Vosges killed in an automobile accident. Two identity cards in his wallet led the police to realize the dead man was really a certain Tachet, sought for collaboration with Vichy and the Nazis. He had become municipal councillor of Wissenbach (1948), maire (1949), and deputy (1951), without anyone guessing his secret. *Le Monde,* Feb. 1, 1952.

13. Edouard Herriot, foreword to Jammy-Schmidt, *Idées et images radicales* (Bar-le-Duc, 1934).

14. *Monde hebdomadaire,* April 4–10, 1957; *Sondages* (1955), no. 1, p. 37; F. Cathala, "Restauration de l'Executif," *Ecrits de Paris,* August, 1955, 43: "Tout le peuple des sans-partis applaudit les hommes qui lui paraissent s'adresser à lui par-dessus le Parlement. Ce fut la raison du succès de M. Mèndes-France comme de M. Pinay."

15. Fauvet, *Les Partis,* 26–27.

16. As late as 1893, *La Libre Parole,* Nationalist and antisemitic, was greeting the election of Socialists like Viviani and Vaillant as a sign of *nationalistic* reaction.

17. See *Ecrits de Paris,* July, 1949 and March, 1952.

18. Charles Morazé, *Les Français et la République,* 252.

19. This alliance could already be glimpsed during the by-election campaign

in the second sector of Paris in early spring of 1958. Alexis Thomas, once a member of the collaborationist Comité France-Allemagne, and president of the Légion française in the Moselle, was elected as an independent "d'Union Nationale," with the support of the R.G.R., Independents, Poujadists, Social Republicans (Gaullists), and U.D.S.R. (Union démocratique et sociale de la Résistance!). Thomas, naturally, was one of the 329 deputies who voted for de Gaulle on June 2, 1958.

20. "Declaration d'Investiture," *Monde hebdomadaire*, May 29–June 4, 1958. This is not the way things have worked out. Deprived of much real power, the deputies of the Fifth Republic indulged in demagogic overbidding even more irresponsible than that of their predecessors.

21. See Dumaine, *Quai d'Orsay*, 387, who notes on June 2, 1949, the orientation of the *colons* of Oran: "Ils sont gaullistes me confie le Préfet, parce qu'ils étaient tous pétainistes. Pour le même motif d'ailleurs; ils veulent rester les grands caciques. . . . Ils proclamaient 'Maréchal nous voici,' ils disent maintenant 'Général nous voilà.'" See also J. Le Cour Grandmaison, in *France Catholique*, June 6, 1958, and the increasingly bitter tone of Algerian *colons* and their representatives.

22. It has been argued that the real electoral showing must be judged by the results of the first ballot, when people indicate their first preference. Since politics is the art of the possible, the way people vote when the chips are down seems a truer indication of political realities; if certain choices have been eliminated by that time it is because they could not hold their own. In such circumstances, it is in the nature of things that the weak will suffer and powerful will benefit. On the other hand, we should do well to bear in mind that the U.N.R. remained a minority party and its preponderance in the Assembly did not reflect a comparable following in the country. Comparing votes cast for the various parties to their parliamentary representation, we find that a Communist deputy represents 374,138 electors, a Socialist 62,110, and a U.N.R. only 25,233.

23. J. H. Clapham, *The Economic Development of France and Germany, 1815–1914* (Cambridge, 1948), 240.

24. Jacques Soustelle, *Monde hebdomadaire*, December 4–10, 1958.

25. Daniel Lerner, "The Hard-Headed Frenchman," *Encounter*, March, 1957, 30.

26. Morazé, *Les Français*, 54.

27. André Siegfried, *Tableau des partis en France* (1930), 169 wrote of the P.C.: "il se compose de révolutionnaires authentiques . . . mais il contient aussi la troupe permanente des irréconciliables et celle—exceptionellement nombreuse aujourd'hui—des mécontents. . . ." The votes of such people are protest votes and many are cast today at both extremes.

28. *Fraternité française*, Oct. 29, 1955; *L'Union* (July, 1954); S. Hoffmann, *Le Mouvement Poujade* (1956), 228, 246.

29. Morazé, *Les Français*, 213. The coincidence is particularly striking between Communist losses in Ille-et-Vilaine and Vendée, Tarn-et-Garonne and Aveyron, Isère and Vaucluse, and Poujadist gains in the same.

30. M. Dogan, "Origine sociale du personnel parlementaire," in *Partis poli-*

tiques et classes sociales en France (1955), 325, even distinguishes between a rural and an urban right. The imaginative might be tempted to establish a correlation between urban-progressive-technocratic-authoritarian and rural-liberal (or Jacobin)-conservative (or reactionary). And this at both extremes.

31. G. Lavau, "Les Classes moyennes," in *Partis politiques et classes sociales*, 66.

32. Dumaine, *Quai d'Orsay*, 40.

33. G. Dupeux, *L'Opinion publique dans le département de Loir-et-Cher de 1848 à 1936* (1962).

34. It may be said that American parties, too, are coalitions of divergent interests and that their effectiveness is often threatened thereby. Apart from anything else, such a statement simply shows that French and American political parties, both, operate in terms of an outworn tradition where the margin for inefficiency was greater than is deemed tolerable today. But the Americans have the advantage that they seldom cared about the ideological crust that has done so much to confuse issues in France. Moreover, the tradition of compromise that keeps them in being is lacking in French politics, where the uncompromising statement of principle is matched only by the intransigence of those particular interests that hide behind it.

35. They may also be called ideological, within the definition of Daniel Lerner, *La Querelle de la C.E.D.* (1956), 182: "Ideology is a product of the degeneration of political language. Between people and facts it interposes the conventions of a vocabulary."

36. Drieu la Rochelle, *Mesure de la France* (1922), *passim*.

37. This what M. Duverger asserts, *Les Partis politiques* (1951), 245; see also A. Siegfried's introduction to *Aspects de la société française* (1954), 24.

3. In Search of the Hexagon

1. Jules Verne, *Géographie illustrée de la France et de ses colonies, précédée d'une étude sur la géographie générale de la France* par Théophile Lavallée (1868), ii.

2. A. de Rougemont, *La France* (New York, 1886), 1.

3. Pierre Foncin, *La Patrie française* (1894), 172. "La France à la forme d'un hexagone légèrement oblong dans le sens du méridien. Elle est, dans ses grandes lignes, symétrique, proportionnée et régulière."

4. Fernand Buisson, *Dictionnaire de pédagogie et d'instruction primaire* (1887), "Géographie," II, 1; i, 801.

5. Elysée Reclus, *Nouvelle géographie universelle 2, La France* (1877), 5; Vivien de Saint-Martin, *Nouveau dictionnaire de géographie universelle* (1884), II, 328.

6. Vidal de La Blache et Caména d'Almeida, *La France*, classe de première, 13th ed. (1915), 6.

7. R. Ozouf et M. Rouable, eds., *Encyclopédie géographique du XXe siècle* (1950), 11.

8. See Léon Mirot's maps of France in 1812, 1814–1815, nineteenth century and twentieth century. Roger Dion's masterful essay on *Les frontières de la France 1947*, updated in a new edition in 1979, makes no reference to the hexagon. The

479 pages of the book put out by the Centre Georges Pompidou, Henry Vayssière's *Cartes et figures de la terre* (1980), make no mention of the hexagon. But see 361– 362 and 466.

9. Emmanuel de Martonne, *Géographie universelle 6, La France* (1947), 1, 4.

10. N. MacMunn and G. Coster, *Europe, A Regional Geography* (Oxford, 1924), 275; but especially *Encyclopaedia Britannica,* 7th ed. (1842), and 9th ed. (1879).

11. Quoted by Bernard Guénée, "Les Limites," in Michel François, ed., *La France et les français* (1972), 62.

12. Vidal de La Blache, *Tableau de la géographie de la France* (1911), 4, 40, 49. See also his *La France,* 103.

13. Nathaniel Smith, "The Idea of the French Hexagon," *French Historical Studies* (Fall 1969), 139–155. I had been unaware of this excellent article until Pierre Nora pointed it out to me in 1982.

14. Victor Morgan, "The Cartographic Image of 'The Country' in Early Modern England," *Transactions of the Royal Historical Society,* 5th ser. 29 (London, 1979), 129–154. See esp. 134–138.

15. Alphonse Dupront, "Du sentiment national," in *La France et les Français* 1459.

16. Morgan, "The Cartographic Image," 153.

17. Vayssière, *Cartes et figures de la terre,* 253.

18. Paul Géoffre de Lapradelle, *La Frontière* (1928), 42, 43.

19. R. V. Tooley, *Maps and Map-makers,* 3rd ed. (London, 1962), 42–43.

20. Ibid., 42.

21. Josef Konvitz, "The National Map Survey in Eighteenth Century France," *Government Publications Review* 10 (1983), 399. It was also delayed and sabotaged by peasants who associated the surveying operations with road-building, hence with corvées, and also with obscurely nefarious practices calling for exorcism. See Vayssière, *Cartes,* 257, 261.

22. Marc Duranthon, *La Carte de France* (1978), 24.

23. Ibid., 64.

24. Konvitz, "National Map Survey," 401.

25. Guénée, "Les Limites," 64.

26. Armand Brette, *Les Limites et les divisions territoriales de la France en 1789* (1970), 1, 79.

27. Colonel Berthaut, *Les Ingénieurs géographes militaires 1624–1831* (1902), II, 2, 65; and *La Carte de France* (1898), 62, 64.

28. Konvitz, "National Map Survey," 400; Berthaut, *La Carte,* 276.

29. Régine Pernoud, *La Formation de la France* (1944; rpt. Paris, 1966), 5.

30. Ernest Lavisse, *A propos de nos écoles* (1895), 86, 101, *passim.*

31. Fr. J.-P. Gibrat published the first edition of his *Traité* at Toulouse in 1787. The revised edition of 1813 was printed in Avignon. It might be worth mentioning that in the *Encyclopédie ou Dictionnaire raisonné des sciences, des arts et des métiers* (Paris, 1751), II, 706–711, 711–715, the slightly more than nine columns of the

article on maps *(Carte)* were followed by the nine columns of the article on playing cards *(Carte [Jeux])*.

32. Pierre Larousse, *Dictionnaire universel du XIXe siècle* (1872), VIII, 1184.

33. *Instruction primaire. Etat de l' instruction primaire en 1864, d'après les rapport officiels des inspecteurs d'académie* (1866), I, 125, 221. See also Lorain, *Tableau de l'instruction primaire en France* (1837), 117, 361, 377.

34. Octave Uzanne, *Le Miroir du monde* (1888), 57.

35. Gaston Bonheur, *Qui a cassé le vase de Soissons?* (1963), 30, 31. But remember that even by the 1890s the map of France was scarcely a commonplace—especially in parish schools. One man, born in 1883, remembers as wall maps "une mappemonde et une carte de Judée"; see Jacques Ozouf, *Nous les maîtres d'école* (1967), 97.

36. Vidal La Blache, *La France*, p. v.

37. See Charles-Joseph Minard, *Des Tableaux graphiques et des cartes figuratives* (1862).

38. E. J. Marey, *La Méthode graphique dans les sciences expérimentales* (1878), 77.

39. Arthur H. Robinson, "The Thematic Maps of Charles Joseph Minard," *Imago Mundi,* 21 (1967), 95–108.

40. Jules Clarétie, *Voyage d'un parisien* (1865), 316.

41. Pitt said, "roll up the map of Europe" after Austerlitz, January 1806. No major French literary figure has written of journeying "over all the universe in a map, without the expense and fatigue of travelling," as had Cervantes in *Don Quixote* (pt. 2, bk. 3, ch. 6).

42. Jules Michelet, *Tableau de la France* (1934), 4, 94.

43. Michelet, *Tableau de la France,* 95; Dupront, "Du Sentiment," 1440; see also Lavisse, *A propos,* 198, who quotes Renan's words with great approval in a speech of 1891. This is not intended to suggest that the sense of national identity itself remained abstract. Only that the tone of the discourse concerning it often tended to abstraction.

44. Saint-Martin, *Nouveau dictionnaire;* for Jaurès's speech at Albi and E. M. de Vogüé's novel, see Raoul Girardet, *Le Nationalisme français 1871–1914* (1966), 95, 123.

45. Ernest Lavisse, *Histoire de la France contemporaine* (1922), IX, 534, 539, 541. Vidal's *La France,* 524, also ends on a reference to "la plus grande France."

46. Marcel-Edmond Naegelen, *Grandeur et solitude de la France* (1956), 193; Louis Merlin, *France, Ton passé . . . le camp* (1966), 20–21.

47. Smith, "The Idea," 151, quoting the *New Yorker,* December 31, 1966, p. 67.

48. See Laurence Wylie in Stanley Hoffmann et al., *In Search of France* (Cambridge, Mass., 1963), 227.

49. Jacques Madaule, foreword to Robert Lafont, *Sur la France* (1968), 20. See also Lafont himself, 257, and Marcel-Edmond Naegelen, *L'Hexagonie,* 10 (1963), 150–151, 156, 219–220.

50. Dupront, "Du Sentiment," 1433.

342 · Notes to Pages 70–76

51. Lavisse, *Histoire de la France contemporaine,* IX, 541.
52. Dupront, "Du Sentiment," 1433.
53. Ibid., 1471.
54. Stephen Bann, *The Clothing of Clio* (Cambridge, 1984), 15.
55. Roland Bacri, *Hexagoneries* (1976), 7.

4. What Is Real in Folk Tales?

1. J. and W. Grimm, *The Grimms' German Folk Tales,* trans. F. P. Magoun, Jr., and A. H. Krappe (Carbondale, 1960), 57–58; hereafter cited as Grimm.
2. Bruno Bettelheim, *The Uses of Enchantment* (New York, 1976), 159.
3. Ibid., 159.
4. Ibid., 160.
5. An attitude which popular storytellers and their public apparently shared. One story told in southwest France begins almost exactly like Hansel and Gretel: "There were once a man and a woman who had a brood of children and little to give them to eat. They were as poor as rats. One night the man said to the wife: 'What will we do with all these brats? We have nothing to give them. We must go and lose them.' The next day the father led them far into the very middle of a forest and said to them, 'Take care of yourselves I'll soon be back to fetch you.'" Daniel Fabre and Jacques Lacroix, "Le Conte de la Fleur," in *Histoires et légendes du Languedoc mystérieux* (1970), 51. More revealingly, the Auvergnat version of Hansel and Gretel, as heard in the nineteenth century and retold in the twentieth, depicts the parents as pressed by need: "They wanted to lose their children so as not to see them die." Marie-Aymée Méraville, *Contes populaires de l'Auvergne* (1970) 152, *passim.* Another story in the same collection, "La Belle aux cheveux d'or," suggests another possibility when a pregnant woman out gathering dead wood promises the child she will bear to a giant she encounters in the forest: "La pauvre femme était bien triste d'abandonner l'enfant qui allait naître, mais elle pensa à cette misère qui l'attendait et n'osa refuser l'offre du géant. Et la maison était si pleine d'enfants, et les parents étaient si pauvres que la petite fille aux cheveux d'or fut apportée au géant dès sa naissance." (Ibid., 28).
6. Bettelheim, *The Uses of Enchantment,* p. 66, and *passim.* Since this essay was written, John Boswell's authoritative study, *The Kindness of Strangers: The Abandonment of Children in Western Europe from Late Antiquity to the Renaissance* (London, 1989) has presented these practices as a normal feature of domestic life in Europe up to the sixteenth century. I suggest that the usage took a long time to peter out.
7. Restif de la Bretonne, *La Vie de mon père,* ed. G. Rouger (1970). There were practical reasons for remarriage. One story about a remarried widow tells us that when her husband died, "the good woman mourned him as she should, but you don't eat regrets in a plate" (Méraville, *Contes,* 51). Roger Devigne, *Le Légendaire de France* (1942), 46, notes the great number of stories and *complaintes* about orphans maltreated by a new wife, or, less often, stepfather. While male mortality was higher overall, deaths in childbed and after made for high female mortality between the ages of 20 and 39, hence an unusually high proportion of maternal

orphans. See François Lebrun, *Les Hommes et la mort en Anjou* (1971), 191. Widowers needed a woman to run the house and shoulder her share of work. Remarriage was frequent at all ages. Thus in 1709, at Sennely in Sologne, Jean Richard, 74, marries Françoise Cochin, 24. His previous wife had died three months before, at 18. Gérard Bouchard, *Le Village immobile* (1972), 18.

8. Jean-Roch Coignet, *Les Cahiers du Capitaine Coignet,* ed. Jean Mistler (1968).

9. Grimm, *Folk Tales,* 41; Bettelheim, *The Uses of Enchantment,* 79, 15.

10. Grimm, *Folk Tales,* 69.

11. Bettelheim, *The Uses of Enchantment,* 11. Compare Governor of Dauphiné to Colbert, 1675: "Il est assuré, Monsieur, et je vous parle pour être informé, que la plus grande partie des habitants de la dite province n'ont vécu pendant l'hiver que de pain, de glandes et de racines, et que présentement on les voit manger l'herbe des près et l'écorce des arbres" (MUS 76, *Journal d'activités du musée dauphinois,* 3). A few years earlier, in July 1663, a missionary described famine conditions in the Maine where one lad had eaten his own hand (Lebrun, *Les hommes,* 333). Jean Vidalenc, *Le Peuple des campagnes* (1970), 351, mentions that in 1847, as in 1816, harvesters would work simply for their food. As late as 1868 subsistence riots broke out over much of France.

12. And Bettelheim makes a point of it, *The Uses of Enchantment,* 62.

13. Grimm, *Folk Tales,* 3.

14. Bettelheim, *The Uses of Enchantment,* 94. He refers to Dante who "found himself in a dark wood where the strait way was lost." But Dante was a highly cultivated burgher, living in one of the most cultivated (and deforested) parts of thirteenth-century Europe.

15. Restif de la Bretonne, *Monsieur Nicolas,* quoted in *La Vie,* 291.

16. See Charles Joisten, *Contes populaires du Dauphiné* (Grenoble, 1971), 2. 19–22. Yves Castan, *Honnêteté et relations sociales en Languedoc* (1974), 470, insists on the peasants' concern for settling crimes and other troubles in ways that would permit continued existence side by side: "La recherche du châtiment ne peut guère rencontrer d'approbation dans un milieu de connivence . . . Humilier le coupable ou le contraindre à une réparation excessive semblent contraires à la prudence. . . . Le bon juge est celui . . . qui fait simplement constater l'échec de l'entreprise de violence ou d'usurpation. Pourvu qu'il obtienne le retour à l'ordre . . ."

17. Méraville, *Contes,* 116–21.

18. Ibid., 75 and *passim.* Note that the trials of so many fairy-tale suitors have to undergo also reflect the very real trials imposed upon outsiders to the village community who sought the hand of a local girl (especially an employer's daughter) in a milieu where endogamy ruled.

19. Vidalenc, *Le Peuple,* 352. Grimm, *Folk Tales,* 200 (also 64, 461). For less desperate but equally convincing motifs, see Charles Joisten, *Contes populaires de l'Ariège* (1965), 111, a story that begins: "C'était un père qui avait trois fils. Alors l'aîné qui avait quinze ans il a dit à son père:—Papa, je veux m'en aller domestique, je veux gagner de l'argent."

20. Denis Roche, *Contes Limousins* (1908), 26, 31. "Le roi ne conserve plus

guère dans les contes patois qu'une ancienne prérogative, qu'il partage avec tous les félons et les bourgeois: il parle français." Also Fabre and Lacroix, *Histoires et légendes,* 166, 173.

21. Castan, *Honnêteté,* 393, 394.

22. Paul Sébillot, *Littérature orale de la Haute-Bretagne* (1880), 110—111. Sébillot also quotes a creole story published in M. J. Thuriault, *Etude sur la langue créole* (Brest, 1874), 222: "il s'agit de nègres qui vont écouter des gens qui parlent le français, et qui apprennent chacun une phrase qui, appliquée maladroitement, les fait finalement aller en prison."

23. Martin Nadaud, *Mémoires de Léonard, ancien garçon maçon* (1895). I have used the excellent edition produced by Maurice Agulhon (1976). For the departure scene see 82. For Nadaud's first accident, 111.

24. Ibid., 94.

25. Ibid., 107.

26. Ibid., 110.

27. "Qaou prèze, lou prézé, lou mèz à là dén." In this context local speech can be suggestive. In the Marche (now northern part of the Creuse) *"voir les anges* se disait pour être affamé, ou simplement être à jeun." Marcel Jouhandeau, *Mémorial* (1955), V, 70. When hungry, one sees angels. Why not fairies?

28. Grimm, *Folk Tales,* 444.

29. We even have a Breton ogress: Saint Beatrix, countess of Talmont, whose husband fought at Bouvines, and who must have scoured thirteenth-century Vendée for fresh meat before she repented and became a saint. See Pierre Saintyves, *Les Contes de Perrault et les récits parallèles* (1923), 89—92, and Louis Buron, *La Bretagne catholique* (1856), 78—83.

30. Grimm, *Folk Tales,* 61.

31. Méraville, *Contes,* 155; Grimm, *Folk Tales,* 424.

32. See Grimm, ibid., 401, "The Jew in the Hawthorn Hedge," for the farm servant whose master pays him "three farthings in cash and counted out right," one for each year of work, and who counts himself wealthy. Other heroes, like Lucky Hans, also ignore the value of money.

33. Sébillot, *Littérature orale,* 67 and *passim.*

34. Castan, *Honnêteté,* 271, 315—317; Jules Lecoeur, *Esquisses du bocage normand* (Condé-sur-Noireau, 1883), 375—384. Even Ravachol, the notorious anarchist bandit (1859—1892), broke into the tomb of the Baronne de Rochetaillée in search of rumored treasure. On the other hand, many died without revealing where they had hidden their savings. Marcel Jouhandeau's grandfather only disclosed it on his death bed: "Au pied du mur qui longe le pré bossu, une seule pierre bouge, Vous la retirerez. C'est là." *Mémorial* (1955), V, 261.

35. *Gazette des Tribunaux,* Feb. 2, 1838, quoted in Stendhal, *Mémoires d'un touriste* (1932), 2, 36, Léonce Chaleil, *La Mémoire du village* (Paris, 1977), 33, 83.

36. Nadaud, *Mémoires,* 275. The fascination of such experiences is confirmed by witnesses six hundred years apart. Early in the fourteenth century, in the Pyrénées, Guillaume Authié had lots of gold and silver in a chest: "From time to

time he and his wife Gaillarde would amuse themselves by putting their heads inside the box and watching the money glitter in the dark." E. Le Roy Ladurie, *Montaillou* (New York, 1978), 339. Around 1900, the son of Alain Le Goff of Plozevet joined the army and sent his enlistment bounty home: "The postman brought it in a sackcloth bag brimming over with 5-*sou* coins. All the riches of Golconda trickled onto the table." P.-J. Hélias, *The Horse of Pride* (New Haven, 1978), 22.

37. Grimm, *Folk Tales,* 518–519, "The Star Dollars."

38. Bouchard, *Le Village,* 320. Not surprisingly, there were many coincidences between real life and fairy magic. In Anjou, the recipes of a *maige,* or healer, sound similar to those found in fairy tales. Thus, to heal the toothache, cut toenails and fingernails and bury them unseen. Lebrun, *Les Hommes,* 404 (also 406).

39. Grimm, *Folk Tales,* 244–248, "The Crofter." The popular (and Christian) view that riches must be stolen has survived among the common people. See Jacques Valdour, *L'Ouvrier agricole* (1919), 90; and of a rich farmer, "he says he earned it by his work, but he's surely stolen a good half of it!" (29) When Proudhon defined property as theft, he was coining a platitude.

40. Some of these fantastic beings have gone down in history, like the goblins who taught certain master-weavers of tapestries the secret of fine colors!

41. Note that men can "pass" outside their class more easily than women, their physique being less significant and the crust of manners more superficial. In eighteenth-century Toulouse, "un simple soldat, de naissance populaire, observateur intelligent des formes civiles des officiers de son régiment, peut en imposer à de nobles familles . . . en se faisant passer sans grands efforts pour un homme né et nourri dans leur société"; Castan, *Honnêteté,* 493.

42. Jean de La Bruyère, *Les Caractères* (1696), chap. 11, "De l'homme," #128.

43. Fabre and Lacroix, *Histoires,* 91. When Johnson and Boswell toured the Western Isles of Scotland in the 1780s, they noted that the villagers of Auchnasheal "were as black and wild in their appearance as any American savages whatever." But complexion was a superficial indication. In Balzac's *Splendeur et misère des courtisanes,* published between 1838 and 1847, cultural characteristics change, but the courtesans cannot alter certain physical traits. Thus, Florine laments the short legs and broad feet inherited from her Breton peasant parents—"obstinate feet" which do not prevent her being a great actress but reveal her origins. Most revealing of all, however, are the instincts of the well born. When the ten-year old Adelaide of Savoy was sent to Versailles to be betrothed to Louis XIV's heir, the Duc de Bourgogne, the wife of the Dutch Ambassador pushed her daughter forward to be kissed by the young princess: "The distinction was beyond her station and, though it was agreed Adelaide could hardly have known, some of the royal family were inclined to blame her, on the assumption that a princess of her birth and standing should have recognized the unkissable by instinct." Lucy Norton, *First Lady of Versailles,* reviewed in *London Times Literary Supplement,* November 24, 1978, 1376. Such sensibilities, reminiscent of "The Princess and the Pea," were certainly more aristocratic than popular.

44. Grimm, *Folk Tales*, 583–585.

45. For Grimm, see 182–185; for Perrault, see his *Contes*, ed. G. Rouger (1967), 103; Bettelheim, *The Uses of Enchantment*, 230.

46. Washington Irving, *The Sketch Book* (Philadelphia, 1848), 50, 51.

47. Méraville, *Contes*, 284. In the Upper Limousin the patois term for combing is *epeuilhar*, which means to delouse. On Christmas night, when the great yule log is burnt out and the household in bed, the Virgin Mary comes to sit by the warm hearth and comb/delouse the infant Jesus. See Albert Goursaud, *La Société rurale traditionnelle en Limousin* (1977), 2, 454.

48. Grimm, *Folk Tales*, "The Gnome," 335; "The King of the Golden Mountain," 340. Le Roy Ladurie tells us that "The mistress deloused her lover, the servant her master, the daughter her mother" (*Montaillou*, 10).

49. Grimm, *Folk Tales*, "The Two Kings' Children," esp. 412–413. Precisely the same motif can be found in a Pyrenean yarn about Jean de Bordeaux in which lice do *not* appear, any more than in a similar tale from central France, "La Montagne rouge." See Joisten, *Ariège*, and Méraville, *Contes*, 187–190. But their stories were collected in the 1950s!

50. Grimm, *Folk Tales*, "The Gnome," 335.

51. Castan, *Honnêteté*, 472, 471, remarks that his Languedoc villagers did not expect to be ill-treated by the magistrates who sat in judgment upon them; "Il faut en vouloir à quelqu'un, pensent-ils, pour le persécuter et quelles raisons auraient ces juges pour le faire?" In folk tales too, when the hero is asked to arbitrate between two parties, the unspoken assumption seems to be that as he is uncommitted to the individuals and the interests at stake, not subject to local influences which alone could make him partial, he will be able to judge the dispute fairly when relatives or neighbors would not.

52. At Mézières (Haute-Vienne), to quicken backward children, they would be laid on the fermenting dough while the oven warmed for baking, and the cover of the kneading trough be briefly lowered on them (Goursaud, *Société rurale*, 313). Several folktale mothers kill their offspring by crushing them with the lid of the *maie*.

53. Joisten, *Dauphiné*, I, 330–337.

54. Other compensating fantasies appear more realistic. Thus, the Grimms' "The Poor Boy in the Grave" (595–598) shows how a wealthy man whose harsh treatment drove an orphan to suicide had his farm burnt down by the sort of accident that happened all the time and died in poverty, as a lot of people did, as a result of what we rather curiously call acts of God. Another (607) tells how a hedgehog fooled a haughty hare into running himself to death, thus pointing the rare moral that no one, however highborn, should make fun of a humble man. Perhaps the most authentically popular tales, those about ghosts, are about transgressors of one sort or another: lawyers, lords, priests, thieving millers or men who had stolen their neighbors' land by shifting landmarks. See Lecoeur, *Esquisses*, chap. 21; and Restif de la Bretonne, *Un village au XVIIIe siècle*.

55. See Grimm, *Folk Tales*, 288 ("The Old Grandfather and the Grandson"), 507 ("The Ungrateful Son"); and Devigne, *Le Légendaire*, 56–57 ("La Couverture

Coupée"), also about harshness to the old and useless. Abbé C. Daugé, *Le Mariage et la famille en Gascogne d'après les proverbes et les chansons* (1916), 282, confirms this attitude: "When one is dead," says the proverb, "there's more bread for another."

56. If a passer-by were invited to eat, the proper thing was to refuse. Castan, *Honnêteté*, 299. For Fairy Bread, see Sébillot, *Littérature orale*, 12–13.

57. A pretty example of this can be found in a Breton version of the three-wish legend, reprinted by Sebillot, ibid., 147, which includes most of our familiar themes: a little orphan boy is oppressed by his stepmother who gives him only crusts of moldy bread to eat, which he has to soak in the village fountain as he goes to work in the fields. One day, as he crouches by the well, soaking his crusts, a beggar asks for some, receives them, and offers him three wishes as a reward. The little boy's first wish is that every time he looks upon his stepmother she will lose all control of her bowels.

58. Geneviève Bollème, *Les Almanachs populaires au XVIIe et au XVIIIe siècles* (1969), 74, 81.

59. This worked in various directions. In the last quarter of the nineteenth century, Sébillot, *Littérature orale*, iv, accused the clergy of suppressing the chief forum of story-telling, the *veillées*: "à force de prêcher, le clergé les a souvent fait disparaître, de même qu'il a supprimé les danses." Writing in M.-L. Tenèze, ed., *Approches de nos traditions orales* (1970), 141, Charles Joisten finds that the Church exerted a major influence on the Alpine legends of the Dauphiné: priests or their catspaws invented tales designed to scare people away from dancing, masquerading, working, or hunting on Sundays and holidays. Similar tales were designed to discredit enemies of the Church: Vaudois, Protestants, in due course masons (like the Carbonari denounced in the bull *Ecclesiam* [1821] whom popular tradition assimilated to fantastic and scary beings).

60. The first to draw attention to the cultural significance of the little blue books was Robert Mandrou, *De la culture populaire au 17e et 18e siècles* (1964), followed by Geneviève Bollème, *La Bibliothèque bleue* (1971). The vulgarization of upper-class cultural themes can also be seen at work in "typical popular images" like that of Lustucru, the mythical blacksmith who cuts off women's heads and forges them better ones—a conceit invented by intellectuals during the seventeenth-century campaign against *précieuses* and bluestockings but soon forgotten behind the avalanche of misogynist stories and engravings that made it "popular." Musée national des arts et traditions populaires, *Cinq siècles d'imagerie française* (1973), 39.

61. By 1953, when Charles Joisten heard the version of "La Mort parrain" (Godfather Death), reprinted in his collection of tales *Ariège* (61), the story begins with a perfectly happy one-child family. The age-old theme of too many urchins has been abandoned, large families are a thing of the past, and parents in search of godfathers face different problems than their forebears did.

62. See, for example, Sébillot, *Littératures orale*, 4, and, more discriminating, Fabre et Lacroix, *Histoires*, 211 ("L'Ami des loups"): "Dans ce temps-là les bêtes ne parlaient plus, mais elles comprenaient encore la langue des hommes."

63. The educated retired fairy tales to the nursery, at least as of 1697, when Charles Perrault (writing under the name of his younger son) had launched the literary fortunes of Mother Goose—a *Mère L'Oye* who was the direct descendant of that *Mère Louisine* (or Mélusine) from which Lusignans and Plantagenets also traced their line.

5. Who Sang the *Marseillaise?*

1. For historical details, see Julien Tiersot, *Les Fêtes et les chants de la Révolution française* (1908); Maurice Dommanget, *De la Marseillaise de Rouget de Lisle à l'Internationale d'Eugène Pottier* (1938); Alfred Chabaud, "La Marseillaise: Chant patriotique Girondin," *Annales historiques de la Révolution française,* September-October 1936, 460–467; and Pierre Cavard, *L'Abbé Pessonneaux et la Marseillaise* (Vienne, 1954).

2. Loire and Rhône became separate departments only one year later, in 1793.

3. Tiersot, *Les Fêtes,* 101.

4. For further details and references, see Eugen Weber, *Peasants into Frenchmen* (Stanford, 1976), especially ch. 6.

5. Laurent Lautard, *Marseille depuis 1789 jusqu'en 1815, par un vieux Marseillais* (1844), I, 134; Jules Michelet, *Histoire de la Révolution française* (1869), III, 238–239; and Joseph Pollio and Adrien Marcel, *Le Bataillon du 10 août* (1881), 389.

6. Alphonse de Lamartine, *Histoire des Girondins,* bk. I, ch. 16.

7. François Mazuy, *Essai historique sur les moeurs et coutumes de Marseille au 19e siècle* (Marseille, 1854), 32.

8. Tiersot, *Les Fêtes,* 38, 42.

9. "Let it be, immortal queen, / He begged her when he left, / That I should love the loveliest / And be of men the best!"

It is a perfect parallel to the stories Robert Mandrou reveals in his study of the *bibliothèque bleue:* as far away as possible from the *concret vécu,* from the *expérience vécue,* of its singers.

10. Batista Bonnet, *Vie d'enfant* (1968), 16, 61.

11. Agricol Perdiguier, *Mémoires d'un compagnon* (1964), 45.

12. Albert Dauzat, *Glossaire étymologique du patois de Vinzelles* (Montpellier, 1915), 18–19.

13. Terry Ranger, *Dance and Society in Eastern Africa* (Berkeley, 1975), 129.

14. Armand Audiganne, *Les Populations ouvrières et les industries de la France* (1860), II, 253. Further details and references in Weber, *Peasants into Frenchmen,* ch. 26.

15. Xavier Thiriat, *La Vallée de Cleurie* (Remiremont, 1869), 381.

16. "The prefect and Monsieur le Maire / Are certainly a pretty pair. / The draft they make us take part in is / Just where our march to death begins." Albert Dauzat, *Le Village et le paysan de France* (1941), 162.

17. *Etat de l'instruction primaire en 1864, d'après les rapports officiels des inspecteurs d'académie* (1866), II, 37.

18. Amédée Reuchsel, *L'Education musicale populaire* (1906), 91. In 1887, Thomas would be commissioned to establish the final official version of the national anthem.

19. Félix Pécaut, "Notes d'inspection," *Revue pédagogique,* October 1894, 307.

20. In 1848, when the peasants of Oyonnax (Ain) heard it sung, they barricaded themselves: "Fremin neutre peurte, y canton la Marseilloise, recha la terreur!" Louis Bollé, *Histoire et folklore du Haut-Bugey* (Bellegarde, 1954), 80. ("Close the doors, they're singing the *Marseillaise,* here's the Terror!")

21. Note that when it did not suit the government's purpose, the song could still get one into trouble. In a pamphlet of 1844, Claude Tillier denounced the government for celebrating the Revolution on July 14, yet setting the gendarmes on anyone who dared to sing the *Marseillaise* during the festive hubbub. See Henry Leslie Maple, *Claude Tillier* (Geneva, 1957), 54.

22. AN (Archives nationales) BB 30370 (Aix, October 16, 1850); Eugène Baillet, *Chansons* (1867).

23. AD (Archives départementales), Ariège, 5M3 (April, 1858).

24. Arsène Vermenouze, "Discours," *La Croix cantalienne,* July 30, 1903.

25. Note also the equivocal German attitude to the hymn. When on September 19, 1870, the Fifth Prussian Army Corps entered Versailles, its bands played it "pour insulter le vaincu." Gustave Desjardins, *Tableau de la guerre des Allemands dans le département de Seine-et-Oise* (1882), 11.

26. "Let's sing of Liberty / Defend our fair city / Let's march, let's march! / Now free of a crowned head / The people shall have bread."

27. *Journal de Montbrison,* September 9, 1877.

28. Similarly symbolic of the *ralliement,* and more visible, was the occasion in 1904 when the leaders of the Action libérale populaire (Albert de Mun and Jacques Piou) entered the grand banquet of their annual party congress to the strains of the Marseillaise.

29. Michelle Perrot, *Les Ouvriers en grève* (1974), II, 549, 562–563; Leo Loubère, *Radicalism in Mediterranean France, 1848–1914* (Albany, 1974), 220; and Roger Béteille, *La Vie quotidienne en Rouergue avant 1914* (1973), 201. Note that the *Carmagnole,* though its tune came from Provence, was also endowed with Parisian lyrics, as was the *Internationale,* set to music in Lille in 1888.

30. "My breast is wholly French, so go, be on your way. / Step not beneath my roof, please take your child away. / My sons will all grow up to sing the *Marseillaise,* / I do not sell my milk to feed a German's son." Pierre Barbier and France Vernillat, *Histoire de France par les chansons* (1961), VIII, 38–39.

31. Maurice Barrès, *Scènes et doctrines du nationalisme français* (1902), I, 3.

6. Religion or Superstition?

1. Albert Mathiez, *Contributions à l'histoire religieuse de la Révolution française* (1907), 32, quoted in Clarke Garrett, *Respectable Folly: Millenarianism and the French Revolution in England and France* (Baltimore, 1975), 17.

2. Not Vauxains, as Garrett has it.

3. Garrett, *Respectable Folly,* 29. For Bishop Pierre Pontard see A. Robert and G. Cougny, *Dictionnaire des parlementaires français* (1891), v. 18.

4. Philippe Muray, *Le 19e siècle à travers les âges* (1984), Auguste Viatte, *Les Sources occultes du romantisme; Illuminisme—théosophie* (1928), and *Victor Hugo et les illuminés de son temps* (Ottawa, 1942). For James Webb see *The Flight from Reason* (London, 1971), republished as *The Occult Underground* (La Salle, Ill., 1974).

5. Muray, *19e siècle,* 142.

6. Ibid., 244.

7. Garrett, *Respectable Folly,* 15.

8. Muray, *19e siècle,* 53.

9. Ibid., 54.

10. Ibid., 13.

11. Louis Reybaud, *Jérome Paturot à la recherche d'une position sociale* (1842), 40.

12. Muray, *19e siècle,* 172. For Fourier, see Jonathan Beecher, *Fourier* (Berkeley, 1986), 166. That Swedenborg, Saint-Martin, and their *illuministe* followers did not affect the left alone, see the testimony of Pierre-Jean Béranger, *Ma Biographie* (1859), 43: "Moquez-vous donc des superstitions de village, lorsque vous voyez des gens d'un monde éclairé infatués de pareilles rêveries."

13. Muray, *19e siècle,* pp. 166–168 *passim.*

14. Ibid., 211.

15. Eliphas Lévi, *Histoire de la magie* (1860), 522.

16. Alphonse Esquiros, *De la vie future au point de vue socialiste* (Marseille, 1850).

17. See Viatte, *Victor Hugo,* 92, *passim,* and Adolphe Constant, *La Mère de Dieu* (1844).

18. Muray, *19e siècle,* 199, 180.

19. Joseph Grasset, *L'Occultisme hier et aujourd'hui, le merveilleux préscientifique* (Montpellier, 1907) quoted in Muray, *19e siècle,* 157; Hugo, *Les Travailleurs de la mer* (1866), 40.

20. J. Bouvéry, *Le Spiritisme et l'anarchie devant la science et la philosophie* (1897), 367. This may be why Anatole France ironically called for the creation of a Chair of Telepathy at the College de France, "for some student of Dr. Charles Richet." *Le Temps,* June 1, 1890.

21. Alphonse Lucas, *Les Clubs et les clubistes* (1851), 183.

22. Viatte, *Victor Hugo,* 126.

23. Eugen Weber, *Satan franc-maçon* (1964); Joanny Bricaud, *La Messe noire* (1924), 50, 58. The relation between Satan and liberating revolt can be glimpsed in the first names some enthusiastic rebels gave their offspring. Paule Mink's son was called Lucifer Blanqui Vercingétorix Révolution; Louis Mézières, future rector of the Academy of Metz, Amour-Satan. See Daniel-Rops, *L'Eglise des révolutions* (1966), 57.

24. Muray, *19e siècle,* 257.

25. Thomas Kselman, *Miracles and Prophecies in Nineteenth-Century France* (New Brunswick, 1983), 138–139.

26. See Jules Bois, *Le Satanisme et la magie* (1895); Arthur Edward Waite,

Devil-Worship in France or the Question of Lucifer (London, 1896); Joanny Bricaud, *J.-K. Huysmans et le satanisme* (Paris, 1913) and *La Messe noire;* Victor-Emile Michelet, *Les Compagnons de la kiérophanie* (1937); André Billy, *Stanislas de Guaita* (1971). For Vintras, see J.-M. Quérard, *Les Supercheries littéraires dévoilées* (1896), iii, 127–167.

27. Muray, *19e siècle,* 301.

28. Michael P. Carroll, *The Cult of the Virgin Mary: Psychological Origins* (Princeton, 1986), 170.

29. See Gérard Cholvy and Yves-Marie Hilaire, *Histoire religieuse de la France contemporaine* (2 vols., Toulouse, 1985–86), I, 280. One might add that a fervent believer like Catherine, plausibly affected by the feast of St. Vincent on 19 July, could be equally impressed by sermons and ceremonies related to a whole series of feasts concerning the Virgin: 2 July, Visitation; 18 August, Assumption; 8 September, Nativity; 7 October, Rosary; 21 November, Presentation. Six out of eight annual fetes of the Virgin Mary fell between her first and last visions. 25 November, two days before the Virgin's crucial command, was the feast of Catherine's own patron saint, St. Catherine of Alexandria.

30. Kselman, *Miracles,* 62–66.

31. Carroll, *The Cult,* 154.

32. See Chapter 5.

33. At La Salette, too, a feast of the Virgin, her Nativity, had been celebrated ten days before her apparition.

34. See Jean Stern, *La Salette: Documents authentiques* (1980), 1, 10–12 and *passim.*

35. Carroll, *The Cult,* 202.

36. For Soeur Nativité see Kselman, *Miracles,* 70–71. And remember that Christ's baptism had been celebrated on 13 January; Candlemas was coming up shortly.

37. For normal peasant indifference see Michael Howard, *The Franco-Prussian War* (New York, 1961), 256.

38. Jules Michelet, *La Sorcière* (1862; 1964 ed.), 91.

39. Kselman, *Miracles,* 147. As an unfriendly observer had commented on Lourdes: "C'est la création d'une industrie exceptionnelle qui n'exige aucune mise de fonds, qui ne connaît ni morte-saison, ni chômage, ni coalition d'ouvriers." *La France nouvelle* (1981 ed.) 19.

40. Ibid., 195.

41. Cholvy and Hilaire, *Histoire religieuse,* 1, 163.

42. Judith Devlin, *The Superstitious Mind: French Peasants and the Supernatural in the Nineteenth Century* (New Haven, 1987), xii.

43. Ibid., 7.

44. Ibid., 182.

45. Ibid., 90.

46. Ibid., 31.

47. Ibid., 9, 16, 19.

48. Ibid., 54.

49. Ibid., 54, 57.

50. Ibid., 101, 83.

51. Ibid., 77.

52. Ibid., 64. For confirmation, see Philippe Boutry, *Prêtres et paroisses dans le pays du Curé d'Ars* (1986), 493.

53. Devlin, *Superstitious Mind*, 71.

54. Ibid., 57, 164, 153.

55. Ibid., 131.

56. Ibid., 127, 136–138.

57. Ibid., 61.

58. Charles Nisard, *Histoire des livres populaires* (1864), 11, 141. Spellbooks also appealed to less feeble imaginations, like those of Huysmans and of Stanislas de Guaita.

59. Lorain, *Tableau de l'instruction primaire en France* (1837), 111, 330.

60. Devlin, *Superstitious Mind,* viii.

61. Emil Dave, *Le Tirage au sort* (Namur, 1934), 4 and *passim.*

62. Michelet, *La Sorcière,* 24, 27, 29, 89, 128, 137. See also Muray, *19e siècle,* 243.

63. Devlin, *Superstitious Mind,* 106.

64. Ibid., 169, 173. J.-K. Huysman's chief motive for believing in contemporary Satanism was the theft of consecrated wafers. See Bricaud, *La Messe noire,* 55–56.

65. Ibid., 153. So did the Holy Virgin who, on Sunday, June 8, 1873 (and again on July 8) appeared to Auguste Arnaud, then working in his vineyard at St. Bauzille (Herault). Dressed all in white, the Lady was wearing a great white veil, a fringed belt, and a high crown like a bishop's mitre. She advised Arnaud (whom she interrupted in the act of lighting his pipe) to worship St. Bauzille and other local saints who felt forsaken, to set up a cross, to organize processions, and *never* to work on Sundays. B. Billet et al., *Notre Dame du Dimanche* (1973). At the time of the apparition, the phylloxera was threatening local vines, and the Virgin knew it.

66. Kselman, *Miracles,* 25.

67. See *Légendaire du Languedoc-Roussillon* (Montpellier, 1972), 5, 51; Georges Rocal, *Croquants du Périgord* (Périgueux, 1934), 41; Lorain, *Tableau de l'instruction,* 356.

68. Devlin, *Superstitious Mind,* 108. She would enjoy the story in Boutry, *Prêtres,* 577: In 1867 the manager of a provincial factory, irritated by the priest's demands that his workers should be free on Sundays, breaks the friendship between his daughter and the priest, "Maman m'a dit que tu étais . . . un méchant, que tu faisais l'orage et tomber le tonnerre, qu'il fallait plus t'aimer."

69. Devlin, *Superstitious Mind,* 215.

70. Ibid., 92.

71. Cholvy and Hilaire, *Histoire religieuse,* II, 238.

72. Ibid., 1, 22.

73. See Jany Rouger and Jean-Louis Neveu, *La Petite Eglise, deux siècles de dissidence* (Parthenay, 1987); Joseph Bertaud, *La Petite Eglise en Poitou* (Poitiers, 1981); Auguste Billaud, *La Petite Eglise dans la Vendée et les Deux-Sèvres* (1961).

74. See notice in Pierre Larousse, *Grand Dictionnaire universel du XIXe siècle* (1866).

75. Cholvy and Hilaire, *Histoire religieuse*, I, 117, II, 113; Kselman, *Miracles*, 16.

76. Quoted by Cholvy and Hilaire, *Histoire religieuse*, I, 42.

77. See Boutry, *Prêtres*, 205.

78. Louis Desprez, *Autour d'un clocher: Moeurs rurales* (Bruxelles, 1884), 66, 80. Antoine Sylvère, *Toinon* (1980), 65–67.

79. P. G. Hamerton, *Round My House* (Boston, 1885), 262; Guillaumin, *The Life of a Simple Man* (London, 1982), 56.

80. Cholvy and Hilaire, *Histoire religieuse*, II, 173.

81. Jacques Léonard, *Les Médecins de l'ouest au XIXe siècle* (1978), III, 1320, 1303–4; *Gazette des tribunaux*, 5 August, 1891. See also Paul Adam, *La Force du mal* (1896), 159.

82. *Gazette des tribunaux*, 17 June, 1883.

83. Abbé Jules Noguès, *Les Moeurs d'autrefois en Saintonge et en Aunis* (Saintes, 1891), 191.

84. Cholvy and Hilaire, *Histoire religieuse*, II, 36, 216; also I, 292.

85. Alban Bensa, *Les Saints guérisseurs du Perche-Gouët* (1978), pp. 40–43.

86. Ibid., 187, 146–147.

87. Ibid., 37.

88. Ibid., 61.

89. Ibid., 63, 140.

90. Ibid., 141–142. Already after the Concordate of 1801, hostility between *curés concordataires* and some village communities clinging to pre-Concordate traditions which the Concordate abolished (Epiphany, for example), had led to schism in some cases, detachment in others, and eventually to Republican and anti-clerical orientation in village politics. See Amblard de Guerry, *Chavagnes* (Toulouse, 1988), 195.

91. Ibid., 111–112, 200.

92. Ibid., 207 and *passim:* a very important point.

93. Ibid., 163, 180.

94. Ibid., 173, 177.

95. Ibid., 60–61.

96. Ibid., 232.

97. Ibid., 76, 234.

98. Ibid., 50, 76.

99. Boutry, *Prêtres*, 506.

100. Bensa, *Les Saints*, 217; Laisnel de La Salle, *Croyances et légendes du centre de la France* (1875), p. xxiv; Emile Littré, *De l'établissement de la 3e République* (1880), 209, 211.

101. The process has found a worthy chronicle in Yves Lambert's marvelous *Dieu change en Bretagne* (1985), which I ignored at the time of writing.

7. The Second Republic, Politics, and the Peasant

1. *The Eighteenth Brumaire of Louis Bonaparte*, in Karl Marx and Frederick Engels, *Selected Works* (Moscow, 1951), I; "The Peasant Question in France and Germany," in ibid., II. True, Marx distinguishes between conservative peasants "in stupefied seclusion" and "the country folk who, linked up with the towns, want to overthrow the old order . . ." But there is little contemporary evidence of an effective linkage with an urban radicalism that was still largely alien to most country folk in Gambetta's day.

2. J. M. Amelin, *Guide du voyageur dans le département de l'Hérault* (1827), 560; *Friedrich Engels auf Reisen* (Berlin, 1966), 141.

3. Eugène Ténot, *Le Suffrage universel et les paysans* (1865), 23. Maurice Agulhon, *1848 ou l'apprentissage de la république* (1973), 130, is less vague. He finds north and northwest France impenetrable to socialism and the Mountain's rural implantation only south of an ideal line from La Rochelle to Metz.

4. Georges Renard, *La 2ᵉ République française*, IX, 223 in *Histoire socialiste* (n.d.).

5. Philippe Vigier, *La Seconde République dans la région alpine* (1963), I, 9–10. For a recent statement of this view see Eric Vigne, "La Nation française, une invention de la Grande Guerre?" *L'Histoire*, 16 (October, 1979), 99. For Vigne, by 1848, the Paris basin, eastern *and southeastern* France "already participated in the industrial revolution and in national political life," while the center and the southwest were first to react against Louis Napoleon's coup d'état, with the peasant southeast relaying their rising. Conclusion: "les conflits politiques nationaux y sont perçus dans toutes leurs conséquences."

6. In Roger Price, ed., *Revolution and Reaction* (London, 1975), 211.

7. As I did in *Peasants into Frenchmen* (Stanford, 1976).

8. Claude Karnoouh, "La Démocratie impossible," *Etudes rurales* (October–December, 1973), esp. 40; Claude Mesliand, "Gauche et droite dans les campagnes provençales sous la 3ᵉ République," *Etudes rurales* (July–December, 1976), esp. 210; J.-C. Boutron, "Transformations et permanences des pouvoirs dans une société rurale," in ibid., esp. 147.

9. Maurice Agulhon in Etienne Juillard, ed., *Histoire de la France rurale* (1976), III, 175.

10. Charles, Louise, and Richard Tilly, *The Rebellious Century, 1830–1930* (Cambridge, Mass., 1975), 289, provide an even more stringent definition of politics, which for them "refers to the pursuit of explicit, long-range programs concerning the distribution and exercise of power at the national or international scale."

11. Charles de Rémusat, *Mémoires de ma vie* (1962), IV, 281, 283.

12. See Jean-François Soulet, *Les Pyrénées au XIXe siècle* (Toulouse, 1987); also

Jacques Godechot, ed., *La Révolution de 1848 à Toulouse et dans la Haute-Garonne* (Toulouse, 1948), 152–154.

13. Agulhon, *1848*, 196.

14. Rémusat, *Mémoires*, IV, 282. George Sand, *Correspondance* (1971), VIII, 349 (March 17, 1848).

15. Rémusat, *Mémoires:* some schoolteachers "transformés par la circulaire de Carnot se mirent à déclamer au hasard contre la réaction, contre la grande propriété, contre moi." According to M. Greslé-Bouignol, "La Révolution de 1848 dans le Tarn," *Revue historique et littéraire du Languedoc*, 19 (1948), 298, the whole southwest, directed from Toulouse, was being covered by official emissaries to private and public teachers, "à l'effet de leur faire connaître, pour ce qui les concernait, les ordres de M. le Ministre de l'Intérieur relativement à l'établissement de la République." For use of *instituteurs* in disseminating official propaganda, see the report of the *commissaire* of the Republic in Meuse to Minister of Interior, May 25, 1848, in *La Révolution de 1848* (January, 1919), 398.

16. Aimé Autrand, *Un Siècle de politique en Vaucluse* (Avignon, 1958), 36.

17. Quoted in Godechot, *La Révolution de 1848*, 216.

18. Ibid. See also Jean Luc Mayaud, *Les secondes républiques du Doubs* (1986).

19. Robert Schnerb, "La Seconde République dans le département du Puy-de-Dôme," *La Révolution de 1848* (1925).

20. That, indeed, was why the voting on April 23 was set in the *chef-lieu de canton*, hoping to remove electors from the influence of their village notables.

21. Georges Rougeron, *Le Révolution de 1848 à Moulins et dans le département de l'Allier* (Moulins, 1950), 17. Arloing would be one of the conservative candidates in the April elections.

22. Sand, *Correspondance*, VIII, 332 (March 9, 1848).

23. Sand, *Correspondance* (1972) IX, 148 (May 16, 1849).

24. Rémusat, *Mémoires*, IV, 417.

25. Sand, *Correspondance*, VIII, 727, 731.

26. AN (Archives Nationales in Paris) BB^{30}361 and BB^{30}378, procureur-général, Limoges, April 1849. Since the peasants spoke patois, articles had to be translated: hence the many attempts to write in dialect. See *La Provence* (Limoges), 7 and 13 May, 1849.

27. Jacques Bouillon, "Les Élections législatives du 13 mai en Limousin," *Bulletin de la société archéologique et historique du Limousin* (1954), 492–493. In *Seconde République*, II, 442, Vigier also attributes real importance to "the wide dissemination of revolt against *les Gros*."

28. Their fears were sometimes very much exaggerated. In May 1848, Nassau Senior, traveling by train from Boulogne to Paris, meets a gentleman who tells him that, in his village near Abbeville, the people "had decided on the impropriety of any man's being richer than his neighbor; and had expressed their intention of pillaging his house and that of his *fermier* . . . In a short time . . . the country would be unsafe for the rich; they must live in the towns, where they could defend one

another." *Journals Kept in France and Italy* (London, 1871) I (May 14, 1848). This was the case even when not all urban radicals respected the niceties of address, unlike the Socialists of Clermont-Ferrand who cried "Vive la République démocratique et sociale! A bas le Préfet! A bas Monsieur le Comte! A bas Monsieur le Marquis!" AN BB[30]365, procureur-général, Riom, March 3, 1849.

29. Elie Reynier, *La Seconde République dans l'Ardèche* (Privas, 1948), 94. Around Paris, at least, the propaganda hewed closer to reality, though not necessarily to possibility: "Le socialisme fait des progrès dans les environs des campagnes de Paris," noted Castellane in May 1849: Its pamphlets do not oppose property, but propose that small property owners and peasants would pay lower taxes, priests would receive salaries sufficient to abandon their resented *casuel,* the *garde-champêtre* would be paid by the state, not the commune, and there would be hospitals and free schools for all. "C'est avec de pareils leurres que le socialisme fait des prosélytes." *Journal du Maréchal de Castellane,* IV (1896), 152.

30. In Price, *Revolution,* 212.

31. For some wise observations on this score see Roger Price, *The French Second Republic* (London, 1972), 298–300.

32. Tilly, *Rebellious Century,* 289.

33. Senior, *Journals,* I, 180–181, 187–189.

34. Henry Chevreau, the republican prefect of Ardèche, in April 1849; the mayors of Borne and of Saint-Etienne-de-Lugdarès, in November 1849; cited by Reynier, *Seconde République,* 48, 88.

35. Procureur-général, Agen, June 30, 1850. AN BB[30]370.

36. Procureur-général, Aix, July 7, 1851. AN BB[30]370. Indifference melted before measures like the new hunting law of August 1851, which raised the cost of a permit to 25 francs, thus depriving most peasants of the chance to hunt legally and creating a host of poachers, makers of gunpowder, and smugglers, all at odds with the law.

37. Autrand, *Un Siècle,* 36. Democracy was not the strongest characteristic of these clubs. In April 1849, the republican list for Ardèche was decided in a meeting held at Privas. The list excluded a great many outlying supporters, much to their displeasure, and led "to divisions that will hurt the party." Felix Bonnaud, *La Révolution de 1848 à Bourg-Saint-Andéol* (Privas, 1905), 11–13.

38. In Peter McPhee, *The Seed-time of the Republic: Society and Politics in the Pyrénées-Orientales, 1846–1852,* (Ann Arbor, 1981).

39. AN F[17]12746. Dossier Morer. The club was dissolved by the authorities in January 1849.

40. Agulhon, *République au village,* 208, 230, 245.

41. Ibid., 264, and especially in Juillard, *Histoire de la France rurale,* III, 509.

42. AN BB[30]370. Feb. 14, 1850.

43. AN BB[30]370.

44. Ted W. Margadant, *French Peasants in Revolt: The Insurrection of 1851* (Princeton, 1980), chaps. 6 and 7, describes in detail the organization and network of *montagnard* societies in the areas where insurrections broke out in December

1851. What strikes me is their fragility, their *friability*, when not sustained by considerations of personal or collective solidarity. Such organizations are sapped by the reluctance of members to pay dues or to continue active in enterprises requiring sustained commitment. See Emile Guillaumin's account of his own syndical adventure half a century later, in *Le Syndicat de Baugignoux* (1912).

45. Pierre Joigneaux, *Souvenirs historiques* (1891), I, 173. Roger Price also has a low opinion of provincial clubs, their influence, and their possible effects on peasants (*Revolution,* 19).

46. François Mazenc, *Le Coup d'état du 2 décembre 1851 dans l'Aveyron* (Albi, 1872), 3–4.

47. Rougeron, *La Révolution,* 78–79, 92.

48. Agulhon, *République au village,* 479.

49. Ibid., pp. 138–142. He concludes, "ces fils, en révolte contre les pères, passent dans le camp ouvrier" (142).

50. Vigier, *Seconde République,* II, 312, 329, 426. It seems to me that, in his contribution to Price, *Revolution,* 269, Ted Margadant takes the point better than Vigier when he shows that where "influential landowners, merchants and professional men" worked for the republic, their public propaganda was effective.

51. Among urban workers too, for that matter. On December 3, 1851, Louis Caussanel, the chief republican leader in Aveyron, fails to find any support in Rodez and moves off telling those for whose support he had hoped: "Les ouvriers de Rodez, vous êtes des merdes. Nous avons voulu nous faire tuer et vous n'avez pas voulu nous suivre. Vous êtes de la canaille." André Aucourt, *Le Coup d'Etat du 2 décembre 1851 et ses répercussions à Villefranche-de-Rouergue* (Rodez, 1953), 16.

52. Aucourt, *Le Coup,* 22 and *passim.*

53. F. Rémi (de l'Yonne), *La Marianne dans les campagnes* (Auxerre, 1881), 11, 18, 23, 27.

54. Ténot, *Le Suffrage,* 19–20, 23.

55. AN BB[30]400. Cour d'Appel Dijon, Affaires de Beaune du 3 au 7 décembre 1851. Sommaire du procureur général, Jan. 29, 1852.

56. Margadant, *French Peasants,* 220–221.

57. Margadant is scrupulous in citing evidence that may appear to counter or to qualify his thesis. But when he remarks that "counterrevolutionary rhetoric concealed political factionalism" (ibid., 314), this can as justly be said of revolutionary rhetoric. My point is that the rhetoric of national political ideology concealed and served very local political interests and that the rhetoric itself played only a limited role compared to more immediate, local inspirations and perceptions. See for example "Le Journal de Romain Bouquets," *La Révolution de 1848* (July–December, 1911), 248–249, 259.

58. Procureur-général, Grenoble, Jan. 9, 1850. Quoted in Jacques Humbert, *Embrun et l'embrunais à travers l'histoire* (Gap, 1972), 440.

59. Gustave Lefrançais, *Souvenirs d'un révolutionnaire* (Bruxelles, 1902), 151. See also AN BB[30]396, procureur-général, Agen, on Republicans and Reds in Gers: "Ils cherchaient à séduire les gens des campagnes, en leur promettant la suppression

des octrois et la diminution des impôts." The men of December 2 understood this and used it to their ends when, on the heels of their coup, they remitted or amnestied fines and sentences pending for *délits forestiers* and other minor offences. See AN F¹ᵉ II 98, préfet Aude, Dec. 20, 1851; and préfet, Bas-Rhin. Dec. 22, 1851, quoted in Paul Muller, "Le Bas-Rhin de 1848 a 1852," *La Révolution de 1848* (January–February, 1910), 363.

60. AN BB³⁰393, on July 8, 1851, at Uvernat (Basses-Alpes), arrdt. Barcelonnette.

61. AN BB³⁰394, Ministère de la Justice, Travail sur le mouvement démagogique antérieur au 2 décembre, lists numerous such occasions. Ibid., procureur-général, Nîmes, September 1851, about the "serious disorders arising from the fêtes votives of Vinezac and Bastide de Virac (Ardèche)," suggests that the authorities may be overreacting.

62. AN BB³⁰393, procureur-général, Montpellier, July 1851.

63. AN BB³⁰393, parquet de Grenoble, June 1851.

64. Quoted in Reynier, *Seconde République,* 92.

65. AN BB³⁰358, procureur-général, Aix, June 1849.

66. AN BB³⁰393, parquet de Besançon, April-June 1851.

67. AN BB³⁰393, parquet de Grenoble, June 30, 1851: "Pour se donner de l'importance, et probablement pour déguiser sous une apparence politique les poursuites qui avaient été dirigées contre lui."

68. AN BB³⁰393, procureur-général, Grenoble, July 21, 1851. Similarly, Antoine Batiffolier, *cultivateur à Champeix, arrondissement d'Yssoire,* was judged at Riom, Dec. 23, 1851, after he had been arrested and charged with seditious cries for having shouted at his mayor and in the street: "A bas les blancs! A bas les blancs!" December 1851 was a bad time to step out of line, but the procureur-général found Batiffolier simply a local troublemaker; a bit wild, already twice condemned for *tapage nocturne,* and much irritated by his village betters. AN BB³⁰396.

69. AN BB³⁰393, parquet de Rennes, June–July 1851.

70. AN BB³⁰401² Loir-et-Cher: 1ᵉ catégorie à transporter; 2³ catégorie a expulser de France. Of the seventeen leaders of rural rebellions who can be identified in the pages of J. Dagnan, *Le Coup d'Etat et la repression dans le Gers* (Auch, 1929), 74–83, two are general-councillors, three are mayors of their village, three are wealthy millers, two are wealthy landowners, among the rest: *aubergistes, huissier, médecin, pharmaciste, épicier, horloger, étudiant.* Compare in Reynier, *Seconde République,* 125–128, the lists of those condemned after the December risings. Margadant (*French Peasants,* chap. 8) devotes an impressive chapter to the democratization of political leadership in the Montagne. But his most convincing arguments bear on the role played by conspicuous and literate artisans and by fairly wealthy farmers.

71. John Merriman, *The Agony of the Republic* (New Haven, 1978), 123.

72. AN F¹⁷9313. The school inspectors' reports indicate that, in any case, it would be difficult, if not impossible, for minor public figures of this order to escape involvement. They would be tempted or forced to side with one local party or another. Most of the *ardèchois* teachers listed by Reynier, *Seconde République,*

79–82, who got into trouble for their political activities, appear to have been in unison with their localities—chiefly Protestant ones. The use of teachers as electoral agents would become standard procedure, at least for the rest of the century: well developed under the Second Empire and, of course, the Third Republic.

73. AN BB^{30}396, procureur-général, Riom, Jan. 27, 1852.

74. AN BB^{30}393, parquet de Pau, August, 1851.

75. Merriman, *Agony,* 119–120.

76. One of his enemies was his brother-in-law, the local justice of the peace. All this is a much condensed account of the information in some ninety manuscripts pages to be found in AN F^{17}12746. In December 1851, Thuir was involved in the widespread but shortlived risings of Roussillon. But many of the *insurgés de Thuir* to whom Horace Chauvet refers (*Histoire du parti républicain dans les Pyrénées-Orientales,* Perpignan, 1919, 110–111) seem to have come from Llupia, a few kilometers to the southeast, where the leader of the local secret society, shouting "Tout est à nous!" urged his followers "to fall upon Thuir." After the rising, the prefect took hostages among the women and children of Thuir (R. Gossez and J. Vienney, *François Arago,* Perpignan, 1952, 43) but not among its notables, and Morer (ill at the time) was not troubled. Chauvet (82–85) lists mayors, teachers, and other officials suspended after the coup. None come from Thuir, though quite a few come from nearby places. Of fifty-seven men of the Pyrénées-Orientales transported to Cayenne, only one came from Thuir: Tignéres Oller-Joseph, aged fifty-one, *ex-commissaire de police,* very likely the Tignéres *fils, ex-huissier de la justice de paix,* listed as a member of the Committee of the Republican Association for Freedom of the Press under the July Monarchy (Chauvet, 16, 124–128).

77. AN BB^{30}396, procureur-général, Riom, Jan. 19, 1852.

78. AN BB^{30}396, procureur-général, Riom, Jan. 15, 1852.

79. Merriman, *Agony,* 204–206.

80. Bouillon, "Elections législatives," 489.

81. Reynier, *Seconde République,* 116–117.

82. Vigier, *Seconde République,* I, 164–165; II, 277.

83. Ibid., I, 191; II, 175, 188, 290.

84. AN F^{1e} II 98, préfet, Huates-Alpes, Jan. 11, 1852.

85. Alternatively, their absence, as in Drôme where the leaders were "men of very ordinary intelligence and energy," can prove decisive too. Eugène Ténot, *La Province en décembre 1851* (1868), 310.

86. Ibid., 36, 274, 275, 332, 132.

87. The following paragraphs are based on accounts in J. Cornillon, *Le Bourbonnais en décembre 1851. Le Coup d'Etat* (Cusset, 1903); E. Mauve, *Le Bourbonnais sous la Seconde République* (Moulins, 1909); Camille Gagnon, *En Bourbonnais sous la Seconde République* (Moulins, 1971); Simone Derrrau-Boniol, "Le Socialisme dans l'Allier, de 1848 à 1914," *Cahiers d'histoire,* 2 (1957), esp. 134.

88. Robert Schnerb, "Seconde République," pp. 717–720.

89. F. Appolis, "La Résistance au coup d'état du 2 décembre 1851 dans l'Hérault," *Actes du 77e Congrès des Sociétés Savantes, Grenoble 1952* (1952), 494.

90. Schnerb, "Seconde République."

91. "Extrêmement populaire et considéré," Lazerme "plaisait aux masses." He was of good nature, competence, sound judgment, family position, "ayant toujours le mot aimable, mais la riposte vive et au besoin la main prompte." Charles de Lazerme, *Carlistes et légitimistes* (Perpignan, 1937), pp. 101–105. Agulhon also recognizes in passing the crucial importance of personal qualities in the choice of "popular" leaders such as artisans, *petits patrons, petits commerçants; République au village*, 480.

92. Gagnon, *En Bourbonnais*, 81.

93. AN BB^{30}396, procureur-général, Limoges, Jan. 23, 1852.

94. AN BB^{30}401^2, commission mixte. Haute-Vienne, Jean-Baptiste Delassis (géomêtre), 44 ans. membre du Conseil Général.

95. Reynier, *Seconde République*, 22, 110–111. See also in AN BB^{30}396, the procureur-général, Agen, testifying how many men of the Gers were unclear why they marched in December: some believed it was to defend Louis Napoleon, others for lower taxes, others because they had been threatened.

96. AN F^{1e} II 98, préfet, Hautes-Alpes, Dec. 11, 1851.

97. AN F^{1e} III, Drôme 8, préfet, Drôme, Jan. 1852.

98. Vigier, *Seconde République*, II, 330, 332.

99. In January 1852, the Archpriest of Béziers, writing to his Archbishop about the bloody riots in his town, discriminated between the *workers* of the faubourg du Pont, "intelligents, doués de ce demi-savoir qui donne un orgueil effréné," and the ignorant peasants of several other faubourgs. Gérard Cholvy, *Religion et société au XIXe siècle: Le diocèse de Montpellier* (Lille, 1973), II, 920. Roger Price draws a similar distinction between the leaders of the insurrection for whom "idealistic political reasons came to the fore," and those who marched behind them. He quotes the grandiloquent proclamation of the Committee of Resistance in the Basses-Alpes and comments: "Thus in the hallowed terminology of bourgeois republicanism was an appeal made to the peasant masses of the economically most backward departments in France." *Second Republic*, 296.

100. Vigier, *Seconde République*, II, 383. Against this view, see Bouquet, "Journal," pp. 248–249, 259, 376–377, for the "futile personal motives" that hid under political guises at La-Tour-du-Pin (Isère).

101. Louis Girard, *La IIe République* (1968), 294: in *bourgs*, "la politique se greffait sur les jalousies ou les haines privées." These, of course, were not the preserve of the eminent alone. Arrested in December 1851, Antoine Rey, a peddler of Saint-Symphorien, is interrogated and declares: "Le maire . . . m'accuse d'avoir insurgé le pays; mais il a une fille modiste et ma femme est marchande de dentelles . . . L'an 1848 je penchais pour la Montagne, parce que j'avais peu de chose: aujourd'hui j'ai hérité d'une trentaine de mille francs et mes idées ont complètement changé." (Quoted in Reynier, *Seconde République*, 128). As Agulhon declared in his *République au village*, 288: "c'est tout le problème des clans, des coteries, des partis au village qu'il faudra bien reprendre un jour. . . ." It is high time we did.

102. Price, *Second Republic*, 309: "Only the upper and middle classes possessed a national ideology."

103. See AN F^le II 98, préfet, Ain, March 3, 1852, concerning a by-election at Trévoux: no political problems, everyone devoted to the Prince, "mais les questions d'intérêts locaux, et par conséquent de personnes, y ont une grande puissance."

104. Eugen Weber, "Peasants and the National State," *Proceedings of the Fifteenth International Congress on Historical Science* (Bucarest, 1980).

105. Paul Cornu, "Grèves des flotteurs sur l'Yonne au 18e et 19e siècles," *Cahiers du Centre,* Jan. 1911.

106. Cholvy, *Religion et société,* I, 721–722. See also Appolis, "La Résistance," 495, on December 4, 1851, at Bédarieux, when local workmen and peasants besieged the gendarmes, "odieux à cette population de braconniers."

107. Margadant, *French Peasants,* 138 and chap. 7 *passim.*

108. Ibid., 152.

109. In *1848,* 179 and *passim.*

110. The latter in a splendid contribution to Price, *Revolution,* 275 and *passim.*

8. Another Look at Peasant Politicization

1. Robert J. Smith, *Kurusu: The Price of Progress in a Japanese Village, 1951–1975.* (Stanford, 1978), 233.

2. Georges Dupeux, *Aspects de l'histoire sociale et politique du Loir-et-Cher, 1848–1914* (1962); Philippe Vigier, *La Seconde République dans la région alpine: Etude politique et sociale,* 2 vols. (1963); Gordon Wright, *Rural Revolution in France: The Peasantry in the Twentieth Century* (Stanford, 1964); and Maurice Agulhon, *La République au village: Les Populations du Var de la Révolution à la Seconde République* (1970).

3. Tilly, "How Protest Modernized in France, 1845–1955," in William O. Aydelotte et al., eds., *The Dimensions of Quantitative Research in History* (Princeton, 1972), 226; see also Ted W. Margadant, *French Peasants in Revolt: The Insurrection of 1851* (Princeton, 1980), esp. 338. Other works have situated this process of economic integration and political participation in a later period. Like Siegfried, who paid great attention to the evolution of economic and social structures, they have recognized the wide diversity of rural experience but have ascribed the crucial changes to the late 1870s and the 1880s. See Pierre Barral, *Les Agrariens français de Méline à Pisani* (1968); Alain Corbin, *Archaisme et modernité en Limousin au XIXe siècle, 1845–1880,* 2 vols. (1975); Theodore Zeldin, *France, 1848–1895,* 2 vols. (Oxford, 1973–1977); and Tony Judt, *Socialism in Provence, 1871–1914: A Study in the Origins of the Modern French Left* (Cambridge, 1979). Even Maurice Agulhon seems to have endorsed this view in the chapters he contributed to Georges Duby and Armand Wallon, eds., *Histoire de la France rurale* (1976–77); see vol. 3: *Apogée et crise de la civilisation paysanne, 1789–1914,* pt. 1, chaps. 1, 3, 5; pt. 2, chaps. 4–5; and pt. 3, chaps. 4–5.

4. Eugen Weber, *Peasants into Frenchmen: The Modernization of Rural France, 1870–1914* (Stanford, 1976).

5. Corbin, *Archaisme et modernité en Limousin,* II, 1004.

6. Judt has suggested that family feuds flourish wherever political and social variety is slight; *Socialism in Provence, 1871–1914,* 206–207. But it could be that such conflicts provide the opportunity for political variety.

7. Tocqueville to Beaumont, June 21, 1842, in Alexis de Tocqueville, *Correspondance d'Alexis de Tocqueville et de Gustave de Beaumont,* ed. André Jardin, vol. 8 of Tocqueville, *Oeuvres complètes,* ed. J.-P. Mayer, 3 pts. (1967), pt. 1, 459.

8. André Siegfried, *Tableau politique de la France de l'Ouest sous la Troisième République* (1913), 96. Laurence Wylie and his co-authors have made a similar point: "Party labels are not meaningless: each party and name have an ideological significance that is well understood in Chanzeaux. But it is a significance that must be understood in local and to some extent historical terms." Wylie, ed., *Chanzeaux: A Village in Anjou* (Cambridge, Mass., 1966), 267.

9. Procureur-général, Roanne, June 18, 1857, AN BB¹⁸1567; and sous-préfet, Parthenay, to préfet, Deux-Sèvres, June 12, 1863, as quoted in Bernard LeClère, *Stephen Liégeard (1830–1925): Essai de réhabilitation du sous-Préfet aux champs* (1968), 73. All subsequent citations of the BB series refer to the reports of attorneys-general attached to the great regional courts of appeal and will be cited simply by the court's regional name.

10. Grenoble, August 9, 1865, AN BB 1717. Such frictions could be of the most futile kind; see Henri Prost, *Charles Dumont et le Jura* (1964), 33.

11. Indeed, the tone of the election was set by the marshall's Bonapartist supporters, like the interior minister, Oscar Bardi de Fourtou, eager to prove himself another Morny. The Bonapartist-style electoral propaganda probably succeeded in mobilizing hitherto indifferent areas even more than republican efforts did. In some departments, 12 percent more voters participated in 1877 than had turned out for the elections of 1876.

12. Mona Ozouf, *La Classe ininterrompue* (1979), 359.

13. See AN BB¹⁸1581 *passim.* Among many examples of the current discrimination between the "intelligent" few and the rest, see préfet, Hérault, April 4 and July 31, 1866, and June 30, 1868, AN Fic III 9.

14. On the elections at Tain (Drôme), see Grenoble, July 6, 1864, AN BB 1717; and, on those at Tarascon (Ariège), see Toulouse, December 10, 1866, AN BB¹⁸, 1692. Vincent Wright and Bernard LeClère have discussed the prominent part played by what a contemporary described as "rivalités locales . . . divisions de clocher . . . rivalités de position, des inimitiés de famille, des antagonismes d'influence et des haines de personnes"; LeClère and Wright, *Les Préfets du Second Empire* (1973), 133. But as one magistrate wrote in 1870, "If some day a true public spirit were to take shape, it will first be born at the municipal level"; Angers, July 4, 1870, AN BB³⁰390.

15. Montpellier, January 10, 1869, AN BB³⁰389; Riom, July 9, 1869, ibid.; and Grenoble, July 21, 1865, AN BB¹⁸1717. To the same point, also see Limoges, August 12, 1865, AN BB¹⁸1717; Montpellier, January 31, 1868, ibid., 1755; and préfet, Hérault, November 11, 1868, AN Fic III 9.

16. Jean Goasguen, "Les Elections de 1871 et les manifestations de l'opinion

publique en Gironde," *Revue historique de Bordeaux et du départment de la Gironde,* new ser. 11 (1962), 11–12, 18, 19; and Jean Merley, *La Haute-Loire de la fin de l'Ancien Régime aux débuts de la Troisième République (1776–1886)* (Le Puy, 1974): 480. On the crucial importance of personalities, also see the evidence of Baron de Bourgoing, AN C 2874; L.-H. Roblin, "L'Administration d'une commune rurale," *Cahiers nivernais* (February, 1909), 8; Michel Denis, *L'Eglise et la République en Mayenne, 1896–1906* (1968), 74, 141; and Guy Thuillier, "Les Historiens locaux en Nivernais de 1860 a 1900," *Actes du 103ᵉ Congrès national des Sociétés Savantes, Nancy-Metz 1978: Section d'histoire moderne et contemporaine,* 2 (1979), 353–354.

17. Brittany, August 14, 1865, AN BB 1717; and Jules Ferry to his wife, June 1877, and to Jules Simon, November 1874, in Ferry *Lettres de Jules Ferry* (1914), 226, 201. Also see July 6, 1861, AN BB³⁰370; and Eugène Ténot, *Le Suffrage universel et les paysans* (1865), 26. On peasant fear, see préfet, Mayenne, to Ministre de l'Intérieur, May 31, 1898, as quoted in Denis, *L'Eglise et la République en Mayenne,* 68; and Françoise Raison-Jourde, *La Colonie auvergnate de Paris au XIXᵉ siècle* (1976), 348. For confirmation by a connoisseur of rural politics of the regard in which local officials were held, see Pierre Joigneaux, *Nouvelles Lettres aux paysans* (1871), vi, 26–27. Also see Inquiry Commission, Gien, 1889, AN C 5468. The C series is devoted to the minutes of and evidence gathered by parliamentary commissions of inquiry into electoral improprieties or fraud and will be cited by the district of inquiry. In a letter of August 4, 1852, Gustave de Beaumont explained to Tocqueville the possible vexations he risked if he did not sit on his municipal council; Tocqueville, *Correspondance,* pt. 3, 66.

18. L. de LaCombe, *Profils parlementaires* (1866), 16. Also see the sketch of Brutus Cazelles, elected since 1852 at Lodève (Hérault), most recently by 28,495 votes out of 28,830 votes cast, and of Alexandre de Bosredon, deputy of Sarlat (Dordogne), "whose good people had confidently elected the man presented to it" by the government, although Sarlat probably "would have elected his competitor with the same confidence"; ibid. (2d ed., 1869), 96, 65. Government support— or its lack—could also influence results in the other direction: François Bel, a lawyer at Montmélian (Savoie), for example, was elected deputy of Chambéry South in 1876 and 1877, after the government had deposed him from his position as mayor; a general councilor of his district since 1860, "his position was very strong," according to Jacques Lovie, "a good example of those men of the second rank—prestigious, experienced, effective—who did more than the great politicians to implant the Third Republic"; Lovie, *La Savoie dans la vie française de 1860 à 1875* (1963), 574.

19. Auguste Lacoin de Villemorin, *Enquête sur la crise agricole* (Blois, 1898), 190; and Jean Lassaigne, *Figures parlementaires* (1950), 27. For the mayor of an Ardèche village in 1908, amid his people "avid to guess his desires and conform to them," see J. d'Indy, "Les Débuts du ski en Vivarais," *Revue du Vivarais* (1953), 24; and, for village politics in the Briançonnais, see Emilie Carles, *Une Soupe aux herbes sauvages* (1977), 211–214.

20. For antipathy, see maire, Colombiès, to préfet, Aveyron, July 11, 1875, as quoted in A. Garric, *Histoire de Boussac* (Rodez, 1973), 83. For hostility, see "Rapport de l'élection d'Edmond Blanc," 24, AN C 5574; and Corbin, *Archaisme et modernité en Limousin,* II, 1000–01. For antagonism, see Joseph Pinard, ed., "Les Mémoires d'un rural déraciné: Journal de J.-F.-S. Pinard," *Mémoires de la Société d'Emulation du Doubs, Besançon,* 12 (1970), 8; and, for dissensions, see Grenoble, August 16, 1864, AN BB 1717; Montpellier, January 30, 1866, ibid.; and Montpellier, January 1864, AN BB¹⁸1685. Such venerable animus waned slowly; see Antonin Lavergne, *Monsieur le Maire* (1905; written in 1893–94).

21. For Saône-et Loire, see Ozouf, *La Classe ininterrompue,* 43. For references to Savoy, see Paul Guichonnet, "La Géographie et le tempérament politique dans les montagnes de la Haute-Savoie," *Revue de géographie alpine,* 33 (1943), 39–86; Simone Hugonnier, "Tempéraments politiques et géographie électorale: Maurienne et Tarentaise," ibid., 42 (1954), esp. 45; and Lovie, *La Savoie dans la vie française,* 528–530.

22. *Réflexions adressées à Messieurs les électeurs de Libourne* (Bordeaux, 1828); Pierre Barral, "Les Forces politiques sous le Second Empire dans le département de l'Isère," *Actes du Soixante-Dix-Septième Congrès des Sociétés Savantes, Grenoble 1952: Section d'histoire moderne et contemporaine* (1952), 172; and Hugonnier, "Témperaments politiques," 49. "The electors want to know and see their representatives in person," wrote one attorney-general; Besançon, June 27, 1861, AN BB 1632. A report of the prefect in Pyrénées-Orientales, dated July 31, 1867, confirms this; the report is quoted in Horace Chauvet, *Histoire du parti républicain dans les Pyrénées-Orientales* (Perpignan, 1909), 188–189. Also see *Revue des candidats au collège électoral de Nevers* (Nevers, 1828), 7.

23. Haute-Garonne, AN C 3158. For similar arguments concerning the elections at Loudun five years later, see Vienne, 1881, AN C 3324.

24. Préfet, Haute-Loire, 1854, AN Fic III, as quoted in Merley, *La Haute-Loire* (1776–1886), 445. For such continuities from the Revolution through 1851 and 1877 and even to the end of the century, see Gwynne Lewis, *The Second Vendée: The Continuity of Counter-Revolution in the Department of the Gard, 1789–1815* (Oxford, 1978), 230–231; and P. M. Jones, "Political Commitment and Rural Society in the Southern Massif-Central," *European Studies Review,* 10 (1980), 337–356.

25. J. Dagnan, *Le Gers sous la Seconde République: La Réaction conservatrice (février 1848–2 décembre 1851)* (Auch, 1928), 170–171; and Mme. Louis (Juliette Bouscaret) Figuier, "Le Franciman," in *Nouvelles languedociennes* (1860), 119. Robert Smith has described village disputes as "waged with the peculiar vehemence of which only people who have known each other for a long time are capable"; *Kurusu,* 237. And he quotes Ronald P. Dore: "Competition within a group which is in theory harmoniously united tends to become fiercer and more emotionally involved than in one where competition is accepted as normal. As such it leaves scars after the event in the resentful humiliation of the defeated." Dore, *Land Reform in Japan* (London, 1959), 343.

26. Lavergne, *Monsieur le Maire*, 318.

27. R. Arambourou, *L'Arrondissement de La Réole au temps de la IIIe République* (Bordeaux, 1962), 152; and André Burguière, *Bretons de Plozévet* (1975), 203. As late as 1945, a Pyrenean elector told a candidate, "I am M.R.P., my poor father was for it already, and so was my poor grandfather." The M.R.P. had just been formed, but the speaker meant it was the "good party" of his family. Quoted in Jacques Fauvet and Henri Mendras, *Les Paysans et la politique* (1958), 502.

28. Albert Quantin, *La Corse* (1914), 263–274. Quantin's information was largely drawn from Paul Bourde's *En Corse* (1887), 10–16, 39–46.

29. Pierre-Jakez Hélias, *Le Cheval d'orgueil: Mémoires d'un Breton du pays bigouden* (1975), 191; and Arambourou, *L'Arrondissement de La Réole*, 170–174.

30. Préfet, Aveyron, to Ministre de l'Intérieur, June 27, 1834, AN Fic III Aveyron, 5; Elie Reynier, *La Seconde République dans l'Ardèche* (Privas, 1948), 18; Marius Faugéras, *Le Diocèse de Nantes sous la monarchie censitaire (1813–1822–1849): La Reconstruction catholique dans l'Ouest après la Révolution* (Fontenay-le-Comte, 1964), I, 232–239; Gérard Cholvy, *Religion et société au XIXe siècle: Le Diocèse de Montpellier*, 2 vols. (Lille, 1973), I, 662, 701–707, and II, 938. For a multitude of cases of conflict between priest and mayor, and of priests leading one of two village parties, see M. Dargaud, "Le Clergé bourbonnais en 1848," in Georges Rougeron et al., eds., *La Révolution de 1848 à Moulins et dans le département d l'Allier* (Moulins, 195?), esp. 240–262. At Neufchâtel (Sarthe), in December 1851, the priest led a group of two hundred lumbermen of the Perseigne forest on Mamers, and the marchers had to be dispersed by gendarmes; Paul Delaunay, *La Société sarthoise sous le Second Empire* (Laval, 1942), 41. For friction between local clergy and imperial authorities in Sarthe, see ibid., 44.

31. Yves-Marie Hilaire, *Une Chrétienté au XIXe siècle? La Vie religieuse des populations du diocèse d'Arras* (Lille, 1977), I, 313; and Cholvy, *Religion et société au XIXe siècle*, II, 560. For similar tensions in the Catholic West, see Michel Denis, *Les Royalistes de la Mayenne et le monde moderne (XIXe–XXe siècles)* (1977), esp. chap. 9. And, concerning instances of clerical self-assertion in Mercourt, Haute-Saône, see Besançon, February 26, 1863, AN BB¹⁸1666; in Chapelle-Blanche, Côtes-du-Nord, see Rennes, July 6, 1863, ibid., 1675; in Hérault, see procureur-général, Montpellier, 1852, 1861, 1864, AN F¹⁹5828; and in Somme, see Amiens, January 12, 1869. Cholvy has cited prefectorial complaints about the oppositional role of the clergy as early as 1857; *Religion et société au XIXe siècle*, II, 938–939.

32. Rennes, February 21, 1865, AN BB¹⁸1692. Also see préfet, Hérault (Montpellier), 1853, AN F¹⁹5828.

33. Goasguen, "Les Elections de 1871," 172; préfet, Hérault (Montpellier), 1883, AN F¹⁹5828; Pierre Pommarède, *La Séparation de l'église et de l'état en Périgord* (Périguex, 1976), 141, 165; and Hilaire, *Une Chrétienté au XIXe siècle*, 313–314, 339.

34. François Delamaire, *Les Catholiques et les élections de 1906* (Périgueux, 1904), 20–21. Also see Pommarède, *La Séparation de l'église et de l'état*, 25. For the activities of a combative prelate like the bishop of Montpellier, Mgr. de Cabrières,

long before that, see, among others, Cholvy, *Religion et société au XIXe siècle*, II, 1118–19. For succulent examples of clerical pressure from 1876 to 1903, see Alexandre Pilenco, *Les Moeurs du suffrage universel en France, 1848–1928* (1930), 169, 197, 200; and for a discussion of electoral pressures in the district of Mauléon (Basses-Pyrénées) in the 1880s, see *Journal Officiel*, December 22, 1889. *La Croix*, May 11, 1903, gives the text of a contract between the Devil and Achille Fould, the banker, ensuring the latter's election in the Hautes-Pyrénées.

35. For fascinating detail on this score, see Cholvy, *Religion et société au XIXe siècle*, II, 1275–76.

36. See, especially, March 19, 1883, AN F^19 5828. Also see Cholvy, *Religion et société au XIXe siècle*, II, 1115. For the *affaire des manuels* at Plozévet, see Burguière, *Bretons de Plozévet*, 240, 284–286. Of course, the Third Republic favored history written for politically didactic ends, like the politicized version of Albigensian history used as an instrument of anticlericalism. Napoléon Peyrat's three-volume *Histoire des Albigeois* appeared from 1870 to 1872. For Peyrat, a Protestant minister, Catharism was a forerunner of Protestantism and of the revolutionary ideal of freedom, with the Albigensian Crusade representing the bloody intolerance of the Roman Catholic Church; see his *Réformateurs de la France et de l'Italie au XIXe siècle* (1860). This was the version of thirteenth-century history that the schools taught for several generations, helping to turn the Midi to radicalism and also reinforcing a resentment against the conquering North that surfaced in the troubles of 1907. See further Thuillier, "Historiens locaux en Nivernais," 358: "Assurément, il existe une histoire locale de droite et une histoire locale de gauche."

37. First Communion was a crucial rite of passage, and some employers long continued to require First Communion certificates before they accepted lads into their service. See, for example, Yves-Marie Hilaire, "Remarques sur la pratique religieuse dans le bassin houillier du Pas-de-Calais dans la deuxième moitié du XIXe siècle," in Louis Trénard, ed., *Charbon et sciences humaines* (1966), 270.

38. J. Calvet, "Une Monographie religieuse d'un diocèse français: Diocèse de Cahors," *Revue catholique des églises* (February 1905), 70; and G. Rouchy, "Monographie religieuse d'un diocèse français: Le Diocèse de St. Flour," ibid. (November 1905), 539, 549–550. It is important to remember that, where the violent rural clashes of the Inventaires occurred in 1906, they reflected rather a clinging to collective traditions (and collective property) than the clash of "modern" political clerical-anticlerical forces; see Jean-Marie Mayeur, "Géographie de la résistance aux Inventaires," *Annales: Economies, sociétés, civilisations*, 21 (1966), 1270–71; and Pommarède, *La Séparation de l'église et de l'état*.

39. Sous-préfet, Béziers, January 1856, AN Fic III, Hèrault 9. In the elections of 1869 one candidate in the Isère asserted that if his opponent won, men would be yoked to the ploughs in lieu of horses, with the iron collars that his opponent's grandfather had used for that purpose before the Revolution; *Moniteur universel*, December 12, 1869, 1596: The crowd cried out, "Nous ne voulons pas labourer." Also see, for the elections of Haute-Garonne in 1873, Charles de Rémusat, *Mémoires de ma vie* (1967), V, 481; and, for the Drôme in 1865, see Grenoble, August 10, 1865, AN BB^18 1717; and, for 1870, Comte Charles de

Lazerme, *Carlistes et Légitimistes* (Perpignan, 1937), 63–64. In general, see Edward Mauve, *Le Bourbonnais sous la Seconde République* (Moulins, 1909), 109–121.

40. Eugène Ténot and Antonin Dubost, *Les Suspects en 1858* (1869). A memo of the minister of the interior, dated March 29, 1864, raises the question of persons condemned after the Vendean risings of the early 1830s, released or granted amnesty since then but still continued under police surveillance in the 1860s; AN BB^{18}1860.

41. Jean Fontane, "Souvenirs d'un paysan," *La Révolution de 1848,* July–August 1909, 165–170. Fontane had organized and briefly raised his friends at Massillargues and Atuech in December 1851. But see Paul Muller, "Autour du coup d'état dans le Haut-Rhin," ibid., September–October 1901, 211; The *démoc-soc* tendencies, so strong in the Haut-Rhin from 1848 to 1850, "were no more than a historical recollection" by 1869.

42. Poitiers, April 6, 1863, AN BB^{18}1671; and Quentin-Bauchart, *Etudes et souvenirs sur la 2ᵉ République et le Second Empire (Mémoires posthumes)*, pt. 2 (1902), 8. For straightforward support of the waning practice, see Evariste Bavoux, *Les Candidatures officielles* (1869).

43. Sous-préfet, Mauriac, 1877, AN BB^{18}1567; and préfet, Poitiers, July 16, 1866, AN BB^{18}1692. Also see Pilenco, *Les Moeurs du suffrage universel*, 58, 89, 112.

44. See AN BB^{30}368 (the years 1855–1863). For confirmation, see Ténot and Dubost, *Les Suspects en 1858*, 22, 23.

45. Pau, April 2, 1866, AN BB^{18}1717; Grenoble, August 10, 1865, AN BB^{18}1755; Pau, April 2, 1866, AN BB^{18}1692; and Lyon, August 8, 1867, AN BB^{18}1755. Margadant has stressed the youth of secret society militants in 1851; *French Peasants in Revolt,* 183. Thus they were still around and available in the later 1860s, when political activity resumed and opportunities for sustained action had much improved.

46. Agulhon, *La République au village;* and Montpellier, July 7, 1858, AN BB^{30}380. For Languedoc, see Cholvy, *Religion et société au XIXᵉ siècle*, II, 1033, 1039, 1053.

47. Rémusat, *Mémoires de ma vie,* 159, 237; Rouen, August 11, 1865, AN BB^{18}1717; and Besançon, June 27, 1861, AN BB^{18}1632.

48. Alexis de Tocqueville noted the story on June 25, 1856, as told to him by Cavaignac himself; *Correspondance,* pt. 3, 419.

49. Besançon, June 26, 1869, AN BB 1784; and L. de LaCombe, *Profils parlementaires, 1863–1869* (rev. ed., 1869), 107. Others adopted similarly vulgar but more ingenious methods of garnering public favor. Thus, for example, the handsome Stephen Liégeard, elected deputy of Thionville (Moselle) in a by-election of 1867, used photographs: "Sa photo . . . largement distribuée par un barbier lorrain a beaucoup contribué à son élection. On l'a nommé sur carte." Ibid., 156.

50. See AN BB 1795^{1} and 1795^{2}, *passim.*

51. Even there, the democratic leadership had its doubts about the workers it wooed. At one public meeting held at Béziers and addressed by Charles Floquet, a workman climbed on the stage and asked to make a statement. The chairman and Floquet prevented him from speaking: "Qu'est-ce qu'il veut?" the chief of police

heard Floquet say to his friends on the platform. "Arrêtez-le, il va nous faire des bêtises." Montpellier, May 7, 1869, AN BB[18]1795[1].

52. Quoted in Paul Guichonnet, "Jules Favre et la bataille politique: Les Elections de 1869 en Haute-Savoie," *Cahiers d'histoire*, 1 (1956), 90. Note that Favre desisted in favor of the "liberal" Monarchist-Catholic candidate, who won. Also see the conclusion of George Baume's novel *M. le député* (1909), about the election in a small country town where, the campaign over, all moan, "What are we going to do now?"

53. Aix, October 7, 1868, AN BB[30]389; Dijon, January 13, 1869, ibid.; and Ténot, *Suffrage universel et les paysans*, 23–24.

54. Limoges, October 1, 1869, AN BB 401[2]. For the traditional theme of calm and tranquility, see Angers, October 1869, ibid.; and Ténot, *Suffrage universel et les paysans*, 23–24.

55. Bordeaux, October 1869, AN BB 401[2]; and Chambéry, October 1869, ibid. On the continuing, crucial role of the rural bourgeoisie, if this needs to be bolstered further, see André-Georges Maury, *Histoire de l'Auvergne* (Toulouse, 1974), 390; and Roger Pierre, *Les Origines du syndicalisme et du socialisme dans la Drôme* (1974), 23.

56. See Ténot, *Suffrage universel et les paysans*, 30, 27; Alfred Massé, *Les Partis politiques dans la Nièvre de 1871 à 1906* (Nevers, 1910), 11–12; Denis, *L'Eglise et la République en Mayenne*, 29; J. Cornillon, *Le Bourbonnais à la fin de l'Empire et sous le gouvernement de défense nationale* (Moulins, 1924), 28; Louis Girard et al., *Les Conseillers généraux en 1870* (1967), 80, 144. Paul Delaunay claimed that Sarthe peasants, who voted heavily for the Empire, were lost between the significance of *yes* and *no* in the plebiscite; *Société sarthoise sous le Second Empire*, 76. *La Feuille du village* of May 21, 1870, describes them as *effarés et ahuris*. One might ponder the remarks of Eric Rouleau on Iran, in an article in *Le Monde*, December 12, 1979, p. 3: "In a country that has practically never lived under a democratic regime, the major part of the population has no sense of living under a dictatorship . . . That is to say, the (sometimes serious) encroachments on their liberty of which liberal intellectuals are sometimes the victims do not especially move most of the Iranians except when [such encroachments] go directly against their interests or aspirations."

57. Fernand Giraudau, *Vingt Ans de despotisme et quatre ans de liberté* (1874), 64–66.

58. As early as 1869, "nobles, once omnipotent in the Vendean countryside are no longer the only masters in their communes"; M. Faucheux, "La Vendée," in Louis Girard, ed., *Les Elections de 1869* (1960), 150. Beginning in the 1860s and accelerating thereafter, more and higher taxes, rising wages, a thinning labor force, and better investment opportunities elsewhere persuaded landowners—noble or bourgeois—first to let and then to sell their properties. A tenant farmer, observed Gabriel Boscary, who could cut costs and live cheaply himself would make a profit on a holding on which the master would ruin himself; Boscary, *Evolution agricole et condition des cultivateurs de l'Aveyron pendant le XIXe siècle* (Montpellier, 1909), 86. Also see Comte de Comminges, *Souvenirs d'enfance et de régiment* (1910), 158; and Cholvy, *Religion et société au XIXe siècle*, II, 1102.

59. Georges Lachaud, *Voyage au pays des blagueurs* (1879), 1. The term "politician" appears to have been reintroduced around 1865, to be used pejoratively about Americans in public life. Emile Littré did not mention it, but the *Supplément* of 1877 explains that the word, until then exclusively used with reference to the United States, was beginning to enter common usage for France; Littré, *Dictionnaire de la langue française* (1876), and *Supplément* (1877), 270.

60. For examples, see Arambourou, *L'Arrondissement de La Réole,* 170–173; Jean Pataut, *Sociologie électorate de la Nièvre au XXe siècle* (1956), 123; sous-préfet, Riom, July 29, 1893, AD Puy-de-Dôme, M. 0162; and *Journal de la Nièvre,* May 8, 22, 1906.

61. Massé, *Les Partis politiques dans la Nièvre,* 12, 23. Alfred Massé, who became a senator of the Nièvre in 1879, was the grandson of a Republican notable and militant of the Second Republic, and hence the scion of a typical local political dynasty. For examples of political didacticism, see the *Supplément au Républicain de l'Allier,* October 4, 1877, which shows in great detail the legislation and civic rights related to elections. Also see AN C 3229. Republicans had also sought to enlighten the rural masses in 1848 and had founded papers "destined to make the political education of our countryside"; *Journal du Tarn,* March 11, 1848. The results had, however, been less than lasting; see M. Greslé-Bouignol, "La Révolution de 1848 dans le Tarn," *Revue historique et littéraire du Languedoc* (1948): 19, 294.

62. See Chapter 9.

63. Massé, *Les Partis politiques dans la Nièvre,* 34 (italics added). It would be interesting to know if Bonapartist efforts in the early 1870s went far beyond the towns. Their *Comité de l'appel au peuple* was designed to create, or re-create, a departmental organization and spread Bonapartist propaganda in the provinces. See [C. Savary] *Rapport de M. Savary sur l'élection de la Nièvre* (1875), *passim.* The Bonapartists attempted, according to Savary, to get people involved in public activities (addresses, petitions, pilgrimages, and so forth), a list of whose participants they published, "which would commit [the participants] in the future"; ibid., 9.

64. 2d district Tulle (Corrèze), 1889, AN C 5470; Pataut, *Sociologie électorale de la Nièvre,* 82; and sous-préfet, Ceret, February 1850, AD, Pyrénées-Orientales, as quoted in Peter McPhee, "The Seed Time of the Republic" (Ph.D., diss., University of Melbourne, 1977), 461.

65. Roblin, *Les Bûcherons du Cher et de la Nièvre: Leurs syndicats* (1903), 96–98, 314.

66. Dunois, "Le Mouvement Bûcheron," *Cahiers nivernais* (March 1909), 13; and Senator Girault of the Cher, speech of December 21, 1891, as quoted in Dunois, "Le Mouvement Bûcheron," 8. For this paragraph in general, see Dunois, "Le Mouvement Bûcheron," *passim;* Roblin, *Les Bûcherons du Cher et de la Nièvre,* 281, *passim;* and Pataut, *Sociologie électorale de la Nièvre,* 42. For an unsympathetic but sober account of rural syndicalism, see Auguste Souchon, *La Crise de la main d'oeuvre agricole en France* (1914), 111, 203–296.

67. Jacques Chevalier, "Chez les paysans du Centre," *Revue catholique des églises* (November 1907), 523–526.

68. Ibid.; and Camille Gagnon, *Histoire du métayage en Bourbonais depuis* 1789 (1920), 102–105. Also see Pierre de Fraix de Figon, *Le Métayage en Bourbonnais du point de vue économique et social* (1911), 223. Writing in 1903, Roblin remarked that, in his day, in the Nièvre "political distinctions [were] just beginning to be grasped, thanks to the influence of the syndicates"; *Les Bûcherons du Cher et de la Nièvre*, 40–41.

69. Finistère, March 1897, AN C 5573. Since the contest was between the Abbé Gayraud, a "red" priest, and the Comte de Blois, a conservative monarchist, one may assume that M. Oliver was a sound republican. Also see the knowledgeable views of Charles Seignobos concerning abstentions in his *L'Evolution de la 3ᵉ République* (Paris, 1912), *passim*.

70. Faucheux, "La Vendée," 148, 152–153; and Arambourou, *L'Arrondissement de La Réole*, 88.

71. *Moniteur universel*, 1847, 574.

72. See Rémusat, *Mémoires de ma vie*, 47–48. Also see Grenoble, August 16, 1864, AN BB 1717.

73. Montpellier, January 1865, AN BB[18]1685; *Moniteur universel*, December 11, 1869, 1509 (Gironde); ibid., December 25, 1869, 1608 (Finistère); ibid., 1609 (Haute-Garonne); and ibid., March 21, 1863, 299 (Gard).

74. At Chézan (Hérault) the ballot box held thirty more bulletins than there had been voters; the magistrate at Béziers decided to do nothing; Montpellier, January 30, 1866, AN BB 1717. In the first district of Marne, a vast variety of frauds were admitted; the government spokesman described them, however, as unremarkable—wat happened there, he said, happened in a hundred other elections; *Moniteur universel*, March 17, 1863, 280–282. For ministerial lack of comment, see *Moniteur universel*, December 11, 25, 1866, 1510, 1612. At least the minister was consistent!

75. Pilenco, *Les Moeurs du suffrage universel*, 176–177. Also see Sherman Kent, *French Electoral Procedure under Louis Philippe* (New Haven, 1937), and *The Election of 1827 in France* (Cambridge, Mass., 1975). For a detailed account of electoral maneuvers and fraud at the village level, see Sylvestre, *Un Scandale électoral: Rapport au Comité Républicain Libéral de l'Ardèche sur les élections municipales de Balazuc* (Aubenas, 1909). The great change came with the introduction of the secret ballot, first used in the elections of 1914. For Luchon, see 2d district St.-Gaudens (Haute-Garonne), 1876, AN C 3158; and, for Pontivy, see Pontivy (Morbihan), 1876, AN C 3159. The Pontivy circular is worth quoting: "M. le Vte de Kergariou fait savoir aux fermiers de M. de Lausanne, de Mme. de Guélen et de Mlle. de Coussin qu'il est chargé par les propriétaires ses parents de faire voter sans exception tous les fermiers pour M. le Comte de Mun. Il doit s'assurer de la façon dont cet ordre sera exécuté pour en rendre compte à leurs propriétaires qui sauront s'en souvenir." To demonstrate that nothing had changed by the elections of 1881, see AN C 3323.

76. For St. Barthélémy, see Pontivy, 1876, AN C 3159. For all other allegations, see Pontivy, 1881, AN C 3323; 2d district Poitiers, 1881, ibid., 3324; and Beaulieu (Corrèze), 1893, ibid., 5573. For an earlier instance at Ballons (Drôme), see Grenoble, August 16, 1864, AN BB 1717.

77. Lorient, 1902, AN C 7306. But Roblin described the voting procedures

of one of his lumbermen at the turn of the century: "He arrives at the *mairie* with his ballot prepared and folded. If he puts in the box a name the mayor wouldn't like, he writes (or has someone write) the name on the ballot paper of the other candidate. And these precautions are not useless in small places!" *Les Bûcherons du Cher et de la Nièvre*, 41.

78. Rion, April 14, 1862, AN BB[18] 1632; and *Moniteur universel*, March 17, 1863, 280. Rémusat noted the change. In the elections of 1863, he spent about 4,000 francs. "It was a lot compared with the elections of the past, which did not cost one hundred francs. It was little besides what elections would henceforth cost." Thereafter, the average election cost him 12,000 francs; but others later spent 35,000 francs and more. "The invasion of elections by democracy has handed France over to wealth." *Mémoires de ma vie*, 161.

79. For Brittany, see Rennes, March 12, 1864, AN BB 1688; for Marne, see *Moniteur universel*, March 17, 1863, 280; for Pontivy, see sous-préfet, Pontivy, AN C 3323; and, for Pyrénées-Orientales, see *Moniteur universel*, December 9, 1869, 1493. The subprefect's surprise reflects more his reaction to such monetary transactions than expert judgment since, up to the elections of 1910, as Pilenco has shown, ten sous (50 centimes) is the figure most often quoted, with a low in the Doubs, where in 1906 a vote could still be had for two sous; *Les Moeurs du suffrage universel*, 213.

80. *Rapport Dejean*, 1893, AN C 5572. A more sophisticated form of the same type of electoral blandishments could be found in those districts wooed by candidates whose chief title was their wealth. That same year, 1893, almost all witnesses in the investigation of Edmond Blanc's election at Bagnères (Hautes-Pyrénées) denied straightforward corruption or fraud. They could, of course, be lying. Electoral Commission Report, Bagnères, 1893, AN C 5574. But one can easily understand how many inhabitants of a poor district might expect to benefit from the election of a rich and helpful representative, even in the absence of personal gratifications. Indeed, a decade later, following the elections of 1902, an anonymous letter was written that denounces Paul Truy, elected at Montreuil-sur-Mer (Pas-de-Calais) for *not* being the millionaire banker that he had claimed to be, which was why people had supported him. Electoral Commission Report, Montreuil-sur-Mer, 1902, AN C 7305.

81. For Kermoroch (and other nearby localities), see 1st district Guingamp (Côtes-du-Nord), 1906, AN C 7305. Protesters claimed that the successful candidate had spent between fifty and sixty thousand francs to buy electors. At Quimper, 1st district, "not a very demanding region until then," bribery and drink in large quantities were denounced as new "Boulangist methods" in 1902. By 1906, at Quimper, 2d district, Republicans estimated that their unsuccessful opponent had spent 250,000 francs in four months of campaigning, during which "the age of gold returned to earth"; Georges LeBail, *Une Election législative en 1906* (1908), 84, 141, 146.

82. 1st district Guingamp, 1902, AN C 7305; and LaCombe, *Profils parlementaires* (rev. ed.), 152.

83. In 1866, a man condemned at Bonneville (Haute-Savoie) for having given

or promised money in exchange for votes explained that his political opponents had provided the peasants with drink. Since he found no inn in one village, he gave the peasants money instead. Chambéry, August 3, 1866, AN BB 1692.

84. 2d district Pau, 1902, AN C 7375; and Robert Mitchell, rapporteur, 1st district, Saint-Malo, in *Journal Officiel*, December 19, 1889. Also see Chambéry, 1902, AN C 7305. The notion that voters should not be allowed to go home without a drink occurs in almost the same words for the elections four years later; LeBail, *Une Election législative en 1906,* 151. Here must lie the origins of the Pyrenean *rastell*, first introduced by Whites *(carlis)* in a cantonal election of 1864, when they offered drinks in a stable before the horse-troughs *(râteliers)*. "This shameful custom [soon came to seem] natural to the natives," as the prefect of the Pyrénées-Orientales complained in 1867, and caused "enormous expense." Horace Chauvet, *La Politique roussillonnaise de 1870 à nos jours* (Perpignan, 1934), 79, and *Histoire du parti républicain,* 189.

85. Henri Vincenot, *Le Billebaude* (1978), 67. Also see Riom, April 14, 1862, AN BB^{18}1632; and Guillaumin to Gabriel Maurière, March 12, 1908, in Roger Mathé, ed., *Cent dix-neuf lettres d'Emile Guillaumin* (1969), 76.

86. For the concept of free men, see Agen, January 9, 1869, AN BB 389; and, for the stolen victory in 1869, see Rémusat, *Mémoires de ma vie,* 249.

87. Louis Latrade, of Corrèze, letter of May 7, 1873, as quoted in Daniel Halévy, *Le Courier M. Thiers* (Paris, 1921), 491–492. On the flattery of the electorate, see Barral, *Les Agrariens, français de Méline à Pisani,* 39–40; and on growing pride, see *Enquête sur l'agriculture française,* AD, Corrèze, 8°T² (13); and Fernand Giraudeau, *Bleus, blancs, rouges* (1873), 187.

88. Letters of Pierre and Joseph Charpentie, in 1st district Brive, AN C 5573. Short of a visit to the monument (or "folly") in Hauterives, the most accessible information lies in Michel Friedman, *Les Secrets du facteur Cheval* (1977).

89. 1st district Brive, 1893, AN C 5572, 5573; and *Journal Officiel,* 1903, 1165, as quoted in Pilenco, *Les Moeurs du suffrage universel,* 255.

90. Haute-Garonne, 1876, AN C 3158; 3d district Puget-Théniers (Basses-Alpes), 1877, ibid., 3229; Pontivy, 1881, ibid., 3323; 2d district Poitiers, 1881, ibid., 3324; Civray, 1881, ibid., Availles, 1881, ibid., J.-P. Charnay, *Le Suffrage politique en France* (1965), 322; and LeBail, *Une Election législative en 1906.*

91. Lacoin, *Enquête sur la crise agricole,* 43–44. Also see Stephen Wilson, "The Antisemitic Riots in France," *Historical Journal,* 14 (1973), 789–806 and Michael Burns, *Rural Society and French Politics* (Princeton, 1984).

92. On credulousness, see Gien (Loiret), 1889, AN C 5468; and Morbihan, Procés-verbal, July 9, 1902, ibid., 7306. Also see Eugen Weber, *Satan, franc-maçon* (1964). For the Ardèche elections, see 2d district Tournon (Ardèche), AN C 5572.

93. Charles Joisten, *Contes populaires du Dauphiné* (Grenoble, 1971): 264, 274–277; and Civray (Vienne), 1881, AN C 3324. Also see 2d district Poitiers, 1881, AN C 3324; and Lacoin, *Enquête sur la crise agricole,* 23, 24, 25, 32, 34, 87, 105.

94. Emile Guillaumin, *Albert Manceau, adjudant* (1906), 9, and "Le Blé

d'Amérique," reprinted in his *Dialogues bourbonnais* (Moulins, 1899): "Ah j'sais ben! leu Mérique! Ca fait rien, quand y aura pus d'farine pour faire du pain, avec leu Mérique j'pense pas qu'o pussient faire quéque chouse de bon."

95. Emile Guillaumin, *Le Syndicat de Baugignoux* (1912), 6, 14, 42. Compare the edifying image of newspaper reading offered in Paul Bert, *L'Instruction civique et morale à l'école* (1881), 67–70.

96. Rouchy, "St. Flour," 550–551. This sometimes produced unpredictable results, as in the Jura, particularly well served by its deputies, which was left with a thick but costly network of narrow-gauge railroads that were completed on the eve of the auto era. Worse still, the influence of Georges Trouillot, who represented Beaufort canton, had got most local youths posted for military service to the closest garrisons, Lons-le-Saunier and Bourg, whose units were especially hard hit in 1914. Beaufort was one of the French cantons with the most war dead. Prost, *Charles Dumont,* 44.

97. Avocat, électeur, *Simple opinion sur les candidatures électorales de l'arrondissement de Troyes* (Troyes, 1846). Also see, for fascinating recollections of electoral politics under Louis-Philippe, *Moniteur universel,* January 12, 1864, 54. Writing at the turn of the century, Georges Clemenceau, scion of an experienced political clan, noted as a matter of course that "local politics in general resolves itself as it does everywhere, into a question of clientele." But, he added suggestively, "the calculation is quickly made of what one vote for one side or the other is worth." Such freedom to calculate had not always been there. Clemenceau, *Figures de Vendée* (Paris, 1930), 117–118. For the view that the reduction to questions of clientele "often, still" happened, see ibid., 235. The testimony suggests that such happenings were less frequent and less commonplace than they once had been.

98. Calvet, "Cahors," 77–78, 83; and *L'Auvergnat de Paris,* August 1882, as quoted in Raison-Jourde, *La Colonie,* 268. *L'Auvergnat de Paris* describes the use an Auvergnat leader, president of the republican-socialist committee in his district, made of politics: "S'il servait la politique avancée, c'était avec l'espoir même pas dissimulé qu'il s'en servirait à son tour . . . pour ses oeuvres, pour son pays d'Auvergne." Ibid., 267.

99. *Le Travailleur rural,* September 1910, reprinted in Emile Guillaumin, *Six Ans de lutte syndicale* (reprint ed., Moulins, 1977), 93–99. Compare Joel S. Migdal, *Peasants, Politics, and Revolution* (Princeton, 1974), with the analysis presented here. Migdal has described the peasants of Coyotepec (Oaxaca), who, after ages of concern about their unruly river, finally sent a spokesman to Oaxaca to ask the government for a footbridge. Migdal argued that "peasant participation in complex political organizations is realized in return for material inducements." Ibid., 4–5. Although I grant his point, I disagree with the miserabilist coloring of the process he has described. His peasants are "overwhelmed"; they are "victims"; they are "forced into an entirely new world"; they are no longer "protected" by "old modes of life and action"; and their "entry into the wider world" is "painful"; ibid., 257–260. This is not my impression of what happened, nor was it that of the Breton peasants; see, for example, Burguière, *Bretons de Plozévet.*

100. See Emile Guillaumin to Georges Valois, October 15, 1908, in Mathé, *Cent dix-neuf lettres*, 82.

9. The Nationalist Revival before 1914

1. See W. C. Buthman, *The Rise of Integral Nationalism in France* (New York, 1939); E. M. Carrol, *French Public Opinion and Foreign Affairs, 1870–1914* (New York, 1931); D. W. Brogan, *Development of Modern France* (London, 1947); A. Capus, *Les Moeurs du temps* (1912); A. Chéradame, *La Crise française* (1912); V. Giraud, *Le Miracle français* (1914); and many others.

2. They accepted the nationalist alliance as they accepted any alliance with right or Center, e.g., as it suited them. Compare maps 13 and 15 in François Goguel, *Géographie des elections françaises* (1951), and André Siegfried, *Tableau politique de la France de l'Ouest* (1913), 417, to understand how lukewarm those western regions where nobility was dominant were in supporting, say, the economic policies of the right, whereas they reacted strongly on issues of national interest or prestige which affected their patriotic outlook.

3. In the Sables d'Olonne, for instance, the Action française allied with Catholic and bourgeois interests in 1914 to secure the defeat of Henri Bazire, successor of Drumont as editor of *La Libre Parole* and leader of a rival movement on the right.

4. Thus we find the Catholics putting up "a free-thinking Republican" as they did at Rennes in 1914 to secure the defeat of a distrusted Catholic like Louis Descamps, or indulging in intramural struggles like those which preceded the election of Paul Simon at Brest against another Catholic candidate. See P. Delourme, *Trente-cinq ans de politique religieuse* (1936), ch. VII, *passim*.

5. Anatole France, *Histoire contemporaine* (1948), 712.

6. Ibid., 743; the similarity to the Poujadist appeal might well be noted.

7. André Siegfried, *Mes souvenirs de la 3ᵉ République* (1946), *passim;* M. Agulhon in P. George et al., *Etudes sur la banlieue de Paris* (1950).

8. Poincarism was the respectable nationalism of 1912–1914, which "allowed all good men to come to the aid of their party" by providing a leader acceptable to good Republicans.

9. Maurice Barrès, *La Terre et les morts* (1899), p. 12.

10. See Charles Maurras, *Action française*, March 3, 1920. One may wonder whether these extreme characteristics were not due, at least in part, to the loss of electoral influence, and to the series of disastrous defeats inflicted upon the Right in general, and upon Nationalist candidates in particular, at all elections after 1898.

11. Maurice Barrès, *Roman de l'énergie nationale;* Jules Romains, *Hommes de bonne volonté;* Anatole France, *Histoire contemporaine; Bulletin de l'Amitié Charles Péguy, passim*.

12. See Ernest Renan, *Réforme intellectuelle et morale; Oeuvres* (1947), I, 347; Roger Thabault, *Mon Village* (1944); France, *Histoire contemporaine*.

13. See some instances of this attitude in P. Hazard, *"L'Ame française à la veille*

de la guerre" in Revue internationale de l'enseignement, 74 (1920); E. R. Curtius, *Die litterarischen Wegbereiter des neuen Frankreichs* (Potsdam, 1920); J. C. Cairns, "Letters and International Politics 1911–1914" in *University of Toronto Quarterly,* 23 (1954); R. S. Bourne, "Maurice Barrès and the Youth of France" in *Atlantic Monthly,* 114 (1914).

14. Agathon, *Les Jeunes Gens d'aujourd'hui* (1913); G. Riou, *Aux Ecoutes de la France qui vient* (1913); E. Henriot, *A Quoi rèvent les jeunes gens* (1913), are the most important.

15. H. Massis, *L'Honneur de servir* (1937), 17; M. Petit, *Histoire de la France contemporaine* (1916), p. 460; E. Weber, "Psichari and God", *Yale French Studies,* 12 (1954).

16. Julien Benda, *Un Régulier dans le siècle* (1938), 136–137.

17. Riou, *Aux écoutes,* 283.

18. Romain Rolland, *Péguy* (1948), I, 246.

19. Paul Acker, *Le Soldat Bernard* (1910); *La Classe* (n.d.).

20. A. Feuillerat, *Paul Bourget* (1937), 245.

21. Roger Martin du Gard, *Jean Barois* (1913); *L'Age critique,* I.

22. See Lavisse's yearly prize-giving speeches at Nouviou-en-Thiérache, reported in *Le Temps;* A. France, *Discours de Réception for Marcel Prévost,* April 21, 1910; H. Bourgin, *De Jaurès à Léon Blum* (1938), *passim.*

23. E. Fournière, *Dépêche de Toulouse,* Feb. 10, 1913; H. Nicolson, *Lord Carnock* (London, 1930), 397–398; *Die Grosse Politik der Europäischen Kabinette* (Berlin, 1922–1927), XL, 190, n. 2; *Amtliche Aktenstücke zur Geschichte der europäischen Politik* (Berlin, 1925), IV, 148; *British Documents on the Origin of the 1914 War* (London, 1926–1938), X, 2, 674; *Un Livre noir* (1922–34), II, 304.

24. R. Heberle, *Social Movements* (New York, 1951), tells us in the introduction what a vague thing a "movement" might be, sometimes a mere trend or tendency, sometimes a factor in producing a trend, sometimes a response to a trend, sometimes a political party, sometimes something much less formal than that. Though to speak of a nationalist party in connection with this period would give the wrong impression, it is correct to speak of a nationalist movement because it qualifies under Heberle's definition as "integrated by a set of constitutive ideas or an ideology."

25. J. Variot, *Propos de Georges Sorel* (1935).

26. *Le Progrès de Lyon,* March 19, 1913; *L'Humanité, May 26, 1913.*

27. *Lettres de la Princesse Radziwill* (Bologna, 1934), IV, 77.

28. *La Libre Parole,* Dec. 13, 1911; May 8, 1912.

29. *La Libre Parole,* Dec. 6, 1911.

30. G. Rozet, *L'Eclair,* September 15, 1911; P. Mulle, *Dépêche de Toulouse,* February 2, 1912; J. Bardouze, *L'Opinion,* December 28, 1912; L. Cury, *L'Echo de Paris,* January 2, 1913; A. Brisson, *Le Temps,* February 24, 1913; V. Marguerite, *Le Goût de l'énergie* (1912); and so on.

31. F. Hertz, *Nationalism in History and Politics* (London, 1944), 35 and *passim.*

32. Heberle, *Social Movements,* 419.

10. Pierre de Coubertin and the Introduction of Organized Sport

1. *Les Sports athlétiques,* late March and April 1896, devoted minimal space to events they described in the most deprecating tone. In 1904 the St. Louis games got a few lines in *l'Auto* and none in *Tous les Sports.*

2. The biographical sketch follows M.-Th. Eyquem, *Pierre de Coubertin: L'Epopée Olympique* (1966), 27, 55, 58, and *passim.* Since these pages were written, two further biographies have appeared: Yves-Pierre Boulongne, *La Vie et l'oeuvre pédagogique de Pierre de Coubertin, 1863–1937* (Québec, 1975) and Louis Callebat, *Pierre de Coubertin* (1988).

3. Coubertin, *Une Campagne de 21 Ans, 1887–1908* (1909), 6–7. His ideal sports for the purpose he had in mind would be rowing, football, and cricket. Running was not a team sport, and anyway, too much of a strain for young boys.

4. See Henri Marion, *L'Education dans l'université* (n.d., 1891?), 292, 294; and the comments of Antoine Prost, *L'Enseignement en France* (1968), 345.

5. Paul Blanchard, *Ma Jeunesse sous l'aile de Péguy* (1961), 112; J. and J. Dumazedier, *Les Jeux Olympiques* (1952), 155; Coubertin, *Pédagogie sportive* (1920), tells of the opposition his notions of "Arnoldian" liberty encountered from the partisans of the old "Napoleonic" discipline.

6. Maurice Barrès, *Les Déracinés,* I (1897), 133.

7. Paul Gerbod, *La Vie quotidienne dans les lycées et collèges au XIXe siècle* (1968), 16–17; Blanchard, *Ma Jeunesse,* 112.

8. See E. Maneuvrier, "Les Associations athlétiques dans l'enseignement secondaire," *Revue Internationale de l'Enseignement,* 15 December 1894. But Maneuvrier probably exaggerated in referring to several hundred such associations. In his *L'Education physique* (1901), xxvii, Philippe Tissié, the dynamic personality behind the athletic expansion of the southwest and an exceptionally well-informed witness, cites an official report of 1899 on the results of the effort made since 1887 to encourage physical education in schools. According to this, out of 112 lycées, 75 (70%) had a sporting club; out of 228 colleges, 81 (35.5%) had one, but only 18 (20.6%) out of 87 *écoles normales* and 18 (9%) out of 201 *écoles primaires supérieures.* These figures confirm the elitist character of sports and games, especially when Tissié asserts that "indifferent at the secondary level, results in the primary school are nil." Tissié attributes the mediocre results *outside the boundaries of the Bordeaux Rectorate* to the fact that some oppose the very notion of games in school; others, for reasons of "false patriotism," dislike their English influence; others plead the difficulty of finding playgrounds; others, finally, fear article 1384 of the Civil Code, concerning school's or teacher's responsibility in case of accidents occuring to children in their care.

9. He is said to have collaborated with R. L. Stevenson on *Treasure Island* and with Jules Verne on *l'Epave du Cynthia.*

10. In January, 1870, a violent exchange between Grousset and Prince Pierre Bonaparte had led the journalist to challenge the prince to a duel. When Pierre Bonaparte shot and killed one of the witnesses, his funeral turned into a vast repub-

lican demonstration (and led to Grousset's imprisonment). Acerbic polemist, Grousset was also a prolific novelist. The articles that concern us are collected in *La Renaissance physique* (1888). See 255 for patriotism, 256 for Olympics.

11. Tissié, *L'Education physique,* xxv. Interestingly enough, Tissié, who advocated Swedish gymnastics, was strongly and repeatedly criticized "on patriotic grounds" by the defenders of "native" gymnastic methods. See *Revue des Jeux scolaires,* 1904–1914, *passim.*

12. Marcellin Berthelot (Senator, 1881–1907) served as Minister of Public Instruction 1886–87, and as Minister of Foreign Affairs under Léon Bourgeois 1895–96. For Clemenceau and the bicycle, see *Le Grand Pan* (1896), quoted in *L'Auto,* 2 November, 1906.

13. G. Bourdon, *La Renaissance athlétique et le Racing Club de France* (1906), 119.

14. E. Maneuvrier, *L'Education de la bourgeoisie sous la République* (1888), 381; *Commission pour l'étude des améliorations à introduire dans le régime des établissements d'enseignement secondaire. 4ᵉ Sous-Comission* (1889); Henri Marion, chairman of the subcommittee on discipline, also saw the problem as affecting "the education of the ruling classes." *L'Education dans l'université* (n.d.), 300.

15. See Demolins, *A Quoi tient la supériorité des Anglo-Saxons?* (1897) and *L'Education nouvelle* (1898); further, Ernest Picard, *L'Education nouvelle à l'école de Guyenne* (Bordeaux, 1905), 12.

16. In actual practice, Coubertin, who had recourse to Darwin and Spencer, did not refer to Nietzsche. Allies like Paul Adam, a more demagogic publicist, did so. Adam's *Morale des sports* (1907), 12–13, 17, quotes Nietzsche on the subject of man being meant to surpass himself, and argues that sport stimulates the "will to power" and invigorates national energy. Adam's (mis) understanding of Nietzsche was characteristic of the way in which the German philosopher was read and used. "Lorsque l'américanisme et le nietzschéisme domineront l'ère prochaine, il n'y aura point d'idées en mesure de prévaloir contre ces phénomènes sociaux . . . Demandons aux sports d'armer nos caractères pour prendre place aux premiers rangs de ceux qui manifesteront leur volonté de puissance avec gloire." No wonder Coubertin kept off Nietzsche!

17. Maurice Barrès, *Du Sang, de la volupté, de la mort* (1884), 268. Thus, the football-playing hero of an autobiographical novel written in the 1920s about school life in prewar days, associated "Nietzsche's conception of . . . the superman with Barrès's culte du moi." Jules Jolinon, *Le Joueur de Balle* (1929), 75: "Réaliser d'abord notre moi athlétique."

18. Maurice Barrès, *Un Programme* (1887), 29.

19. Louis Barron, *Les Jeux* (n.d., 1891?), 217–219.

20. *Revue de Paris,* 15 June 1894.

21. Roger Caillois, *Les Jeux et les hommes* (1958), 193–194, refers to the magic of the sporting star who triumphs by skill, stubbornness and strength—means *apparently* available to all—and also by luck, which enables the humblest admirer to dream that he, too, might perhaps do as much. For Caillois this is one of the essential compensation-fantasies of democratic societies.

22. A. P. Stanley, *Life of Dr. Arnold* (London, 1839), I, 158. Compare Jean Giraudoux, *Le Sport* (1928), 60, who praises the particularity of sporting papers: "Loin de vouloir nous apprendre ce qui se passe dans le monde, ils nous retirent du bain de nouvelles où trempe lamentablement le pauvre Européen."

23. In E. M. Earle, *Modern France* (1951), 32–43.

24. Jolinon, *Joueur de Balle*, 75. Géo André (1889–1943), French champion in high jump, was second in the Olympic Games of 1908; Jean Bouin (1888–1914), runner, was second in the 5000-metre race in the Olympic Games of 1912; Georges Carpentier, the boxing champion, needs no introduction.

25. Jean Bobet, brother of cycling champion Louison Bobet, *Les Lettres françaises*, 2 October 1957: "pour améliorer le rendement de l'homme, on n'a plus le droit de s'amuser."

26. For enduring social and intellectual prejudice, see B. Guillemain, *Le Sport et l'éducation* (1955), 31. An international UNESCO study, *La Place du sport dans l'éducation* (1956), 5, notes that where most Western nations consider sport as part of their national heritage and an integral part of school curricula, the French look on it as "a form of play without much purpose, likely to make the child lose hours precious for his studies." Compare the disenchanted comments in *Exposition Universelle Internationale de 1900 à Paris. Concours internationaux d'exercices physiques et de sports. Rapports* (1901), II, 341–342.

11. Inheritance, Dilettantism, and the Politics of Maurice Barrès

1. Barrès remains little known, despite an immense bibliography. See Alphonse Zarach, *Bibliographie barrèssienne. 1881–1948* (1951), 358, and several more recent works.

2. He turned against Dreyfus to the chagrin of friends like Léon Blum, who had expected him to follow the band of believers in Dreyfus's innocence. Blum, *Souvenirs sur l'Affaire* (1935), 84–89; on p. 86: "Puisqu'il était notre chef, eh bien! il allait nous suivre. Nous avions tellement senti comme lui qu'il ne pouvait pas penser autrement que nous."

3. For an excellent treatment of this see Zeev Sternhell, *Maurice Barrès et le nationalisme français* (1972).

4. Louis Aragon, preface to *L'Oeuvre de Maurice Barrès* (1965, henceforth cited as OMB), vol. II; Léautaud, *Journal littéraire*, I (1954), 30–31, 35, 36, 75; then a change of mind, 255, 258–259.

5. J. E. Blanche, *Mes modèles* (1928), 16. Barrès, Preface to Maurice Beaubourg, *Contes pour les assassins* (1890), xiv–xv. In 1919 André Breton and his friends had asked Barrès to provide a preface for Jacques Vaché's *Lettres de guerre*. Barrès "almost promised," reported Breton in a letter to Tzara, but the published volume includes no such thing. There is no knowing how far this was a prank. But the "trial" has about it the air of a massacre of what was to some a literary father-figure. See Michel Sanouillet, *Dada à Paris* (1965), 258 and *passim*.

6. See Jacques Julliard, *Fernand Pelloutier* (1971), 92, 93. Augustin Hamon to

Pierre Monatte: "C'est moi qui introduisis F. P. auprés des écrivains anarchistes parisiens tels que Bernard Lazare et Maurice Barrès." And, a little later: "Je considère Barrès, avec ses ouvrages comme le *Jardin de Bérénice,* anarchiste à cette époque-là."

7. "Il se penchait du haut d'une tour . . . sur la vie. Il y voyait grouiller les Barbares, il tremblait à l'idée de descendre parmi eux." *Sous l'oeil des barbares* (1888). OMB, I, 116. Pierre Lasserre, *Portraits et discussions* (1914), 216, also compares Barrès's notion of fame to the desire for a good seat from which to watch the passing show.

8. Jérome and Jean Tharaud, *Mes années chez Barrès* (1928), 10.

9. René Jacquet, *Notre maître, Maurice Barrès* (1900), 207–208, places this on Dec. 10, 1890, preceding a performance of *Tartuffe.* In 1892, a mention in the newly published *Toute Licence sauf contre l'amour* announced as forthcoming a preface to Loyola's *Spiritual Exercises.* According to André Maurel, *Souvenirs* (1925), 206, this was suppressed so as not to put off Barrès's left-wing electors in 1893 and 1896.

10. 1875, 42,620 lycées and collègiens, 1.87% of their age group; 1881, 53,277, 2.37% of their age group; 1900, 58,800, 2.59% of their age-group. The proportion was still the same in 1920. See V. Isambert-Jamati, *Crises de la société, crises de l'enseignement* (1970), 376.

11. The vice-rector of the Academy of Paris provides some indications of the social origins of Paris lycées in 1880: 33% of their fathers are *rentiers,* 13% in liberal professions, 16% in public administration, 7% in private administration, 30% in industry and commerce. The categories are vague, especially the last, but they are all we have. See Octave Gréard, "L'Enseignement secondaire à Paris en 1880," *Revue bleue,* 1880, 313–322; Isambert-Jamati, *Crises,* 111; and commentary of the situation in Edmond Goblot, *La Barrière et le niveau* (1967), a book written around 1912 but first published in 1925.

12. Jules Bertaut, *Ce qu'était la province française avant la guerre* (1918), 125.

13. He did actually hold the office of tax-collector *(receveur)* of Charmes. But this was almost a sinecure, like his later position as *ordonnateur de l'hospice,* an appointment to which the prefect made no opposition after the mayor of Charmes assured him that "Monsieur Barrès n'a jamais eu les idées de son fils." AD, Vosges, 8M64¹(Oct. 28, 1892). On country-town *receveurs* and their *commis,* see Paul David, *La Commune rurale* (Toulouse, 1863), 424: "Un jeune paysan, leveur d'impôts au nom du gouvernement, employé lui-même d'un bourgeois titulaire qui a 20 km. de là humait les délices d'un repos acheté à peu de frais."

14. Victor Méric, *A travers la jungle politique et littéraire* (1930), 37, 56, 233: "La République—la vraie—a ses traditions, ses vieilles familles, ses titres de noblesse." Note that when Barrès talks of Puvis de Chavannes (who, he thinks, has taken and expressed the best of Impressionism!) he notes that Puvis comes "from an old and one of the best families in Burgundy." *Cahiers,* 1898, OMB, XIII, 128–165.

15. J. Tharaud, *Mes années,* 22. In effect, both Barrès (b. 1862) and Jaurès (b. 1859) were the offspring of honorable but hardly *grandes* provincial bourgeois families.

16. See note 10, above, and Antoine Prost, *L'Enseignement en France, 1880–1967* (1968), 230, 346. A prize-giving speech in a small western town made the situation clear: "Un jeune homme qui se respecte et dispose par-dessus le marché de quelques mille francs de rentes, ne saurait, sans forfaire à son rang, se passer du diplome de licencié." Léon Déries, *L'Etudiant* (La Roche sur Yon, 1890), 14. Parchments were part of the social uniform.

17. OMB, I, 93.

18. Henri Gouhier, *Notre ami, Maurice Barrès* (1928), 49. See in Barrès, *Le Départ pour la vie* (1961), 143–144, 146–147, 223, his long march, begun in 1882, to launch the review he yearned for: *Les Taches d'encre* (themselves probably made possible by an inheritance) sold for 1 franc, at a loss, though the price was equivalent to 4 pounds of bread or the daily wage of a female haymaker.

19. *Les Taches d'encre*, no. 3, January 1885, OMB, I, 462: "notre *révolte de roseau pensant contre la nécessité*." Barrès's italics. For *désoeuvrés*, see OMB, I, 444. For an eminent representative of the genre, see Daniel Halévy's neighbor, Cavé, depicted in *Pays parisiens* (1932), 82 ff, "outstanding in having done nothing all his life." Cavé's family had pressed him to find a position, he had asked to be a Colonel, had settled for a job as theater censor, gave up the job in exchange for the Legion of Honor, and retired.

20. *Examen de trois romans idéologiques* (1892), OMB, I, 38. In April 1892, when Charles Maurras published his story "Les Serviteurs" in the *Revue bleue,* he used this as an epigraph, but the *Revue* excised it. See C. Maurras–M. Barrès, *La République ou le Roi* (1970), 62. Léon Blum, "Méditations sur le suicide d'un de ses amis," *Le Banquet,* 4 June 1892, echoes the same view. His generation lacks enthusiasm, is indifferent and *blasée,* its senses are exhausted, its sensibilities indolent. Barrès's John the Baptist had been Paul Bourget who, in his 1886 preface to the *Nouveaux Essais de psychologie contemporaine,* vi, had called for someone who would speak the words that would drag youth out of the uncertainty from which it suffered. Presumably he referred to middle-class youth, since others had little time left over from work.

21. "Le Dernier Soir d'une année qui s'accomplit," *Revue contemporaine,* Oct. 1885: "Attendons . . . de nous seuls le bonheur . . . Tâter le pouls à nous émotions, c'est un digne et suffisant emploi de la vie; du moins faut-il que rien de l'extérieur ne vienne troubler cet apaisement: ayez de l'argent et soyez considéré." This piece, joined to a story already published in *Les Taches d'encre* (Feb. 1885) and to some autobiographical material, would become his first book, *Sous l'oeil des barbares* (1888).

22. OMB, I, 260, 265. Note that money could provide other advantages, too. In a letter of 12/12/1888 Maurras mentions that he will write to a young man who doesn't know where to publish a 15-page study on the *Barbares,* and tell him that Barrès will take care of its publication. *La République ou le Roi,* 23.

23. OMB, I, 164.

24. Ibid., 109.

25. Ibid., 377.

26. Ibid., 107. Perhaps that is why he preferred dogs, and never stopped liking them.

27. "Temperamentally, he would have attacked any party in power just as vigorously." Louis Madelin, "Barrès le bon Lorrain." *Pays lorrain,* March 1924.

28. *Le Figaro,* February 2, 1890.

29. *Courrier de l'Est,* October 27, 1889.

30. *Courrier de l'Est,* April 27, 1890; *Figaro,* April 27 and 28, 1888. AD, Meurthe-et-Moselle, série wM/757bis, April 1888 and April 1890.

31. *La République ou le Roi,* 134.

32. *Courrier de l'Est,* January 19, January 26, July 13, March 16, February 2, 1890; *La Cocarde,* 1894–95, *passim; L'Ennemi des lois* (1893); *De Hegel aux cantines du Nord* (1904).

33. See Aragon's revealing comment in his preface to the second volume of Barrès's collected works, OMB, II, xiv: "J'ai le regret de dire que, pour étroit qu'il soit, le nationalisme de Barrès est plus proche de ce que je ressens, et sans doute de ce que ressent aujourd'hui l'avant-garde ouvrière dans notre pays, que l'internationalisme, disons de M. Guéhenno." The fact is that between 1880 and 1900 "socialism" was so ill-defined in France that men like Barrès on the one hand and Guesde on the other could both honestly call themselves socialists. Just how vague contemporary notions were, can be seen in Péguy's wry remarks on his own Orléans group's joining Guesde's Parti Ouvrier Français—"La Crise du parti socialiste," *Revue blanche,* Sept. 15, 1899, and "Compte-Rendu de mandat," *Oeuvres en prose, 1898–1908* (1965), 347 and *passim.* Yet there is no gainsaying that Barrès's socialism went back to a humanitarian and romantic tradition closer to 1848 than to 1900, to Hugo, Lamartine, and Proudhon than to Marx. Thibaudet has noted this Proudhonian quality of Barrès's socialism, which Marxists naturally scorn as petty-bourgeois. As Marxists gained ground in French socialism, Barrès was bound to move away from it.

34. Tharaud's offhand remark on the subject is revealing: "Il était antisémite comme tout le monde l'était à la Chambre, où les Juifs étaient nombreux." *Pour les fidèles de Barrès* (1944), 67.

35. *Le Figaro,* February 22, 1890. On the other hand, while state socialism suggests a beautiful dream, antisemitism suggests the slogans that could attract workers into the national community, and reconcile them to it by papering over class divisions at someone else's experience.

36. At Neuilly, not at Nancy as in J.-M. Domenach, *Barrès par lui-même* (1954), 184. On that same page, another error: Barrès married in 1891, not 1893. See the letter of Mme. Barrès in Bibliothèque Nationale, Manuscrits français, AN 13712, March 23, 1918. Cécile Delhorbe, *L'Affaire Dreyfus et les écrivains français* (1932), 162, also makes the error of placing the electoral failure of 1893 in Nancy.

37. See reports in Archives de la Préfecture de Police, Paris, B a/1149, for 4e circonscription, Saint-Denis.

38. Paule Couche-Lebreton came from a family of soldiers and *polytechniciens.* The name of one of her forebears, General Lebreton, is inscribed on the Arc de Triomphe. Her father was Directeur des Eaux de la ville de Paris. The girl was determined to escape her milieu, attended the lectures of the Sorbonne, planned to marry an artist. But one of the lectures she attended outside the Sorbonne, with her mother, was one that Barrès gave at the Odéon in 1890. A year later she had indeed

married an artist, and one in whose work she maintained a lively interest for the rest of their life together. Their son, Philippe, was born on July 8, 1896.

39. *Cahiers,* Dec. 1897, OMB, XIII, 147.

40. Ibid., 146. Interestingly, the first article Barrès wrote on the subject (in this latest phase) insisted only on the risk that the rising uproar presented to the good name of the army and, particularly, of an officer corps which was so different from the incompetent and defeatist traitors of the war of 1870–71. But the article reads more like an indictment of the generals of 1870 than as a defense of those of the day. "La Foi dans l'armée," *Le Journal,* Nov. 20, 1897. This may have been what Barrès's mother-in-law, who was sympathetic to Dreyfus, referred to when she asked him how he could be for the generals after having assailed them so. In the end, though, as she put it: "Et puis, je ne vais pas me brouiller avec vous pour un petit juif." (Comm. M. Philippe Barrès, Dec. 1972.)

41. Girardet, *Le Nationalisme français* (1966), 17.

42. René Michaud, *J'avais vingt ans: Un jeune ouvrier au début du siècle* (1967), 14.

43. OMB, I, 338–340.

44. J. Tharaud, *Pour les fidèles,* 193.

45. AD, Meurthe-et-Moselle, series wM/762 ter. February 9, 1889. Comp. Georges Sadler, *Barrès mosellan* (Metz, 1939), 42.

46. Hence, no doubt, his insistence on manners as a shield, his very French café-terrace view of the world, his prescription that "il faut opposer aux hommes une surface lisse, leur livrer l'apparence de soi-même, être absent." *Jardin de Bérénice,* OMB, I, 350.

47. "Philosophie d'héritier . . . pédagogie d'héritier" writes Albert Thibaudet, *La Vie de Maurice Barrès* (1921), 57, and Micheline Tison-Braun repeats this in her *Crise de l'humanisme,* I (1958), 253. But neither explains quite what this can mean, and the heritage, under their pens, appears rather a cultural one to be preserved than a social and material one to be enjoyed and lived on.

48. *Les Déracinés* (1947), I, 142–143; II, 13. The Duc Albert de Broglie, MacMahon's chief minister, had also pointed out the implications of a situation that obviously did not leave the *possédants* unmoved: "Le diplôme de bachelier est une lettre de change souscrite par la société: elle doit être payée en fonctions publiques: si elle n'est pas payée à l'échéance, nous avons cette contrainte par corps qu'on appelle une révolution." Quoted by Louis Maggiolo (retired rector of the Academy of Nancy). *Les Ecoles en Lorraine avant et après 1789,* 3e partie, (Nancy, 1891), 94.

49. OMB, II, 453–454. The pamphlet quoted, *Sensations de Paris: Le Quartier Latin* (1888), was a rewriting of two articles published in *Voltaire,* Nov. 2, 1887, and *Revue illustrée,* Feb. 15, 1888. Barrès may have encountered the theme while reading Taine. He took it up again in *Les Déracinés,* and still again in *Les Annales,* July 2, 1911: "Les Etudiants: Ces Messieurs?" Fear and resentment of middle-class *déclassés,* threatening the material heritage and the elitist culture, must have been strong indeed.

50. *Les Déracinés* (1947), II, 220.

51. Georges Sorel, *Matériaux d'une théorie du prolétariat* (1919), 97–98, quoted in George Lichtheim, *Marxism in Modern France* (New York, 1966), 28.

52. For the two major speeches in which he defined the term (Auxerre June 6, 1874 and Paris, January 20, 1881), see Joseph Reinach, ed., *Discours et plaidoyers politiques de M. Gambetta* (1881–85), IV, 156 and IX, 118.

53. *La République ou le Roi,* 670; "La mort d'un ami," *Le Gaulois,* September 13, 1903. Compare Lucien Herr, "A. M. Maurice Barrès," *Revue bleue,* Feb. 15, 1898, 241–245.

54. OMB, VI, 69, 70. Another Lorrainer, Hubert Lyautey, also worried about the danger and the drain on outlying provinces, forced "to hurl their best children into the Paris pit." Letter of June 17, 1895, in Pierre Lyautey, *Les plus belles lettres de Lyautey* (1962), 41.

55. OMB, VI, 293, 294. This is the sort of remark that infuriated Paul Claudel, who, in any case, objected to Barrès's treatment of his old philosophy professor, Burdeau, whom he had liked. Claudel, *Journal, 1933–1955* (1969), 303, 383–384.

56. E. and J. de Goncourt, *Journal* (1956), IV, 674 (December 2, 1894).

57. Pierre Barral, *Les Fondateurs de la 3e République* (1968), 12–13.

58. Sternhell, *Maurice Barrès;* C. Stewart Doty, *The Politics of Maurice Barrès* (Athens, 1976).

59. OMB, II, 257, 263.

60. Significantly, Sturel who in *Les Déracinés* had sacrificed his mistress, Astiné, to his personal relations with her murderers, and the murderers in turn to his own interest, does the same thing in *Leurs figures* when he sacrifices Fanfournot, the anarchist whom he had moved to political action, to meet the request of another personal relation, his ex-mistress, Mme. de Nelles. Throughout, moral and political action (or rather, inaction) are dominated by private considerations; and this is explicitly stated. See Jean Lionnet, *L'Evolution des idées chez quelques uns de nos contemporains* (1903).

61. *Les Déracinés,* I, 270, 271. There are frequent references to the dilettantism of Barrès's politics, sometimes from Barrès himself, who admits he entered to "participate in the passions of my epoch." See Jules Huret, "Les Littérateurs à la Chambre," *Le Figaro,* July 31, 1893 and *Enquête sur l'évolution littéraire* (1891), 16–24 and *passim.* One founds a review or goes into politics for the experience. For Jules Renard, see his *Journal* (1965), 206, 347, 405.

13. Nationalism, Socialism, and National Socialism

1. Together with four other defendants on bail pending trial, Susini disappeared on December 4, 1960, a few hours after having addressed the annual banquet of *Aspects de la France,* heir of royalist *Action française.*

2. These are some of the publications and groups, many ephemeral, *not* mentioned here: La France ouvrière, Front national du travail, Front national-syndicaliste, Ligue nationale-populaire, Ligue de la Révolution nationale, Milice socialiste nationale, Mouvement socialiste monarchiste, Travail et Nation, Group national-syndicaliste, Parti national-populaire, Parti socialiste national, La Révolte populaire, La Révolution nationale, L'Union nationale et sociale.

3. *La Cocarde* (Paris, 1910), p. 23.

4. In the darkest days of war we find Maurras, who has long appreciated the "national socialist spirit" of Socialists like Albert Thomas and Marcel Sembat, expressing hope that they might succeed where Hervé had failed and teach French workers "the social and national doctrine which is that of the future." *Action française,* August 21, September 1, October 2, 1917.

5. "Le Fascisme et son avenir en France," *Revue universelle,* January 1, 1936.

6. See Thierry Maulnier, "Charles Maurras et le socialisme," *Revue universelle,* January 1, 1937.

7. Just how intriguing can be seen by a glance at the members of its editorial board: Emile Baumann, René Benjamin, Vincent d'Indy, Paul Jamot, Georges Sorel, J. and J. Tharaud, Jean Variot. Add to these Elémir Bourges in 1912 and, in 1913, Maurice Barrès, Paul Bourget, Maurice Donnay, Henri Clouard, Maurice Denis, and Francis Jammes.

8. "Urbain Gohier," *L'Indépendance,* 21, Jan. 1, 1912, 305–320.

9. See *L'Indépendance,* June 1, 1912, 336 when, at the end of a long, three-installment article on "Quelques prétentions juives," Sorel declares that "The defense of French culture is today directed by Charles Maurras."

10. *Combat,* Feb. 1936.

11. Jean Saillenfest, "Fascisme et syndicalisme," *Combat,* Oct. 1936. By Jan. 27, 1937, Thierry Maulnier and J.-P. Maxence's virulent *L'Insurgé* was proclaiming: "Syndicalistes nationalistes de tous les pays, unissez-vous!"

12. Gaston Marcellin, *Lettres d'un disparu* (1925); II, 25. For Georges Valois, see his own fascinating and prejudiced works, especially *L'Homme contre l'argent* (Paris 1928); *Basile, ou la politique de la calomnie* (Paris, 1927).

13. After the Second World War, Lamour became member of the Conseil Supérieur du Plan, President-Director of the Compagnie Nationale d'Aménagement de la Région Bas-Rhône-Languedoc, and one of France's great economic managers.

14. It was said that Renaud hired his party members among the Paris unemployed, especially North African laborers. But see Henry Coston, ed., *Partis, journaux, et hommes politiques* (1960), 61–64, for another view of Solidarité française's importance.

15. *Le Franciste,* April and July, 1934.

16. Marcel Bucard, *Le Francisme* (1934), 9; see also 11: "Nous ne sommes pas, en effet, des hommes d'ordre au sens bourgeois qu'on attache à ce mot . . . Nous sommes résolument et violemment contre la notion de l'ordre établi."

17. We might take this opportunity to correct the entry concerning Henry Coston in the Fourth edition of *Who's Who in France,* where his editorial talents appear to have been exercised throughout the thirties for the benefit of an inexistent *Parole Libre.* Actually, and with much ingenuity, Coston sought to carry forward the labors of Drumont, either in the daily "independent-nationalist" *La Libre Parole* (1930–1932), or in the pages of parallel monthlies like *La Libre Parole anti-judéo maçonnique* (roughly 1930–1935) and *La Libre Parole populaire, Organe du parti français national-communiste* (roughly 1933–1934). In 1935, we find *La Libre Parole* amalgamating with *Le Porc-Epic,* the new publication being no less *anti-judéo maçonnique* than the old. In 1937, this is replaced by *Le Siècle nouveau,* clearly

inspired by Valois' *Nouveau Siècle*. Coston's copycattism is striking: first Drumont, then Valois; while his postwar books irresistibly remind one of A. Hamon's prewar *Maîtres de la France*.

18. *Action nouvelle*, Aug. 18, 1933. Debu-Bridel, sometime of Action française and of the Faisceau, became during the war a member of the Conseil National de la Résistance and, after it, Senator of the Seine and *Gaulliste de gauche*.

19. Bertrand de Jouvenel, *Doriot* (1936), 12.

20. See Maurice Duverger, *Jeunesse de France*, May 30, 1937; compare Mosley's words quoted in James Drennan, *Oswald Mosley and British Fascism* (London, 1934), 12: "Before we leave the mortal scene we will do something to lift the burdens of those who suffer. Before we go we will do something great for England."

21. Marcel Déat, *Néo-Socialisme? Ordre, autorité, nation* (1933).

22. Pol Vandromme, *Robert Brasillach* (1956), 218–220.

23. *Revue universelle*, July 15, 1938; compare with Pietro Nenni, *Vingt ans de fascismes* (Paris 1960), p. 58.

24. See, in order, *Grande Revue*, March 1934, *Combat*, Feb. 1936, and *L'Insurgé*, Aug. 4, 1937.

25. François Berry, *Le Fascisme en France* (1926), 20. It was too soon, then, to remark that, the immediate menace past, the need for such organizations no longer felt, money for them dried up until new crises in 1933 (and, more especially, 1936) set it flowing once more.

26. It would, of course, be false to suggest a necessary opposition between industrial capitalism and *étatisme*. The industrial capitalist has always supported and demanded state intervention on the economic and legislative planes—subvention, protection, antiunion or restrictive legislation, and so on—and for this purpose sought to capture or dominate the state. See, for example, Jean Lhomme, *La Grande bourgeoisie au pouvoir* (1960). In the last 150 years, all political groups which centralized when in power have called for decentralization when out of power.

27. *Action française*, Feb. 6, 1917. In Léon Daudet's words, "Il souffrait réellement de l'injustice sociale, il tenait à son role de plébéien, fils de plébéien . . . un homme de bibliothèque et de rêverie."

28. Many early Socialists seem to have felt, like Drumont, that nineteenth-century economic history could be summed up as "the bourgeoisie exploiting the people and being despoiled in turn by the Jews." (*La Fin d'un monde*, Paris 1888, quoted in *Combat*, Jan. 1938). It was only the Dreyfus affair that forced Socialists to discard their demagogic antisemitism and admit that racial, if not religious, identification of their class enemies was impossible.

We should note, however, that the statement coming from the Duc d'Orléans, immediately taken as antisemitic and repeated *ad nauseam,* had already appeared under Louis-Philippe in Montalembert's attacks on the new and unstable forms of industrial property coming to challenge the power (and socioeconomic significance) of a gentry based on landed property. This illuminates not only the changing aspects of reaction, but indicates that capitalists on the defense from the turn of the century will adopt some of the moral-traditional arguments that had been opposed to them two generations before.

29. In this connection, see Marcel Proust's letter to Georges de Lauris (dated 1905) in *Revue de Paris,* June 15, 1938, 757, in which he refers to his uncle, assistant to the mayor of Illiers, an anticlerical who never greets the *curé* and reads the then-intransigent *Intransigeant,* but who since the Dreyfus affair also reads the *Libre Parole* . . .

30. Edouard Drumont, *Le Secret de Fourmies* (1892), 33–34.

31. The tale of this sort of activity remains to be told and, necessarily, ill-told because it leaves little trace. Its most persistent analyst, E. Beau de Lomenie, himself a veteran of the Action française and the national-social movement, has been largely ignored and dangerously underrated. *His Responsabilités des dynasties bourgeoises,* 3 vols. (1943–1957), deserve attention for the suggestive (though very one-sided) light they throw on the history of contemporary France.

32. Compare Gabriel Péri's clandestine *Non, le nazisme n'est pas le socialisme,* posthumously published in 1942 after his execution by the Germans, 29–30: "Nazi leaders . . . turned popular anti-capitalism into a rough and barbarous anti-semitism. Jew was identified with banker, 5-and-10 cent store owner, Anglo-Saxon creditor . . . There as everywhere, anti-semitism has been the cunning way of turning away popular anger from the struggle against the régime of oligarchical exploitation." And, on p. 13, on French national-socialists: "Ils vitupèrent la ploutocratie; c'est pour mieux sauver ses privilèges." This was not always true; but, whatever the intentions, "objectively"—as Péri would have said—the result was the same.

33. *Le Monde,* Nov. 20–21, 1960.

34. *Le Monde,* May 17, 1960.

14. Jews, Antisemitism, and the Origins of the Holocaust

1. The term "antisemitism" seems to have been coined by the German journalist, Wilhelm Marr, in the popular pamphlet, *The Victory of Judaism over Teutonism,* published in the wake of the German stock exchange crash of 1873. It really means antijudaism, of course; but I shall use it in its accepted sense.

2. Théodore Reinach, *Textes d'auteurs grecs et romains rélatifs au judaisme* (Hildesheim, 1963), 295.

3. Ibid., 27, 14–15.

4. Ibid., 17, 30. This would be repeated by many Greek authorities on the Jews and, after them, by Romans as late as Rutilius Namatianus in the fifth century.

5. Posidonius of Apamea, quoted in ibid., 57.

6. Ibid., 56. See also Angelo Segré, "Antisemitism in Hellenistic Alexandria," *Jewish Social Studies,* VIII, 2 (1946), 127–136.

7. Ibid., 176.

8. Juvenal, satire XIV, in Reinach, *Textes,* 293.

9. Cicero, *Pro Flacco* #67, cited in ibid., 238.

10. Religious indoctrination against the Jews has been thoroughly treated in Jules Isaac, *Jésus et Israel* (1948); Léon Poliakov, *Du Christ aux Juifs de cour* (1955)

and a host of other works. For a swift treatment, see George La Piana, "The Church and the Jews," *Historica Judaica*, XI, 2 (October, 1949), 117–144.

11. For example, see inter alia Robert Jalley, *Le Folklore du Languedoc* (1971), 151; Dieudonné Dergny, *Images, coutumes et croyances ou livre des choses curieuses* (Brionne, 1885), I, 330–342; Charles Beauquier, *Traditions populaires: Les Mois en Franche-Comté* (1900), 44. In Corsica, in 1914, "Le Jeudi saint, à la lecture de l'évangile de la Passion, on voit des hommes entrer en fureur quand Ponce-Pilate livre Jésus aux Juifs. Ils injurient le pusillanime procurateur de Judée; ils tapent sur les bancs à casser leurs bâtons." Albert Quantin, *La Corse* (Paris, 1914), 257. In the opening scene of his novel, *The Last of the Just,* André Schwartz-Bart has described the effect of good Friday services on the Jews of rural Poland.

12. The Feast of St. Verney, patron of the winegrowers of Beaumont (Puy-de-Dôme) was a great annual event. See Francis Gostling, *Auvergne and Its People* (New York, 1911), 25–26. In March 1925, the parish magazine of Ornans (Doubs) recalled the story of St. Vernier, the vintners' patron: "Modèle accompli des vertus de son âge, [the 13-year old] excita la haine des juifs, ces ennemis séculaires du nom chrétien . . . Ayant résolu son abjuration ou sa mort, ils l'attirèrent dans un lâche guet-apens et le massacrèrent le 19 avril, 1287, après avoir tout essayé pour le faire abjurer sa foi."

13. Anatole Leroy-Beaulieu, *Israel chez les nations* (1893), 16.

14. Hannah Arendt, *The Origins of Totalitarianism* (New York, 1958), 108.

15. Ibid., 94.

16. Rudolph Loewenstein, *Christians and Jews* (New York, 1951), 11.

17. This may have been due to "the philosemitism of the liberals" of the circle in which he moved (Arendt, *Origins,* 335). Lucien Rebatet exaggerates when he claims that in the four or five years before the war "Paris était antisémite à 80% de sa population capable d'une idée," but he cannot have exaggerated much and Arendt, *The Origins,* 108, seems to confirm him. As Rebatet says, simplistic anti-semitism was much more widespread "dans la petite bourgeoisie, dans les couches populaires, que chez les intellectuels." *Cahiers de l'Herne,* Special number on Céline (1963), 44.

18. Arendt, *Origins,* 116–117.

19. Emile Zola, "Lettre à la France," January 6, 1898, in René Rémond, *L'Histoire de l'anticléricalisme* (1976), 206.

20. François Bournand, *Les Juifs et nos contemporains* (1898), 215.

21. For more detailed treatment of all this see Edmund Silberner's numerous writings, notably, "French Socialism and the Jewish Question, 1865–1914," *Historia Judaica*, XVI, 1 (1954), 3–38, and, more recently, Zeev Sternhell, *La Droite révolutionnaire, 1885–1914* (1978).

22. Silberner, "French Socialism," 21–24. Some Socialists, like Réne Viviani who once remarked that "antisemitism is the best form of social struggle," had picked up their antisemitism in Algeria, which was a hothouse of anti-Jewish feeling. See *Journal Officiel, Chambre des députés, Débats* (February 21, 1895), 592–593. For the influence of Algerian antisemitism on metropolitan socialists see Charles Robert Ageron, *Les Algériens musulmans et la France* (1968), I, 583.

23. For Jaurès, see Ageron, *Les Algériens;* Stephen Wilson, *Wiener Bulletin,* 3/4 (1972), 34; also *Dépêche de Toulouse,* May 1 and May 8, 1895.

24. See, for example, in Robert Tucker, ed., *The Marx-Engels Reader* (New York, 1972), 46–51.

25. Bernard Lazare, *Entretiens politiques et littéraires* (1890), I, 177, 179, 232 and *passim.*

26. P. Quillard, *Le Monument Henry* (1899), 476. For Charles Péguy, writing in 1900, three-quarters of the Jewish upper bourgeoisie, half of the Jewish middle class, a third of petty bourgeois Jews are antisemitic: *Oeuvres en prose, 1898–1908,* 290. This appears confirmed when Arthur Meyer, *Ce que mes yeux ont vu* (Paris, 1910), 124, 134, expresses his admiration for Drumont and insists that nowadays "one can, one must be antisemitic." For this and more see Stephen Wilson, "Antisemitism and the Jewish Response in France during the Dreyfus Affair," *European Studies Review,* 6 (1976), 237.

27. Leroy-Beaulieu, *Israel chez les nations,* 175–176.

28. Quoted by Hugh Lloyd-Jones, "The Books That Marx Read," *Times Literary Supplement,* February 4, 1977, 119.

29. Leroy-Beaulieu, *Israel chez les nations,* 253–254.

30. Arendt, *Origins,* 118. Compare with the remarks of E. F. Gautier, *Un Siècle de colonisation* (1930) on the "exemple quotidien et contagieux du mépris musulman pour le Juif!" On top of which Algerian Jews are "natives." Ageron, *Les Algériens musulmans,* 589, also speaks of their "nativeness" *(indigénat),* which prevented the *colons* from accepting them as equals, and refers to "the atavistic contempt of the Muslims . . . which surrounded them with a sort of blemish, constantly renewed."

31. Leroy-Beaulieu, *Israel chez les nations,* 31, makes much of this. See Joseph Lémann, *L'Entrée des israélites dans la société française* (1886), ch. 1.

32. Thus Alsatians (and Lorrainers), who despised Jews as much as Algerians did, settled heavily behind the Gare de l'Est, around La Villette where in the 1880s and thereafter Parisian antisemites recruited their toughest supporters. Emile Durkheim, born at Epinal in 1858, could testify that in 1870 it was the Jews who were blamed for the defeat, just as in 1848 in Alsace they suffered from the Revolution. See his contribution to Henri Dagan, *Equête sur l'antisémitisme* (1899), 60.

33. While trying to hold on, meanwhile, the Catholic Church sponsored a lively revival of anti-Jewish fantasies brought up to date. See Pierre Sorlin, *La Croix et les Juifs* (1967), and Pierre Pierrard, *Juifs et catholiques français* (1970). Catholic publications supported Drumont and spread the wildest antisemitic accusations. Antisemitic literature was widely used in Catholic schools.

34. In 1898, Jules Guérin's Ligue antisémitique advocated a "Saint-Barthélemy des juifs" and invited the French to imitate those Galicians who had burnt a Jewish family alive. Wilson, *Wiener Bulletin,* 35.

35. Compare this with certain explanations of Algerian antisemitism. Agéron, *Les Algériens musulmans,* 589, explains that Algerian Jews, long isolated in their *mellahs,* lived in narrowly endogamic communities and were recognized as a Jewish "nation" governed by its own law.

36. *An Anthology of Historical Writings on the Armenian Massacres of 1915* (Beirut, 1971), 118.

37. Ibid., 126, 194.

38. Herbert Adams Gibbons, *The Blankest Page in Modern History* (New York, 1916), 15–17; Arnold Toynbee, *Armenian Atrocities* (New York, 1917), 22.

39. *The Turkish Armenocide: An Open Letter to President Wilson,* by Armin T. Wegener (reprinted AHRA, 1965), 76.

40. *Anthology,* 123.

41. Ibid.; *Armenian Atrocities,* 70. For many details, see the British White Book, *The Treatment of Armenians in the Ottoman Empire, 1915–16,* edited by Viscount Bryce (London, 1916); and, further, Henry Morgenthau, *Secrets of the Bosphorus* (London, 1918), chs. 23–27.

42. Note that the Turkish persecution of Armenians sacrificed even military interests and the efficient pursuit of war to the superior aim of their destruction: blocked roads, spreading typhus, loss of rare skilled personnel—doctors, government and railroad officials, bank clerks, drivers, artisans, even army effectives, were sacrificed to a higher passion. The German Ambassador commented: "It looks as if the Turkish government wants to lose the war!" Johannes Lepsius, "The Armenian Question," *Muslim World,* 10 (London, 1920), 350. Morgenthau, *Secrets of the Bosphorus,* 223, quotes Talaat Pasha: "We care nothing about the commercial loss."

15. Revolution? Counterrevolution? What Revolution?

1. Max Gallo, *Gauchisme, réformisme et révolution* (1968), 133. Despite all this, he explains, May 1968 was not the revolution.

2. André Découflé, *Sociologie des révolutions* (1968). There is no point in taking intellectual issue with the lunatic fringe. Découflé is used for reference because he represents the more respectable French students of the subject.

3. Quoted in John Anthony Scott, *The Defense of Gracchus Babeuf* (Amherst, 1967), 42.

4. Découflé, *Sociologie,* 40.

5. Ibid., 7, also 11–12. One might ask in passing whether popular interest in or sympathy for social bandits and some of the other outlaws described by Eric Hobsbawm, who often prey more on their own kind than on the powerful and the rich, reflects even the most primitive form of social revolt. The solidarity of common folk against lawmen and tax collectors is rooted in human and local experience, not in social awareness, however dim. Take the case of smugglers, whom peasants took for granted, buying the salt or matches they sold, accepting their activities as part of the local economy, aiding them when they could. Though differently motivated, such attitudes no more reflect social revolt than our occasional sympathy for those who cheat the Customs or Internal Revenue.

6. Ibid., 13–14.

7. Thus, for example, Cardinal de Retz, a seventeenth-century expert on the matter, writes in his *Mémoires* concerning "les émotions populaires": "Les riches n'y viennent que par force; les mendiants y nuisent plus qu'ils n'y servent, parce que la

crainte du pillage les fait appréhender. Ceux qui y peuvent le plus sont les gens qui sont assez pressés dans leurs affaires pour désirer du changement dans les publiques et dont la pauvreté ne passe toutefois pas jusque'à la mendicité publique."

8. See Herbert Marcuse in J. A. Scott, *The Defense,* 103. Saint-Just had already declared: "The miserable are the power of the earth." (Speech of 8 Ventôse/March 1794).

9. Just how wrong, can be seen from the remark a working man made to Ramon Fernandez, the literary critic, after the Sixth of February riots of 1934: "Il nous faudrait des fusils et descendre vers les quartiers riches! . . . Avec, à notre tête, un chef, un homme enfin: tenez, un type dans le genre de Gide!" Reported by Ramon Fernandez, "Politique et littérature," *Nouvelle revue française* (1935), 286.

10. Michel Clouscard, *Néo-fascisme et idéologie du désir* (1973), 49.

11. Right and left differ simply in the subject of their messianic fantasies: nation or race for the one, proletarians or intellectuals for the other. Both can be fascinated by heroes. And both, recently, have turned their attention to youth, last brittle hope of those who have bet on so many other horses and lost. But youth (like ideology) is a product of adult society, as the industrial proletariat is a product of capitalist society, and seems as destined for assimilation as its predecessors; even more so.

12. René de Chateaubriand, *Essai sur les révolutions* (1797), vol. II (Bruxelles, 1826), 280–281.

13. See Jacques Ellul, *Métamorphose du bourgeois* (1967), 158. I have greatly benefited from the reading of this book and others by him. Ellul, with whom I do not always agree, is one of the really original thinkers in France. The mass of those to whom the term is often applied are more liable to run in schools, like fish.

14. Gallo, *Gauchisme,* 107.

15. There was White Terror, of course. But the use of terror does not define a counterrevolutionary regime, any more than a revolutionary one. Both may use it and generally do. Yet violence and terror can be found in other regimes as well, with no particular ideological overtones. And let it be understood, once and for all, that the attempt to treat certain phenomena from a detached point of view, does not imply approval.

16. Guillermo Lora, *Bolivie: De la naissance du POR à l'Assemblée populaire* (1971), 203; Ruben Vasquez Diaz, *La Bolivie à l'heure du Che* (1968), 99.

17. Découflé, *Sociologie,* 18. Note the implication of deliberate policy ("project"), where the most one could assert might be an "objective" role; and the objection that a counterrevolution must have a rival revolution to counter with a revolution of its own, suggesting (a) that the United States (and Canada?) represent a *sui generis* revolutionary cause, yet (b) that the only revolutions deserving the name are those that North Americans oppose.

18. Clouscard, *Néo-fascisme,* 9–10, 72. Clouscard has excellent precedents. Much bandied about during the Terror, the term was even applied to Robespierre, in the Committee of Public Safety, after the vote of the law of 22 Prairial, year II. One danger of such confusionism was pointed out by Eugene Varga in his study of

the economic crisis of the 1930s, *La Crise* (1935), 264–265. Communists, he warned, have made the mistake of calling fascist dictatorship what was only "the accentuated fascisation of bourgeois regimes." This weakened the antifascist struggle, because workers said that if that was fascism, then fascism is not as terrible as all that . . .

19. Découflé, *Sociologie,* 122–123.

20. Arno J. Mayer, *Dynamics of Counterrevolution in Europe,* (New York, 1971), 115, 116.

21. Ibid., 78.

22. Compare Branco Lazitch, *Lénine et la 3e Internationale* (Neuchâtel, 1951), 211. In 1923 the KPD conference at Frankfurt defined fascism as "a preventive counterrevolution in that it uses pseudoradical slogans."

23. Mayer, *Dynamics,* 62. On p. 63 Mayer remarks that the counterrevolutionary project "is far more militant in rhetoric, style and conduct," where it can be likened to its revolutionary competitors, "than in political, social or economic substance," when in effect the political, economic, and, in some ways, social substance of (say) the Nazi politics of the 1930s was more radical and innovative than that of most contemporary socialists.

24. Ibid., 62: "As of the 1870s it became increasingly clear that to be effective, the struggle against Socialism required a distinct popular ideology."

25. In any case, how intense was the class struggle in France, when Georges Sorel had to initiate a hopeless though brilliant campaign to revive it?

26. There is no vouching for Boulanger. He was certainly an opportunist, and hardly straightforward in his political dealings. But he was not intelligent enough to conceive a manipulative ideology, and hardly a typical revolutionary *or* counterrevolutionary leader.

27. A case where the encounter between straightforward (conservative) and camouflaged counterrevolutionaries is clear appears in Miklos Szinai and Laslo Szucs, eds., *The Confidential Papers of Admiral Horthy* (Budapest, 1965), 112–118, reprinting a January 14, 1939, memorandum of Count Istvan Bethlen and the "rightist" opposition he represented. Bethlen criticizes the pro-Nazi Imredy for being too sympathetic to the Germans and stirring up a hornets' nest with his overbidding. As for the revolutionary Arrow Cross itself, Horthy's lines of October 14, 1940, addressed to the then Prime Minister Pal Teleki, are revealing (150–151). Horthy says he has always been antisemitic, but he wants no precipitate measures that would only ruin the country: "In addition, I consider for example the Arrow Cross men to be by far more dangerous and worthless for my country than I do the Jew. The latter is tied to this country from interest, and is more faithful to his adopted country than the Arrow Cross men, who, like the Iron Guard, with their muddled brains, want to play the country into the hands of the Germans."

28. See Jean-Michel Etienne, *Le Mouvement rexiste jusqu'en 1940* (1968).

29. One can go further and ask if Pétain's National Revolution of 1940, overturning a republic that all, including the left, proclaimed was rotten, was more or less of a revolution than General de Gaulle's raping her faintly consenting successor

in 1958, or Revlon's introducing a revolutionary shade of nail polish in 1973.

30. Mayer, *Dynamics*, p. 2.

31. I mean the sort of usage as when Mayer speaks of the "revolutionary opposites" of counterrevolutionary leaders (ibid., 66).

32. Ibid., p. 20.

33. Jacques Ellul, "Le Fascisme, fils du libéralisme," *Esprit*, 53 (February 1937), 762–763, defines fascism by its formal will to react against liberalism, and not as a true reaction. But that applies to communism too, "also formal negation of Liberalism and perhaps also its offspring."

34. Daniel Lerner and Harold D. Lasswell, *World Revolutionary Elites* (Cambridge, Mass., 1966), 230, 461, 463–464 and *passim*.

35. Mayer, *Dynamics*, 89.

36. It was, of course, against this trend that Mao waged his Cultural Revolution, and lost.

37. André Malraux, "S.O.S.," *Marianne*, October 11, 1933.

38. The Fourth Congress of the Communist International (1922), while recognizing that fascists sought a mass base "in the peasant class, in the petty bourgeoisie, and even in certain sections of the proletariat," insisted that the combat organizations they set up were counterrevolutionary, and thus arrogated to itself the coveted revolutionary label. Was the label thus preempted, or was it fascist opportunism and its incidental (as well as doctrinal) hostility to socialism and communism that gave the label up?

39. See Mayer's remark, *Dynamics*, 66, that counterrevolutionaries favour the conspiratorial rather than the critical-analytic view of history. Is not this characteristic of many creeds addressed to masses? What about the left's use of bankers, "merchants of death" and, multinational conglomerates?

40. Notably in "The Men of the Archangel," *Journal of Contemporary History*, I, no. 1 (December 1965). And Maurice Thorez, "holding out his hand" in 1936 to the militants of fascist leagues, "sons of the people" like the Communists, seems to bear out my point.

41. See Malraux speaking in 1929 about the revolutionary characters of his novel, *Les Conquérants*, who were recognized as typical revolutionaries by experts like Trotsky. The revolutionary leader, says Malraux, "doesn't have to define Revolution, but to make it." Quoted in Jean Lacouture, *André Malraux* (1973), 136. Similarly, the Second Havana Declaration quoted in Régis Debray, *Essais sur l'Amérique latine* (1967), 131, proclaims: "The duty of a revolutionary is to make the revolution."

42. See, for example, Talcott Parsons' famous essay of 1942, "Some Sociological Aspects of the Fascist Movements," in *Essays in Sociological Theory* (Glencoe, Ill., 1954).

43. Note that the question of private property, central both in Marxist doctrine and in categorizing fascism, was regarded as a secondary issue, incidental to major aims: productivity, employment, order, restructuring the society and the productive process. In this respect too, fascists (in theory) and Nazis (in practice) showed themselves more flexible than their rivals.

44. Likewise, petty bourgeoisie and new middle classes, regarded by Communists as the chief source of fascist support, are considered to play a positive role when they participate in the national revolutions of the Third World.

45. Jules Monnerot, *Sociologie de la révolution* (1969), 553. His italics.

46. See above, note 40, and Rogger and Weber, eds., *The European Right* (Berkeley, 1965).

47. Ellul, *Autopsie de la révolution* (1969), 338.

48. Philippe Ardant, "Le Héros maoïste," *Revue française de science politique* (1969). The hero is characterized by his lack of personal selfishness. He is above all devoted to the collectivity, the fatherland, and Mao. As to how exciting it all seemed to the Germans, we can read about in Nora Waln, *Reaching for the Stars* (Boston, 1939) or Emmanuel Mounier, *Esprit,* 49 (October 1936), 36: "la fidélité dans la joie . . . le sourire du régime . . . Si vous voulez étonner un nazi, dites-lui qu'il vit sous une dictature."

49. *Journal officiel de la Commune,* quoted in Découflé, *Sociologie,* 37: "Paris a fait un pacte avec la mort." Guevara, quoted in *Le Monde,* 27 April, 1967, calls for two, three, several Vietnams, "with their share of death and immense tragedies," for the sake of the blows they can deal to imperialism. As for death, "let it be welcome provided that our warcry reaches a receptive ear, that another hand takes up our weapons, and that other men rise to strike up the funeral march and the crackling of machine guns and new cries of war and victory." See also his *Créer deux, trois . . . de nombreux Vietnams, voilà le mot d'ordre* (1967), 12, 13. Debray is quoted in Ellul, *De la révolution aux révoltes* (1972), 139.

50. Debray, in Ellul, *De la révolution;* Béguin, *Esprit,* October 1948, quoted in Lacouture, *Malraux,* 339; Gonzalez and Sanchez Salazar, *Che Guevara en Bolivie* (1969), 237. The sympathetic Salazars entitle one of their chapters "A Twentieth-Century Don Quixote." This is as revealing as the legend that has grown around another hero of the revolutionary left, the Colombian priest who died as a guerrillero, Camilo Torres. A self-sacrificing and devoted Christian populist, Torres hardly seems a revolutionary leader of the classic pattern: rather, the idealistic chief of primitive rebel bands. See the book by his friend, Mgr. German Guzman-Campos, *Camilo Torres* (1968).

51. Raymond Aron, *Le Développement de la société industrielle et la stratification sociale* (1957), I, 105, points out that in the nineteenth century optimism was on the liberal side: "Le pessimisme était socialiste." You could call a catastrophic pessimism (or optimism) the belief that things would have to get much worse before a vast explosion can open the door to betterment. This could, thanks to some confusion, provide a meeting ground for the socially pessimistic right and the doctrinally "pessimistic" left.

Frequently, what one sought in one camp was more readily available in the other. Thus, in his *Chiens de paille,* written in the spring of 1943, revised in April 1944, finally published in 1964, Drieu La Rochelle notes his disillusion with Hitlerism, too much of a *juste milieu:* "Mon idéal d'autorité et d'aristocratie est au fond enfoui dans ce communisme que j'ai tant combattu" (110). About that same time, Konstantin Rodzevski, head of the émigré All Russian Fascist Party, handed himself over to Soviet authorities and wrote to Stalin that Stalinism was exactly what he had erroneously called fascism, but purged of the exaggerations, errors and illusions of fascism. Rodzevski was to be condemned to death and executed in Moscow in 1946, but his opinion remains suggestive. See Erwin Oberlander, "The All-Russian Fascist Party," *Journal of Contemporary History,* I, no. 1 (1965).

52. Ellul, *De la révolution,* 202.

53. I happen to disagree with them now, as I did then. But that is by the way.

54. The question has been raised how revolutionary such holidays really were. Not only Nuremberg but 1968 suggest equivocal answers. The documentary film, "Français si vous saviez," shows newsreels of Pétain and de Gaulle being cheered by hundreds of thousands of enthusiastic Parisians at a few weeks' interval.

55. Mayer, *Dynamics,* 65.

56. See his statements, in *Dynamics,* 6–7. To have done so "would involve diluting the heuristic construct, leaving it with a blunted cutting edge . . ."

57. François Bourricaud, *Pouvoir et société dans le Pérou contemporain* (1967); Louis Constant, *Avec Douglas Bravo dans le maquis vénézuélien* (1968), 7; Carlos Romeo, *Sur les classes sociales en Amérique latine* (1968), 27 and *passim.*

58. Debray, *Essais,* 86, 202; Lora, *Bolivie,* 188, 203, 204.

59. Salazar, *Che Guevara,* 29. Even Trotskyists agreed that "the MNR is indisputably the greatest popular party Bolivia has known." Lora, *Bolivie,* 210.

60. Compare Lora, *Bolivie,* 185 ff; Pablo Torres, *La Contre-insurrection et la guerre révolutionnaire* (1971), 39 and *passim.* Writing to Fidel Castro in 1965, Guevara equated revolution, "the most sacred of tasks," with "the struggle against imperialism of whatever kind." The Salazars, *Che Guevara,* 42, quote the letter in full. In it we also meet, not for the first time, the Castrist slogan "Revolution or Death"—another traditional revolutionary reference, hardly restricted to fascists.

61. Edgar Morin, *Introduction à une politique de l'homme* (1965), 92–93. Half-failures all, Morin remarks, "but isn't half-failure also a formula of life? Isn't that what we call success?"

62. I use the term in the Sorelian sense, to describe a combination of unifying images capable of instinctively evoking the feelings and ideas corresponding to a sociopolitical movement of the purpose of action.

63. Thus returning, *mutatis mutandis,* to Bossuet's description of an earlier situation: "Les révolutions des empires . . . servent à humilier les Princes." *Discours sur l'histoire universelle,* pt. 3, ch. I.

64. I wonder whether the real revolutions of our time are not our wars. Burckhardt, in 1868, noted that "modern wars are but an element in modern crises; they do not carry in themselves and do not produce the effects of a true crisis; beside them, bourgeois life goes on its way." Their short duration, Burckhardt explained, fails to mobilize the forces of despair from which alone could come "the total renewal of life, the expiatory destruction of what was and its replacement by a new living reality." The revolutionary projects of the time sought to remedy this. Yet Burckhardt's remark could now apply to their descendants, if we replaced the term "bourgeois life" with "bourgeois values." Meanwhile, the great wars of the twentieth century have proved effective midwives to the "destruction of what was and its

replacement by a new living reality," even without the help of deliberate revolutions. Perhaps Burckhardt's Basel colleague, Nietzsche, was right when he predicted our entry into "the classic era of war," an era in which the functions that the nineteenth century attributed to revolution would be carried out by other means. See Jakob Burckhardt, *Considérations sur l'histoire du monde* (1938), ch. IV, especially 159–160.

Acknowledgments

The following is a list of the original titles, places, and dates of previously published essays in this collection; they are listed in order of appearance in the book and are reprinted by permission of the publishers.

Chapter 2 originally appeared as "New Wine in Old Bottles: *Les Familles spiri-tuelles de la France,*" *French Historical Studies,* 1, 2 (Fall 1959), 200–224.

Chapter 3 originally appeared as "La Formation de l'hexagone républicain" in Pierra Nora, ed., *Les Lieux de mémoire. Vols. 2: La Nation* (Gallimard, 1986), and in English as "In Search of the Hexagon," *Stanford French Review* (Fall–Winter 1988), 367–385.

Chapter 4 originally appeared as "Fairies and Hard Facts: The Reality of Folktales," *Journal of the History of Ideas,* 42, 1 (January 1981), 93–113.

Chapter 5 originally appeared as "Who Sang the *Marseillaise?*" in Jacques Beauroy and others, eds., *Popular Culture in France* (Anma Libri, 1977) pp. 161–173.

Chapter 6 originally appeared as "Religion and Superstition in Nineteenth-Century France," *The Historical Journal,* 31, 2 (Cambridge University Press, 1988), 399–423.

Chapter 7 originally appeared as "The Second Republic, Politics, and the Peasant," *French Historical Studies,* 11, 4 (Fall 1980), 521–550.

Chapter 8 originally appeared as "*Comment la Politique vint aux paysans:* A Second Look at Peasant Politicization," *American Historical Review,* 87, 2 (April 1982), 357–389.

Chapter 9 originally appeared as "Some Comments on the Nature of the Nationalist Revival in France Before 1914," *International Review of Social History,* 3, pt. 2 (Autumn 1958), 220–238.

Chapter 10 originally appeared as "Pierre de Coubertin and the Introduction of Organised Sport in France," *Journal of Contemporary History,* 5, 2 (1970), 3–26.

Chapter 11 originally appeared as "Inheritance and Dilettantism: The Politics of Maurice Barrès," *Historical Reflections,* 2, 1 (Summer 1975), 109–131.

Chapter 12 originally appeared as "About Marc Bloch," *The American Scholar,* 51, 1 (Winter 1981–1982), 73–82.

Chapter 13 originally appeared as "Nationalism, Socialism, and National-Socialism in France," *French Historical Studies*, 2, 3 (Spring 1962), 273–307.

Chapter 14 originally appeared as "Jews, Antisemitism, and the Origins of the Holocaust," *Historical Reflections*, 5, 1 (Summer 1978), 1–17.

Chapter 15 originally appeared as "Revolution? Counterrevolution? What Revolution?" *Journal of Contemporary History*, 9, 2 (1974), 3–47.

Index